TRANSNATIONAL CORPORATIONS
AND WORLD ORDER

TRANSNATIONAL CORPORATIONS AND WORLD ORDER
Readings in International Political Economy

EDITED BY
George Modelski
UNIVERSITY OF WASHINGTON

W. H. Freeman and Company
San Francisco

Sponsoring Editor: Richard J. Lamb; *Project Editor:* Pearl C. Vapnek; *Manuscript Editor:* Jeanne Duncan; *Designer:* Marie Carluccio; *Production Coordinator:* Linda Jupiter; *Illustration Coordinator:* Cheryl Nufer; *Compositor:* Lehigh/Rocappi, Inc.; *Printer and Binder:* The Maple-Vail Book Manufacturing Group.

Library of Congress Cataloging in Publication Data

Main entry under title:

Transnational corporations and world order:
readings in international political economy.

    Includes bibliographical references and index.
    1. International business enterprises—
Addresses, essays, lectures. 2. Investments,
Foreign—Addresses, essays, lectures. I. Modelski,
George A.
HD2755.5.T68   338.8'8   78-12964
ISBN 0-7167-1026-9
ISBN 0-7167-1025-0 pbk.

Printed in the United States of America
9 8 7 6 5 4 3 2 1

CONTENTS

PREFACE

This volume is intended to meet a felt need for a comprehensive treatment of transnational corporations. It is designed for use in upper division courses in international relations, especially those emphasizing international political economy and transnational relations. In addition, it should be of interest to anyone concerned about the impact of transnational corporations on the contemporary world.

As part of the rapidly growing literature on international political economy, this collection emphasizes the political and social impact of transnational corporations, as well as the consequences of their activity for world order. The book brings together the most significant classic writing on this subject, reflecting the principal schools of thought (both positive and negative).

The book is organized around five major topics, each introduced by a comprehensive essay. First, it lays out the basic descriptive material necessary for understanding the recent growth and present world position of transnational corporations. Then it goes on to offer representative theoretical explanations of this phenomenon. In the core of the book, several types and sets of political and social consequences of corporate activity are examined: consequences on international relations, on peace and war, on East–West relations, on labor, on "dependency," and on the Third World. Given these effects, the problems of regulation at the international level are then looked at in some detail as they affect both the industrialized and the developing countries. The survey concludes with some contrasting estimates of the future role of transnationals.

My interest in multinational corporations and their place in international relations began more than a decade ago at the University of Washington. During this period, I was fortunate to have had my interest strengthened by that of a number of students in the graduate program of the Department of Political Science; I should like to mention in particular Fuad Ajami, Gary Gallwas, David Osterberg, and Keith Orton. A year's sabbatical spent at Harvard University's Center for International Affairs as a member of the Transnational Relations and Politics Seminar in 1973–1974 helped me to gain additional perspective.

In the final analysis, the value of a book such as this rests upon the quality of the contributions. It has been a pleasure to try to knit into a meaningful whole the work of so rich and diverse a group of authors.

For the translation of several chapters I am grateful to my wife, Sylvia. Her participation made this a more lively assignment.

Over the years, I have been encouraged to pursue this project by two successive directors of the University Programs of the Institute for World Order, Inc., of New York—Michael Washburn and Burns H. Weston. I thank them for their steady support without wishing to implicate them in my editorial comments or judgments.

October 1978   *George Modelski*

TRANSNATIONAL CORPORATIONS
AND WORLD ORDER

OVERVIEW

The theme of this volume is the world impact of transnational corporations. That such impact exists and is widely felt few now doubt; but opinions differ as to its precise nature. It will be our purpose here to review a variety of materials in order to better understand this impact, to assess both its benign and its negative features, and to explore ways of dealing with it on a global scale.

Our subject is, therefore, a global social assessment of an important transnational institution. We shall not be concerned, for instance, with questions of business management or administration, or with optimal decision strategies of the corporation; nor will we be primarily concerned with questions of economic theory or foreign investment analysis. Even though we cannot ignore these narrower questions, our own focus is broader and more properly interdisciplinary. We shall analyze contributions from the literature of economics and business, political science and international relations, law and sociology, to illuminate what is a crucial problem for the student of world order.

Terminology

We define the transnational corporation broadly (using corporation in the non-technical sense) as a network of enterprises that controls activities and assets in more than one state, and most often three or more states. In choosing this particular term for the title of this volume we do not wish to suggest that it is necessarily preferable to the myriad other terms that have been used in the past decade or two. In fact, many of our selections use the popular term "multinational corporation"; others use the "multinational enterprise" or simply the "multinational"; and still others refer to the "international corporation," or the "large international firm." In our commentary we shall use these terms interchangeably without intending to convey any shift of emphasis.

1

The reason why we chose "transnational corporations" for the title is that in the past few years the United Nations has chosen to use that term, and it is appropriate that a volume that emphasizes world order should employ the same terminology. The Group of Eminent Persons that reported on this subject at the request of the Economic and Social Council in 1974 preferred "transnational" to "multinational." They expressed the "strong feeling that the word transnational would better convey the notion that these firms operate from their home bases across national frontiers"—the implication being that "multinational" suggests a higher degree of international content and control than is justified.

For Constantine Vaitsos, an influential Latin American economist, there is a semantic difference between the terms: "The firms we are talking about are not multinational in the sense that they have multinational allocation to research and development, in terms of top management, in terms of ownership. They are transnational firms."[1] But one may wonder whether the terms are in fact precise enough to convey these finer shades of meaning. In our commentary, unless such terms are specifically defined in another sense, such precision is not aimed for and the terms are used in their most general sense. Moreover, the use of either term in reference to a particular firm does not imply that the firm wishes to be so described.

The other term employed in our title is "world order." By using that term we mean to suggest that the scope of this work is global, and that transnational corporations do not affect merely one particular society or nation-state. Their impact is world-wide. Transnational enterprises are now active in most countries. They are international organizations of great variety and wide scope. They are the structural elements that are the basis of today's world order.

We also wish to suggest that the way in which the world is organized is not the only way it might be ordered; there is a wide range of choices for those who might wish to discuss the options for change or for reform. A useful concept here is that of a "preferred world," defined as "an image of a reformed world stated in fairly precise behavioural detail."[2] In discussions of transnational corporations, we should bear in mind that their role as important world structures will help to determine the future of world order, and that the world order of tomorrow will in turn shape the future of transnational enterprises.

Global Political Economy

Although our approach is broadly interdisciplinary, it does fall within the scope of global political economy. We define political economy as the field of study that is concerned with the interrelationship of politics and economics. Indeed, different concepts of political economy might be distinguished according to whether economics *should* determine politics (liberalism), or whether it *does* determine politics (Marxism) or, finally, whether politics determines economics (neomercantilism).[3] But to posit the existence of such a field we need not start with the assumption that either politics or economics plays a superior role; we might in fact prefer to take an eclectic position in which, depending on the issue and the facts of the case, either economics or politics, or both or neither, might be of primary interest.

Global political economy is concerned with the organization and performance of economic functions within, and as part of, the world order. Here too, we find a two-way relationship. The international economy (the pattern of relationships concerned with such matters as world trade, money, and finance) operates within a political framework that is determined by the activities of the major powers and international organizations. They establish the trade rules, tariffs, and exchange rates and determine the flow of public and nonpublic funds in the form of aid, loans, and investments. They set what François Perroux has called "the framework of exchange." But the international economy also affects the global political structure. Economies rise to dominance and fall as global growth centers and firms prosper and decline and as cycles of innovation and discovery alter the positions and relations of the powers and the prospects for international organization.

In this sense we see transnational corporations as entities that are primarily economic. The basic thrust of their activities is toward the performance of economic functions, some of them crucial to various national economies (such as the manufacture of automobiles) and others, more interesting perhaps, essential to the fulfillment of global requirements (such as world-wide distribution of oil). But in performing primary economic functions such corporations also affect and are affected by the global order. First, they benefit from the support the political framework provides them and they are regulated by that framework. Second, they in turn contribute to shaping that framework by making sources of wealth and power available to nation-states and (potentially) to international organizations, and thus they themselves contribute to international order.

Transnational Relations and Interdependence

Today's students of international relations have become familiar with the proposition that their subject covers more than intergovernmental exchanges as symbolized by the diplomatic and strategic complex of traditional international politics.[4] They now recognize transnational enterprises as one of the significant components of transnational relations, existing side by side with an increasingly dense network of international organizations. Multinational firms that coordinate production on a global scale and distribute their output throughout the world are one of the most striking recent manifestations of global interdependence. As such they put into question the value of models of world politics that proceed from the assumptions of national self-sufficiency and of the exceptional character of cross-boundary relationships.[5] But they are not the only such manifestation or the first one. The world has known significant elements of such interdependence for at least 500 years, and has known long-distance trade for more than a millennium. But twentieth-century corporations have brought significant new elements into the picture. They not only engage in trade or conduct their own investment projects; they now coordinate industrial production, marketing, finance, and research and development on a global scale and in accord with a concerted strategy. According to one view, they are the international counterpart of the nineteenth-century industrial revolution; according to another, they may be the skeleton of the world economy of the future. On all counts they lend depth and texture to international relations.

Transnational corporations enter international relations in two ways. They are autonomous and powerful organizations carrying out their functions and pursuing their interests in a world of other strong organizations. As such they may be essential elements of the global economic system—in effect, global problem-solvers, important actors the world might not be able to do without. But they may also be problem-makers in the world at large; their activities may have to be watched and to be regulated. Hence they may also have to be acted upon by other actors, and in particular by political actors.

In describing transnational corporations as a manifestation of global interdependence we are saying that they are the form the need for world-wide economic exchange assumes in today's world. The world cannot do without business exchanges of some kind, and transnational corporations fill this need today more or less adequately. Relatively autonomous forms of global business exchange seem more likely to be efficient than forms of enterprise that are tightly and narrowly controlled or that are uniformly state owned. Yet the precise form and direction that international business should assume is always an open question. Over the centuries, long-distance economic exchanges have taken a variety of forms; and of firms there have been legions. Hence on the basis of past experience we cannot say that the form assumed by the need to coordinate markets and production in the 1970s (the transnational corporations with predominantly industrial interests, supported by multinational banks and other services) will necessarily still be the dominant form early in the next century. Indeed we can be quite sure that important changes are already in the making and that unanticipated ones are inevitable. Hence contemporary forms of interdependence are not necessarily embodiments of eternal verities, and even some reversions toward forms of more circumscribed interdependence are not inconceivable.

Approaches to Transnational Corporations

The field of international business is composed of a number of important and partly antagonistic interest groups, and its analysis must necessarily consider the interests and the world views of such groups. Without wishing to be excessively deterministic in this matter we might maintain for the sake of clarity of exposition that the field includes at least four important groups: corporations (represented by management), employees (both union and nonunion), home-country governments, and host-country governments.

In the present volume we have tried to assemble studies and expositions of views that adequately express the distinct outlook and approach toward multinational corporations of each of these groups. The corporate and management view, in addition to being expounded by industry and company spokesmen, tends to prevail in schools of business administration; it argues the case for economic liberalism but is not averse to accommodation of interests within precise boundaries of national regulation. This position is represented by contributions such as those of Kindleberger, Vernon, and Perlmutter. The labor view is identified with the interests of unions. Cox discusses it at some length. The home-country point of view is most clearly represented by the contributions of Gilpin; it is a view that tends to support national firms and asserts that strong links bind multinational firms to their home base. But it also asserts that the benefits accruing to the home country should be weighed in the light of the not inconsequential costs they might be creating. In this respect the view might lean toward neomercantilism. The host-country point of view sometimes considers attraction of foreign investment to be the universal remedy for all national ills, but also generally tends to be suspicious of foreign intrusions and inclines toward control and regulation. Third World supporters usually tend to express a pure host-country position, sometimes in the formal manner of legal analysis, as in Orrego's article, sometimes in international documents such as the Report of the Group of Eminent Persons, and sometimes in the more specialized theories of dependency and imperialism (Sunkel, Galtung, Amin).

The effort to be representative also has a geographical dimension, and thus we have brought together, in addition to contributions from the United States, contributions from Latin America (Sunkel, Orrego), Europe (Perroux, Galtung), and Africa (Amin), as well as articles that review the situation in Eastern Europe and in Southeast Asia, and articles that reflect the positions that have evolved within the United Nations system.

However, this effort does not exhaust the range of views to be considered. We must also admit the possibility of an analysis capable of reconciling all of these intrinsically valid positions and reaching a synthesis at the level of global public interest and optimal world order. The volume as a whole might be regarded as an approach toward such a synthesis—a synthesis finally to be accomplished in the mind of the reader.

A Preview of the Contents

We have grouped our collection of materials on transnational corporations in five areas of major interest.[6] Part I is descriptive and empirical. Excerpts from the report of the United Nations Secretariat provide basic data about the state of the multinational corporate world as of the early 1970s. The report describes the activities of corporations of the United States, Western Europe, and Japan, both in the industrialized and the developing worlds. The basic data from the United Nations report are supplemented by a glance into the past in the article by Gilpin, who persuasively advances the view that over the past few decades the emergence of the United States as a world power has been the necessary condition for the rapid growth of multinational corporations. Perlmutter proposes a useful classification of multinational companies and sees the prospects bright for enterprises that are "geocentric." Modelski takes a close look at the workings of the world's fifty largest industrial companies during the period 1955–1975 and confirms that global firms with high international content seem indeed to have done quite well during that time. The empirical orientation of the initial selections reflects the view, expressed throughout the volume, that the study of the impact of corporations demands a knowledge both of general propositions and of the history, identity, and future of individual corporations. That is why the names of some corporations keep recurring over and over again.[7] They are indexed at the end of this volume.

Part II is theoretical in orientation and examines the principal concepts in terms of which multinational corporations must be understood and studied. Kindleberger and Vernon analyze the basic concept of monopoly and the effects of innovation in national product markets. Blair uses the example of the international oil industry between 1945 and 1973 to illustrate the concept of concentration, and finds the methods of oligopolistic market control that operated in that industry during that period more sophisticated than the earlier explicit cartel arrangements. Perroux's "theory of the dominant economy" concerns the effects of domination in the world economy. Galtung (writing some two decades later) sought to conceptualize the influence of the developed countries (the Center) on the rest of the world (the periphery). Both the Perroux and the Galtung models attempt to explain the role played by and the influence wielded by enterprises based in the active zones of the world.

In Part III we examine the impact of the large firm on the world at large and on world-order values in particular. Here political and economic causal analysis is particularly useful. Frank Tannenbaum argues that international business is a force for peace, and Staley's analysis makes it clear that disputes over foreign investment are not likely to disturb relations among the major powers or create a threat to the peace at that level. The study of Gutman and Arkwright confirms this for Eastern Europe. Staley does show, however, that international investment activities may create certain problems between the major powers and the developing countries, and our three other selections illustrate several aspects of that situation, particularly in Latin America. Sunkel argues that the activities of foreign businesses help to maintain a condition of dependency. This point is clarified in the Senate study of ITT activities in Chile (selection 14). Müller suggests that the effect of corporate activity, based on some Latin American data, might be poverty rather than wealth.

If transnational corporations are indeed responsible for negative effects that are not automatically corrected through the play of market or other forces—and the power of large firms makes this less likely—then regulation, the subject of Part IV, is a way to respond to such problems. The past few years have seen a rapid expansion of regulatory activity, and much of it has been stimulated by the analyses of negative impact we have just mentioned. Indeed, the experience of Latin American countries has had remarkable influence on the regulatory activities of international bodies (in particular, the United Nations). Orrego's article, the Report of the Group of Eminent Persons, and the Charter of the Economic Rights and Duties of States are testimony to that influence. But in addition to the United Nations regulatory system, which seems to be concerned mainly with the problems of the developing countries, a second system of regulation has evolved through the Organization of Economic Cooperation and Development (OECD) for the harmonization of policies among the developed states. Keohane and Ooms discuss this policy trend, which has found expression in the recent OECD Declaration on International Investment and Multinational Enterprises. But Weinstein's contribution carries the warning that the implementation of regulatory designs sometimes confronts severe problems, especially in countries where such regulation is most needed.

Part V consists of a number of selections designed to help students of transnational corporations organize their thinking about the future. The point is made that thinking about preferred images of the world is in part, and in the strict sense of the word, wishful thinking. It is an effort to create a world to our liking, a world that would respond better to our interests. A disciplined effort at analysis of the future must synthesize a number of such images as they bear on transnational corporations and combine them with some more general conceptions of future world order. Gilpin, Macrae, Hymer, Amin, and Cox all attempt this feat, and the reader must form his own synthesis, even while allowing for the fact that the world inexorably keeps moving ahead in its own way. Although none of these projections includes a world that has no international business, none overlooks the possibility that the years ahead might be years of challenge and new adjustment for all those who work with and who try to think about transnational enterprises.

NOTES

1. In Don Wallace, Jr., ed. *International Control of Investment* (New York: Praeger, 1974), p. 127.
2. Saul Mendlowitz, ed. *On the Creation of a Just World Order* (New York: The Free Press, 1975), p. xiii.
3. Robert Gilpin, *U.S. Power and the Multinational Corporation* (New York: Basic Books, 1975), pp. 26 ff.
4. George Modelski, *Principles of World Politics* (New York: The Free Press, 1972), Introduction.
5. Robert O. Keohane and Joseph S. Nye, Jr., eds. "Transnational Relations and World Politics," *International Organization*, 25(3): Summer 1971.
6. In general, we have omitted the more specialized footnotes.
7. That is also why a useful student class project would be an in-depth study of one selected transnational enterprise and its impact on the world.

PART I

DESCRIPTION

INTRODUCTION

Knowledge of the world of business and of its impact on the world at large is to a substantial degree independent of knowledge of the theories that have been spun about business activities. The business world exists in large part irrespectively of the numerous concepts and theories that can be and have been applied to its understanding. Ultimately, and fundamentally, of course, such a clear-cut division between theory and reality cannot be maintained: what we perceive and what we know depend in turn on the validity of our theories and the strength of our concepts; but for practical purposes the division can be defended as a helpful expository device. This pool of empirical knowledge is in fact the common resource on which most observers of transnational business draw in their search for explanation and meaning.

A student of transnational enterprises, then, should acquire a store of basic information about:

1. How and where transnational enterprises operate.
2. The names and backgrounds of the most important of these corporations.
3. How changeable the world of business really is and how the fortunes of companies rise and fall.
4. The world order within which these enterprises function, and the historical circumstances from which they have emerged.

In 1972, the United Nations launched its own inquiry into the role and current situation of multinational corporations. According to the report of the Secretariat in New York which was used as a source of background information by the Group of Eminent Persons, whose recommendations we shall note in Part IV, multinationals are a global phenomenon. Even though the investment of United States firms is largest in volume, the firms of other countries are also active in this important field, and in some parts of the world, such as Africa and parts of Asia, they are more numerous and more important. The major part of all transnational business is located in the developed areas of North America, Western Europe, and Japan. Although only about one-third of all transnational corporate activity is conducted in the developing countries of the Third World, the political significance of that activity is greater than the proportion would suggest. Manufacturing accounts for about two-fifths of the total, all phases of the oil industry account for another third. Multinational banking, too, has grown spectacularly in recent years. International production, that is, the output of branches of transnational firms located outside the national base, is now a substantial proportion of the world product—possibly as high as one-fifth if the centrally planned economies are omitted from the calculation. Although these are global figures, an accurate picture of the situation must also include country-by-country variations; for instance, the extremely strong investment position of multinational firms (and in particular American firms) in Canada, and, by contrast, their rather weak position in Japan. There are also differences by industry; for example, multinationals invest heavily in petroleum refining and advanced technology, but not at all in public utilities or transportation, which were in earlier decades important fields for foreign investment. Finally, the role of multinationals in the centrally planned economies of the Soviet Union, Eastern Europe, and possibly even China, should not be ignored. But we should also bear in mind the necessity of keeping such a picture up to date, because the world, and international business conditions, are capable of rapid change.[1]

Students of transnational corporations will at some stage encounter the problem of definitions, and will find that a variety of terms are used to refer to what is basically one phenomenon. The United Nations study opens with a useful survey of definitions, which indicates that multinational activities require the physical presence of the corporation in a number of national jurisdictions, hence raising problems of supervision and control.

A classification scheme that has attracted considerable attention was described in an article by Howard V. Perlmutter of the Wharton School of Business at the University of Pennsylvania, which was published in 1968. Perlmutter proposes that firms be classified according to the attitudes and policies of their executives toward their international operations. He labels corporations either as "ethnocentric," "polycentric," or "geocentric," and these terms have proved useful in distinguishing among companies whose behavior might at first seen undistinguishable. Perlmutter himself is an enthusiast for geocentric enterprises; he sees them as a "new kind of institution" and views those building them as "the most important social architects of our time."

George Modelski, a specialist in international relations, demonstrates with the help of discriminant analysis that Perlmutter's notion that firms with large-scale international operations are likely to show greater viability over the long run was true for the world's fifty largest industrial firms in the period 1955–1975. He points out, too, that these large-scale international operations have yet to have a corresponding degree of international control (that is, non-national participation in decision-making). This article may also prove useful for the empirical information it makes available about those very large companies. For large corporations are not unlike countries: they have a history and an identity of their own, and to be understood, each of them needs to be known on its own terms. The most important and the most interesting among them are the global firms, that is, those with high international content. Familiarity with these principal actors of world business is as necessary as knowledge of the major powers and the important states is to the student of world politics.

Robert Gilpin describes the historical background of transnational corporations and the conditions of world order within which all transnational corporations have to operate. After reviewing the various positions with regard to the interdependence of political and economic relations at the global level, he concludes that politics determine economic activity, and that therefore, transnational actors are influenced by peculiar patterns of international politics. In the nineteenth century, Britain provided the political context within which free traders, bankers, railroad builders, and other investors could successfully engage in a considerable degree of transnational activity. More recently, Gilpin argues, multinational corporations have flourished because it has been in the best interest of the United States that they should do so and within the power of the United States to ensure that they do. He clearly implies that a change in the interests or the power of the United States would have a severe effect on transnational enterprises.

Gilpin (who teaches political science at Princeton University), an exponent of what might be described as the "politics in command" thesis, sees multinational corporations principally as the product, or the resultant, of a pre-existing structure of world order. Although he acknowledges the power of the oil companies, for instance, he tends to underplay their influence on world politics. We should take note of this view, for we shall wish to return to it later for some additional and qualifying observations.

Mira Wilkins's *The Emergence of Multinational Enterprise*[2] is a study of the international involvement of American business in 1914, on the eve of World War I and prior to the assumption of a world role by the United States, and may be consulted as an alternative to Gilpin's broad generalizations. A business historian, she shows how remarkably active American business was transnationally even at the beginning of this century. She points out that, in proportion to gross national product, overseas investment probably was as great in 1914 as it was to become after 1945. For her, it would seem, American multinationals loom large today because the United States economy too has become larger and more productive; but relatively speaking, multinationals are no more important today than they were two or three generations ago. American firms flourished in 1914 because the United States economy was buoyant and because its innovative products (such as electrical equipment, cars, and petroleum) were sought the world over and the supplies needed to produce them were also sought all over the globe. Her model is one of "autodetermination" of transnational economic activity. Such processes unfold as an expression of the strength of particular economies and of their characteristics as areas of growth. Such "active zones" also give rise to strong transnational interpenetration.

But before the reader fully accepts such a position, he should look in some detail at the data. Transnational business cannot be so easily separated from world politics. In 1914 United States enterprises prospered generally in what was then still the British system of world order, even though that system had by that time already lost most of its vitality. The historical affinities between New York and London, and the growing convergence of United States and British diplomatic positions, also meant that American firms were particularly strong in the English-speaking parts of the world: in Britain itself (still the premier economy then), and in Canada, Australia, India, South Africa, and such important outposts as Hong Kong and Shanghai. In other words, American enterprise found congenial the conditions of the later phase of *Pax Britannica,* and could thus negotiate with some success the transition from the British to the American system of world order. Neither Gilpin nor Wilkins intends to imply that the role of firms other than American should be ignored. The companies of Britain and other European countries flourished and competed in the years before 1914, but not all weathered well the period of the world wars.

The last step in attempting to understand how transnational corporations behave and decide in various contexts is to study a few individual corporations in some detail. To accomplish this objective we need accurate and interesting "biographical" studies of crucial firms, but considerations of space preclude the inclusion of selections on this subject. Histories commissioned by firms tend to concentrate on business problems at the expense of social and political insights. C. Wilson's *History of Unilever*[3] is a sober business history based upon company records, but as an account of the world's largest food and soap manufacturer it could have been written with more emphasis on the implications of such a role. Ida M. Tarbell's *History of the Standard Oil Company* (1904), on the other hand, remains to this day a classic radical critique of business enterprise and an example of the influence of pungent writing on the fortunes of business. No biographies of the transnational business leaders of the post-1945 era have so far been written, but the careers of such nineteenth-century pioneers of multinational enterprise as the Rothschilds, Vanderbilts, John D. Rockefeller, Friedrich Krupp, the Siemens brothers, the Nobels, and the McCormicks are worth remembering.

Among those readable and perceptive works that might be recommended as an introduction to the study of transnational corporations are popular books by Anthony Sampson. *The Sovereign State of ITT* (1973) is a fast-moving account of the history of one of the largest international corporations. In the early 1970s ITT attracted world-wide attention for its role in Chile and in the pay-off scandals that led to Watergate. Sampson notes the symbiotic relationship between this communications company and the world of international politics, and the crucial role of ITT's chief executive officers in molding the company's personality. *The Seven Sisters* (1975) tells the story of the large international oil firms, from the discovery of oil in Pennsylvania in 1859 to the victory of the Organization of Petroleum Exporting Countries in 1973-1974. Brief descriptions of the great oil companies and their leading personalities alternate with occasionally scathing comments on oil company and government policies. This is an excellent introduction to the oil giants and the world they built. Sampson's most recent book, *The Arms Bazaar* (1977), is a timely report on the international trade in arms—"of all industries the most global." Much of it is devoted to a description of the Lockheed bribery scandals, which gave rise to world-wide investigations into the unethical practices of multinational business, and to a call for new rules to control unethical practices.

NOTES

1. An update of the 1973 survey was brought out by the United Nations in 1978 *(TNCs in World Development: A Re-examination,* Publication E/C.10/38). Among the findings of this new report are the following:

    (1) The world stock of direct foreign investment grew by 80 percent between 1971 and 1976, at about the same rate as the GNPs of the developed market countries, hence somewhat slower than in the 1960s. Estimated at about $105 billion in 1967, it rose to 158 billion in 1971 and reached 287 billion by 1976.
    (2) Between 1967 and 1976 the United States' share of the world stock of direct foreign investment fell from 54 to 48 percent and that of the United Kingdom from 17 to 11 percent; Japan's share rose from 1 to 7 percent.
    (3) In the same period, foreign direct investment in the developing countries declined from about one-third to no more than about one-quarter of the total. This smaller share is now concentrated in a few of the larger countries, so that by 1975 Brazil, Mexico, India, Malaysia, and the OPEC countries accounted for just over one-half of all such investment.
    (4) The service sector (such as banking and advertising) made up about one-quarter of all TNC assets.

2. Cambridge, Mass.: Harvard University Press, 1970. See in particular Chapter X: "The Status of American International Enterprise in 1914."

3. London: Cassell, 1954–68 (three vols.).

1 / Multinational Corporations in World Development

United Nations

The upsurge in interest in the multinational corporation has been accompanied by an expansion of the vocabulary relating to it. The various terms and concepts used have often been developed to suit particular purposes at hand and are subject to individual preferences. In empirical research, moreover, which in most cases has to rely on data derived from administrative records in which the concepts are not uniform, differing definitions have been employed. A review and clarification of these concepts and definitions will help to avoid unnecessary controversy and facilitate an understanding of the true dimensions of multinational corporations.

Any description, however, of the dimensions of multinational corporations faces manifold problems. The difficulties stem not only from the limited availability of conventional data, but also from the fact that even when they are available the data do not adequately measure the phenomenon of multinational corporations. Neither the number, sales nor earnings of affiliates, nor capital flows and investment stock, particularly taken separately, can fully measure the size of the operations of the multinational corporation. The large incidence of inter-affiliate transactions and attendant transfer pricing can distort the real picture, as can other practices involving capitalization, accounting procedures and control of local resources. Until sufficient methodological work and collection of standard information has been carried out the figures must be treated with caution and their interpretation is subject to a considerable margin of uncertainty.

Definitions

While the terms "corporation," "firm" and "company" are generally used interchangeably, the term "enterprise" is sometimes preferred as clearly including a network of corporate and non-corporate entities in different countries joined together by ties of ownership. In the present context, "corporation" is not used as a legal term but rather in accordance with common usage as reflected in the wording of the Economic and Social Council resolution 1721 (LIII).

From United Nations Department of Economic and Social Affairs, *Multinational Corporations in World Development* (New York: United Nations, 1973), pp. 4–23. Some notes have been omitted, and the remainder renumbered in sequence. Figures have been renumbered.

The term "multinational" signifies that the activities of the corporation or enterprise involve more than one nation. Certain minimum qualifying criteria are often used in respect of the type of activity or the importance of the foreign component in the total activity. The activity in question may refer to assets, sales, production, employment, or profits of foreign branches and affiliates.

A foreign branch is a part of an enterprise that operates abroad. An affiliate is an enterprise under effective control by a parent company and may be either a subsidiary (with majority or sometimes as little as 25 percent control of the voting stock by the parent company) or an associate (in which case as little as 10 percent control of voting stock may be judged adequate to satisfy the criterion). In the broadest sense, any corporation with one or more foreign branches or affiliates engaged in any of the activities mentioned may qualify as multinational. More strictly, a particular type of activity (e.g. production), a minimum number of foreign affiliates (e.g. six), or a minimum foreign share of activity (e.g. 25 percent of sales or assets) may be added as conditions for qualifying for the definition.

Such concepts are amenable to further variations according to the main characteristics and motivations of multinational corporations and may be rather theoretical in character. Some authors emphasize the fact that, despite the growing importance of foreign activities, many corporations are basically home-country oriented concerns that operate abroad, and prefer the terms "international" or "transnational." On the basis of their orientation, corporations are also distinguished into "ethnocentric" (home-country oriented), "polycentric" (host-country oriented) or "geocentric" (world-oriented). When internationalism is taken to the limit the corporation may be considered "anational" and hence be referred to as "denationalized," "supranational" or a "cosmocorp."

Because of the broad frame of reference of this survey, in accordance with the terms of the Economic and Social Council resolution, the term "multinational corporation" is used here in the broad sense to cover all enterprises which control assets—factories, mines, sales offices and the like—in two or more countries. This definition has the advantage that no important aspect of the phenomenon (e.g. finance or services) or of the problem (e.g. questions associated with nationally oriented enterprises or small firms) is arbitrarily excluded. It also permits maximum and flexible use to be made of existing data which are variously defined and not generally amenable to reclassification to suit a more restricted definition. At the same time, as the data that follow will indicate, there is a very high degree of concentration in multinational corporations, with a relatively few firms accounting for the bulk of their activities. Thus, a fairly good picture of the situation can frequently be obtained by concentrating on the largest and most important firms, especially those engaged in extractive and manufacturing activities.

One implication of the present definition is that multinational corporations are responsible for most foreign direct investment. Nevertheless, a study of multinational corporations must be distinguished from the study of foreign direct investment, chiefly because the most important questions to be asked in connection with multinational corporations are not limited to and in some cases are even independent of financial flows. They concern a host of other activities also, such as the transfer of technology as well as goods, the provision of managerial services and entrepreneurship and related business practices, including co-operative arrangements, marketing restrictions and transfer pricing. As the operations of multinational corporations have expanded and evolved, the elements not directly related to the provision of capital have become increasingly important. Moreover, these operations can only be understood as components of an international corporate system. As will be demonstrated below, parent companies that own foreign-based enterprises typically control these enterprises' activities and determine the way in which financial, technical and managerial resources are allocated around the world and the resulting mix of the entire package.

Size, Patterns and Trends

Size and Concentration

Although quantitative information on multinational corporations leaves much to be desired and the wide disparities in methods of estimation among corporations, economic sectors and countries introduce a considerable margin of error in the interpretation of all the essential economic magnitudes, a few general characteristics are discernible. A central characteristic of multinational corporations is the predominance of large-size firms. Typically, the amount of annual sales runs into hundreds of millions of dollars. Each of the largest four multinational corporations has a sales volume in excess of $10 billion, and more than 200 multinational corporations have surpassed the one billion level.

Indeed, for most practical purposes, those with less than $100 million in sales can safely be ignored. [1] The very size of these corporations as compared with other economic entities, including the economies of many nations, suggests an important source of power. Moreover, there are strong indications that the multinational corporations have grown dramatically, especially during the last decade. As a result, both their absolute and relative size has expanded.

Closely related to their large size is the predominantly oligopolistic character of multinational corporations. [2] Typically, the markets in which they operate are dominated by a few sellers or buyers. Frequently they are also characterized by the importance of new technologies, or of special skills, or of product differentiation and heavy advertising, which sustains or reinforces their oligopolistic nature.

Another characteristic of the very large multinational corporation is their tendency to have a sizeable cluster of foreign branches and affiliates. Although almost half of some 7,300 multinational corporations have affiliates in one country only, nearly 200 multinational corporations, among the largest in the world, have affiliates in twenty or more countries. The establishment of subsidiaries or the making of foreign investments, particularly in industries in which there is a high degree of industrial concentration, generally tends to be bunched in periods of relatively strong economic activity. These activities frequently reflect the need to react to or counter the activities of other multinational corporations.

A further central characteristic of multinational corporations is that they are in general the product of developed countries. Although the non-availability of statistical information on multinational corporations in many developing countries obscures the over-all picture, this fact in itself reflects the high degree of concentration of the location of parent companies in the developed countries. Eight of the 10 largest multinational corporations are based in the United States. All in all, the United States alone accounts for about a third of the total number of foreign affiliates, and together with the United Kingdom, the Federal Republic of Germany and France, it accounts for over three-quarters of the total.

The high degree of concentration of the origin of multinational corporations in the developed countries is even more clearly revealed by the distribution of the stock of foreign direct investment as measured by estimated book value. Of a total estimated stock of foreign investment of about $165 billion, most of which is owned by multinational corporations, the United States accounts for more than half, and over four-fifths of the total is owned by four countries, the United States, the United Kingdom, France and the Federal Republic of Germany.

Moreover, foreign direct investment tends to be concentrated in a few firms within each home country. For the United States, about 250 to 300 firms account for over 70 percent. For the United Kingdom, over 80 percent of the total is controlled by 165 firms. For the Federal Republic of Germany, 82 firms control over 70 percent and the nine largest foreign investors alone control 37 percent of the total. In the case of Japan, although there are some giant firms active abroad, many small firms appear to have participated in foreign investment activities.

The size of affiliates varies with the sector and area of operation. In the natural resources sector, for example, affiliates appear to be three to four times larger than in manufacturing. In the petroleum sector and in trade the average size of affiliates is somewhat larger in developing countries than in developed. In manufacturing, the size of affiliates in developing countries is only half that in developed, whereas in public utilities it is double.

Some changes in this pattern appear to have occurred over the last two decades. The size of United States affiliates in developed market economies doubled between 1950 and 1966. In the European Community the increase was almost threefold and in Japan more than fourfold. On the other hand, no change was recorded in the average size of United

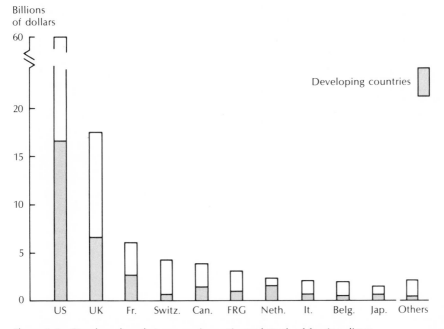

Figure 1-1 Developed market economies: estimated stock of foreign direct investment by country of origin and area of investment, end 1967.

States affiliates in developing countries, except in Africa where the United States presence had previously been very limited. A similar trend suggests itself among United Kingdom affiliates, where an increase in average size in the developed market economies has not been matched by an increase in the size of affiliates in developing countries. The pattern reflects the fact that affiliates in developing countries often serve the local markets only, especially in the case of import-substituting manufactures, while the relatively larger affiliates in developed countries frequently serve bigger regional as well as national markets.

The dramatic growth of multinational corporations in the postwar period has been accompanied by unprecedented growth in the number of affiliates, the levels of capital flow and the stock of investment. Between 1950 and 1966, the number of United States affiliates increased three times, from 7,000 to 23,000. The number of affiliates of the 187 main United States multinational manufacturing corporations increased almost 3.5 times during the same period. The growth of United Kingdom affiliates during this period was less dramatic, possibly a reflection, among other factors, of the sluggish growth of the economy and the longer history in the United Kingdom of direct investment abroad. In the first twenty years after the Second World War, the number of affiliates less than

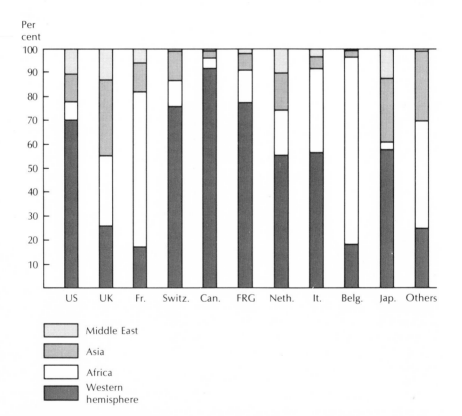

Figure 1-2 Developed market economies: distribution of estimated stock of foreign direct investment by developing region, end 1967. (Percentage distribution.)

doubled. In contrast, the more recent entry of Japan into the field has been marked by a rapid rate of growth in the number of affiliates. Although no precise data exist, there are indications that the growth of French affiliates was somewhat higher than those of the United Kingdom, while affiliates of the Federal Republic of Germany are growing more rapidly than those of the United States.

The growth of foreign affiliates has been accompanied by an increase in direct investment and the accumulated stock of foreign direct investment. During the last decade, the flow of direct investment from 13 countries of the Organization for Economic Co-operation and Development rose from $2.9 billion to $7.9 billion a year. Among the countries with an above-average rate of increase were Japan, the Federal Republic of Germany, Italy, the Netherlands and the Scandinavian countries.

The growth of investment flow has been reflected in the increase in its cumulative stock. Between 1960 and 1971, the book value of United States direct investment increased from $33 to $86 billion and that of the United Kingdom from $12 to $24 billion. The most dramatic increase, from less than $300 million to approximately $4.5 billion, was registered by Japan—a fifteenfold rise. Recent indications show that this pace has continued if not accelerated. Almost equally impressive was the performance of the Federal Republic of Germany, which exhibited an almost tenfold increase of investment stock to $7.3 billion by 1971.

Geographical Distribution

Although the network of multinational corporations is world-wide, the bulk of their activities is located in the developed market economies. Over two-thirds of the estimated book value of foreign direct investment is located in this area where the advanced economic level and similarities in institutional and social structures have facilitated the spread of the multinational corporate system.

Although the developing countries have received only about a third of the total estimated stock of foreign direct investment, that is, only half as much as the developed countries, the presence of foreign multinational corporations in the developing countries is generally of greater relative significance, since their economies account for much less than half of that of developed market economies.

Among the developing countries, the western hemisphere has attracted an estimated 18 percent of the total stock of foreign direct investment, Africa 6 percent, and Asia and the Middle East 5 and 3 percent, respectively. The distribution of affiliates (links) is roughly similar. Country variations reveal certain special relationships between the multinational corporations of some developed market economies and countries of investment.

The corporations of some of the smaller European countries with no colonial experience, such as Austria, Switzerland and the Scandinavian countries, have a limited spread in the developing world. Faced apparently with a limited domestic market, and at times with trade barriers, corporations in these countries have invested in other developed countries with a view to enlarging the market for their products. On the other hand, the developing countries' share in the number of affiliates as well as the estimated stock of investment is relatively high for Portugal, France, the United Kingdom, Italy, Belgium and the Netherlands. This pattern of distribution reflects the importance of former colonial ties. Thus, two-thirds of the French and Belgian affiliates in developing countries are in Africa, most of them in French-speaking countries. The more balanced distribution of the network of affiliates and stock of investment of the United Kingdom parallels to a large extent the geographical spread of the Commonwealth. One third of United Kingdom affiliates, for instance, are in developing countries, 40 percent of them in Africa and 32 percent in Asia. Of the total stock of United Kingdom direct investment, 38 percent is in developing countries and is similarly geographically diversified. Sixty percent of it is equally distributed between Asia and Africa, 26 percent is in the western hemisphere and 13 percent—above the average of 9.5 for all Development Assistance Committee countries—is in the Middle East. The Japanese presence in the developing countries is also pronounced. Sixty percent of affiliates and investment stock is located in these countries, with a strong concentration in Central and South America and Asia. Central and South America is also the preferred region for affiliates as well as book value of investment in the case of the Federal Republic of Germany. Canada, in particular, and Switzerland also, shows a high concentration in the developing countries of the western hemisphere, while the Australian presence is felt almost exclusively in Asia.

A little more than one-quarter of United States affiliates and of the stock of direct investment is located in developing countries. Central and South America account for about 70 percent of the number of United States affiliates and of the book value of investment in developing countries, with the rest more or less equally distributed among Africa, Asia and the Middle East.

Further light can be shed on this distribution of foreign direct investment among developing areas and the pattern of relationships between home and host countries by examining the distribution of investment by industrial sector.

Distribution by Industry: Natural Resources and Manufacturing

Historically, the activity of multinational corporations developed in the extractive and public utility areas before it became prominent in manufacturing. By the turn of the century, European and North American investors, attempting to secure their markets in petroleum, a field in which oligopolistic conditions were soon formed, had extended their vertical integration from the source of the supply to marketing. The entrenched United Kingdom and French positions in the Middle East were successfully challenged by United States corporations. Cartel arrangements concluded between multinational corporations before the Second World War were weakened in later years as the discovery of rich new fields in various parts of the world, in developing countries especially, encouraged the entry of new corporations into the field and brought about a large degree of market interpenetration among the largest multinational corporations in petroleum.[3] As the technology of production has become standardized and patents have expired, national corporations in developing countries, operating independently or in joint ventures with foreign multinational corporations, have been moving increasingly towards downstream vertical integration.

Market interpenetration and partnership have diluted the pre-war international cartels in other extractive industries also, but the growth of multinational corporations experienced in the petroleum sector has not been matched by most metal industries. Where technology, economies of scale and market control by the multinational corporations do not constitute formidable barriers, and the geographical distribution of the raw material source is limited, as in the case of copper, host countries have at times succeeded in increasing their participation or even wresting control from foreign multinational corporations. In other industries, such as aluminium, where not all these conditions are present, multinational corporations continue to play a primary role.

Manufacturing activities abroad, on the other hand, appeared later than operations in natural resources, either as the processing of raw materials or as the production of consumer goods. It appears that, initially, manufacturing operations increased faster in developed countries, later in developing countries, and in the last ten years their growth has again been more dynamic in developed countries, especially in western Europe. Industrial sectors involving high technical skills have witnessed the fastest growth.

Manufacturing is at present the major activity of multinational corporations. It represents a little more than 40 percent of the total estimated stock of foreign direct investment of the main developed market economies. Petroleum accounts for 29 percent, mining and smelting for 7 percent and other industries for 24 percent. A similar picture emerges from the distribution of United States affiliates among industrial sectors.

There is an asymmetry in the industrial distribution of multinational corporation activities in developed and developing countries. Whereas in developing countries half of the estimated stock of investment is in extractive industries and a little more than a quarter in manufacturing, in developed market economies half of it is in manufacturing, and about 30 percent is in extractive industries. [4]

Within a particular industrial sector, pronounced concentration in a few home countries is evident. Four-fifths of the estimated stock of investment in petroleum and in manufacturing originates in the United States and the United Kingdom.

Significant variations exist among major investing countries in the distribution of the stock of investment by sector. Although the largest investing countries, namely the United States and the United Kingdom, have a similar pattern in industrial distribution (one-third in extractive industries and 40 percent in manufacturing) both Japan and the Federal Republic of Germany show a different pattern of concentration; the former in trade and extractive industries, the latter in manufacturing. Japan's foreign direct investment appears to be aimed at securing raw material sources and export markets for the parent corporations. Even its investment in manufacturing (one quarter of the total) is relatively heavily concentrated in lightly processed raw materials such as lumber and pulp and low technology industries such as textiles and steel and non-ferrous metals. In contrast to the Japanese structure, almost 80 percent of the foreign direct investment of the Federal Republic of Germany is in manufacturing and high technology products such as chemicals, electrical products and transport equipment. When compared with the

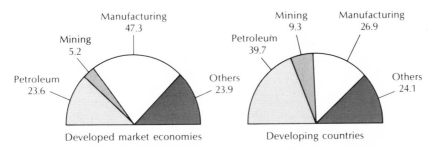

Figure 1-3 Developed market economies: estimated distribution of estimated stock of foreign direct investment by sector and area, end 1966. (Percentage distribution.)

dominant position of the United States and the United Kingdom in petroleum, the Federal Republic of Germany's investment in this area is almost negligible (3 percent in petroleum and 5 percent in mining).[5]

Concentration in high technology industries is also a characteristic of United States investment and to a lesser extent that of the United Kingdom. Chemicals, machinery, electrical products and transport equipment account for half of all the manufacturing investment of the United Kingdom and almost 60 percent of that of the United States. The technological strength of United States multinational corporations in the major chemical and automotive industries has given that country a dominant position in these fields. Much of the expansion of United States manufacturing affiliates abroad has been in the production of "skill-oriented" products, in which research and development is relatively a high percentage of sales and where an oligopolistic structure is prevalent.[6]

Multinational corporations have also been active recently in the service sector, especially in banking, tourism and consulting. Banking in particular has grown spectacularly in recent years. Between 1965 and 1972, United States banks more than tripled their foreign locations from 303 to 1,009. In 1972 alone, United States banks opened 106 foreign locations (i.e. branches, representative offices and agencies, affiliates and subsidiaries) while in the same year Japanese banks opened 25 new facilities, bringing the total to 145. The total number of foreign facilities of United Kingdom banks in 1972 amounted to

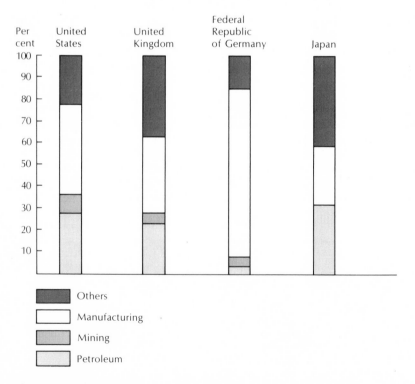

Figure 1-4 Selected developed market economies: stock of foreign direct investment by sector, 1970. (Percentage distribution.)

192, those of the Federal Republic of Germany to 103 and those of France to 91. Foreign deposits represent an increasing share of total deposits of United States multinational banks. For example, for the larger New York-based banks foreign deposits increased from 8.5 percent of the domestic deposits in 1960 and 33.6 percent in 1968 to 65.5 percent in 1972.[7]

The expansion of the Eurocurrency market to $100 billion by the end of 1972, coupled with the phenomenal expansion of overseas branches, especially of United States banks, provides a readily available source of funds that can be shifted internationally, as well as the mechanism through which such shifts can be made. At the same time, they provide an important source of credit in several areas of the world, over and above what can be supplied by local banks. . . .

Ownership Patterns

By and large, multinational corporations exercise effective control over their foreign affiliates through complete or majority ownership, although at times such control can be exercised from a minority position. At least 80 percent of United States affiliates and 75 percent of United Kingdom affiliates are either wholly owned or majority-controlled. In terms of stock of investment, these two countries have placed about 90 percent in affiliates which are at least majority-owned. This desire for majority ownership and control appears to be a general characteristic of multinational corporations from other home countries, except in the case of Japanese multinational corporations, where a somewhat more sizeable proportion of affiliates and stock of investment are minority-owned joint ventures. This difference in the ownership pattern is apparently influenced by differences in methods of control as well as in the industrial and the geographical distribution of foreign activities. The predominance of trading activities and light industries in the case of Japanese multinational corporations suggests that relatively small affiliates may be adequate in many cases. Moreover, since a relatively high proportion of Japanese investment— made mostly in recent years—is located in developing countries, the ownership pattern may also have been influenced by a tendency of some Japanese multinational corporations to maintain a relatively low profile in some of those countries. This geographical influence on ownership patterns is also suggested by the somewhat lower share of wholly owned affiliates in the total number of affiliates of United States corporations in developing countries as compared with that in developed countries. Over the last three decades, a slight increase in the proportion of minority ownership, particularly in developing countries, is suggested by United States data. There is also an indication that the longer the life of an affiliate, the more likely is it to be wholly owned. This tendency can, of course, be offset by pressures from host countries, as exemplified by recent trends toward increased local ownership in the OPEC and other countries.

Dimensions in the World Spectrum

The enormous size and steadily growing importance of multinational corporations are clearly revealed when viewed in the context of world economic activities. Although the usual comparison of gross annual sales of multinational corporations with gross national product of countries exaggerates the relative importance of the activities of multinational corporations, the general conclusion that many multinational corporations are bigger than a large number of entire national economies remains valid. Thus, the value added by each of the top ten multinational corporations in 1971 was in excess of $3 billion—or greater than the gross national product of over 80 countries. The value added of all multinational corporations, estimated roughly at $500 billion in 1971, was about one-fifth of world gross national product, not including the centrally planned economies.

International production, defined as production subject to foreign control or decision and measured by the sales of foreign affiliates of multinational corporations has surpassed trade as the main vehicle of international economic exchange. It is estimated that international production reached approximately $330 billion in 1971.[8] This was somewhat larger than total exports of all market economies ($310 billion).

Since the rate of growth of international production is estimated to have exceeded that of world gross domestic product or world exports, an increasing share of world output would be generated by the foreign production of multinational corporations if recent trends were to continue.[9] However, future developments will depend very much on the extent to which the problems raised by the operations of multinational corporations are dealt with by appropriate national and international measures which will permit continued growth in desired areas and directions, or by restrictive measures which will obstruct further growth. In addition, changing relationships between different groups of countries, for example increased co-operation and exchange between developed market economies and centrally planned economies, will influence the direction of multinational corporation activities.

Dimensions in Developed Market Economies

If the world-wide integrative role of the multinational corporation is debatable, its importance to the interrelationship of the developed market economies is beyond doubt. Most of the developed market economies serve simultaneously as home and host countries. The United States, however, acts primarily as a home country, while certain others, such as Cyprus, Greece, Spain, Turkey, New Zealand and South Africa, are almost exclusively hosts to foreign multinational corporations.

During the period 1968-1970, inward direct investment flows were on the average only 20 percent of the outward flows for the United States, 30 percent for Japan, 63 percent for the United Kingdom and the Federal Republic of Germany and 90 percent for the Netherlands. The reverse is the case with most of the other countries. In France inward direct investment flows were almost twice as high as the outward flows, in Italy and Canada a little more than twice, in New Zealand, three times higher, in Belgium, four times and in Australia, Spain, Portugal and South Africa, 7.5 to 12 times greater than outward flows.

As far as the United States is concerned, the preponderant position in the economy is occupied by domestic multinational corporations, rather than foreign multinational corporations whose presence is not as yet significant. More than one-third of the manufacturing output of the United States is represented by the top 187 United States multinational manufacturing corporations. In certain industrial sectors, such as automotive, pharmaceutical and fabricated metal products, the consolidated sales of these corporations account for more than three-fourths of the sales of all United States firms, and in petroleum refining, chemicals, rubber and electrical machinery, for more than one-half. A larger group, of 264 multinational corporations, is responsible for half of all United States exports of manufactures. In 1971, United States multinational corporations generated an outflow of capital of $4.8 billion for direct investment abroad and an inflow of approximately $9 billion in interest, dividends, royalties and management fees. Furthermore, given the practice of extensive local borrowing, their control of overseas assets is substantially higher than the book value of long-term equity and debt held abroad. [10]

In contrast, the relative importance of foreign multinational corporations in the United States is limited. Foreign investment in the United States, while far from negligible, is mainly portfolio investment. The European investment in the United States, for instance, is about as high as the United States investment in Europe; but whereas 80 percent of the latter is in direct investment, 70 percent of the European investment in the United States is in portfolio form, almost equally divided between stocks and bonds. Thus, the book value of United States direct investment in other developed countries, with the exception of the Netherlands, is several times higher than the book value of direct investment of those countries in the United States. [11] Multinational corporations from the United Kingdom, the Netherlands and Switzerland are the leading investors in the United States, accounting for about 60 percent of total direct foreign investment. Although European and, more recently, Japanese corporations have penetrated the petroleum industry, manufacturing and the service sector in the United States, there is no single industry in which they have assumed a preponderant role.

With the exception of Japan, the reverse is true in the case of the other developed economies, where foreign affiliates account for an important share of output, investment, employment or exports.

In Japan, where regulatory policies have restrained foreign entry, firms with foreign capital participation represented in 1968 only 2.3 percent of total fixed assets and 1.65 percent of total sales in manufacturing. The share was much higher in the oil industry (60 percent) and in rubber (19 percent). [12] Given the recent Japanese liberalization measures, the share of foreign affiliates (more than half of which are joint ventures) must certainly have increased.

In Canada, at the other end of the spectrum, the presence of foreign multinational corporations is pervasive, representing one-third of total business activity. Foreign affiliates account for 60 percent of manufacturing output and 65 percent of output in mining and smelting. The United States accounts for 80 percent of total direct foreign investment and the United Kingdom for most of the rest. In the United Kingdom, United States affiliates represent almost 70 percent of the total stock of foreign direct investment. They account for 13 percent of total manufacturing output, employ 9.2 percent of the labour force and are responsible for one-fifth of all manufacturing exports. [13] In Belgium, foreign affiliates are responsible for a quarter of the gross national product, one-third of total sales, 18 percent of employment and 30 percent of exports. More than half of the total foreign direct investment is accounted for by United States-controlled affiliates. [14] In the Federal Republic of Germany, Italy and France, foreign penetration is less pronounced, with the United States accounting for at least half of it, except in the case of France where its share is less than a third. [15]

The importance of multinational corporations in the developed market economies varies considerably by industrial sector. There is a high concentration in a fairly small number of industrial sectors characterized by fast growth, export-orientation and high technology, sectors which are also regarded as key sectors by the host countries. It appears that in most of the developed market economies foreign-owned firms own very high (75–100 percent) or high (50–75 percent) sector shares in industries characterized by high technology. Thus, there is very high or high foreign presence in the oil refining industry in Canada, the Federal Republic of Germany and Japan. Chemicals are under very high foreign ownership in Canada, high in Australia, and medium (25 to 50 percent) in the Federal Republic of Germany and Norway. The computer and electronics industries are under very high foreign ownership in the Federal Republic of Germany and the United Kingdom. Transport equipment is under very high foreign ownership in Canada and Australia, and medium in the United Kingdom. Electrical machinery is highly owned by foreign corporations in Austria, the Federal Republic of Germany and Canada.

The presence of United States multinational corporations is also more pronounced in some sectors than in others. For instance, they control more than half of the petroleum industry in Belgium, approximately three-fifths of the food, tobacco, oil-refining, metal manufacturing, instrument engineering, computer and technical manufacturing industries in the United Kingdom, and more than 15 percent of the production of semiconductors and 80 percent of computers and electronic data-processing equipment in the European Community. In the service sector, the United States presence is considerable in the hotel and recreation industries, consulting, public relations and banking. It is estimated that in 1970 there were more than 30 United States banks operating in Europe, many of them having established affiliates jointly with European banks.

Another indication of the importance of United States affiliates in developed countries is their share in the gross fixed capital formation of these countries. In Canada in 1970 it amounted to one-third, in the United Kingdom to one-fifth, in Belgium and Luxembourg and the Federal Republic of Germany to between 12 and 13 percent, and in France 6 percent. In certain industries, the share was much higher, e.g. in Canada it was more than 50 percent in chemicals, fabricated metals, machinery and transportation equipment.

Dimensions in Developing Countries

In 1968 developing countries accounted for about one-third of the book value of foreign direct investment as opposed to only one-sixth of world gross domestic product and one-fifth of world exports, not including centrally planned economies. Half of foreign direct investment in developing countries was in the development of natural resources, a little less than one-third in manufacturing and the rest in trade, public utilities, transport, banking, tourism and other services.

Generally speaking, the relative importance of the multinational corporation in developing countries is rising in the manufacturing and services sectors and declining in the primary industries, in particular those connected with agriculture (plantations). On balance, the overall importance of the multinational corporation is growing. As a source of the net flow of resources to developing countries, private direct investment flows from such corporations represented about one-fifth of the total in the 1960s. During the same period, this flow increased at an average annual rate of 9 percent. In 6 out of the 12 developing countries for which data were available, the stock of foreign direct investment increased faster than that of gross domestic product. In the second half of the 1960s, the slow growth of investment in some countries is attributable to the liquidation of foreign investment through nationalization.

54276

The relative size of the accumulated stock varies by industrial sector and country, and the share of foreign affiliates' activity in output, employment or exports varies accordingly. In some countries, the foreign content of the local economy is very high and at times concentrated in one sector, while in others it is less significant or more diversified.

In the Middle East, which accounts for 9.4 percent of the total foreign direct private investment in developing countries, petroleum accounts for approximately 90 percent of the total stock of foreign investment. [16] In South America (36 percent of the total), on the other hand, 39 percent of foreign investment is in manufacturing, 28 percent in petroleum and 10 percent in public utilities. In Africa (20 percent of the total), 39 percent is in petroleum, 20 percent in mining and smelting and 19 percent in manufacturing. In Asia (15 percent), manufacturing has attracted 30 percent, petroleum 22 percent and agriculture 18 percent of the total foreign investment stock. In Central America (19 percent of the total), manufacturing has attracted 31 percent, petroleum 16 and trade 13 percent of the total.

This aggregate picture, however, does not reveal the fact that multinational corporations have tended to concentrate in a few developing countries. Only a few developing countries have a stock of direct investment of more than $1 billion. Thus, Argentina, Brazil, India, Mexico, Nigeria, Venezuela and certain Caribbean islands, [17] account for 43 percent of the total stock of investment in developing countries, which is roughly the same proportion as that of their combined gross domestic product to the estimated total for all developing countries. According to OECD estimates for the end of 1967, in another 13 countries [18] in various developing regions the stock of investment was between $500 million and $1 billion, accounting for nearly another 30 percent of the total stock of investment in developing countries. This concentration is related to the sector in which foreign investment is predominant. In African countries and in Central and South American and Middle Eastern countries (Algeria, Libya, Nigeria, Zambia, Jamaica, Netherlands, Antilles, Trinidad and Tobago, Peru and Venezuela, Iran, Kuwait and Saudi Arabia), it is the extractive industries which predominate. In all these countries, the stock of investment in either petroleum or mining exceeds $200 million. In several other countries, manufacturing is the predominant sector, more than $200 million being invested in manufacturing in Argentina, Brazil, India, Mexico and the Philippines. In India and Malaysia, investment in agriculture exceeds $200 million.

The activities of United States multinational corporations represent half of the total stock of foreign direct investment in developing countries. In certain regions, however, such as Central and South America, the United States accounts for almost two-thirds of the total stock of foreign direct investment. The rest of the stock is represented by the United Kingdom (9 percent), Canada (7 percent), Netherlands (5 percent) and the Federal Republic of Germany (4 percent). In Africa, on the other hand, the United States accounts only for one-fifth of the total stock; the United Kingdom predominates with 30 percent, France following with 26 percent. Belgium, the Netherlands and Italy account for 7, 5 and 4 percent respectively. In the Middle East, the United States accounts for 57 percent, the United Kingdom for 27 percent and the Netherlands and France for approximately 5.5 percent each. In Asia, the United Kingdom has the largest share (41 percent), the United States follows with 36 percent, France with 7 percent and the Netherlands with 5 percent.

In some developing countries where the stock of investment exceeds $500 million, the foreign affiliates of a single developed market economy account for more than 80 percent of the stock of total investment. [19]

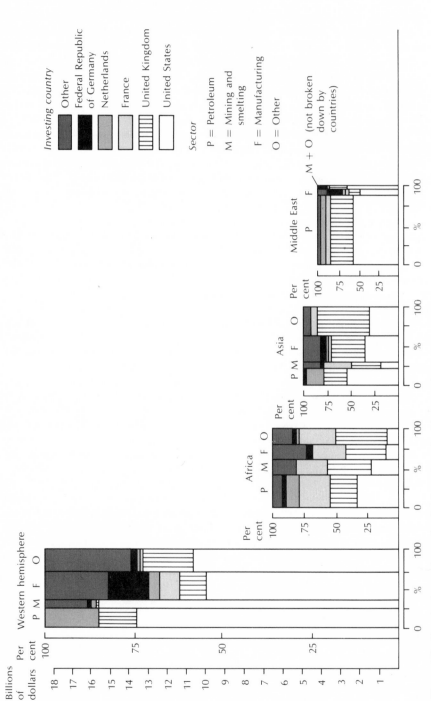

Figure 1-5 Developing regions: distribution of stock of foreign direct investment by sector and country of origin, end 1967. (Billions of dollars and percentage shares.)

Data on the share of foreign multinational corporations in local production is limited. In Singapore, in 1966, affiliates from the main investing countries are estimated to have contributed one-third of the total value added in manufacturing. [20] It has been estimated that in the mid-1960s, sales of United States enterprises alone represented 17 percent of the gross value of industrial production of Mexico, 13 percent of that of the Philippines and 11 percent of that of Argentina and Brazil. [21] In Central America, the output of foreign affiliates is estimated at 30 percent of the output of the manufacturing sector. Among the 500 largest manufacturing firms in Brazil, foreign affiliates controlled 37 percent of total assets. [22] In Mexico, among middle and large-sized firms, weighted average foreign participation reached 45 percent in 1970. Foreign participation in the output of Mexican manufacturing industries, however, reached 100 percent in rubber products and transportation materials, and a weighted share of more than 75 percent in industrial chemicals and tobacco in 1970, while foreign participation in textile production was only 8 percent. [23]

Expenditures of multinational corporations on plant and equipment represent a varying share of the total gross fixed capital formation of developing countries. In 1970, the share of such expenditures by United States manufacturing affiliates was 9 percent in Mexico and 18 percent in Brazil. In some cases, such as electrical machinery in Brazil, the expenditure of United States affiliates on plant and equipment accounted for more than half of the total fixed capital formation in the industry. [24]

In addition to their dominant role in the export of products of the extractive industries, multinational corporations are in general playing an increasingly important part in the export of manufactures from developing countries. [25] There is evidence of an overall increase in the exports of affiliates, both as a share of total sales and as a share of total exports by the host country.

Thus, exports of United States manufacturing affiliates in Central and South America accounted for 4 percent of their total sales in 1957, 7.5 percent in 1965 and 9.4 percent in 1968. [26] Their share in the total exports of manufactures from these regions, which was 12 percent in 1957, reached 41 percent in 1966. This share varies by country; thus, in Argentina, between 1965 and 1968, exports of United States affiliates accounted for 14.5 percent of total exports. In Mexico, in 1966, United States manufacturing affiliates accounted for 87 percent of exports of manufactures, and in Brazil they represented 42 percent.

Sporadic data suggest that despite their visibility and presence in key sectors, the contribution of foreign affiliates to the total gross domestic product of developing countries remains relatively small in most host countries. This is because the bulk of the gross domestic product of most developing countries originates in agriculture and the service industries where, on the whole, the presence of the multinational corporation is relatively limited.

Dimensions in Centrally Planned Economies

Although the centrally planned economies have attracted only a very small amount of direct investment and very few affiliates of multinational corporations, they are more involved in the activities of these corporations than a cursory examination of the standard data might indicate. The form in which the multinational corporations extend their operations in these economies differs from that taken in others. Equity participation in countries in which the private ownership of means of production is not congruent with the system is naturally uncommon. The major exceptions are a limited number of sales offices of multinational corporations and some minority participation, which is permitted by law in Romania and, on a very limited basis, in Hungary. [27]

Yet, apart from straightforward trade, the relationship between multinational corporations and the centrally planned economies has often involved co-operative arrangements in production, the development and transfer of technology, and marketing. Most of these arrangements are relatively recent in origin, reflecting the general trend in the centrally planned economies towards more outward-looking policies and a new emphasis on economic co-operation. Typically, a complex set of arrangements provides for technical help by the multinational corporation in plant construction (e.g. Occidental Petroleum and the proposed fertilizer complex in the USSR), exports and imports (e.g. the purchase by Occidental of the products of the plants, and sales to the USSR of Occidental products) and trade credit.

It has been estimated that there were about 600 industrial co-operation agreements with the developed market economies in force in Eastern European countries at the beginning of 1973. About one-third of these agreements have been concluded within the last two or three years, and continued fast growth is indicated. On the whole, these agreements account for a relatively small proportion of total trade with developed market economies. In some Eastern European countries, however, they already account for 10 to 15 percent of exports to the developed market economies in some branches of industry. In Hungary, for example, they are responsible for one-sixth of engineering exports to developed market economies. [28]

Similarly, while these agreements do not account for a significant share of the total output of Eastern European countries, they are important for certain branches. These are mostly industries requiring high technology or large investment. For example, over half of passenger automobile production in the USSR in 1975 is expected to come from Fiat, under one of the first industrial co-operation agreements negotiated with Italy. The current figure for Poland is two-fifths.

More recently, the role of multinational corporations in the exploitation of natural resources in the USSR has assumed particular importance. The copper project in Eastern Siberia being negotiated with multinational corporations would involve an investment of $1 to $2 billion, with an annual production of several hundred thousand tons. The natural gas project in Siberia, also involving the active participation of multinational corporations, would account for a major part of the entire natural gas production of the USSR by 1980. Moreover, as exports of these natural resources would continue to flow long after the initial foreign investments were paid off, import capacity would be correspondingly expanded. A further implication of these projects is that because of the vast outlay and the scope of activities involved, they will probably require the participation of very large multinational corporations or consortia of a number of them. Moreover, since many of these arrangements involve large deferred payments beyond the capacity of multinational corporations to finance, they will require finance from banks or export credit institutions.

Similar co-operative agreements have also been made between enterprises of the centrally planned economies and developing countries. Here, on the other hand, the centrally planned economies are usually the providers of technical aid, machinery and equipment and credits, to be paid off with the products of the newly set-up plant.

In recent years, such co-operation has become a rapidly growing source of development assistance from socialist countries. Among the socialist countries' main partners are

India and the countries of North Africa. Since 1971, there has been a tendency for a rapid spread to new partners in other regions and continents.[29]

NOTES

1. Raymond Vernon, *Sovereignty at Bay: The Multinational Spread of United States Enterprises* (New York, 1971), p. 4.
2. Frederick T. Knickerbocker, *Oligopolistic Reaction and Multinational Enterprise* (Boston, 1973).
3. The nine largest United States multinational corporations in petroleum had crude oil operations in 1938 in 40 countries and in 1967 in 96 countries. Over the same period their subsidiaries in all types of operations related to petroleum increased from 351 to 1,442. Vernon, *op. cit.,* p. 32.
4. Investment in petroleum in developed market economies is mainly in refining and distribution.
5. The radically different foreign direct investment structures of these countries reflect, to a certain extent, differences in endowments of factors and natural resources, in industrial competitiveness and in business traditions and orientation. In the case of Japan, the re-emergence of large trading companies and the desire to secure raw materials have played a determining role; in the case of the Federal Republic of Germany, the major factors were the competitive strength of the IG-Farben successor corporations and apparent disinterest in building up a major domestically owned petroleum industry (approximately 90 percent of the petroleum industry of the Federal Republic of Germany is foreign-owned).
6. Vernon, *op. cit.,* p. 63.
7. Frank Mastrapasqua, *U.S. Expansion via Foreign Branching: Monetary Policy Implications* (New York, 1973), pp. 23-25.
8. Estimates of international production made in the literature vary according to the methodology used. J. Polk, on the basis of sales associated with direct investment and portfolio investment, estimates international production at $420 billion for 1968. See Judd Polk, "The Internationalization of Production," mimeo (United States Council of the International Chamber of Commerce, 1969); J. Behrman, on the basis of sales associated with direct and portfolio investment as well as licensed rights, estimates international production at $450 billion for 1971. See J. N. Behrman, "New Orientation in International Trade and Investment," in Pierre Uri, ed. *Trade and Investment Policies for the Seventies: New Challenges for the Atlantic Area and Japan* (New York, 1971).

    Both authors, without adjusting for value added, evaluate the internationalized gross domestic product of market economies to be 23 percent for 1968 (Polk) and 22 percent for 1971 (Behrman). If the adjustment is made these shares would be considerably lower. S. Robock and K. Simmonds in calculating foreign production do not include portfolio investment or licensed rights; their figure for foreign production for 1970 is $230 billion, representing approximately 11 percent of market economies' gross domestic product. See S. H. Robock and K. Simmonds, *International Business and Multinational Enterprises* (Homewood, Illinois, 1973).
9. Whereas between 1961 and 1971 gross domestic product of market economies at current prices rose at an annual average rate of 9 percent, international production, estimated on the basis of sales at current prices of United States foreign affiliates between 1962 and 1968, rose at an annual average rate of about 13 percent.
10. United States net capital exports for direct investment abroad as a share of investment outlays of United States affiliates vary considerably by year, sector and area of investment. In 1968, in western Europe, the share was less than one-third; in a sample of 125 large multinational corporations (representing one-sixth of United States industry's ex-factory sales) only 6.7 percent of gross foreign investment was financed through a net capital

outflow from United States parent companies, the principal source being foreign depreciation reserves, earnings and borrowings. Business International, *The Effects of United States Corporate Foreign Investment, 1960–1970* (New York, 1972).

11. The United States' stock of direct investment in the European Community is 3.5 times higher than the Community's investment in the United States; it is 7 times more in the case of Canada and almost 70 times more in the case of Latin America. Rainer Hellmann, *The Challenge to United States Dominance of the Multinational Corporation* (New York, 1970).

12. Japanese Trade and Industry Ministry, *Special Report on Foreign Owned Firms in Japan* (Tokyo, 1968).

13. John Dunning, *United States Industry in Britain* (London, Economists' Advisory Group Research Study, Financial Times, 1972).

14. D. Van den Bulcke, *The Foreign Companies in Belgian Industry* (Ghent, Belgian Productivity Centre, 1973).

15. The foreign share in the total nominal capital of firms in the Federal Republic of Germany was 19 percent at the end of 1968, and in Italy in 1965 15 percent. In France, out of a total of $707 million of direct foreign investment in 1967, the United States accounted for 30 percent, the European Community countries for 29 percent, and Switzerland for 22 percent. G. Bertin, "Foreign investment in France," in *Foreign Investment: The Experience of Host Countries,* I. Litvak and C. Maule, eds. (New York, 1970).

16. The discussion on the distribution of stock of foreign direct investment in developing countries is based on rough estimates made by the Organization for Economic Co-operation and Development. See OECD, *Stock of Private Direct Investments by DAC Countries in Developing Countries, end 1967* (Paris, 1972).

17. Leeward Islands, Windward Islands, Bahamas, Barbados and Bermuda.

18. Algeria, Libya, Jamaica, Panama, Trinidad and Tobago, Chile, Colombia, Peru, Iran, Kuwait, Saudi Arabia, Malaysia and the Philippines.

19. In 1968, in Chile, Colombia, Panama, Peru, Philippines and Saudi Arabia, more than 80 percent of the stock of foreign investment was owned by United States affiliates. In Zaire, 88 percent of total investment was made by Belgian affiliates.

20. H. Hughes and You Poh Seng, eds., *Foreign Investment and Industrialization in Singapore,* (Canberra, Australian National University Press, 1969), p. 192.

21. Economic Commission for Latin America, *Economic Survey of Latin America* (United Nations publication, Sales No. E.72.II.G.1), p. 293.

22. F. Fajnzylber, *Sistema industrial y exportación de manufacturas: analisis de la experiencia brasilera,* Economic Commission for Latin America, November 1970.

23. See C. Vaitsos, "The changing policies of Latin American Governments towards economic development and direct foreign investment," forthcoming in *Journal of World Trade Law;* Carlos Bazdzeseh Parada, "La politica actual hacia la inversión extranjera directa," *Comercio Exterior* (Mexico City, 1972), p. 1012.

24. United States Senate, Committee on Finance, *Implications of Multinational Firms for World Trade and Investment and for United States Trade and Labor* (Washington, D.C., 1973).

25. The relative contribution of foreign affiliates may be affected by their orientation towards import substitution, which is enhanced by the restrictive tariff policies of host countries, and by the type of products manufactured in developing countries in connection with the global requirements of multinational corporations.

26. United States Department of Commerce, *United States Business Investment in Foreign Countries, 1960* (Washington, D.C. 1960); and *Survey of Current Business,* October 1970.

27. Yugoslavia is a special case. It was the first socialist country to permit minority participation by foreign enterprises. A constitutional amendment of 1971 goes so far as to offer a guarantee against subsequent expropriation and nationalization, once a joint venture contract has come into effect.

28. United Nations Economic Commission for Europe, *Analytical Report on Industrial Co-operation among ECE Countries* (mimeographed document, E/ECE/844, 14 March 1973).

29. For further information, see "Centrally Planned Economies and the International Development Strategy," in *Implementation of the International Development Strategy: Papers for the First Overall Review and Appraisal of Progress during the Second United Nations Development Decade,* vol. II (United Nations publication, Sales No. E.73.II.A.3).

2 / The Tortuous Evolution
of the Multinational Corporation

Howard V. Perlmutter

Four senior executives of the world's largest firms with extensive holdings outside the home country speak:

> *Company A:* "We are a multinational firm. We distribute our products in about 100 countries. We manufacture in over 17 countries and do research and development in three countries. We look at all new investment projects—both domestic and overseas—using exactly the same criteria."
>
> *Company B:* "We are a multinational firm. Only 1% of the personnel in our affiliate companies are nonnationals. Most of these are U.S. executives on temporary assignments. In all major markets, the affiliate's managing director is of the local nationality."
>
> *Company C:* "We are a multinational firm. Our product division executives have worldwide profit responsibility. As our organizational chart shows, the United States is just one region on a par with Europe, Latin America, Africa, etc., in each product division."
>
> *Company D (non-American):* "We are a multinational firm. We have at least 18 nationalities represented at our headquarters. Most senior executives speak at least two languages. About 30% of our staff at headquarters are foreigners."

While a claim to multinationality, based on their years of experience and the significant proportion of sales generated overseas, is justified in each of these four companies, a more penetrating analysis changes the image.

The executive from Company A tells us that most of the key posts in Company A's subsidiaries are held by home-country nationals. Whenever replacements for these men are sought, it is the practice, if not the policy, to "look next to you at the head office" and "pick someone (usually a home-country national) you know and trust."

The executive from Company B does not hide the fact that there are very few non-Americans in the key posts at headquarters. The few who are there are "so American-

From Howard V. Perlmutter, "The Tortuous Evolution of the Multinational Corporation." Reprinted with permission from the January–February 1969 issue of the *Columbia Journal of World Business.* Copyright © 1969 by the Trustees of Columbia University in the City of New York. Tables have been renumbered.

ized" that their foreign nationality literally has no meaning. His explanation for this paucity of non-Americans seems reasonable enough: "You can't find good foreigners who are willing to live in the United States, where our headquarters is located. American executives are more mobile. In addition, Americans have the drive and initiative we like. In fact, the European nationals would prefer to report to an American rather than to some other European."

The executive from Company C goes on to explain that the worldwide product division concept is rather difficult to implement. The senior executives in charge of these divisions have little overseas experience. They have been promoted from domestic posts and tend to view foreign consumer needs "as really basically the same as ours." Also, product division executives tend to focus on the domestic market because the domestic market is larger and generates more revenue than the fragmented European markets. The rewards are for global performance, but the strategy is to focus on domestic. His colleagues say "one pays attention to what one understands—and our senior executives simply do not understand what happens overseas and really do not trust foreign executives in key positions here or overseas."

The executive from the European Company D begins by explaining that since the voting shareholders must by law come from the home country, the home country's interest must be given careful consideration. In the final analysis he insists: "We are proud of our nationality; we shouldn't be ashamed of it." He cites examples of the previous reluctance of headquarters to use home-country ideas overseas, to their detriment, especially in their U.S. subsidiary. "Our country produces good executives, who tend to stay with us a long time. It is harder to keep executives from the United States."

A Rose by Any Other Name . . .

Why quibble about how multinational a firm is? To these executives, apparently being multinational is prestigious. They know that multinational firms tend to be regarded as more progressive, dynamic, geared to the future than provincial companies which avoid foreign frontiers and their attendant risks and opportunities.

It is natural that these senior executives would want to justify the multinationality of their enterprise, even if they use different yardsticks: ownership criteria, organizational structure, nationality of senior executives, percent of investment overseas, etc.

Two hypotheses seem to be forming in the minds of executives from international firms that make the extent of their firm's multinationality of real interest. The first hypothesis is that the degree of multinationality of an enterprise is positively related to the firm's long-term viability. The "multinational" category makes sense for executives if it means a quality of decision making which leads to survival, growth and profitability in our evolving world economy.

The second hypothesis stems from the proposition that the multinational corporation is a new kind of institution—a new type of industrial social architecture particularly suitable for the latter third of the twentieth century. This type of institution could make a valuable contribution to world order and conceivably exercise a constructive impact on the nation-state. Some executives went to understand how to create an institution whose presence is considered legitimate and valuable in each nation-state. They want to prove that the greater the degree of multinationality of a firm, the greater its total constructive impact will be on host and home nation-states as well as other institutions. Since multinational firms may produce a significant proportion of the world's GNP, both hypotheses justify a more precise analysis of the varieties and degrees of multinationality. However, the confirming evidence is limited.

State of Mind

Part of the difficulty in defining the degree of multinationality comes from the variety of parameters along which a firm doing business overseas can be described. The examples from the four companies argue that (1) no single criterion of multinationality such as ownership or the number of nationals overseas is sufficient, and that (2) external and quantifiable measures such as the percentage of investment overseas or the distribution of equity by nationality are useful but not enough. The more one penetrates into the living reality of an international firm, the more one finds it is necessary to give serious weight to the way executives think about doing business around the world. The orientation toward "foreign people, ideas, resources," in headquarters and subsidiaries, and in host and home environments, becomes crucial in estimating the multinationality of a firm. To be sure, such external indices as the proportion of nationals in different countries holding equity and the number of foreign nationals who have reached top positions, including president, are good indices of multinationality. But one can still behave with a home-country orientation despite foreign shareholders, and one can have a few home-country nationals overseas but still pick those local executives who are home-country oriented or who are provincial and chauvinistic. The attitudes men hold are clearly more relevant than their passports.

Three primary attitudes among international executives toward building a multinational enterprise are identifiable. These attitudes can be inferred from the assumptions upon which key product, functional and geographical decisions were made.

These states of mind or attitudes may be described as ethnocentric (or home-country oriented), polycentric (or host-country oriented) and geocentric (or world-oriented). While they never appear in pure form, they are clearly distinguishable. There is some degree of ethnocentricity, polycentricity or geocentricity in all firms, but management's analysis does not usually correlate with public pronouncements about the firm's multinationality.

Home Country Attitudes

The ethnocentric attitude can be found in companies of any nationality with extensive overseas holdings. The attitude, revealed in executive actions and experienced by foreign subsidiary managers, is: "We, the home nationals of X company, are superior to, more trustworthy and more reliable than any foreigners in headquarters or subsidiaries. We will be willing to build facilities in your country if you acknowledge our inherent superiority and accept our methods and conditions for doing the job."

Of course, such attitudes are never so crudely expressed, but they often determine how a certain type of "multinational" firm is designed. Table 2-1 illustrates how ethnocentric attitudes are expressed in determining the managerial process at home and overseas. For example, the ethnocentric executive is more apt to say: "Let us manufacture the simple products overseas. Those foreign nationals are not yet ready or reliable. We should manu-

Table 2-1 Three Types of Headquarters Orientation Toward Subsidiaries in an International Enterprise

Organization Design	Ethnocentric	Polycentric	Geocentric
Complexity of organization	Complex in home country, simple in subsidiaries	Varied and independent	Increasingly complex and interdependent
Authority; decision making	High in headquarters	Relatively low in headquarters	Aim for a collaborative approach between headquarters and subsidiaries
Evaluation and control	Home standards applied for persons and performance	Determined locally	Find standards which are universal and local
Rewards and punishments; incentives	High in headquarters low in subsidiaries	Wide variation; can be high or low rewards for subsidiary performance	International and local executives rewarded for reaching local and worldwide objectives
Communication; information flow	High volume to subsidiaries orders, commands, advice	Little to and from headquarters. Little between subsidiaries	Both ways and between subsidiaries. Heads of subsidiaries part of management team
Identification	Nationality of owner	Nationality of host country	Truly international company but identifying with national interests
Perpetuation (recruiting, staffing, development)	Recruit and develop people of home country for key positions everywhere in the world	Develop people of local nationality for key positions in their own country	Develop best men everywhere in the world for key positions everywhere in the world

facture the complex products in our country and keep the secrets among our trusted home-country nationals."

In a firm where ethnocentric attitudes prevailed, the performance criteria for men and products are "home-made." "We have found that a salesman should make 12 calls per day in Hoboken, New Jersey (the headquarters location) and therefore we apply these criteria everywhere in the world. The salesman in Brazzaville is naturally lazy, unmotivated. He shows little drive because he makes only two calls per day (despite the Congolese salesman's explanation that it takes time to reach customers by boat)."

Ethnocentric attitudes are revealed in the communication process where "advice," "counsel," and directives flow from headquarters to the subsidiary in a steady stream, bearing this message: "This works at home; therefore, it must work in your country."

Executives in both headquarters and affiliates express the national identity of the firm by associating the company with the nationality of the headquarters: this is "a Swedish company," "a Swiss company," "an American company," depending on the location of headquarters. "You have to accept the fact that the only way to reach a senior post in our firm," an English executive in a U.S. firm said, "is to take out an American passport."

Crucial to the ethnocentric concept is the current policy that men of the home nationality are recruited and trained for key positions everywhere in the world. Foreigners feel like "second-class" citizens.

There is no international firm today whose executives will say that ethnocentrism is absent in their company. In the firms whose multinational investment began a decade ago, one is more likely to hear, "We are still in a transitional stage from our ethnocentric era. The traces are still around! But we are making progress."

Host Country Orientation

Polycentric firms are those which, by experience or by the inclination of a top executive (usually one of the founders), begin with the assumption that host-country cultures are different and that foreigners are difficult to understand. Local people know what is best for them, and the part of the firm which is located in the host country should be as "local in identity" as possible. The senior executives at headquarters believe that their multinational enterprise can be held together by good financial controls. A polycentric firm, literally, is a loosely connected group with quasi-independent subsidiaries as centers—more akin to a confederation.

European multinational firms tend to follow this pattern, using a top local executive who is strong and trustworthy, of the "right" family and who has an intimate understanding of the workings of the host government. This policy seems to have worked until the advent of the Common Market.

Executives in the headquarters of such a company are apt to say: "Let the Romans do it their way. We really don't understand what is going on there, but we have to have confidence in them. As long as they earn a profit, we want to remain in the background." They assume that since people are different in each country, standards for performance, incentives and training methods must be different. Local environmental factors are given greater weight (see Table 2-1).

Many executives mistakenly equate polycentrism with multinationalism. This is evidenced in the legalistic definition of a multinational enterprise as a cluster of corporations of diverse nationality joined together by ties of common ownership. It is no accident that many senior executives in headquarters take pride in the absence of non-nationals in their subsidiaries, especially people from the head office. The implication is clearly that each subsidiary is a distinct national entity, since it is incorporated in a different sovereign state. Lonely senior executives in the subsidiaries of polycentric companies complain that: "The home office never tells us anything."

Polycentrism is not the ultimate form of multinationalism. It is a landmark on a highway. Polycentrism is encouraged by local marketing managers who contend that: "Headquarters will never understand us, our people, our consumer needs, our laws, our distribution, etc. . . . ."

Headquarters takes pride in the fact that few outsiders know that the firm is foreign-owned. "We want to be a good local company. How many Americans know that Shell and Lever Brothers are foreign-owned?"

But the polycentric personnel policy is also revealed in the fact that no local manager can seriously aspire to a senior position at headquarters. "You know the French are so provincial; it is better to keep them in France. Uproot them and you are in trouble," a senior executive says to justify the paucity of non-Americans at headquarters.

One consequence (and perhaps cause) of polycentrism is a virulent ethnocentrism among the country managers.

A World-Oriented Concept

The third attitude which is beginning to emerge at an accelerating rate is geocentrism. Senior executives with this orientation do not equate superiority with nationality. Within legal and political limits, they seek the best men, regardless of nationality, to solve the company's problems anywhere in the world. The senior executives attempt to build an organization in which the subsidiary is not only a good citizen of the host nation but is a leading exporter from this nation in the international community and contributes such benefits as (1) an increasing supply of hard currency, (2) new skills and (3) a knowledge of advanced technology. Geocentrism is summed up in a Unilever board chairman's statement of objectives: "We want to Unileverize our Indians and Indianize our Unileverans."

The ultimate goal of geocentrism is a worldwide approach in both headquarters and subsidiaries. The firm's subsidiaries are thus neither satellites nor independent city states, but parts of a whole whose focus is on worldwide objectives as well as local objectives, each part making its unique contribution with its unique competence. Geocentrism is expressed by function, product and geography. The question asked in headquarters and the subsidiaries is: "Where in the world shall we raise money, build our plant, conduct R&D, get and launch new ideas to serve our present and future customers?"

This conception of geocentrism involves a collaborative effort between subsidiaries and headquarters to establish universal standards and permissible local variations, to make key allocational decisions on new products, new plants, new laboratories. The international management team includes the affiliate heads.

Subsidiary managers must ask: "Where in the world can I get the help to serve my customers best in this country?" "Where in the world can I export products developed in this country—products which meet worldwide standards as opposed to purely local standards?"

Geocentrism, furthermore, requires a reward system for subsidiary managers which motivates them to work for worldwide objectives, not just to defend country objectives. In firms where geocentrism prevails, it is not uncommon to hear a subsidiary manager say, "While I am paid to defend our interests in this country and to get the best resources for this affiliate, I must still ask myself the question 'Where in the world (instead of where in my country) should we build this plant?' " This approach is still rare today.

In contrast to the ethnocentric and polycentric patterns, communication is encouraged among subsidiaries in geocentric-oriented firms. "It is your duty to help us solve problems anywhere in the world," one chief executive continually reminds the heads of his company's affiliates (see Table 2-1).

The geocentric firm identifies with local company needs. "We aim to be not just a good local company but the best local company in terms of the quality of management and the worldwide (not local) standards we establish in domestic and export production." If we were only as good as local companies, we would deserve to be nationalized."

The geocentric personnel policy is based on the belief that we should bring in the best man in the world regardless of his nationality. His passport should not be the criterion for promotion.

The EPG Profile

Executives can draw their firm's profile in ethnocentric (E), polycentric (P) and geocentric (G) dimensions. They are called EPG profiles. The degree of ethnocentrism, polycentrism and geocentrism by product, function and geography can be established. Typically R&D often turns out to be more geocentric (truth is universal, perhaps) and less ethnocentric than finance. Financial managers are likely to see their decisions as ethnocentric. The marketing function is more polycentric, particularly in the advanced economies and in the larger affiliate markets.

The tendency toward ethnocentrism in relations with subsidiaries in the developing countries is marked. Polycentric attitudes develop in consumer goods divisions, and ethnocentrism appears to be greater in industrial product divisions. The agreement is almost unanimous in both U.S.- and European-based international firms that their companies are at various stages on a route toward geocentrism but none has reached this state of affairs. Their executives would agree, however, that:

1. a description of their firms as multinational obscures more than it illuminates the state of affairs;

2. the EPG mix, once defined, is a more precise way to describe the point they have reached;

3. the present profile is not static but a landmark along a difficult road to genuine geocentrism;

4. there are forces both to change and to maintain the present attitudinal "mix," some of which are under their control.

Forces Toward and Against

What are the forces that determine the EPG mix of a firm? "You must think of the struggle toward functioning as a worldwide firm as just a beginning—a few steps forward and a step backward," a chief executive put it. "It is a painful process, and every firm is different."

Executives of some of the world's largest multinational firms have been able to identify a series of external and internal factors that contribute to or hinder the growth of geocentric attitudes and decision. Table 2-2 summarizes the factors most frequently mentioned by over 500 executives from at least 17 countries and 20 firms.

From the external environmental side, the growing world markets, the increase in availability of managerial and technological know-how in different countries, global competition and international customers, advances in telecommunications, regional political and economic communities are positive factors, as is the host country's desire to increase its balance-of-payments surplus through the location of export-oriented subsidiaries of international firms within its borders.

In different firms, senior executives see in various degrees these positive factors toward geocentrism: top management's increasing desire to use human and material resources optimally, the observed lowering of morale after decades of ethnocentric practices, the evidence of waste and duplication under polycentric thinking, the increased awareness and respect for good men of other than the home nationality, and, most importantly, top

Table 2-2 International Executives' View of Forces and Obstacles Toward Geocentrism in Their Firms

Forces Toward Geocentrism		Obstacles Toward Geocentrism	
Environmental	Intra-Organizational	Environmental	Intra-Organizational
1. Technological and managerial know-how increasing in availability in different countries	1. Desire to use human vs. material resources optimally	1. Economic nationalism in host and home countries	1. Management inexperience in overseas markets
2. International customers	2. Observed lowering of morale in affiliates of an ethnocentric company	2. Political nationalism in host & home countries	2. Nation-centered reward and punishment structure
3. Local customers' demand for best product at fair price	3. Evidence of waste and duplication in polycentrism	3. Military secrecy associated with research in home country	3. Mutual distrust between home country people and foreign executives
4. Host country's desire to increase balance of payments	4. Increasing awareness and respect for good men of other than home nationality	4. Distrust of big international firms by host country political leaders	4. Resistance to letting foreigners into the power structure
5. Growing world markets	5. Risk diversification in having a worldwide production & distribution system	5. Lack of international monetary system	5. Anticipated costs and risks of geocentrism
6. Global competition among international firms for scarce human and material resources	6. Need for recruitment of good men on a worldwide basis	6. Growing differences between the rich and poor countries	6. Nationalistic tendencies in staff
7. Major advances in integration of international transport & telecommunications	7. Need for worldwide information system	7. Host country belief that home countries get disproportionate benefits of international firms profits	7. Increasing immobility of staff
8. Regional supranational economic & political communities	8. Worldwide appeal of products	8. Home country political leaders' attempts to control firm's policy	8. Linguistic problems & different cultural backgrounds
	9. Senior management's long term commitment to geocentrism as related to survival and growth		9. Centralization tendencies in headquarters

management's own commitment to building a geocentric firm as evidenced in policies, practices and procedures.

The obstacles toward geocentrism from the environment stem largely from the rising political and economic nationalism in the world today, the suspicions of political leaders of the aims and increasing power of the multinational firm. On the internal side, the obstacles cited most frequently in U.S.-based multinational firms were management's inexperience in overseas markets, mutual distrust between home-country people and foreign executives, the resistance to participation by foreigners in the power structure at headquarters, the increasing difficulty of getting good men overseas to move, nationalistic tendencies in staff, and the linguistic and other communication difficulties of a cultural nature.

Any given firm is seen as moving toward geocentrism at a rate determined by its capacities to build on the positive internal factors over which it has control and to change the negative internal factors which are controllable. In some firms the geocentric goal is openly discussed among executives of different nationalities and from different subsidiaries as well as headquarters. There is a consequent improvement in the climate of trust and acceptance of each other's views.

Programs are instituted to assure greater experience in foreign markets, task forces of executives are upgraded, international careers for executives of all nationalities are being designed.

But the seriousness of the obstacles cannot be underestimated. A world of rising nationalism is hardly a precondition for geocentrism; and overcoming distrust of foreigners even within one's own firm is not accomplished in a short span of time. The route to pervasive geocentric thinking is long and tortuous.

Costs, Risks, Payoffs

What conclusions will executives from multinational firms draw from the balance sheet of advantages and disadvantages of maintaining one's present state of ethnocentrism, polycentrism or geocentrism? Not too surprisingly, the costs and risks of ethnocentrism are seen to out-balance the payoffs in the long run. The costs of ethnocentrism are ineffective planning because of a lack of good feed-back, the departure of the best men in the subsidiaries, fewer innovations, and an inability to build a high calibre local organization. The risks are political and social repercussions and a less flexible response to local changes.

The payoffs of ethnocentrism are real enough in the short term, they say. Organization is simpler. There is a higher rate of communication of know-how from headquarters to new markets. There is more control over appointments to senior posts in subsidiaries.

Polycentrism's costs are waste due to duplication, to decisions to make products for local use but which could be universal, and to inefficient use of home-country experience. The risks include an excessive regard for local traditions and local growth at the expense of global growth. The main advantages are an intensive exploitation of local markets, better sales since local management is often better informed, more local initiative for new products, more host-government support, and good local managers with high morale.

Geocentrism's costs are largely related to communication and travel expenses, educational costs at all levels, time spent in decision-making because consensus seeking among more people is required, and an international headquarters bureaucracy. Risks include those due to too wide a distribution of power, personnel problems and those of re-entry of international executives. The payoffs are a more powerful total company throughout, a better quality of products and service, worldwide utilization of best resources, improvement of local company management, a greater sense of commitment to worldwide objectives, and last, but not least, more profit.

Jacques Maisonrouge, the French-born president of IBM World Trade, understands the geocentric concept and its benefits. He wrote recently:

"The first step to a geocentric organization is when a corporation, faced with the choice of whether to grow and expand or decline, realizes the need to mobilize its resources on a world scale. It will sooner or later have to face the issue that the home country does not have a monopoly of either men or ideas. . . .

"I strongly believe that the future belongs to geocentric companies. . . . What is of fundamental importance is the attitude of the company's top management. If it is dedicated to 'geocentrism,' good international management will be possible. If not, the best men of different nations will soon understand that they do not belong to the 'race des seigneurs' and will leave the business."

Geocentrism is not inevitable in any given firm. Some companies have experienced a "regression" to ethnocentrism after trying a long period of polycentrism, of letting subsidiaries do it "their way." The local directors built little empires and did not train successors from their own country. Headquarters had to send home-country nationals to take over. A period of home-country thinking took over.

There appears to be evidence of a need for evolutionary movement from ethnocentrism to polycentrism to geocentrism. The polycentric stage is likened to an adolescent protest period during which subsidiary managers gain their confidence as equals by fighting headquarters and proving "their manhood," after a long period of being under headquarters' ethnocentric thumb.

"It is hard to move from a period of headquarters domination to a worldwide management team quickly. A period of letting affiliates make mistakes may be necessary," said one executive.

Window Dressing

In the rush toward appearing geocentric, many U.S. firms have found it necessary to emphasize progress by appointing one or two non-nationals to senior posts—even on occasion to headquarters. The foreigner is often effectively counteracted by the number of nationals around him, and his influence is really small. Tokenism does have some positive effects, but it does not mean geocentrism has arrived.

Window dressing is also a temptation. Here an attempt is made to demonstrate influence by appointing a number of incompetent "foreigners" to key positions. The results are not impressive for either the individuals or the company.

Too often what is called "the multinational view" is really a screen for ethnocentrism. Foreign affiliate managers must, in order to succeed, take on the traits and behavior of the ruling nationality. In short, in a U.S.-owned firm the foreigner must "Americanize"—not only in attitude but in dress and speech—in order to be accepted.

Tokenism and window dressing are transitional episodes where aspirations toward multinationalism outstrip present attitudes and resources. The fault does not lie only with the enterprise. The human demands of ethnocentrism are great.

A Geocentric Man—?

The geocentric enterprise depends on having an adequate supply of men who are geocentrically oriented. It would be a mistake to underestimate the human stresses which a geocentric career creates. Moving where the company needs an executive involves major adjustments for families, wives and children. The sacrifices are often great and, for some families, outweigh the rewards forthcoming—at least in personal terms. Many executives find it difficult to learn new languages and overcome their cultural superiority complexes, national pride and discomfort with foreigners. Furthermore, international careers can be hazardous when ethnocentrism prevails at headquarters. "It is easy to get lost in the world of the subsidiaries and to be 'out of sight, out of mind' when promotions come up at headquarters," as one executive expressed it following a visit to headquarters after five years overseas. To his disappointment, he knew few senior executives. And fewer knew him!

The economic rewards, the challenge of new countries, the personal and professional development that comes from working in a variety of countries and cultures are surely incentives, but companies have not solved by any means the human costs of international mobility to executives and their families.

A firm's multinationality may be judged by the pervasiveness with which executives think geocentrically—by function, marketing, finance, production, R&D, etc., by product division and by country. The takeoff to geocentrism may begin with executives in one function, say marketing, seeking to find a truly worldwide product line. Only when this worldwide attitude extends throughout the firm, in headquarters and subsidiaries, can executives feel that it is becoming genuinely geocentric.

But no single yardstick, such as the number of foreign nationals in key positions, is sufficient to establish a firm's multinationality. The multinational firm's route to geocentrism is still long because political and economic nationalism is on the rise, and, more importantly, since within the firm ethnocentrism and polycentrism are not easy to overcome. Building trust between persons of different nationality is a central obstacle. Indeed, if we are to judge men, as Paul Weiss put it, "by the kind of world they are trying to build," the senior executives engaged in building the geocentric enterprise could well be the most important social architects of the last third of the twentieth century. For the institution they are trying to erect promises a greater universal sharing of wealth and a consequent control of the explosive centrifugal tendencies of our evolving world community.

The geocentric enterprise offers an institutional and supra-national framework which could conceivably make war less likely, on the assumption that bombing customers, suppliers and employees is in nobody's interest. The difficulty of the task is thus matched by its worthwhileness. A clearer image of the features of genuine geocentricity is thus indispensable both as a guideline and as an inviting prospect.

3 / International Content and Performance Among the World's Largest Corporations

George Modelski

The present study[1] reports on the experience of firms that, in 1955 and in 1975, were ranked the fifty largest industrials in the world's market economies. It draws attention to the fact that by 1975 most of the world's biggest firms had acquired a substantial degree of international content and were, in fact, transnational enterprises; it also demonstrates, by means of discriminant analysis, that high international content has been one of the characteristics distinguishing high-performance firms from others.

The world's fifty largest industrial corporations, which we propose to describe and analyze here, are so substantial in scale that they alone constitute a tangible portion of global industrial capacity. A conservative estimate is that they contributed, in 1975, between 10 and 15 percent of the industrial output of the market economies (which is the United Nations term for the world outside the Soviet Union, Eastern Europe, and China) and that they alone might control as much as one-third of all international investment. Although such figures cannot, by their nature, be guaranteed, they do indicate that the fifty companies are a significant population among world firms and as such deserve close study. Because "the predominance of large-scale firms [is] . . . the central characteristic of multinational corporations,"[2] this study is of particular importance to those interested in transnational enterprises and in the special problems arising from the regulation of large-scale businesses.

In focusing on large firms we need not accept the view that the largest firms are also necessarily the most interesting, the most enterprising or innovating, or the fastest growing. Quite the contrary, experience shows that the mature giants of industry tend also to be among the more cautious and conservative of firms; they tell us less about the frontiers of innovation than about the average trends of the world economy. But the big firms are also certain to be among the most prominent and visible, they are likely to set the tone for much of business activity, and they are also likely to be among the politically most influential.

Table 3-1 The World's Fifty Largest Independent Industrial Companies, 1975

Rank 1975	Company	Incorp. Founda-tion	Headquarters	Sales[a] ($ US	Net Income[a] Millions)	Industry Group
1	Exxon	1882	New York	44,865	2,503	Oil
2	General Motors	1908	Detroit	35,725	1,253	Auto
3	Royal Dutch-Shell	1906	London/The Hague	32,105	2,111	Oil
4	Texaco	1902	New York	24,507	831	Oil
5	Ford Motor	1903	Dearborn, Mich.	24,009	323	Auto
6	Mobil Oil	1882	New York	20,620	810	Oil
7	National Iranian Oil	1951	Tehran	18,855	16,947	Oil
8	British Petroleum	1909	London	17,286	369	Oil
9	Standard Oil of Calif.	1879	San Francisco	16,822	773	Oil
10	Unilever	1907	London/Rotterdam	15,016	332	Consumer
11	Int. Business Machines	1911	Armonk, N.Y.	14,437	1,990	Electronics
12	Gulf Oil	1907	Pittsburgh	14,268	700	Oil
13	General Electric	1880	Fairfield, Conn.	13,399	581	Electrical
14	Chrysler	1925	Highland Park, Mich.	11,699	(260)	Auto
15	Internat. Tel. & Tel.	1920	New York	11,368	398	Electronic
16	Philips	1891	Eindhoven, Netherlands	10,746	152	Electronic
17	Standard Oil of Indiana	1889	Chicago	9,955	787	Oil
18	Cie Francaise des Petroles	1924	Paris	9,146	168	Oil
19	Nippon Steel	1970	Tokyo	8,797	122	Steel
20	August Thyssen-Huette	1890	Duisburg, GFR	8,765	100	Steel
21	Hoechst	1863	Frankfurt on Main	9,462	101	Chemical
22	ENI	1953	Rome	8,334	(135)	Oil
23	Daimler-Benz	1926	Stuttgart, GFR	8,194	126	Auto

24	U.S. Steel	1901	Pittsburgh	8,167	560	Steel
25	BASF	1865	Ludwigshafen on Main	8,152	153	Chemical
26	Renault	1895	Boulogne-Billancourt	7,831	(129)	Auto
27	Siemens	1847	Munich	7,760	201	Electrical
28	Volkswagenwerk	1938	Wolfsburg, GFR	7,681	(64)	Auto
29	Atlantic Richfield	1881	Los Angeles	7,308	350	Oil
30	Continental Oil	1875	Stamford, Conn.	7,254	331	Oil
31	Bayer	1863	Leverkusen, GFR	7,223	128	Chemical
32	E.I. du Pont de Nemours	1802	Wilmington, Del.	7,222	272	Chemical
33	Toyota Motor	1937	Toyota City, Japan	7,194	251	Auto
34	ELF-Acquitaine	1945	Paris	7,165	200	Oil & Gas
35	Nestle	1866	Vevey, Switzerland	7,080	309	Consumer
36	Imperial Chemical Ind.	1926	London	6,884	424	Chemical
37	Petroleo Brasileiro	1953	Rio de Janeiro	6,626	704	Oil
38	British-American Tobacco	1902	London	6,146	314	Consumer
39	Procter & Gamble	1890	Cincinnati	6,082	334	Consumer
40	Hitachi	1920	Tokyo	5,916	94	Electrical
41	Westinghouse Electric	1872	Pittsburgh	5,863	165	Elect. Eq.
42	Mitsubishi Heavy Ind.	1950	Tokyo	5,694	41	Steel
43	Union Carbide	1917	New York	5,665	382	Chemical
44	Tenneco	1947	Houston, Texas	5,600	343	Oil
45	Nissan Motor	1933	Tokyo	5,480	116	Auto
46	Goodyear Tire & Rubber	1898	Akron, Ohio	5,452	162	Auto
47	Montedison	1888	Milan	5,418	(184)	Chemical
48	British Steel	1967	London	5,340	172	Steel
49	International Harvester	1879	Chicago	5,335	79	Auto
50	Occidental Petroleum	1920	Los Angeles	5,334	172	Oil

a Rounded; losses in Brackets.

We must also remember that the universe of transnational enterprise extends far beyond the circle of manufacturing and mining corporations and comprises several other important classes of global business, among them (1) multinational banks such as Morgan Guarantee, and financial service companies; (2) global transportation, including air and shipping lines and hotel chains; (3) trading companies, including the important Japanese firms and the grain traders; (4) the insurance world, including Lloyd's of London; (5) advertising and accounting firms that serve the transnational corporations, and construction firms, architects, and general contractors that also serve governments; (6) global utilities, such as COMSAT, and (7) world media, including newspapers such as *The Economist*. Trends discernible among the industrial corporations need not be exactly duplicated in these other fields, and in the aggregate more than one-half of world output originates outside industry.

The Method and the Data

Our method is to compare the fifty largest firms in 1975 with those fifty that were largest in 1955 as a means of describing basic trends over a period of two decades that constitute the core of post-World War II developments.

In Table 3-1 we present information concerning the fifty largest firms of 1975; the criterion of size is the volume of sales because it is the best available measure of a firm's output. In addition to sales, we show information on the year of incorporation (or constitutive merger), headquarters' location, net income (or loss), and industry group. The principal source for Table 3-1 is the *Fortune* directory of corporations.[3] The companies in Table 3-1 will be systematically compared with a similar list for 1955.[4]

Table 3-1 requires careful study. It shows a good cross-section of world industry and all major industrial areas are represented in it. Many of the names it includes are "household words": Exxon or Shell for gasoline, Ford or Toyota for cars, Nestle for instant coffee and ITT for its problems (Watergate and Chile). The foundation dates show these to be mature organizations each with a history of its own. They are substantial building blocks of the world economy.

Basic Trends

The first conclusion to be drawn from a comparison of the list of 1975 with that of 1955 is the impermanence of rank and the ubiquity of change. No company can claim guaranteed tenure of the room at the top.

Table 3-2 presents the data in diagrammatic form and shows how we can distinguish three groups of companies. In Group One we have twenty-seven companies that held top-fifty rank in 1955 but no longer did so twenty years later. Five of these no longer maintain independent existence and altogether disappeared through amalgamations in the great merger era of the late 1960s, even though some are still recognizable as divisions of the corporations that absorbed them (e.g., Armour in Greyhound, or Jones & Laughlin in LTV). Twenty-two other companies dropped out of top-fifty rank; some have retained near-fifty status (e.g., Eastman Kodak and Krupp); and others have slid far down the list of leading corporations. Over this period of twenty years, therefore, the probability that a company would hold top-fifty rank was less than one in two (.46).

Table 3-2 The Top-Fifty in 1955 and 1975

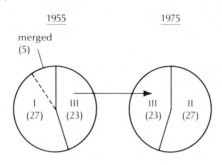

Group One	Group Two	Group Three
Esmark	Nat. Iranian Oil	Exxon
Bethlehem Steel	IBM	General Motors
[a] Armour	ITT	Royal Dutch Shell
Kraft	Philips	Texaco
Republic Steel	CPF	Ford Motor
Firestone Tire	Nippon Steel	Mobil Oil
[a] Sinclair Oil	A. Thyssen	British Petroleum
RCA	Hoechst	Standard of Calif.
Uniroyal	ENI	Unilever
Cities Service	Daimler-Benz	Gulf Oil
Phillips Petr.	BASF	General Electric
[a] Douglas Aircraft	Renault	Chrysler
Boeing	Siemens	Standard of Ind.
Dunlop Rubber	Volkswagenwerk	US Steel
Aluminium Co. of America	Atlantic Richfield	Nestle
	Continental Oil	DuPont
General Foods	Bayer	ICI
[a] North American Aviation	Toyota Motor	BAT
Borden	Elf-Acquitaine	Procter & Gamble
International Paper	Petrobras	Westinghouse Elec.
B.F. Goodrich	Hitachi	Union Carbide
Hawker Siddeley	Mitsubishi H.I.	Goodyear Tire
Krupp	Tenneco	Int. Harvester
American Can	Nissan Motor	
Eastman Kodak	Montedison	
United Technologies	British Steel	
[a] Jones & Laughlin	Occidental Petr.	
Armco Steel		

[a] Merged.

In Group Two, we have those corporations that in 1975 were new to the list of top industrials; twenty-seven such companies raised their world status significantly in that space of twenty years. Among these are the computer giant, IBM—the prototypical high-technology firm; several West European and Japanese firms, and two Third World companies, in Brazil and Iran. This was the high-growth section of world industry.

In Group Three, we have another group of high achievers, firms that ranked high in 1955 and still held their status in 1975. They were, and remain, among the most powerful in the world, and have been the core of the Anglo-American world economy of the past few decades: Exxon and Royal Dutch-Shell, and the rest of the "Seven Sisters" of international oil (Texaco, Mobil Oil, British Petroleum, Standard of California, and Gulf); General Motors, Ford and Chrysler in autos, DuPont and ICI in chemicals, Nestle and Unilever in foods. All of them are mature firms of global reach, established quality and endurance.

However, if we look at all three groups (a total of seventy-seven firms), the significant fact seems to be the relative transience of world status. In spite of all that we hear about the new industrial state and the imposing power of large companies, the facts seem to indicate that life at the top is unstable and that, in world proportions, the turnover is quite substantial.

This high turnover (which is characteristic not only of top industrials but of corporations in general)[5] occurs among companies that are not exactly young or newly formed. In 1975, the average age of top-fifty companies since incorporation (which in some cases understates the length of time since the foundation of a business) was seventy years. More than half of them had been in business in the nineteenth century. In other words, the large corporations are well-established organizations, having behind them several generations of growth. Generally speaking, the longer a corporation remains in existence, the better its chances of continued survival (among Group Three companies, the average age was over eighty); but age itself is no guarantee of success or even survival; among the five that had disappeared, two were more than 100 years old.

Industrial Change

As we compare the firms that were prominent in 1955 with those that are dominant twenty years later, the first set of questions concerns industrial structure: how has world industry changed in that period? Broadly speaking, in 1955 the powerful firms were in the steel, motor, and aviation industries; by 1975 the locus of activity in world industry has shifted to the oil, chemical, and electrical industries.

The shift may be observed in Table 3-3, which records the proportions of the large industrials found among the leading industries, and the distribution of the total sales among these several industrial categories. As the table demonstrates, in these twenty years, no single industry stood still; each has either risen or fallen back.

Clearly, the major gainer has been the oil industry. Fully one-third of the world's major industrials are now oil companies, and close to one-half of the total sales of the top-fifty in 1975 were in oil and related energy fields (coal, natural gas, uranium). Several of the oil companies also had strong chemical divisions and have shared with the chemical companies (which in turn also depend on oil) in the expansion of chemical production. Energy-related too are the electrical engineering and electronics industries, the third

Table 3-3 Major Industry Groups among the Top Industrials: 1955, 1975

Industry Group	No. of Firms among Top-Fifty Firms		Per Cent Share of Top-Fifty Sales		Per Cent Change in Sales, 1955–1975
	1955	1975	1955	1975	
Oil	11	17	27	46	+ 19
Electrical, etc.	3	7	6	12	+ 6
Chemical	3	7	5	9	+ 4
Steel	6	5	10	6	− 4
Aerospace	5	—	4	—	− 4
Auto & Tire	9	10	30	21	− 9
Consumer	9	4	15	6	− 9

major area of recent industrial growth. The common thread linking the three expanding fields is nuclear energy; most of the high-growth firms also share interests in the nuclear field. Given the significance of the energy sector in the world industrial spectrum, it is little wonder that disturbances that occur there (such as the oil price rises, the problems of nuclear power, and possibilities of an oil embargo) become, in the form of an energy crisis, major questions for the stability of the world economy and important world problems.

Contrasting with the rising importance of the energy complex are a group of industries that have been losing out: the slow-growth steel, auto, aviation, and food industries. The decline in the prominence of the auto and tire firms is quite striking, as is the fading of the steel industry, no longer the key sector of industrial growth. None of the five aviation firms among the top-fifty in 1955 has maintained its rank—a consequence of the falling off in military orders.

We could summarize the change over the two decades quite broadly, and very loosely, as a shift from an economy whose center of gravity was a World War II-type military industrial complex (motors, steel, aviation) to an economy in which the bulk of major firms and two-thirds of their sales is in the energy field, with emphasis on oil, nuclear power, and computers. These firms have also become the sinews of more contemporary military power. In this way the evolution of the top-fifty reflects changes in world industrial structure. We can also expect that twenty years hence, new processes will be under way, and the mix of firms serving them will be a new one.

Regional Distributions

As a general rule, we would expect major industrial firms to be distributed among regions roughly in the same proportions as industrial production (as distinguished from gross national product, which is a measure of overall economic activity). In other words, we would expect shifts in regional industrial power to be reflected in shifts in the distribution of industrial firms.

As we can see from Table 3-4, important changes in regional distribution of industrial power did occur between 1955 and 1975. Four of these changes are particularly noteworthy.

Table 3-4 Distribution of Top-Fifty Industrials Compared with Industrial Production: 1955, 1975

	(1) Per Cent Share of Top-Fifty Industrials (by volume of sales)		(2) Per Cent Share of Industrial Production[a]		(3) Index of Representation (1:2)
North America	1955	83	1955	51.1	1.6
	1975	55	1975	37.2	1.5
Western Europe	1955	17	1955	28.5	0.6
	1975	34.5	1975	35.5	1.0
Japan	1955	—	1955	2.4	—
	1975	6	1975	9.0	0.6
Developing Areas	1955	—	1955	8.8	—
	1975	4.5	1975	14.8	0.6

[a] Of market economies; based on *United Nations Statistical Yearbooks* for 1965 and 1976.

1. A dramatic increase in Japan's share of the industrial output of the market economies, from just over 2 percent to 10 percent. That is how, since World War II, Japan has risen to be the world's third major industrial power.

2. An augmentation in Western Europe's industrial capabilities, from less than 30 percent to 35 percent—basically a catching up on the war losses that were still in evidence in 1955.

3. A slow rise in the industrial potential of the Third World countries; a rise, not insubstantial, from 9 to nearly 15 percent, and an indication that industrialization is making some progress, however slow.

4. A decline in the share of North America (United States and Canada), from a level in excess of 50 percent in 1955 to 37.2 percent in 1975—a result of the erosion of the advantages gained in World War II, the slower rate of industrial growth since, and the advance of the service economy.

Corresponding to these basic shifts in industrial power have been changes in the national affiliation of the world industrials.

1. The Japanese contingent in 1975 is smaller (in sales volume, though not in the number of firms) than what we could expect, given Japan's share of industrial output. For Japan, the index of representation among large industrials is therefore 0.6.

2. Western Europe has moved from a condition of "underrepresentation" in 1955 (0.6) to a condition of full representation in 1975 (1.0). Once again, Western Europe is strong in large firms, and Britain and West Germany are particularly well represented.

3. The Third World is the area that is the most underrepresented (0.3). But we also note that its share of large enterprises has risen since 1955, and that that share is likely to continue to rise (as the result of Venezuelan takeovers of oil enterprises in 1976 and, more generally, as the result of continued, and in particular oil-linked, industrialization).

4. The considerable overprepresentation of North America (and particularly the United States) in 1955 (1.6) has declined only a little, to 1.5 (despite a significant drop in United States share of world industrial output). This is due to the continued pre-

dominance of United States firms among the very large firms, especially among the oil companies. The relative advantage of the early postwar years, derived from industrial strength but aided by political factors,[6] has been maintained. America's stake among the major industrials is now about equal to that of Western Europe in terms of number of firms, though not in terms of sales volume. The world impact of the Europeans still suffers from the dispersion among a number of national affiliations and the lack of political unity at the regional level. The American firms, on the other hand, remain the largest single group and still produce over one-half of the total output of the major firms. Their visibility remains high.

Engagement in International Interdependence

Industrial specialization and regional specialization may be two of the major factors accounting for the variability of corporate fortunes and for the differences in performance and growth. Let us now look at a third set of factors that might be involved but that are not commonly linked with international interdependence: a company's engagement in international interdependence.

So far we have discussed large industrial firms as global phenomena without regard to whether they might or might not operate transnationally. As a matter of fact, most of them do function transnationally and that is why, given our interest in transnational corporations, we want now to pay greater attention to this part of the problem.

We shall distinguish between two sets of characteristics that can describe a firm's engagement in international interdependence: (1) international content, and (2) international control.

International Content

The concept of international content refers to the character of corporate operations, and in particular to the extent to which an enterprise engages in operations outside the confines of its home market. These international operations may be supply- or production-oriented, as when a British oil company pumps oil in Iran or Nigeria for shipment to Britain, or when Ford produces components in Europe, in part for use in the United States. Or, the operations may be principally demand- or market-oriented, as when a firm sells a proportion of its output on world markets. Such international sales may be comprised in part of exports from national plants, as when Nippon Steel ships overseas about one-third of its output, or of sales abroad of foreign subsidiaries, as when General Motors sells from its plants in Britain, Germany, or Australia. Or, imports may be purchased for home plants or for the national market; for example, the Brazilian oil company Petrobras depends for more than half of its refinery operations and home sales on oil acquired from overseas oil firms.

Information on international production and international sales has in recent years been made available in company annual reports (though no information is given on imports). Table 3-5 displays such information, expressed as a percentage of total production or total sales for each firm. In the case of oil companies, there are separate entries for primary (oil, natural gas, and coal mining) and secondary (refining) operations.[7]

Table 3-5 International Content: The Top-Fifty Industrials, 1975

Company	Status		International Content, 1975		
	1955	1975	Sales	Production	Crude Oil, Nat. Gas, & Coal Production[f]
Exxon	G	G	69	73	74
General Motors	M	M	32	27	
Royal Dutch Shell	G	G	75[E]	64[e]	89
Texaco	M	G	59	65[g]	68
Ford Motor	M	G	34	50[d]	
Mobil Oil	G	G	63	64	43
National Iranian Oil	G	G	93	14[g]	
British Petroleum	G	G	83	71[g]	98
Standard California	M	G	60		80
Unilever	G	G	91	72[a]	
IBM	M	G	50	45[a]	
Gulf Oil	G	G	54	55	85
General Electric	M	M	26	27[a]	
Chrysler	M	M	34	35	
ITT	G	G	51	53[a]	
Philips	G	G	89	78[a]	
Standard Indiana	Nat	M	15	16[g]	40
CPF	G	G	63	38	100
Nippon Steel	Nat	M	31		
Aug. Thyssen Huette	Nat	M	29	12[a]	
Hoechst	M	G	68	32	
ENI	M	G	24	23[g]	52
Daimler-Benz	M	G	56	22	
US Steel	Nat	Nat	3	1[b]	
BASF	M	G	50	26[a]	
Renault	M	M	48	29	
Siemens	M	G	51	42[a]	

Statistics on international sales and international production may be used to classify corporations according to their degree of international content, on the general assumption that firms high in international content may tend to behave differently from firms whose operations are basically national. Their international content may then be used to establish their "transnational status."

Thus in Table 3–5 each company is assigned, on the basis of the strength of its international content, both in 1955 and in 1975, to one of the three types of transnational status: global, multinational, or national. A company whose international sales or international production exceeds 50 percent is labeled global. Both Exxon and IBM are, by this definition, global companies: Exxon because both in sales and in production the international content exceeds fifty percent; and IBM because, even though its production capacity (as measured by percentage of the labor force at overseas plants) has only 45 percent international content, its international sales supplied 50 percent of revenues in 1975. An

Table 3-5 *(cont.)*

Company	Status		International Content, 1975		
	1955	*1975*	*Sales*	*Production*	*Crude Oil, Nat. Gas, &* *Coal Production[f]*
Volkswagenwerk	M	G	65	37	
Atlantic-Richfield	M	M	13	14[g]	29
Continental Oil	Nat	M	37	30[g]	29
Bayer	M	G	68	47	
DuPont	M	M	27	21[a]	
Toyota Motor	Nat	M	43		
Elf-Acquitaine	G	G	20	21[g]	77
Nestle	G	G	99	96[E,a]	
ICI	M	G	58	38	
Petrobras	Nat	Nat	4	3[c]	
British-American Tobacco	G	G	94	78[a]	
Procter & Gamble	M	M	22	12[b]	
Hitachi	Nat	M	13		
Westinghouse Electric	M	M	30	22[a]	
Mitsubishi H.I.	Nat	M	33		
Union Carbide	M	M	34	46[a]	
Tenneco	Nat	M	13	10[b]	
Nissan Motor	Nat	M	33	8	
Goodyear Tire	M	M	39	47[a]	
Montedison	Nat	M	33	8	
British Steel		M	17	10	
International Harvester	M	M	39	32[a]	
Occidental Petroleum	Nat	M	43	38	

G Global
M Multinational
Nat National
E Estimated
[a] Employment
[b] Assets

[c] Capital Expenditures
[d] Excluding Canada
[e] Outside Europe
[f] Oil Companies Only
[g] Refinery Runs

enterprise rating less than 10 percent according to both of these criteria (such as United States Steel, with 3 percent international sales and 1 percent production assets) is regarded as national. Finally, those firms, of which there are quite a few, that exceed 10 percent on either international sales or production but do not exceed 50 percent on either, are residually classified as multinational. In this intermediate group are such firms as General Motors, whose international activities are quite substantial in themselves and quite significant for the countries where their principal facilities are located but for which, because of the relative weight of the home market, the center of activity tends to be in the national territory.

This classification of transnational enterprise departs in one particular from some common methods of classification: it assigns transnational status in part on the basis of international sales, and these include both home-country exports and international production proper (that is, host-country sales from local facilities). In other words, both exports and production of foreign subsidiaries are treated as equally important sources of transnational status. The reason for doing this is that both exports and affiliate production are ways of performing global functions in the economic sphere. They are in part interchangeable, and for industrial firms they are quite intimately linked; the setting up of subsidiaries and the commencement of foreign production quite often follow, in the product cycle, upon the establishment of export markets. In practice, moreover, most corporations with large export sales also have a substantial network of affiliates; this export status cannot be removed from the consideration of multinational activity.[8]

Changes in International Content

On the basis of the classification and the information we have just noted we can identify a third basic trend among the world industrials: a significant recent rise in international content, hence in this particular form of international interdependence. Table 3-6 summarizes this finding.

It is evident that in those twenty years an important change has occurred in the character of the most prominent of the world industrials. It is not that international content was unknown in 1955 and made a strong showing only in 1975. On the contrary, in both years firms of intermediate international content constitute about one-half of the total. But an important shift has occurred in the relative roles of national and global companies. Whereas two decades ago the national companies fielded a strong contingent and global companies ranked third, by 1975, the national companies had nearly disappeared from the top-fifty industrials, and one-half of the list is now comprised of global firms.

There are two reasons for this last development: the national companies that dropped from the list were also companies in industries that had lost ground (steel, air, tire, food), and they were also United States companies; global companies that gained were in the energy area, and were non-American companies. In part, the process is therefore explained in terms of factors we have previously considered (industrial and regional specialization). But international content seems also to be playing an additional role; this is evidenced both by the high staying power of these companies that were global in 1955 (eight out of nine of these that were global maintained top-fifty rank to 1975) and by a good deal of "status change" by companies that improved their rankings.

What has occurred then is both a good degree of success by companies that had a high international content in the first place, and also a considerable amount of status change—the deliberate raising of international content as the result of company policy. As may be seen from a comparison of the "Status 1955" and the "Status 1975" column in Table 3-5,

Table 3-6 Transnational Status among the Top-Fifty Industrials: 1955, 1975

Companies Classified as	1955	1975
National	15	2
Multinational	26	23
Global	9	25

nearly one-half of the top-fifty companies of 1975 experienced an increment in international content that was significant enough to effect promotion to a higher status category; hence there was a "status change" in those two decades. On the other hand, not one single firm can be observed to have moved toward lower transnational status.

A comparison of the international content figures for American and non-American companies is revealing. With regard to international production, the figures are quite similar: American firms, 37 percent; European and Japanese firms, 36 percent. With regard to international sales, however, the figures differ: American firms, again, 37 percent; European and Japanese firms, 51 percent. It would thus seem that the large industrials now have, on the average, about one-third of their production facilities outside their home market, but that European and Japanese companies also perform strongly in export markets.

We may thus conclude that the postwar decades have witnessed what must be termed, for want of a better word, universalization of the international content, to a degree unprecedented in the experience of industrial corporations. The high degree of international content, and of the international sales of the average company, and the fact that hardly any large firm today can dispense with international operations, indicate that most large industrial firms today are transnational enterprises.

International Control

International content may be all-pervasive and surprisingly strong, but the same cannot be said about international control. Let us define international control as the degree to which the ownership or managerial control is shared with non-nationals.

Here we find that the dominant condition, and the rule, is control by nationals; the instances of even marginal and tentative participation by non-nationals are the exception. Even though information on this subject is scattered and incomplete, there is no reason to believe that internationally dispersed or cross-nationally shared patterns of participation are anything but rare.

As regards ownership, the prevalent pattern is national. This is most obvious in companies that are state-controlled: either owned outright, in a majority mode, or through a minority share. Among the top-fifty of 1975, ten firms (20 percent) had state participation of significant proportion. This shows that transnational activity is not an exclusive preserve of private firms. All French and Italian firms in that group were either owned outright (such as ENI, or Renault where 94.5 percent state ownership is combined with a 5.5 percent holding by employees), or had strong state minority holdings (Montedison had some 15 percent). State ownership is also gaining ground in Britain (British Steel, nationalized in 1967; British Petroleum, 51 percent state-owned), and in the Third World countries (such as Iran and Brazil). Although it is not entirely incompatible with foreign shareholdings (as in British Petroleum where some 5 percent of the stock is held in the United States), state ownership is basically a method of establishing and maintaining national control.

Aside from state ownership, three other ownership patterns may be discerned. First, *bank or company ownership* through large shareholdings or through debt instruments, as in Japan (Nippon Steel or Mitsubishi Heavy Industries) or in Germany (where Deutsche Bank owns some 30 percent of Daimler-Benz). Second, *family ownership* by such families as the DuPonts (28 percent of DuPont is family-owned), the Siemens, or the Leverhulme Trust in the case of Unilever. (However, no one individual and no single family seems to hold a majority stake in any of these companies, even though family control is sometimes safeguarded by such devices as special voting rights.) Third, *dispersed ownership,* characteristic of many large companies, in which no single interest is predominant and a controlling coalition is organized by the directors and executives. None of these patterns shows characteristics of international control.

Available data do not clearly indicate any trends, but the following propositions may be put forward: (1) No top-fifty company is majority-owned by non-nationals—that is, in no case is the nationality of headquarters employees different from that of majority shareholders (though we might note the case of the Thyssen family, who own 25 percent of ATH and are now living in Argentina). (2) A considerable if unknown number of firms have minority foreign shareholdings—some United States companies as well as the Anglo-Dutch companies (Royal Dutch-Shell, Unilever, Philips), which have significant proportions of United States, French, Swiss, German and other holdings. But these are instances of dispersed ownership. (3) The only noteworthy recent change in the ownership patterns of major companies at the international level has been that linked with the influx of "oil money." Among the top-fifty, Kuwait acquired 15 percent of Daimler-Benz, and a syndicate headed by a Saudi Arabian financier purchased 7 percent of Occidental Petroleum in 1974; Iran now owns 17 percent of Krupp (one of the top-fifty of 1955). None of these constitute controlling holdings and now seem less significant than they were thought to be at the time.

Managerial Control

In no top-fifty company did the nationality of management (the chief executive officer, full-time directors, other senior executives) diverge significantly if at all from what one would expect, given the location of headquarters. The only recent indication of increased sensitivity to extranational interests has been the practice of appointing one or two non-nationals to the board of directors. No non-nationals were members of the boards of state-owned enterprises, or Japanese boards in 1955, but as of 1975, nineteen of the top-fifty companies (that is, close to two-fifths of the total) had either one or two non-nationals on their boards. Global companies were twice as likely to have such representation as multinational firms, and national companies had none. United States, West German, and Anglo-Dutch companies were particularly prominent among them; for example, IBM, Exxon, Volkswagen, ICI, and Royal Dutch. There were some instances of cross-national interlocking directorates, such as the board linkages among ICI, Unilever, BASF, and Chrysler, or between Exxon and British-American Tobacco. (In the latter case, there was also a second-order link between Exxon and British Petroleum.) A few companies seemed to serve as central nodes of communication; IBM had links to five other top-fifty firms; Siemens was the central node of the West German firms.[9]

Although it is an interesting phenomenon, this modest though possibly growing degree of transnational representation in the managerial process of large firms does not contradict the basic fact of national control.[10]

International Content and Performance

We began by noting the impermanence of rank and the variability in the fortunes of even the largest of the industrial companies. Their rank in the industrial hierarchy can never be taken for granted for long, and the fall from grace has been swift for many. We have also noted that such variability is explained largely by processes of industrial change and the differential development of regional and national economies.

But we have also seen that one basic process that occurred between 1955 and 1975 has been the internationalization of large industrial concerns. A significantly large share of their output is now sold internationally (thus escaping the confines of the national economy), and many of these concerns have raised their transnational status, no doubt in response to deliberate policy and in expectation of superior performance. Did those firms do better than those that refrained from change? In other words, is internationalization related to superior performance? Do corporations with high international content have a record of performance that is better than that of firms with low international content? And if there is a difference, is it significant when compared with the influence of the other factors we have noted?

Perlmutter's Hypothesis

One set of answers to these questions was given in 1968 by Howard Perlmutter. Having coined the term "geocentric corporation" for the "world-oriented enterprise," he also advanced the proposition that, in the future, geocentric firms might be expected to be more successful than ethnocentric or polycentric corporations. He argued that "the degree of multinationality of an enterprise is positively related to the firm's long-term viability . . . [because] it means a quality of decision-making which leads to survival, growth, and profitability in an evolving world economy."[11]

For Perlmutter, the qualities that explained such performance were basically attitudinal: "the way executives think about doing business around the world," "the pervasiveness with which executives think geocentrically," and derivatively, the policies they pursue on the basis of such inclinations. As attitudes favoring such performance Perlmutter listed the following: capacity to work with a variety of politicians, capacity to acquire and integrate smaller firms, capacity to recruit and train personnel for international service, capacity to stay in contact with world-wide product uses; and above all, capacity to build trust and confidence among managers of many nations.[12]

It might be argued that a good indicator of the existence and effectiveness of the attitudes Perlmutter was describing is "status change," that is, change in the international content of the company over a period sufficiently long to establish its effect on long-run viability. (As was seen earlier, a substantial proportion of large firms did experience such status change over a period of two decades.) Another indicator of abiding commitment to international operations is, of course, the proportion of international sales and of international production to total output.

With the available information we should, therefore, be able to test the expectation that firms with a record of status change or firms that have a high international content can be shown to have performed better than other firms. We would not expect international content level, or changes in it, to be the sole determinant of business performance. But we should like to know whether the effects of the international content variables could be isolated as statistically significant.

Two Criteria of Performance

To conduct such an analysis we need criteria by which to judge long-term corporate performance. One such criterion of performance has been implicit in the preceding discussion—namely, the capacity to attain, and to retain, top-fifty rank among the world industrials. Let us call this *Rank Performance* (RANKPER). According to this criterion, we can use the distinctions made earlier among the three groups of companies, and retain their labelings respectively as Group One (the "drop-outs"), Group Two (the "achievers"), and Group Three (the "high-fliers"), as seen previously in Table 3–2. With regard to the variable of Rank Performance our seventy-seven firms thus divide easily into three groups. This is a crude and rather simple but basic and conservative measure that favors the very large firms that have succeeded in maintaining their rank.

An alternative measure of performance is growth of output. We know that the top-fifty firms in 1975 produced for sale output whose value (in monetary terms) was six times higher than that produced by their counterparts in 1955. (Real output probably increased no more than three times.) Knowing this average growth rate, we can assign to each firm a score expressing the rate of growth in sales in relation to that mean (sixfold) rate of increase. A firm whose sales rose precisely sixfold over the period of twenty years (as did those of ICI) would receive a score of 1.0; a firm with a below-average sales record would score less than one (General Motors had a score of 0.46); and growth companies expanding at several times the mean would score more than one (IBM had a score of 4.3). (Firms that merged are scored zero.)

On the basis of this *Growth Factor* (GROFAC) the seventy-seven firms cluster into two groups: the low-to-average group with scores of 0–1.5, and the high-growth group with scores of 1.5–8. As a measure of performance, Growth Factor is only weakly correlated (.16) with Rank Performance. It singles out high-growth firms irrespective of previous rank. Smaller firms that have risen fast tend to have higher scores. The two measures, Rank Performance and Growth Factor, thus tap two different aspects of business success.

Discriminant Analysis

We have now classified seventy-seven firms into three groups according to the RANKPER variable and into two groups according to the GROFAC variable. What independent variables best explain differences in performance between these groups? What factors discriminate most efficiently among these groups?

A statistical method that can be used to distinguish between two or more groups of cases is discriminant analysis.[13] To distinguish between the groups we need a collection of discriminating variables that measure the characteristics on the basis of which the groups are expected to differ. In our case these are: (1) the industry variable, basically dichotomized into high-growth (INDHGR) and low-growth (INDLGR); (2) the location variable, also dichotomized into USA and EECJAP; (3) the status change variable

(STATCHG), dichotomized into yes or no; and (4) international sales in 1975 (INSAL75). We shall want to know if these variables are significant for this purpose.

The mathematical objective of discriminant analysis is to weight and linearly combine the discriminating variables in some fashion so that the groups are as statistically distinct as possible. We want to discriminate among the groups in the sense of being able to tell them apart. Discriminant analysis attempts to do this by forming one or more combinations of the discriminating variables into discriminant functions where each variable in the analysis is qualified by a weighting coefficient and the sum of them is combined into a discriminant score. The maximum number of functions is one less than the number of groups. Ideally the discriminant scores for the cases within a particular group will be quite similar (that is, close to the mean, or group centroid). The functions are also formed so as to maximize the distance between groups. Once the discriminant functions have been derived they help to measure the success with which discriminating variables can actually be discriminated when combined into such functions. The weighting coefficients serve to identify the variables that contribute most to differentiation into the respective functions. As a check on the adequacy of the discriminant function we can classify the original set of cases to see how many are correctly classified by the variables that are being used, and we can also use graphic displays of cases in a space defined by the discriminating functions.

Results for Rank Performance Groups

Results of discriminant analysis of the three RANKPER groups (direct method) show that the four variables, in order of discriminating power (as measured by Wilks's Lambda), were: USA, INSAL75, INDHGR, and STATCHG. Two discriminant functions were formed. For function one, the coefficient making the greatest, though negative, contribution was USA (-1.27), followed by INDHGR (.90) and STATCHG (.34). For function two, the factor loading most heavily was INDHGR (-.1.15), followed by INSAL75 (-1.05). The canonical correlation[14] for discriminant function one was .72, and for function two, .57. The classification routine correctly classified 75.3 percent of the cases as members of the groups to which they actually belong. All but one of these results are significant at a level better than one in a thousand.

The plot of discriminant scores (Figure 3–1) shows some of the results of this analysis. Here the numbers (1, 2, 3) represent cases from the group with a corresponding number (some numbers represent more than one firm), and they are placed in a space defined by the two discriminant functions (function 1, horizontal; function 2, vertical). The first function serves to separate US from non-US firms, low- from high-growth firms, and those that have had status change from those that have not. The second function distinguishes high international sales firms (down) from those that are lower in international content (up). A few firms have been identified, including Exxon (whose discriminant scores are $(-.726; -2.462)$, which is a US but high-growth firm of considerable international content.

The three large dots in the figure are the "group centroids" (or group means), which are the most typical locations of a case from that group. A comparison of the group centroids shows how far apart the groups are, and the figure indicates that they are quite far apart. The plot of the cases also shows that the three groups cluster quite well into these distinct sectors *and* with only a minority of cases found outside group "boundaries" (that is, misclassified). (For instance, General Motors, a Group Three company, is in Group One "territory" because it is a relatively slow-growth US firm, with fewer international sales than a Group Three firm would be expected to have.)

Results for Growth Factor Groups

Discriminant analysis of the two GROFAC groups gives only slightly different results. The variables of greatest discriminating power (Wilks's Lambda) were USA, STATCHG, and INDHGR. The coefficient for the one discriminant function (because there were two groups, only one function was formed) gave heaviest weight to USA, followed by INDHGR and STATCHG. The canonical correlation for the discriminant function was .70, and the classification routine correctly classified a satisfactorily high 87 percent of all the cases. All the results were statistically significant (0.001).

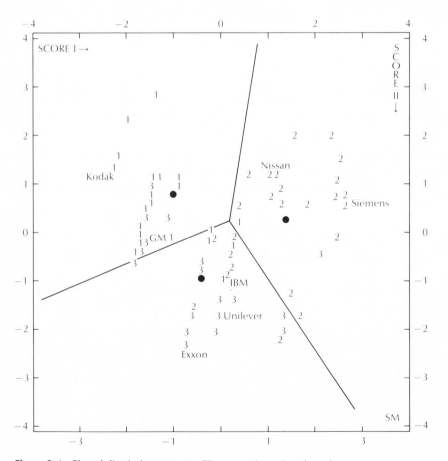

Figure 3-1 Plot of discriminant scores, 77 corporations, 3 rank performance groups.

Discussion

The relatively sophisticated statistical technique of discriminant analysis was used here to sustain the argument about the importance of international content variables, hence as a means of supporting Perlmutter's hypothesis. For the period 1955–1975, change in transnational status and international sales have been shown to be factors that discriminated effectively between rank-performing and high-growth factor firms, and others. In other words, international content, and policies designed to raise international content, have been shown to be significant in accounting for corporate performance during that period, and ranked in importance next to such basic factors as industry and location. In fact, the analysis demonstrated, more clearly, that RANKPER gave greater weight to international sales, indicating that the performance of the very large and mature firm was favorably influenced by high international content. GROFAC, on the other hand, lent greater weight to change in transnational status, thus tending to show that the not-so-very large, but nevertheless rising, firms might benefit, in their movement into top rank, from status change.

How do we explain these findings? According to Perlmutter, the basic mechanisms are quality of management decision-making, awareness of opportunities that exist globally, and capacity for exploiting them. We could expand this to say that one aspect of that mechanism, defensive in character, could be risk-spreading. A large firm whose production and supply facilities and sales and marketing networks are well distributed globally is less likely to be affected by disturbances or slowdowns in the growth rate of one economy or area. A firm with a far-flung network of such arrangements is better able, over a longer run, to absorb the shocks and ups and downs all economies are likely to experience. In any event, all firms attempting to serve global needs, as the international oil companies do, know that such world-wide networks are indispensable to success. That is why on Rank Performance, the measure of the very large firm, international sales scores high and show up as a separate dimension. A positive and more outgoing aspect of possibly the same mechanism is the need to participate in high-growth areas, and generally to take advantage of world-wide opportunities. In the two decades under discussion, West European and Japanese economies grew faster than that of the United States. Firms, including American ones, with a high European or Japanese content and a stake in those countries, had a chance of participating in that growth. Quite likely the areas of high growth will be different in the next two decades, but those firms capable of moving into them (by undergoing status change) will be more likely to benefit from that growth and may prove capable of managing a variety of new political conditions. That is why, in this respect, Growth Factor, which scores the smaller, but more aggressive firms, also brings out status change, and status change in turn measures a company's flexibility, the ambition of its executives, its adaptability to change, and its capacity to benefit from new developments.

Conclusions

For a student of transnational corporations and world order the following concluding remarks would seem to be significant.

1. Gain some familiarity with the names and the record of major firms, both American and non-American. These names will crop up again and again in discussions of transnational corporations.

2. Do not be overimpressed with the size and the power of those large firms that constitute the bulk of the transnational business community. Their fortunes wax and wane, and over a period of years quite a few of them will have passed from the high state and new ones will have risen.

3. Remember that most large industrial companies have significant international content, which makes nearly all of them transnational corporations, and that the number and importance of global firms has grown perceptibly in the past two decades, as one aspect of increasing international interdependence.

4. Firms rise and decay because the industries they are in grow or cease to grow, or because the economies of which they are a part also grow at varying rates. But they also tend to perform better when their international content is high or rising, as they change to take advantage of international interdependence. That is why transnational corporations are also important to a prosperous world order, and likely to be prominent within it. That is also why we need world-wide arrangements to support them and to regulate them.

NOTES

1. Earlier versions of this study were presented at the "Colloquium on Multinational Management, Interdependence and the Pacific" at the University of Washington, and in the series "The Politics of Interdependence" at Stanford University, in April–May 1977. The paper has benefited from financial assistance of the Department of Political Science of the University of Washington, the research assistance of Gary Gallwas, and the suggestions of Rick Johnston, who also helped administer programs at the university's Center for Quantitative Studies in the Social Sciences.

2. United Nations, *Multinational Corporations in World Development* (New York, 1973), p. 6.

3. "The Fifty Largest Industrial Companies in the World," *Fortune,* August 1976, p. 243. Shell Oil and Western Electric have been omitted because they do not meet the test of independence (both are subsidiaries of other firms), and International Harvester and Occidental Petroleum have been substituted in their place.

4. The top-fifty companies of 1955 are listed in Table 3-2 (add together Groups One and Three). Sources for the top-fifty 1955 list include *Fortune* Directories for 1955–1958 and *Moody's Industrial Manual,* 1956–1958.

5. In the period 1954–1974, 159 of the 500 United States industrials disappeared through mergers. *Fortune,* August 1974, p. 163.

6. Discussed in R. Gilpin, "The Politics of Transnational Economic Relations" (selection 4).

7. Table 3-5 is based principally on company reports for 1975, and on some private communications (a letter was sent to every top-fifty 1975 company). The first column (Status 1955) is an estimate based on Nicholas K. Bruck and Francis A. Lees, "Foreign Investment, Capital Controls and the Balance of Payments," *The Bulletin,* No. 48–49 (April 1968), Appendix, pp. 69–93 (New York University, Graduate School of Business Administration, Institute of Finance). Appendix lists international content figures for United States companies for 1965).

8. Indicators not used here for arriving at international content are foreign earnings (because they fluctuate considerably from year to year, and because net income abroad is an accounting concept that is susceptible to a degree of manipulation and that may be influenced by tax considerations) and the number of foreign subsidiaries (because their significance is hard to assess).

9. Board members of IBM, Siemens, and Unilever were appointed in 1977 to a "Group of Persons" to assist in the work of the United Nations Commission on Transnational Corporations.

10. Joint ventures are another form (and measure of) joint control and international management. Data on hand do not suggest that joint ventures contradict our basic findings.

11. Howard V. Perlmutter, "The Tortuous Evolution of the Multinational Corporation" (selection 2).

12. Howard Perlmutter, "Supergiant Firms of the Future," *Wharton Quarterly* (Winter 1968), pp. 13-14.

13. This section is based on Norman H. Nie, *et al., SPSS: Statistical Package for the Social Sciences,* 2d ed. (New York: McGraw-Hill, 1975), Chapter 23 and pp. 435-436.

14. Canonical correlation *squared* may be interpreted as the proportion of variance in the discriminant function explained by the groups. *Ibid.,* p. 442.

4 / The Politics of Transnational Economic Relations

Robert Gilpin

Robert Gilpin

I

. . .International society, we are told, is increasingly rent between its economic and its political organization. On the one hand, powerful economic and technical forces are creating a highly integrated transnational economy, blurring the traditional significance of national boundaries. On the other hand, the nation-state continues to command men's loyalties and to be the basic unit of political decision. As one writer has put the issue, "The conflict of our era is between ethnocentric nationalism and geocentric technology."[1]

• • •

The issues raised by these contrasting positions are central to any evaluation of the impressive growth of transnational economic relations since the end of the Second World War. In specific terms the issue is whether the multinational corporation has become or will become an important actor in international affairs, supplanting, at least in part, the nation-state. If the multinational corporation is indeed an increasingly important and independent international actor, what are the factors that have enabled it to break the political monopoly of the nation-state? What is the relationship of these two sets of political actors, and what are the implications of the multinational corporation for international relations? Finally, what about the future? If the contemporary role of the multina-

Reprinted by permission of the publishers from *Transnational Relations and World Politics*, edited by Robert O. Keohane and Joseph P. Nye, Jr. Cambridge, Mass.: Harvard University Press, 1972. Copyright © 1970, 1971 by the President and Fellows of Harvard College. Some notes have been omitted, and the remainder renumbered in sequence.

tional corporation is the result of a peculiar configuration of political and economic factors, can one foresee the continuation of its important role into the future?

Fundamental to these rather specific issues is a more general one raised by the growing contradiction between the economic and political organization of contemporary international society. This is the relationship between economic and political activities. While the advent of the multinational corporation puts it in a new guise, the issue is an old one. It was, for example, the issue which in the nineteenth century divided classical liberals like John Stuart Mill and the German Historical School represented by Georg Friedrich List. Whereas the former gave primacy to economics and the production of wealth, the latter emphasized the political determination of economic relations.[2] As this issue is central to the contemporary debate on the implications of the multinational corporation for international relations, I would like to discuss it in brief outline.

The classical position was, of course, first set forth by Adam Smith in *The Wealth of Nations*.[3] While Smith appreciated the importance of power, his purpose was to inquire into the nature and causes of wealth. Economic growth, Smith argued, is primarily a function of the extent of the division of labor which in turn is dependent upon the scale of the market. Much of his attack, therefore, was directed at the barriers erected by feudal principalities and mercantilist states against the free exchange of goods and the enlargement of markets. If men are to multiply their wealth, Smith argued, the contradiction between political organization and economic rationality had to be resolved in favor of the latter.

Marxism, the rebellious ideological child of classical liberalism, erected the concept of the contradiction between economic and political relations into a historical law. Whereas classical liberalism held that the requirements of economic rationality *ought* to determine political relations, the Marxist position was that the mode of production *does* determine the superstructure of political relations. History can be understood as the product of the dialectical process—the contradiction between evolving economic forces and the sociopolitical system.

Although Karl Marx and Friedrich Engels wrote amazingly little on the subject of international economics, Engels in his famous polemic, *Anti-Dühring*, dealt explicitly with the question of whether economics or politics was primary in determining the structure of international relations.[4] Karl Dühring's anti-Marxist theory maintained that property relations resulted less from the economic logic of capitalism than from extraeconomic political factors. Engels, on the other hand, using the example of the unification of Germany in his attack on Dühring, argued that economic factors were primary.

Engels argued that when contradictions arise between economic and political structures, political power adapts itself to changes in the balance of economic forces and yields to the dictates of economic development. Thus, in the case of nineteenth-century Germany, the requirements of industrial production had become incompatible with feudal, politically fragmented Germany. Though political reaction was victorious in 1815 and again in 1848, it was unable to prevent the growth of large-scale industry in Germany and the growing participation of German commerce in the world market.[5] In summary, Engels argued that "German unity had become an economic necessity."[6]

In the view of both Smith and Engels the nation-state represented a progressive stage in human development because it enlarged the political realm of economic activity. In each successive economic epoch the advancing technology and scale of production necessitates an enlargement of political organization. Because the city-state and feudalism were below the optimum for the scale of production and the division of labor required by the

Industrial Revolution, they prevented the efficient utilization of resources and were super-seded by larger political units. Smith considered this to be a desirable objective; for Engels it was a historical necessity.

In our era this Marxist emphasis on the historical law of development has been made by many writers—Marxists and non-Marxists—in discussing the contemporary contradiction between the nation-state and the multinational corporation. This position that economic forces are determining the structure of international relations has been put most forcibly by the economist, Stephen Hymer. In an intriguing article entitled "The Multinational Corporation and the Law of Uneven Development" Hymer has argued that contemporary international relations are rapidly being reshaped by "two laws of economic development: the Law of Increasing Firm Size and the Law of Uneven Development."[7]

The law of increasing firm size, Hymer argues, is the tendency since the Industrial Revolution for firms to increase in size "from the *workshop* to the *factory* to the *national corporation* to the *multi-divisional corporation* and now to the *multinational corporation.*" The law of uneven development, he continues, is the tendency of the international economy to produce poverty as well as wealth, underdevelopment as well as development. Together these two economic laws will produce the following consequence:

> A regime of North Atlantic Multinational Corporations would tend to produce a hierarchical division of labor between geographical regions corresponding to the vertical division of labor within the firm. It would tend to centralize high-level decision-making occupations in a few key cities in the advanced countries, surrounded by a number of regional sub-capitals, and confine the rest of the world to lower levels of activity and income, i.e., to the status of towns and villages in a new Imperial system. Income, status, authority, and consumption patterns would radiate out from these centers along a declining curve, and the existing pattern of inequality and dependency would be perpetuated. The pattern would be complex, just as the structure of the corporation is complex, but the basic relationship between different countries would be one of superior and subordinate, head office and branch office.

In contrast to the position of liberals and Marxists alike who stress the primacy of economic relations nationalists and the so-called realist school of political science have emphasized the primacy of politics. Whereas the liberal or Marxist emphasizes the production of wealth as the basic determinant of social and political organization, the realist stresses power, security, and national sentiment. Thus, whereas [George W.] Ball predicted to a session of the Canadian House of Commons that economic logic would lead to the eventual total integration of Canada and the United States, [Kari] Levitt and other Canadian nationalists prefer national independence to a higher standard of living.

Although himself a proponent of economic liberalism, the late Jacob Viner made one of the best analyses of the relationship of economic and political factors in determining the structure of international relations and concluded that political and security considerations are primary. In his classic study, *The Customs Union Issue,* Viner analyzed all known cases of economic and political unification from the perspective of whether the basic motivation was political or economic.[8] Thus, whereas Engels interpreted the formation of the Zollverein as a response to the industrialization of Germany and the economic necessity of larger markets, Viner argued "that Prussia engineered the customs union primarily for political reasons, in order to gain hegemony or at least influence over the lesser

German states. It was largely in order to make certain that the hegemony should be Prussian and not Austrian that Prussia continually opposed Austrian entry into the Union, either openly or by pressing for a customs union tariff lower than highly protectionist Austria could stomach."[9] In pursuit of this strategic interest it was "Prussian might, rather than a common zeal for political unification arising out of economic partnership, [that] had played the major role."[10]

Whereas liberalism and Marxism foresee economic factors leading to the decline of political boundaries and eventually to political unification, Viner argued that economic and political boundaries need not coincide and may actually be incompatible with one another. The tendency today, he pointed out, to take the identity of political and economic frontiers for granted is in fact a quite modern phenomenon and is even now not universal. With respect to tariffs, the concern of his study, the general rule until recently was that political unification was greater than the area of economic unification. Furthermore, any attempt to further economic unification might undermine political unification; this was the case with respect to the American Civil War and is the case today in Canada.[11]

Viner concluded his argument that economic factors are of secondary importance to political unification with the following observation which is highly relevant for the concerns of this essay:

> The power of nationalist sentiment can override all other considerations; it can dominate the minds of a people, and dictate the policies of government, even when in every possible way and to every conceivable degree it is in sharp conflict with what seem to be and are in fact the basic economic interests of the people in question. To accept as obviously true the notion that the bonds of allegiance must necessarily be largely economic in character to be strong, or to accept unhesitatingly the notion that where economic entanglements are artificially or naturally strong the political affections will also necessarily become strong, is to reject whatever lessons past experience has for us in this field.[12]

The contemporary argument that interstate relations will recede in face of contemporary technological developments and will be replaced by transnational relations between large multinational corporations was anticipated in the 1930s by Eugene Staley. In a fascinating book, *World Economy in Transition,* Staley posed the issue which is our main concern: "A conflict rages between technology and politics. Economics, so closely linked to both, has become the major battlefield. Stability and peace will reign in the world economy only when, somehow, the forces on the side of technology and the forces on the side of politics have once more been accommodated to each other."[13]

While Staley believed, along with many present-day writers, that politics and technology must ultimately adjust to one another, he emphasized, in contrast to contemporary writers, that it was not inevitable that politics adjust to technology. Reflecting the intense economic nationalism of the 1930s, Staley pointed out that the adjustment may very well be the other way around. As he reminds us, in his own time and in early periods economics has had to adjust to political realities: "In the 'Dark Ages' following the collapse of the Roman Empire, technology adjusted itself to politics. The magnificent Roman roads fell into disrepair, the baths and aqueducts and amphitheatres and villas into ruins. Society lapsed back to localism in production and distribution, forgot much of the learning and the technology and the governmental systems of earlier days."[14]

II

This rather lengthy discussion of the relationship between economics and politics argues the point that, although the economic and technical substructure partially determines and interacts with the political superstructure, political values and security interests are crucial determinants of international economic relations. Politics determines the framework of economic activity and channels it in directions which tend to serve the political objectives of dominant political groups and organizations. Throughout history each successive hegemonic power has organized economic space in terms of its own interests and purposes.

Following in this vein, the thesis of this essay is that transnational actors and processes are dependent upon peculiar patterns of interstate relations. Whether one is talking about the merchant adventurers of the sixteenth century, nineteenth-century finance capitalists, or twentieth-century multinational corporations, transnational actors have been able to play an important role in world affairs because it has been in the interest of the predominant power(s) for them to do so. As political circumstances have changed due to the rise and decline of nation-states, transnational processes have also been altered or ceased altogether. Thus, as the French economist François Perroux has observed, the world economy did not develop as a result of competition between equal partners but through the emergence and influence of great national economies that successively became dominant. [15]

From this perspective the multinational corporation exists as a transnational actor today because it is consistent with the political interest of the world's dominant power, the United States. This argument does not deny the analyses of economists who argue that the multinational corporation is a response to contemporary technological and economic developments. The argument is rather that these economic and technological factors have been able to exercise their profound effects because the United States—sometimes with the cooperation of other states and sometimes over their opposition—has created the necessary political framework. By implication, a diminution of the Pax Americana and the rise of powers hostile to the global activities of multinational corporations would bring their reign over international economic relations to an end.

The basic point was made some years ago by E. H. Carr when he wrote that "the science of economics presupposes a given political order, and cannot be profitably studied in isolation from politics." [16] An international economy based on free trade, Carr sought to convince his fellow Englishmen, was not a natural and inevitable state of affairs but reflected the economic and political interests of Great Britain. The regime of free trade had come into existence and was maintained by the exercise of British economic and military power. With the rise after 1880 of new industrial and military powers with contrasting economic interests, namely, Germany, Japan, and the United States, an international economy based on free trade and British power became less and less viable. A proponent of appeasement, Carr advocated in defense of the Munich Pact that England work with these challenging powers, particularly Germany, to create a new international system which reflected the changed balance of economic and military power and interests in the world.

Perhaps the most effective way to defend the thesis that the pattern of international economic relations is dependent upon the structure of the international political system is to review the origins of the Pax Britannica, its demise with the First World War, and the eventual rise of a Pax Americana after the Second World War. What this history clearly reveals is that transnational economic processes are not unique to our own age and that the pattern of international economic activity reflects the global balance of economic and military power.

Each successive international system that the world has known is the consequence of the territorial, diplomatic, and military realignments that have followed history's great wars. The origins of the Pax Britannica lie in the complicated series of negotiations that followed the great upheavals of the Napoleonic wars. The essential features of the system which were put into place at that time provided the general framework of international economic relations until the collapse of the system under the impact of the First World War.

The first essential feature of the Pax Britannica was the territorial settlement and the achievement of a balance of power among the five Great Powers.[17] This territorial re-alignment can be divided into two parts. In the first place, on the continent of Europe the territorial realignments checked the ambitions of Russia in the east and France in the west. Second, the overseas conquests of the continental powers were reduced at the same time that Great Britain acquired a number of important strategic overseas bases. As a result the four major powers on the Continent were kept in check by their own rivalries and by offshore Britain which played a balancing and mediating role.

British naval power, the second essential feature of the Pax Britannica, was able to exercise a powerful and pervasive influence over global politics due to a fortunate juncture of circumstances. Great Britain's geographical position directly off the coast of continental Europe and its possession of several strategic naval bases enabled it to control Europe's access to the outside world and to deny overseas colonies to continental governments. As a consequence, from 1825 when Great Britain warned France not to take advantage of the revolt of the Spanish colonies in America to the latter part of the century, the greater part of the non-European world was either independent or under British rule. Moreover, the maintenance of this global military hegemony was remarkably inexpensive; it thus permitted Great Britain to utilize its wealth and energies in the task of economic development.

Third, using primarily the instruments of free trade and foreign investment in this political-strategic framework, Great Britain was able, in effect, to restructure the international economy and to exercise great influence over the course of international affairs. As the world's first industrial nation, Great Britain fashioned an international division of labor which favored its own industrial strengths at the same time that it brought great benefits to the world at large. Exchanging manufactured goods for the food and raw materials of other nations, Great Britain was the industrial and financial center of a highly interdependent international economy.

One may reasonably argue, I believe, that in certain respects the regime of the Pax Britannica was the Golden Age of transnationalism. The activities of private financiers and capitalists enmeshed the nations in a web of interdependencies which certainly influenced the course of international relations. In contrast to our own era, in which the role of the multinational corporation in international economic relations is unprecedented, the private institutions of the City of London under the gold standard and the regime of free trade had a strategic and central place in world affairs unmatched by any transnational organization today. Prior to 1914 the focus of much of international relations was the City of London and the private individuals who managed the world's gold, traded in commodities, and floated foreign loans. Though this interdependence differs radically in kind from the internationalization of production and the immense trade in manufactured goods which characterize our own more industrialized world economy, this earlier great age of transnationalism should not be overlooked. In exaggerated acknowledgment of the political importance of the transnational actors which dominated this age J. A. Hobson in his book on imperialism asked rhetorically whether "a great war could be undertaken by any European State, or a great State loan subscribed, if the house of Rothschild and its connexions set their face against it." [18]

The foundations underlying the Pax Britannica and the transnational processes it fostered began to erode in the latter part of the nineteenth century. On the Continent the industrialization and unification of Germany profoundly altered the European balance of power. France, too, industrialized and began to challenge Great Britain's global supremacy. Overseas developments of equal or potentially greater magnitude were taking place. The rapid industrialization of Japan and the United States and their subsequent creation of powerful navies ended British control of the seas. No longer could Great Britain use its naval power to deny rivals access to the globe. With the decline of British supremacy the imperial struggle for the division of Africa and Asia began, leading eventually to the outbreak of the First World War.

The war completed the destruction of the pre-1914 system. As a consequence of the duration and intensity of the conflict one sector after another of economic life was nationalized and brought into the service of the state. The role of the state in economic affairs became pervasive, and economic nationalism largely replaced the laissez faire traditions upon which so much of prewar transnationalism had rested. Not until the Second World War would political relations favor the reemergence of extensive transnational activity.

The failure to revive the international economy after the First World War was due to many causes: the policies of economic revenge against Germany; the ill-conceived attempt to reestablish the gold standard; the nationalistic "beggar-my-neighbor" policies pursued by most states, etc. In terms of our primary concern in this essay one factor in particular needs to be stressed, namely, the failure of the United States to assume leadership of the world economy, a role Great Britain could no longer perform. Whereas before the war the City of London provided order and coordinated international economic activities, now London was unable and New York was unwilling to restructure the international economy disrupted by the First World War. The result was a leadership vacuum which contributed in part to the onset of the Great Depression and eventually the Second World War.

For our purposes two developments during this interwar period hold significance. The first was the Ottawa Agreement of 1932 which created the sterling area of imperial preference and reversed Great Britain's traditional commitment to multilateral free trade. The purpose of the agreement between Great Britain and the Commonwealth, an action whose intellectual roots went back to the nineteenth century, was to establish a regional trading bloc effectively isolated from the rest of the world economy. Germany in central Europe and Japan in Asia followed suit, organizing under their hegemonies the neighboring areas of strategic and economic importance. "This development of trading blocs led by great powers," one authority writes, "was the most significant economic development of the years immediately preceding the second World War. As always the breakdown of international law and economic order gave opportunity to the ruthless rather than to the strong." [19] Such a system of law and order the international gold standard had provided. Under this system transnational actors could operate with little state interference. With its collapse nation-states struggled to create exclusive spheres of influence, and trade relations became instruments of economic warfare.

The second important development from the perspective of this essay was the passage of the Reciprocal Trade Agreements Act in June 1934. The purpose of this act was to enable the United States government to negotiate reductions in tariff barriers. Followed in 1936 by the Tripartite Monetary Agreement, the act not only reflected the transformation of the United States into a major industrial power but also represented the first step by the United States to assert its leadership of the world economy. Furthermore, it demonstrated the potential of bilateral negotiation as a method to achieve the expansion of multinational trade even though the immediate impact of the act was relatively minor. World trade continued to be dominated by preference systems, especially the sterling area, from which the United States was excluded. The importance of this prewar situation and the determination of the United States to overcome this discrimination cannot be too greatly emphasized. The reorganization of the world economy was to be the keynote of American postwar planning.

III

American plans for the postwar world were based on several important assumptions. In the first place, American leadership tended to see the origins of the Second World War as largely economic. [20] The failure to revive the international economy after the First World War and the subsequent rise of rival trading blocs were regarded as the underlying causes of the conflict. Second, it was assumed that peace would be best promoted by the establishment of a system of multinational trade relations which guaranteed to all states equal access to the world's resources and markets. Third, the main obstacles to the achievement of such a universal system, Americans believed, were the nationalistic and discriminatory measures adopted in the 1930s by various European countries—trade preferences, exchange controls, quantitative restrictions, competitive currency depreciations, etc.

The importance of economic considerations in American postwar planning has led in recent years to a spate of writings by revisionist historians who interpret these efforts as part of a large imperial design. [21] While this literature does serve to correct the simpleminded orthodox position that the cold war originated as a Communist plot to achieve world domination, it goes much too far and distorts the picture in another direction.

There is no question that the creation of a system of multilateral trade relations was in the interests of the United States. Preference systems ran directly counter to American basic interests as the world's dominant economic power and a major trading nation. It does not follow from this fact, however, that American efforts to achieve such a system were solely self-serving and unmotivated by the sincere belief that economic nationalism and competition were at the root of the Second World War. Nor does it follow that what is good for the United States is contrary to the general welfare of other nations.

The American emphasis on postwar economic relations represented a long tradition in American thought on international relations. The American liberal ideal since the founding of the Republic has been the substitution of commercial for political relations between states. [22] In the best free trade tradition trade relations between nations are considered to be a force for peace. Furthermore, as a nation which felt it had been discriminated against by the more powerful European states, the United States wanted a world in which it would have equal access to markets. Universal equality of opportunity, not imperial domination, was the motif of American postwar foreign economic planning.

This naive American faith in the beneficial effects of economic intercourse was reflected in the almost complete absence of attention to strategic matters in American postwar plans. In contrast to the prodigious energies devoted to the restructuring of the international economy little effort was given to the strategic and territorial balance of the postwar world. This neglect is explicable in large part, however, by the prevailing American assumption that a universal system based on an integrated world economy and on the United Nations would replace the traditional emphasis on spheres of influence and the balance of power.

If one accepts the revisionist argument that imperial ambition underlay American postwar plans, then the cold war should have been between the United States and Western Europe, particularly the United Kingdom, rather than between the Union of Soviet Socialist Republics and the United States. The bête noire of American planners was European discrimination and especially the imperial preference which encompassed a high percentage of world trade and exercised considerable discrimination against American goods. American plans for the postwar era were directed against the British in particular. Beginning with the framing of the Atlantic Charter in 1941 and continuing through the negotiation of the Lend-Lease Act (1941), the Bretton Woods Agreement (1944), and the British loan (1945), the thrust of American policy was directed against Commonwealth discrimination.

In light of the intensity of these American efforts to force the United Kingdom and other European countries to accept a multilateral system it is important to appreciate that they were abandoned in response to growth of Soviet-American hostility. As American leadership came to accept the Soviet diplomatic-military challenge as the major postwar problem, the United States attitude toward international economic relations underwent a drastic reversal. In contrast to earlier emphases on multilateralism and nondiscrimination the United States accepted discrimination in the interest of rebuilding the shattered West European economy.

The retort of revisionists to this argument is that the American-Soviet struggle originated in the American desire to incorporate Eastern Europe, particularly Poland, into the American scheme for a global empire. This effort, it is claimed, clashed with the legitimate security concerns of the Soviet Union, and the cold war evolved as the Soviet defensive response to the American effort to expand economically into the Soviet sphere of influence. If the United States had not been driven by the greed of its corporations, American and Soviet interests could easily have been accommodated.

There are sufficient grounds for this interpretation to give it some plausibility. Certainly, American efforts to incorporate Eastern Europe and even the Soviet Union into the world capitalistic economy raised Soviet suspicions. Although the American view was that the withdrawal of the Soviet Union from the world economy following the Bolshevik Revolution had been a contributing factor to the outbreak of the Second World War and that a peaceful world required Soviet reintegration, the Russians could easily interpret these efforts as an attempt to undermine communism. No doubt in part they were. But it is a long jump from these American efforts to trade in an area of little historical interest to the United States to a conflict so intense and durable that it has on several occasions taken the world to the brink of thermonuclear holocaust.

A more realistic interpretation, I believe, is that the origins of the cold war lie in the unanticipated consequences of the Second World War. The collapse of German power in Europe and of Japanese power in Asia created a power vacuum which both the United States and the Soviet Union sought to fill to their own advantage. One need not even posit aggressive designs on either side to defend this interpretation, although my own position is that the Soviet Union desired (and still desires) to extend its sphere of influence far beyond the glacis of Eastern Europe. To support this political interpretation of the cold war it is sufficient to argue that the power vacuums in Central Europe and the northwestern Pacific created a security dilemma for both powers. In terms of its own security neither power could afford to permit the other to fill this vacuum, and the efforts of each to prevent this only increased the insecurity of the other, causing it to redouble its own efforts. Each in response to the other organized its own bloc, freezing the lines of division established by the victorious armies and wartime conferences.

One cannot understand, however, the pattern of the cold war and its significance for international economic relations unless one appreciates the asymmetric situations of the United States and the Soviet Union. Whereas the Soviet Union is a massive land power directly abutting Western Europe and the northwestern Pacific (primarily Korea and Japan), the United States is principally a naval and air power separated from the zones of contention by two vast oceans. As a consequence, while the Soviet Union has been able with relative ease to bring its influence to bear on its periphery at relatively much less cost in terms of its balance of payments, the United States has had to organize a global system of bases and alliances involving an immense drain on its balance of payments. Moreover, while the Soviet system has been held together largely through the exercise of Soviet military power, economic relations have been an important cement holding the American bloc together.

These economic and strategic differences between the two blocs have been crucial determinants of the postwar international economy and the patterns of transnational relations which have emerged. For this reason some attention must be given to the interplay of economic and political factors in the evolution of relations between the three major components of the contemporary international economy: the United States, Western Europe, and Japan.

Contrary to the hopes of the postwar economic planners who met at Bretton Woods in 1944, the achievement of a system of multilateral trade was soon realized to be an impossibility. The United Kingdom's experience with currency convertibility, which had been forced upon it by the United States, had proven to be a disaster. The United Kingdom and the rest of Europe were simply too weak and short of dollars to engage in a free market. A further weakening of their economies threatened to drive them into the arms of the Soviet Union. In the interest of preventing this the United States in cooperation with Western Europe had to rebuild the world economy in a way not envisaged by the postwar planners.

The reconstruction of the West European economy involved the solution of three problems. In the first place, Europe was desperately short of the dollars required to meet immediate needs and to replenish its capital stock. Second, the prewar European economies had been oriented toward colonial markets. Now the colonies were in revolt, and the United States strongly opposed the revival of a world economy based on a colonial preference system. Third, the practices of economic nationalism and closed preference systems between European states and their overseas colonies had completely fragmented the European economy.

The problem of rehabilitating the economy of the Federal Republic of Germany (West Germany) was particularly difficult. The major trading nation on the Continent, its division into Soviet and Western zones and the Soviet occupation of Eastern Europe had cut industrial West Germany off from its natural trading partners in the agricultural German Democratic Republic (East Germany) and the East. The task therefore was to integrate the industrial Western zones into a larger West European economy comprising agricultural France and Italy. The failure to reintegrate industrial Germany into the larger world economy was regarded to have been one of the tragic errors after World War I. A repetition of this error would force West Germany into the Soviet camp.

The American response to this challenge is well known. Through the Marshall Plan, the Organization for European Economic Cooperation (OEEC), and the European Coal and Steel Community (ECSC) the European economy was revived and radically transformed. For our purposes one point is significant. In the interest of security the United States tolerated, and in fact promoted, the creation of a preference area in Western Europe which discriminated against American goods. At first the mechanism of discrimination was the nonconvertibility of European currencies; then, after the establishment of the European Economic Community (EEC) in 1958, discrimination took the form of one common external tariff.

The economic impact of economic regionalism in Western Europe was not, however, completely detrimental to United States-European trade. One can in fact argue that regionalism gave Europe the courage and security to depart from traditions of economic nationalism and colonialism. The establishment of a large trading area in Europe turned out to be more trade-creating than trade-diverting. As a consequence American and European economic ties increased and the United States continued to enjoy a favorable balance of trade with its European partners.

With respect to Japan the United States faced a situation similar to that presented by West Germany. Although Japan was not severely damaged by the war, it was a densely populated major trading nation exceptionally dependent upon foreign sources of raw materials, technology, and agricultural products. With the victory of the communists on the Chinese mainland Japan's major prewar trading partner came under the control of the Soviet bloc. Furthermore, Japan suffered from discrimination by other industrialized states both in their home markets and in their overseas colonial empires. The exclusion of the Japanese from South and Southeast Asia practiced by the Dutch, French, and British had been a major cause of Japan's military aggression, and the continued existence of these preference systems threatened its economic well-being. Separated from the Soviet Union by a small body of water and economically isolated, Japan's situation was a highly precarious one.

As in the case of West Germany the task of American foreign policy was to integrate Japan into the larger world economy and lessen the attraction of markets controlled by the Communist bloc. While this history of American efforts to restructure Japan's role in the world economy is less well known than is the history of its European counterpart, the basic aspects deserve to be emphasized. In the first place, the United States brought pressures to bear against Dutch, French, and British colonialism in South and Southeast Asia and encouraged the integration of these areas into a larger framework of multilateral trade. Second, over the strong opposition of Western Europe the United States sponsored Japanese membership in the International Monetary Fund (IMF), the General Agreement on Tariffs and Trade (GATT), and other international organizations. [23] Third, and most significant, the United States in the negotiations leading to the Treaty of Peace with Japan granted Japan privileged access to the American home market. [24]

At the same time that these developments in the economic realm were taking place, through the instrumentalities of the North Atlantic Treaty Organization (NATO) and the Treaty of Peace with Japan, Western Europe and Japan were brought under the protection of the American nuclear umbrella. In Europe, Japan, and around the periphery of the Soviet Union and the People's Republic of China (Communist China) the United States erected a base system by which to counter the Soviet advantage of geographical proximity. Thus, with their security guaranteed by this Pax Americana, Japan, Western Europe, and, to a lesser extent, the United States have been able to devote the better part of their energies to the achievement of high rates of economic growth within the framework of a highly interdependent transnational economy.

Just as the Pax Britannica provided the security and political framework for the expansion of transnational economic activity in the nineteenth century, so this Pax Americana has fulfilled a similar function in the mid-twentieth century. Under American leadership the various rounds of GATT negotiations have enabled trade to expand at an unprecedented rate, far faster than the growth of gross national product in the United States and Western Europe. The United States dollar has become the basis of the international monetary system, and, with the rise of the Eurodollar market, governments have lost almost all control over a large segment of the transnational economy. Finally, the multinational corporation has found the global political environment a highly congenial one and has been able to integrate production across national boundaries.

The corollary of this argument is, of course, that just as a particular array of political interests and relations permitted this system of transnational economic relations to come into being, so changes in these political factors can profoundly alter the system and even bring it to an end. If, as numerous writers argue, there is a growing contradiction between the nation-state and transnational activities, the resolution may very well be in favor of the nation-state or, more likely, of regional arrangements centered on the dominant industrial powers: Japan, the United States, and Western Europe.

IV

This argument that contemporary transnational processes rest on a peculiar set of political relationships can be substantiated, I believe, if one analyzes the two most crucial relationships which underlie the contemporary international economy. The first is the relationship between the United States and West Germany, the second is that between the United States and Japan.

While the American-West German special relationship is based on a number of factors including that of mutual economic advantage, from the perspective of transnational activities one factor is of crucial importance. In simplest terms this is the exchange of American protection of West Germany against the Soviet Union for guaranteed access to EEC markets for American products and direct investment. In both agricultural commodities and manufactured goods the United States continues to enjoy a very favorable trade balance with Western Europe. With respect to direct investment the subsidiaries of American corporations have been able to establish a very powerful position in Western Europe since the beginning of the EEC in 1958.

Without this overall favorable trade balance with Western Europe and West German willingness to hold dollars, the American balance-of-payments situation might, the West Germans fear, force the United States to reduce its troop strength in West Germany. As such a move could lessen the credibility of the American nuclear deterrent, the West Germans are very reluctant to make any moves which would weaken the American presence in Western Europe. Consequently, while the significance of American direct investment in Europe for the American balance of payments is unclear, the West Germans are unwilling to take any action regarding this investment which might alienate American opinion and lessen the American commitment to Western Europe.

The importance of the military dependence of West Germany on the United States for continued access to EEC markets for subsidiaries of American corporations was revealed several years ago. In the early 1960s President Charles de Gaulle of France launched an offensive against increasing American economic penetration of Western Europe. While the major part of this effort was directed against "the hegemony of the dollar," a parallel attempt was made to arrest and possibly reverse the flow of American direct investment in Western Europe. [25]

The initial move of the French government was to prevent further American direct investment in France. This effort, however, soon proved to be self-defeating. Denied permission to establish or purchase subsidiaries in France, American corporations were welcomed into one of France's partners in the EEC and thus still had access to the French market. That France acting alone could not solve the problem was driven home to the French when General Motors Corporation, denied permission to locate in France, established one of the largest automobile assembly plants in Western Europe across the border in Belgium.

In response to this situation de Gaulle sought to obtain West German cooperation against American investment in EEC countries. Together these two most powerful of the six could dictate a policy which the others would be forced to accept. Through the instrumentality of the Franco-German Friendship Treaty of 1963, therefore, de Gaulle sought to form a Bonn-Paris axis directed against American hegemony in Western Europe. While the terms of this treaty go beyond our immediate concerns, two aspects are important. In the first place, de Gaulle wanted West Germany to join France in taking a stand against American investment. Second, he wanted to see joint West German–French cooperative efforts in science, technology, and industry in order to lessen European dependence upon the United States in these areas.

Although there was sentiment in West Germany favorable to taking measures to limit the rapidly growing role of American subsidiaries in EEC countries, the West German government refused to take any action which might weaken the American commitment to defend Western Europe. The United States government not only reminded the West Germans that a continued American military presence was dependent upon West German support of measures to lessen the American balance-of-payments deficit, West Germany was also pressured to increase its military purchases from the United States and to avoid competitive arrangements with France. Largely as a result of these American pressures the Friendship Treaty was in effect aborted and the first serious counteroffensive of the nation-state against the multinational corporation collapsed. It is clear, however, that the outcome of this tale would have been altogether different if West Germany had desired greater military and economic independence from the United States.

Turning to the other pillar of the contemporary transnational economy, the American-Japanese special relationship, mutual economic interest is an important bond, but the primary factor in this relationship has been the security issue. In contrast to the American-West German situation, however, this relationship involves American protection and a special position for the Japanese in the American market in exchange for United States bases in Japan and Okinawa. The asymmetry of this relationship compared with that between the United States and West Germany reflects the differences in the economic and military situations.

As mentioned earlier the basic problem for American foreign policy with respect to Japan was how to reintegrate this highly industrialized and heavily populated country into the world economy. Given communist control of mainland Asia and the opposition of European countries to opening their markets to the Japanese this meant throwing open the American economy to Japanese exports. As a consequence of this favored treatment the Japanese have enjoyed an exceptionally favorable balance of trade with the United States. For security reasons the United States has not only tolerated this situation but with a few exceptions, has not restricted Japanese imports or forced the Japanese to open their economy to American direct investment.

In contrast to the situation prevailing in Europe the purpose of American military base structure in Japan is not merely to deter local aggression against the Japanese; rather, it is essential for the maintenance of American power and influence throughout the western Pacific and Southeast Asia. Without access to Japanese bases the United States could not have fought two wars in Asia over the past two decades and could not continue its present role in the area. Largely because of this dependence upon Japanese bases for its strategic position around the periphery of Communist China, the United States has been willing to tolerate in a period of balance-of-payments deficit the $1.5 billion annual trade surplus Japan enjoys vis-à-vis the United States.

In the case of both the American-European and the American-Japanese relationships new forces are now at work which threaten to undermine the foundations of contemporary transnational relations. In the case of United States–European relations the most dramatic change is the decreased fear of the Soviet Union by both partners. As a consequence both Americans and Europeans are less tolerant of the price they have to pay for their special relationship. The Europeans feel less dependent upon the United States for their security and are more concerned with the detrimental aspects of close economic, military, and diplomatic ties with the United States. The United States, for its part, is increasingly sensitive to European discrimination against American exports and feels threatened by EEC moves toward the creation of a preference system encompassing much of Western Europe, the Middle East, and Africa. As the Mansfield amendment to reduce United States military forces in Europe reveals, Americans, too, are less willing to pay the cost of maintaining a large military force abroad.[26]

With respect to the relationship of Japan to the United States, strategic and economic changes are undermining the foundations of transnationalism. At the same time that Communist China is receding as a security threat to the United States and Japan, economic strains are beginning to aggravate relations between the two countries. In the eyes of the United States Japan's economy is no longer weak and vulnerable, necessitating special consideration by the United States. As a consequence the demands of American interests for import curbs against Japanese goods and for the liberalization of Japanese policies on foreign direct investment are beginning to take precedence over foreign policy and strategic considerations. Nor does the United States continue to accept the fact that the defense burden should rest so heavily on it alone. Underlying the Nixon Doctrine of American retrenchment in Asia is the appreciation that a greater Japanese military effort would not only reduce American defense costs but would also cause the Japanese to divert resources from their export economy and relieve Japanese pressures in the American market.

The Japanese for their part resent the fact that they are almost totally dependent upon the United States for their security and economic well-being. While they of course want to maintain a strong position in the American market and feel particularly threatened by protectionist sentiment in the United States, they are growing increasingly concerned about the price they must pay for their close association with the United States. Moreover, they feel especially vulnerable to American economic pressures such as those that have been exerted to induce Japan to permit direct investment by American corporations. But the dominant new factor is the Japanese desire to play a more independent role in the world and to enjoy the prestige that is commensurate with their powerful and expanding economy.

In the cases of both American-European and American-Japanese relations new strains have appeared which threaten to undermine the political framework of transnational economic activity. Diplomatic and military bonds tying Europe and Japan to the United States have weakened at the same time that economic conflicts have intensified and have become less tolerable to all three major parties. As a result the favorable political factors that have facilitated the rapid expansion of transnational processes over the past several decades are receding. In their stead new political forces have come into play that are tending to isolate the United States and to favor a more regional organization of the international economy.

On the other hand, one must readily acknowledge that the multinational corporation and transnational processes have achieved tremendous momentum. It is not without good reason that numerous authorities have predicted the demise of the nation-state and the complete reordering of international life by 200 or 300 "megafirms." [27] Perhaps, as these authorities argue, the multinational corporation as an institution has sufficiently taken root in the vested interests of all major parties that it can survive the vicissitudes of political change. History, however, does not provide much comfort for this train of thought. As Staley and Viner have suggested, the contradiction between the economic and political organization of society is not always resolved in favor of economic rationality. Moreover, whatever the outcome—the preservation of multilateral transnational processes, a reversion to economic nationalism, or the division of the globe by economic regionalism—the determining consideration will be the diplomatic and strategic interests of the dominant powers.

V

Prior to concluding this essay one crucial question remains to be treated: What, after all, has been the impact of transnational economic activities, especially the multinational corporation, on international politics? In answer to this question both Marxists and what one might call the transnational ideologists see these transnational processes and actors as having had a profound impact on international relations. Some go much further. By breaking the monopoly of the nation-state over international economic relations the multinational corporation is claimed to have altered the very nature of international relations.

Under certain circumstances and in relation to particular states there can be little doubt that the multinational corporation has, and can exercise, considerable influence over domestic and international relations. One could mention in this connection the international petroleum companies, for example. But in general there is little evidence to substantiate the argument that the multinational corporation as an independent actor has had a significant impact on international politics. As Staley has convincingly shown in his study of foreign investment prior to World War II, where business corporations have exercised an influence over political developments they have tended to do so as instruments of their home governments rather than as independent actors. [28]

Contemporary studies on the multinational corporation indicate that Staley's conclusion continues to hold true. While the evidence is indisputable that the multinational corporation is profoundly important in the realm of international economic relations, its political significance is largely confined to its impact on domestic politics where it is an irritant to nationalistic sentiments. In part the resentment has been due to the unwarranted interference by foreign-owned corporations in domestic affairs; this has especially been the case in less developed countries. More frequently, nationalistic feelings have been aroused by the predominant positions multinational corporations may hold in the overall economy or in particularly sensitive sectors.

Despite all the polemics against multinational corporations there is little evidence to support the view that they have been very successful in replacing the nation-state as the primary actor in international politics. Where these business enterprises have influenced international political relations, they have done so, like any other interest group, by influencing the policies of their home governments. Where they have tried to influence the foreign and economic policies of host governments, they have most frequently been acting in response to the laws of their home countries and as agents of their home governments. In defense of this argument it should be noted that a Canadian study of American direct investment in Canada focused its concern almost exclusively on the extraterritorial application of American law (antitrust laws, the Trading with the Enemy Act, and balance-of-payments regulations). [29] As Canada has a higher percentage of foreign ownership than any other industrialized country and as this study was one of the most thorough which any government has conducted on foreign direct investment, its conclusions are especially significant.

Contrary to the argument that the multinational corporation will somehow supplant the nation-state, I think it is closer to the truth to argue that the role of the nation-state in economic as well as in political life is increasing and that the multinational corporation is actually a stimulant to the further extension of state power in the economic realm. One should not forget that the multinational corporation is largely an American phenomenon and that in response to this American challenge other governments are increasingly intervening in their domestic economies in order to counterbalance the power of American corporations and to create domestic rivals of equal size and competence.

The paradox of the contemporary situation is that the increasing interdependence among national economies, for which the multinational corporation is partially responsible, is accompanied by increased governmental interference in economic affairs. What this neo-mercantilism constitutes, of course, is one response to the basic contradiction between the economic and political organization of contemporary international society. But in contrast to the opinion of a George Ball who sees this conflict resolved in favor of transnational processes, the internationalization of production, and actors like the multinational corporation, nationalists in Canada, Western Europe, and the less developed world favor upholding more powerful states to counterbalance large multinational corporations.

Similarly, the impetus today behind the EEC, Japan's effort to build an economic base less dependent on the United States, and other moves toward regionalism reflect in part a desire to lessen the weight of American economic power; in effect, these regional undertakings are essentially economic alliances between sovereign governments. Although they are altering the political framework within which economic forces will increasingly have to operate, the basic unit is and will remain the nation-state. For better or for worse it continues to be the most powerful object of man's loyalty and affection.

NOTES

1. Sidney Rolfe, "Updating Adam Smith," *Interplay*, November 1968 (Vol. 2, No. 4), p. 15.
2. An analysis of the argument is provided by Edmund Silberner, *The Problem of War in Nineteenth Century Economic Thought,* trans. Alexander H. Krappe (Princeton, N.J.: Princeton University Press, 1946).

3. Adam Smith, *An Inquiry into the Nature and Causes of the Wealth of Nations,* ed. Edwin Cannan (New York: Modern Library, 1937).

4. The relevant sections appear in Ernst Wangermann, ed., *The Role of Force in History: A Study of Bismarck's Policy of Blood and Iron,* trans. Jack Cohen (New York: International Publishers, 1968). The best exposition of Marxist theories of economic relations is P. J. D. Wiles, *Communist International Economics* (New York: Frederick A. Praeger, 1969).

5. Wangermann, p. 13.

6. *Ibid.,* p. 14.

7. The article appears in J. N. Bhagwati, ed., *Economics and World Order* (New York: World Law Fund, 1970). [Reprinted in this volume.]

8. Jacob Viner, *The Customs Union Issue* (Studies in the Administration of International Law and Organization, No. 10) (New York: Carnegie Endowment for International Peace, 1950).

9. *Ibid.,* pp. 98–99.

10. *Ibid.,* p. 101.

11. *Ibid.,* pp. 95–101.

12. *Ibid.,* p. 105.

13. Eugene Staley, *World Economy in Transition: Technology vs. Politics, Laissez Faire vs. Planning, Power vs. Welfare* (Publications of the Council on Foreign Relations) (New York: Council on Foreign Relations [under the auspices of the American Coördinating Committee for International Studies], 1939), pp. 51-52.

14. *Ibid.,* p. 52.

15. Perroux's theory of the dominant economy is set forth in his "Esquisse d'une théorie de l'économie dominante," *Economie appliquée,* April–September 1948 (Vol. I, Nos. 2-3), pp. 243-300. [Reprinted in this volume.]

16. Edward Hallett Carr, *The Twenty Years' Crisis, 1919-1939: An Introduction to the Study of International Politics* (2nd ed.; New York: St. Martin's Press, 1954), p. 117.

17. Albert H. Imlah, *Economic Elements in the Pax Britannica: Studies in British Foreign Trade in the Nineteenth Century* (Cambridge, Mass: Harvard University Press, 1958), chapter I.

18. J. A. Hobson, *Imperialism: A Study* (3rd rev. ed.; London: G. Allen & Unwin, 1938), p. 57.

19. J. B. Condliffe, *The Commerce of Nations* (New York: W. W. Norton & Co., 1950), p. 502.

20. The basic source for this period is Richard N. Gardner, *Sterling-Dollar Diplomacy: The Origins and Prospects of Our International Economic Order* (expd. ed.; New York: McGraw-Hill Book Co., 1969).

21. The most ambitious statement of this thesis is Gabriel Kolko, *The Politics of War: The World and the United States Foreign Policy, 1943-1945* (New York: Random House, 1968).

22. See the study by Felix Gilbert, *To the Farewell Address: Ideas of Early American Foreign Policy* (Princeton, N.J: Princeton University Press, 1961).

23. For the history of these efforts see Gardner Patterson, *Discrimination in International Trade: The Policy Issues, 1945-1965* (Princeton, N.J: Princeton University Press, 1966), chapter 6.

24. Frederick S. Dunn, in collaboration with Annemarie Shimoney, Percy E. Corbett, and Bernard C. Cohen, *Peace-Making and the Settlement with Japan* (Princeton, N.J: Princeton University Press, 1963), chapter 7.

25. For this history see Robert Gilpin, *France in the Age of the Scientific State* (Princeton, N.J: Princeton University Press [for the Center of International Studies, Princeton University], 1968), chapter 3.

26. United States, Congress, House, *Amending the Military Selective Service Act of 1967 to Increase Military Pay; To Authorize Military Active Duty Strengths for Fiscal Year 1972; And for Other Purposes,* H.R. 6531, 92nd Cong., 1st sess., 1971, Amendment No. 86.

27. Howard V. Perlmutter, "Some Management Problems in Spaceship Earth: The Megafirm and the Global Industrial Estate," *Academy of Management Proceedings, 29th Annual Meeting, Chicago, August 24-27, 1969,* pp. 59-93.

28. Eugene Staley, *War and the Private Investor: A Study in the Relations of International Politics and International Private Investment* (Garden City, N.Y: Doubleday, Doran & Co., 1935). [Chapter 13 reprinted in this volume.]

29. *Foreign Ownership and the Structure of Canadian Industry,* Report of the Task Force on the Structure of Canadian Industry (Ottawa: Queen's Printer, January 1968).

PART II
THEORIES

INTRODUCTION

The empirical description of transnational corporate activity is not enough; it must go hand in hand with theoretical analysis based on explicit concepts and leading up to significant generalizations. Establishment of the "fact" that this global phenomenon is important and omnipresent does not suffice; further explanation, leading to a better understanding, is required.

Explanations of the activity of multinational corporations are answers to such questions as "why foreign investment?" "Why does the world need business enterprises that cross national frontiers?" For in this world of nation-states we inhabit it is not immediately obvious why corporations need to extend transnationally and why business organizations domiciled in one nation-state should take it upon themselves to impinge on the lives and livelihoods of peoples in other nation-states. The answers to such questions are explanations of the basic purposes and the functions of corporate enterprise at the global level, and at bottom these explanations are in fact arguments about the legitimacy of such enterprise. Why should transnational corporations be regarded as legitimate institutions in the world today? What are the grounds on which they are granted special privileges and on which their "intrusions" into everyday life may be justified? These questions are also of great political importance.

At the risk of considerable oversimplification we might say that two different sets of answers can be given in response to these questions: (1) answers that stress the *economic functions* of transnational enterprise (its contributions to production and to efficiency, to streamlining distribution and marketing, and to research and product innovation and to economic development in general); and (2) answers that seek to come to grips with *power*—in other words, with the political consequences of the concentration of functions and resources that is the hallmark of the corporate phenomenon. For, as we have already noted, a basic characteristic of multinational corporations is that they are large and powerful; they are capable of inspiring awe, respect, and suspicion on this ground alone. They are large in part because they operate on a large (that is, global) scale, and size in turn becomes a condition of power. Because they are large they cannot easily be ignored; they obtrude on their surroundings. In a world accustomed to thinking of nation-states as the only rightful wielders of concentrated power, they are eyed with jealousy and apprehension.

The explanation of the economic functions of multinational corporations is the work of students of business. Yet even economists no longer explain transnational corporate activity as the product of the operation of the global marketplace. Some economists would even argue that in a perfect market, local entrepreneurs could always be found to perform the necessary managerial and investment functions, rendering transnational activity redundant. Charles Kindleberger, a professor of economics at the Massachusetts Institute of Technology, reviews recent theories of direct foreign investment (explanations of why firms gain and maintain control over assets, including subsidiaries and affiliates, in other countries) and arrives at the firm conclusion that a satisfactory explanation cannot proceed from the premise of the perfect market but must be couched in terms of a theory of monopolistic competition. For him, foreign investment is the product of the monopolistic advantages that might accrue because of departures (either in supply or in marketing) from free market conditions, or because of economies of scale, or because of governmental action. Much of the benefit linked with multinational enterprise is seen as deriving from its contribution to innovation and technology.

Kindleberger here adopts the monopolistic theory of foreign investment first advanced by Stephen Hymer, a student of his, in 1960. But Kindleberger adds to it a paradoxical corollary: although large transnational firms may swallow up competitors and exploit their monopolistic advantages, their main impact is the widening of the area of competition. Kindleberger therefore argues that large international firms lead the world toward greater economic efficiency, even though the road passes through the dangerous terrain of monopolistic control. But he concludes by indicating that general statements about the desirability of foreign investment tend not to be useful and that any analysis must be on a case-by-case basis, fortified by acquaintance with individual corporations.

Given the facts that foreign investment problems are large-scale (in great part because the corporations that give rise to them are themselves large) and that they vary with the corporations involved, Kindleberger's conclusion seems eminently reasonable. One wonders, though, how generally acceptable is Kindleberger's view concerning the liberating effect of transnational business activity. Hymer himself (of whom more in Part V) probably would not have accepted it. For another corollary of the monopolistic theory of foreign investment might be that in a world of perfectly free markets, transnational activity would be redundant and nation-states, rather than foreign business, might be the agents exploiting market imperfections that are largely the result of the existence of states and of governmental regulations. Yet it can also be argued that even in a world of perfect competition, specifically global functions (such as the distribution of oil, satellite communications, or the production of new knowledge) would have to be performed, and the confrontation of foreign and domestic enterpreneurs, a problem that occupies Kindleberger most of all, would be less important than the efficient performance of an essential service.

Raymond Vernon's theory of the product cycle (based on research conducted at the Harvard School of Business) might be described as an application or a variant of the monopolistic theory of foreign investment, exemplified by the experience of United States-based multinational corporations in the past one hundred years. Experience in introducing innovative products into the largest and the highest-income market in the world gave these firms a monopolistic advantage that enabled them to increase their exports and to expand, setting up manufacturing establishments in other areas of the world. It is also a necessary part of this argument that after a time the novelty of the products wears off and local competitors arise and meet the challenge on their own terms. According to this model, a successful firm would be required to produce a steady stream of innovative products, or at least would want to market a steady flow of differentiated products. If it did not, or could not, the firm would be well advised to cease international activity at the point of the cycle where it no longer had the advantage.

Theodore Moran[1] has used the product cycle model to explain the "strong pressures for foreign investment" that he believes so strongly affect "American corporate capitalism." He sees the concept of "institutional necessity" as capable of replacing traditional Marxist models of surplus capital, or underconsumption, that have generally received scant empirical support. Vernon, however, believes that by 1970 the product cycle model had begun to be less convincing as an explanation of American corporate behavior.

The monopolistic theory of direct foreign investment, including the product cycle variant, hints at the facts of power. The most important consequence of restraints to competition is market power, that is, the power all monopolitic enterprises (and also oligopolitistic firms, for oligopoly—a market structure dominated by a few firms—is a form of monopoly) have over the conditions in which they operate, the supplies they buy, the markets they serve, and above all, the price and output decisions that are made with regard to their products. Market power translates into profits, profits create wealth, and wealth is a form of power.

Kindleberger's model, as he presents it, applies to national markets, where international corporations serve local needs and enjoy a monopolistic advantage. But the market power of transnational enterprises may also be exercised at the global level, in world markets. An excellent and most important illustration of such a process is John Blair's description of how the major oil companies controlled world oil prices between 1945 and 1973. Blair served for many years as a government economist in Washington and spent the last years of his life writing what is considered the definitive work on *The Control of Oil* (published in 1976). This case study is obviously significant because oil is by far the most important single commodity in international trade today, and because disruptions in its flow, as during the 1973-1974 oil embargo with its attendant price increases, can bring havoc to the world economy. His study is also a textbook example of the market power of transnational corporations, exercised in this case not through explicit cartel agreements but rather through the informal coordination of production so as to achieve a predictable growth rate for world oil supplies. Since 1973 the market power of the Organization of Petroleum Exporting Countries (OPEC) has been added to the power of the oil majors, and it has been argued that OPEC governments could not have carried out their daring price increases without exerting control over the world markets that had been built up by the oil transnationals in previous decades.

Blair's analysis is not noncontroversial; oil industry spokesmen have reacted sharply in opposition to it. They point out, among other things, that major oil corporations' share of crude oil production outside North America and the communist countries fell from 82 percent in 1963 to 30 percent in 1975, and that similar if less drastic declines also occurred in their participation in refining and marketing operations. During this period, governments boosted their percentage of crude output to 62 percent.[2] This seems to indicate that the global oil industry is now moving toward a condition of lesser concentration and, if that industry is typical of other transnational economic structures, other global industries may be moving in the same direction as the result of such processes as nationalization, and the entry of new firms.

The studies in this part focus on the power of multinational corporations and the ways that power may be exercised. Such corporations exercise not only their own power; but as we noted in Part I, in Gilpin's article in particular, they are influential and effective in part because they are part of "dominant economies."

François Perroux is an eminent French economist who presented a series of lectures on a theory of the "dominant economy" in 1947 at a time when American economic influence in Europe was at its all-time peak and when Europeans were facing the problem of coming to terms with the fact of American dominance. Even though the United States remains the world's largest economy, this fact is no longer so salient today, and the immediate problems Perroux analyzed are no longer current; yet because of the basic questions he raises and the clarity of his arguments, his study remains a classic discussion of the elements of international political economy. For those who have no background in elementary economics this selection requires especially careful reading and some use of the Glossary at the end of this volume, but the extra effort is worthwhile.

The core of Perroux's analysis is the effect of power on economies in general and the universality of what Perroux calls the domination effect. Between two economic units (such as firms, or national economies) the domination effect may be present, either because of differences in size and/or bargaining power, or because the units participate in different zones of economic activity. Just as firms might dominate markets, so national economies can also be dominant in the world at large, and a similar analysis can be applied to both. Firms associated with a dominant economy reap a number of advantages, depending in part on the unity of decision-making in the dominant economy. They are favored in part also because macro-decisions about the "rules of the game" of international economics (including the rules governing the monetary and trade systems) become an object of negotiation in which the superior size and bargaining strength, and the active role of the dominant economies, become salient points. The processes initiated by and the advantages accruing to such firms, and to the dominant economy, are irreversible. Given the existence of the nation-state system, which is a system of national monopolies (Perroux purposely refers to the State as "the monopolist of public constraint" in order to emphasize the analytical parallel between the economic monopoly of certain firms and the political monopoly of the legitimate use of force claimed by the State), the domination effect is an unavoidable feature of the world political economy.[3]

Perroux may have overestimated the irreversibility of the domination effect he described and underestimated the reciprocal interdependencies that exist in the world economy, but his analysis has stood the test of time. It has been recognized as the intellectual backbone of postwar French international economic policy. In recent years it has been an inspiration for students of Third World problems and has influenced the shaping of Third World policies toward new rules of the game of international economics.

In the theoretical literature the concept of imperialism frequently arises in the discussion of transnational actors as instruments of domination. In the literature of the social sciences imperialism is a concept of venerable age, for it has been used in studies of international economic activity since the end of the nineteenth century; but it is also a concept of some imprecision. An entire period of modern history, the years between 1873 and 1914, is often referred to as one of economic imperialism, and the Great War of 1914–1918 is sometimes cited as one of its consequences. Names such as Hobson, Lenin, and Hilferding have been associated with it for many decades.

Although Perroux eschewed the concept even while dealing effectively with the reality that it describes, in recent years (since the mid-1960s in particular) the concept of imperialism has regained currency, drawing strength both from the classical sources and from more recent studies of dependency undertaken primarily in Latin America (about which more in Part III). As formulated by Johan Galtung (who is Director of the International Peace Research Institute in Oslo, Norway, and who also spent some time in Chile), the structural theory of imperialism is based on a world conceived as divided between the "center" and the "periphery" but held together by a global system of dependence. Although the two terms (center and periphery) remain undefined in Galtung's article, we may recognize them as referring to the "developed" and the "developing" worlds, respectively, and to the problem of equitable relations between them. The problems that Perroux addressed (United States-European relations) having passed the stage of urgency, "imperialism" now refers primarily to the system of relations between the developed and the developing countries and to the role that transnational corporations play within that system.

In Galtung's scheme, multinational corporations are among the international organizations that link the center to the periphery in the contemporary phase of imperialism. They are a form of economic imperialism because the relations they facilitate promote harmony between the center and the governments of the developing countries (the centers of the periphery) but create disharmony between the governments and the people of the developing countries. They create such disharmony because they are asymmetrical. They are essential parts of two of the mechanisms of imperialism—the mechanism of vertical relations across gaps in processing levels (such as in exports of raw materials), and the mechanism of "feudal interaction structures" (which create a condition of dependency because of trade partner and commodity concentration); hence both mechanisms are exploitative.

Structural problems call for structural change. According to Galtung, strategies for structural change in the "international dominance system" therefore include "horizontalization" (exchange on more equal terms, less vertical interaction, and more self-reliance) and "defeudalization," including the destruction of multinational asymmetrical organizations and "the establishment of global or transnational organizations."

As a model of Third World problems Galtung's scheme appears overly simple. His major proposition, that imperialism (domination) creates or causes inequality (and underdevelopment), needs to be supplemented by the consideration that gaps in development (or inequality, that is, differences, in size, bargaining power and activity rates) in turn give rise to domination. Prescription for change must therefore be directed both to structural change at the international level, through manipulation of center-periphery relations, and also to change directed at dealing with such causes of domination as underdevelopment, lack of bargaining power, and inactivity. One wonders too whether the success of OPEC in raising so dramatically the price of oil (an unprocessed material), in part through the successful manipulation of asymmetrical international corporations, could have been predicted from this model, two years after its formulation. Like Perroux's theory, this one holds that processes and advantages are irreversible. Yet the concepts of core and periphery have gained currency in recent years and are useful in a variety of contexts.[4]

NOTES

1. "Foreign Expansion as Institutional Necessity for U.S. Corporate Capitalism: The Search for a Radical Model," *World Politics,* Vol. 25(3), April 1973, pp. 369-386.
2. Geoffrey Chandler, "The Innocence of Oil Companies," *Foreign Policy* 27 (Summer 1977): 52-71.
3. A more recent, but also more general, statement of Perroux's views on the relationship of power to the economy may be found in *Pouvoir et Economie* (Paris: Dunod, 1973). It does not diverge, in its essentials, from the analysis presented in selection 8 (but see note 1 at the end of that selection).
4. For a discussion of these concepts, see Karl Deutsch, "Imperialism and Neocolonialism," *Papers, Peace Science Society International,* Vol. 23 (1974), pp. 11-15.

5 / The Monopolistic Theory of Direct Foreign Investment

Charles Kindleberger

Direct Investment as a Capital Movement

Direct investment used to be thought of by economists as an international capital movement. Capital movements take place in a variety of forms—through the issue of new securities, largely bonds; through purchases and sale of outstanding securities, both stocks and bonds, on security exchanges; through a variety of short-term credit instruments and forms; and through direct investment. Direct investment differed from other kinds of international capital movements in that it was accompanied by varying degrees of control, plus technology and management. But it was a capital movement.

For some purposes, and especially in the concerns of the United States, the capital movement features of direct investment remain paramount. . . . There is, in addition, renewed interest in the capital aspects of direct investment from a theoretical point of view, and particularly in the way national capital markets can be joined internationally through the markets for whole companies, in contrast with securities traded in organized markets. . . . But economists trying to interpret direct investment as a capital movement were struck by several peculiar phenomena. In the first place, investors often failed to take money with them when they went abroad to acquire control of a company; instead they would borrow in the local market. Capital movements would take place gross—the acquisition of an asset (an outflow) and the incurring of a liability (an inflow)—but not net. Or the investment would take place in kind, through the exchange of property—patents, technology, or machinery—against equity claims, without the normal transfer of funds through the foreign exchange associated with capital movements. And direct investment would proceed by the reinvestment of profits, with the capital outflow matched by earnings on past investment, but again no movement of funds through the foreign-exchange market. On this showing the clue to direct investment lay in capital formation, not in capital movement. [1]

In the second place, direct investment often takes place simultaneously in two directions. United States companies invest in Europe, and European companies invest in the

From Charles Kindleberger, *American Business Abroad* (New Haven, Conn.: Yale University Press, 1969), pp. 1-36. Lecture I, originally titled "The Theory of Direct Investment." Reprinted with permission of the publisher. Some notes have been omitted, and the remainder renumbered in sequence.

United States. Such two-way movements occur to some degree in securities, as investors seek to diversify their portfolios on the one hand, or to escape taxation, confiscation, or other real or imagined evils on the other. Europe and Canada own a lot of United States corporate stocks. The contrast is rather with bonds, where, prior to the imposition of the Interest Equalization Tax in 1963 which cut off the flow, foreign debtors would issue bonds in New York, but United States debtors would not issue bonds abroad to raise funds for expenditure in this country.

Direct investment may thus be capital movement, but it is more than that.

Control

Direct investment has long been defined as a capital movement involving continuing control by the investor. Sometimes this is put in legal terms, depending upon whether the equity ownership amounts to 10, 25, 48, 51, 95, or 100 percent of the foreign subsidiary. The 1968 mandatory restrictions on foreign direct investment, for example, choose 10 percent as the criterion. To the economist, of course, the test is not the extent of ownership, but the locus of decision-making power. It is said that one 100 percent British-owned subsidiary of an American company has carried decentralized decision-making so far that it tells its parent, rather than asks it, even on the focal issues of dividends, capital budgeting, new products, research, and top personnel appointments, which decentralized corporations ordinarily reserve for centralized decision. If this is true, it is no different from an ordinary portfolio investment.

The economist, moreover, is interested in control only insofar as it affects behavior. In their study, *Canadian-United States Economic Relations,* Irving Brecher and S. S. Reisman are inclined to deprecate the importance of United States direct investment in Canada.[2] They argue that two companies, one foreign, one Canadian, operating in the same circumstances, both presumably rational and both seeking to maximize earnings, will operate in the same way. Things equal to the same thing are equal to each other. But a Canadian corporation and a foreign corporation in the same industry in Canada, even if both are unaffected by government, are not necessarily the same thing. If the Canadian corporation were an international firm of the same size and extent as the foreign, this might be so. For a company of a given volume and structure of assets and earnings it would make little difference economically whether the ownership were Canadian or United States. But assume that the Canadian is a national and the American an international corporation. They will scan different horizons in space, and possibly in time, and maximize different objective functions. The international corporation may take depreciation allowances out of Canada to invest in a cheaper new source of output, whereas the Canadian firm's choice would be between expanding production in Canada or not expanding at all. Or in the event of world depression, the international corporation might cut back production in its various locations on the basis of the grief it foresaw from various national institutions—governments, unions, public opinion—rather than cutting back high-cost units first so as to equalize the marginal cost of production in each operation. With a narrower spatial and a shorter time horizon, the Canadian firm, because it is national and smaller, maximizes income in a Canadian context in the short run, the international firm in a world context in the long run. They may well then behave differently.

The control aspect of direct investment, which economists have been inclined to dismiss, is increasingly assuming political significance. In part this is the result of an unresolved conflict in international law; in part the result of what we may loosely characterize as pure nationalism. On the first score, for example, the United States assumes that it has the right to require parent companies to direct the operations of their subsidiaries in ways that conform to American purposes, while foreign governments, sovereign over the territory where these subsidiaries are located, deny the existence of such a right. What I have called pure nationalism is the uneasiness that many people instinctively have when they contemplate the fact that the activities of institutions within their economy and polity are "controlled" from outside the political unit. I shall argue that this feeling, like so many of the instincts direct investment or the international corporation arouses over the globe, is not to be trusted. The international corporation should be judged by how it operates, not for what it is. Scratch any of us deeply enough and you will find instincts of nationalism or xenophobia, overlain though they may be with layers of civilizing repression, and equally, instincts of peasant attachment to the soil; also populist fear of outside capital, mercantilist pleasure in expanding exports, on which I expatiate below, and perhaps others. The reactions are understandable, but they are not on that account to be approved.

The political, as distinct from the economic and legal, issue of control is thus made up of two elements, one involving attempts by governments to achieve national purposes through international corporations with headquarters in their jurisdictions and of other countries to resist them, and one of what I have called pure nationalism. It will be difficult to keep them distinct.

Growth of the Firm

There is a variety of theories about the firm, but the essence, at least in a number of theories, is growth. Firms manage and allocate resources; they innovate in new products; they are legal people; but primarily they grow. In growing they may well go abroad; in going abroad, they grow abroad.

In one formulation associated with the reinvestment of earnings, this comes close to a gambling theory of foreign investment. It has been observed that roughly half the earnings on foreign investment are reinvested abroad. From this a decision rule is deduced that firms bring home half their winnings and plow back the other half.[3] The fact that there is an average reinvestment of half of their foreign earnings by United States companies cannot be doubted, but the existence of a rule of thumb that ascribes such conduct to individual corporations can be. A rule of thumb makes sense only when the benefits from its adoption in the reduction of costs of decision-making exceed the possible losses in poor investment choice. It is hard to believe that any firm is so irrational as to invest abroad by rule of thumb.[4]

Reinvest they do, when they have both profits and prospects for further profits.[5] The rate of reinvestment evidently depends on both profits and profitability. Nor is there any basis for suggesting that new investment is limited, after the initial start, to profits on past investment, on some sort of compound-interest formula. Investment goes forward on the basis of past earnings, new funds from the parent company, and new borrowings at home and especially abroad.

Within the total view that direct investment is a function of the growth of the firm are two strands, one emphasizing the market, the other the internal source of finance. The first is very much in vogue among businessmen. Direct investment, they say, is stimulated not by profits but by markets. Not only separate business spokesmen, like Mr. Richard Fenton formerly of Pfizer International, but the business community as a whole, as recorded in the questionnaires of the National Industrial Conference Board, insist that business investments seek markets. From markets a firm can imply a market share, a volume of sales, and an earnings-to-sales ratio. A senior executive is quoted as saying: "If we can look forward to a certain *level of sales* we won't hesitate to invest, for our profit will justify any amount of investment needed to support an operation."[6] It is easy, of course, to find counterexamples, where companies have a large foreign market supplied by exports, and with investment limited to distribution facilities and inventories, if any investment is needed at all. An outstanding example is the Volkswagen company which enjoys substantial sales in the United States, but deliberately refrains from domestic manufacture, having in fact first bought and then sold a former Studebaker plant at Linden, New Jersey. But the explanations which businessmen give of their thought processes must not be taken with literal seriousness. Like Monsieur Jourdain in Molière's *Le Bourgeois Gentilhomme* who spoke prose all his life without having been aware of it, they doubtless maximize profits rather than merely follow markets.

One factor accounting for the gap between business behavior and business perception of it may be the initial lag between investment and profits, resulting from "breaking-in" or "teething" troubles. A chemical firm established overseas for forty years found that its pre-World War II investment, which accounted for 42.5 percent of overseas assets, produced 53.5 percent of total earnings and 82 percent of dividends.[7] Subsequent investments are putatively as profitable as the earlier, with a time profile for earnings which starts low, or even negative, and rises to a normal long-run rate after a considerable interval. But the terrible possibility must be considered that businessmen actually do as they say they do and invest where markets are, without sufficiently considering long-run profits margins. The troubles of Chrysler with Rootes and Simca and of General Electric with Machines Bull in French computers raise the specter of such an outcome. But the returns are far from in.

Linking direct investment to markets and market position leads to an organic view of the process, as opposed to what we might call a mechanical one. The issue arises in connection with balance-of-payments restrictions, . . . But the theory is clear. Direct investment is tied to markets. If markets grow, the firm must grow. If the firm stops growing, it dies. Anything that interferes with the growth of the firm, such as balance-of-payments restrictions, while the organic life of the market goes its way will kill the firm. But the issue can wait.

The second view connects direct investment not with markets but with the cost of capital to the firm. Many economists regard retained earnings as not only cheaper capital than borrowings or the sale of new equities, but so cheap as to approach a negative cost. Extra dividends for stockholders only lead them to expect more. So long as there is any reasonable basis for expansion, the firm should reinvest rather than pay out profits above some long-run, and very slowly rising, amount. In addition, ploughed-back earnings escape the personal income tax and can be cashed in, if need be, at the lower rates on capital gains. If opportunities for growth at home are limited, look abroad. In any event, grow.

There is something to this doctrine, but how much cannot be tested quantitatively with current Department of Commerce data, which lump open-book claims with equity as "direct investment." In 1957, when the latest published survey of United States foreign investment was undertaken, foreign sources of capital provided 40 percent of total assets, largely in debt, and 25 percent of the total debt financing was furnished from the United States. Since 1957, however, and especially since 1963, United States companies have been borrowing in the Euro-bond market and the Euro-dollar market at rates of interest that may be small compared with expected profit possibilities and with the rates at which European companies borrow but are high by United States capital market standards. Direct investment involves much more than the reinvestment of funds that United States business is reluctant to distribute to shareholders. Firms grow, and may grow abroad rather than at home for one reason or another, but direct investment involves entering into commitments and taking risks, not merely investing earnings for which no better use is handy.

Monopolistic Competition

Each of these explanations—capital movement packaged with decision-making and associated with technology, former of capital, consequence of the growth of the firm—has an element of the truth but none provides an entirely satisfactory explanation of the phenomenon. The United States government is currently fostering direct investment while seeking to limit the capital outflow involved. The thesis that asserts firms are irrational and invest as if they were gambling is hardly persuasive, possibly not a priori, but at least in a Darwinian sense. As long as some foreign markets continue to be served by imports, as well as by production near the market, the notion that direct investment is a function of markets alone is unconvincing. Control may lie at the root of the problem presented by direct investment, but why do some firms want to control and not others?

A more general theory—originally propounded in a thesis at the Massachusetts Institute of Technology by Stephen H. Hymer—is that direct investment belongs more to the theory of industrial organization than to the theory of international capital movements. [8] The investing company can earn a higher rate of return abroad than at home—as it must if it undertakes the risks and overcomes the costs of operating in a different political and legal environment, at a distance from its decision-making center. It is not enough for the return to be higher abroad than at home. If this were all, capital would move through organized capital markets rather than through firms that specialize in the production and distribution of goods. Capital markets specialize in moving capital, and under competitive conditions they are better at it than firms engaged in other lines. In addition to earning more abroad than at home, the investing firm must be able to earn a higher return in the market where it is investing than local firms earn. There are costs of operating at a distance, costs not only of travel, communication, and time lost in communicating information and decisions, but also costs of misunderstanding that leads to errors. [9] For a firm to undertake direct investment in a foreign country it must have an advantage over existing or potentially competitive firms in that country. If not, those firms, operating more cheaply in other respects because nearer the locus of decision-making and without the filter of long lines to distort communication, would put the intruder out of business. One is tempted to say that foreign firms which specialize in market-oriented products will be able successfully to establish subsidiaries in a country that does not produce the goods. But this is not so unless the firms possess some advantage which they can transfer from one country to another but which cannot be acquired by local firms. With perfect international markets for technology, management, labor skills, components, and other material input, the market abroad will be served by a local firm.

Put the matter another way: in a world of perfect competition for goods and factors, direct investment cannot exist. In these conditions, domestic firms would have an advantage over foreign firms in the proximity of their operations to their decision-making centers, so that no firm could survive in foreign operation. For direct investment to thrive there must be some imperfection in markets for goods or factors, including among the latter technology, or some interference in competition by government or by firms, which separates markets.

This theory may be illustrated by contrasting it with another. In their interesting *Federal Tax Treatment of Foreign Income,* Krause and Dam assert: "Another reason for investing abroad is that production costs may be lower than in the United States because of favorable wage rates, raw material prices, or interest rates . . . or because of the opportunity to reduce transportation costs, distribution costs, inventory and servicing costs to the markets for which the outputs are intended." [10] In the present view, cheaper costs abroad than at home are not enough. What must be explained is why the production abroad is not undertaken by local entrepreneurs, who have an inherent advantage over outside investors. There must be a more than compensating advantage on the part of the foreigner before direct investment will be called forth.

The nature of the monopolistic advantages which produce direct investment can be indicated under a variety of headings:

1. departures from perfect competition in goods markets, including product differentiation, special marketing skills, retail price maintenance, administered pricing, and so forth;

2. departures from perfect competition in factor markets, including the existence of patented or unavailable technology, of discrimination in access to capital, of differences in skills of managers organized into firms rather than hired in competitive markets;

3. internal and external economies of scale, the latter being taken advantage of by vertical integration;

4. government limitations on output or entry.

It may be useful to illustrate these separate advantages briefly.

Goods Markets

That product differentiation breeds direct investment is indicated by its prevalence in branded products such as pharmaceuticals, cosmetics, soft drinks, and specialty foodstuffs, and in concentrated industries such as automobiles, tires, chemicals, electrical appliances, electronic components, farm machinery, office equipment. It does not occur in standardized goods produced by competitive industries such as textiles, clothing, flour milling, and distribution (except for Sears, Roebuck in Latin America). In oligopolistic industries there is likely to be two-way investment, with Lever Brothers and Royal Dutch Shell in the United States and Procter and Gamble, Esso, and other United States oil companies in Britain, or Campbell Soup and Heinz in Europe and Knorr and Nestlé in the United States. Indeed, in concentrated industries there is pressure for each firm to develop a position in each important or potentially important market—regardless of the rate of profit obtainable in absolute terms—to prevent any of its few competitors from obtaining a substantial advantage which it would put to use over a wider area. The threat of competition by a foreign firm in the home market may be reduced if the domestic firm stands ready to retaliate through an existing subsidiary in the market of the threatener. A major drug company is said to admit that it loses on its investment in Brazil but has to be there to cover the actions of the competition.

Marketing skill was what brought one of the earliest types of United States invest-ment—life insurance—to Europe and is what Americans and Europeans alike believe is the major contribution of many American companies today. It is closely associated, of course, with product differentiation through advertising and with administered pricing (though European competitors complain of price cutting). Incidentally, the experience of the life insurance companies supports the theory that direct investment is based on an advantage of one kind or another and is impossible where such advantage does not exist. United States companies taught their marketing secrets to European insurance companies and then withdrew to the confines of this country. Theories that rely on the growth of the firm have little explanation for withdrawal. Servan-Schreiber states, "United States troops will leave Vietnam, but United States industry will not leave Europe."[11] Hymer, on whose theory this analysis relies, puts it colorfully: "Corporations do not die like ordinary trees; they are like California redwoods." But these pronouncements do not take account of some failures, such as those American companies which tried to introduce cake mixes and bowling into Europe in the last decade, or of withdrawals other than that of the life insurance companies—General Electric, Rexall (Boots drug), and Woolworth—from Britain at the end of the 1930s.

Factor Markets

Superiority of management may be the advantage that many companies bring to foreign investment, though it usually must be combined with monopoly advantages in goods markets or increasing returns to scale to convert it into a basis for operating in foreign markets. The nature of that superiority is elusive, being said variously to consist in central-ization of decision-making and in decentralization, in scientific cost-benefit analysis and in merely a concern for marketing, in the maintenance of high standards on technical per-formance, tolerances, delivery dates, and so on, at the same time that it runs afoul of local practices and especially of trade union tradition. . . .

There is little or no advantage to the foreign investor in access to labor other than management and technical staff.

The advantage of the large international company in raising capital is another topic that arises in specific contexts later.

This leaves us, at this stage of the proceedings, to discuss patents and industrial secrets, which are a major advantage of the large international corporation in differentiated products. Patents and restricted technology limit entry. The question that inevitably arises, however, is whether to exploit the advantage through licensing foreign firms or to undertake foreign production oneself. Examples can be found of each—and in the same industry. St. Gobain, a French company, developed a new process for producing plate glass and undertook to build a plant in Tennessee, which was called upon its completion "the most modern obsolete plant in the world." The reason for this obsolescence was that the British Pilkington company developed a newer and superior method of producing plate glass, the float process. But rather than undertake production in the United States Pilkington decided to license existing producers—Pittsburgh Plate Glass, Libby-Owens-

Ford, and the Ford Motor Company. The choice was presumably made on the basis of fine calculations of costs and prospective profits. A further factor seems to have been that the Pilkington company is a family concern which hesitated to borrow enough capital to start production on the scale necessary to compete with the three American companies (which requires a full line of automotive glass products) and which perhaps was concerned that it would let loose the demon of cut-throat oligopolistic competition.

If we assume that a firm is not constrained by unwillingness to raise capital or by fear of the consequences of breaking into a foreign market, what will the choice between licensing and direct investment depend on? Where the license fee fails to capture the full rent inherent in technical superiority, the advantage lies in direct investment. There may be other considerations: whether the patent or industrial secret is adequately protected by the license, or whether at the expiration of the arrangement the licenser will find his secret gone; whether the licensee is likely to provide competition in other markets—possibilities which it might be illegal to protect against through agreement but which are safeguarded through ownership. Research is needed to amass a series of cases in which the choice between licensing and direct investment has been made in one sense or the other, in order to formulate exactly the nature of the governing considerations. Since both methods are used, however, it is evident that the calculation is a close one. Licenses tend to bring in a lower return, directly and indirectly, but are less expensive in capital, time, and energy.

One apparently irrational feature of the choice appears in statements gathered by interview from two American firms that they are willing to enter into joint ventures with foreign participants if the foreigners provide some advantage in kind—technical knowledge, marketing skills, or "some other valuable and unique service"—but not otherwise. [12] The irrationality, to which we return, is that admission of local participants to the equity of a foreign investment should be a function of the price they pay, not the character of the payment. If the local capitalists pay a high enough price for a small enough portion of the equity, money is as good as real considerations, or better. The higher the price the greater the extent to which the foreign investor capitalizes the advantage, or a portion of it, that he brings to the venture, rather than drawing an income from it.

Economies of Scale

Economies of scale are very much in people's minds today in Europe where attention is focused on the large size of American companies compared with the relatively small size of European concerns. The advantages of large-scale production internal to the firm are self-evident, although it is useful to point out that there are counterbalancing diseconomies of scale in administration, which at some point, different in different industries and for different methods of management, set limits to the optimum scale of operations. Long-term cost curves turn up somewhere, or competition would reduce the number of firms in each industry to one.

Economies of scale must be distinguished from the profits available through horizontal integration which extends to the point where the firm has some control over price. The benefit to the firm from extending operations overseas may lie not in producing greater numbers at a cheaper cost per unit, but in raising the price at which units are sold. When this occurs, direct investment involves a loss for the world, though perhaps a gain for a country. Production is reduced rather than expanded, and price is raised above marginal cost, which remains at least as high as before. In the short run, the direct investment that obtains a larger share of the market and market power may be equally profitable—no more, no less—than the direct investment that lowers cost through internal economies of scale achieved through horizontal integration. In the long run, however, monopoly profits persist, whereas in the competitive situation profits return to the long-run level.

While internal economies of scale—and monopoly—account for horizontal integration, external economies of scale lead to vertical integration. In a number of lines where production is bulky, inventories are expensive, and coordination of decision is required at several stages of the process, the firm may be a better means of organizing production than the competitive market. In oil, for example, it is possible for separate firms to produce crude petroleum, transport it, refine it, and market the products, dealing with each other at arm's length through markets. But there are substantial economies, it appears, in coordinating decisions at various stages of production, so much so that direct investment in the petroleum industry is the rule, both backward to sources of crude petroleum supplies and forward to consumer markets for refined products. In some industries, such as metals, vertical integration goes only to the source of raw materials. Steel companies own iron mines, copper companies produce copper ore abroad, aluminum companies own bauxite (and electricity), so that they may better coordinate the output and shipment of ore with the needs of metal refining. Their advantage over other firms with equal technology, managerial skill, access to capital, and so on is that they coordinate mining operations with transport and marketing—with an eye to minimizing both interruptions in flows and the piling up of unwieldy inventories. Like governmental planning in Rosenstein-Rodan's 1943 article on balanced growth, vertical integration converts external economies to internal profits. [13] But the capital needed for operations on this scale tends to limit entry into these industries, and to provide at least the possibility of oligopoly which raises price above marginal cost. And the existence of separate stages of production in different countries within the same company gives rise to problems of transfer pricing, discussed below.

Vertical integration can also serve an economic purpose in helping to avoid the risks of technological change or new channels of trade, which require coordinated new investments at various stages of the movement of a commodity from production to consumption. I became aware of this in studying the economic history of Britain, noting that tenant farmers found it difficult to shift from wheat to dairy products because of the difficulty of dividing the risks of investment, and the profits, between the owners of East Anglian farms and their tenant-operators, or that the failure to change from small coal cars on the British railways to larger, more efficient ones was because the cars were owned by the coal mines but new investment by both the mines and the railroads was needed to arrive at the new size. A current illustration given by my colleague, Morris Adelman, is the profitability of large new investments—in coal mines, railroad cars, and loading facilities in the United States, large ships and unloading and distribution equipment in Europe—to bring West Virginia coal to Europe at half the cost that coal can be mined there. It proves impossible to undertake the investments needed at each stage of the process without vertical integration which would coordinate it.

Vertical integration can also be a pathological condition. Competition, like matter and games, is subject to entropy. Even where there are no economic advantages in coordinating production at various stages, or of coordinating new investments at different levels of production to carry through innovation, companies may feel safer with assured access to sources of inputs and to outlets for products. In these circumstances the industry will shift from numerous firms which are small and competitive at each stage to one of a few large, vertically integrated concerns. Once started, the process acquires momentum. When the oil company that used to sell gas feed stocks to petrochemical companies acquires a petrochemical subsidiary of its own, other chemical firms it used to supply feel constrained to acquire their own sources of supply. A striking example is the purchase by Alcan Aluminium Limited of Canada of a half interest in the government-owned Aardal og Sunndal Verk (A.S.V.) aluminum smelter in Norway, a move that expanded the former's "aluminum capacity by almost 20 percent and eliminated a source of price competition that had vexed the entire industry." [14] Alcan's interest in acquiring A.S.V.—to reduce competition—is made evident in this remark. But the newspaper account goes on to indicate that the Norwegian government felt that A.S.V. needed a tie-up with a producer of alumina to assure future deliveries. "Norway feared that the trend toward integrated production . . . might leave a lone smelter without supplies or customers." [15] In some industries, such as automobiles, vertical integration proves inefficient in the long run, and the industry proceeds to disintegration and the establishment of separate firms for component manufacture which deal at arm's length. The Cummins Engine Company of Indiana sought to obtain a foothold in the diesel-engine industry in Europe but found itself unable to develop markets since truck producers in Europe (Fiat, Berliet, Mercedes) all produced their own diesel engines—a stage in the development of truck production regarded as behind the disintegrated structure of the United States and Britain. Vertical integration can thus either make for direct investment reducing competition in goods markets and the markets for inputs, or it can frustrate direct investment.

A special form of imperfectly competitive market for factors is in capital. I have claimed that direct investment does not represent a capital movement, and this is largely true. But on occasion, in industries that need large amounts of capital, a foreign firm will have an advantage over a domestic firm because of its superior credit standing. The international capital market is not perfect, and even to the extent that capital markets are joined, different rates are charged to borrowers of different credit standing. Many borrowers cannot command the large sums necessary for capital-intensive investments at all. I do not mean to limit this to access to the New York capital market or the Euro-dollar bond market. Even before the restraints on United States investment abroad, United States firms were borrowing abroad despite higher nominal interest rates: in case of difficulty, the asset and the liability would be in the same currency basket and the net risk of loss thereby diminished. Since the restrictions, the propensity to borrow abroad has increased. And not only in New York and in Euro-dollars but abroad and in foreign currencies, American firms of worldwide credit standing typically have an advantage over domestic firms with only a national credit rating and limited liquidity. In some countries, foreign capital markets are particularly underdeveloped, and capital must be brought from the United States or transferred from one foreign operation to another. But this is not the essense of direct investment. With perfect capital markets, and assuming the borrowers are of equal credit standing, the domestic entrepreneur abroad could borrow in New York as easily as the American entrepreneur. The fact is that where the direct investor has an advantage over his local competition based on capital availability, this is the result not of his nationality, but of his better credit rating in all parts of the international capital market. Whatever the source of capital, the international firm with its large cash flow and high liquidity is a better credit risk than local enterprise and, in imperfectly competitive markets, gets lower rates on loans and preferred access to limited funds.

Let me present the pith of this theory of direct investment with the use of the simple formula for capitalizing a stream of income, $C = I/r$ where C is the value of a capital asset, I is the stream of income it produces, and r is the rate of return on investment. Thus, for example, an investment producing a $5 flow of income is worth $100 at a 5 percent rate of profit. This theory of direct investment insists that ordinary capital movements take place between countries when interest rates differ, but that direct investment corresponds for the most part to differences in I that can be earned by entrepreneurs from abroad over local entrepreneurs. I is higher for the foreigner than for the local entrepreneur because of some advantage in goods markets such as a differentiated product or assured outlets or marketing skill; in factor markets, such as specialized technology or management skill; or in both goods and factor markets through coordinating operations at several stages of production. When the advantage in factor markets is access to cheap capital, because of either the larger cash flow of depreciation and profits in internal funds or a preferred position in capital markets as a borrower, differences in r may contribute to the result. Primarily, however, the theory asserts that direct investment occurs when the foreign firm can earn a higher I than the local firm, whereas ordinary capital movements reflect a lower r. The exception for imperfect capital markets will be developed later. The theory can be illustrated with the far from hypothetical example of a European family seeking to sell out a family firm. A foreign firm, typically from the United States, is able to bid more for the going concern than its European competitors, i.e. pay a higher C, not because of a lower r—or perhaps better not solely, or even mainly because of a lower r—but because it can earn a higher I on the firm's assets.

Government

Finally government. The role of government does not affect the choice between local and foreign firms, except when it refuses to sanction direct investment. If we assume that foreign firms have an advantage over local firms, the question is whether the goods are provided by imports or by a direct investor. Here government enters with tariffs. Government may impose a tariff in the hope of stimulating production by nationals, only to find that it has encouraged the entry of foreign firms.

Brash, for example, claims that increases in tariffs have been decisive in stimulating American investment in Australian manufacturing industry. [16] This statement can be broken down into two stages. Australian tariffs stimulate investment behind the tariff walls. The advantage of American manufacturing concerns over Australian firms result in the entry into Australian manufacturing of American rather than Australian firms. The same stimulation to direct investment presumably came from the formation of the European Economic Community, and again in two stages. The formation of the customs union favored firms inside the common tariff over those outside. Foreign firms that were discriminated against by the customs union set up subsidiaries within the customs area if they had an advantage that enabled them to compete successfully with local firms.

Government intervention to cut off imports and substitute domestic production may lead foreign firms into what has been called "defensive investment", i.e. investment that produces a less than average return, but where the difference between the gross return plus and the loss that would have resulted from exclusion gives the necessary rate of return on a marginal basis. [17] A firm threatened with a loss of 4 percent a year on an existing investment may find it worthwhile to undertake new investment at a below-average return to prevent the loss. The behavior is viable in the short, but not of course in the long run, when all costs are variable and average costs become marginal costs.

In my judgment, however, the major impact of the Treaty of Rome was not to create new opportunities for outside firms to invest within the Community or to threaten exporters with losses against which they sought to defend. More significant, I think, was the treaty's calling attention to opportunities for profitable investment which had until then been ignored. Europe had lain over the horizon of most American companies, out of sight. Opportunities for profitable investment existed, but company managements in the United States were unaware of them. Coming as it did when major domestic postwar investment programs had been completed, the Rome treaty, plus its forerunner, the European Coal and Steel Community, and successive steps toward integration which followed it, had little importance in altering the bases on which close calculations of alternative profit opportunities were made. What they did was to lift the attention of United States business to a wider horizon and to focus interest on the fast-growing European market with its unfolding investment opportunities. Government's role was minimal. The major stimulus to direct investment in Europe in the late 1950s and the 1960s was a discontinuous enlargement in the horizon scanned by United States corporate management. The Common Market may have triggered it. It did not produce it. [18]

Corollaries of the Monopolistic Theory of Direct Investment

The fact that the foreign corporation has some advantage over the local corporation, which makes direct investment possible, has a number of corollaries. It is a strong reason in the eyes of the investor against sharing his equity. The world of affairs abounds in the apparently reasonable suggestion that the overseas investor enter into joint ventures with local interests. Instead of buying 100 percent of a domestic firm, buy half. But the overseas investor asks why he should give half the scarcity value of his advantage away. This reasoning assumes, as I have indicated, that there are barriers to adjusting the price paid for half the enterprise which would enable the foreign investor to capitalize on the scarcity value of his contribution. It may be difficult for the local investor to appreciate the profitability of the prospective enterprise, so that he would be unwilling to make his monetary contribution at an implicit valuation of the foreign contribution which accorded with the foreigner's view. To an economist, as I have said, the problem has an air of irrationality or imperfect knowledge about it. In a broad market there should be no difficulty in varying the price of the foreign contribution of a special advantage such as technology, relative to the domestic contribution of money, land, facilities, or whatever is involved, so as to represent something like its market real scarcity value.

There is, of course, one other aspect to a foreign investor's reluctance to share control, or even to tolerate a substantial interest, and in many cases it may be the controlling one. The interests of the partners may differ. The foreign investor may wish to accumulate capital, whereas the domestic investor wants dividends. In this case they would disagree on the appropriate rate of reinvestment of profits, or in readiness to undertake new investments to make good losses or to take advantage of new opportunities. Thus Heinz bought a higher share of its Japanese subsidiary after its partners in that country were reluctant to expand at the rate they thought was required; and Coca-Cola found it difficult to persuade its partner bottlers abroad to undertake the necessary investment to move from 6-ounce to 10- and 12-ounce bottles. Or the international corporation may have a wide number of interests, in a variety of countries, which are related to its interest in a particular subsidiary, while the partner in that subsidiary has only one. The most usual source of a conflict of interest arises where the international corporation is integrated over a number of stages of production and the local subsidiary covers one. How intercompany transactions are priced may become a bone of contention in this case, as it affects whether profits are earned in the wholly owned parent or the partially owned child. Transfer pricing is an important question for that other partner of every company in every country, the tax collector, who clearly has an interest in ensuring that profits are earned and taxed in the jurisdiction where they ought to be. [19]

The economic answer to the tax collector is easy to formulate, difficult to apply. Payments for all goods and services sold within a corporation, including rents, royalties, and fees for patents, industrial knowledge, and management services, should be set at the prices that would prevail in a competitive market, with all element of monopoly or monopsony eliminated. In the well-known case of oil tanker charges, however, one must be careful not to apply the single-voyage charter rates, which are highly competitive but cover such a small part of the market that they tend to fluctuate in exaggerated fashion as changes in total demand and supply are brought to bear against a limited segment of the market. In this and similar cases, some other criterion must be used. The market for short- and long-term charters is competitive, so that it is relatively easy to get a good approximation to a short- or long-term price which would be reached with competitive arm's-length bargaining. In the crude oil market, which is very imperfect and where actual transactions are known only to a limited degree, it is perhaps possible to calculate a proxy competitive price. But in highly complex mechanical, chemical, or electrical goods, such calculation becomes impossible since there is no market from which "competitive" prices can be estimated or approximated. Tax commissioners and private partners may be able in one way or another to "construct" a profit which makes crude legal or bargaining sense perhaps, but it is difficult to devise an economically justifiable criterion.

The answer given by the large international companies to the demand for local participation is hardly satisfactory. They urge the local investor to buy shares in the parent company. But the local investor wants a piece of the monopoly profits from the corporation's advantage in the local market, profits which, in the nature of direct investment, are higher than those in the main place of business.

Where takeovers occur, or a minority shareholding is bought out, as in the Ford of Dagenham minority purchase in 1960, the local owner of assets or shareholder can capitalize a portion of the prospective gains by selling his assets for more than they are worth to him or to his countrymen. When Ford of Detroit offered the 40 percent minority shareholders of the British company 145 shillings a share, the market quotation was in the low 90s, and the local shareholder got a capital gain of more than 50 percent. Ford of Detroit, which had more than $1 billion in idle cash in the home office and which anticipated no better use for it than buying up the remaining interest in its already controlled but prospectively profitable British subsidiary, was willing—or, perhaps it should be said, was obliged—to share the anticipated profits to a considerable extent in order to acquire the shareholding.

International corporations thus prefer 100 percent ownership to joint ventures or minority holdings. To the extent that they need additional finance, they seek it abroad, and through debt. This is to limit risk by holding assets and liabilities in the same currency and avoid the possibility of losing assets while liabilities remain. The reason for obtaining capital in debt form is to protect the company's equity. In 1957 United States firms owned 60 percent of the assets in their foreign subsidiaries, but this consisted of 85 percent of the equity capital and only 25 percent of the creditor capital. By subtraction, foreign investors had 15 percent of the equity and 75 percent of the debt. There are instances where United States corporations prefer to take a limited interest in foreign operations. The Kaiser company, for example, is said to limit itself to a 25 or 30 percent interest, wanting a voice in management, some earnings, but a quiet life. Again some governments, notably that of India, require foreign corporations, as a condition of entering the market, to undertake to sell as much as 30 percent of their equity to local investors. In these circumstances, the foreign investor naturally seeks to spread the stock widely so as to prevent the coalition of a strong minority voice in management. And . . . there have been strong measures proposed in Canada to get a substantial proportion of foreign equity in Canadian corporations into Canadian hands. But where the investment is based on an advantage over local competitors, and there are difficulties in getting the full capitalized value of this advantage in advance by selling it at its value to the holder, foreign equity owners may be expected to resist these pressures, quite apart from the complication of loss of control.

The second corollary is less evident. Direct investment belongs to the theory of monopolistic competition. But while direct investment may gobble up competitors and exploit its monopolistic advantages, its main impact is in widening the area of competition. Domestic markets are protected, if not by tariffs, at least by distance, ignorance, lethargy. The small, inefficient domestic producer is typically more of a monopolist than the large, monopolistically competitive wide-ranging firm. Such a domestic market thrives on high prices and low volume. Sometimes, as in France before the European Coal and Steel Community and the European Economic Community, a handful of large firms holds a high price umbrella each over an entourage of small and inefficient coexisting or symbiotic firms in the rest of the industry. The French call this sort of market Malthusian.[20] Retail price maintenance, understandings that no firm will rock the boat, "conscious parallel action" even if no explicit agreement (to use the United States Supreme Court's phrase), make the local market before the entry of the international corporation much more monopolistic than the monopolistically competitive intruder. The cost advantages of the intruder are so great, even when its conduct is not aggressively competitive, that prices are reduced, volumes are expanded, and the monopolistic phenomenon extends the area of competition.

A strong case against this competition can be based on infant-industry argument. Given a chance to develop, to acquire technology, penetrate markets, learn management skills, and so forth, national firms may grow to compete effectively with the large international firm, and it is useful to give them the chance. This is so not for nationalistic reasons or for sentiment, but for efficiency. This exception apart, however, the presumption is that the international firm, unregulated except where necessary to keep entry free, will lead to greater world economic efficiency. The small local firm will object to "unfair" competition; it is really objecting to competition. . . .

The International Corporation and Efficiency

Compare the growth of the international corporation in the 1950s and 1960s with the rise of the national corporation in the 1880s and 1890s in the United States. There was great concern for abuses of competition, culminating in the passage of the Sherman Anti-Trust Act of 1890. Muckrakers inveighed against big business. Populists attacked the domination of Wall Street. But the national corporation, emerging out of the growth of the local corporation and the regional corporation, made an important contribution, over time, to economic efficiency in the United States. Prior to 1900, factor markets in the United States were less perfect than they are now. Wage rates were higher in the New England and Middle Atlantic states and the West than in the South and Middle West. Capital was cheaper in financial centers than in the rural areas of the West and South. Capital markets of New York, Philadelphia, Boston, Chicago and the major cities were joined after a fashion, but the connections between them and the rest of the country were limited and fragile.

The rise of the national corporation provided a new institution alongside the imperfect factor markets, which worked toward factor-price equalization and economic efficiency. Where capital failed to move easily to other cities, national corporations established financial offices and raised capital in New York. Where labor failed to move to the high wage areas in the North and East, corporations brought capital to labor in the South and West. There were other pulls on national corporations than factor-price differences— pulls, moreover, that also worked toward efficiency by attracting corporations to sources of supply, thus saving transport costs on heavy materials or by pulling them to the market, thus saving transport costs on bulky assembled products. But owing to the immobility of labor and land and to barriers to the free movement of capital, factor markets by themselves were inadequate to produce the efficient optimum implied by equality of factor prices. The national corporation provided an economic institution, unforeseen by the classical economists, which, while it carried the threat of monopoly, brought the United States closer to the classic competitive world. To achieve this result it may have been necessary to maintain a strong antitrust movement to ward off the evils of monopoly while moving toward the blessings of greater factor mobility.

The national corporation, it should be made clear, was a product of the railroad, telegraph, and telephone, which made it possible for a decision-making center to operate over wide distances without too great cost. The jet aircraft, the radio-telephone, and the rapid rate of growth in postwar Europe have lifted the horizons of many national corporations to the world scene, to join the limited number of pioneers who go back to 1900 and earlier. The development of corporations which scan the world for investment opportunities does offer the possibility, along with the spread of monopoly, of equalizing factor prices, even in the face of the international barriers to the movement of capital and of labor, in strictly analogous fashion to the rise of the national corporation in the United States after 1880.

Circumstances Alter Cases

If direct investment may expand or reduce competition it follows that it is impossible to draw general conclusions about its desirability, assuming that competition is desirable. It is necessary, rather, to settle matters on a case-by-case basis. This is not unknown in the antitrust field. In the United States prospective mergers are submitted to the Department of Justice to see whether the character of the firms, or their resultant size, is judged—case by case—to restrain trade. In Europe, it is claimed that business agreements, or cartels, . are not objectionable in themselves, but that there are good cartels and bad cartels, just as there are permissible and impermissible mergers in the United States. This is an uncomfortable position for the law. The economist, on the other hand, has long been used to deriving different conclusions from the same action, depending upon whether other things were equal (*ceteris paribus*) or altered (*mutatis mutandis*).

Equal treatment under the law requires the world to be indifferent to whether International Business Machines or the General Electric Company buys Machines Bull Compagnie, the French computer concern. But if I.B.M. were to acquire it, competition in the computer field would be reduced; for G.E. to team up with Machines Bull and Olivetti, on the other hand, or for Radio Corporation of America to join with Siemens, holds out the hope—although not, as it turned out, a very bright one—of widening the range of world competition in the computer field.

Direct investment is, then, a subject in which it is necessary to judge case by case, on the basis of the relevant circumstances, before coming to conclusions about the effects of one or another action. All the while countries, companies, and academic economists search for rules of thumb which can be generalized. "Investment for new enterprises, but not for takeovers"; or for "production, but not control"; or "in manufacturing, but not in distribution," and so forth. . . .

The necessity for companies and countries to proceed case-by-case, depending upon circumstances, is not only offensive to Anglo-Saxon notions of jurisprudence; administrative discretion raises the possibility of rapid changes in rules of conduct and of arbitrary disagreements between countries. The beauty of the market, as economists extol it, is that it operates through the direction of the invisible hand. When the French government changes its mind three times in five years on general rules for foreign investment and ends up with administrative discretion lacking procedures for appeal or even for pushing for decision, the directing hand is painfully visible. Moreover, two hands, attached to two different countries, may push in different directions, letting the international company slide between them in one case, or punishing it doubly in another. . . .

NOTES

1. Jack N. Behrman, "Promoting Free World Economic Development Through Direct Investment," *American Economic Review, 50,* No. 2 (May 1960), 271–281.
2. Ottawa, Queen's Printer, 1957.
3. E. R. Barlow and J. T. Wender, *Foreign Investment and Taxation* (Englewood Cliffs, N.J., Prentice-Hall, 1955).
4. For another rule of thumb, see Jean-Jacques Servan-Schreiber, who quotes a survey by a company named Donaldson and Lufkin which says that United States business considers it normal to invest 20 to 30 percent of its assets in Europe (*The American Challenge* [New York, Atheneum, 1968], p. 11). But the variance around such numbers, even if they should be valid averages, is so wide as to make the statement of little interest.
5. E. T. Penrose, "Foreign Investment and the Growth of the Firm," *Economic Journal, 66* (June 1956), 220–35.
6. Judd Polk, Irene W. Meister, and Lawrence A. Veit, *U.S. Production Abroad and the Balance of Payments: A Survey of Corporate Investment Experience* (New York, National Industrial Conference Board, 1966), p. 67.
7. From a master's thesis at M.I.T. by G. V. Lydecker, "Direct Foreign Investment and the Balance of Payments: A Study of the President's Program of Voluntary Restraint" (1966), p. 106.

Another company (ibid., p. 98) stated that the bulk of its dividends came from the mature investments "as would be expected."

See also "Cummins Trimming Ventures in Europe," New York Times (January 22, 1968), which states that losses to date are about $8.4 million on $17 million invested in three plants in Britain, one opened in 1957 and two in 1966.

8. Stephen H. Hymer, "The International Operations of National Firms: A Study of Direct Investment" (doctoral dissertation, Cambridge, Mass., M.I.T., 1960).

9. Answering a question at a business conference, a banker stated: "Most American companies expect and do get a higher return on their capital abroad than they do in the U.S. This is justified if only because the risk of investment outside your own country is greater. This is not so much a political risk in Europe as the risk of not being able to see business opportunities as clearly as the local company." See E. Russell Eggers, Manager, The Chase Manhattan Bank, Paris, "The Pattern of American Investment in Europe," Record of Proceedings Second International Investment Symposium, New College, Oxford, July 1964, in The Changing World (London, P. N. Kemp-Gee, 1965), p. 287. For this last risk, of course, it is necessary to have a higher original rate of return than foreign, not domestic, companies.

10. Lawrence B. Krause and Kenneth W. Dam, Federal Tax Treatment of Foreign Income (Washington, D.C., The Brookings Institution, 1964), p. 64.

11. The American Challenge, p. 275.

12. Lydecker, pp. 98, 112.

13. P. N. Rosenstein-Rodan, "Problems of Industrialization of Eastern and South-eastern Europe," Economic Journal, 53 (June–September 1943).

14. "Alcan Aluminium Active in Norway," New York Times (March 31, 1957).

15. Ibid.

16. Donald T. Brash, American Investment in Australian Industry (Cambridge, Mass., Harvard University Press, 1965), p. 40.

17. A. Lamfalussy, Investment and Growth in Mature Economies (Oxford, Blackwell, 1963).

18. For a demonstration that the tariff was less of a stimulus to U.S. investment in the European Economic Community than industrial growth there, though the effects were additive rather than mutually exclusive, see Lawrence B. Krause, European Economic Integration and the United States (Washington, D.C., The Brookings Institution, 1968), pp. 126–31.

19. See James A. Shulman, "Transfer Pricing in Multinational Business" (doctoral dissertation, Cambridge, Mass., Harvard Graduate School of Business Administration, August 1966).

20. As an interwar example of resistance to direct investment based on fear of competition, see Alfred Sauvy, Histoire économique de la France entre les deux guerres (Paris, Fayard, 1967), p. 372. The Czech shoe company, B'ata, planned to construct a factory in France. Immediately, the so-called Poullen Law of March 22, 1936, was passed to forbid the opening of new factories or ateliers for shoe manufacture, or the enlargement of existing ones.

6 / The Product Cycle Model

Raymond Vernon

It is a good deal easier to describe the investment behavior of U.S.-controlled enterprises in the census-taker's terms than to determine the stimulus for that behavior. Still, the motivation and response of U.S. enterprises during the century or so in which they set up and operated their overseas subsidiaries have had such persistent regularities that there is a certain efficiency in looking at the process in terms of a behavioral model. Such a model, like any observed generalization, constitutes a deliberate simplification of reality. Apart from simplifying the economic aspects of the process, the model makes no pretense at capturing the even more complex sociological, political, and idiosyncratic factors.

Still, there is a basis for picturing the development of overseas manufacturing facilities in the following terms: To begin with, U.S.-controlled enterprises generate new products and processes in response to the high per capita income and the relative availability of productive factors in the United States; they introduce these new products or processes abroad through exports; when their export position is threatened they establish overseas subsidiaries to exploit what remains of their advantage; they retain their oligopolistic advantage for a period of time, then lose it as the basis for the original lead is completely eroded.

The first stage in the sequence involves a unique stimulus and a unique response. During most of the past century, businessmen in the United States were exposed to such a stimulus because they confronted a set of problems and opportunities distinctly different from those facing the business interests of the other main industrial powers.[1] None could compare with the United States in terms of accessibility and cheapness of water and fossil power, forest products, and arable land. But labor in the United States has always been scarce, especially labor skilled in production techniques. In terms of comparative advantage, labor has been scarcer and more costly in the United States in relation to the country's other endowments than it was in other advanced countries in relation to their other endowments.

Despite the limited capabilities of U.S. labor as measured by their production skills, incomes in the United States have been high. A rich supply of raw materials in the early part of the period and ample supplies of capital in the latter part, coupled with a high level of general literacy and education, more than made up for the lack of production

From Raymond Vernon, *Sovereignty at Bay: The Multinational Spread of U.S. Enterprises,* pp. 65-77, 107-109. © 1971 by Basic Books Inc., Publishers, New York, and Longman Group Limited, England. Tables and notes have been renumbered.

skills. High productivity went hand in hand with high per capita income, and high per capita incomes generated a high level of internal demand. To satisfy this demand, U.S. entrepreneurs had to find a way of producing the wanted goods by means that used little skilled labor.[2] Sewing machines sharply increased the productivity of scarce seamstresses during the 1850s. Drip-dry shirts reduced the need for services of scarce laundresses during the 1950s.

But why was it U.S. producers that responded to these special U.S. needs? Why not European producers? In the open and frictionless world of classical economic theory, of course, there would be no special reason to assume that the demand for new products in the United States would be met in the first instance by U.S. producers; European producers, sensing the opportunity for profit, might have been expected to respond, especially if their production costs were lower.

Experience suggests that in the early stages of introducing a new product, producers have usually been confronted with a number of critical, albeit transitory, conditions that deeply affect the choice of a production site. If the first use of a product was for the U.S. military, as it sometimes was, a U.S. location was often indispensable. When producing for nonmilitary buyers in the United States, however, there were also reasons to produce at home. First, there was no particular incentive during the early stages for a producer to look outside the consumer country for a location where production costs were low. Because of the demand conditions that producers confronted at those stages, they were less concerned with costs than they were likely to be later on. (The pioneer radio fan of the early 1920s, for instance, was much less sensitive to the price of his product than was the suburban family of the 1970s.) This phenomenon, well-explored among marketing specialists, seems to stem from the high degree of product differentiation or the existence of monopoly in the early stages.[3] Second, there was an especially urgent need at this early stage for swift and effective communication inside the enterprise, and with customers, suppliers, and even competitors outside the enterprise. Producers have been uncertain regarding the ultimate dimensions of the market, the efforts of rivals to preempt that market, the specifications of the inputs needed for production, and the specifications of the products likely to be most successful in the effort.[4] These considerations have tended to argue for a location in which communication between the market and the executives directly concerned with the new product was swift and easy. In the choice of location, flexibility and swift response were given more weight than capital and labor cost.[5]

By specializing in the development of labor-saving innovations and high-income products, U.S. businessmen found themselves with product lines that had real promise in foreign markets. After 1879 or so, the rest of the world found itself tracking over an economic terrain that U.S. businessmen had already traversed. During the latter half of the nineteenth century, the price of labor in Western Europe was rising rapidly relative to the price of other factors and per capita incomes were moving parallel with the price of labor.[6] Thus, in Great Britain from 1850 to 1910, money wages rose by about two-thirds while prices were generally stagnant. After World War II, money wages continued to outrun prices all over Europe.

According to the product cycle concept, innovation has provided a basis for the export of manufactured goods from the United States. The utility of the product cycle concept as an explanatory device can be tested, therefore, in the patterns of trade of the United States and other countries. Here, the evidence in support of the view that some such phenomenon has existed is fairly impressive.

Various studies indicate that the United States has tended to specialize in the export of products from industries that employ a relatively high proportion of scientists and engineers in their labor force and that spend relatively large proportions of their income on research and development. These analyses . . . show that U.S. export concentration on products of this sort has systematically been greater than the export concentration of other countries in such products.[7] As added confirmation of the distinctive character of U.S. exports, other analyses suggest that the price elasticity of demand for U.S. exports has tended to be considerably lower than for U.S. imports or for the exports of other countries.[8]

Though the cumulative persuasiveness of these studies is considerable, one has to recognize that the underlying data in such analyses tend to be fairly aggregative, perhaps too much so to provide the kind of sure footing that is needed to test the product cycle concept. Besides, inasmuch as most analyses are based on cross-sectional data reflecting a single point in time, they suffer from the vulnerabilities usually involved in testing a dynamic concept with static evidence. It is reassuring, therefore, to find that confirmation for the existence of the sequence appears in a number of studies that do not suffer from these particular disabilities, analyses that trace the experiences of specific narrowly defined products over periods of time.

To begin with, studies of individual products in the U.S. market confirm the assumption that products commonly go through a cycle of initiation, exponential growth, slowdown, and decline—a sequence that corresponds to the process of introduction, spread, maturation, and senescence suggested earlier.[9] Moreover, there has been some systematic testing of export patterns for individual products. One analysis, for instance, measures the change in U.S. exports of twenty well-established consumer durable products between the early 1950s and the early 1960s. The anticipation, based on the product cycle concept, was that the U.S. export position during those years would be best sustained in products whose ownership was associated with high income and whose introduction to the market was comparatively recent. Thus, the United States was seen as having a less vulnerable export position in vacuum cleaners or electric mixers—products that are comparatively new and associated with high incomes—than in radios or gas cookers. The data confirm these expectations very nicely.[10]

Still another analysis has traced the experience of the United States and other countries in the production and exportation of nine major petrochemical products from their genesis to the year 1966. Here, too, the data confirmed the existence of a pattern which began with innovation in the United States, moved on for a time to growth of U.S. exports to other markets, and finally displayed a visible braking or actual reversal of such export growth.[11]

Innovation and export, according to the product cycle hypothesis, have eventually induced many U.S. enterprises to produce abroad and to serve their markets from a foreign location. How has that decision been reached? For the period after World War II, the foreign investment decision is a much-studied field.[12] It has at times been probed by investigators who were looking at the phenomenon from the viewpoint of the capital-exporting country, at other times from the viewpoint of the capital-importing areas, at still other times from the viewpoint of the decision-making firms. Some of the studies have used the extensive survey approach, some the intensive in-depth analysis of individual cases.

Studies that were based on the extensive survey approach have generally not been designed to test a hypothesis as elaborate as the product cycle sequence. Still, they are helpful. Superficially, studies of this sort generally report that the overseas subsidiaries of manufacturing enterprises were set up primarily to increase sales, serve an expanding market, meet local competition, overcome an import barrier, increase profits, and so on. It is only when these replies are interpreted in light of some of the more intensive analyses of individual cases that they begin to take on meaning in terms of the product cycle sequence. [13]

As noted earlier, the decision to set up manufacturing facilities abroad has commonly been triggered by the perception of a threat to an established export market. The exact form of the galvanizing threat has differed from one case to the next. Over time, however, there has been a remarkable similarity in some of the patterns. Table 6-1 presents a summary of the motivations of ten major U.S. parents that by 1900 had already established a major presence overseas. Their motivations in doing so do not appear to have been very different from those of the producers who would follow them fifty or sixty years later. In the case of . . . nine petrochemicals . . . for example, the original producers did not set up a plant outside their domestic market without first being threatened by the appearance abroad of some uncontrolled competitor. More generally, unlicensed imitators or parallel innovators have commonly provided the immediate threat that has led to the initial overseas investment.

The decision of U.S. businessmen to invest abroad has often been made easier by the fact that by the time the step was taken, the technology of production had settled down sufficiently to be transferable to a foreign facility without considerable cost and inconvenience to the U.S. enterprise, especially if the transfer was being made to a fairly advanced country. It is true that at times, especially after World War II, some backward areas have offered special governmental inducements to the U.S. investor. Much more important, however, has been simple growth in national demand. That growth opened up the possibility that the average delivered cost for an overseas production facility would no longer be disadvantageous by comparison with the marginal cost of output from the United States. Big markets, therefore, tended to be attractive sooner than small.

The readiness of multinational enterprises to cross the threshold from exports to direct investment may well have been enhanced by the realization that once the production process was free of its dependence on the specialized inputs of the U.S. economy—once the conventional costs of capital and labor came to dominate the calculation—foreign locations might be more attractive than U.S. production sites. As far as the financial costs of capital are concerned, these are often presumed to be uniform by multinational enterprises, irrespective of where a facility might be located. Even when the national capital costs are allowed to vary by location or when local borrowing at different interest rates is contemplated, the effect of capital cost differences on total costs of production is not generally significant enough to be crucial for the locational decision. Therefore, labor has often proved the source of the real difference between costs in the United States and those abroad. [14] Once the question of costs has become important, that consideration has tended to draw industry away from a U.S. location.

The readiness of U.S. enterprises to search out a lower cost location abroad at some point in the development of their products has probably been enhanced as well by the fact that the profit margins associated with the manufacture of fabricated industrial products commonly decline as the early monopoly stage begins drawing to a close. [15] The reasons for the decline stem partly from change on the supply side: As products mature, the average costs of production tend to drop, and as the oligopolistic structure of the industry weakens, the decline in cost is reflected in the price. Price declines have also been induced

Table 6-1 Characteristics of Foreign Manufacturing Plants Established before 1900 by Specified U.S. Parents

U.S. Parent	Principal Products	Location of Foreign Plants	Substantial U.S. Exports Prior to Foreign Investment?	Asserted Reasons for Foreign Investment[a]
Colt	Firearms	Great Britain	Yes	Local competitive threat
Singer	Sewing machines	Great Britain/ Austria/Canada	Yes	Local competitive threat, lower costs
ITT	Communications	Great Britain/ Belgium/Germany/ Austria/France/ Italy/Russia/Japan	Yes	Local competitive threat, lower costs
General Electric and its predecessors	Electrical products and equipment	Great Britain/ France/Germany/Canada	Yes	Local competitive threat, lower costs, national pressures
Westinghouse Air Brake	Air brakes and signal equipment	Great Britain/ France/Germany/ Russia	Yes	Local competitive threat, lower costs, national pressures
Westinghouse Electric	Electrical products and equipment	Great Britain/ France/Russia	Yes	Local competitive threat, lower costs
Eastman Kodak	Photographic goods	Great Britain	Yes	Local competitive threat, lower costs
United Shoe Machinery	Shoe machinery	Great Britain/ France/Germany/ Switzerland	Yes	Not determined
Parke, Davis	Pharmaceuticals	Canada	Yes	Lower costs
American Radiator and Standard Sanitary's predecessor	Radiators	France	Yes	Lower costs, larger demand

[a] The asserted reasons given in this column are inescapably a matter of interpretation to some extent, subject to the usual biases that go with such a process.
Sources: Principally Mira Wilkins, *Emergence of Multinational Enterprise* (Cambridge: Harvard University Press, 1970), and company annual reports.

by change in the structure of demand: As the markets for new products widen, the added buyers generally tend to be more price responsive than the pioneer buyers. These changes make the original producers increasingly sensitive to the question of production costs.

Once a U.S. producer has decided to place his production facilities closer to a foreign market in order to reduce his costs, this decision seems to provide a stimulus for parallel behavior among the producer's oligopoly partners.[16] . . . To reestablish the equilibrium of the oligopoly market, leading enterprises have sometimes felt compelled to take a position that matched the advances of a rival firm.

The decision of innovators to try to prolong their hold on overseas markets by direct investment has induced not only their rivals but also their suppliers to take similar action. Here again, threat has vied with promise as the stimulus for action. Whenever a U.S. supplier of industrial materials has been invited by a major customer to set up a supplying facility in some foreign location, the danger in rejecting the invitation has generally not been missed by the supplier. As a result, automobile component suppliers in the United States have been drawn abroad by the major automobile companies, chemical producers by the processors of petrochemicals and plastics, packaging material producers by the food companies.

One added variant on the familiar product cycle sequence bears mentioning, a variant that has repeatedly been observed in the history of U.S. foreign direct investment. In many cases, the first competitive edge that a U.S. businessman thought of himself as possessing was one that could not be tested by export. Food-processing companies, for instance, have commonly thought of themselves as having a special capacity for mobilizing, financing, and directing the activities of independent farmers; for standardizing and controlling quality in the mass production of complex organic materials; and for controlling the distribution of perishable products in ways that reduced the threat of deterioration. The bulk character of the final product, however, has generally prevented the producing firms from testing and developing large foreign markets by way of exports from the United States.[17] In these cases, because no prior market test was available through exports, the U.S. businessman's decision to use his apparent advantage as a basis for setting up an enterprise in a foreign country has sometimes involved special risks.

The sequence sketched out in the last few pages carries the product cycle to the threshold of its final stage. The enterprise, having lost its oligopoly advantage, finds that it can no longer claim any cost or other advantage over its imitators, local and foreign; even its overseas subsidiaries, operating in an economic environment no different from their competitors, begin to feel the pressure. At this stage, diseconomies associated with large size and an elaborate organizational apparatus threaten to outweigh the economies. Confronted with a loss of market, U.S.-controlled enterprises have been observed responding in a number of different ways.

One such response has been to slough off the product as no longer of much interest, as a commodity in the pejorative parlance of the food and chemical trades. A second has been to try to create new oligopoly advantages by making changes in the product or in the services associated with it. A third, barely distinguishable from the second, has been to try to create the illusion of such advantages through stepped-up advertising. Finally, there have been efforts to find a very much lower-cost production site for the product where competitors could not easily pursue, a site whose costs would be low enough to offset the disadvantages of scale of the large organization.

All these reactions, separately and in combination, have appeared in the responses of multinational enterprises. The first three reactions, involving such stratagems as the trivial manipulation of drug molecules and the repackaging of food products, have not entailed new locational decisions on the part of the multinational enterprise. But when the reaction of the enterprise has been to look for lower-cost production sites, the location issue has been raised again. In part, it is this process that accounts for the spread of multinational enterprises beyond locations in advanced countries into less-developed areas and for the rise in international cross-hauling among their constituent units.

• • •

Toward Another Model

The product cycle sequence may have seemed an efficient concept by which to describe the activities of U.S.-controlled multinational enterprises during most of the decades of their existence. But by 1970, the concept was frequently exhibiting procrustean tendencies—that is, tendencies to discard or distort information in order to have the facts conform rather more nicely to the theory. For instance, the product cycle sequence relies heavily on the assumption that the special conditions of the U.S. environment—especially factor costs and consumer tastes in the United States—will set in train a sequence that leads step by step to international investment. Though this may be an efficient way to look at enterprises in the U.S. economy that are on the threshold of developing a foreign business, the model is losing some of its relevance for those enterprises that have long since acquired a global scanning capacity and a global habit of mind.

By the late 1960s there were plenty of illustrations that U.S. manufacturing enterprises were already capable of a considerable degree of global scanning. U.S. parents were better equipped than they had ever been to evaluate foreign opportunities and assess foreign threats, and to respond to these opportunities and threats by developing complex logistical networks among their affiliates. IBM was producing integrated circuits in France, and mounting materials for the circuits in Germany; it was concentrating one type of computer assembly in its French plant, another in its German; and it was producing hybrid circuits for both at still a third location.[18] Bendix was using the cheap labor of Taiwan to assemble automobile radios for world markets. Ford was making fender steel in Holland for car production in the rest of Europe and tractor components in Germany and motors for compact models in Britain to be used in U.S. assembly plants.[19] Singer was cross-hauling its many makes and models of sewing machines between Scotland, Canada, Japan, and the United States, concentrating the production of different types where markets and factor costs suggested. More generally, the networks established by U.S.-controlled multinational enterprises, by the late 1960s, were handling an international trade in manufactured goods of impressive proportions: about $9,000 million annually in exports from the United States; $12,000 million from Europe and Canada; and $1,400 million from the less-developed parts of the world.

By 1970, the product cycle model was beginning in some respects to be inadequate as a way of looking at the U.S.-controlled multinational enterprise. The assumption of the product cycle model—that innovations were generally transmitted from the U.S. market for production and marketing in overseas areas—was beginning to be challenged by illustrations that did not fit the pattern. The new pattern that these illustrations suggested was one in which stimulation to the system could come from the exposure of any element in the system to its local environment, and response could come from any part of the system that was appropriate for the purpose.

Of course, before an organization could be thought of as global in outlook, one would expect it to have shed any nonrational preferences for U.S. money, personnel, or markets. It would be an exaggeration to say that this has yet happened to any great extent. But it is no exaggeration to note the palpable existence of that tendency. With large sums of long-term money being raised in foreign markets, with key personnel being hired in foreign countries, and with major fixed assets being established in foreign jurisdictions, the trend could hardly be avoided.

Despite the tendency toward a global outlook, it is safe to assume that U.S.-controlled multinational enterprises will generally think of themselves as American companies for a long time to come, long after the concept has lost some of its meaning in day-to-day operational terms. That, of course, is understandable. To accept some measure of confusion about one's national identity is not an easy thing for anyone raised in a system of nation states. But the American identification will not prevent U.S.-controlled enterprises from ranging widely through the globe in search of inspiration, capital, labor, materials, and markets. [20]

NOTES

1. For an extended discussion of the ties between market conditions and industrial innovation, see Jacob Schmookler, *Invention and Economic Growth* (Cambridge: Harvard University Press, 1966).

2. These are treacherous concepts, to be handled with care. An invention need not substitute one factor for another; on the contrary, it can be saving of both labor and capital at the same time. See W. E. G. Salter, *Productivity and Technical Change* (Cambridge University Press, 1960), pp. 43-44. Under classical conditions, this fact undermines the justification for assuming the existence of any particular factor bias in cost-saving innovations. But if innovation is thought of as a scarce factor that commands a monopoly rent and if the innovating activity is thought of as involving a lumpy commitment with resulting economies of scale, then the probability that there will be factor-saving bias in innovation is once more rendered plausible. For more on this issue, see Nathan Rosenberg, "The Directions of Technological Change: Inducement Mechanisms and Focusing Devices," *Economic Development and Cultural Change 18*, no 1, pt. 1 (October, 1969) 1-24.

3. Some products inherently lend themselves to standardization less than others. See G. C. Hufbauer, "The Impact of National Characteristics and Technology on the Commodity Composition of Trade in Manufactured Goods" in Raymond Vernon, ed., *The Technology Factor in International Trade* (New York: Columbia University Press, 1970), pp. 145-231. The statement in the text is therefore to be thought of as an intertemporal statement for a given product, not one to be applied in comparing different products.

4. A. T. Knoppers, "American Interests in Europe," in Eric Moonman, ed., *Science and Technology in Europe* (Harmondsworth, Middlesex, Eng.: Penguin Books, 1968); W. P. Strassmann, *Risk and Technological Innovation* (Ithaca: Cornell University Press, 1959), pp. 32-34, 221; D. A. Schon, *Technology and Change* (New York: Delacorte Press, 1967), pp. 19-41, 103-111; OECD, *Gaps in Technology between Member Countries: Sector Report, Plastics* (Paris, 1968), p. 102; P. R. Lawrence and J. W. Lorsch, *Organization and Environment: Managing Differentiation and Integration* (Boston: Harvard Business School, 1967), pp. 88-96; A. J. Harman, "Innovations Technology, and the Pure Theory of International Trade," unpublished Ph.D. thesis, MIT, September 1968, p. 131.

5. This is, of course, a familiar point elaborated in George F. Stigler, "Production and Distribution in the Short Run," *Journal of Political Economy*, 47 (June 1939): 305 ff.

6. H. M. Croom and R. J. Hammond, *An Economic History of Britain* (London: Christophers, 1938), p. 293; H. O. Meredith, *Outlines of the Economic History of England* (London: Pitman & Sons, 1908), p. 352; S. B. Clough and C. W. Cole, *Economic History of Europe* (Boston: Heath, 1952), p. 662. In France, wages and prices followed a roughly similar trend; wages rose rapidly whereas prices scarcely increased over the period. Institut National de la Statistique et des Études Économiques, *Annuaire statistique de la France, 1966: Résumé rétrospectif* (Paris, 1967), pp. 373, 422, 425.

7. W. H. Gruber, Dileep Mehta, and Raymond Vernon, "The R & D Factor in International Trade and International Investment," *Journal of Political Economy*, 75, no. 1 (February 1967): 24-25; G. C. Hufbauer, "The Impact of National Characteristics and Technology on the Commodity Composition of Trade in Manufactured Goods," in Raymond Vernon, ed., *The Technology Factor in International Trade* (New York: Columbia University Press, 1970); W. H. Gruber and Raymond Vernon, "The Technology Factor in a World Trade Matrix," in the same source; J. H. Dunning, "European and U.S. Trade Patterns, U.S. Foreign Investment, and the Technological Gap," *Proceedings of the International Economic Association*, September 1969, mimeograph.

8. H. S. Houthakker and S. P. Magee, "Income and Price Elasticities in World Trade," *Review of Economics and Statistics*, 51, no. 2 (May 1969): 111-125; F. M. Adler, "The Relationship between the Income and Price Elasticities of Demand for U.S. Exports," Columbia University, November 1969, mimeograph; W. H. Branson, *A Disaggregated Model of the U.S. Balance of Trade*, Federal Reserve System Staff Economic Study (Washington, D.C.: Federal Reserve System, 1968).

9. Rolando Polli and Victor Cook, "Validity of the Product Life Cycle," *Journal of Business*, 42, no. 4 (October 1969): 385-400.

10. L. T. Wells, Jr., "Test of a Product Cycle Model of International Trade," *Quarterly Journal of Economics*, 83 (February 1969); 152-162.

11. R. B. Stobaugh, "The Product Life Cycle, U.S. Exports, and International Investment," unpublished D.B.A. thesis, Harvard Business School, June 1968. See also OECD, *Gaps in Technology* (Paris, 1968), six industry sectoral studies; also studies on the plastics, electronics, and chemical process plant industries, respectively, all directed by Christopher Freeman, *National Institute Economic Review*, 26 (November 1963), 34 (November 1965), and 45 (August 1968).

12. See R. S. Basi, *Determinants of United States Private Direct Investments in Foreign Countries* (Kent, O.: Kent State University Bureau of Economic and Business Research, 1963); A. N. Hakam, "The Motivation to Invest and the Locational Pattern of Foreign Private Industrial Development in Nigeria," *Economic and Social Studies*, 8, no. 1 (March 1966): 50; G. L. Reuber and Frank Roseman, *The Takeover of Canadian Firms, 1945-1961: An Empirical Analysis*, 1968, mimeograph; National Industrial Conference Board, *U.S. Production Abroad and the Balance of Payments* (New York, 1966), p. 63; Arthur Stonehill and Leonard Nathanson, "Capital Budgeting and the Multinational Corporation," *California Management Review*, 10, no. 4 (Summer 1968): 39-55; R. F. Mikesell, ed., *U.S. Private and Government Investment Abroad* (Eugene, Ore.: University of Oregon, 1962), p. 89; *Overseas Operations of U.S. Industrial Enterprises, 1960-1961* (New York: McGraw-Hill, 1960); National Planning Association, *Case Studies of U.S. Business Performance Abroad* (Washington D.C.: National Planning Association, 1955-1961), eleven case studies; H. J. Robinson, *The Motivation and Flow of Private Foreign Investment*, Investment Series no. 4 (Menlo Park, Calif.: Stanford Research Institute, 1961), p. 24; D. M. Phelps, *Migration of Industry to Latin America* (New York: McGraw-Hill, 1936), pp. 43-87; Michael Kidron, *Foreign Investments in India* (London: Oxford University Press, 1965), pp. 253-256; B. L. Johns, "Private Overseas Investment in Australia: Profitability and Motivation," *Economic Record*, 43 (June 1967): 257-261; Whatarangi Winiata, "United States Managerial Investment in Japan, 1950-1964," unpublished Ph.D. thesis, University of Michigan, 1966, p. 110.

13. Especially fruitful sources are Yair Aharoni, *The Foreign Investment Decision Process* (Boston: Harvard Business School, 1966), esp. chaps. 3-7; E. P. Neufeld, *A Global Corpora-*

ration (Toronto: University of Toronto Press, 1969); Mira Wilkins and F. E. Hill, *American Business Abroad* (Detroit: Wayne State University Press, 1964). For a good source of business histories repeatedly consulted, see L. M. Daniells, *Studies in Enterprise* (Boston: Harvard Business School, 1957).

14. Mordechai Kreinin, "The Leontief Scarce-Factor Paradox," *American Economic Review,* 55 (March 1965): 131; T. R. Gates, *Production Costs Here and Abroad* (New York: National Industrial Conference Board, 1958), pp. 26–27.

15. See G. C. Hufbauer, *Synthetic Materials and the Theory of International Trade* (London: Duckworth, 1966), p. 59; OECD, *Gaps in Technology between Member Countries: Plastics* (Paris, 1968), p. 104; R. B. Stobaugh, "Systematic Bias and the Terms of Trade," *Review of Economics and Statistics,* 49 (November 1967); 617–619; R. B. Stobaugh, "Away from Market Concentration: The Case of Petrochemicals," Marketing Science Institute working paper, October 1970.

16. This phenomenon is being explored by F. T. Knickerbocker in a D. B.A. dissertation at the Harvard Business School.

17. These cases are not confined to food products. A recent decision by Armco Steel to manufacture preengineered steel building systems in Germany, despite the fact that a market for such systems had not yet appeared in Europe, is illustrative of the same phenomenon. "U.S. Industry Ties Keep German Producer Independent," *The New York Times,* December 26, 1969, p. 49. It is doubtful if the market for such a product, which notably conserves skilled labor, could be developed by exports from the United States.

18. A. J. Harman, *"The International Computer Industry: Innovation and Comparative Advantage,* (Cambridge: Harvard University Press, 1971), pp. 131–134.

19. Royal Commission on Farm Machinery, *Special Report on Prices* (Ottawa: Queen's Printer, 1969), p. 92; "A Ford Aide Fears Minicar Cost Rise," *New York Times,* August 21, 1970, p. 1.

20. For an articulation of a typical set of such views on the part of businessmen, see F. G. Donner, *The World-Wide Industrial Enterprise* (New York: McGraw-Hill, 1967).

7 / Concentration in International Oil

John M. Blair

History of Petroleum Industry

In the history of concentrated industries, the usual sequence has been a progression from market control through collusion, conspiracy, and cartels to the nonprice competition of oligopolistic interdependence.

．　．　．

From a broad historical point of view, the period beginning in the late 1920's and extending somewhat beyond the end of World War II could be thought of as the cartel era in international oil. Most of the postwar era might properly be regarded as the period of oligopolistic interdependence. And, in light of very recent developments, we could now be entering into a third phase—an era of bilateral monopoly, with the producing countries acting as sellers and the companies as buyers, possessing, however, the exclusive right to purchase.

．　．　．

Concentration in International Oil

The fundamental requirement for market control by noncollusive means is of course a concentrated industrial structure. For many years it has been an accepted tenet of economic thinking that the behavior of prices, profits, and output will differ from that expected under classical—and neoclassical—theory where the industry is oligopolistic; that is, a major share of its output is accounted for by a small number of its leading, and usually large, firms. As can be seen [in Table 7-1], this is the structural form of international oil:

From the testimony of John M. Blair at the Hearings before the Subcommittee on Multinational Corporations of the Committee on Foreign Relations, United States Senate, 93rd Congress, 2nd Session, *Multinational Corporations and United States Foreign Policy* (Washington, D.C.: Government Printing Office, 1975), July 25, 1974, Part 9, pp. 192–230. Some notes have been omitted, and the remainder renumbered in sequence. Tables and figures have been renumbered.

Table 7-1 Concentration Ratios of World Crude Oil Production, 1972 [In percent]

	Mideast	OPEC countries	United States	Free world supply
4 largest companies	64.4	52.9	30.3	48.3
7 largest companies	90.9	77.2	39.1	70.0

Source: Subcommittee on Multinational Corporations, Hearings, pt. 4, p. 68.

If economists had to select one figure as representing the point at which oligopoly begins, there would probably be a consensus that it is in the neighborhood of control by the top four companies of around half the output. In recent years this judgment has been corroborated by a number of empirical studies finding that above a 50-percent concentration ratio—that is, control by the four largest companies of 50 percent or more of the industry's output—the behavior of prices, profits and margins does in fact differ noticeably from that at decidedly lower levels of concentration. By this standard, the international oil industry would clearly qualify as oligopolistic. Incidentally, the lower concentration ratios shown for the United States understate the effective control of the market since the private means of control have been supplemented by governmental intervention—"market demand" prorationing and the import quota—which, as demand has now come to exceed capacity, have become unnecessary.

· · ·

Five of the seven international majors are American firms, and two are British-Dutch. The U.S. firms are in turn made up of two segments: Subsidiaries of the old Standard Oil Trust (Exxon, Mobil, and Socal) and "non-Standard" majors, Texaco and Gulf, which obtained concessions in areas from which the original Middle East operators had been effectively excluded by the Red Line agreement.

The 1972 market shares of the seven companies are shown [in table 7-2] in accordance with these company groupings.

The 3 "Standard" companies alone produced nearly two-fifths of the Mideast output and almost a third of the OPEC total; that is the total produced by the 11 countries that are members of the Organization of Petroleum Exporting Countries. The five American companies, it can be seen, accounted for nearly three-fifths of production in the Mideast

Table 7-2 Concentration of Free World Crude Oil Production, 1972 by Company Groups [In percent]

	Mideast	OFEC countries	United States	Free world supply
Exxon, Mobil, and SoCal	39.8	30.5	18.7	28.3
Gulf and Texaco	18.7	19.0	13.9	17.7
BP and Shell	32.4	27.7	6.5	24.0
Total	90.9	77.2	39.1	70.0

Source: Derived from Subcommittee on Multinational Corporations, Hearings, pt. 4, p. 68.

and nearly half in all OPEC countries. The British-Dutch companies accounted for just under a third of the Mideast output and more than a quarter of the OPEC total. The control of the market indicated by these impressive market shares has been further strengthened by joint ownership of oil-producing companies and other interlocking relationships.

Common Assumptions on Growth Rate

In addition to a concentrated structure, the achievement of noncompetitive behavior in a rapidly growing industry also requires the sharing of a common point of view concerning the rate at which the industry should expand. Differing assumptions on the desired growth rate would lead to differing expansion plans and thus to the danger of an oversupply, defined by industry spokesmen as the coming on to the market of a supply in excess of demand at the existing price. Referring to conditions during the 1960's, Subcommittee Counsel Henry asked Howard W. Page, senior vice president of Exxon, "Was your major problem having more oil than you could market at acceptable prices?" Page responded by saying, "That was one of the problems we had, yes, along with the rest of the industry."[1] Page's response to a similar question by Senator Percy was to the same effect. The Senator asked, "If you had been using the production capacity up to the fullest extent, obviously it would have driven prices down considerably," to which Page replied, ". . . I mean if we had used any one to capacity, then we would have to shut the other back. There was no place to go with it. You can't dump it in the sea. There is a law against it." In other words, any expansion from one source that would cause overall supply to grow at an unduly rapid rate must be compensated for by a corresponding decrease somewhere else. George T. Piercy, also a senior vice president of Exxon, stated, "Well, I think that if some capacity was brought on anywhere else in the world, as Mr. Page has said, it is like a balloon and you brought it on one place—you push it in one place, something has to give somewhere else because the fact that oil was brought in here or there does not in any way mean there is any more consumption.

One way of dealing with the problem is not to develop new sources in the first place. Page recounted the dismay occasioned by the discovery of a potential new source of supply, Oman:

> Just at this time, the producing department brought in their geologist who had just come back from Oman, and he stated, "I am sure there is a 10 billion oil field there;" and I said, "Well, then, I am absolutely sure we don't want to go into it, and that settles it." I might put some money in it if I was sure we weren't going to get some oil, but not if we are going to get oil because we are liable to lose the Aramco concession, our share of the Aramco concession, anyway, if we were going to back up any further on it by going into new areas.

. . .

In the oil industry the discipline of the market is further weakened by the fact that, being fully integrated, the major companies can more or less apportion their profit and their cost to that stage which happens to be of greatest benefit to them. In the past that has been the production level because of the tax features. It is at the stage of production that a firm derives the greatest benefit from percentage depletion, expensing intangible drilling costs and foreign tax credits. The whole structure of the oil industry is quite different from what would have evolved without the special tax benefits granted to the industry by the U.S. Congress.

. . .

There are always objections that can be made to the operation of the competitive market. The competitive market subjects enterprises to a very hard form of discipline. It has, however, certain important advantages that no other form of public policy possesses; not only does it bring about a price which is economically desirable, that is, it calls for the supply needed to meet the existing level of demand, but—and this is often overlooked— it exerts a constant downward pressure on costs. Under public utility regulation the rates of a public utility may be set in such a way as to yield only a fair or reasonable markup above cost, but there is no way of seeing to it that the utility constantly reduces cost and keeps abreast of new technological developments. Only competition provides that incredibly valuable discipline.

A further function performed by competition—no other form of public policy provides a reward to the enterprise that introduces an innovation, a new technology, or product that either exploits a demand that had not been tapped before or results in a reduction in cost. One of the great problems in the Soviet economy has been the lack of such incentives operating within state enterprises. Their technological backwardness, which they are now acknowledging, is not the result of an inadequate supply of trained engineers and technicians. In fact, they turn out a greater number of engineers than the Western World, than the United States each year. The problem is that their new ideas, their new concepts, that would contribute to industrial progress are not received. There is no place for them. Rather than trying something new, which might interfere with production, the plant managers seek to achieve their production norms by relying upon the existing and older technologies. That is the fundamental reason why the economies of the Communist countries are lagging increasingly behind the Western World.

. . .

A Stable Growth in Supply

The achievement of a consensus among rival oligopolists on a desired growth rate would, of course, be greatly facilitated if the rate were assumed to be relatively stable over an extended period of time. In the Mideast, Africa, and similar environs, a leadtime of several years is usually required between a decision to make a substantial expansion in productive capacity and the installation of the production, storage, and transportation facilities necessary to bring it onstream. And the leadtime becomes even longer if new refining capacity is required. Under such circumstances, widely varying assumptions from 1 year to the next as to the rate of increase in supply would make it difficult, if not impossible, for each oligopolist to plan for precisely that increase in his output which would maintain his share of the market but not produce an oversupply.

Whether simply a means of implementing mutual interdependence or the product of collusive agreement, world petroleum supply has exhibited a remarkably stable annual growth rate, as reflected in the output of the leading producing countries—outside North America and the Communist bloc. This is revealed in chart 1 which shows for 1950-72 the yearly average increase in aggregate output of the 11 members of OPEC—Saudi Arabia, Iran, Kuwait, Iraq, Abu Dhabi, Qatar, Venezuela, Libya, Nigeria, Algeria, and Indonesia.

The compound growth rate and a measure of the "closeness of fit" have been computed by—

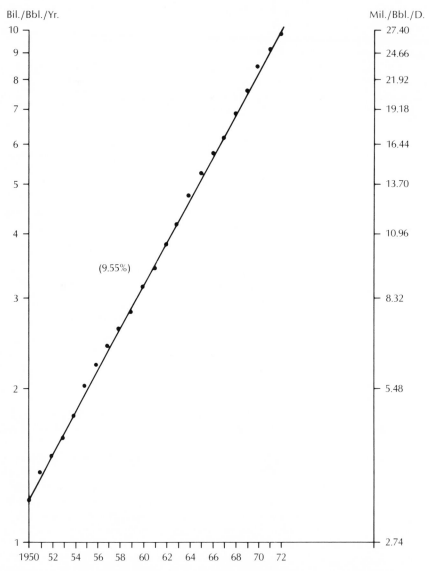

Figure 7-1 Crude oil production: actual vs. estimated growth rate, 1950–72. (*Source:* Derived from Organization of Petroleum Exporting Countries, Statistical Bulletins.)

(a) plotting the actual increase in aggregate output;

(b) fitting a regression line to these observations;

(c) determining therefrom the compound rate of increase in output—the "average growth rate"—and

(d) measuring the deviations between the regression line and the actual observations, thereby indicating by a coefficient of determination (R^2) the extent to which the actual increases are "explained" by the estimated growth rate.

This chart [Figure 7-1], like the others used in this analysis, has been drafted on semilogarithmic paper by means of which a given percentage change occupies the same vertical distance anywhere on the chart.

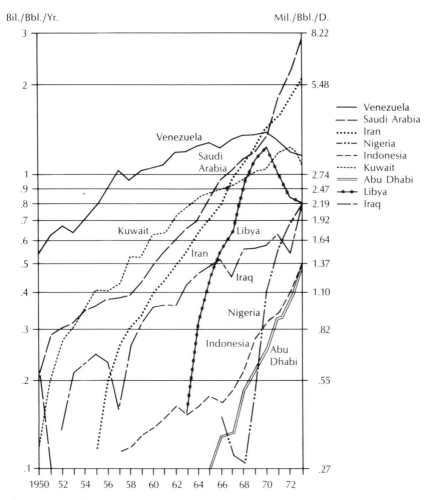

Figure 7-2 Production of crude oil: 9 leading producing countries, 1950-73. (*Source:* Derived from Organization of Petroleum Exporting Countries, Statistical Bulletins.)

For the 11 countries as a group, the average annual percentage increase in output during 1950-62—the "estimated" growth rate—works out to be 9.55 percent. The measure of the closeness of fit of the regression line to the actual observations—the coefficient of determination or R^2—is an astonishing 99.9 percent. In other words, an assumption that oil production would increase at an average annual rate of 9.55 percent explains all but one-tenth of 1 percent of the actual change.

. . .

If each of the producing countries had been increasing its output at about the same rate, the steady rise in overall supply could be explained as merely the sum total of the behavior of the individual countries. But this explanation obviously falls if the different sources of supply have been expanding at widely varying rates and, even more strikingly, if some have been characterized by actual declines. That such has been the pattern of the international oil industry is apparent from [Figure 7-2] which shows for 1950-73 the yearly change in total production for each of the nine leading producing countries. The international supply picture is revealed as a composite of long-sustained steady increases—Saudi Arabia and Iran—of much slower rates of increase—Venezuela, Kuwait, and Iraq—of precipitous rises—Libya until 1970, Nigeria, Abu Dhabi, Indonesia—and of occasional pronounced declines—Iran in 1951-54; Iraq in 1957, 1967, and 1972; Nigeria in 1968; and Venezuela and Libya since 1970. Somehow the major oil companies have been able to orchestrate these and other aberrations into a smooth and uninterrupted upward trend in overall supply.

. . .

The Underestimation of Demand

Not only have the international majors been able to secure a remarkable stability in the growth rate of supply; they have also underestimated demand, as is usually the case where an industry secures the power to adjust supply to its own demand forecasts. The penalty of producing too much, that is, a lower price resulting in decreased revenues on all sales, is far greater than the loss from producing too little; that is, a failure to secure revenues on just these sales that are foregone because of supply. Moreover, forecasts are generally constructed on the basis of past relationships between a product's use and measures reflecting demand (for example, GNP, per capita income, population trends, et cetera). What this technique does not, and cannot, adequately allow for is the discovery of new uses for a product which, in the case of petroleum, have followed one upon the other in a bewildering procession, both as fuel (for example for powerplants) and as materials (for example plastics, synthetic fibers, fiberglass, and most recently graphite fibers). Nor, incidentally, can this technique accurately allow for the effect on demand of a price change when its extent, as in 1973, is well beyond the range of recorded experiences.

. . .

Although qualified by a variety of explanations, oil industry spokesmen have conceded that demand has been underestimated. Responding to persistent questioning, Piercy of Exxon acknowledged:

We did underestimate energy demands. That shortfall was reflected in oil. That, coupled with a loss of ability to produce in two or three nations which we have already mentioned has resulted in this all-out tight situation that we have today.

Oligopolistic Interdependence

Despite a concentrated industry structure and a consensus on the growth rate, noncompetitive behavior could still not be achieved unless each oligopolist could depend on the others to avoid undertaking expansions that would significantly increase their shares of the market. What is involved here is an extension of a psychological consideration inescapably inherent in the structure of oligopolistic industries. In the classic formulation by Edward H. Chamberlain:

> If each seeks his maximum profit rationally and intelligibly, he will realize that when there are only two or a few sellers his own move has a considerable effect upon his competitors, and that this makes it idle to suppose that they will accept without retaliation the losses he forces upon them. Since the result of a cut by anyone is inevitably to decrease his own profits, no one will, and although the sellers are independent, the equilibrium result is the same as though there were a monopolistic agreement between them.[2]

In a competitive industry this psychological awareness is absent because each seller recognizes that his share of the market is so small that nothing he can do will affect his rivals. It is also absent in a monopoly since, by definition, there are no competitors to be concerned with. But in an oligopoly each of the leading producers has a sufficient share of the market to make him acutely conscious of the injurious consequences on himself of reactions by his rivals to any competitive move that he might initiate. Observing that the term "oligopoly" is "altogether appropriate" to the oil industry, Paul H. Frankel notes that in addition to militating against the occurrence of price competition, oligopoly has other consequences:

> Where there are only a few competitors, it is much easier for them to band together in order to fix and maintain prices and, if appropriate, to agree on market shares for each of them, than either course would be if a great number of competitors were involved. Furthermore the chosen few can in certain circumstances act in parallel even in the absence of explicit agreements to that effect.[3]

Imperfect competition theory was developed against the economic setting of the Great Depression. At the time price resistance to depressed economic conditions was widely regarded as a contributing cause of underconsumption. Hence it is understandable that this new contribution to theory was focused on short-term price behavior. Since World War II the conduct of large companies in oil and other industries raises the further question of whether the same type of psychological considerations would also apply to an expansion of capacity that in time would make a price reduction inevitable. In other words, would an oligopolist abstain from expanding his capacity because of his expectation that his expansion would be matched by his rivals, thereby creating a future supply in excess of what the market could absorb at the then existent price. Certainly, the aggressive expansion by a rival would induce an oligopolist to expand his capacity simply to maintain his share of the market, even though he fully recognizes the consequences of what he is doing on overall supply. Only if each oligopolist is confident that the expansion plans of his rivals will do no more than roughly maintain their established market shares can he reasonably be expected to limit his own expansion. How, short of collusive agreements, is such a state of confidence to be achieved?

Information on Rivals' Plans

In world oil a number of sources of information are available on the basis of which each of the seven international majors should be able to arrive at a fairly accurate judgment of his rivals' plans. One is knowledge of the growth rates of the principal producing countries. Obviously, the steadier the growth rate, the greater its reliability as a means of predicting a country's probable future production and thus of the supplies going to its concession-owning companies. For example, with nearly two-fifths of total OPEC production Iran and Saudi Arabia have exhibited extremely stable growth rates. The assumption that supply from these sources would continue to expand at their historical rates would not have been seriously in error.

Control Through Joint Venture

As it has evolved in oil, the jointly owned operating company has not only provided a means of implementing a jointly held concession but, for a given country, puts the power of implementation into the hands of fewer than half of the seven majors. . . .

Of the five countries with a dominant joint venture, majority stock control was attained in 1971 by only two companies in Saudi Arabia, Kuwait, and Indonesia and by three in Iraq and Abu Dhabi (the two leading firms holding 48 percent). In terms of production more than half of the output was accounted for by only two firms in all but one of the countries, the exception being Iraq.

Because so much of each country's output is produced by so few of the majors, none of the oligopolists need be particularly concerned that any of the countries will be the source of a price-weakening surplus produced by independents. What is more important, none need be greatly concerned that any of the countries will be the source of such a surplus produced by any of the other majors, since its increased profits resulting from greater production in a given country would probably be more than offset by reduced profits in the other countries in which it also operates. The extra dimension introduced by the joint venture into imperfect competition theory is an awareness by each oligopolist of the probable consequences on all of his areas of production of a competitive move he might initiate in any one of them.

· · ·

Adjusting for Aberrations

The ability of the oil companies to maintain a smooth and steady rate of increase in overall supply despite extreme changes in important supplying countries can be illustrated, on the one hand, by the loss of output resulting from Iran's nationalization of

Anglo-Iranian's properties and, on the other, by the rapid emergence of Libya as an important source of supply. As can be seen from [Figure 7-1], neither the former, which affected supply during 1951-54, nor the latter, which became important during 1965-70, had any discernible effect on the growth rate of overall supply.

After several years of fruitless negotiations with the Anglo-Iranian Oil Co., the Iranian Government on May 1, 1951, nationalized the industry under the leadership of its Prime Minister, Dr. Mossadegh. The last straw was the discovery by the Iranians that the companies had offered better terms to other Mideast producing countries, notably Aramco's 50-50 profit-sharing agreement with Saudi Arabia. But unhappiness with oil revenues was not the only cause of dissatisfaction. According to Mikdashi, "a crucial factor, not yet amenable to economic analysis, was Persian dissatisfaction with the predominance of a major British interest (viz AIOC) in the country. Dr. Mossadegh himself acknowledged the importance of this social-political factor."

The oil companies promptly reacted by imposing a collective boycott on Iranian oil: Prospective buyers were informed that legal action would be taken against them on the grounds that without a compensation agreement the oil was still the property of Anglo-Iranian. "The embargo . . . was very effective due to the cooperation of the eight major oil companies. . . . This embargo had, as intended, a punitive effect on Persia economy."

Oil exports dropped from over $400 million in 1950 to less than $1.9 million in the 2-year period from July 1951 to August 1953.

Little difficulty was experienced in making up the deficit with oil from Arab countries:

> Oil was available—even to AIOC—in abundance in neighboring countries, and world surplus production capacity of crude oil was estimated then at about 1.5 million barrels per day pressing from outlets.

As can be seen from [Figure 7-2], unusually sharp increases between 1951 and 1955 were registered by Kuwait and Iraq, while the production of Saudi Arabia was also accelerated above its long-term trend. If between 1951 and 1955 Iranian production had held at its 1950 level, the net loss, after deducting 290 million barrels actually produced, would have totaled 910 million barrels. Some 800 million barrels would have been made up by the expansion above what would appear to be the long-term growth rates of Kuwait, 300 million; Iraq, 200 million; and Saudi Arabia, 300 million. Miscellaneous increases from smaller Middle East countries, for example, Qatar, would have completely closed the gap. In Mikdashi's words, Anglo-Iranian's total production "was substantially replaced by the end of 1954 with oil produced by subsidiaries from outside Persia."

An aberration in the opposite direction was the rapid emergence in the 1960's of Libya as a large-scale producer. Like the virtual disappearance of Iranian output in the previous decade, compensatory changes in production were made to offset the sudden appearance of this sizable increment. In this case the adjustment process was facilitated by the inveterate tendency of the companies to underestimate demand. Had it not been for this fact the Libyan expansion, in the words of an internal Exxon document, would have caused the growth in Middle East output to have been "inordinately low." Under those circumstances the document observed,

> No known method of allocating the available growth is likely to simultaneously satisfy each of the four major established concessions; i.e., Iraq, Iran, Kuwait, and Saudi Arabia.

From the very outset Exxon emphasized that the anticipated rapid growth in Libyan production would necessitate curtailments in the Middle East. The company's 1961 forecast noted:

> During the middle of the 1960–68 forecast period, the advent of large-scale production in Libya and increases in Sahara and other supply sources may restrict the growth of Middle East outlets.
>
> Libyan crude oil and NGL production is expected to increase dramatically in the next years, achieving a level of 3.5 million barrels per day by 1971. This level is sufficient to make Libya the foremost producing country in the Eastern Hemisphere in 1971, displacing Iran to second place and Saudi Arabia to third. In contrast with historical ownership patterns in North Africa and the Middle East, the bulk of the new increments of production will be produced by companies considered "newcomers" to the international oil trade without established captive outlets and without a significant stake in the Middle East. Since Libyan oil is favorably situated with respect to the major European markets and has desirable low sulfur qualities, relatively little difficulty in capturing third party markets is expected.

A similar pessimistic appraisal is to be found in an internal document of Standard Oil of California. In a memorandum of December 6, 1968, S. E. Watterson, assistant manager of its economics department, warned:

> . . . it will become exceedingly difficult, if not impossible, to maintain relatively rapid growth in the high level producing countries of the Middle East and still accommodate reasonable growth of crude production from new as well as old fields in many other countries outside of the Middle East.

The heart of the problem lay in the fact that so much of the Libyan output was in the hands of independents who had neither the incentive to moderate their output nor the capability of offsetting it with reductions elsewhere:

> The downward revisions or adjustments of crude production in Libya and Nigeria for 1969 were made on the assumption that major companies with large interests in the Middle East would be required to moderate their liftings from Libya and Nigeria in order to maintain politically palatable growth in their liftings from the Middle East. Some companies, however, such as Occidental, Continental and others, without large interests in the Middle East, will be under heavy pressure to expand production rapidly and, therefore, are not likely to limit their Libyan liftings. Their Libyan oil will be competing vigorously with the majors' oil from the Middle East and Africa.

Responding to questions based on this memorandum, G. L. Parkhurst, former vice president of Socal, testified:

> . . . we were going to have an awful time meeting the demands of the Iranians and the Saudis . . . my only reaction was to tell the people who were trying to move Saudi Arabia and Iranian crude oil. "Get to work even harder than you have been working because we just can't let this thing happen."

In 1970, mirabile dictu, the problem which had given rise to such deep concern within Exxon and Socal—and undoubtedly within the other majors as well—was resolved. Libyan production, which had been growing rapidly, turned sharply downward, dropping from its peak of 3,318 million barrels per day in 1970 to 2,761 in 1971, to 2,239 in 1972, and to only 2,100 in 1973. In its 1972 forecast Exxon promptly revised its Middle East growth rate upward from 4.2 percent to the historical rate of 10 percent.

The International Control Mechanism

Over the years there has developed an intricate mechanism of controlling international production which, with certain necessary differences, bears a striking resemblance to the control mechanism long operative in the United States. In each, the initiating action is a forecast of overall supply. Although termed a forecast of demand, the forecast for the United States, prepared by the Bureau of Mines, really measures supply to be produced and historically has run somewhat below actual demand. An example was cited by a congressional committee:

> When the Bureau of Mines through their monthly forecasts of demand, under-estimated the demand by close to 2 percent for each of the years 1946 and 1947, the spot shortages followed as night the day. The mechanism was wound too tight.

For the world oil trade outside the United States somewhat similar forecasts, in the form of annual growth rates, are prepared by most, if not all, of the seven international majors. And they have also tended to run somewhat below actual demand. As Piercy of Exxon acknowledged, "We did underestimate demand. . . ."

Forecasts are made for the "free world"—excluding the United States, Canada and the Communist countries—for the Eastern Hemisphere and, of greatest importance, for the Middle East. The growth rate during 1958-72 for the five principal Mideast countries averaged 9.91 percent a year, which incidentally, turns out to be the identical figure cited by Exxon in its 1970 forecast:

> The region's (Mideast) oil production is forecast to average 9.3 percent per year growth through 1980, about the same as the 9.9 percent per year growth since 1960.

After determining the size of the pie, the next step is to divide it up among the governmental bodies with jurisdiction over the oil producing areas. In the United States this function has been performed by the Interstate Oil Compact Commission at which representatives of the various oil-producing States agree on the amount to be produced by each. In the world oil trade the function is performed directly by the seven majors which determine the rate at which oil is to be produced in each of the oil-producing countries. Since the latter 1950's the pivotal rate appears to have been that of Iran. To bring Iranian production back into the flow of supply an agreement in 1954 was negotiated under which Iranian output after 3 years was to keep pace with the "average growth rate" of the Mideast. Although no exact rate was specified, the desire of the U.S. Government to build up Iran as a bastion against Communist influence was recognized by all.

It is, therefore, not surprising that of all the major producing countries, Iran during 1958-72 enjoyed the highest growth rate—12.46 percent a year, which, incidentally, happens to be almost exactly the rate cited by Exxon. Iranian production . . . would expand 12.5 percent per year during 1967 and 1968, in accordance with agreements already made with the government. An annual growth rate of 12.46 percent for Iran is well above the rate for the Mideast as a whole—10.24 percent—and, among the long-established producing countries, is approached only by the 11.49 percent rate of Saudi Arabia.

With a high growth rate established for Iran, the owners of Aramco were faced with the necessity of maintaining a roughly comparable rate for Saudi Arabia. To Exxon, Socal, Texaco, and Mobil, the Aramco concession was far more important than their participation in the Iranian consortium. Emphasizing the necessity of maintaining good relationships with King Ibn Saud, Page testified:

> . . . If we hadn't played ball with him, we could have lost the Aramco concession, which is not something for us to lose. It is the biggest concession in the world, and we had 30 percent of it as against a concession one-quarter as big in which we had 7 percent. So you know what you had better do in these cases.

Under the circumstances it is not surprising that production in Saudi Arabia moved up almost in tandem with Iranian output. Again, deviations from the growth rate (11.49 percent) were few and far between.

With output growing at such an extraordinary pace in both Iran and Saudi Arabia, the area's existing "glut of productive capacity"—to use Page's term—would soon have reached formidable proportions had production in the other Mideast countries been allowed to rise at anything like the same rates. But during 1958-72, the increase in production of Iraq and Kuwait averaged only 5.12 percent and 5.93 percent, respectively, less than half the rates of Saudi Arabia and Iran and well below their own previous rates. Reflecting the rapid expansion in Libya, in Iraq the growth rate fell from an average of 8.11 percent during 1958-64 to only 3.71 percent during 1965-70; in Kuwait it declined from 11.98 percent to 4.45 percent.

According to Page, the relatively slow growth rate in Iraq stemmed from a dispute between the oil companies and the Iraqi Government. Feeling that efforts to develop their country's oil resources had left much to be desired, the Iraqi Government in 1961 enacted the so-called law 80 of the Kassim regime, restricting the concession held by the Iraq Petroleum Co. to areas in which it was then producing and foreclosing it from a number of extremely promising fields. But this controversy was certainly not the only reason for the low rate of production. In response to the question, "what would have happened if Iraq production had also surged during the 1960's," Page responded:

> I admit we would have been in one tough problem, and we would have had to lower our liftings from the (Iranian) Consortium down to the minimum we could possibly take there and meet the agreement. Remember we were taking more than agreement called for out of Iran, you see, and we were taking an equal amount, though, from Saudi Arabia, we would have had to cut back on both of those and we would have had to slow down on our development of Libya, which nobody wanted to do, but this was discussed at a time when people came to me and said, "Can you swallow this amount of oil?" and "of course, with Iraq down," the answer was, "Yes, I am going to have a lot of problems and some tough problems, but I will "undertake to do it."
>
> And I was successful, that is all I can say. But if Iraq had come on, it would have been that much harder.

According to Exxon's yearly forecasts Kuwait has been used as an "evener" by means of which actual Mideast output is brought into balance with the supply called for by the overall growth rate. Thus, "Kuwait production is estimated by difference after reviewing possible company supply positions" (1963) and "Kuwait output is determined to be the difference between Eastern Hemisphere demand and supplies from all other sources" (1964). Quite apart from such major disturbances as the Libyan expansion, the international oil companies are constantly confronted with unexpected occurrences, such as unusually mild—or severe—winters, interruptions in pipeline and tanker transportation, delays and breakdowns in refinery operations and a multitude of problems involved in trying to achieve a nice articulation of supply with markets thousands of miles away. To prevent such interruptions from upsetting the smooth and orderly increase in overall supply, production in Kuwait has not infrequently been contracted when supplies from other sources appeared excessive and expanded when they seemed insufficient.

The performance of this function can be seen most clearly in [Figure 7-2]; unlike the steady undeviating upward trends of Iranian and Saudi Arabian output increases in Kuwait's output have been recurrently interrupted by years of slow growth or actual declines.

In short, for countries producing some three-fifths of total OPEC output the international majors would be provided with reasonably accurate foreknowledge of their rival's supplies by assuming growth rates of 10 percent for the Mideast in a whole, 11-12 percent for Iran and Saudi Arabia and 5-6 percent for Iraq and Kuwait. Countries with slow growth rates are also unlikely to be the sources of unexpected increases in supplies. During 1958-72 Venezuelan production grew at an average rate of only 2 percent and indeed, since 1970 has moved noticeably downward. The addition of Venezuela and Qatar—with a growth rate of 7.95 percent—to the four Mideast countries brings to 73 percent the share of OPEC production which can be said to have been readily predictable.

Two of the remaining OPEC countries—Nigeria and Abu Dhabi—have registered spectacular growth rates—33.36 percent and 35.59 percent respectively—while production in a third, Indonesia has also been moving up sharply since the midsixties. Two factors, however, militate against the emergence of these countries as sources of uncontrollable excess supply. For one thing, independent producers are virtually nonexistent, accounting in 1972 for only 6 percent of the production in Nigeria; 3 percent in Abu Dhabi and none in Indonesia. Moreover, it would appear that companies bringing on new sources of supply are expected to make more or less compensating reductions in their liftings from other sources. Thus, Exxon's 1964 forecast observes, "Major participants in the IPC group, the Iranian consortium, and Nigerian production, are also the major offtakers of Kuwait crude. Therefore, to the extent the former fails to achieve offtake estimates, Kuwait would acquire most of the alternative outlet." And the forecast for 1967 states, "the downward revision for Persian Gulf production is primarily reflected in Kuwait's outlet and to a minor extent in Iraq's. Kuwait's growth would be retarded because major offtakers of that crude are developing new production in Africa and elsewhere."

• • •

There remain only the two North African countries, Libya and Algeria. Accounting together for only one-eighth of OPEC output; their days as international oil's principal area of uncertainty appear to be over.

In the United States the control mechanism has been implemented by the force of law. Production by individual wells in excess of their "allowables" is in violation of State law; shipments in interstate commerce of oil produced in excess of those allowables is in violation of Federal law. And the apportionment of total supply among the various oil-producing States is, by statute, exempt from the antitrust laws. But, except for a few restrictions made in the name of "conservation," the control mechanism outside the United States operates without the force of law. What makes it operational is not the legal power of some international authority—which does not exist—but the recognition by each oligopolist that his self-interest is best promoted by limiting his expansion to the extent and in the manner delineated above and by his expectation that the other oligopolists will be guided by the same considerations and act in the same manner.

It should be clear that the seven international majors have succeeded to a remarkable degree in limiting to a predetermined rate the growth of overall supply. Essential to the achievement of this result must be the attainment of a second objective, that is, preventing significant changes in market shares, since pronounced gains by any one of the oligopolists would inevitably lead to defensive expansions by the others, thereby causing total supply to exceed the predetermined growth rate. How stable has the pattern of market shares proved to be?

As can be seen from [Table 7-3], the trend in the concentration ratio for the seven companies as a group has been remarkably stable. Over the 5-year period, 1968-72, their share of total OPEC output changed by less than 1 percentage point, the proportion moving narrowly within the range of a high of 79 percent and a low of 77.1 percent. In view of the many dramatic changes that have taken place within the international oil industry during recent years, complete stability in market shares among the individual companies is hardly to be expected, and indeed noticeable changes were registered by Exxon and Gulf—decreases—and by BP and Socal—increases.

Yet, the principal explanation for such changes as did occur appears to lie not so much in the expected gains and losses arising from the normal rivalry of firms competing with each other in the market as in the widely varying growth rates of the different countries in which the different firms happened to hold concessions. . . .

The decline in Exxon's share of OPEC operations is in a sense a cost of the farflung nature of its operations. It was the leading producer in countries which for one reason or another have chosen to reduce their rate of production, to nationalize the properties of concession holders, or both. Above-average increases registered by Exxon in . . . Saudi Arabia and Iran were more than offset by below-average performance in Venezuela, Libya, and Iraq. In recent years the Government of Venezuela has been following a deliberate policy of restrictionism to conserve its resources; the Government of Libya

Table 7-3   Changes in Shares of Production of OPEC Countries by Companies, 1967–72 [In percent]

	Exxon	Mobil	SoCal	Texaco	Gulf	BP	Shell	Seven companies	Other companies[a]
1972	15.1	5.5	9.8	10.0	9.0	16.9	10.8	77.1	11.0
1971	15.9	5.4	8.7	9.0	9.9	17.7	12.4	79.0	12.6
1970	16.8	5.3	8.1	8.5	9.7	16.7	12.4	77.5	15.4
1969	17.8	5.2	7.9	8.5	10.1	15.9	12.0	77.4	15.4
1968	19.2	5.4	7.7	8.4	11.1	14.4	11.7	77.9	15.8

[a] Exclusive of CFP and government-owned and nationalized companies.
Source: Organization of Petroleum Exporting Countries, Annual Statistical Bulletins.

restricted output in an effort to increase its revenues and the Government of Iraq nationalized the Iraq Petroleum Co., of which Exxon was part owner. The loss by Gulf was also due to an exogenous factor but of a different character. Most of Gulf's foreign output consists of Kuwait crude which, because of its high sulfur content, has encountered environmental resistance in Western markets.

In contrast, the improvements in market share registered by Socal—as well as the lesser gain by Texaco—are traceable to the simple fact that nearly all of their foreign production comes from nations enjoying rapid growth rates—Saudi Arabia. Iran, and Indonesia. Production in the first two also benefited Mobil, but the loss in Iraq prevented Mobil from increasing its share of the OPEC total. Responsible for the improvement in BP's market share were its gains in Iran—where it has an equity ownership of 40 percent—and the even more precipitous rises in the newer producing countries of Nigeria and Abu Dhabi. Thus, had it not been for factors exogenous to the relationship of the companies with each other, the changes in market shares, limited though they were, would have been virtually nonexistent, which, of course, is to be expected of the "live and let live" policies of a tight and mature oligopoly.

The exception was Libya where, earlier, concessions had deliberately been granted to independents who were not important producers elsewhere. Thus, an important increment to supply fell into the hands of firms willing and anxious to secure a "market position" even, if necessary, through price competition. . . . In 1970, however, the growing strength of the independents, was reversed. Restrictions by the Libyan Government and nationalization in Algeria combined to reduce the output of "other companies" from 3,573,000 barrels per day in 1970 to 2,253,000 in 1972 and their share of OPEC production . . . from 15.4 percent to 11.0 percent. Thus far, one effect of the drive toward nationalization would appear to be the removal of a troublesome thorn from the side of the majors.

• • •

There is a widespread and common misapprehension that in dealing with the oil-producing countries the companies have been in the role of buyers—that their posture has been more or less analogous to that of, say, Sears, Roebuck in purchasing tires to be sold under the Allstate label from the various tire manufacturers. As a purchaser, Sears seeks to obtain the best quality of tire possible at the lowest price. That has not been the position of the major oil companies in dealing with the producing countries of the world. They have not been buyers, but holders of concessions. The rewards to themselves are a function of the quantity and the price obtained for the product. In other words, the higher the price, the greater their profit. It is not merely that they have not been buyers, it is that their incentive has been the reverse. Instead of trying to secure lower prices, their revenues have been enhanced by securing a higher price. As long as this situation continues any hope that the oil companies will operate as monopsonistic buyers utilizing their monopoly power to obtain price concessions which in turn can result in lower prices to consumers is, of course, nothing more than wishful thinking.

• • •

It is difficult to speculate about what might happen in the future. However, it would be my expectation that if a given oil-producing country were to welcome and entertain solicitations from any and all buyers, we would be presented with something approaching the market of competitive theory. If demands in relation to supply were strong, the price would be bid up. At other times if there were a glut, as you mentioned exists at the present time, the price would fall. Consequently, one of the essential steps to the establishment of anything approaching competitive conditions in international oil would be the proffering of oil by the oil-producing countries to any buyers that were interested in securing it.

．　．　．

NOTES

1. Hearings before the Senate Subcommittee on Multinational Corporations, Mar. 28, 1974, pt. 7.
2. Edward H. Chamberlain, *The Theory of Monopolistic Competition,* 5th ed., Harvard University Press, 1946, p. 48.
3. Paul H. Frankel, *Mattei: Oil and Power Politics,* Frederick A. Praeger, 1966, p. 82.

8 / An Outline of a Theory of the Dominant Economy

François Perroux

The Dominant Economic Unit and Equilibrium Theory

. . . We do not, at present, have a coherent general theory of what I propose to call the "domination effect" in economics. Such a theory would give us the necessary first synthesis leading to the greater synthesis between a theory of economics and a theory of force, power and coercion.[2] Even less do we possess a theory of the internationally dominant economy based on the twin relationship between the morphology of domination effects and the influence of the domination effect upon the international equilibrium.

The world is such that we pay, in experience, a rather high price for such gaps in our knowledge. We are used to thinking of economics in terms of pure exchanges between equals, yet the concrete problems that we have to solve are obviously of a different nature. This is surely one of the areas where the lag between our theories and our practice is most clearly manifested. We vainly try to remain on top of new experiences by means of theories based on ancient and completed experiences. Many aspects of today's world might lead us to believe (had we the taste for quick generalizations) that it is just as opportune to see the economic world as an aggregate of patent or concealed relations between dominants and dominated as it is to picture it as an aggregate of relations between equals. . . . As soon as the whole economy is understood as a *heterogeneous* entity made up of parts (zones or sectors) which are more or less dominant and more or less dominated and capable of actions that do not result in reactions of equal force, the picture of the mechanism offered to us by the theories of general equilibrium becomes unsatisfactory. Thus political economy asks questions which theory, for the time being, is not only unable to answer, but for whose solution it uses tools of doubtful appropriateness.[3]

This serious flaw in domestic economics has become a scandal, today, in the area of international economic relations The historian and the sociologist would render a valuable service if they showed how the growth of the world economy was accomplished by the action of successive dominant national economies (continental or maritime). They would have to draw up a table of the causes and mechanisms of rise and fall, with detailed accounting of the sacrifices borne and the benefits bestowed upon the dominated economies.

From "Esquisse d'une Théorie de l'Economie Dominante," *Economie Appliquée*, Vol. I, No. 2-3 (April-September, 1948), pp. 245-284. With permission of the author.[1] Translated by Sylvia Modelski.

Today's economist is beset by much more narrowly defined and urgent tasks. The United States of America has become, and for a long time to come is likely to remain, a dominant economy in the world. While carefully avoiding all sterile polemics, rejecting all fiery language, and being purely scientific, it is necessary to know exactly what we mean by that. The solutions to the central difficulties of our time depend upon the correctness of our reply. . . .

To start with, then, take a random selection of economic units defined as aggregates of material and human elements under one management that tend to maximize any result judged to be advantageous. These units are in exchange relationships with each other. (1) What is the nature and extent of the domination effect? (2) What are the typical elements causing it?

Taking two units only, we shall say that A exerts a domination effect on B when, regardless of any particular intention of A's, A exerts a definite influence (asymmetrical effect) on B without reciprocation (retroaction) or with unequal reciprocation (retroaction). An asymmetry or irreversibility of principle or degree is basic to the effect under examination.

This is true whether the links are intentional or unintentional.

1. *Unintentional links.* The most elementary and general form is the following: unit A increases or decreases, that is, expands or contracts in volume, for reasons that are completely innocent of any wish to affect B. B, under A's influence, increases or decreases, that is, it expands or contracts in volume. There is no reverse influence (retroaction), at least not of the same degree. We will say that A exerts an unintentional domination effect over B.[4]

Even at this high level of generality, we must immediately consider an unintentional influence of A on B of a totally different kind. We demonstrate it by supposing that A changes its structure. Let A be a complex of needs (units of consumption), a complex of factors (units of production), or a complex of related economic activities (supplies and demands). Let A and B be constant. If a change in A's structure induces a change in B's structure without the reverse occurring, at least not to the same degree, we shall have a pure case of domination effect of A on B through *change of structure.* If A and B are variable, it is easy to see how the domination effect through volume change combines with the domination effect through structural change. . . .

2. *Intentional links.* Unit A, that is, the authority ruling over it, decides to exert a domination effect on unit B. Given that A and B have trade relations, the most general expression of the maximization of the result sought by both parties is the equalization of the marginal advantage gained and of the marginal advantage ceded. The effective result sought (which is not necessarily or exclusively the same as the net return) is maximized when:

$$\frac{\text{marginal advantage gained}}{\text{marginal advantage ceded}} = 1$$

If A buys and sells services and products to B, A will tend to impose on B a price superior to the marginal value of the product sold. The advantage external to pure exchange, i.e., the quantity by which the marginal advantage gained will deviate from equality with the marginal advantage ceded, will measure the success of the domination effect. This is easily applied to cases such as the seller of a factor, the buyer of a factor, the seller of a product, and the buyer of a product. Given that the only determination of a general scope described by economic theory is that of pure exchange, i.e., the equalization of the marginal advantage gained and the marginal advantage ceded, the domination effect is measured by the area of indeterminacy it introduces in the economic universe of pure exchange, as well as by the advantage external to pure exchange.

Perfect and pure competition, besides the definitions it has been given, could therefore be understood as the economic state from which all element of domination is excluded, in other words, as the world of *contrat sans combat*.[5]

If exchange relations in the economic world are or are not established only through equalization of the marginal advantage gained and the marginal advantage ceded, it is, from the theoretical point of view, irrelevant whether the economic calculations are made by the interested parties themselves or by a third party. The same results would be arrived at by a third party rigorously applying the rules of the game and consequently dictating how the interested parties should behave. It would be doing nothing more nor less than what economic units do spontaneously. Arbitrage is unthinkable in the economic world of *contrat sans combat*.

If, instead of considering two units only we were to take a larger number: A on the one hand, and B,C,D,E . . . N on the other, our analysis would remain essentially the same. A exerts a domination effect on one of the other units, say, B for example, when a change in its size or structure imposes a change in the size or structure of B, without the reverse occurring to the same degree. A exerts a domination effect over the totality of the other units when a change in its size or structure forces a change in the size or structure of the totality of the other units B,C,D,E . . . N without the reverse being true, or true to the same extent. And so the problem arises of the distribution of the global effect of domination between the various dominated units. Obviously, this distribution can deviate, and in fact most often does deviate, from a design for equal or proportional distribution.

It is appropriate, even at this level of abstraction and generalization, to introduce a notion which is pivotal in the concrete study of domination effects on the most complex and realistic models. *A* can transmit its domination effect on B,C,D directly or indirectly. If the transmission takes place through an intermediate unit T, the latter can amplify or cushion (even stop) the initial effort.

What are the other typical ingredients of the domination effect, besides its definition and measurement? By this, we mean linkage concepts that enable us to master correctly, for the sake of a theoretical analysis, the immense diversity of real-world phenomena at the origin of the concrete effect of domination.

These typical ingredients are two:

One is *difference in bargaining power*. . . . A and B being ostensibly equal in size, A exerts a domination effect over B because its bargaining power (in its elements other than size) is greater. The other is *difference in size*. . . . The bargaining power being held rigorously equal for every unit in all its elements other than those proceeding from size differences, the said difference in size produces its effect. It is the familiar case of the difference in the relative share of each unit in the total supply and demand.

Our analysis reconstructs, from a perspective dictated by its very purpose, the most fundamental outlines of the modern theory of monopoly in so far as they are elaborated from the point of view of monopolistic units and their relations.[6] Bearing this in mind, we have the greatest interest in proceeding immediately to the level of aggregate quantities. Since we were careful to define the domination effect in its most general terms, it will be easy to point out the new applications of it here.

Consider a national economy consisting of *active* and *passive zones*. Zone A is said to be active when it exerts an irreversible effect on zone B, the irreversibility being either of principle or of degree. Zone B sustains the effect without reaction or without reaction of an intensity or degree sufficient to correct or compensate for the initial action. The relations of influence of A over B and of B over A are not symmetrical.[7]

Obviously, the domination effect functions not only from unit to unit by reason of their respective size and bargaining power, but also from zone to zone because of their respective sizes and structures. Thus we express in general terms, and for our own purpose, phenomena already noted by modern economic theory, even though they may not have been singled out for detailed scrutiny and their connection not fully understood.

Aside from any reference to one of the Keynesian orthodoxies, many modern economists are probably ready to admit that investment exerts more influence on savings than savings on investment. . . . that the centers and units making the decisions on investment or its conditions are dominant in relation to the centers and units that decide on savings and its conditions.

Furthermore, in cases of what is sometimes termed "entrepreneurial activism," "the tyranny of supply" or simply "the induced shift of the demand curve to a firm," the supply of a product exerts more influence over its demand than its demand exerts over its supply. . . .

Taking into account all the incidental and structural causes for asymmetry, it is probably much more accurate to treat an economy as an aggregate of zones or quantities that are diversely active and passive rather than as an aggregate of zones or quantities whose relations of influence are reciprocal or characterized by an equal degree of activity or passivity.

Consequently, a unit exerts a domination effect not only because of its size or bargaining power, but also because of its membership in this or that zone or, if you will, because of the nature of its activity within a whole. If this conclusion is combined with what has been said about the domination effect transmitted through an intermediary, the resulting proposition is perhaps not without interest. Companies belonging to an active zone consisting of an aggregate of investment activities are in a position, provided they fulfill the other necessary conditions, to develop a domination effect combining the three elements of bargaining power, size and nature of activity.

The general propositions used throughout the remainder of this analysis may be summed up as follows. The domination effect, whether intentional or not, is an asymmetric and irreversible influence. It is measured by the advantage external to the bargain or by the margin of indeterminacy derived from it, as compared with the equilibrium of pure exchange. Its elements are (1) the bargaining power of the unit, (2) its size, and (3) the fact that it belongs to an active zone in the economy. Its action is transmitted directly or through an intermediary. In the latter case, one finds the most diverse combinations: production unit A acting by way of production unit B on production unit C; production unit A acting through a bank to influence production unit C; production unit A acting through a bank or a financial intermediary to influence consumption unit C, etc. In this last case are also found the most diverse mechanisms of amplification or cushioning by an intermediary of an effect of a given initial intensity.

The asymmetry and irreversibility which constitute the domination effect are in logical opposition to the reciprocal and universal interdependence on which rests the theory of general equilibrium and of its re-establishment or correction in case it is disturbed.

If, in a given whole, certain units can impose, during period p_0, an exchange based on an advantage external to the exchange and if, for the new conditions thus created, in the course of periods p_1, p_2, p_3 . . . the same domination effect is not eliminated, we are faced with a sustained and cumulative deviation from the equilibrium of pure exchange. We will never again meet the necessary conditions for an elimination or correction of this deviation.

If active zone A exerts an influence over passive zone B, the changes that occur in A might well lead to an adjustment of the equilibrium in B, but the changes induced in B will not provoke the necessary adjustments in A. In both series of cases, readjustment through general and reciprocal interdependence is excluded.

More precisely, if n dominant units fix the price and sustain it from period to period, the other units having to adjust their quantities and prices to it, the general level of price equilibrium and the form of the equilibrium as a whole are determined by the dominant units, not by the relations of general and reciprocal interdependence between all units.

The domination effect cannot logically be "deduced" from the rigorously expressed premises of a general equilibrium based on conditions of general and reciprocal interdependence. Conversely, as soon as we take the domination effect as given, the links with which we have been made familiar by the representation of economics in terms of general and reciprocal interdependence are broken. From these links, we go to typical sequential chain effects which eventually allow for the growing and irreversible domination of one unit or zone over all the others.

A whole dynamics may be drawn from the domination effect. When it is completely formulated, it might perhaps deservedly be called the *dynamics of inequality,* just as the dynamics of J. Schumpeter could be called the *dynamics of innovation.* Whereas the latter opposes the mechanics of innovation to those of routine, the other one would oppose the mechanics of domination to those of the *contrat sans combat.*

Surely one may already perceive, in embryo form, some of the distant consequences of these preliminary explanations for the internationally dominant economy and its effect on the balance of world trade.

The principle of international economic interdependence is repeated like a slogan of foreign trade policy. Its significance, as explanation of the real world in which we live can only be determined through a careful application, to the relations between national economies, of the analytical tool which we have just set forth. The uneasily reversible movements and troublesome disproportions that plague the relations between the United States and the rest of the world are undoubtedly due, in part, to historical accident: they also have an economic logic which the traditional interpretations of the balance of foreign transactions seem unable to account for. On the other hand, the analysis of asymmetries and irreversibilities which we have noted might perhaps guide us towards a general interpretation of these phenomena in the domestic as well as the international economies.

To test this, we must refine and particularize the general theory which we have elaborated in the most abstract terms. Our first need will be to try to establish a parallel between the dominant firm and the dominant national economy. Thus we will be studying the domination effect for two very different definitions of the units between which this effect is established.

The Dominant Firm and the Dominant National Economy

Let us analyze the domination effect, which we have described in its broadest aspects, by asking how it is put to work, be it by a firm or by a national economy.

If, at the outset, we decided to treat the national economy as a firm, an expedient to which the theory of international trade is often forced to resort (as it is to so many other conventional and simplifying devices), this distinction would still be justified to the full degree to which external exchanges differ from internal exchanges. But it will be one of our theses that the comparison of the national economy to an enterprise, if it must (for want of a better alternative) be retained at a high level of abstraction, prevents us from perceiving, at the heart of international exchanges, the domination effect in all its richness and complexity. The understanding of the dominant firm merely opens the way to the understanding of the dominant national economy. The comparison is not without interest.

The theory of the dominant firm has had contributions from many sources. But, on the one hand, the link between these diverse contributions is generally not made and, on the other hand, the analyses remain static; they do not prepare the way for an understanding of the mechanism by which, in the course of successive periods, a firm can become more and more dominant. This last interpretation is at least as necessary as the previous one in order to arrive at the facts of the real world.

The domination effect occurs: (1) between production units and consumption units and (2) between production units A and production units B. From the static point of view, it will be sufficient to show that even though it cannot strictly be said that the domination effect is automatically present in every model of a monopolistic situation, it does exist in one or the other of the two forms just mentioned in the majority of monopolistic situations; and it becomes more and more difficult to avoid the closer the situations are to reality.

. . . Starting from a state of perfect competition that characterizes pure exchange, it is not possible to imagine the emergence of a dominant firm. For this event to take place, a new fact must be introduced. The choice is between: (1) a massive move (already noted, for example, by J. Schumpeter who drew his inspiration from the history of capitalism) by the dynamic entrepreneur or firm, (2) an extraneous historical event, the element of "luck" which is unrelated to any historical point of view, which will cause the initial inequality in favor of a firm, and (3) an imperceptible deviation which admits that perfect equality of the means of action between companies is a limited situation which the theory has no reason to consider as the only correct and representative one, on the contrary. As soon as the slightest inequality between firms is acknowledged, the breach through which the cumulative effect of domination insinuates itself is made.

A firm (or firms) having become dominant, that is, having attained a position to exercise more influence than it receives from other economic units, its growth is a matter of passing successively from one equilibrium position to another. Each time, the adjustment is imposed on the environment instead of proceeding from it. It must follow from this that inequality kills competition even if, strictly speaking, competition does not kill competition, because the economic world around us is a world of dominant firms and dominated firms and not of firms of equal power and dimensions. Even if, which is not the case, the general tendency were unequivocably toward a minimal inequality, there still would remain the task of digging up the economic logic according to which inequality has grown and prevailed over long periods.

Now, if a rigorously "pure" theory of the cumulative effects which are the basis of the dominant firm's growth from period to period does not come easily, at least the typical concatenations which account for these effects can be described systematically.

The dominant firm is a firm with a surplus. By that we do not mean that it makes super profits, which are by nature temporary, but that under minimum conditions (which observation proves are quite common) it is the center of a persistent tendency, from period to period, toward a long drawn-out excess of sales over purchases, in quantity and value. To the extent that the dominant firm achieves integration, it produces within itself part of the goods and services which, nonintegrated, it would have to buy outside. It buys from the outside lesser quantities and by virtue of this alone, for a given price level, the relative importance of its external purchases tends to decrease. Furthermore, it can impose on its partners a purchasing price for its inputs which is inferior to the free market price and a selling price for its output which is superior to the free market price. For this reason alone, therefore, for given quantities bought and sold, it tends to sell more in value than it buys.

If we were to transpose the international market vocabulary to the domestic market, we might perhaps say: the dominant firm benefits from a chronic export (sales) surplus over its imports (purchases). Its terms of trade, that is, the ratio between the cost of its purchases and the cost of its sales, become more favorable or can be made favorable by its own decision.

The dominant firm uses its surplus to invest internally, to consolidate its technical and commercial superiority while achieving independence from the capital market, and to make external loans to other production and consumption units. This latter connection (about which the least that can be observed is that it is historically based) amounts to saying that the company with a surplus is a creditor firm which, besides the weapon of independence of choice about price and output, possesses also the powerful weapon of credit.

Through the distribution of credit it acts in three directions: (1) it finances the demand for its product, it shifts its sales curve to the right; (2) it penetrates rival companies by buying some of their shares or, through a different distribution of credit, it can impose changes in their structures to suit its own interests; (3) it acts through intermediary financial or political centers to exert domination effects which would otherwise have been difficult to achieve.

In disposing of its surplus, the dominant firm acts as a credit-dispensing company, using procedures the repercussions of which are not demonstrated in static analysis. One can certainly find many instances of these theoretical connections in the history of modern capitalism, from the dominant industrial and commercial firms which are involved in banking activities, to the effect of these firms upon banks which have become more or less specialized organs by way of the *Verlagsystem* (putting-out system). There is no doubt, either, that the parallel between these processes and those of the internationally dominant economy is persistently suggestive. To give only one example: the day when a nation (say, Italy, but just to focus our ideas) which is rich in labor but poor in consumption goods and capital is turned into a center for the transformation of raw materials supplied by a dominant economy, using machinery also supplied by it, for re-exportation, at least partly influenced by it, the *Verlagsystem* once practiced from firm to firm is, in its essential features, reproduced on a larger scale.

It is useful to note the impossibility of compensating or corrective actions in the case of the dominant firm. Take a firm whose production represents 40 percent of the total output of an economy, and its purchase of factors 40 percent of the total purchase of factors, i.e., of the income distributed throughout the whole economy. An unexpected breakdown in that firm's payments mechanism or a forecasting error on the part of its management cannot be compensated whereas, in all probability, the effects of the same breakdown would be dispersed in many diverse ways among a large number of independent firms and the mistakes of a large number of independent managements need not happen at the same time and in the same manner. These incidents assume a massive importance in the dominant economy and make their impact felt all at once on the flow of payments, on adjustments and sales in the economic unit under consideration.[8]

The reactions, in time, of the dominated firm toward the dominant firm are not easy to capture in a simple framework. The dominant firm develops an attraction and repulsion effect. Apart from companies which are partly controlled by the dominant firm, one must also consider as indirect satellites those firms which establish durable business relations with it, and also sometimes long-term contracts or arrangements, be it to accomplish the very object of these operations or to gain the advantages which such a powerful connection offers. The dominated firms (or units) also have two other reactions which are more often than not combined: the coalition and the association with a view to resisting the influence of the dominant firm, to diverting the traffic away from the dominant firm's orbit, to stopping or threatening to stop traffic with the dominant firm. On all these points, the analogy with the dominant national economy is so plain to see as to make it unnecessary to dwell on it.

The difficulty and the interest begin precisely at the point of departure from the analogy. A firm is a center for the maximization of an economic result and it is managed by one authority; this is not the case for a national economy except when it is subjected to state planning. If, not unreasonably, it can be considered as one center for maximization of political power in so far as it is represented by one State, in our individualistic society it is the companies and their association that, maximizing their net profit in a relatively independent way, contribute to the maximization of national welfare.

Furthermore, a dominant firm does not manipulate the currency in which exchanges are made; it does not publicly control the other firms; it does not have, at least officially, an army and a navy to confront other dominant firms with or with which it threatens them. If the old orthodoxy according to which there is no "supply and demand" of America, England, Germany, but only the supplies and demands of Americans, Englishmen and Germans, were absolutely correct, all study of the dominant national economy and, in a wider sense, all study of relations between national economies, would be pointless. This conceptual model of the world would be of little use in our effort to live and act in the world as we see it. The economic theory of international relations has wavered between two extremes: at times it assumed that nations themselves were "individuals," "units," firms, whose aggregate indifference curves or other aggregate curves can be manipulated; at other times, it is as if the whole world were made up of individuals or, if you like, of firms and households whose particular curves alone matter, the "grid" of national boundaries being superimposed upon phenomena it cannot control. For a long time to come, these two types of analysis will continue to be used, by us too. But the time seems ripe to take notice of the fact that it is in between the two, the area which neither one nor the other can, by definition, cover, that the heart of the matter lies.

A correct representation of the national economy determines a correct representation of the domination effect exerted by a national economy as well as its forms and the conditions under which it is applied.

Even if, in order to study their working, we are forced to consider national economies as firms, units or individuals, we have the greatest interest in understanding the formation and impact of the domination effect and to see them for what they are: complexes or systems that are adaptable through the combined action of governmental decisions and the decisions of entrepreneurs and consumers. Each of two of n national units will therefore present itself as a group of private firms arbitrated by a "monopolist of public constraint," that is, by the state. It follows immediately from this that the domination effect occurs (1) in the relations of complex A groups with complex B groups; (2) in the relations of the State in A with the State in B; (3) in the relations between the State in A and the private groups in A and the corresponding relations in B.

This picture of the nation is very different, both in principle and in its repercussions, from the customary representation of an area of perfect mobility of factors beyond whose frontier this mobility becomes nil. Instead of focusing on the imperfections of mobility and the resulting mechanical links, it puts at the very center of the international market's imperfections the facts of national organization and the strategies of the groups and of the monopolists of public constraint. All at once, it brings about a coupling of the modern theory of noncompetitive economic systems with that of world trade. It throws a rude light on all the reasons why international trade is by nature the locus of imperfectly competitive economic systems and consequently for which it would be useless to conceive of possible and practical competition other than as a deliberately constructed system, a victory for the ingenuity and will of men and not at all the result of spontaneous reactions and natural forces.

For pure competition to rule on a world scale, it would actually be necessary that: (1) the sales of each firm inside national group A be perfectly dependent on prices established by other firms of the same national group and of the other national groups B,C,D,E . . . N; (2) each firm inside a national group be incapable of influencing the price-output decisions of the other firms belonging to the same national group and of other national groups. This twin feature of homogeneity and nonmonopolistic competition alone can give substance to the parametric function of the international price. For this feature to emerge, the necessary structural conditions would be, on the one hand, a very large number of firms of which none can influence the price-output decisions of its neighbor and, on the other hand, either a single World State which does not alter the relations between constituent firms or a large number of small Nation-States whose presence and actions add or substract nothing to the existing relations between the firms they contain.

Such a universe without domination effect sharpens, by contrast, our understanding of the real international world where relations between the dominant and the dominated are established for reasons of both the structure of modern capitalism and the very existence of the Nation-States.

The elements of asymmetry and irreversibility which constitute the domination effect can from now on be studied with more precision at the level of national economies. Let us first consider the national economy as a total system or complex; then we will turn to any part of this system or complex, and characterize the domination effect in the two cases.

First, then, *the total system or complex making up a national economy*. If we have the right to speak about aggregate imports and exports, the aggregate (national) supply and demand for goods, capital, and services, it is because the units making up the region called nation (1) come, in certain specified areas, under the jurisdiction of the same executive authority, that of the monopolist of public constraint, the State, or (repeating R. F. Harrod's just remark) that of the central bank in the case where the latter is relatively independent of the State; (2) have a specific solidarity with each other or a specific degree of external interdependence which stems from the national currency and from external economies on the national scale; (3) are managed by company executives and groups which, in a particular number of cases, behave in a similar fashion, i.e., their attitude toward waiting or ex-post reactions move in the same direction in advance of or in response to domestic or external political events.

The elements of the domination effect—bargaining power, size, nature of activity—are therefore transposable to the total aggregate that is the national economy. The aggregate effect is all the more striking because the bargaining power of the State and of the groups and firms within it, the size of the State and that of the groups and firms, the proportion of strategic activities to the whole, instead of neutralizing or contradicting each other, work in the same direction to engender an asymmetric or irreversible influence over other national economies, that is, other aggregate systems.

Let us take a closer look at the modalities of the domination effect as it is exercised by one national economy over another. Let us set aside, because they are relatively simple, the cases of basic asymmetry. In a given field, national economy A exerts an influence on national economy B; the reverse is not true to any degree in the field in question. This is obviously the case in relations between a creditor country and a debtor country, the first being able to lend to the second and the reverse not being true to any degree. This is also the case of a country which, it is assumed, has exclusive use of a war secret or a revolutionary economic invention and which can keep this monopoly to itself alone or share it with selected partners. Such monopolies, it may be noted, are only seemingly localized; the monopoly of investment services or of a political-economic secret exerts a diffuse influence over the totality of economic choices of the parties.

Having said this, let us try to classify the asymmetries in the influence exerted by dominant economy A on dominated economies B,C,D . . . N. First, take *the alteration of a parameter that is characteristic of the whole* of the national economy, for example the gross national product or income. The increase in A's national product induces an increase in B's national product, be it directly through an increase of external traffic between A and B, or indirectly through an increase of external traffic between B and C, D, etc. If, for any reason, the increase in A's national product brings about a given increase in B's national income, the reverse effect being of lesser intensity, we have the asymmetry in question. One of the two national products will be the mover, the other will be moved.

Second, *the alteration of a parameter external* to a national economy and its effect upon an aggregate quantity representing a fraction of that economy's activity. A uniform 10 percent decrease in the price of goods traded induces an increase of 10 percent or more in B,C,D imports from A, but a less than 10 percent increase in A's imports from B,C,D; or again, a uniform rise of 10 percent in the income in B,C,D causes an increase of imports from A of 10 percent or more; a uniform 10 percent increase in A's aggregate income induces a growth of imports from B,C,D of less than 10 percent. The double correction by way of the movement of prices and balances is threatened and the disequilibrium of balances in favor of the dominant economy is maintained or aggravated.

Finally, let us take *the alteration of a parameter internal* to a national economy and its effect upon a quantity representing a fraction of that economy's activity. A given level of under-employment or unused capacity in A of, say, 10 percent induces a decrease of 10 percent or more in imports from B,C,D to A. A given level of underemployment or unused capacity in B of 10 percent causes a decrease of less than 10 percent in B imports from A because these are perhaps inelastic imports which B cannot renounce.

The examples abound; they all come within the framework of asymmetry in the reciprocal elasticity of incomes and products, and in the inelasticity of an aggregate quantity to the same change occurring in an internal or external parameter. The dominant economy's aggregate quantities have largely autonomous variations; the dominated economies' aggregate quantities are plastic in relation to the dominant ones. If the effect were pushed to the limit, the adjustment process would run from the dominant economies to the dominated one and not in the reverse direction. The dominant economy, an autonomous nodal point, would induce, by its very movements and apart from any premeditated plan, an activity in other economies which would be little else than a motion of adjustment. Notably, the result would be that the choice of the rate or level of aggregate investment in this same economy would determine the levels of consumption and of investment in the dominated economies. This is the technical sense which might be given to the formula according to which the decisions of domestic political economy of certain nations are decisions of world political economy.

Up to now, we have considered the total economic system or complex which is the national economy. Let us now take one part of that system or complex—for example, one of the groups of firms composing it. The A_1 group of national economy A can exert, by virtue of its size, its bargaining power, or both, a domination effect on the B_1 group of national economy B. Let us say, for example, that it can influence B_1's price-output decisions without retroaction or without equal retroaction. This domination effect of the A_1 group, which results from its relative structure vis-à-vis the B_1 group and from the strategy chosen by its leaders, is itself increased or decreased by the relations it maintains with the monopolist of public constraint in A and B. These monopolists determine the general framework (tariff, credit) within which exchanges between group A_1 and group B_1 take place.

It is obvious that the domination effect is maximized and the area of indeterminacy in international exchanges is at its peak when an economy has, for strategic goods and services, the relatively most powerful oligopolistic groups aided by the bargaining power of one of the greatest world monopolists of public constraint, in the midst of an economy which, through its overall structure, tends to exert a domination effect over numerous other economies.

To analyze the domination effect in detail, one would have to have a detailed table, on the one hand of the structure of economy A and of the structure of economy B and, on the other hand, of the nature and characteristics of the external relations binding them. Structural equations would have to be matched with coupling equations. The domination effect, in so far as it is exercised by economy A, cannot be reduced to a situation of independence of this economy A with regard to foreign trade; in so far as it is received by economy B, it cannot be reduced to a situation of dependence of this economy B on foreign trade.

A national economy which is very much dependent on foreign trade can be strongly dominant because of its structure; this was the case of England in the nineteenth century: largely dependent on external transactions, yet dominant through its commercial and financial apparatus. An economy that is strongly dependent on foreign trade, even if it does not have a center such as London was about 1900, may be only slightly dominated because its imports and exports are divided and shared among a great number of countries.

Finally, a totally autarchic economy which, contrary to all probability, has no foreign transactions, would be totally independent, but also, at the level of world trade it would not be dominant at all; it would have achieved perfect isolation vis-à-vis the world.

. . . Our own field being the examination of the domination effect (whether intentional or not) of one national economy acting principally through means congruent with the market economy,[9] we shall now push the analysis further. Looking at the characteristic economic systems of bilateral monopoly, oligopoly and monopolistic competition, we shall ask if and how the specific effects of these economic systems are found in the behavior of the dominant economy. This theoretical survey will lead us to a brief description of these effects on the contemporary North American economy.

The Dominant Economy and Types of Monopolistic Situations

The domination effect is connected to every main type of monopolistic situation. It is therefore natural to describe it in connection with them at the level of international relations. In what sense can it be said that national economies have, vis-à-vis each other, relations of unilateral or bilateral monopoly, oligopoly or monopolistic competition?[10] Is the application of such analytic tools to national economies (rather than to businesses) useful in extracting interesting regularities? And what are these? How, thanks to these uniformities, is the domination effect of one national economy over another or several others transformed and given new meanings?

Given a national economy in a monopolistic situation, the difficulties we experience when applying to it the tools used to study monopolistic firms and their relations are precisely the ones that the theory of foreign trade sweeps under the carpet when it treats the national economy as if it were one firm and assumes it to exchange one product or one representative product. These difficulties must be preliminarily and carefully scrutinized in order to see what can be extracted from any application to our field of the knowledge acquired from the study of monopolistic situations in the domestic market.

A nation's resources are put to economic use through the marshaling of various forces or the exercise of public authority, such as that of the heads of private firms that maximize their net income by means of the market, or of the State representatives who maximize the national power, or the social welfare, or a combination of both, through public policy or by means of the market or a combination of these.

The unity of decision logically needed to give the attributes of a monopolistic situation to the entire national economy is never perfectly achieved. Considered in the totality of its elements, this decision is always "mixed" or "semipublic," and it is admitted once and for all that one must have recourse to the arbitrary and the metaphor each time there is question of the monopolistic situation of a "national economy." But this metaphor has this peculiarity that it is really indispensable for the understanding of the facts imposed upon us by observation and action. It is all the more expressive of a reality where individual and State plans within the same economy set themselves the same objectives and use compatible and cooperative means. We are then approaching a state of affairs where the decisions, within the nation, are not unlike the decisions of the various services of a single firm which aim at the same goal and come under a common management. In abstract terms, this synergy obtains when the firms agree to pursue the objectives of national power or if the State accepts the task of maximizing net incomes, or if, in a given situation, the goals of maximizing national income, national power and social welfare coincide, or if agreement can be practically arrived at or imposed by a compromise between these different objectives. Let us say, in more concrete terms, that to the extent to which the balance of power between private groups is exactly reflected within the State, that to the extent to which the unanimous decision resulting from a determinate hierarchy of private forces is mirrored in the decision of public authorities, the unwanted allegorical element almost disappears. We are then left with cases where, in fact, unity of decision prevails over the aggregate of the national economy. An important consequence follows. The domination effect, born of A's monopolistic situation vis-à-vis B,C,D . . . will not vary solely with the relative share of A's supply nor with the elasticity of money supply, but also with *the degree of unity of decision,* with the national economy considered as one monopolist. This unity will always be appreciated in pure fact. Under the most democratic institutions and a largely liberal private economic system, it will happen as a result of a unanimous agreement over an ideal welfare goal and the voluntary acceptance of its requirements, or because, in a given historical situation, an increase in national power coincides with the social welfare.

There is another reason why it is convenient not to abandon the analysis of the behavior and overall situation of a national economy; it is the existence, in all systems at all times, and the growing importance today in observable economic systems, of macro-decisions. The competition, in the area of foreign trade, may be analyzed (1) as a struggle for business which is (barring an increasing number of exceptions) carried out by private firms [they seek to deliver a certain output at a certain price], and (2) as a struggle for fixing the framework for business exchanges which is (with all due regard to consultations, lobbying and other pressures) the work of the monopolists of public constraint heading the various national economies, that is, the States. This fixing of the framework within which the exchange takes place has a double objective: on the one hand, the determination of durable or relatively durable rules—say, the choice of a customs duty or an exchange parity; on the other hand, the choice of certain characteristic aggregate quantities—for example, the amount of aid provided through an international investment plan, the amount of contribution to an international monetary fund or an international bank.

These two levels of macro-decisions are, relatively to the micro-decisions of private units, of variable importance according to whether the economies are more or less planned, and also—during the process of historical evolution—according to whether the basic macro-decisions are revised and adapted, or on the contrary the whole system of macro-decisions is changed, as happens during reconstruction. But, taking this difference in degree into consideration, it must nevertheless be said that one of the truly regrettable paradoxes of the traditional theory of international trade is to have demoted and minimized *the struggle for the fixing of the rules of the game* and to have concentrated all the attention on *the game.* The struggles for the frame of reference of the contract are also decisive, sometimes more decisive than the struggles for the quantity and price inscribed in the agreement.

There is, as we know, on the contract curve drawn in the analysis of bilateral monopoly, a point of equal concessions marking the equality of the contractual forces. Similarly, one can imagine a "framework of exchange" which gives the two national economies a perfect "equality of opportunity," that is, it establishes their relations on such a basis that neither can outdo the other except through economic performance. That this framework is purely ideal and imaginary is not too important: it only helps us to understand how the real framework of exchange differs from the ideal to the extent that the strengths of the two monopolists of public constraint, whose ambitions conflict, differ in fact from forces that in theory are supposedly equal.

It must not only be said that there is an element of bilateral monopoly in all international trade transactions. One should add that the preliminary struggle for the framework of exchange is, commonly, the result of a contest between State powers. Each partner fields all its political and economic assets. The combination of the differences in sizes, of national economic structures, with the diversity of military and diplomatic resources of each, renders totally improbable the equality of strength of the parties, even if there were no glaring disproportions. In the struggle for the fixing of the framework of exchange, the domination effect is the rule.

It is not easy to have to admit that the national economy is at the mercy of a composite of heterogeneous decisions. The difficulty is compounded by the fact that the national economy does not trade one product or a representative product as the theory claims, but through firms or groups of firms, an infinite variety of products which, from the point of view of relations with the outside world, come under very diversely competitive or monopolistic systems. The monopolistic situation of a national economy and of the dominant economy will therefore have to be evaluated by groups or families of products. But, paradoxically enough, to evaluate the relative position of a national economy and particularly the dominant economy, it will also be necessary to take into account the whole complex—that is, a kind of up to now not well-examined general complementarity between groups of activities from which the domination effect emerges and through whose proximity to and amalgamation with the national economy's bargaining power the total complex acquires meaning from our point of view. A dominant firm, we know, is such not only because of its bargaining power and the relative size of its supply and demand, but also because of the zone to which it belongs or the nature of the activity it pursues. Similarly, a national economy possessing great bargaining strength, as well as a large share of the supply and demand of several world products, will exert domination effects of a different kind and degree according to the nature of the products with regard to which its monopoly is defined. Those multiple complementarities which are the key production services in a given period of industrial development, and the complementarities of bargaining power which are the goods and services of political interest (oil, to name only one), play a critical role in this respect. The consequences of the connection between monopolistic situations causing special domination effects and those of the relative "weight" given to products in relation to which the monopolistic situation defines itself, are naturally and a priori held to be beyond its scope by an analysis which treats the national economy as producer and trader of one product or of one representative product.

It is fairly obvious why there can be no question of transposing the diagrams and detail of monopoly analysis to the relationships between two or several national economies. The modern theory of monopolistic companies in the domestic market should rather be considered as a pool of "interpretative themes" from which we draw for a free understanding (while never succumbing to the temptation of an automatic borrowing) of the "analogous" relations established between national economies.

If a national economy practically has control of supply (or demand, monopsony) of a good or service on the global scale (e.g., long-term credit services), it will not be incorrect or entirely accurate to speak of unilateral monopoly. The unity of decision in the matter of distribution of long-term credit abroad would be perfect only if it were the exclusive function of the State. But, at the moment at least, it would be even more unrealistic to base our argument on the scattered activities of private lenders rather than on a monolithic action by the State.

The reality lies in between. The private lenders accept the direction and supervision of their activity by State agencies. The decisions and the direction with regard to foreign loans are unitary enough to make it legitimate to attribute the reactions and powers of a monopolist to the total aggregate represented by the national economy in question. It sorts out its debtors, determines the overall quantity of credit to be distributed at a time; it chooses the forms of a loan (from government to government, in the private market, through semiofficial agencies) and balances the proportions of quantities lent in each form; it exerts a preponderant influence in the choice of rates and conditions. It practices, under its most varied forms, the politics of differentiation which is one of the normal consequences of monopoly. Its ambitions are limited only by the elasticity of demand for credit, itself organized and coordinated within the borrowing national economy.

This situation of a joint and supervised supply of goods or services brought face to face with a joint and supervised demand for the same goods and services outlines the "diluted" applications of the analysis of bilateral monopoly. The same model has been drawn upon since the dawn of the modern theory of international trade. What is wrong, it seems to us, is not to have dwelled upon some of its less obvious forms. It is true that if two States, with planned economies, carry out their entire foreign trade with each other, the model of bilateral monopoly applies in its pure form and it would probably not be too difficult to show, on this basis, that the foreign transactions between two collectivist States are determined solely by the bargaining power of the two parties, that is, inequality being the rule, the domination effect will hold sway. Of course, even if the two socialist States were strongly decentralized economies but came into contact only through foreign trade monopolies, a similar conclusion would remain valid. But the argument can be carried quite a bit further. Take a free economy. The sole fact that the latter deals with a partner whose economy is rigorously planned makes it almost impossible to think that it can do without official or semiofficial planning of its exchanges with the collectivist partner. The relations will be established, seemingly, between a monopolist and a free market, but in reality the situation will approximate that of bilateral monopoly where one of the monopolistic positions is induced by the other. If to this case is added that of national economies exchanging goods and services within limits fixed by the macro-decisions of import and export planning, the list of plurinational bilateral "monopoloids" lengthens. And if one remembers that foreign trade has never taken place otherwise than between countries establishing, through the choice of their tariffs and exchange rates, a sort of flexible and unofficial planning of their external exchanges, the applicability of one of the most typical models of indeterminacy and of the domination effect becomes truly overwhelming.

A similar interpenetration of zones where, in order that the traditional theory of international trade remain valid, competition should reign, is the phenomenon of oligopoly (here understood as the system where unit A can influence unit B's price-output decision without the latter remaining passive).

As soon as the national economy is seen as an aggregate of groups overseen by a monopolist of public constraint, some facts (obvious in practice) are brought to light which were not visible as long as it was represented as a juxtaposition of atomistic firms or as one big firm.

In a great number of important cases, oligopolistic private firms in country A enter into relations with similar firms in country B. Let us assume, for the time being, that the possibility of A firms influencing the price-output decisions of B firms arises from the number, size and structure of these firms and proceeds not at all from State intervention.

The very presence of these multinational private oligopolies introduces a partial dominance in the relations between the two economies in question.

Nor is this all. Assume private firms in A and in B whose number, dimensions and structure are such that they can reciprocally influence their price-output decisions. The State on each side organizes them in groups under its control, at least as far as their import-export activities are concerned. It puts at the disposal of these groups all or part of its bargaining power. There is every reason to believe that the bargaining strength of every State is not the same and that the combination of the State's bargaining power with the interested groups varies from country to country. Special indeterminacies and privileged opportunities that are vulnerable to the domination effect are therefore characteristic of these quasi-public multinational oligopolies.

Finally, take the national economies themselves, the total aggregates A,B,C . . . N. The competition between these total aggregates would be more efficient, their power more comparable, their independence with regard to the world price more perfect, the greater their number is. Setting aside these conditions, we have duopolistic or oligopolistic relations between the total aggregates themselves. A great economy of continental dimensions which has become the wealthiest in the world puts its pressure on another economy supported by satellite economies. The struggle "within" the contract is about the exchange and the fixing of the framework of the exchange. The stakes are the aggregates of relations between the Big Two on the one hand, and on the other, between the Big Two and the rest of the world. Their respective situation is such that the strategy of elimination is not desirable while the strategy of entente is not possible. What remains are the resources and perils of a strategy of influence. By distinguishing the "strategies" from the "objective constellations" of the market, by emphasizing the plurality of possible outcomes of the oligopolistic contest, the theoreticians of the domestic market may not have foreseen the scruples they would create among their more attentive colleagues in the field of international trade. . . .

Those who seek inspiration from monopolistic competition, provided they understand its technicalities, will encounter special difficulties in the analysis of foreign trade. Decreasing costs, the slope of the sales curve, unused capacity, the experience of many producers whose market is imperfect only because of product differentiation, are the many conditions not, or not necessarily, found in the relations between national economies. Bilateral monopoly and oligopoly are far more suggestive.

Yet, without wishing to be at all paradoxical, we will maintain that two familiar themes of monopolistic competition are indispensable to the understanding of the domination effect between national economies. These are: (1) product differentiation; and (2) the shifting to the right, through calculated policy, of the sales curve (demand curve to the firm).

On the first point, we are aiming at something quite different from the familiar "national" differentiation of the product of a *dominant* national economy. The product of such an economy automatically has, for the buyer, side advantages proceeding from the fact that it is the product of the dominant economy or of a dominant economy. In acquiring this product, the buyer also acquires the hope that he will receive good or better treatment as an applicant for credit, special opportunities to develop his business relations with an "active" zone of the world economy, powerful political friendships. This specific differentiation and these elements of *nonprice competition* have always played a pre-eminent role in international trade; today they exert an influence which should be of interest to all those who stand to gain from the promotion of a reasonable interpretation of the (GATT) rule of nondiscrimination.

Without presuming to elaborate this point fully here, let us draw four lines along which this might be done:

1. The curve of the aggregate demand of the "rest of the world" is nothing else, to the dominant economy, than the export curve of the dominant economy to the "rest of the world" (or import curve of the "rest of the world" coming from the dominant economy). [11] In choosing the level of its investment, of its employment, of its national income, the dominant economy (for a given trend in imports) fixes the maximum amount of imports that the "rest of the world" will be able to pay for by exporting to the dominant economy. If the "rest of the world" imports more than it exports, the gap cannot be filled to achieve long-term equilibrium, except through long-term credits granted by the dominant economy and whose amounts are determined by it. The most general decisions of political economy taken by the dominant economy therefore decide which curve will finally prevail among the family of curves expressing the possible levels of aggregate external demand.

2. As regards the creation of aggregate demand in the distant future, the dominant economy exerts a mainly irreversible influence. There are, at any one time, several systems for the creation of new markets (characterized by their geographical position, their volume, their structure and their period of maturation) which can be ideally classified according to the relative advantages they bring to the great national economies. The dominant economy can induce or help induce the realization of the system which is most advantageous to itself and to its satellites.

3. The dominant economy may be able to remain dominant only under the condition that the basic essentials of the free economy are maintained nationally and internationally. It can afford the necessary costs of (a) bringing its partners around to accept the basic type of economy suitable to itself (incidentally, this could be the best economically, I am not disputing this *here*); (b) preventing the national economies with which it deals from assuming structures (nationalizations, planned economies) harmful to it.

4. Through loans for specified objectives or through tied loans which must be used for purchases on its own territory, the dominant economy can create demand or demand in a direction easy to foresee.

• • •

. . . The application of the concept of the dominant economy, as we have just described it, to the American case presents few difficulties. So few, in fact, that one would be tempted to consider this concept as a theoretical edifice inspired by one concrete example, or as an aggregate of transparent allusions. This would be a misunderstanding of our central intention and, we hope, of one of the major results of our analyses. These tend to throw light on a *general* domination effect [12] which, besides its interest on the level of the philosophical interpretation of economics, forces us to correct the teachings of universal and reciprocal interdependence and clarifies a great number of domestic market situations, as well as the structure and function of all dominant national economies. Historically, dominant national economies have been those economies in which we can observe, at a high degree of concentration and intensity, an effect which very commonly and ordinarily characterizes the relations between all national economies *(structural inequality)*.

. . . Let us assume that the United States economy is an aggregate of groups of firms that exert domination effects with regard to various key products. These groups are linked to banking and financial centers that (1) when considered one by one enjoy dimensions and bargaining power that put them in a favorable position as regards similar foreign centers; (2) taken as a whole, benefit from three exceptional factors of influence: the bargaining power of the United States, the size of the American investment supply as a ratio of world investment supply, the fact that investment is, at all time and in particular in times of reconstruction, an eminently active economic "zone."

The struggle for the framework of exchange and the calculated shift of the aggregate demand curve, the propaganda and pressure over structures—such are the main features of the unequal and peaceful competition between the United States and its partners.

The total aggregate making up the U.S. economy is a relatively autonomous center of expansion or contraction. At the origins of this basic fact are not only the accidents of history, but also economic logic. This logic is a permanent problem, remaining the same in its fundamental features, despite the diversity of its manifestations during the Great Depression, for instance, or on the occasion of the revival of the world economy.

The distinction of this economic logic and of the historical contingencies, uneasy and delicate though it may be, gives the key to the transition from an abstract model to the observable reality and even yields insights of great practical utility.

An economically dominant complex, in its theoretical purity, exerts more influence than it receives solely on the basis of its size and its superiority with regard to labor returns and least-cost production. This minimum requirement is sufficient to explain the tendency toward integration, the cumulative concatenation of economic and technical progress, the possibility of the said economy to improve the terms of trade in its favor, the possibility of the State controlling it deploying bargaining strength whose value is set by the economic advantages and superiorities of the complex it represents. This pure model of the dominant economy, needless to say, cannot be found anywhere in the real world. More often than not, it will be overladen with adventitious features which do not flow from it logically or which could only be made to fit through too clever a dialectic. These features reinforce and specify the domination effect reduced to its strictly economic content. History offers examples of them in as great a variety as there are types of dominant economy. It is in order to base a general theory on actual[13] conditions that we will choose examples relevant to the American case.

1. A dominant economy can be (but need not be) an economy of refuge where capital is deposited temporarily or for a duration. An economy of refuge is identified by the presence, sometimes in combination, of various features. The fundamental rules of capitalism (respect for private property) are least likely to be violated there; the opportunities for speculative gain there are, within a period, maximized. These characteristics can, of course, come together within an economy which is not at all dominant, and conversely, they are not necessarily combined in such an economy. When they are present, they accentuate the influence of that economy in the matter of investment and eventually aggravate the consequences of the sudden shifts of the dominant economy with respect to foreign investments.

2. A dominant economy may (or may not) enjoy a giant temporary "collective rent" due to the fact that it has or has not fully and directly sustained the shock of a great war.[14] The domination effect is strongly reinforced by this; it could even be that

permanent elements likely to consolidate and extend it might result from this; but it is not useful to confuse this "surplus" with the strictly economic conditions and content of the domination effect in the long run.

3. A dominant economy may or may not benefit from certain intermediary monopolies, may or may not establish a vast collective monopoly through legislation and immigration quotas, for the benefit of its labor force. The domination effect it exercises as a total complex is thereby aggravated, but even if these elements were absent, we could still observe it at work.

Unless we are mistaken, the study of the domination effect at the international level is the condition and basis of an *objective* and *scientific* examination by all parties of the exigencies of a realistic reorganization of the world economy. The United States, through its official representatives, claims the economic leadership for itself. The necessary and possible content, the viable form of this leadership, can only be defined by a very clear and precise representation of the irreversible influence which the American economy exerts on the "rest of the world" and on its constituent parts. The extent of the dominant economy's responsibilities will therefore be equivalent to the extent of adjustment acceptable to the dominated economies. These measurements are not available to us as long as we continue to repeat, in the face of a new world, the traditional theory of international equilibrium as it was formulated in the nineteenth-century world which it interpreted incompletely, but which it depicted at least in some of its deep structures and tendencies.

The domination effect at the international level is not only linked to the development of noncompetitive systems of private firms in modern capitalism. It is not only linked with a certain form (authoritarian and planned) of modern State. It is linked to the very *existence* of the Nation-State, and in order to reduce it, it is necessary to go beyond the complicated and solid historic reality of the Nation-State. . . .

NOTES

1. *Author's Note:* I thank very much Professor George Modelski of the Department of Political Science of the University of Washington for having this essay translated. It was presented in English as part of a series of lectures delivered at Balliol College, Oxford, upon the invitation of Professor Thomas Ballogh (Economics Department) in 1947. Subsequently, without any change in the *general* hypothesis, the analysis developed in two directions: first, the general *asymmetric effects* were specified and formulated as (a) *influence;* (b) *dominance;* (c) *partial domination.* Second, two entire books were presented to offer a detailed formulation: *Pouvoir et Economie,* 2d ed. (Paris: Dunod, 1974); and *Unités Actives et Mathématiques Nouvelles. Révision de la Théorie de l'Equilibre Général* (Paris: Dunod, 1975), 275 pp. Might I suggest that the interested reader consult the last-mentioned works. In order to simplify this task, I have introduced some explicit references in the notes to the text.
   May I express my gratitude to Ms. Sylvia Modelski, who has translated this essay.
2. For a comprehensive development of such a theory, see *Pouvoir et Economie* and *Unités Actives.*
3. *Unités Actives,* pp. 25–43.
4. For the later distinction between *influence, dominance, propelling effect, partial domination* and *absorption* (major), see *Unités Actives,* pp. 113–121.
5. A sale or deal closed without argument or haggling over the price, i.e., without bargaining.

6. For detailed elaboration, see *Unités Actives,* pp. 128–146.

7. Compare with François Perroux, "Note on the Concept of 'Growth Pole'," in *Economic Policy for Development,* I. Livingstone, ed. (Penguin Modern Economics Readings, 1971).

8. For greater precision, see François Perroux, "La Firme Motrice dans une Région Motrice," in *Cahiers de l'I.S.E.A.* (Paris, 1961).

9. Clearly, our interpretation lies outside the bounds of a theory of imperialism. Besides the reservations we might have about the accuracy of all the ones that have been proposed, we think that the emotional vocabulary which they all use is not conducive either to the acquisition of knowledge or to the progress of peaceful relations among nations. By contrast, the analysis of the domination effect offers a ground of scientific neutrality acceptable to all interested parties.

10. For the author's most recent positions on the analytical theory of monopoly, oligopoly, partial monopoly and monopolistic competition, see *Unités Actives,* pp. 128–157.

11. According to the well-known scheme of reciprocal demand:

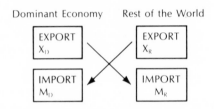

12. Let us not forget the distinctions between (a) influence, (b) dominance, (c) partial domination presented by the author subsequent to the delivery of his lectures at Balliol College (1947). In the text, "period of reconstruction" designates the reconstruction of those countries damaged in World War II.

13. 1948

14. Written in 1948.

9 / A Structural Theory of Imperialism

Johan Galtung

Introduction

This theory takes as its point of departure two of the most glaring facts about this world: the tremendous inequality, within and between nations, in almost all aspects of human living conditions, including the power to decide over those living conditions; *and* the resistance of this inequality to change. The world consists of Center and Periphery nations; and each nation, in turn, has its centers and periphery. Hence, our concern is with the mechanism underlying this discrepancy, particularly between the center in the Center, and the periphery in the Periphery. In other words, how to conceive of, how to explain, and how to counteract inequality as one of the major forms of *structural violence*. Any theory of liberation from structural violence presupposes theoretically and practically adequate ideas of the dominance system against which the liberation is directed; and the special type of dominance system to be discussed here is *imperialism*.

. . .

Thus, imperialism is a species in a genus of dominance and power relationships. It is a subtype of something, and has itself subtypes to be explored later. Dominance relations between nations and other collectivities will not disappear with the disappearance of imperialism; nor will the end to one type of imperialism (e.g. political, or economic) guarantee the end to another type of imperialism (e.g. economic or cultural). Our view is not reductionist in the traditional sense pursued in marxist-leninist theory, which conceives of imperialism as an economic relationship under private capitalism, motivated by the need for expanding markets, and which bases the theory of dominance on a theory of imperialism. According to this view, imperialism and dominance will fall like dominoes when the capitalistic conditions for economic imperialism no longer obtain. According to the view we develop here, imperialism is a more general structural relationship between two collectivities, and has to be understood at a general level in order to be understood and counteracted in its more specific manifestations—just like smallpox is better under-

From Johan Galtung, "A Structural Theory of Imperialism," *Journal of Peace Research* No. 2 (1971), pp. 81–98. Reprinted by permission of the author. Notes have been omitted. Tables and figures have been renumbered.

stood in a context of a theory of epidemic diseases, and these diseases better understood in a context of general pathology.

Briefly stated, imperialism is a system that splits up collectivities and relates some of the parts to each other in relations of *harmony of interest,* and other parts in relations of *disharmony of interest,* or *conflict of interest.*

• • •

Defining 'Imperialism'

• • •

Imperialism is a relation between a Center and a Periphery nation so that

(1) there is *harmony of interest* between the *center in the Center* nation and the *center in the Periphery* nation,

(2) there is more *disharmony of interest* within the Periphery nation than within the Center nations,

(3) there is *disharmony of interest* between the *periphery in the Center* nation and the *periphery in the Periphery* nation.

Diagrammatically it looks something like Figure 9-1. This complex definition, borrowing largely from Lenin, needs spelling out. The basic idea is, as mentioned, that the center in the Center nation has a bridgehead in the Periphery nation, and a well-chosen one: the center in the Periphery nation. This is established such that the Periphery center is tied to the Center center with the best possible tie: the tie of harmony of interest. They are linked so that they go up together and down, even under, together. How this is done in concrete terms will be explored in the subsequent sections.

Inside the two nations there is disharmony of interest. They are both in one way or another vertical societies with LC gaps [that is, gaps in living conditions between a center

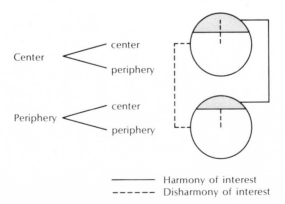

Figure 9-1 The structure of imperialism.

and a periphery]. Moreover, the gap is not decreasing, but is at best constant. But the basic idea, absolutely fundamental for the whole theory to be developed, is that *there is more disharmony in the Periphery nation than in the Center nation.* At the simplest static level of description this means there is more inequality in the Periphery than in the Center. At the more complex level we might talk in terms of the gap opening more quickly in the Periphery than in the Center, where it might even remain constant. Through welfare state activities, redistribution takes place and disharmony is reduced for at least some LC dimensions, including income, but usually excluding power.

If we now would capture in a few sentences what imperialism is about, we might perhaps say something like this:

In the Periphery nation, the center grows more than the periphery, due partly to how interaction between center and periphery is organized. Without necessarily thinking of economic interaction, the center is more enriched than the periphery—in ways to be explored below. However, for part of this enrichment, the center in the Periphery only serves as a transmission belt (e.g. as commercial firms, trading companies) for value (e.g. raw materials) forwarded to the Center nation. This value enters the Center in the center, with some of it drizzling down to the periphery in the Center. Importantly, there is less disharmony of interest in the Center than in the Periphery, so that *the total arrangement is largely in the interest of the periphery in the Center.* Within the Center the two parties may be opposed to each other. But in the total game, the periphery see themselves more as the partners of the center in the Center than as the partners of the periphery in the Periphery—and this is the essential trick of that game. Alliance-formation between the two peripheries is avoided, while the Center nation becomes more and the Periphery nation less cohesive—and hence less able to develop long-term strategies.

Actually, concerning the three criteria in the definition of imperialism as given above, it is clear that no. (3) is implied by nos. (1) and (2). The two centers are tied together and the Center periphery is tied to its center: that is the whole essence of the situation. If we now presuppose that the center in the Periphery is a smaller proportion of that nation than the center in the Center, we can also draw one more implication: *there is disharmony of interest between the Center nation as a whole and the Periphery nation as a whole.* But that type of finding, frequently referred to, is highly misleading because it blurs the harmony of interest between the two centers, and leads to the belief that imperialism is merely an international relationship, *not a combination of intra- and inter-national relations.*

· · ·

The Mechanisms of Imperialism

The two basic mechanisms of imperialism both concern the *relation* between the parties concerned, particularly between the nations. The first mechanism concerns the *interaction relation* itself, the second how these relations are put together in a larger interaction structure:

(1) the principle of *vertical interaction relation*
(2) the principle of *feudal interaction structure.*

The basic point about interaction is, of course, that people and nations have different values that complement each other, and then engage in exchange. Some nations produce

Table 9-1 An Interaction Budget

	A ("developed")		B ("developing")	
	Inter-actor effects	Intra-actor effects	Inter-actor effects	Intra-actor effects
Positive (in)	Raw materials	Spin-offs	Manufactured goods	Little or nothing
Negative (out)	Manufactured goods	Pollution, exploitation	Raw materials	Depletion, exploitation

oil, other nations produce tractors, and they then carry out an exchange according to the principles of comparative advantages. Imagine that our two-nation system has a prehistory of no interaction at all, and then starts with this type of interaction. Obviously, both will be changed by it, and more particularly: a gap between them is likely to open and widen if the interaction is cumulatively asymmetric in terms of what the two parties get out of it.

To study whether the interaction is symmetric or asymmetric, on equal or unequal terms, *two* factors arising from the interaction have to be examined:

(1) *the value-exchange between the actors—inter-actor effects*
(2) *the effects inside the actors—intra-actor effects*

In *economic* relations the first is most commonly analyzed, not only by liberal but also by Marxist economists. The inter-actor flow can be observed as flows of raw material, capital, and financial goods and services in either direction, and can literally be measured at the main points of entry: the customs houses and the national banks. The flow both ways can then be compared in various ways. Most important is the comparison in terms of *who benefits most*, and for this purpose intra-actor effects also have to be taken into consideration.

In order to explore this, the interaction budget indicated in Table 9-1 may be useful. In the Table the usual exchange pattern between a 'developed' nation A and a 'developing' nation B, where manufactured goods are exchanged for raw materials, is indicated. Whether it takes place in a barter economy or a money economy is not essential in a study of exchange between completely unprocessed goods like crude oil and highly processed goods like tractors. There are negative intra-actor effects that accrue to both parties, indicated by the terms "pollution" for A and "depletion" for B, and "exploitation" for either. So far these negative spin-off effects are usually not taken systematically into account, nor the positive spin-off effects for A that will be a corner-stone in the present analysis.

It is certainly meaningful and important to talk in terms of unequal exchange or asymmetric interaction, but not quite unproblematic what its precise meaning should be. For that reason, it may be helpful to think in terms of three stages or types of exploitation, partly reflecting historical *processes* in chronological order, and partly reflecting types of *thinking* about exploitation.

In the first stage of exploitation, A simply engages in looting and takes away the raw materials without offering anything in return. If he steals out of pure nature there is no human interaction involved, but we assume that he forces "natives" to work for him and do the extraction work. It is like the slave-owner who lives on the work produced by slaves—which is quantatively not too different from the land-owner who has land-workers working for him five out of seven days a week.

In the second stage, A starts offering something "in return." Oil, pitch, land, etc. is "bought" for a couple of beads—it is no longer simply taken away without asking any questions about ownership. The price paid is ridiculous. However, as power relations in the international systems change, perhaps mainly by bringing the power level of the weaker party up from zero to some low positive value, A has to contribute more: for instance, pay more for the oil. The question is now whether there is a cut-off point after which the exchange becomes equal, and what the criterion for that cut-off point would be. Absence of subjective dissatisfaction—B says that he is now content? Objective market values or the number of man-hours that have gone into the production on either side?

There are difficulties with all these conceptions. But instead of elaborating on this, we shall rather direct our attention to the shared failure of all these attempts to look at *intra-actor* effects. Does the interaction have enriching or impoverishing effects *inside* the actor, or does it just lead to a stand-still? This type of question leads us to the third stage of exploitation, where there may be some balance in the flow between the actors, but great differences in the effect the interaction has within them.

As an example let us use nations exchanging oil for tractors. The basic point is that this involves different levels of processing, where we define "processing" as an activity imposing Culture on Nature. In the case of crude oil the product is (almost) pure Nature; in the case of tractors it would be wrong to say that it is a case of pure Culture, pure *form* (like mathematics, music). A transistor radio, an integrated circuit, these would be better examples because Nature has been brought down to a minimum. The tractor is still too much iron and rubber to be a pure case.

The major point now is the *gap in processing level* between oil and tractors and the differential effect this gap will have on the two nations. In one nation the oil deposit may be at the water-front, and all that is needed is a derrick and some simple mooring facilites to pump the oil straight into a ship—e.g. a Norwegian tanker—that can bring the oil to the country where it will provide energy to run, among other things, the tractor factories. In the other nation the effects may be extremely far-reaching due to the complexity of the product and the connectedness of the society.

There may be ring effects in all directions, and in Table 9-2 we have made an effort to show some types of spin-off effects. A number of comments are appropriate in connection with this list, which, needless to say, is very tentative indeed.

First, the effects are rather deep-reaching if this is at all a correct image of the situation. And the picture is hardly exaggerated. It is possible to set up international interaction in such a way that the positive intra-actor effects are practically nil in the raw material delivering nation, and extremely far-reaching in the processing nation. This is not in any sense strange either: if processing is the imprint of Culture on Nature, the effects should be far-reaching indeed, and strongly related to development itself.

Second, these effects reinforce each other. In the nine effects listed in Table 9-2, there are economic, political, military, communications, and cultural aspects, mixed together. Thus, the nation that in the international division of labor has the task of providing the

Table 9-2 Intra-Actor Effects of Interaction Across Gaps in Processing Levels

Dimension	Effect on center nation	Effect on periphery nation	Analyzed by
1. Subsidiary economic effects	New *means of production* developed	Nothing developed, just a hole in the ground	Economist
2. Political position in world structure	Central position reinforced	Periphery position reinforced	International relationists
3. Military benefits	*Means of destruction* can easily be produced	No benefits, wars cannot be fought by means of raw materials	
4. Communication benefits	*Means of communication* easily developed	No benefits, transportation not by means of raw materials	Communication specialists
5. Knowledge and research	Much needed for higher levels of processing	Nothing needed, extraction based on being, not on becoming	Scientists, technicians
6. Specialist needed	Specialists in *making,* scientists, engineers	Specialist in *having,* lawyers	Sociologists of knowledge
7. Skill and education	Much needed to carry out processing	Nothing needed, just a hole in the ground	Education specialists
8. Social structure	Change needed for ability to convert into mobility	No change needed, extraction based on ownership, not on ability	Sociologists
9. Psychological effects	A basic psychology of self-reliance and autonomy	A basic psychology of dependence	Psychologists

most refined, processed products—like Japan with its emphasis on integrated circuits, transistors, miniaturization, etc. (or Eastern Europe's Japan: the DDR, with a similar emphasis)—will obviously have to engange in research. Research needs an infra-structure, a wide cultural basis in universities, etc., and it has obvious spill-over effects in the social, political, and military domains. And so on: the list may be examined and all kinds of obvious types of cross-fertilization be explored.

Third, in the example chosen, and also in the formulations in the Table, we have actually referred to a very special type of gap in processing level: the case when one of the nations concerned delivers raw materials. But the general point here is the *gap,* which would also exist if one nation delivers semi-finished products and the other finished products. There may be as much of a gap in a trade relations based on exchange between textiles and transistors as one based on exchange between oil and tractors. However, and this seems to be basic: we have looked in vain for a theory of economic trade where this gap is meaningfully operationalized so that the theory could be based on it. In fact, *degree of processing,* which is the basic variable behind the spin-off effects, seems absent from most thinking about international exchange.

This, and that is observation number *four,* is not merely a question of analyzing differences in processing level in terms of what happens inside the factory or the extraction plant. It has to be seen in its social totality. A glance at the right-hand column of Table 9-2 immediately gives us some clues as to why this has not been done: academic research has been so divided that nowhere in a traditional university set-up would one come to grips with the totality of the effects of an interaction process. Not even in the most sophisticated inter-, cross- or trans-disciplinary research institute has that type of research been carried so far that a meaningful operationalization has been offered. Yet this is indispensible for a new program of trade on equal terms to be formulated: *trade, or interaction in general, is symmetric, or on equal terms, if and only if the total inter- and intra-actor effects that accrue to the parties are equal.*

But, and this is observation number *five:* why has the idea of comparing the effects of interaction only at the points of exit and entry been so successful? Probably basically because it has always been natural and in the interest of the two centers to view the world in this way, not necessarily consciously to reinforce their position in the center, but basically because interaction looks more like *"inter*-action only" to the center. If the center in the Periphery has based its existence on being rather than becoming, on ownership rather than processing, then the inter-action has been very advantageous to them. What was formerly Nature is through the 'beneficial interaction' with another nation converted into Money, which in turn can be converted into many things. *Very little effort was needed:* and that this was precisely what made the exchange so disadvantageous, only became clear after some time. Japan is, possibly, the only nation that has really converted the absence of raw materials into a blessing for the economy.

Some implications of the general principle of viewing intra-actor in addition to inter-actor effects can now be spelled out.

One is obvious: *asymmetry cannot be rectified by stabilizing or increasing the prices for raw materials.* Of course, prices exist that could, on the surface, compensate for the gap in intra-actor effects, convertible into a corresponding development of subsidiary industries, education industry, knowledge industry, and so on (although it is hard to see how the psychology of self-reliance can be bought for money). Much of this is what raw material producing countries can do with the money they earn. But this is not the same. One thing is to be *forced* into a certain pattern of intra-actor development *in order to* be able to participate in the inter-actor interaction, quite another thing to be free to make the decision without having to do it, without being forced by the entire social machinery.

• • •

In short, we see vertical interaction as the major source of the inequality of this world, whether it takes the form of looting, of highly unequal exchange, or highly differential spin-off effects due to processing gaps. But we can also imagine a fourth phase of exploitation, where the modern King Midas becomes a victim of his own greed and turns his environment into muck rather than gold, by polluting it so strongly and so thoroughly that the negative spin-off effects from processing may outstrip all the positive effects. This may, in fact, place the less developed countries in a more favorable position: the lower the GNP, the lower the Gross National Pollution.

But this phase is still for the (near?) future. At present what we observe is an inequality between the world's nations of a magnitude that can only be explained in terms of the cumulative effect of *strong* structural phenomena over time, like the phenomena described here under the heading of imperialism. This is not to deny that other factors may also be important, even decisive, but no analysis can be valid without studying the problem of development in a context of vertical interaction.

If the first mechanism, the *vertical interaction relation,* is the major factor behind inequality, then the second mechanism, the *feudal interaction structure,* is the factor that maintains and reinforces this inequality by protecting it. There are four rules defining this particular interaction structure:

    (1) interaction between Center and Periphery is *vertical*
    (2) interaction between Periphery and Periphery is *missing*
    (3) multilateral interaction involving all three is *missing*
    (4) interaction with the outside world is *monopolized* by the Center, with two implications:
        (a) Periphery interaction with other Center nations is *missing*
        (b) Center as well as Periphery interaction with Periphery nations belonging to other Center nations is *missing.*

This relation can be depicted as in Figure 9-2. As indicated in the Figure, the number of Periphery nations attached to any given Center nation can, of course, vary. In this Figure we have also depicted the rule "if you stay off my satellites, I will stay off yours."

Some important *economic* consequences of this structure should be spelled out.

First, and most obvious: the *concentration on trade partners.* A Periphery nation should, as a result of these two mechanisms, have most of its trade with "its" Center nation. In other words, empirically we would expect high levels of *import concentration* as well as *export concentration* in the Periphery, as opposed to the Center, which is more free to extend its trade relations in almost any direction—except in the pure case, with the Periphery of other Center nations.

Second, and not so obvious, is the *commodity concentration:* the tendency for Periphery nations to have only one or very few primary products to export. This would be a trivial matter if it could be explained entirely in terms of geography, if e.g. oil countries were systematically poor as to ore, ore countries poor as to bananas and coffee, etc. But this can hardly be assumed to be the general case: Nature does not distribute its riches that way.

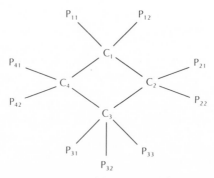

Figure 9-2 A feudal center-periphery structure.

There is a historical rather than a geographical explanation to this. A territory may have been exploited for the raw materials most easily available and/or most needed in the Center, and this, in turn, leads to a certain social structure, to communication lines to the deposits, to trade structures, to the emergence of certain center groups (often based on ownership of that particular raw material), and so on. To start exploiting a new kind of raw material in the same territory might upset carefully designed local balances; hence, it might be easier to have a fresh start for that new raw material in virgin territory with no bridgehead already prepared for imperialist exploits. In order to substantiate this hypothesis we would have to demonstrate that there are particularly underutilized and systematically underexplored deposits precisely in countries where one type of raw materials has already been exploited.

The combined effect of these two consequences is a *dependency* of the Periphery on the Center. Since the Periphery usually has a much smaller GNP, the trade between them is a much higher percentage of the GNP for the Periphery, and with both partner and commodity concentration, the Periphery becomes particularly vulnerable to fluctuations in demands and prices. At the same time the center in the Periphery depends on the Center for its supply of consumer goods. Import substitution industries will usually lead to consumer goods that look homespun and unchic, particularly if there is planned obsolescence in the production of these goods in the Center, plus a demand for equality between the two centers maintained by demonstration effects and frequent visits to the Center.

However, the most important consequence is political and has to do with the systematic utilization of feudal interaction structures as a way of protecting the Center against the Periphery. The feudal interaction structure is in social science language nothing but an expression of the old political maxim *divide et impera*, divide and rule, as a strategy used systematically by the Center relative to the Periphery nations. How could—for example—a small foggy island in the North Sea rule over one quarter of the world? By isolating the Periphery parts from each other, by having them geographically at sufficient distance from each other to impede any real alliance formation, by having separate deals with them so as to tie them to the Center in particularistic ways, by reducing multilateralism to a minimum with all kinds of graded membership, *and* by having the Mother country assume the role of window to the world.

However, this point can be much more clearly seen if we combine the two mechanisms and extend what has been said so far for relations between Center and Periphery *nations* to relations between center and periphery *groups* within nations. Under an imperialist structure the two mechanisms are used not only between nations but also within nations, but less so in the Center nation than in the Periphery nation. In other words, there is vertical division of labor within as well as between nations. And these two levels of organization are intimately linked to each other (as A. G. Frank always has emphasized) in the sense that the center in the Periphery interaction structure is also that group with which the Center nation has its harmony of interest, the group used as a bridgehead.

Thus, the combined operation of the two mechanisms at the two levels builds into the structure a subtle grid of protection measures against the major potential source of "trouble," the periphery in the Periphery.

• • •

Obviously, the more perfectly the mechanisms of imperialism within and between nations are put to work, the less overt machinery of oppression is needed and the smaller can the center groups be, relative to the total population involved. *Only imperfect, amateurish imperialism needs weapons; professional imperialism is based on structural rather than direct violence.*

The Types of Imperialism

We shall now make this more concrete by distinguishing between five types of imperialism depending on the *type* of exchange between Center and Periphery nations:

(1) *economic*
(2) *political*
(3) *military*
(4) *communication*
(5) *cultural*

The order of presentation is rather random: we have no theory that one is more basic than the others, or precedes the others. Rather, this is like a Pentagon or a Soviet Star: imperialism can start from any corner. They should all be examined regarding the extent to which they generate interaction patterns that utilize the two *mechanisms* of imperialism so as to fulfill the three *criteria* of imperialism, or at least the first of them.

The most basic of the two mechanisms is *vertical* interaction, which in its modern form is conceived of as interaction across a gap in processing level. In other words, what is exchanged between the two nations is not only not the same things (which would have been stupid) but things of a quite different kind, the difference being in terms of where the most complex and stimulating operations take place. One tentative list, expanding what has been said above about economic interaction, might look like Table 9-3. The order of presentation parallels that of Table 9-2, but in that Table cultural imperialism was spelled out in more detail as spin-off effects from economic imperialism.

The vertical nature of this type of *economic* interaction has been spelled out in detail above since we have used that type of imperialism to exemplify definition and mechanisms. Let us look more at the other types of vertical interaction.

The *political* one is clear: the concept of a "mother" country, the Center nation, is also an indication of how the decision-making center is dislocated, away from the nation itself and towards the Center nation. These decisions may then affect economic, military, communication, and cultural patterns. Important here is the division of labor involved:

Table 9-3 The Five Types of Imperialism

Type	Economic	Political	Military	Communication	Cultural
Center nation provides	Processing, means of production	Decisions models	Protection, means of destruction	News, means of communication	Teaching, means of creation— autonomy
Periphery nation provides	Raw materials, markets	Obedience, imitators	Discipline, traditional hardware	Events, passengers, goods	Learning, validation— dependence

some nations produce decisions, others supply obedience. The decisions may be made upon application, as in 'bilateral technical assistance,' or in consultation—or they may simply emerge by virtue of the model-imitator distinction. Nothing serves that distinction quite so well as unilinear concepts of "development" and "modernization," according to which Center nations possess some superior kind of structure for others to imitate (as long as the Center's central position is not seriously challenged), and which gives a special aura of legitimacy to any idea emanating from the Center. Thus, structures and decisions developed in the "motherland of liberalism" or in the "fatherland of socialism" serve as models by virtue of their place of origin, not by virtue of their substance.

The *military* implications or parallels are also rather obvious. It cannot be emphasized enough that the economic division of labor is also one which ensures that the Center nations econonomically speaking also become the Center nations in a military sense: only they have the industrial capacity to develop the technological hardware—and also are often the only ones with the social structure compatible with a modern army. He who produces tractors can easily produce tanks, but he who delivers oil cannot defend himself by throwing it in the face of the aggressors. He has to depend on the tank-producer, either for protection or for acquisition (on terms dictated by the Center). And just as there is a division of labor with the Center nation producing manufactured goods on the basis of raw materials extracted in the Periphery nation, there is also a division of labor with the *Center nations processing the obedience provided by the Periphery nations into decisions that can be implemented.* Moreover, there is also a division of labor with the Center providing the protection (and often also the officers or at least the instructors in "counterinsurgency") and the Periphery the discipline and the soldiers needed—not to mention the apprentices of 'military advisors' from the Center.

As to the fourth type, *communication* imperialism, the emphasis in the analysis is usually turned towards the second mechanism of imperialism: the feudal interaction structure. That this largely holds for most world communication and transportation patterns has been amply demonstrated. But perhaps more important is the vertical nature of the division of labor in the field of communication/transportation. It is trivial that a high level of industrial capacity is necessary to develop the latest in transportation and communication technology. The preceding generation of *means of communication/transportation* can always be sold, sometimes second-hand, to the Periphery as part of the general vertical trade/aid structure, alongside the *means of production* (economic sector), the *means of destruction* (military sector), and the *means of creation* (cultural sector). The Center's planes and ships are faster, more direct, look more reliable, attract more passengers, more goods. And when the Periphery finally catches up, the Center will already for a long time have dominated the field of communication satellites.

One special version of this principle is a combination of cultural and communication exchange: *news communication.* We all know that the major agencies are in the hands of the Center countries, relying on Center-dominated, feudal networks of communication. What is not so well analyzed is how Center news takes up a much larger proportion of Periphery news media than vice versa, just as trade with the Center is a larger proportion of Periphery total trade than vice versa. In other words, the pattern of partner concentration as something found more in the Periphery than in the Center is very pronounced. The Periphery nations do not write or read much about each other, especially not across bloc borders, and they read more about "their" Center than about other Centers—because the press is written and read by the center in the Periphery, who want to know more about that most "relevant" part of the world—for them.

Another aspect of vertical division of labor in the news business should also be pointed out. Just as the Periphery produces raw material that the Center turns into processed goods, *the Periphery also produces events that the Center turns into news.* This is done by training journalists to see events with Center eyes, and by setting up a chain of communication that filters and processes events so that they fit the general pattern.

The latter concept brings us straight into *cultural* imperialism, a subtype of which is scientific imperialism. The division of labor between teachers and learners is clear: it is not the division of labor as such (found in most situations of transmission of knowledge) that constitutes imperialism, but the location of the teachers, and of the learners, in a broader setting. If the Center always provides the teachers and the definition of that worthy of being taught (from the gospels of Christianity to the gospels of Technology), and the Periphery always provides the learners, then there is a pattern which smacks of imperialism. The satellite nation in the Periphery will also know that nothing flatters the Center quite so much as being encouraged to teach, and being seen as a model, and that the Periphery can get much in return from a humble, culture-seeking strategy (just as it will get little but aggression if it starts teaching the Center anything—like Czechoslovakia, who started lecturing the Soviet Union on socialism). For in accepting cultural transmission the Periphery also, implictly, validates for the Center the culture developed in the center, whether that center is intra- or inter-national. This serves to reinforce the Center as a center, for it will then continue to develop culture along with transmitting it, thus creating lasting demand for the latest innovations. Theories, like cars and fashions, have their life-cycle, and whether the obsolescence is planned or not there will always be a time-lag in a structure with a pronounced difference between center and periphery. Thus, the tram workers in Rio de Janeiro may carry banners supporting Auguste Comte one hundred years after the center of the Center forgot who he was. . . .

In science we find a particular version of vertical division of labor, very similar to economic division of labor: the pattern of scientific teams from the Center who go to Periphery nations to collect data (raw material) in the form of deposits, sediments, flora, fauna, archeological findings, attitudes, behavioral patterns, and so on for data processing, data analysis, and theory formation (processing, in general) in the Center universities (factories), so as to be able to send the finished product, a journal, a book (manufactured goods) back for consumption in the center of the Periphery—after first having created a demand for it through demonstration effect, training in the Center country, and some degree of low level participation in the data collection team. This parallel is not a joke, it is a *structure*. If in addition the precise nature of the research is to provide the Center with information that can be used economically, politically, or militarily to maintain an imperialist structure, the cultural imperialism becomes even more clear. And if to this we add the *brain drain* (and body drain) whereby "raw" brains (students) and "raw" bodies (unskilled workers) are moved from the Periphery to the Center and "processed" (trained) with ample benefits to the Center, the picture becomes complete.

The Phases of Imperialism

We have mentioned repeatedly that imperialism is *one* way in which one nation may dominate another. Moreover, it is a way that provides a relatively stable pattern: the nations are linked to each other in a pattern that may last for some time because of the

Table 9-4   Three Phases of Imperialism in History

Phase	Period	Form	Term
I	Past	*Occupation,* cP physically consists of cC people who engage in *occupation*	Colonialism
II	Present	*Organization,* cC interacts with cP via the medium of international *organizations*	Neo-colonialism
III	Future	*Communication,* cC interacts with cP via international communication	Neo-neo-colonialism

many stabilizing factors built into it through the mechanism of a feudal interaction structure.

The basic idea is that the center in the Center establishes a bridgehead in the Periphery nation, and more particularly, in the center of the Periphery nation. Obviously, this bridgehead does not come about just like that: there is a phase preceding it. The precise nature of that preceding phase can best be seen by distinguishing between three phases of imperialism in history, depending on what type of concrete method the center in the Center has used to establish the harmony of interest between itself and the center in the Periphery. This is enumerated in Table 9-4.

From the Table we see that in all three cases, the Center nation has a hold over the center of the Periphery nation. But the precise nature of this grip differs, and should be seen relative to the means of transportation and communication. No analysis of imperialism can be made without a reference to these means that perhaps are as basic as the means of production in producing social dynamics.

Throughout the overwhelming part of human history, transportation (of human beings, of goods) did not proceed at a higher speed than that provided by pony expresses and quick sailing ships; and communication (of signals, of meaning) not at higher speed than that provided by fires and smoke signals which could be spotted from one hilltop to another. Precise control over another nation would have to be exercised by physically transplanting one's own center and grafting onto the top of the foreign body—in other words, colonialism in all its forms, best known in connection with "white settlers." According to this vision, colonialism was not a discovery of the Europeans subsequent to the Great Discoveries: it could just as well be used to describe great parts of the Roman Empire that through textbooks and traditions of history-writing so successfully has dominated our image of racial and ethnical identity and national pride.

Obviously, the quicker the means of transportation could become, the less necessary would this pattern of permanent settlement be. The break in the historical pattern came when the steam engine was not only put into the factory to provide new *means of production* (leading to conditions that prompted Marx to write *Das Kapital*) but also into a vessel (Fulton) and a locomotive (Stephenson): in other words, *means of transportation* (the book about that is not yet written). This gave Europeans a decisive edge over peoples in other regions, and colonialism became more firmly entrenched. Control could be accurate and quick.

But decolonialization also came, partly due to the weakening of cC, partly due to the strengthening of cP that might not challenge what cC did, but want to do so itself. Neo-colonialism came; and in this present phase of imperialism, control is not of the direct, concrete type found in the past. It is mediated through the means of transportation (and, of course, also communication) linking the two centers to each other. The control is less concrete: it is not physical presence, but a link; and this link takes the shape of international organizations. The international organization has a certain permanence, often with physical headquarters and a lasting general secretary in the mother country. But above all it is a medium in which influence can flow, with *both* centers joining as members and finding each other. Their harmony of interest can be translated into complete equality within the international organization, and vice versa. Their identity is defined relative to the organization, not to race, ethnicity, or nationality. But with differential disharmony *within* nations, this actually becomes an instrument of disharmony *between* nations.

These organizations are well-known for all five types of imperialism. For the economic type, the private or governmental multinational corporations (BINGOs) may serve; for the political type, many of the international governmental organizations (IGOs); for the military type, the various systems of military alliances and treaties and organizations (MIGOs?); for communication the shipping and air companies (CONGOs?), not to mention the international press agencies, offer ample illustration; and for cultural imperialism, some of the international nongovernmental organizations (INGOs) may serve as the conveyor mechanisms. But this is of course not to say that international organizations will necessarily serve such purposes. According to the theory developed here, this is an empirical question, depending on the degree of division of labor inside the organization and the extent to which it is feudally organized.

Next, the third phase. If we now proceed even further along the same line of decreasingly concrete (but increasingly effective?) ties between the two centers, we can envisage a phase where even the international organizations will not only go into disrepute, but dissolve. What will come in their place? *Instant communication,* whereby parties who want to communicate with each other set up ad hoc communication networks (telesatellites, etc.) that form and dissolve in rapid succession, changing scope and domain, highly adjustable to external circumstance, guided by enormous data-banks and idea-banks that permit participants to find their 'opposite numbers' without having them frozen together in a more permanent institutional network that develops its own rigidities.

In other words, we envisage a future where very many international organizations will be threatened in two ways. First, they will be exposed to increasing criticism as to their function as a tie between two centers, communicating and coordinating far above the masses in either country, which will in itself lead to a certain disintegration. Second, this does not mean that the centers, if they are free to do so, will cease to coordinate their action, only that they will do so by other means. Instead of going to ad hoc or annual conventions, or in other ways instructing a general secretary and his staff, they may simply pick up their videophone and have a long distance conference organized, where the small group of participants can all see and talk to each other—not like in a conference, but in the more important adjoining lobbies, in the coffee-houses, in private quarters—or wherever they prefer to carry out communication and coordination.

To penetrate more deeply into the role of international organization as an instrument of imperialistic dominance, let us now distinguish between five phases in the development of an international organization. As example we take one economic organization, General Motors Corporation (GMC) and one political organization, the International Communist Movement (ICM)—at present not organized formally as an international. The stages are indicated in Table 9-5. Needless to say, these two are taken as *illustrations* of economic and political imperialism—this is not a *study* of GMC and ICM respectively.

Table 9-5 Stages in the Development of an International Organization

	General Motors Corporation (GMC)	International Communist Movement (ICM)
Phase 1: National only	In one country only ("mother country")	In one country only ("fatherland")
Phase 2: National goes abroad	Subsidiary, or branch office, established by "agents"	Subversive organization, established by "agents"
Phase 3: Multi-national, asymmetric	Other national companies started, with "mother country" company dominating	Other national parties established, with "fatherland" party dominating
Phase 4: Multi-national, symmetric	Total network becomes symmetric	Total network becomes symmetric
Phase 5: Global, or transnational organization	National identities dissolve	National dissolve

In the beginning, the organization exists only within national boundaries. Then comes a second phase when it sends representatives, at that stage usually called "agents," abroad. This is a critical stage: it is a question of gaining a foothold in another nation, and usually subversive, from below. If the other nation is completely new to this economic or political pattern, the "agents" often have to come from the "mother country" or the "fatherland" upon the invitation of dissatisfied individuals who find their own mobility within the system blocked *and* who think that the present system does not satisfy the needs of the population. But this phase is not imperialist, for the center in the mother country has not established any bridgehead in the *center* of the offspring country—yet.

The agents may be highly instrumental of social change. They may set into motion patterns in economic life that may reduce significantly the power of feudal landlords and introduce capitalist patterns of production; or they may set into motion patterns in political life that may reduce equally significantly the power of industrialists and introduce socialist patterns of production. Both activities are subversive of the social order, but not imperialist, and are, consequently, examples of other ways in which one nation may exercise influence over another.

But in Phase 3 this development has gone a significant step further. The agents have now been successful, so to speak: national companies/parties have been established. Elites have emerged in the Periphery nations, strongly identified with and well harmonizing with the Center elites. The whole setting is highly asymmetric; what we have identified as mechanisms and types of imperialism are now discernible.

There is *division of labor:* the 'daughter' company in the Periphery nation is particularly concerned with making raw materials available and with securing markets for the mother company in the Center nation. If it enters into processing, then it is often with a technology already by-passed by "development" in the Center country, or only leading to semi-finished products. Correspondingly, the company/party in the mother country makes more decision and the parties in the Periphery provide obedience and secure markets for the implementation of orders. Thus, in both cases the implicit assumption is always that the top leadership of the international organization shall be the top leadership of the company/party in the Center country. Headquarters are located there and not elsewhere; this location is not by rotation or random choice.

Further, the *general interaction structure is clearly feudal:* there is interaction along the spokes, from the Periphery to the Center hub; but not along the rim, from one Periphery nation to another. There may be multilateral meetings, but they are usually very heavily dominated by the Center, which takes it for granted that it will be in the interest of the Periphery to emulate the Center. And this then spans across all five types of interaction, one way or the other—in ways that are usually fairly obvious.

We have pointed to what seem to be basic similarities between the two international organizations (GMC and ICM). Precisely because they are similar, they can do much to impede each other's activities. This similarity is not strange: they both reflect the state of affairs in a world that consists of (1) nation-states, of (2) highly unequal power and level of development along various axes, and is (3) too small for many nation-states to stay within their bonds—so they spill over with their gospels, and patterns are established that are imperialist in nature. *For phase 3 is clearly the imperialist phase;* and because so many international organizations are in this third phase, they at present stand out as vehicles of asymmetric forms of center-center cooperation.

This is the present state of most international organizations. Most are extensions of patterns developed first in one nation, and on assumptions that may have been valid in that country. They are usually the implementation in our days of the old missionary command (Matthew 28: 18–20): "Go ye all forth and make all peoples my disciples." This applies not only to economic and political organizations, but to the other three types as well. Typical examples are the ways in which cultural patterns are disseminated. In its most clear form, they are even handled by official or semi-official institutions more or less attached to the diplomatic network (such as USIS, and the various cultural activities of the Soviet and Chinese embassies in many countries; and to a lesser extent, the British Council and Alliance Française). But international organizations are also used for this purpose by Center nations who firmly believe that their patterns are good for everybody else because they are good for themselves.

However, the Periphery does not necessarily rest content with this state of affairs. There will be a dynamism leading to changes towards Phase 4, so far only brought about in very few organizations. It will probably have its roots in the division of labor, and the stamp as second-class members given to the Periphery in general, and to heads of Periphery companies and parties in particular. Why should there be any written or unwritten law that GMC and ICM heads are located in the United States and the Soviet Union, respectively? Why not break up the division of labor completely, distribute the research contracts and the strategic planning evenly, why not rotate the headquarters, why not build up interaction along the rim and build down the interaction along the spokes so that the hub slowly fades out and the resulting organization is truly symmetric? This is where the Norwegian GMC president and the Rumanian ICM general secretary have, in a sense, common interests—and we predict that this movement will soon start in all major international organizations following some of the very useful models set by the UN and her Specialized Agencies. It should be noted, however, that it is not too difficult to obtain equality in an international organization where only the elites participate, since they already to a large extent harmonize with each other.

But this is not the final stage of development, nothing is. The multi-national, symmetric form will always be artificial for at least two reasons: the nations are not symmetric in and by themselves—some contribute more than others—and they form artificial pockets relative to many of the concerns of the organizations. Any multi-national organization, however symmetric, is a way of reinforcing and perpetuating the nation-state. If nation-states are fading out in significance, much like municipalities in many parts of the world, multi-national organizations will also fade out because they are built over a pattern that is becoming less and less salient. What will come in its place? The answer will probably be what has here been called a hypothetical Phase 5—The global or world organization.

•   •   •

PART III

EFFECTS

INTRODUCTION

The concepts and theories we have reviewed thus far are, in part, predictions of what social and political impacts might be expected from the world-wide operations of large corporations. Both the monopolistic theory of direct investment, with its connotations of market power and integration of the world economy, and the concepts of the dominant economy and of imperialism, which link business activities and the political order, make clear that a significant impact is to be expected and predict the general impact that might be forthcoming.

The effects of transnational corporate activity being the central concern of this volume, now require closer analysis. The effects we shall single out for special attention do not constitute the full range of consequences to be expected. Our analysis will be limited to the effects of such activity on world values. We shall ask: does transnational enterprise contribute to a better world order, and if not, why not? What particular effects account for such influence? How might a balance of positive and negative effects be reached?

An effective political system might be defined as one that optimizes, for the relevant society, the production of the basic values of order and justice.[1] A "preferred world" might be defined as one in which the common goal is "the promotion and realization of four central values: (1) the minimization of large-scale collective violence; (2) the maximization of social and economic well-being; (3) the realization of human rights and conditions of political justice; and (4) the rehabilitation and maintenance of environmental quality, including the conservation of resources."[2]

In one way or another, large international firms affect all four of these values. The theories of foreign investment, of the dominant economy and of imperialism, alert us to some of these effects, especially in relation to the values of economic well-being and of political order (minimizing violence). The maintenance of human rights and conditions of political justice depends in part upon the conditions of governance within each large corporation because each such corporation is in itself a political system. It also depends in part upon the opportunities for free choice in the national political system, and here we might ask about the contribution of corporate activity to creating and maintaining such conditions. That question has been posed in the case of Chile and ITT, and we shall analyze this case in some detail, and also consider its representativeness. Nor, finally, is the question of environmental quality far removed from the study of corporate activity. Pollution is most often (though not exclusively) directly linked to the activity of the large firm. The transnational corporation, being so prominently engaged in the world distribution of petroleum by means of tankers and through off-shore mining and refinery operations, can hardly escape responsibility for pollution of the oceans, one of the key aspects of environmental deterioration and one that is rapidly becoming a major world problem. Other threats to the quality of the waters are chemical plants and their products, paper mills, and, of course, urban sewage. It is equally plain that the major cause of air pollution is auto emissions and that the auto makers, so prominent among the large firms, and among the major consumers of petroleum products, cannot be absolved from responsibility either. Steel works and power plants are other contributors to the deterioration of environmental quality, and the rising nuclear industry raises the specter of yet another set of problems. The slow progress of measures setting limits on pollution and halting the process of deterioration is a reflection of the power of the corporations.

The first selection in Part III was written in 1968, at the peak of a period of rising corporate self-confidence, by Frank Tannenbaum, then a Professor of Latin American Affairs at Columbia University. It may still be the most far-reaching set of claims for the beneficent effects of transnational economic activity on world order. Tannenbaum's main premise is that "an enduringly effective international order" cannot be built "on the political unit we know as the nation-state." The alternative base for a world order is, for him, "the extranational corporate body"—the corporation carrying out global functions. This "body," to his mind, has demonstrated vigorous growth and the capacity to fulfill such basic international functions as communications, banking, and distribution. Its ability to carry out these functions is so great as to render the nation-state functionless in its external role of providing national security. If the international corporation were to succeed in establishing itself firmly at the global level, then problems of national security would cease to exist.

Tannenbaum's theory might be regarded as an application of the functionalist thesis[3] to the case of the international firm. The functionalist sees economic, technical, and other functional tasks as necessitating the creation of international structures that would surmount the problems posed by the existence of warring nation-states. In this same way, for Tannenbaum, the fundamental tendency of an expanding global corporate system is to create the preconditions for peace, and the effect of such a system is therefore to promote basic values of world order. The international enterprise holds together the industrialized world, increases production, creates new cross-national loyalties, and exercises political powers more effectively than the nation-state.

Tannenbaum's arguments appear somewhat sanguine. They bring to mind the claims by mid-nineteenth century free traders such as Richard Cobden that broad and unfettered expansion of international commerce was the surest road to world peace. This view has also been expressed eloquently by George Ball,[4] among others, and seconded by Arnold Toynbee, the historian. Toynbee saw multinational corporations as "world citizens" already "running the world's economy because there is not a world state to run it"; this, he said, "is the way a world political organization is going to come into existence," just as the world of the *Pax Romana* came into existence some four centuries before the Roman Empire, when businessmen began operating as an economic unit.[5]

But the precise effects of international business upon the state of international relations are a matter not only of bold forecasts but also of careful analysis and cautious prognostication. Eugene Staley's *War and the Private Investor,* written in 1935, still is the most careful and the classic study of its kind—an excellent example of events analysis (see especially Chapter 13).

Staley's book was part of the University of Chicago's project on "The Causes of War"—probably the first substantial social science research enterprise in the study of international relations.[6] Staley wrote it in response to the literature on imperialism referred to in Part II. That literature had suggested the importance of the economic causes of war, and in particular that the investment process played a role in the mechanism of causation. Staley's first major finding, presented in this section, is that as a cause of war, the use (and misuse) by investors of governmental influence on their own behalf is less important and less frequent than the opposite tendency, governmental use of investors for their own purposes. His thesis casts serious doubt upon some common generalizations about the causes of war.

Staley's other important finding, based on an analysis of some three dozen cases of intergovernmental friction associated with foreign investment, is that relations among the Great Powers are not seriously affected by such problems. The profile of an investment most frequently found to be a cause of "investment friction" shows that it is made (1) by citizens of Great Powers, (2) in developing countries, (3) with special concessions, (4) for political purposes, and (5) in transportation and communication. On the whole, Staley would not expect transnational business projects to be among the significant causes of wars among the Great Powers, but he would expect them to aggravate relations between the developed and the developing countries.

This basic finding has not been challenged by contrary evidence and is as important today as it was more than four decades ago. The materials used and the events mentioned in that analysis may appear dated but they are not really so. A careful look at Table 11-1 reveals that about one-third of the companies involved in the 34 cases of international political friction are still active and indeed very much in evidence—particularly the oil companies whose history is replete with political friction. Some examples that are to this day important to an understanding of the world oil scene are the Mesopotamian oil controversy, of which the Iraq Petroleum Company was born—formed jointly by Anglo-Persian (now B.P.), Shell, New Jersey Standard (now Exxon), and the French oil major; the Mexican oil problems (Shell), the Persian troubles (Anglo-Persian), and the Soviet property confiscations (Shell, New Jersey). Staley shows (Table 11-2) that oil mining as an extractive industry should have been added to the list of types of firms likely to become objects of political friction.

The article on "Multinationalization and the Countries of Eastern Europe" is an analysis of the impact of multinationals upon the relations between the developed countries of different economic systems. It picks up the references to the dimensions of the problem in the section on "centrally planned economies" in the United Nations report in Part I but goes beyond the industrial cooperation agreements mentioned there (such as the Fiat plant construction and the Occidental Petroleum fertilizer projects) and looks at problems arising in joint production ventures that involve Western firms directly in manufacturing operations in Eastern Europe (for instance, Renault or Control Data in Rumania). Drawing in part on Marxist thought, Gutman and Arkwright (young researchers associated with a Paris center for the study of foreign policy) present a European perspective on the process of multinationalization and take into consideration the views of East European economic planners. Without too much reference to empirical data, they give an informed explanation of several of the problems arising out of this surprising (to Marxists and others) implantation of Western capitalist firms in Eastern Europe and the ways in which this process might be controlled.[7] They also draw attention to proposals made by a Hungarian economist for creating "socialist multinationals," and they raise the question: why are there no such firms in the countries of Eastern Europe? Although no progress has been made in the creation of "socialist multinationals" in Eastern Europe itself, Soviet firms (especially in shipping, banking, and oil distribution) have, in recent years, in a manner "resembling the offshoots of a Western conglomerate," begun to enter Western markets, but there is as yet no manufacturing.[8]

The value of this article lies in its analysis of the various political impacts of "multinationalization." In broad terms, the détente between the Soviet Union and the West is viewed as the manifestation of an economic necessity, and the activities of multinationals is viewed as an expression of that necessity. The effect of multinationalization on relations among the Great Powers is, therefore, as predicted by Staley, nonproblematic and possibly stabilizing. But further dissection of the problem by Gutman and Arkwright discloses some possible "domination effects" (in Perroux's terms) that might arise from the presence of multinationals in Eastern Europe.

A more complete statement of problems of the "domination effect" as seen in the context of dependency theory and as they affect Latin America is the article by Osvaldo Sunkel, a Chilean economist presently with the Institute of Development Studies, University of Sussex, England. As is now clear (and as predicted by Staley), the effects of transnational corporate activity are peculiarly evident in the developing countries. Sunkel points out that large global corporations, far from diminishing the significance of nation-states (as Tannenbaum asserted they might), have had the effect of inflaming nationalism by creating the conditions of "dependent state capitalism." Without totally excluding cooperation of the nation-state government with foreign firms, Sunkel sees the solution to the problem to be to allow greater national autonomy in order to achieve economic development without dependency in a reformed international economic system.

Sunkel's article is exemplary of the substantial literature that in the past decade or so has begun to accumulate on the subject of *dependencia*. That literature originated in Latin America, and Sunkel argues that as a result of post-1945 development policies in that area, transnational corporations have been shown to be an element in the structure of dependence, hindering development and fostering autocracy. Like Galtung, he sees changes in the present "asymmetric" international system as a prerequisite of development.

The *dependencia* theory tends to paint the big picture in broad strokes. We might mention at this point two empirical studies of the role of corporations in the economies of Latin America that suggest greater complexity. Theodore Moran's longitudinal study of relations between Chile and the copper mining corporations[9] shows that the balance of advantage might sometimes be with one party and, at other times, with the other; but in the long run, the corporations' bargaining power tends to wane. Charles Goodsell's sober if somewhat circumscribed testing of the imperialism-dependency model in the context of Peruvian politics yields similarly mixed results.[10] Goodsell shows that American corporations in Peru certainly have not shied away from politics and have sometimes sought United States diplomatic intervention on their behalf. They have also influenced public policies in a variety of ways, to their own advantage. But Goodsell claims that there was neither "grossly imperialistic domination nor politically innocent negotiation."

At the time of Goodsell's research (c. 1970), a small number of subsidiaries of American firms were among the largest in the Peruvian economy and were the biggest taxpayers. They were thus judged by Goodsell sufficiently critical to generate a considerable degree of economic dependence. But the military-revolutionary regime led by General Velasco (1968–1975) brought about a sweeping change in the treatment of American corporations, and the bulk of the irritants (including affiliates of Exxon, General Motors, Gulf, Utah International—now merged with General Electric—and ASARCO) were either nationalized or forced out of the country. By 1976, under a new government, most of the established mining activities and the local communities where they were located were state controlled, and the situation that had been described by Goodsell had changed drastically. Yet at the same time new agreements were being made for a large new copper project and for an oil venture by Occidental Petroleum. In other words, the earlier sources of dependence have been eliminated but new problems are sure to arise because of the new decisions.

Selection 14 is a detailed account of the *cause célèbre* of multinational activity of the 1970s—the involvement of the International Telephone and Telegraph Corporation (ITT), one of the world's largest and most successful transnational corporations, in the political affairs of Chile. The affair became public in March 1972, when Jack Anderson, the columnist, published a series of documents indicating that ITT was interfering in the Chilean political process. A subcommittee of the Committee on Foreign Relations of the United States Senate investigated the matter and issued the well-documented report that is reproduced here. A further repercussion of the affair was that on Chilean initiative, the subject of multinational corporations was for the first time placed on the agenda of the United Nations. In due course a new system was established to regulate the activities of multinational corporations.

The ITT-Chilean situation in 1970-1972 bore *all* the marks of "trouble" as predicted by Staley: it involved (1) citizens of a Great Power and a corporation based in the United States; (2) a developing country; a firm (ITT) (3) operating under special licenses from the host government, (4) being used by (or at least linked with) United States government agencies, (5) in the communications industry.

What the record of this case shows is that a large corporation is capable of conducting its own foreign policy: it has its own intelligence system; it has agents it can use on political missions; and it may have allies in governmental agencies and among other corporations that find themselves in similar circumstances. That ITT attempted to interfere with the Chilean electoral process is now well established.[11] What is less clear is how representative this case is of the general behavior of such corporations. The reluctance of other firms to collaborate with ITT in the Chilean venture suggests that such collaboration might be infrequent. On the other hand, corporate payments to politicians and to political parties in furtherance of somewhat illicit corporate purposes have since been revealed to be not uncommon. The several Lockheed cases (especially in Japan, Italy, and the Netherlands) involving bribery of leading political personalities, and the large political payments (by Gulf in Korea and by Exxon in Italy) show that the impact of large corporations on politics can be been quite serious and suggest the need for clearer expression and implementation of norms of corporate activity.

The ITT study is based on close analysis of company documents combined with extensive use of interview techniques (powerfully aided by the investigatory powers of a Senate subcommittee). Ronald Müller's controversial argument that poverty is the product of multinational activity draws on a large number of specialized studies by Latin American scholars and by United Nations agencies, based largely on the experience of the 1960s, to describe the effect of corporate operations on the economic welfare of institutionally weak countries south of the Rio Grande.

Müller is a professor of economics at the American University in Washington, D.C., and his basic proposition in this article is that the lesser bargaining power of the developing countries translates into excessive and exploitatitive gains for the large multinationals, and generally worsens rather than ameliorates the living conditions of the poorest 60 percent of the population of those countries. Müller cites studies done in the three specific fields where Latin American research has raised serious questions about multinational operations: technology transfer, transfer pricing, and restrictive business practices. The vaunted contribution of the great corporation, its ability to transfer technology, is shown to be a cause of unemployment and increased social inequality. The financial contribution of the corporation, on close analysis, is really a financial drain, aggravated by corporate practices that manipulate intercompany transfer prices in the interests of the maximation of global profit; a number of other corporate practices diminish export performance and have negative effects on the balance of payments.

These last three selections (all, interestingly enough, based on events and experiences in Latin America)—Sunkel on *dependencia,* the evidence on the ITT case, and Müller's analysis of the economic impacts—allow us to make a statement concerning the effects of multinationals that represents the core of the developing countries' criticism of multinationals: the need for an international system of regulating the behavior of multinational corporations is demonstrated by the problems that have largely been created by their presence.

NOTES

1. George Modelski, *Principles of World Politics* (New York: The Free Press, 1972), p. 11.
2. Richard A. Falk, *A Study of Future Worlds* (New York: The Free Press, 1975), p. 11.
3. David Mitrany, *A Working Peace System* (Chicago: Quadrangle Books, 1966).
4. "The Promise of the Multinational Corporation," *Fortune,* June 1, 1967, p. 80.
5. "Are Businessmen Creating A New Pax Romana?" *Forbes,* April 15, 1974, pp. 68-70.
6. See Quincy Wright, *A Study of War* (Chicago: Chicago University Press, 1942), Appendix A.
7. In November 1976, Vietnam announced that capitalist investment in the country would eventually be allowed and would take the form of joint ventures producing specifically for export and for the development of natural resources including oil and gas (*The Economist,* March 5, 1977, pp. 91-92). The proposed new investment code evidently drew on East European experience.
8. Herbert E. Meyer, "The Communist Internationale has a Capitalist Accent," *Fortune,* February 1977, pp. 134-148; the proposal for "socialist multinationals" was advanced by Egon Kemenes in *Acta Oeconomica,* No. 1 (1971), translated in *Problèmes Economiques* (Paris), No. 1260, February 23, 1972.
9. *Copper and Chile* (Princeton, N.J.: Princeton University Press, 1975).
10. *Peruvian Politics and American Corporations* (Cambridge, Mass.: Harvard University Press, 1974), esp. Chap. 9.
11. In addition to the measures taken by ITT, listed in the Senate Report (Conclusion), it has been revealed that "the ITT, after receiving direct advice from the C.I.A. on how to proceed, forwarded $350,000 in cash to a leading conservative candidate" before the election of 1970. *New York Times,* December 23, 1976, pp. 1, 7.

10 / The Survival of the Fittest

Frank Tannenbaum

Efforts to organize the world for peace past and present have always broken down in the end. This is a simple statement of the historical record. One cannot argue lack of good will or honesty of purpose, lack of or a genuine desire to achieve an effective international body that would take on itself the role of peace-keeping. But, as the whole world knows, successive efforts have been frustrated. The League of Nations was the latest great failure. Unhappy though it is to say, the United Nations may be headed in the same direction.

There are many reasons why this has happened. Human affairs are complicated matters. They have been shaped and influenced by a myriad of "causes" which taken together have given us our present dubious heritage—a threat of human annihilation, and an apparent inability to stem the drift towards converting the threat into an imminent convulsion. A casual evaluation of the daily record suggests that man seems to have no instrumentality at hand to reverse the armaments race or to stop him from the last decision he would probably ever be called upon to make—give the signal that would release thermonuclear warfare.

Such a possibility would only seem consistent with a world gone mad or held in the grip of individuals who lack "reason," conscience, Christian charity or ordinary common sense. In fact, there are good but worried people now in the United States who are prepared to put the 200,000,000 population underground as a security measure against such a war, and there are others who seem to accept the prospects of a loss of 20 to 30 million American lives in an effort to defeat the enemy.

The mere statement of these matters as possibilities, as reasonable things that prudent men are trying to comprehend and plan for, so as to mitigate what seems to them even greater horrors, raises fundamental questions of why this possibility is upon the world. It will not do to blame it on the scientists who learned how to split the atom and manufacture the atomic bomb. The problem is not a scientific one. It is not even primarily military. It is political because it involves the nature and function of the state itself.

The modern nation-state is of relatively recent origin. Some historians place its emergence as a result of the Reformation. Others mark its beginnings at about the time of the French Revolution, or as one of its major consequences. Be that as it may. The primary definition of the modern nation-state is that it can protect its citizens from external attack and maintain internal order. The emphasis upon protection from external aggression has most clearly set the tone and defined the character of the modern state. Nationalism, in fact, and all that goes with it require the ability to keep the state absolutely sovereign, which in essence means the ability to impede any intrustion upon its territory, interests or dignity.

In a world of competitive nation-states, such as Europe represented after the Reformation when France and Spain were expanding and consolidating their future at the expense of their neighbors, and after the French Revolution when France was trying to impose its rule upon the rest of Europe, questions of national security became the prime consideration. The First and the Second World Wars were logical by-products of this system; so is the Cold War; so is the armaments race; so are the struggles in various parts of the world that have followed the Second World War. In each case the attack is against a "sovereign nation" to subjugate it, to impose upon it another loyalty, and even another system. Fear of conquest governs the political attitude of all nation-states toward the rest of its world.

The many alliances, treaties, understandings, mutual defense pacts, disarmament meetings, peace congresses, and international courts undertaken because of security considerations have all failed in the end. The history of the sovereign state is a bloody one and it could not be otherwise. A state absolutely sovereign as Thomas Hobbes saw it, accepting no infringements on its rights, confined in a geographic boundary, beset by enemies equally sovereign, equally ambitious and presumably equally well or better armed could only be at war or preparing for war. The nation-state system is intrinsically unstable and the prospect of war is ever present. The improved weapons placed in its hands by the new technology have merely increased the size and the human and material costs of warfare.

The attempts to form international organizations have not seriously changed the nature of the system or the relations of the states to each other. The League of Nations witnessed Mussolini's attack upon Ethiopia, Japan's invasion of China, the Chaco War in South America and other conflicts as well. The United Nations have seen numerous small wars, the blockade of Berlin, the Korean War, the war in Vietnam, the very real danger of a war between Greece and Turkey and the conflagrations in the Middle East, to mention only a few of the more evident examples. And one should not forget the confrontation over Cuba between the United States and Russia.

An organization of the world made up of sovereign states is not a satisfactory base for maintaining international stability. Each member in any real crisis, or even in lesser matters, behaves as a nation-state; when it takes a position in the United Nations on any subject, it does so in accord with its conception of its own interests. Every debate, every vote, every speech reflects this outstanding fact. Anyone who listened to the debate over the recent war in the Middle East will testify that not a single state put the international order before its own national interest, nor could it do so. The nation-state system by the very nature of its overriding involvement in the question of national security cannot act otherwise. Unfortunate though it may be, there is no evidence that an enduringly effective international order can be built on the political unit we know as the nation-state.

It is not that having described the impasse men and nations find themselves in that I have the answer. I wish I did. The question is of an order to which no answer can be invented. The history, traditions and manner of thought of the last five hundred or more years underlie the present situation. The horror it implies for human destiny is the ossification and obliteration of mankind. Surely not even the vision of the Apocalypse was more convulsive than the horror hidden in the "balance of terror" between the great powers. And all of this is upon us because of the state's search for absolute security—which it is still pursuing and which it must pursue while it exists. How much longer will the national political state survive—(if it is not destroyed by the atomic bomb)—another five hundred years? Probably not. If it can *not* supply protection for its citizens, it has lost its major reason for being. This applies to both the little and the big nation. Nor as we have seen, can the state build a viable international order. Its nationalism stands in the way. It has no possibility of doing so.

If, as some assume, the movement towards European unity suggests a decline of nationalism, then in the present state of affairs it would simply be replaced by a larger nationalism. The appearance of an all-European nationalism would not necessarily advance an international organization; it might even make it more difficult to approve the surrender of a larger sovereignty which would be involved. The point really is that international organization cannot be built on the nation, or a combination of nations with national characteristics; it must have a different genesis.

An Alternative Base

If such a base could be found upon which to build an extra-national political institution, then indeed the external role of the nation-state would decline and gradually disappear and the problems of security—national security—would become meaningless. Security for the nation would exist because no one would bother about it just as no one now fusses about religious orders, even those that have an ancient military history. This must sound like the wildest sort of dream, like the emanations of some Utopian prophet with no sense of the real world and therefore irrelevant. I wish it were irrelevant. Then the problem it tries to deal with would no longer exist. But it does exist and it cannot be solved. It can only be bypassed and allowed to wither away. The threat to the security of the nation-state must first become meaningless before the present danger of atomic weapons can come to seem irrelevant to the needs of mankind. The arms cannot be destroyed as long as there is danger to the security of the state. The threat to national security must become meaningless before the sword will be beaten into plowshares.

This seemingly impossible idea, of a disappearing security problem because the nation-state can no longer provide it, is a daily growing phenomenon going unnoticed. If the nation-state can no longer protect its own against annihilation from the outside, it in fact becomes functionless but that in itself would not create the supra-national order. If we are ever going to have an international order, then it will have to rest upon some other base, preferably one that is extra-national by its very nature; one that bypasses the problem of national security. Such a base does exist and is growing stronger and more inclusive with every day that passes. It comes from an existing and expanding body of international organizations which are multiplying daily in function and number. They are supra-national in their very existence, plan and purpose. Their managers, governors, authorities think in extra-national terms; their personnel is indifferent to the nation-state except as an impediment.

This extra-national body is the corporation—the extra-national corporate body as I would prefer to call it. Others have called it the multinational corporation—or even the "cosmocorp." It is natural because it has its origin in performing a needed function. It is as natural as was the slow growth of a trading and commercial community that in the end created the nation-state as a substitute for medieval order.

Other extra-national institutions have long existed. Religious bodies like the Roman Catholic Church, the Greek Orthodox Church, scientific bodies, the International Red Cross and hundreds of other corporate bodies exercise jurisdiction over property, have thousands of employees, have contractual relations in a hundred different countries, have their own internal systems of discipline, their own police force and administrative arrangements. They make rules and regulations that affect the lives, comfort, convenience and fortune of thousands of people in many parts of the earth. These bodies govern the enterprise under their control and in doing so, exercise powers that border on the sovereign.

None of these religious or eleemosynary organizations have demonstrated the vitality and growth of the ubiquitous business corporation. An international telephone company provides a good example of a business penetrating national considerations. It is indifferent to national boundaries and unconcerned about national security. It becomes aware of the state for the most part as an impediment, an obstruction. Its servants are only involved in fulfilling a function wherever it needs to be satisfied: in the Sahara, Switzerland, Vietnam or Paraguay. This is equally true of the international airline company. Its pilots, mechanics, ticket agents, financiers, passengers, may come from any and all places. Its concern is with speed, safety, schedules, costs, landing fields, trained pilots, weather control, absolutely effective communication. The questions that bother the nation-state—security, national interest, customs, tariffs, fear of invasions, danger of violations of the border are in this instance matters of irritation or indifference. Those same considerations apply to international banks, to some of the large manufacturing and distribution companies like Unilever, Philips Lamp, Standard Oil Company (New Jersey), Shell and others.

When an international airline company decides to establish a terminal in a new "nation" for the first time, it has performed an act of greater import to the body politic of that nation than most acts of the government. When an international bank decides to make a loan, it exercises a judgment, the political consequences of which may prove great indeed—it may save the government from being overthrown, or it may stimulate an industry that will provide employment for many, increase the national income and raise the standard of living of all.

When an international oil company opens up an oil field, as has happened in Venezuela or Iran, it may change the face of the nation and lay the foundations of a modern society. In doing so it exercises authority equal to, or in some instances greater than, the local government. It makes contracts, acquires land, lays pipelines, brings in shipping, develops communications, roads, builds schools, brings in a great variety of skills which are gradually passed on to the local population, changes the social structure of the body politic, stimulates a labor movement, a skilled working class, a middle class of distributors, a wealthy class of lawyers, politicians and local participants; and by the royalties and taxes it pays permits the government for the first time in its history to perform those services expected of it in a modern society. The government can build schools, expand its university, develop a national road system, etc. The powers of the corporate body are very great but its influence upon the society in which it operates may be greater. The acts of a supranational corporate body have in effect the characteristics of a sovereign state; they may be unavoidable—such as the need for the right of way for a pipeline which has to be provided or the corporate body will not be able to function in this place, just as the government cannot build a highway unless its legislature will authorize the funds and the courts uphold the rights of eminent domain.

The international oil corporation, the international communications corporation, the international bank are natural bodies. They are called into being by the need in our time for the function which they and they alone can perform. The modern world is their presence. They are the essence of the extra-national system that has grown and expanded at a rate faster than the population explosion, or literary output or whatever. In that sense they perform functions more essential than that of sovereignty, or better perhaps, functions that only they can perform and without which the modern state would be seriously crippled. And these functions have to be performed by an international corporate body and cannot be performed by any other agency. The nation-state cannot run the international tele-communications system, or the international airline system, or the international distributing system.

These are private institutions operating for a profit. The profit is the wage that keeps the system going. The function is public, essential and indispensable if the people living in the nation are to share the growing exchange of goods, ideas and people. The picutre is obscured by the presence of a few large nation-state powers like the United States or Russia. They seemingly could do many things for themselves, perhaps not as efficiently or effectively, but the smaller political bodies in Latin America, in Europe, in Africa and Asia are completely dependent upon the "sovereign" corporate body—the international banking system, the international oil industry, the international communications system—for their participation in the world. And when an international corporate body decides to build an airfield in a small African or Asian country, it in fact exercises an act of sovereignty—no one can compel it to do so and local government can only stop it from doing so to its own disadvantage and increasing isolation in the modern world. Such an act would be equivalent to a defeat in a war.

An Extra-National Commitment

This corporate body of which we have been speaking is increasing in number, in power, in prestige, in size, in the areas of modern enterprise that it embraces. Its purpose is service—in response to manifest needs—and it has a "life everlasting" as long as the service needs to be performed. Its ownership is irrelevant, for the owner does not either manage or control it except in legal fiction, and it can be owned by people all over the globe. Its management can be drawn from wherever competence is to be found; its profits may be distributed among owners in all nations; its technical personnel and labor force can be, and often are, completely international.

Equally, or more significant, the international corporate body is devoted to the performance of an international function. Its total commitment is extra-national. It has no concern with boundaries, national interest, local cultural pride, regional idiosyncrasies except only as they favor or hinder the performance of the function for which the corporate body has come into existence. This international corporate body is thus autonomous within the state where it operates. It draws its capital, finance, skill, material from wherever it finds it. It is at the service of the nation but is not of it. Its life will go on when the present government has fallen, when the state even has changed its character by merger, annexation, defeat or whatever.

The international communication corporations will go on no matter what the political map will look like fifty years from now. The functional service is more durable than the political form or territorial prescription. The telephone system operates in both East and

West Germany, in both North and South Korea. The international corporate body is in fact extra-national and stands indifferent to it. Its personnel thinks, plans, and operates on a supra-national basis. The international corporate body "governs" functionally across all borders wherever it has found a natural role, a service it alone can provide.

We thus really have two systems of "sovereignty" in the world: the state, large and small, and the supra-national corporate body. The first is on the defensive, probably on the decline, troubled by fear, anxious over its security, living by permission of those who could annihilate it on any day. Even the great powers stand in fear that the "balance of terror" will break down or that some fallible human being will miscalculate and blunder to produce a cataclysm which may see the end of all life on the face of the earth.

The nation-state has tried to build an international system for its own salvation but has always failed. Its commitment to absolute sovereignty has impeded its ability to contrive an extra-national body which would submerge and limit the state. If we live by the experience of the past, the modern nation-state cannot build an extra-national body to its own undoing as a nation-state bent on security above all else.

The second "sovereignty" is the extra-national corporate body. It is growing in number, size, influence, power, functions and independence. Excepting for the very great powers, the smaller nations are increasingly dependent upon the extra-national corporate body for the means of economic development, if not for survival. These corporate bodies are service organizations that perform their essential functions for a fee—such as interest on a bank loan, or a profit on oil distribution. They are apolitical but possess great political influence if not political power. Their international character makes them indifferent to local political squabbles. Their supra-national structure places them beyond the need for national security so essential to the state. They have one great vulnerability.

Clearly, if the state manages to blunder into a holocaust which consumes the races of men that people the earth, then the international corporate bodies will go down the stream and be washed away as if they had never existed. But if we assume that life is carried by some creative impulse that will not die, that man has always contrived a new structure when the old one was worn out, when it could no longer provide for, and protect those whom it was meant to serve, then one would expect what has happened in the past to be repeated in the present impasse. The extra-national corporate body would seem the logical basis for the contrivance of a non-military supra-national order.

Precedents

This is a strange destiny for the corporation. But primitive instances of it have been seen in the past: the Knights Templar and the Hanseatic League, for example. These functioned well for a time within the boundaries of the then known world. The reduction of the earth to the size of a large ancient parish with many autonomous governments makes the supra-national corporate body the natural bond between them. The speed of communication, the increased mobility and proliferation of the sciences make corporate organization increasingly evident, necessary and inevitable.

An industrialized world is held together by the large number of corporate bodies and by their widening role. The corporation groups the nationals into a new loyalty—a functional identity across all borders. The day may well come when the majority of people in all nations will have their functional loyalties to one or more supra-national corporate bodies. They may well become conscious of basic commitments, values and interests unrelated to the state or the nation.

This is probably inevitable if the industrial and technological upheaval works its way as it seems bound to do. The international corporate bodies would have differences with other similar organizations. But the differences would have little to do with nationalism or military security. What seems implicit in this development is a new supra-national order based not upon the state obsessed by security needs but resting on the naturally extra-national bodies that are visibly enveloping men and states over a large portion of the globe.

Time is the essence of change and transition. How long will it take for the corporate body to be so evidently the international structure as to make the formal legal organs contrived by the nation-state irrelevant because the state itself will become irrelevant to international dealings? It took many centuries before the commercial revolution gradually evolved a middle class that found the feudal order unacceptable and gradually contrived the nation-state to serve its ends. One cannot assume that so profound a structural change as here envisaged can go on without political implications, and without a shift in political power. It is difficult to see the way this shift of political power will occur—but that it will take place there can be no doubt. It would have been equally difficult to foresee the modern state in the glories of a feudal society.

How long will it take? Will the nation-state hold on long enough to permit this to occur or will it destroy itself and mankind as well? What about Russia and China? The answer here, I think, is clear. If Russia and China are going to become industrialized in the sense that the United States is industrialized, then they will go the same way—the international corporate body will reach over into the closed state as in some measure it already does. The international corporate body is a natural functional institution and it can only be kept from its role if there is no extensive industrial development. In either case the closed communist or the non-communist states will either destroy each other or persevere long enough to allow the unforeseen growth of the international corporate body to take on the requisite political role and bypass the problem of security while leaving to the state the police powers for internal civil needs.

This is the major issue confronting mankind. It is a question of time and no one can say whether man will allow himself the mercy of surviving long enough to find a way of transferring international political powers to the corporate bodies that have come into being unwittingly and whose commitments are primarily functional, to render service where it is needed—indifferent and untroubled by the issues of national security and sovereignty.

11 / Conditions Under Which Investments Are Most Frequently Involved in Political Friction

Eugene Staley

Under what circumstances do private investments most often become involved in international political difficulties, and why? What are the basic conflicts back of the investment aspects of the so-called economic causes of war? Why do these conflicts sometimes take the form of clashes between organized national states? These are some of the theoretically interesting and tremendously practical questions with which it is proposed to deal. . . . The present chapter will examine the circumstances under which private investments have been centers of political friction, with the object of ascertaining why certain situations and certain types of investment produce more such difficulties than others.

First, . . . has the use of private investments in the service of diplomacy tended to create more dangerous or less dangerous situations than the use of diplomacy in the service of private investments? A careful answer to this question cannot be made without the important qualification that the distinction between investments as tools of foreign policy and as determinants of foreign policy, when presented in sharp focus for the sake of clarity of analysis, inevitably departs more or less from reality. We know . . . that these two political rôles of private investment are usually interwoven to some degree. It would be a mistake, therefore, to imply that a clear-cut distinction can be made between investment friction[1] arising out of the use of private capital as a tool of diplomacy and investment friction connected with the use of diplomacy as a tool of private capital. The foreign policies of states and the foreign investments of their citizens mutually influence and condition one another. Nevertheless, there are certain observations about this mutual conditioning in relation to international political friction which are important, partly because, while based on concrete case studies, they are not altogether in line with what some theoretical writers on the "economic causes of war" have prepared us to expect.

There have been many more serious cases of investment friction between strong states where the predominant rôle of the investments has been that of tools than where private capital has played the part of instigator of a friction-causing policy. Recall the Franco-

From Eugene Staley, *War and the Private Investor* (Chicago: The University of Chicago Press, copyright © 1935), pp. 357–388. Reprinted by permission of the publisher. Some notes have been omitted, and the remainder renumbered in sequence. Tables have been renumbered.

Italian clash over Tunis, the Turco-Italian war over Tripoli, the penetration of the Yalu by Russia before the Russo-Japanese War, the tensions between England and Russia in Persia, Japanese operations in Manchuria, and many similar cases. . . . Cases of the other type—that is, in which investors, for the sake of profits, have directly brought major powers into serious political friction—are much more rare. Samoa seems to offer one. The German private debts may be, to a limited extent, another. Perhaps the Boer War might be included here (with its preliminaries of the Jameson Raid, etc.), though we have noted that it would be very questionable to classify the leader of the South African financiers, Cecil Rhodes, as predominantly profit-seeker rather than political empire builder. Furthermore, the Boer War was not between two major powers, though it did have European repercussions, especially on Anglo-German relations. Should the political friction among Germany, France, England, and Russia which centered about the Bagdad railway be counted as instigated by the activities of profit-seeking investors? Certainly that was part of the complex of causes, but it can hardly be called the predominant one. The political fears, ambitions, and strategies of statesmen, which made the railway a pawn in the game of *haute politique* and the balance of power, were much more decisive in determining that it should become a friction center than were any interests or attitudes of the capitalists themselves. Indeed, these latter could have reached compromises among themselves several times had it not been for the political interests of their governments. The Mannesmann brothers with their mining claims in Morocco, and the Lynch Brothers with their navigation monopoly in the Near East, were material factors in making it difficult for governments to settle certain disputes, but in both cases the political clashes stemmed from quite other roots than investment conflicts, while in one if not both the investments had begun as tools of diplomacy and later began to add their own aggravations to the situation. Numerous interventions, like those practiced by the United States in Nicaragua, Cuba, and the Caribbean generally, have had a mixed background of investment and strategic political interest, but these have usually not involved clashes between major powers. Where there has been really serious friction between major powers over investment matters, examination will disclose in most instances that the political opposition existed before the investment issues arose, and either expressed itself through them or crystallized around them.

Also, conflicts over private investment matters between strong states have rarely, almost never, reached a state of dangerous international tension except in cases where the states involved have been pursuing some political policy (extraneous to the investment affair itself) which has led them into conflict. Investments have become involved in dangerous international disputes mainly where political clashes existed already, and the investments offered a field of battle, or new weapons, for the further prosecution of the already existing conflict. In other words, private investments seeking purely business advantage (i.e., unmotivated by political expansionism, balance of power strategy, military considerations, or other reasons of state) have rarely of themselves brought great powers into serious political clashes. It is where an aura of political ambitions has attached to the investments, and especially where the investments have been pushed in for political reasons from the start, that most of the dangerous investment frictions between great states have occurred.

This is the factual situation, revealed by the investigation of concrete cases. If one seeks to account for these facts, the most useful explanation will run in terms of the way in which those in charge of foreign policies apply the principle of national advantage. Desires of investors in harmony with established lines of national foreign policy receive enthusiastic governmental support. Desires of investors which run counter to established lines of national foreign policy receive hesitant or grudging support, no support at all, or active opposition. This is an important general principle of wide application. Now, it is characteristic of modern international relations that those lines of foreign policy which the governors of national states at any particular time conceive to be in the highest national interest are almost certain to be based on considerations of power. National power is generally regarded not only as the *sine qua non* of prideful national existence, but as a sacred necessity in order to provide security against attack. Just as the military and naval expenditures of states comprise the largest items in their governmental budgets, so power ranks highest among the conscious or unconscious objectives of statesmen who determine foreign policy. This gives greatest weight to questions of military and naval strategy (including territorial bases, lines of communication, and the like), alliance politics, and "prestige" in general. This latter is an extremely important phase, not only of national pride, but of actual power, for it enables statesmen to win battles without fighting and is generally believed by them to constitute the best insurance against military attack or political pressure from without. Prestige is a compound of such various elements as military strength, past history, political alliances, colonial conquest, industrial productivity, and success of nationals in foreign commerce—those things which nationalists regard as essential to prevent their country from becoming a "second-rate" nation. Economic development, including economic expansion abroad, has been increasingly recognized by governments as a cardinal factor in a nation's prestige and hence in its power, not to speak of the direct relationship between certain aspects of economic development and military power itself. Economic expansion abroad, however, is only one phase of that complex called national prestige and power, and the interests of particular private investors abroad may be minor items in the whole. When the vigorous promotion and protection of private investment interests abroad seems to the governors of national states to offer an occasion for increasing the general power and prestige of the nation, they are ordinarily eager to assist. They are often more eager than the investors themselves, as we have seen in a great many cases. But when for any reason a clash arises between the particular investment interests of citizens abroad and some of the other constituents of national power enumerated above, the least "vital" will be sacrificed. Private investment interests have usually, in actual practice, been subordinated by governments to factors of general political or military strategy which have a more direct bearing on power. Thus it is that private investors have received strong, even outrageously exaggerated governmental backing where they have been tools and agents of power and prestige politics; while other investors, whose projects seemed to run counter to the government's line of political endeavor, have experienced official indifference or even active opposition. A few concrete examples follow:

> The British government, for the sake of the political advantage of maintaining the goodwill of the United States, in 1913 influenced its oil magnate, Lord Cowdray, to drop projects on which he had embarked in Mexico, Columbia, and other Latin-American countries. At the same time the same government was encouraging its oil men in other parts of the world, and had previously been aiding Cowdray, also, who had a contract for supplying oil to the British navy. The pressure from the United States was bound up with general questions of Mexican policy, which then were acute due to the revolution, with the Panama Canal tolls question, and with President Wilson's doctrine enunciated in his Mobile speech (October 27, 1913)

that economic concessions as well as territorial acquisitions might imperil a country's autonomy and would have to be considered by the United States in upholding
its Monroe Doctrine. It was Ambassador Page in London through whom these
views were pressed upon the British government, and he wrote to Wilson that "the
real meaning of concessions" at last began to get into the heads of those in control,
whereupon they "pulled Cowdray out of Columbia and Nicaragua—granting the
application of the Monroe Doctrine to concessions that might imperil a country's
autonomy." To Colonel House, Wilson's confidential adviser, Page reported: "Lord
Cowdray has been to see me for four successive days. I have a suspicion (though I
don't know) that, instead of his running the Government, the Government has now
turned the tables and is running him. . . . He told me this morning that he (through
Lord Murray) had withdrawn the request for any concession in Colombia." Later
Page added that "Cowdray has, I am sure, lost (that is, failed to make) a hundred
million dollars that he had within easy reach by this Wilson Doctrine, but he's
game."

It appears that the American government was ready to show a similar consideration toward the British when in 1927 the Kingdom of Abyssinia moved to extricate itself from the political domination of England, Italy, and France by drawing
in "neutral" American capital for the construction of a dam at Lake Tana on the
headwaters of the Blue Nile. Dr. Martin Workener, as a personal representative of
the Abyssinian sovereign, Ras Raffari, journeyed to New York, where he interested
the White Engineering Corporation. In Washington he talked with Secretary of
State Kellogg and was told that the American government could regard the project
favorably only if assurances were given that no slave labor would be employed and
if it were agreeable to Great Britain. Britain had a special interest in the Tana
Lake region as strong or stronger than that claimed by the United States in Latin
America, for out of it flowed the waters that gave life to Egypt. The appeal to
American capital probably did improve Abyssinia's bargaining position when final
arrangements came to be made, but the United States showed no inclination to
support its investors in any arrangements that would alarm Britain.

．　．　．

In France, "above and beyond all other considerations which induced French
official intervention with the movement of French capital abroad was the wish to
make the investment serve the political purposes of the state." The Minister of
Foreign Affairs, announcing the rejection of an application by French bankers for
official listing of bounds of the Crédit Foncier Cubain, explained, "When a request
is addressed to the government, it is examined with an appreciation of the financial
interest and French political interests . . . in all requests the French interest should
take precedence over the financial interest. . . ." Likewise, in the protection of
investments once made, heavy losses to investors caused by the action of certain
Latin-American states where France had no pressing political concerns brought
only mild measures, while much less serious interference with French private interests in Turkey were seized upon as the occasion for a naval demonstration and
political demands. "Eager as it was to protect its investors, influential as these
investors were in official circles, it was in a measuring of political advantage or
disadvantages that the government found its primary guide.

．　．　．

The illuminating article on "The Relation of Government to Foreign Investment" by a former United States Assistant Secretary of State . . . expounds frankly

the doctrine which has been followed in practice by most governments. Subtle calculation of national advantage, which depends, of course, upon the political objectives of the government, "is the first measure, as the citizens' right is the second measure of the government's support. The government's obligation is its duty to the citizen, but the coefficient of that duty is its duty to the nation." Thus, an American who jumps into a pet preserve of Great Britain or France and engages in enterprises subversive of some policy of theirs would not be abandoned entirely to his fate if his enterprise suffered, but the United States would merely seek equitable damages for him, not specific performance. When American financial advisers were forced out of Persia by Russia and England, a case of this kind arose, and since American influence in Persia was not an important national interest the proper policy was to secure an equitable adjustment doing justice in a general way to the American citizens. "If, on the other hand, those advisers had been in a country where American influence was of national importance, the American government must have resisted their dismissal and insisted upon specific performance, although the contracts were no more binding in the one case than in the other."[2] This explains why the difficulties of American investors in the region of the Panama Canal are much more likely to bring strong action from Washington than exactly similar difficulties elsewhere. "In the encouragement of American enterprises abroad," writes E. M. Borchard, "the government lends its support to such as are legitimate and nationally beneficial, the degree of support being measured by the national advantage to be expected."[3]

Thus far the discussion has concerned international investment friction among the major powers, that is, usually, between capital-exporting countries. The situation is not exactly the same with respect to the relationship between a capital-importing and a capital-exporting country, particularly where that relationship has been in practice, one between a relatively weak and a relatively strong country. The political relations of capital-importer with capital-exporter seem to have been more subject to disturbance by the direct influence of investment difficulties than have the relations between rival capital-exporters. That is, the relations between the United States and Mexico, for example, have been influenced much more powerfully and directly by the interests of private investors than have the relations between the United States and Great Britain. Thus, private investments have been important as instigators (as distinguished from tools) of diplomatic action mainly in connection with the relations of relatively weak capital-importing countries with relatively strong capital-exporting countries.

The reason for this is twofold. In the first place, governments apply the test of political expediency in their decisions as to the extent and manner of the support which shall be given to investors abroad, and political expediency is much more likely to approve strong measures where the resistance will come only from a relatively weak, capital-importing country, than where strong support of the investor would mean a clash with another major power (another capital-exporting country). Secondly, the potential sources of investment conflict between capital-investing and capital-receiving regions or groups are themselves more numerous, intense, direct, and lasting than those between rival capital-investing regions or groups. The reference here is to basic economic conflicts. Rival lending regions may find themselves in conflict over opportunities for the profitable investment of their capital or over priority of repayment, but the process of international investment establishes between a capital-importing and a capital-exporting country a relatively permanent capital-labor conflict, a creditor-debtor conflict, a conflict of vested interests with groups interested in social reform or revolution, not to speak of cultural conflicts unleashed by the industrialization which accompanies capital investment. . . .

It is also true that those cases of international investment friction involving mainly diplomacy in the service of private investment (as distinguished from private investment in the service of diplomacy) have as a rule tended toward less serious disturbances of the peace than have cases of the other type. This follows simply from the fact that the powers of resistance of the relatively undeveloped capital-importing countries have not been great enough to produce wars of major magnitude, while foreign policy has been most subject to investment influence in connection with conflicts involving just such countries. Interventions to protect lives and property, imposition of laws and governmental policies favorable to alien investors, arbitrary settlement of investment conflicts by ultimatum, outright conquest, colonization, or political subjection, have often taken place in the past without resulting in disturbances called by the name of war, because one party was too weak to put up a noteworthy resistance against the other.

The relative importance of the two processes by which international private investments become involved in political frictions—that is, as tools of diplomacy and as instigators of diplomacy—may be different in the future. In the first place, the momentum of political expansionism by the great powers, leading to the acquisition of colonies and spheres of influence, achieved by methods of penetration which involve private investments, may be running down. Most of the politically "vacant" territory which Western national states have been engaged in appropriating for themselves during the last half-century is now occupied. Secondly, the capital-importing countries are growing stronger, and as their powers of defense and attack increase with increasing industrialization the disputes which arise between them and the capital-exporting countries will cease to be petty. Since political expansionism by the great powers typically involves private investments as tools of policy, while the instigation of political friction by private investments is relatively more frequent between capital-exporting countries and those that receive capital, the two developments mentioned above may magnify the rôle of private investments as determinants rather than tools of policy.

Thus far we have been asking, What processes have brought private investments into international political friction? Now we turn to a second question, to which the remainder of this chapter is devoted: What types of private investments have been most frequently and characteristically associated with international political friction?

First of all, it is well to make explicit the easily observable fact that the mere size of the foreign investments in a particular country has no direct relationship to the political significance of the investments or to the political friction which may develop around them. In fact, if the coefficient of correlation could be calculated between the intensity of international investment friction in different regions and the amounts of foreign investment in those regions, the coefficient would certainly be negative. That is, the countries with the largest amounts of foreign capital within their borders have, on the whole, the least political trouble over that capital. . . . Note that the largest total sums of foreign capital are found in Canada, the United States, and Australia. Then recall some of those areas which have figured most strikingly in . . . investment friction cases . . .: Morocco, Tunis, Egypt, Haiti, China, Persia, Nicaragua, Turkey, Samoa, Mexico, Albania. In most of these countries the total amount of foreign investment has been relatively small, in some quite insignificant compared with world totals. It should not be implied, however, that the connection between relatively small amounts of foreign capital and political friction over investments, or between larger amounts and the absence of such friction, is a causal one. Rather, some of the same circumstances which set the stage for political friction over investments also operate to keep the total amount of investment small. The point is that the political significance of international investments in any particular country does not depend upon the amounts invested, but upon the conditions which surround the investments.

As an aid to the discovery of significant surrounding conditions which determine whether investments are likely to be involved in political friction or not, an analysis of some thirty friction cases . . . is tabulated in Table 11-1 and summarized in Table 11-2. The method for the selection of these cases was simple and free from conscious bias. It consisted . . . of listing for examination as nearly as possible all the cases in recent times— roughly, within a half-century or so—in which anyone has alleged that international private investments played a significant part in international political friction. Those cases on which enough information was available and which seemed on examination to be rather serious instances of investment friction (involving *private* investments . . .) found their way into this tabultaion. The result is presented here in full consciousness of the unavoidable defects in such an attempt at quantitative analysis—the problem of weighting, for example, and the necessary reliance upon personal judgment in deciding how a given case should be classified. Yet what are the alternatives to the conscious compilation and open presentation of such an analysis? Either no attempt at all to decide what types of private investment have been most characteristically involved in political friction, or the presentation of conclusions arrived at by some unconscious process not clear to the reader (or to the author) and probably more dogmatically asserted because less carefully scrutinized.

Table 11-1 lists thirty-four instances of international investment friction from all parts of the world, some of them single episodes, others long-continued tensions, and shows what types of private investment were mainly involved in each instance. . . . The summary in connection with Table 11-2, . . . will serve as a key to the symbols at the head of the columns in Table 11-1.

The cases of Tables 11-1 and 11-2 designated by the letter "A" are those in which the political friction existed mainly between two or more capital-exporting countries interested in one and the same investment area, while the letter "B" designates cases of trouble between a capital-import area and the country or countries from which it has received capital. Of course, in some cases (marked "AB" in Table 11-1) both kinds of political friction appeared in connection with private investments from abroad. The cases containing "A" friction (22 in number), and the cases containing "B" friction (also, as it happens, 22 in number) are summarized separately in Table 11-2, . . .

Certain striking facts emerge from an inspection of these tabulations. In the first place, all the cases of international investment friction included in this analysis, with two exceptions, center about the holdings of citizens of the major powers. The cases were not intentionally so selected. Such a result follows, no doubt, from the fact that the major powers have been the chief capital exporters, but it is still noteworthy that the rather considerable investments of citizens of Switzerland, Holland, Denmark, Sweden, and other countries not major political and military powers have hardly ever been centers of serious international political friction.[4] Secondly, international investment friction has occurred almost exclusively in connection with investments in nonindustrialized areas of weak, unstable government—the so-called "backward" countries. This has been true of

Table 11-1 Types of International Private Investment Chiefly Involved in Thirty-four Cases of International Political Friction

Types of Investment Chiefly Involved (See classification in text for symbols)

	Type of Friction (A—Between Capital-Export Countries; B—Between Capital-Export and Capital-Import Countries)	I Migration of Management				II Politico-Economic Character of Receiving Area			III Employment of Investment					IV Political Character of Providing Area		V Objects Sought by Investment			
		1	2a	2b	2c	1	2	3	1	2	3	4	5	1	2	1	2a	2b	2c
Abyssinia	AB			×				×	×	×				×		×	×	×	
Albania	A			×				×	×	×				×		×	×	×	
Bagdad Railway	A			×				×	×	×			×	×		×		×	×
Balkan Railways	A			×				×	×	×				×		×			
China—Japan in Manchuria	AB			×	×			×	×	×			×	×			×	×	
China—Russia in Manchuria	AB			×	×			×	×	×		×		×			×		
China—Germany in China	AB		×	×				×	×	×	×			×				×	
China—Britain in China	AB		×	×				×	×	×	×			×			×	×	
China—United States in China	AB		×	×				×	×	×			×	×		×		×	
China—French in South China	AB		×	×				×	×	×	×		×	×		×		×	
China—Strikes, boycotts, friction connected with industrialization	B		×						×	×		×		×		×			
Colombia—oil	B			×				×	×	×	×			×		×			
European expansion in Central Africa	A				×			×	×	×	×			×	×	×		×	×

German Private Debts	B
Italy and Rival Alliances	A
Mesopotamian oil	A
Mexico—oil and land laws	B
Mexico—isthmus of Tehuantepec	B
Morocco	A
N'Goko Sangha, etc. in Congo	A
Nicaragua	B
Persia—tobacco concession	B
Persia—Anglo-Russian Rivalry	A
Persia—Anglo-Persian oil difficulties (1932-3)	B
Rumania—oil and land laws	B
Saar District	AB
Samoa	A
South Africa—Jameson Raid, Boer War	B
Soviet Russia—Friction with Powers over Property Confiscation	B
Tripoli	AB
Tunis	A
United States "Economic Imperialism" and resulting Ill-Will in Latin America	B
Venezuela—European Intervention, United States Assertion of Monroe Doctrine	AB
Yalu—Russo-Japanese Conflict	A

Table 11-2 Frequency of Occurrence of Various Types of International Private Investment
in the Friction Cases of Table 11-1

	Number of times found associated with friction	
	Of Type "A"	Of Type "B"

Types of investment
Classified according to:

	Of Type "A"	Of Type "B"
I. Migration or Non-Migration of Management		
1. Loans not conferring control—"portfolio investment"	1[a]	1[b]
2. Direct investment (total of sub-types a, b, c when duplications eliminated)	22	22
a. Under general laws	(9)	(15)
b. Under special concessions	(18)	(17)
c. Under government by investor, in unorganized territory (Chartereds)	(5)	(2)
II. Politico-Economic Characteristics of Investment Area		
1. "Old" countries—industrialized, politically highly organized, capitalistic	2[c]	3[d]
2. "New" countries—undeveloped, but possessing industrial techniques, relatively stable political organization of Western European type	0	3
3. "Backward" countries—non-industrialized, lacking techniques and political organization of Western European type, having weak or unstable government	20	17
III. Employment of Investment		
1. Trade and commerce	9	11
2. Transportation and communication	15	13
3. Extractive industries (mining, lumber, oil)	13	15
4. Manufacturing	2	5
5. Finance (banking, mortgage companies, etc.)	9	8
IV. Political Characteristics of Capital-Providing Area		
1. Investments by citizens of great powers	22	22
2. Investments by citizens of lesser powers	1[e]	1[b]
V. Objects Sought by Investment		
1. Private profit, business only	14	18
2. Patriotic investments (total of sub-types a, b, c, when duplications eliminated)	20	15
a. Subsidized by investor's government	(11)	(6)
b. Stimulated by it, not subsidized	(18)	(13)
c. Stimulated by patriotic, expansionist visions of individuals, colonial societies, etc.	(3)	(1)

[a] *Italy and rival alliances.*
[b] *German private debts.*
[c] *Saar, Italy and rival alliances.*
[d] *Soviet Russia, Saar, German private debts.*
[e] *Belgian investments in Congo.*

the "B" cases and still more true of the "A" cases. Only four cases out of the thirty-four here studied, in fact, have involved private investments in "advanced" countries.

Third, the tabulations under heading I of Table 11-2 show that those private investments in which management and entrepreneurship, as well as capital itself, crossed national boundaries (direct investments) have been much more prolific of political disputes than have loans to foreign corporations or foreign entrepreneurs. This finding is associated with the previous observation that investment friction characteristically develops in "backward" countries, for management and entrepreneurship always accompanies private capital exports to such regions, while the purchase of foreign corporation bonds or of less than controlling interests in foreign enterprises is typical only of capital exports to relatively "advanced" countries. Of the direct investments themselves, those made under special concessions or franchises are found more frequently in our friction cases than those which operate under the general laws of the capital-receiving country applicable to all business enterprises. Operation under special concession, again, represents another characteristic difference between investments in "backward" and "advanced" countries. It is also associated particularly with public utility enterprises of high strategic value, such as transportation and communication developments. It will be noted that those direct investments which operate under general laws are more important as centers of friction between capital-importing and capital-exporting countries than between rival capital-exporting countries.

Fourth, investments employed in all of the five uses tabulated under heading III have been involved, at least occasionally, in political friction. Transportation and communication investments appear most frequently in our cases where friction between rival capital-exporting powers is in question; extractive operations (oil, plantations, minerals, all considered together) come second. The same two types of investment have also provided the most occasions for contention between capital-importing and capital-exporting nations, but with extractive investments leading slightly in order of frequency. Trading investments have not been far behind as centers of trouble; banking and loan operations follow; while manufacturing investments have as yet provided relatively infrequent occasions for international friction. This ranking according to political involvement corresponds closely with the probable ranking according to amounts of international capital invested in these various employments. The conclusion seems to be that the particular employment of an investment has less to do with its potentiality as a friction center than other conditions surrounding it, though the strategic nature of transportation and communication investments as well as the large share of international capital invested in these forms may be thought to account for their frequency in friction cases.

The fifth and final observation relates to heading V of the tabulations. The motives behind particular private investments cannot, of course, be determined objectively, nor is reliable information on which to base a judgment easy to obtain. Therefore, a high degree of accuracy cannot be claimed for the classification of individual cases,[5] but the general situation is undoubtedly depicted with fair accuracy by the totals of Table 11-2, heading V, which show that "purely business" investments were involved 14 and 18 times in "A" and "B" types of friction, respectively, while "patriotic" investments were involved 20 and 15 times. When one considers that without doubt purely business investments predominate greatly over patriotic investments in the capital exports of the world as a whole, it is evident that private investments in which patriotic motives play a significant rôle are many times more likely to become involved in political friction than investments made for private profit only. All but two of the 22 "A" cases here studied involved patriotic invest-ments in some form—either under governmental subsidy, governmental stimulation, or the stimulation of patriotic political visions such as are entertained by colonial societies. The conclusion suggested is essentially sound, and accords with the observations and the reasoning presented earlier in this chapter: Private investments made for purely profit-seeking ends rarely become subjects of dispute between strong, capital-exporting powers, except where they are associated in time and place with "patriotic" investments which indicate a political ambition on the part of the capital-exporting country's government or an influential group within it. Purely profit-seeking private investments, on the other hand, even when not associated with "patriotic" investments, are more frequent centers of trouble between capital-importing and capital-exporting countries.

One might summarize the results of our tabulation in the form of a recipe or formula for the preparation of international private investment difficulties. The ideal case would seem to involve investments:

1. By citizens of a great power;

2. In a non-industrialized country with a weak and unstable government, or in a partly industrialized or even an advanced country about to experience a social revolu-tion (e.g., pre-revolutionary Russia), or in a region of disputed sovereignty (e.g., the Saar District just after the World War);

3. Under conditions which bring migration of management and entrepreneurship as well as migration of capital, especially in connection with special concessions of franchises rather than under the general laws of the capital-receiving country;

4. With the object, in addition to profit-making, of serving the strategic political and military purposes of the investing country, as expressed by its government in the form of subsidies or some less direct stimulus to investments deemed of national value;

5. In projects connected with the development of transportation and communica-tion routes, especially those having great strategic value from both the political and economic standpoint, or in the extractive industries associated with the early stages of industrial exploitation in non-industrialized countries.   ◆

The observations above attempt to portray the factual situation as our analysis of concrete cases of international friction has revealed it. If a satisfactory explanation of these facts is to be evolved it will consist in part, of course, of the line of reasoning advanced earlier. . . . That is, political expediency, reasons of high policy extraneous to the invest-ment affair as such, play a major rôle in determining whether a given investment will become involved in political friction or not. This goes far to explain the striking immunity of investments by citizens of the lesser political and military powers to serious interna-tional friction. It is not expedient for such states to press investment conflicts to the point of political crises. The same principle of political expediency helps to explain the particu-lar susceptibility to political friction of investments in areas of weak government, of trans-portation and communication investments, of certain extractive investments, and of investments involving special concessions or franchises, and of "patriotic" investments, for these characteristics often mean that the investments having them are especially service-able to foreign policy. Two other principles will be introduced at this point, and, together with what has gone before, they provide the best theoretical explanation of the factual situation revealed by our tabular analysis of investment friction cases. These two princi-ples are, first, that *the likelihood of investment friction varies inversely with the assimilability of the capital to the institutions of the capital-receiving country,* and, second, that *the likelihood of investment friction also varies inversely with the political determinateness of the investement area.* It will first be shown how these factors usually operate to render investments between "advanced" countries peaceful, and then how the relative absence of assimilability and political determinateness in "backward" countries makes such countries likely centers of investment friction. Finally, it will be shown how exceptions to the general rule—that investments between "advanced" countries are not likely to produce political friction while those in "backward" countries are likely to do so—may be accounted for on the basis of these two principles.

Two examples will serve to emphasize the generalization that investments between "advanced" countries do not usually give rise to political friction and will afford a concrete basis for the application of our explanatory principles. First, consider the large investments built up abroad by German electrical firms, particularly the German General Electric and Siemens and Halske, in the decades following 1890.[6] These firms controlled street railway companies, power plants, and related enterprises in Russia, Italy, South Africa, Austria, Poland, Argentina, Brazil, and elsewhere. They cooperated with French, English, and Russian banks. Yet their enterprises in the countries named never gave rise to any serious diplomatic controversy, so far as one is able to learn, though they had characteristics which we have found peculiarly subject to political friction, being direct investments, often under special franchises, in the public utility field. Compare the lack of friction over such investments in these relatively stable, westernized countries with the situation in countries like Morocco and Persia, where, as a German diplomat of wide experience remarked "as soon as a man sets up a shoe shop it becomes involved in international politics." Or consider, as the second example, the very large capital imports of Canada. Since 1900 Canada has been one of the great borrowers of the world. It has been estimated that by 1928 there were, roughly, five and one-half billion dollars of outside capital invested in the country. Of this more than two billion was British, more than three billion American, and the rest came from other countries. The total foreign investment in Canada was at that time about one-fifth of the estimated Canadian national wealth. American capital has entered in large amounts in the form of direct investments—branch plants, enterprises under American management—while that from other countries has been mainly in the form of loans. No political issues have arisen from outside investments in Canada, and none of any great importance are likely to arise. Canada has a stable, reliable government, an orderly judicial system, and the same methods of doing business as has the United States. The American business man and other investors in Canada do not require the political support of their own governments to make sure that their investments will be protected. They receive the same treatment in Canadian courts as Canadian business men and never think of involving diplomatic pressure.

The fundamental reasons for the absence of investment friction in cases typified by these examples are the high degree of assimilability for foreign capital and the political determinateness of the receiving area. The countries of the world which have been important exporters of capital in the modern era, up to the present time, have shared broadly the same culture, insofar as that culture impinges directly upon investment enterprise. This culture has been characterized by certain legal principles and practices for the interpretation of obligations and the enforcement of contracts, certain principles of private property and public order, and other fundamental modes of thinking and acting with respect to economic enterprise which we associate with modern industrialized, capitalistic, western civilization. The countries in which we have found capital imports rarely involved in political friction—those countries that we, with a good deal of ethnocentrism, call "advanced" countries—have substantially the same cultural characteristics as those just described for the capital-exporting countries. Their modes of governmental supervision over business do not differ radically from those of the capital-export regions, they follow roughly similar rules in the organization and control of their courts, they do not entertain any great prejudice against the industrial and other practices of the investors from abroad, which are not too unlike their own. They take roughly the same things for granted as do the capital exporters themselves, live on similar fundamental assumptions, have comparable value scales, regard roughly the same actions as fair or unfair. These circumstances give to private investments that come in from abroad what is here termed a high degree of assimilability, which implies relatively infrequent clashes with the people or the government of the capital-receiving area.

Furthermore, these "advanced" countries where foreign investments seldom get into political trouble are characterized, even when small, by relatively stable, established, and respected governments; while the potential capacity of the population to offer military resistance against an invader or to bring world public opinion and perhaps a political ally to its aid, is not insignifcant. In other words, there is no political vacancy, no political vacuum, in such countries. [7] The question of sovereignty is not an open question, and therefore the governments of foreign investors are not tempted to turn the investments of their citizens to account as devices of political penetration. This is the "political determinateness" which is here suggested as the second factor in explanation of the rarity of investment friction in industrialized, politically stable countries.

These two factors, the capacity to assimilate investment capital, and political determinateness, combine in "advanced" countries to produce a situation in which foreign investors never think of relying for the security of their undertakings upon diplomatic pressure from their home governments, while the governments of the great capital-exporting nations, on their part, entertain no ideas of achieving territorial expansion or political domination by means of the investments of their citizens. In other words, investments from abroad under such circumstances lose their political earmarks; they are, for most purposes, de-nationalized. The governments of the capital-importing countries do not anticipate, nor need they seriously fear, efforts of outside powers to dictate changes in their laws and customs or to influence the granting of economic privileges; hence, they can contemplate the entrance of foreign capital with some degree of complacency, or even hospitality, rather than with the antagonism inspired by apprehension. All these statements are untrue, in fact their opposites are usually true, when we turn to the consideration of capital investments and political friction in "backward" countries.

The institutional arrangements which prevail in those countries that, from the modern western viewpoint, are industrially and commercially retarded and politically unstable or insecure, are such as to provide a low degree of assimilability for capital which comes from the institutional background of England, France, Germany, America, and the other capital-exporting regions. The legal traditions and the courts of such countries are not well adapted to the defense of contractual obligations and private property rights, at least not in the sense essential to the smooth functioning of western business methods. There may be "law and order" of a kind, but the kind of public order which appeals to a folk society of the South Seas or to such radically un-western civilizations as those which confronted the first modern investors in Morocco, Persia, or China is not "law and order" at all from the standpoint of a western business man. He finds frequent occasion to desire the aid and protection of his home government, which may be accorded through extra-territoriality, interventions, diplomatic interposition, and other political means. Not only the absence of the institutional foundations necessary to profitable foreign investment leads to political implications in such countries, but the absence of certain essential technical services— considered public services and ordinarily supplied by government in western countries— has the same tendency. This has been one factor leading, for example, to the construction of railway and telegraph lines in "backward" territories under subsidies from foreign states, with attendant political complications. The migration of capital to regions unaccustomed to the institutional basis of modern western capitalism, in other words, almost inevitably implies a concomitant migration of *government*—"law and order" and public services—of the type familiar to the industrialized west. At least, governmental ideas adapted to the functioning of capital investments must go with the capital, and the situation is obviously one suited to the development of political friction. Concrete examples to illustrate the relative unassimilability of private capital in "backward" countries, with resulting political difficulties, are hardly necessary here, since most of the descriptive matter in this volume bears on the point. The aids which governments may give to private investors abroad . . . are almost without exception applicable to investments in politically weak and industrially undeveloped countries rather than in "advanced" ones. . . .

As for the factor of political determinateness, it is almost too obvious to need stating that in non-industrialized, politically weak countries the temptation for strong, capital-exporting powers to indulge in imperial expansion is at its maximum. Some "backward" areas are true political vacuums when the first investor arrives; they are politically vacant, in the sense that they have no government whatever of the European type, but perhaps only a loose and local tribal organization. Others have a government, but one too feeble to offer serious resistance to a modern western power. Still others are in a state of chronic revolution. In all these cases, quite contrary to the situation in "advanced" countries, the question of sovereignty is an open question, and the political significance of foreign investments tends to become very great.

We have already observed that the factors of assimilability and political determinateness which characterize "advanced" countries tend to de-nationalize foreign investments made in such countries. Just the opposite is true in the "backward" regions of the world. This was strikingly illustrated when the French Foreign Office in 1902 undertook through its consular officers to arrive at an estimate of the amount of French capital invested abroad. "In the poorly policed countries where our nationals have daily need for recourse to consular protection," read the resulting report, "the constant manifestation of French interests continues to make it possible to estimate their value. But where liberal institutions assure public security, the same interests avoid, rather than seek, official attention, and an inquiry like this finds itself deprived of its best source of information."[8] The assimilability or non-assimilability of private capital to the institutions of a country in which it is invested, and the political stability or instability of government in that country, thus determine very largely the degree to which it remains national, and therefore the degree to which any conflicts in which it becomes involved are likely to take an international, political form.

What of the exceptions to the general rule that private investments in "backward" countries do, and in "advanced" countries do not, become involved in international political friction? It will be recalled that among the cases of Table 11-1 there were four such exceptions: investments in Russia, in the Saar District, in Italy at the time rival alliances were building, and recent difficulties over German private debts. It is an important validation of the principles of assimilability and political determinateness that they not only explain the general rule but also account rather neatly for these exceptions. In Russia, friction over private investments arose as a result of the social revolution which took place there in 1917. Russian institutions suddenly came to have almost nothing in common with those of the capital-exporting nations, insofar as the treatment of private investments is concerned. Russia, in other words, passed from a condition which represented a fairly high degree of assimilability for private foreign capital, to extreme unassimilability, and political friction arose over foreign investments which were in Russia and could not be withdrawn. In the Saar District it was not the factor of assimilability, but political determinateness which was involved. The Treaty of Versailles left the ultimate sovereignty over the Saar District an open question, to be settled by a plebiscite in 1935. It was under such conditions of political indeterminateness that some of the characteristic phenomena of politico-economic "penetration" developed. In the Italian case the open question was not one of sovereignty, but which of the two rival alliances then forming in Europe should count Italy in its membership—political indeterminateness in another form. German investments went to Italy to strengthen the Triple Alliance; French investments were withdrawn as an expression of political tension over Italy's desertion of her former friends. In the German private debt case it is again a sudden decrease in assimilability, due this time to the national socialist revolution, which is responsible for the friction. Not merely default as such, but an apparent determination to redefine property and contract rights of non-Germans in ways that subordinate them to "national" purposes, has particularly aroused outside powers.

There are also exceptions of another sort to the general rule that private investments in "backward" countries do, and in "advanced" countries do not, become involved in international political friction. Certain "backward" countries, that is, show relatively little tendency to become centers of investment friction. That is true, for example, of the less developed Latin-American countries with respect to the investments of European nationals. Friction has developed between these capital-receiving countries and the European capital-exporters (the "B" type of friction) on many occasions, to be sure, but political difficulties among the European capital-exporting nations themselves over investments in this region (the "A" type) have been almost entirely absent. Neither type of friction has compared in intensity, furthermore, to the political difficulties that have developed around European investments in northern Africa, the Near East, and China. The explanation turns on the principle of political determinateness. By reason of the Monroe Doctrine of the United States this particular region, though its governments were often weak, could never be considered politically vacant by European nations, and as a result relatively little political friction developed over their investments in the region.[9] Similarly, once a "backward" country has been incorporated into the colonial empire of a great power and the accomplished fact has been accepted by the other powers this country usually ceases to be the seat of serious investment friction. This result is partly due to the installation of political and economic institutions by the imperial power which increase the assimilability of private capital from abroad, partly to the fact that the entry of capital from other sources then the imperial nation may be discouraged in various ways, but mainly, perhaps, to the fact that the political fate of this particular "backward" area has definitely been determined. Let the question of sovereignty be reopened, as by the development of a strong indepence movement, and foreign private investments may once more become centers of political friction.

There are other ways by which the assimilability of an area for capital from abroad may be increased, or its political status rendered more definite. Thus, certain countries which not so long ago were "backward" are rapidly adapting themselves to the industrial culture of the West and at the same time are losing their political weakness. Persia might be mentioned as an example. If the analysis in this chapter is correct, such developments should tend to decrease the likelihood of investment friction arising in these countries. The political determinateness of capital-importing countries is also increased by every development which tends toward the building up of a strong world federation which can effectively guarantee the territorial integrity and political independence of its members.

Summary

The conclusions of this chapter may now be surveyed: In actual cases of investment friction the two rôles of private investment in diplomacy are usually intertwined; that is, the investments serve both as tools and as determiners of policy. Nevertheless, in serious disputes between strong states the rôle of private investments as tools has been the predominant one. Conflicts between great powers over private investment matters have rarely, almost never, reached a state of dangerous international tension except in cases where the powers have been led into conflict by the pursuit of political policies extraneous to the investment affair itself. The best explanation for these facts runs in terms of the way in which those in charge of foreign policies interpret national advantage. Where investments can be regarded as economic aids to established lines of foreign policy, they are supported most vigorously; investments receive least vigorous political backing where they are not in any sense tools of national policy or where they run counter to national policy.

When we turn to the consideration of political friction between strong, capital-exporting states and weak, capital-importing states, on the other hand, difficulties directly incited by investment conflicts are relatively more important. There are more potential economic conflicts between capital-receiving and capital-lending regions than between rival lending regions, and political expediency more readily permits conflicts with weak opponents to develop into acute forms than similar conflicts with strong opponents. Up to the present day, investments have been involved in more serious friction as tools than as instigators of diplomatic policy, but there are reasons for thinking that the situation may be changing.

As for the types of private investment most frequently involved in political friction, our tabulation points to investments (1) by citizens of great powers, (2) in non-industrialized, politically weak countries, (3) under special concessions or other forms of foreign entrepreneurship, (4) for political purposes, (5) in transportation and communication projects. The institutional characteristics of the capital-receiving area, which determine the assimilability of capital from the western, capitalistic world, and the political determinateness of the capital-receiving area, go far to determine whether or not private foreign investments will bring political friction.

NOTES

1. Note on terminology: This expression "investment friction" will be used as a substitute for the lengthy and awkward locution, "international political friction between national

states either caused by or associated with the investment of private capital abroad." Similarly, the expression "international investment conflict," or simply "investment conflict" will be used to mean clashes of interest or attitude associated with the investment of private capital abroad, insofar as these clashes involve private persons and groups, not states. Thus, antagonism between the native population of a Chinese province and foreigners who are building a railroad through the province is "investment conflict." If foreign governments send threatening notes to the Chinese government in connection with these matters, or if they quarrel among themselves over the railroad, then we have "investment friction."

2. F. M. Huntington Wilson, former Assistant Secretary of State under Knox in the Taft administration, in the *Annals of the American Academy of Political and Social Science,* 68 (November, 1916), 303.

3. *The Diplomatic Protection of Citizens Abroad,* p. 400.

4. No doubt cases of political friction involving the investments of these smaller countries can be found, though most of them would be in close connection with investments of major powers. For example, the Royal Dutch-Shell oil interests have derived their international political significance from their British rather than their Dutch connections, and Belgian investments in China became involved politically because much of the capital which went out from Brussels was really French and was regarded as such.

5. Sometimes, as in the investment of German capital in Shantung, private investments have been made in a given region under governmental auspices, with direct or indirect governmental stimulation, and at the same time *other* private investments have been made in the same region from purely business motives. This explains the frequent appearance of x-marks in more than one column of heading V (Table 11-1) with reference to the same case, for "patriotic" investments of different types and "purely business" investments may be involved in the same political friction.

6. Cf. Karl Helfferich, *Georg von Siemens* (Berlin, 2d edn., 1923), II, 99, 128, 132-3.

7. Cf. R. G. Hawtrey, *Economic Aspects of Sovereignty* (London and New York, 1930), pp. 33, 52-57.

8. In Argentina and Uruguay, for example, the evaluation of French holdings presented considerable difficulties. Frenchmen who migrate to such countries arrive with modest capitals, become rich, "but the fortune thus acquired can be counted only partially as an asset of the mother country, for in the great majority of cases it is destined to be denationalized. French firms, French industries, are in the hands of Frenchmen who make Argentina their country by adoption and whose children will usually be Argentine citizens." Not so, however, in countries like China. (*Journal Officiel,* September 25, 1902, report on the French fortune abroad, by the Ministry of Foreign Affairs.)

9. The same cannot be said of the investments of the United States, of course.

12 / Multinationalization and the Countries of Eastern Europe

Patrick Gutman and Francis Arkwright

We are at the moment witnessing a change in East-West economic cooperation, an enrichment of traditional exchanges through the implementation of coproduction programs and the formation of "joint ventures" within the world economic system where the multinational firm is called upon to play a leading role—be it by implantation of multinational companies of capitalist origin or by the eventual emergence of multinational companies of socialist origin within the COMECON. Actually, the development of détente between East and West is but the political expression of an economic necessity, namely, the need to overcome the difficulties and contradictions inherent in the two systems.

Multinationalization and the Countries of the East

From Cooperation to Multinationalization

Since relations between multinational companies and nation-states are commonly studied within the familiar framework of center-periphery relations, this study focuses attention on the flow back to the center and the discovery of the countries of East Europe: the movement of multinational productive and financial capital away from the developing countries and toward European counties, and in particular toward socialist countries. It is interesting to note, at this juncture, that Americans and Europeans are in keen competition for the setting up of multinational subsidiaries in countries of the East and that, for once, the West Europeans enjoy a relative advantage over the Americans due to geographic proximity. Furthermore, and as opposed to the developing countries, the socialist economies offer practically no risk of nationalization in the immediate future since they need the advanced technology and economies of scale characteristic of the big multinational corporation.

Until about 1970, and excluding Yugoslavia, the agreements that were negotiated and put into effect made no provision for western implants in the East. The accords merely postulated the execution of production programs which the two sides implemented separately, the western partner in the West, the socialist partner in the East; there never was,

From Patrick Gutman and Francis Arkwright, "Multinationalisation et les Pays de l'Est," *Politique Etrangère,* No. 4-5 (1974), pp. 517-538. By permission of the publisher. Translated by Sylvia Modelski.

as there is now in joint venture agreements, the possibility of joint production in the East, requiring the capitalist partner to bring to the socialist countries its technical know-how, not only in production methods, but also in distribution, management and marketing. Multinationalization now brings about an enrichment in East-West trade, because the multinational subsidiary, by its implantation for purposes of production and technology, tends to substitute the manufacture of goods within the socialist countries for traditional trade flows. It has thus become increasingly difficult to talk of East-West trade when describing the reality beneath the process of multinationalization, and this must alter our perception of the relations between East and West.

This new form of cooperation, the joint venture, answers the East European countries' need to make a profit, exploit their resources rationally, develop their lands, utilize advanced technology and realize economies of scale in production. The acceptance of multinationalization by the design of appropriate legal frameworks corresponds to the socialist countries' desire to take advantage of a creative and imaginative capitalist formula, the multinational firm, that is capable of extracting profits unattainable through traditional practices that were entirely dependent on the merchandizing angle whereas the multinational brings together the production and merchandising angles.

Charles Levinson, Secretary General of the International Federation of Chemical and General Workers, in defining the multinationalization process, has shown that

> the necessity to make profits has led to a new form of enterprise, completely forbidden under the ideological mythologies upheld by the elites on both sides: a partnership in co-production between an anti-capitalist state trust and an anti-communist enterprise. Production is divided in two and to recoup its investments and profits the western firm takes charge of the world marketing of the part destined for export and makes its profit in overseas sales. This ingenious synthesis has made it possible to by-pass traditional legal and institutional obstacles and to open eastern markets to western profits.

This multinationalization assumes two forms: (1) The equity joint venture or joint enterprise with equal participation of capital. This form implies that the joint firm is an independent enterprise with equal participation of two or several partners, each of whom has rights and obligations commensurate with their share of capital (49 percent to the capitalist partner, 51 percent to the socialist partner). (2) The contractual, also called nonequity, joint venture, so-called because a major part of the financial resources is brought in by the western partner, in compensation for which the risks taken by the common enterprise are offset by a higher allocation of profit, or payment in the form of goods.

We have here the possibility of an unequal, majority participation by the western partner, which is very favorable to the East European partner because not only does it not prevent it from controlling the joint enterprise, but it diminishes its capital contribution. In this way the multinational firm leads to an optimum allocation of the factors of production: raw materials and labor furnished by the socialist countries; technology and capital furnished by the western countries.

While multinationalization thus goes beyond the limits of traditional accords on industrial cooperation, some observers express doubts as to the multinational character allowed by such joint ventures.

Is the Multinational Character Maintained?

In other words, does a multinational firm cease to be one when it extends its activities from the West to the East? For some observers the mere fact that the western partner is a subsidiary of a multinational firm is not sufficient reason to give the resultant unit multinational character; the existence of a multinational purpose at the level of decisions of the subsidiary must be proven; ownership is not enough.

1. The critics maintain that the multinationalization process is not genuine because production decisions are not made by the parent firm but by the subsidiary in the East, and, furthermore, that they would more likely follow the developmental goals of the socialist economies, according to their own priorities, than the imperative of internationalization of production and commercial exchanges. Actually, they tend to ignore or underestimate the effects of the establishment of the multinational firm's subsidiary, and the real integration of the production process that follows. For the socialist partner may use the name, trademark, the prestige of the multinational and its distribution network to dispose of products made in the East under the terms of the joint venture; and the capitalist partner may eventually utilize the implant as a springboard for the sale of surplus production (part of the output not used directly in the development of the socialist economies which the capitalist multinational can dispose of in the West, on its own account). In addition, this could promote the cause of further implantations from the first socialist country to other ones, as these constitute a potentially strong and sound market.

2. Other observers think that the majority control enjoyed by the socialist side turns the multinational subsidiary into an ordinary enterprise that has lost its multinational character because the parent company no longer has other than a minority voice in its management. Though it is true that, in other parts of the world, majority participation tends to be the rule because the parent company prefers complete control of the units making up the multinational firm, it must also be remembered that we are here in a transition phase of multinationalization. But, as Michalet puts it, "a minority investment reduces the risk of loss"; a small initial investment allows penetration into many markets in the field of advanced technology. Finally, the main strategic reason is that "the risk is diversified and the probability of not missing out on a profitable investment is increased."

Strict or Limited Multinationality?

Although the mere fact of placing what is happening in the East side by side with the numerous definitions of the multinational firm offered by economists may not allow us to say that the implementation of capitalist multinational subsidiaries carries with it all the characteristics of multinationality, this exercise might enable us to grasp the reality and to determine whether it is possible to speak of multinationalization in the large sense or in the restricted (or limited) sense.

A multinational company may be defined broadly as an enterprise engaged in production activities in several countries. Most theoreticians nevertheless give it a narrower definition, and reviewing these definitions, we notice that each economist sees the concept of the multinational firm as a tool of his own reasoning—his definition is a personal working concept needed for the presentation of his theory. Thus the "international enterprise" of one becomes the "transnational enterprise" of another. Because of this, economists are using different analytical categories for the same economic fact: the process of multinationalization.

If, by multinationalization in the East, we mean the process leading to the implantation of subsidiaries of western firms in socialist economies, and if we include in the term "multinationality" the criteria and characteristics which identify an enterprise as a multinational firm, we have two ways of reacting to the definitions:

1. Either we accept the narrower definitions and therefore approach the subject in terms of "strict multinationality." If we choose this path we may decide not to recognize multinationalization ostensibly because the multinational character is not fully maintained. By using a normative approach, we may succeed in denying the positive facts; even though the firms in question might be multinational in the West, their implants in the East no longer maintain this character.

2. Or else we challenge the usefulness of some of the criteria used (requiring, for example, ownership of, say, 25 percent of the assets) without ignoring the reality (of contractual, or nonequity joint ventures). The approach is then one of "limited multinationality" because it is difficult to deny that, within the world economic system, the multinational does cross the capitalist barrier when it implants itself in the East. We cannot agree to characterize the process of multinationalization according to definitions which do not take into account the socialist world.

The existence of a world economic system allows multinationalization to go on from one mode of production to the other, from capitalism to socialism; this does not amount to a convergence of systems (or modes of production) but more precisely to an "entente." Multinationalization brings about a state of peaceful coexistence between bureaucratic and plutocratic élites for the better management of their respective problems, whether they be the sharpening of capitalist competition or the slackening of socialist economic development due to lack of integration within COMECON.

Hence according to Pierre Goetschin, we observe that "a number of multinational enterprises are less preoccupied with ensuring total control of their subsidiaries and that they agree to local partnerships. The increasing weight of the socialist economies tends to alter the content of multinationalization: the capitalist multinational companies seem obliged to place less emphasis on ownership and control and more on contractual relations implying some executive authority."

Thus the "strict multinationality" approach (which consists of determining, by means of subjective and unadjusted criteria, whether the multinational implant in the East possesses all the characteristics of multinationality) rests on a false statement of the problem and must give way to a "limited multinationality" approach that will seek to define the compatibility or lack of it between the aims of the multinational and those of the socialist economy.

Problems of Economic Compatibility

Statement of the Problem and Political Interpretation

The western (American or European) multinational corporations which implant themselves abroad know very well that the countries where they operate are jealous of their economic sovereignty. Such sensitivity is even greater in Eastern Europe because the relationship there is one between elements belonging to two different modes of production.

Consequently, the somewhat restricted legal framework which we have described has one essential function: to reconcile and make economically compatible the capitalist and socialist purposes and to limit the risks of friction between the field of activities of the multinational firm and the economic sovereignty of the socialist country; that is, to avoid the domination effect. On this subject, let us ask the following questions:

1. Can the logic of socialist development be made compatible with the capitalist objectives of multinational firms which tend to exploit differences in the levels of development? In other words, are there areas of compatibility between multinational corporate planning and socialist planning?

2. Will the influence of the multinational firms lead to a weakening of state power or will it serve as an excuse for reinforcing the role of the state?

3. How far can capitalist multinationalization go in Eastern Europe? What are the risks of a backlash by socialist authorities? To what extent is the risk taken by the latter a real one? If it is real, can we see relief in the emergence of the socialist multinational?

Insofar as the multinational firm is a tool for rationalizing production, management and marketing, and in so far as its structure, subject to a plan though it is, allows it greater flexibility, and a better appraisal and forecast of possible futures, one can agree that it has a role to play in the development of socialist economies: not only is it compatible with the socialist mode of production, it is even indispensable to it by reason of its size and its technology. Furthermore, considering that the growth of socialist countries now depends on a development strategy based on the benefits of unbalanced growth, the multinational firm can be conceived of as the economic tool capable of launching the socialist economy into growth with emphasis on priority sectors and privileged "poles of development." The firm will achieve this more easily than the socialist state itself because the latter is burdened with excessive centralization.

Conversely, the multinational firm may be viewed as an element foreign to the socialist mode of production because, in addition to creating problems of control for socialist planners, its logic is capitalist. It amounts to a systematic exploitation of the differences in levels of development. Its economic influence and its unintended consequences are greater than what is envisaged by the legal framework of the contractual associations actually in force. The fact that it only holds 49 percent of the assets does not mean that it may not exercise a control greater than 49 percent, the juridical limit of capital ownership. The problem of the multinational firm's dominance over the socialist economy is therefore more an economic than a juridical one, and the problems of economic compatibility are of much greater concern to the socialist authorities than ideological problems. One must therefore acknowledge that the multinational's eastern branch will be able to prosper only if it keeps to the goals of socialist development and to the priorities laid down by the authorities, which may still allow the exploitation of East European workers through the appropriation of "socialist surplus value."

Consequently, we think that the contractual character given by the socialist authorities to joint companies with foreign capital contribution is a compromise: it sets the rules within which the game is to be played, and it must allow the satisfaction of the interests of both parties. This is the ideology of mutual advantage and "reciprocity" dear to Samuel Pisar and to financial and industrial circles that benefit from extolling "peaceful coexistence." The multinational fact is a manifestation of this peaceful coexistence. It justifies the intrusion of capitalism in the socialist economies as follows:

1. In the East, the western multinational is used as an economic instrument toward a political end, namely, reaching communism more speedily, but above all, bridging the technological gap.

2. In the West, détente is spoken of as the political expression of an economic end, namely, the expansion of markets and, by the same token, an extension of the activities of multinational firms.

In each case it is really the economic interest that determines politics, but the ostensible reason given varies to conform to ideological imperatives.

Finally, although it is true that there now exists a world economy resulting from the internationalization of production and the emergence of the multinational company, it cannot be concluded that there is congruence of economic systems. All there is is an understanding, "peaceful coexistence," between the elites who manage the two blocs.

Domination or Sovereignty?

Having analyzed the first manifestations of capitalist multinationalization in socialist economies, we must ask questions as to its further evolution. To do this, we shall look for evidence of its compatibility with the socialist mode of production.

The Multinational Firm, the Socialist Mode of Production and Planning

At the moment, only a few multinational firms participate in joint ventures. Given their relatively small number, "eastern implants" have a chance of taking root, especially since they assist in the development of socialist economies. What would happen if this movement grew considerably? Would there not be a risk that multinationalization might alter the socialist mode of production? Given that the multinational firm is an element perfected by the capitalist system, that it introduces the reflexes of the market economy through its implant in the East, it is fair to ask if, in the long run, it might not become incompatible with a planned economy characterized by rigid control. This could become a source of contradictions for a system wishing to be genuinely socialist—contradictions which could become quite serious if the technological contribution and the growth of minority sectors and of privileged "poles of development" depended on the multinational. If this risk were real, it is up to the socialist planners to take charge of it so as to minimize it and control it as well as possible since (to quote Lenin) their task is "to develop trade by all means possible because the place assigned to it in our country is rather limited."

This control consists of harmonizing the implant's production plan with the national plan of the socialist country, otherwise—and this is understandable—there could be no joint ventures. This would seem inescapable in terms of logic, but it is too simplistic in so far as the multinational firm can still exercise economic domination even though the objectives of the two plans coincide. By the way, this congruence is made possible only if decentralization is effected by socialist planners. If the planning of the multinational firm and the socialist country meet, this does not eliminate the possibility of domination by the implant over the socialist economy. Technological superiority can lead to instances of domination, for example, the impact upon production proving greater than the socialist planners could have foreseen. The explanation for this lies, in our opinion, in the nature of the multinationalization allowed by the joint venture agreement. Dependence can result from the multinational firm effecting a genuine integration of the process of production across frontiers, thereby justifying the expression "world economic system," which becomes a reality containing within itself possibilities of domination.

If this is the case, perhaps we should measure the effect of a subsidiary, in the East under a coproduction agreement, by means of a table of interindustry transactions involving a detailed study in input-output terms, as in cost-benefit analysis, to determine the actual effect on the socialist plan as compared with its proposed aims. In sum, we would apply economic criteria of compatibility through the adoption of a battery of warning signals. It is probable that such a measure (even if technically different, it would be undertaken in the same spirit) is now being used by the socialist planners in order to enable them to weigh the usefulness of introducing this or that multinational firm. However, we must not exaggerate the macroeconomic importance of the activities of the subsidiary within joint venture accords because they represent, at this time, little in comparison with national production, but its qualitative importance in economic development, regional planning and the elimination of disparities between regions, is enormous. Furthermore, if its relationship to the production sectors in which it is operating were considered, we see that these are sectors with a high degree of capitalization, requiring an advanced technology. This is no accident and we must carefully consider the problems relating to multinationalization in socialist economies by using sectoral and microeconomic approaches.

Differentiation at the Plant Level

We must proceed to an even more refined analysis. We must define the nature of the production operation carried out by the multinational subsidiary under the joint venture accord. Knowing as we do what is being produced (this could be a component part or the complete product), let us analyze possible domination effects of the affiliate over socialist planning and vice versa.

First Case. If the subsidiary in question is the only one producing this type of component (i.e., if no other affiliate of the multinational firm is producing it), the multinational increases its dependence on the socialist economy and makes it easy for the eastern planning authority to control its activity. It has a weak position vis-à-vis the host economy, thus it will tend to bend to its will. However, this is not its interest and, therefore, in order to have an incentive to implant itself in the East to produce the component part of a finished product, it must arrange to be the only possible buyer of that component. Otherwise it would be at the mercy of a troublesome work stoppage and could easily suffer higher costs. It could be forced to produce the component elsewhere and would no longer enjoy the relative advantage offered by implantation in the East. Take the case of Renault, which produces all "R12" rear axles and the transmissions for its mini-vans in the Dacia works at Pitesti. It is essential that Renault be confident that the Rumanian affiliate will follow its given plan, which is likely since Renault is the only potential buyer. This might be viewed as an example of what Howard Perlmutter calls the ethnocentric multinational, since production is for the country of origin, in this case France, but permits a diversification of production satisfactory to both parties. Renault gets lower production costs, and Rumania, in addition to foreign exchange, gets component parts for its own car assembly lines.

Second Case. If the affiliate in question manufactures the whole product (for instance, the complete car), the element of control over planning is less important inasmuch as the affiliate is more integrated with the host country, i.e., the socialist country. But this advantage must be qualified by the risk of nationalization of the affiliate. This risk increases when the finished product can be put into use directly. But a socialist country that would take such a course would automatically cut itself off from future technical innovations of the parent company. Moreover, it assumes (1) that the socialist partner has digested the technology used thus far under the joint venture agreement and (2) that it is capable of putting it into operation.

Multinational Productivity, Employment and Labor Organization

The emergence of multinationals in socialist economies through western implants poses some problems for multinational labor organizations. Let us examine the reactions of their best-known leader, Charles Levinson, to a practical case: "Recently an Austrian glassworks had trouble with its labor union the majority of whose members belonged to the Austrian Communist Party; what did the boss do? He decided to fire his 200 workers and transferred his factory to Hungary where wages are lower and strikes are no problem. The president of the Austrian union made a special trip to Hungary to ask fraternal support from its Hungarian counterpart, but the latter replied: this is an economic and not a union problem." Levinson adds: "Well, let us be logical: these thousands of millions which are going to be invested in the USSR, Hungary, Rumania and Yugoslavia, what are they? They are—as Marxism told us many times—the surplus value accumulated from the exploitation of American and European workers. And the mixed enterprises are a grave menace to multinational labor unions: there are no independent unions in the East, except for Yugoslavia; the right to strike does not exist there, and the manager more often than not belongs to the same party as the union secretary and is watchful that the union pushes production ahead. The international proletariat is thus limited to the capitalist world."

At first glance, this may seem a partisan reaction, but it must be realized that capitalist multinationalization in the East constitutes an extraordinary opportunity for the multinational firms, which, in the face of a growing multinational unionism, are thus able to find lower production costs and, above all, untroublesome workers in the socialist economies. Not only is there in the East, at the onset, a relatively attractive level of cost, but in addition, there is this considerable relative labor advantage. This competition among workers enrages American and European trade unions affiliated with multinational labor organizations. A job drain is in effect that trade unionists find hard to accept, and it may explain Levinson's reaction. But it should not be forgotten that the foreign currency earned by the socialist workers, as a result of the multinational implantation, allows them in turn to import products and consumer goods manufactured by the same multinationals, which creates new jobs. There is thus a feedback effect in this process as far as the creation of jobs is concerned: the multinational firm gains on both fronts, in the East as well as in the West.

The problem of socialist labor remains to be discussed. For we must ask ourselves if, on the one hand, socialist workers involved in production have a special status, and if, on the other hand, they are able to control their output (as in Yugoslavia). It is to be expected that there will be distortions in or changes of status according to whether the worker participates in a typical state enterprise or in a joint venture—there must be salary differences since working conditions vary appreciably from one to the other. Another problem is to determine if the socialist labor force is able to control the output of a joint production effort in conformity with socialist principles, and if it exercises any genuine control over the distribution of the profits thus earned. This train of thought leads to the question of whether, for example, the Yugoslav experience in self-management might not be losing force as the management committee, consisting of Yugoslav leaders and capitalist representatives of the multinational, tends to replace the workers' committee, the real organ of self-management. Marx was right when he declared that the relations of the means of production are determined by the evolution of techniques, and independently of the will of the individuals. But it is precisely this "technological superiority" aspect which has brought about the process of multinationalization in the East. Some, in particular members of the school of thought represented by Bettelheim, go as far as to assert that there is a strengthening of the corporate state in eastern economies because capitalist multinationalization is nothing but the dissemination of capitalist techniques in Eastern Europe. The eastern leaders take a gamble when they think they can allow implants in socialist economies by way of joint ventures without changing the nature of their mode of production. This is a gamble which events alone will be able to justify, but we think it will be a difficult one to win because the characteristic of the multinational is to exploit the differences between technological levels. This is the partial conclusion that can be drawn now; but it seems that it should be reconsidered when we turn to the question of the eventuality of a socialist multinationality within the COMECON.

When Shall We Have a Multinational of Socialist Origin?

In the end it would appear that capitalist multinationalization in socialist economies is a stop-gap measure: a device capable of smoothing over the difficulties of transition while awaiting the development of the socialist multinational. The lack of multinationals of socialist origin is the more striking if we observe that East-West joint ventures grow more easily than do companies linking several COMECON countries. Contrary to expectation, multinationals of socialist origin are extremely rare, not to say nonexistent, which proves the difficulty of socialist integration. What one finds, at most, are forms of binational and sometimes transnational industrial cooperation for the realization of projects and programs necessitating substantial investments.

This does not stop certain socialist economists from advocating the multinational enterprise of socialist origin. Let us examine the thesis of one of them, the Hungarian Egon Kemenes, who defines such a firm as follows:

> By socialist multinational enterprises, we mean socialist state enterprises which are also active on the territory of another socialist country. It is useful to distinguish them from collective or mixed ownership companies, which are the collective property of several socialist states and are active on the territory of one or more socialist states. The need to set up one or the other of these types will depend on the particular situation. Due to a number of reasons, the running of socialist or collectively owned multinational firms should in many respects be simpler and easier than the operation of this type of enterprise in capitalist countries: in the socialist countries, the political and economic systems are on the whole very similar, and what is more, most of their constituent elements are homogeneous; the cultural and technical systems in these countries are also very compatible. Their homogeneity is

greater than that of capitalist countries within the capitalist world. Resistance of the environment to the creation of multinational or collectively owned companies which results from differences in systems is therefore less in the socialist countries than can be seen in some capitalist countries. . . . The conclusion can therefore be drawn that the political, economic and legal harmony of the market formed by the member states of the Council for Mutual Economic Cooperation should in principle afford more favorable conditions for the operations of multinational or collectively owned enterprises than can the environment of the capitalist world, although the judicial system of these states does not as yet specify the rules governing the creation of such enterprises.

Although we agree with Egon Kemenes in believing that the success of socialist integration depends on socialist multinationalization, we nevertheless think that his analysis must be looked at again and qualified because the multinational, since this time it is socialist, is presented by him as a rational tool incapable of exerting domination over the host structure. He lightly dismisses the problems or difficulties that may arise from multinationality as such, and presents only its advantages. His argument therefore calls for some observations:

1. When the socialist multinational is defined as a socialist state enterprise, all the characteristics of the socialist mode of production are preserved. This amounts to an anointment of the multinational which, because it is socialist, ceases to exploit the differences in levels of development or technology (which is what its capitalist equivalent does) and which, because it is a state enterprise, no longer poses problems of domination effects in the host country's plan. In this fashion Kemenes pictures a perfect multinational which does not exist.

2. Furthermore, all the clashes that might occur between multinational firms on the one hand and nation-states on the other are left in the background. This is a revealing lapse in so far as the "Complex Program" of economic integration adopted in 1971 by COMECON, while purporting to promote integration and restructuring of production, did not aim to achieve supranationality. Does that mean that we must speak of an eventual socialist multinationalization of the other socialist countries under Moscow's leadership? The question arises: How is it that by virtue of its technology ITT could implant itself in the U.S.S.R. with the agreement of the Soviet authorities while at the same time it was undermining the foundations of Chilean socialism?

This criticism should not give the impression that we do not believe that socialist multinationalization is capable of taking over from capitalist multinationalization in the East, but we doubt that this can be done by the enterprise described by Kemenes. Multinationalization could be the key to socialist integration, but it remains to be seen how this will be achieved because domination inheres in the multinational firm, whether capitalist or socialist.

From the cold war to peaceful coexistence, East-West relations have changed and have evolved profoundly because of the economic necessity of rapprochement. This tendency will probably continue as long as the autonomous multinationalization of the countries of the East, within the COMECON, is not realized; that is, as long as the difficulties inherent in socialist integration have not been surmounted. Hence we have, for the moment, more or less skillful ideological justifications for the intrusion of capitalism in East Europe. In spite of everything, multinational implants in socialist countries continue and contain within themselves the possible effects of domination over the economies of the East, particularly over planning. They constitute the spearhead of the capitalist system which the communist bloc rejects, but which it nevertheless accepts as a source of the technology of which it is in dire need. Détente is thus the political expression of an economic necessity: multinationalization.

13 / Big Business and "Dependencia"

Osvaldo Sunkel

The winds of economic nationalism are blowing strong in Latin America. . . . The recent burst of nationalism is in fact a reaction to long-term and increasingly intolerable dependence on foreigners. The development strategy of industrialization as a substitute for imports was supposed to free the economy from its heavy reliance on primary exports, foreign capital and technology. It has not only failed to achieve these aims, but has in fact aggravated the situation and nature of "dependencia."

In its initial period, from 1930 to around 1955, the strategy stimulated the growth of a significant manufacturing industry and of the corresponding national entrepreneurial class. But subsequently industry was taken over to a large extent by foreign subsidiaries, with the result that much of the benefit expected from industrialization has gone abroad in payment for capital equipment and in a transfer of profits, royalties and other financial payments. This has effectively denationalized and eroded the local entrepreneurial class. Although the massive penetration of foreign firms has accelerated growth rates, especially industrial, it has also accentuated the uneven nature of development: on the one hand, a partial process of modernization and expansion of capital-intensive activities; on the other, a process of disruption, contraction and disorganization of traditional labor-intensive activities.

Disguised and open unemployment—that process of internal polarization and segregation which has been termed "marginalization"—has therefore been rising; together they account for levels estimated at over 25 percent, and they are still increasing. Owing to this and to the fact that the development strategies pursued aimed at the formation and strengthening of a reliable middle class, income seems at least as heavily concentrated in the hands of the wealthy as it was 20 years ago, allowing them consumption levels and patterns similar to those of the middle classes of developed countries, while the gap between high and low incomes in towns and in the countryside appears in most cases to have widened.

Things obviously went wrong with the development policies and strategy pursued after the Second World War. In a nutshell, the essence of its logic was that rapid economic growth could be achieved by protecting and stimulating industry, which eventually, and with the aid of appropriate government action, would induce the modernization of other sectors of the economy. This, in turn, would improve the social conditions of the people,

From Osvaldo Sunkel, "Big Business and 'Dependencia': A Latin American View," *Foreign Affairs* (1972), pp. 517-531. Reprinted by permission of the publisher.

more or less following the pattern of the industrial revolution in Western Europe and North America.

Apparently something important had been overlooked which hindered both the implementation and even an adequate understanding of the process. In the conventional approach to underdevelopment, the unit of analysis has always been the national economy in isolation, treated as if it existed in an international vacuum. Myrdal, Singer, Nurkse, as well as Prebisch and numerous economists from underdeveloped countries and U.N. agencies such as the Economic Commission for Latin America and the United Nations Conference on Trade and Development (UNCTAD) have emphasized the significance of the foreign trade structure of these countries—raw material exports and manufactured imports—as causing instability, stagnation, deteriorating terms of trade and balance-of-payments difficulties. They have also pointed to foreign financing and technical aid as having a significant influence on the rate of growth and the equilibrium of the underdeveloped economy.

New studies of "dependencia" in industry and related sectors have led to a greater recognition of its nature and effects. To begin with, local development and modernization are seen not in isolation but as part of the development of an international capitalist system, whose dynamic has a determining influence on the local processes. Therefore, foreign factors are seen not as external but as intrinsic to the system, with manifold and sometimes hidden or subtle political, financial, economic, technical and cultural effects inside the underdeveloped country. These contribute significantly to shaping the nature and operation of the economy, society and polity, a kind of "fifth column" as it were. Thus, the concept of "dependencia" links the postwar evolution of capitalism internationally to the discriminatory nature of the local process of development, as we know it. Access to the means and benefits of development is selective; rather than spreading them the process tends to ensure a self-reinforcing accumulation of privilege for special groups as well as the continued existence of a marginal class.

In other words, this approach considers the capitalist system as a whole, as a global international system, within which national economies—nation-states—constitute subsystems. These are not completely separated from each other but partially overlapping, owing to the fact that national economies interpenetrate each other to some extent in terms of productive facilities, technologies, consumption patterns, ideologies, political parties, cultural activities, private and government institutions. According to this approach, it is no longer possible to assume that underdevelopment is a moment in the evolution of a society which has been economically, politically and culturally autonomous and isolated.

The present international panorama of countries at different levels of development is not simply an aggregate of individual historical performances; the development process is not simply a race which started somewhere before the industrial revolution and in which some countries reached advanced stages while others stagnated or moved slower. The "dependencia" analysis maintains that one of the essential elements of the development of capitalism has been, from the outset, the creation of an international system which brought the world economy under the influence of a few European countries, plus the United States from the late nineteenth century onwards. Development and underdevelopment, in this view, are simultaneous processes: the two faces of the historical evolution of the capitalist system.

II

During the colonial period, in order to extract the precious metals and obtain the tropical products needed by the metropolis, Europeans interfered with existing social relationships and reorganized local economies on the basis of slavery and other forms of forced labor. This created the basis for agrarian structures and institutions which have survived in some form until today. During the nineteenth and first half of the twentieth century, the industrial revolution in Europe and later in the United States created a world economic system where Europe and the United States invested heavily in the production of food and raw materials in the rest of the world, while specializing at home in the production of manufactures. In Latin America, to the agrarian colonial heritage was added specialization in the export of staples and raw materials and with it another set of socio-economic and political structures and institutions, including the new dominant élites.

The breakdown of the nineteenth-century model of international economic relations during the two World Wars and the Great Depression opened for Latin American economies the period of import-substituting industrialization. This meant, in the larger countries of the region, the formation by the middle of the 1950s of a significant manufacturing sector, complete with its entrepreneurial class, professional and technical groups and industrial proletariat, as well as the necessary and ancillary government and private financial, marketing and educational agencies.

But during this period, while Europe was being ravaged by war and economic crisis, the U.S. economy developed into the most powerful center in the capitalist world and expanded into the economies of both developed and underdeveloped countries, bringing about very substantial changes, particularly in the latter. At the same time the U.S. economy experienced important changes in its internal structure. Government intervention expanded considerably within the United States, accelerating growth, reducing cyclical fluctuations and contributing to a fantastic development of science and technology; all this helped produce large business conglomerates. Vast economic, technological and therefore political power has enabled the multinational corporation, through the control of the marketing and communication processes, to induce consumers and governments to buy the products which it is technologically able to produce in ever-growing quantities. Within certain limits it is thus able to plan the development of consumption.

These institutional developments in the United States are reflected abroad as the new multinational corporations spread throughout the international economy. Their activities follow a fairly definite pattern: first, they export their finished products; then they establish sales organizations abroad; they they proceed to allow foreign producers to use their licenses and patents to manufacture the product locally; finally, they buy off the local producer and establish a partially or wholly owned subsidiary. In the process a new structure of international economic relations is emerging, where trade between national firm Z of country A and national firm Y of country B is replaced by the internal transfers of firm Z to countries A and B, while firm Y vanishes from the picture.

As a consequence, free-market forces and/or national policies are gradually superseded by the multinational firm's plans. It is estimated that for the decade 1960-70 around a fourth of all manufacturing exports from the United States were intra-firm transfers, and this proportion is rising quickly. Moreover, while previously only the international primary product market was an oligopoly, this is now also becoming true of the international market in manufactures. For the underdeveloped countries this means that outside control, formerly applied only to their exports is also increasingly exercised over their imports. Lastly, the intervention by government agencies in the developed countries, which paved the way for business expansion in their national markets, now is being repeated internationally, as these agencies intervene increasingly in "world markets"—

which is really a euphemism for other countries' markets—to support and protect the expansion of their firms.

The greatly extended economic role of the state takes essentially two forms: direct, bilateral, government-to-government relationships on the one hand, and international, multilateral economic organizations on the other. The bilateral relationship between a dominant and a dependent country corresponds closely to mercantilistic formulas. The dominant country tries to establish, enlarge and preserve exclusive privileges for its business interests, granting in exchange support of various kinds to the local social groups with which it is associated. The instruments of domination in bilateral relationships are well known: tied loans, technical aid, preferential arrangements with regard to transportation, communications, foreign investment, tariffs and so on. The multilateral relationship consists of a maze of international economic organizations. Some would like to see these set up in a hierarchical system, with organizations like the World Bank and the International Monetary Fund (IMF), where developed countries have a decisive influence, at the top. Regional organizations like the Organization of American States (OAS), which exist within one hegemonic system, and organizations among the developed countries such as the European Community would be kept independent from outside influence. World organizations where each country has one vote would be relegated to a rather weak position, much as are the organizations among underdeveloped countries of one region, the Latin American Free Trade Association (LAFTA) and the Organization of African Unity (OAU). Meanwhile, it has not been possible to create a formal global organization of underdeveloped countries—only the informal UNCTAD group, originally 77, now over 100.

Efforts to reorganize international relations to correspond to the transformation in the structure of the world economy have been clearly discernible in recent reports dealing with international coöperation. This is not surprising, since it should be the function of the superstructure to provide the ideological rationale for the system, as well as to lay down the rules of the game and provide the institutional means for policing its implementation. The following quotation constitutes a good statement of an apologist for these trends:

> The international corporation is acting and planning in terms that are far in advance of the political concepts of the nation-state. As the Renaissance of the fifteenth century brought an end to feudalism, aristocracy and the dominant role of the Church, the twentieth-century Renaissance is bringing an end to middle-class society and the dominance of the nation-state. The heart of the new power structure is the international organization and the technocrats who guide it. Power is shifting away from the nation-state to international institutions, public and private. Within a generation about 400 to 500 international corporations will own about two-thirds of the fixed assets of the world. [1]

III

Following the transformations that have occurred in the new centers of the capitalist world—the U.S., European and Japanese economies—the system of international economic relations has experienced fundamental institutional and structural changes. As a consequence, the internal economic, social and political structures of the dependent underdeveloped countries have also experienced fundamental transformations. These transformations are the main factors behind the rising nationalism in Latin America.

As mentioned earlier, the large expansion of the U.S. multinational corporation in Latin America really gained momentum around the mid-1950s; but only in the late 1960s did it reach the stage of the wholesale process of buying up local firms and integrating affiliates closely with headquarters and with each other. A study of the operations of 187 transnational corporations in Latin America shows that while in 1945 there were only 74 of these firms with manufacturing subsidiaries in the region, in 1967 the number of their subsidiaries in the region had increased from 182 to 950, and the total number of subsidiaries from 452 to 1,924. [2]

This process has profoundly affected the Latin American economy and society. While in the earlier period foreign investment in these countries manifested itself mainly in primary production and public utilities, in the postwar period extractive subsidiaries grew from only 38 to 56. The fundamental impact has therefore been in the manufacturing and related sectors, which have expanded considerably since the 1930s. In their growth they were faced with the need of starting almost from scratch to obtain a specialized labor force, highly qualified technicians, entrepreneurs, equipment, raw materials, financial resources, organizations for marketing, distribution, publicity, sales and credit, as well as technical ability to carry out all these tasks. In the process of industrial growth and diversification, these countries have been increasingly incorporating these elements from foreign sources.

From the nineteen-thirties through the early nineteen-fifties, particularly in the larger countries, immigrants and local entrepreneurs provided most of the skilled personnel; capital and financing came mainly from public sources, both national and foreign; know-how and technology were acquired through the purchase of licenses and technical assistance. All these producers contributed to the formation and strengthening of private entrepreneurship and industry. But in recent years there has been a reversal of these trends. Subsidiaries of foreign firms have provided a complete package of entrepreneurship, management, design, technology, financing and marketing. This has been the local counterpart of the institutional transformations indicated earlier in the mature capitalist countries and in the international economy.

On a more general level, import-substituting industrialization constitutes another way of setting the underdeveloped economies within the framework of a reorganized world economic system. The new system is formed, as before, on the basis of dominant (developed) economies and dependent (underdeveloped) economies, increasingly linked to each other through growing transnational interlocking of production structures and consumption patterns.

In the plants, laboratories, design and publicity departments, as well as in the planning, decision-making, personnel and finance organizations that constitute its headquarters—always located in an industrialized country—the transnational corporation develops: (1) new products; (2) new ways of producing those products; (3) the new machinery, equipment and innovative methods necessary to produce them; and (4) the publicity needed to create their markets. In the underdeveloped country, the corporation establishes the subsidiaries necessary for the marketing, assembling or routine production of those goods. The import-substitution process of industrialization has therefore become the corporation's stretegy for penetration of foreign protected markets, supported by external public and private credit, international technical assistance and ideological advice in respect to the development policies and strategies.

Let us look at some of the economic effects of this process through the words of Professor Harry Johnson:

The corporation . . . has no commercial interest in diffusing its knowledge to potential native competitors, nor has it any interest in investing more than it has to in acquiring knowledge of local conditions and investigating ways of adapting its own productive knowledge to local factor/price ratios and market conditions. Its purpose is not to transform the economy by exploiting its potentialities (especially its human potentialities) for development. . . . The main contribution of direct foreign investment will be highly specific and very uneven in its incidence.[3]

A.O. Hirschman, on his part, has pointed out that direct private foreign investment, by taking over local firms and displacing local entrepreneurship, may be harming the quality of local factors of production. Moreover, given the "complete package" character of subsidiaries, the foreign contribution may not be complementary but may instead be competitive with local factors of production, retarding or preventing their growth, and therefore decreasing the quantity of local inputs. His conclusion: "Private foreign investment is a mixed blessing, and the mixture is likely to become more noxious at the intermediate stage of development which characterizes much of present-day Latin America."[4]

The massive expansion and branch-plant nature of direct foreign investment has in fact some highly negative effects. In the first place, there is the process of vertical integration between the subsidiary and the headquarters. This means that flows of goods, finance, technology, etc. generally take place within firms, which have a natural tendency to prefer their own branches or affiliates as partners in any transaction, even if the country's interests are different. Their tendency is not to integrate with local suppliers or to share or adapt their technology, as Johnson points out. Furthermore, there is usually a market-sharing agreement among headquarters and the various subsidiaries and affiliates, which often means that branch plants are not allowed to export. Even the integration process in LAFTA or the Central American Common Market gives the subsidiaries located in the member countries a further opportunity to diminish the position of national firms.

Secondly, subsidiaries within one country tend to integrate horizontally, to conglomerate among themselves. Gaining control of finance, credit, markets and publicity means a considerable capacity to influence consumption patterns, not only of the higher income groups which can afford their goods, but also of lower income groups by way of the "trickling down" effect, thereby completely distorting their consumption patterns.

The control of the commanding heights of the economy also means, of course, the capacity to influence the allocation of resources in the public sector, frequently in the direction of providing the infrastructure needed for subsidizing the expansion of the foreign subsidiary. It also implies the capacity to acquire significant financial resources, private and public, with which to finance local expansion and foreign remittances, almost without the need of net additional foreign capital. In fact, between 1963 and 1968 only nine percent of the total funds used by the Latin American subsidiaries of U.S. corporations came from abroad. This, together with their negligible contribution to exports, inevitably leads to a serious balance-of-payments problem.

In the third place, foreign subsidiaries are usually able to extract oligopolistic profits from the exploitation of consumer and supplier markets. Moreover, as they keep most of their international transactions within the boundaries of the firm, there is a strong tendency to remit excess profits by manipulating the prices, kinds and quantities of these transactions.

Finally, the activities of subsidiaries in underdeveloped countries follow a definite life cycle. At the beginning the foreign firm may make a substantial contribution in capital, skilled personnel, technology, management, etc. But over time the cash outflow becomes larger than the inflow. Moreover, among the various alternative ways of obtaining external coöperation, direct foreign investment in the form of wholly owned subsidiaries is the one that has the smallest educational effect because of its policy of retaining its monopoly of skills and technology. It is only as a consequence of the process of the country's development that local personnel learn modern management and technological skills. Eventually, the corporation's net contribution to the development capabilities of the country becomes negligible or even negative. When the technology of the activities in which the firm operates becomes standardized and well known, the subsidiary becomes an "obsolete" form of foreign ownership from the point of view of its contribution to the resources, abilities and technology of the country.

IV

While these and other negative economic effects illustrate clearly the "mixed blessing" that private foreign investment represents, it is the socio-political consequences that are of far greater importance and of a much more explosive character.

The massive penetration of subsidiaries of foreign firms into the industrial, financial, marketing and distribution activities has fundamentally changed the ownership pattern in most Latin American countries. Foreign firms have acquired a dominant position among medium and large firms in many if not all the main sectors of private economic activity. This implies a basic change in the social structure and the political system. As the economist Celso Furtado has pointed out:

> The process of forming a local entrepreneurial class has been interrupted. The best talents that emerge from local industries are being absorbed into the new managerial class. . . . National independent entrepreneurship is . . . restricted to secondary activities or to pioneering ventures which, in the long run, simply open up new fields for the future expansion of the multinational corporation. . . . The elimination of the national entrepreneurial class necessarily excludes the possibility of self-sustained national development, along the lines of the classical capitalist development.[5]

In other words, a significant part of the national bourgeoisie is being transformed into a private transnational technocracy, losing legitimacy as part of a national ruling class.

But Furtado's observation may be extended to all groups and social classes to gain a clearer perception of the crisis which is affecting the nation-state in Latin America. At the level of production, this crisis makes itself felt through the massive and extraordinarily dynamic penetration of the transnational firm with its subsidiaries and affiliates; at the technological level, by the large-scale introduction of highly capital-intensive techniques; at the cultural and ideological level, by the overwhelming and systematic promotion and publicity of conspicuous consumption capitalism; and at the concrete level of development policies and strategies, by the pressure of national and international interests in favor of an industrialization process aimed basically at providing consumer goods for the high-income groups.

This process of so-called modernization implies the gradual replacement of the traditional production structure, which is labor-intensive, by another of much higher capital intensity. Under these conditions, the process incorporates into the new institutions and structures the individuals and groups that are apt to fit into the kind of rationale which prevails there. It also expels those individuals and groups that have no place in the new productive structure or lack the ability to adapt to it. Therefore, this process not only prevents the formation of a national entrepreneurial class, but also limits and erodes the middle class generally (including intellectuals, scientists and technocrats) and even creates privileged and underprivileged sectors within the working class, adding another serious difficulty to the creation of a strong labor movement.

In this process, some national entrepreneurs are coöpted as executives into the new subsidiaries; some professionals, forming part of the technical staff, and some specially trained employees are incorporated. The rest are left out. Part of the qualified labor supply will be brought in and the remainder excluded, adding to the growing problem of unemployment and underemployment. The effects of the disintegration of each social class have important consequences for social mobility. The marginal entrepreneur will probably be added to the ranks of small businessmen, or will abandon independent activity and become a middle-class employee. The segregated sectors of the middle class will probably form a group of frustrated lower-middle-class people trying to maintain appearances without much possibility of upward mobility and terrified by the prospect of proletarianization. The unemployed or underemployed workers will increase the numbers of those marginal to the economy and society, as in the lower middle class. Growing pools of resentment and frustration will certainly accumulate in both middle and lower classes.

Corresponding to this downward mobility there is also an upward mobility of a selective and discriminatory character. Some unemployed or underemployed are incorporated into the working class, some workers rise to the lower ranks of the middle classes and some sectors of the middle classes become small or medium-sized entrepreneurs. This upward movement probably tends to depress the wage levels, at least of unskilled workers and employees, and increases the anguish of the lower-middle and working classes.

Corresponding to this internal mobility is an international mobility between the internationalized sectors of developed and underdeveloped countries; these constitute in fact an international market for skilled labor. One side of this mobility is the outward "brain drain;" the obverse is the flow of experts and administrators sent into the underdeveloped countries to oversee the process of modernization and development described earlier. There may also be a flow of underemployed from Latin America in response to demands for low-salaried employees in developed countries.

V

The crisis of the nation-state which has been outlined above also affects the main institutions of society: the state, the armed forces, political parties, the universities, the Church. In Latin America, different countries have reacted in various ways to this crisis. In Brazil, leading groups and classes seem to have accepted "dependencia" and marginalization as inevitable and necessary ingredients of the process of development and modernization. An increasing share of the ownership and control of national resources and activities is being turned over to foreign firms and the government apparatus is being put at their disposal. This means not only the provision of infrastructural investments necessary for their expansion, but also the political and police repression needed to suppress the growing reaction and resentment to advancing denationalization, widening inequality and increasing marginalization. This development model could perhaps best be described as Dependent State Capitalism.

In other countries, owing to the different nature of preëxisting local conditions and other elements which cannot be analyzed here, certain social classes have reacted to the crisis by trying to oppose the above-mentioned trends. To do this they are trying to regain control over the economy. But this implies, in the first place, taking away the control of the state from the social groups which are more closely associated with the development strategy of Dependent State Capitalism. In the case of Peru this has been done by the nationalist elements among the military, and in Chile by a government elected with the support of large sectors of the working class and important sections of the middle class.

Having taken over the control of the state, these groups face three essential development tasks in correcting the main malformation inherited from the historical process of interaction with the international system: in the first place, this means transforming the agrarian structure, which is the fundamental root of inequality, marginalization and stagnation; second, using the primary export sector, which represents an underdeveloped country's most important source of capital accumulation, to support the expansion of heavy and consumer industries; and, finally, the reorganization of the industrial sector, essentially in order to orient it away from satisfying the conspicuous consumption of the minority into satisfying the basic needs of the majority.

In this process of structural reform, many well-established local and foreign interests will be affected. If there are foreign investments in the agricultural sector, they will be affected by agrarian reform. If there are foreign investments in the primary export sector, whether agricultural or mining, they will be affected by the need to control these fundamental sources of foreign financing. If there are foreign investments in the industrial and related sectors, as there increasingly are, the reorientation of industrial policy will affect subsidiaries of foreign firms. As the present level of industrial development has rested to a large extent on the power structures built around the main local and foreign industrial and commercial monopolies and the banking system, they are also bound to be taken over by the state. This will mean nationalizations and renegotiations with foreign interests.

It is interesting to note that international public opinion has more or less become accustomed to the idea that structural reforms are necessary in agriculture, so much so that underdeveloped countries are urged to go ahead with agrarian reform. If foreign interests are involved, there may be protests but they would be considerably attenuated by the recognized need for an agrarian reform.

Even in the field of primary export activities it is being accepted that our nations have the right to control their most essential resources, and that the policies of subsidiaries of foreign firms do not necessarily conicide with the best long-term interests of the country. It seems, as Hirschman points out, that at a certain level of industrial and general development, our countries are also beginning to reassert their own interests in the fields of manufacturing, commerce and banking, where the foreign penetration is now greatest. The conflict of interest with foreign private investment in these sectors will be more or less intense according to whether the country will choose a socialistic development path, as in Chile; some rather progressive variety of state capitalism, as seems to be the case in Peru; or some less well-defined and more moderate variety, as in most other countries.

Whatever the case, the era of "creating favorable business conditions for direct foreign investment" as a general policy seems to be coming to an end. But even then, as is seen more and more with the socialist countries, possible coöperation with foreign firms is not totally excluded, even though there will certainly be little place for wholly owned subsidiaries of foreign firms or private foreign investment of the traditional kind. What is opening up is a new era of hard bargaining and negotiations, of pragmatic and detailed considerations of specific cases, of weighing the conditions offered by Japan, Europe, the socialist countries and the United States, of building up alliances with countries with similar interests (the Andean Pact, the Special Co-ordination Commission of Latin America, the Organization of the Petroleum Exporting Countries), etc. In short, what we are seeing is the assertion of the national interest of our countries in their international economic relations. The aim is greater autonomy, in order to achieve development without "dependencia" and without marginalization. To achieve this goal, the asymmetrical nature of the present system of international economic relations must first undergo a thorough reform.

NOTES

1. R. Barber, "Emerging New Power: The World Corporation," *War/Peace Report,* October 1968, p. 7.

2. J. W. Vaupel and Joan P. Curham, "The Making of Multinational Enterprise." Boston: Harvard University Division of Research, 1969.

3. Harry G. Johnson, "The Multi-National Corporation as an Agency of Economic Development: Some Exploratory Observations," in Barbara Ward, Lenore d'Anjou and J. D. Runnalls, "The Widening Gap: Development in the 1970's." New York: Columbia University Press, 1971, p. 244 and 246.

4. Albert O. Hirschman, "How to Divest in Latin America, and Why," *Essays in International Finance,* No. 76, Princeton University, November 1969.

5. Celso Furtado, "La concentración del poder económico en los EE. UU. y sus proyecciones en América Latina," *Estudios Internacionales,* Año I, No. 3-4, Santiago, 1968.

14 / The International Telephone and Telegraph Company and Chile, 1970–1971

United States Senate

Introduction

On March 21, 1972, syndicated columnist Jack Anderson wrote that the International Telephone and Telegraph Corporation was involved in "a bizarre plot to stop the 1970 election of leftist Chilean President Salvador Allende." Mr. Anderson further alleged that the company was in regular contact with the Central Intelligence Agency and that the Agency participated in the plot. His allegations were based on documents he had obtained from the corporation's files.

Following the publication of the Anderson columns, the Senate Foreign Relations Committee asserted its paramount jurisdiction over "intervention abroad" and voted to investigate the allegations. At the same time, the Committee voted to establish a Subcommittee on Multinational Corporations and directed the Subcommittee to undertake a broad study of multinational corporations and their impact on American foreign policy.

The Subcommittee was asked to make the investigation of the Anderson allegations its first order of business. Further, to insure a fair and balanced investigation, the Subcommittee was asked to postpone hearings until after the 1972 Presidential election.

This, the Subcommittee's first report, covers, and is limited to, its investigation of the Anderson allegations.

In September 1972 the Subcommittee staff began an intensive investigation of the activities of the United States Government and American owned private corporations in connection with the 1970 Chilean Presidential election. The staff interviewed dozens of businessmen, present and former government officials, and present and former ITT employees. In addition, the staff requested and received numerous documents relating to the Chilean situation from ITT and other companies. These were considerably more extensive than the original documents on which the Anderson columns were based. The Subcommittee also requested access to documents from the Department of State, but this was refused. This lack of cooperation by State left an important gap in the record, as will be noted later.

From the Report to the Committee on Foreign Relations, United States Senate, by the Subcommittee on Multinational Corporations, June 21, 1973, *The International Telephone and Telegraph Company and Chile* (Washington, D.C.: Government Printing Office, 1973), pp. 1-20.

The Subcommittee heard testimony from witnesses during two days of hearings in executive session and seven days of hearings in public sessions. The witnesses included ITT employees, ITT outside directors, Government witnesses, and witnesses representing other companies and financial institutions which had interests in Chile, or which were mentioned in the documents.

The Hearing Record

Synopsis of Chilean Presidential Election

In 1970 Chile was in the midst of a presidential election campaign. President Eduardo Frei Montalvo, Christian Democrat, had been elected president in 1964. After completion of his six-year term in 1970 he was ineligible for re-election. The three major candidates were:

1. Dr. Salvador Allende Gossens, Socialist, candidate of the Popular Unity coalition of Communists. Socialists, Social Democrats, Radicals and dissident Christian Democrats.
2. Jorge Alessandri Rodriguez, Independent, candidate of the right-wing National Party, a fusion of the Conservative and Liberal parties.
3. Radomiro Tomic Romero, candidate of the ruling Christian Democrat Party.

The Popular Unity candidate, Dr. Allende, a long-time Senator and founder of the Socialist Party, making his fourth try for the presidency, campaigned for a program of extensive land reform and the rapid nationalization of basic industries, banks, and communications systems, many of which were controlled by foreign capital.

The Christian Democrat, Mr. Tomic, a former Ambassador to the United States, campaigned for a continuation of Frei's program of gradual "Chileanization" of key sectors of the economy—a sort of middle way between capitalism and full socialism.

Conservative former President Alessandri, was the only candidate to give whole-hearted support to the private free enterprise system.

The results of the September 4 popular election were:

	Votes	Percent
Allende	1,075,616	36.3
Alessandri	1,036,278	35.3
Tomic	824,849	28.4

Although Dr. Allende won with a margin of 39,000 votes, no candidate had an absolute majority. In such a case, the Chilean constitution required that a joint session of Congress choose between the first and second place finishers. The Congressional election was held October 24, 1970. Salvador Allende Gossens received 153 of the 195 votes. He was sworn in one week later.

The analysis of the hearing record is in three parts: Part I, the period before September 4, 1970, the date of the Chilean popular election for president; Part II, the period between September 4 and the Congressional election of October 24, 1970; and Part III, the post-October 24 period, after Salvador Allende Gossens had been elected President of Chile.

Part I. The Period Preceding the Popular Election of September 4, 1970

McCone and Helms—May/June 1970

The Chilean political situation was discussed at an ITT Board meeting in the spring of 1970 (Rohatyn testimony) and at the June 1970 board meeting the opinion was expressed that Dr. Salvador Allende Gossens, the Marxist candidate, would win the popular election. (McCone testimony.)

On his own initiative, Mr. John McCone, a former Director of the Central Intelligence Agency, at the time a consultant to the Agency and a Director of ITT, held a number of conversations about Chile with Richard Helms, then CIA Director. At least two conversations took place in Langley, Virginia, and one at Mr. McCone's home in San Marino, California. (McCone testimony.) During these conversations, Mr. McCone told Helms that ITT expected Dr. Allende to win the election. He pointed out that Allende was campaigning on a platform calling for the expropriation of American business, including ITT's properties, and expressed the opinion that the American national interest, as well as business interests were involved, "because there were, as you know, several hundred million dollars of OPIC guarantees, of which approximately 100 million dollars were ITT's." (McCone testimony.)

Mr. McCone asked Mr. Helms whether the United States intended to intervene in the election to encourage the support of "one of the candidates who stood for the principles that are basic in this country." (McCone testimony.) Mr. McCone indicated that the two candidates he had in mind were Mr. Radomiro Tomic Romero, the candidate of the Christian Democratic Party and Mr. Jorge Alessandri Rodriguez, an independent and the candidate of the conservative National Party. (McCone testimony.) Incumbent Christian Democratic President Eduardo Frei Montalvo was prevented by law from succeeding himself.

Mr. Helms told Mr. McCone that the matter had been considered by the "Forty Committee," the Executive Branch interdepartmental committee, at that time chaired by Dr. Henry Kissinger, which approves CIA covert actions, and that a decision had been made that nothing of consequence should be done. (McCone testimony.) Helms indicated that some minimal effort would be mounted which "could be managed within the flexibility of their own budget" that is, without seeking additional appropriated funds. (McCone testimony.) Mr. Helms was very pessimistic about the chances of Mr. Alessandri and was of the personal opinion that Dr. Allende would win. This opinion was contrary to the official reports of the U.S. Embassy. Based upon polls commissioned or undertaken by the CIA, the Embassy was reporting that Alessandri would win a plurality with approximately 40 percent of the vote. (Korry testimony.)

McCone said that he informed Mr. Geneen of the decision by the Agency not to intervene beyond the "normal budget flexibility" in the Chilean election and that Mr. Geneen was disappointed by the news. (McCone testimony.)

Geneen and Broe—July 16, 1970

During one of the conversations, Mr. McCone suggested to Mr. Helms that someone on Helms staff contact Mr. Geneen, and this suggestion led directly to a meeting between Mr. Geneen and Mr. Broe, the Chief of the CIA's Clandestine Services (also known as the Directorate of Plans), Western Hemisphere Division, on July 16, 1970, in the Sheraton-Carlton Hotel, Washington, D.C. In response to Mr. McCone's request, Mr. Helms told Mr. Broe that Mr. Geneen, ITT's Chief Executive Officer, would be in Washington on July 16, 1970, and that he should get in touch with Geneen to arrange a meeting. (Broe testimony.) Thus it was McCone, through his suggestion to Helms, who set in motion a series of contacts between the ITT and CIA in connection with Chile.

Mr. Broe was contacted by William Merriam, head of ITT's Washington office, who told him that Mr. Geneen wanted to meet late in the evening. Mr. Broe waited for Mr. Geneen in the lobby of the hotel. Mr. Merriam arrived, introduced himself and then took Mr. Broe up to Mr. Geneen's suite to wait for him. Mr. Merriam left the suit before the conversation began. (Broe testimony.) Mr. Geneen asked Mr. Broe for information on the electoral situation, the status and potential of the candidates and their parties. (Broe testimony.) Then Mr. Geneen offered to assemble an election fund for Jorge Alessandri Rodriguez, one of the Chilean candidates. Mr. Geneen said the fund would be "substantial" and that he wanted the fund controlled and channeled through the CIA. (Broe testimony.) Mr. Broe refused the offer and told Mr. Geneen that the CIA was not supporting any candidate in the Chilean election. The meeting lasted about an hour.

Mr. Geneen accepted Broe's account of the meeting as accurate, although he said he could not remember making the offer of a campaign fund. (Geneen testimony.) He testified that he made a similar offer to the CIA in 1964 and the offer was rejected by the Agency. (Geneen testimony.) Following the meeting, Mr. Geneen told Mr. Broe to contact ITT Vice President Ned Gerrity if Geneen was out of town.

Mr. Broe called Mr. Geneen on July 27th to tell him there was no change in the Chilean situation. The conversation was very brief and dealt with the progress of the candidates.

Part II. The Period Between September 4 and the Congressional Election of October 24, 1970

The Alessandri Formula

On September 4, 1970, Salvador Allende Gossens won a narrow plurality of the vote. On September 9, Mr. Alessandri announced that if elected by the Congress, he would immediately resign. This maneuver would open the way for President Frei to run again. In a two-way contest between President Frei and Dr. Allende, many believed Frei would win. This plan became known as the "Alessandri formula."

The Million Dollar Offer

On September 9, 1970, the ITT Board of Directors met for its monthly meeting in New York City. Mr. Geneen expressed his concern to John McCone over the political situation in Chile. In Mr. McCone's words: "What he told me at that time was that he was prepared to put up as much as a million dollars in support of any plan that was adopted by the government for the purpose of bringing about a coalition of the opposition to Allende so that when confirmation was up, which was some months later, this coalition would be united and deprive Allende of his position." (McCone testimony.) Mr. Geneen asked Mr. McCone to support his proposal. Mr. McCone agreed and came to Washington several days later and met with Henry Kissinger, Assistant to the President for National Security Affairs, and Richard Helms. He communicated to both Kissinger and Helms Mr. Geneen's offer of a $1,000,000 fund for the purpose of assisting any government plan designed to form a coalition in the Chilean Congress to stop Allende. Dr. Kissinger, according to Mr. McCone, thanked him and said he would hear from him. Mr. McCone did not receive a call back from Dr. Kissinger and therefore assumed no government plan had been developed. (McCone testimony.)

On September 11, 1970, at roughly the same time Mr. McCone was meeting with Dr. Kissinger and Mr. Helms, Jack Neal, the International Relations Director in the ITT Washington office, telephoned Viron P. Vaky, Dr. Kissinger's assistant for Latin American Affairs. He informed him that Mr. Geneen was willing to come to Washington to discuss his interest and that the company was willing to contribute a sum of money in seven figures. He also advised Mr. Vaky that the company was aware of Ambassador Korry's position with respect to the Alessandri formula and that he, Neal, hoped that the White House would remain neutral in the event other attempts were made to "save the situation in Chile." Mr. Neal claimed that on the following day, September 12, he delivered the same message to Assistant Secretary of State Charles Meyer. (Neal testimony.) Meyer however testified that, although he had spoken with Mr. Neal on that date he could not recall the offer of a sum of money. (Meyer testimony.)

There is little doubt that the ITT fund of "up to seven figures" was offered in support of any U.S. government plan to form a coalition in the Chilean Congress capable of stopping the election of Salvador Allende. Mr. Geneen testified that even if the plan did not block Allende's election, he hoped it would create a situation in which Allende would go slowly on the nationalization of American property in Chile. (Geneen testimony.)

During the hearings Ned Gerrity, ITT's Vice President in charge of corporate relations told the committee that the fund was offered for a constructive purpose such as housing and was designed to be a display of good will by ITT towards the Allende government. (Gerrity testimony.) But this contention strains credulity. Neal denied any knowledge of the use to which the money was to be put. (Neal testimony.) Gerrity admitted that he had never communicated any constructive purposes for use of the funds to Merriam, who gave Neal his instructions. (Gerrity testimony.) Nor could Gerrity recall whether he had ever explicitly discussed such proposals with Geneen. (Gerrity testimony.) Vaky testified that he understood the offer of funds by Neal to be in the context of blocking Allende from becoming president. (Vaky testimony.) And, in all of the documents submitted, there is no evidence of a constructive purpose for the $1 million fund.

Finally, since the end of World War II, the U.S. provided in excess of $1.4 billion in foreign aid funds to Chile. The idea that $1 million for housing, technical assistance, or agriculture could have an influence on Allende, a dedicated Marxist for the past 30 years, is not credible. As Senator Case stated: "The whole body of evidence, memoranda, internal communications in the company, communications among all of you shows great disillusionment on the part of ITT with a program of aid to Chile, . . . this adds to the difficulty of believing that a relatively small amount of additional aid would be of any value." (Gerrity testimony.)

In short, Gerrity's assertion that the company intended a constructive use of the $1 million fund has all of the earmarks of an afterthought. As Senator Percy put it: "The implausibility of this story is what bothers us. It just does not hang together. It does not make any kind of sense for reasonable, rational men . . . to really feel that this assistance could have an impact." (Gerrity testimony.)

Hendrix and Berrellez in Santiago

In addition to regular reports from the line officers of ITT subsidiaries, ITT receives reports from its Corporate Relations Department which go directly to company head-quarters in New York. Two ex-newspaper men, Hal Hendrix and Robert Berrellez, were responsible for reporting for ITT's Corporate Relations Department on Chilean political developments. Mr. Hendrix, who was based in New York made frequent trips around Latin America, as did Mr. Berrellez who was based in Buenos Aires. The reports filed by Messrs. Hendrix and Berrellez were among the most suggestive documents received by the Subcommittee and the background of their reports was the subject of intensive investigation.

In August 1970, Mr. Hendrix was instructed by Mr. Gerrity to make a commitment to increase the advertising of the ITT-controlled Chilean telephone company (Chiltelco) in conservative Chilean newspapers by 50%. Mr. Hendrix explained that he made the recommendation because the newspapers were losing advertisers who thought Dr. Allende would win. The advertising program was designed to bolster the newspapers to "keep their editorial voices alive." Mr. Gerrity testified that he later learned the commitment had never been honored. It was vetoed by Benjamin Holmes, Chiltelco's local manager, as being too obviously political.

The Company instructed Mr. Berrellez to make reporting on the election his number one priority. On the night of the popular election, he filed cables to New York every few hours as the votes were tabulated. On September 7, Mr. Berrellez filed his first post-election report which was based largely on an interview with Arturo Matte, Mr. Alessandri's brother-in-law and closest political adviser. Berrellez summed up the situation as follows:

(a) any attempt to implement the Alessandri formula would lead to a bloodbath; (b) prospects for successful implementation of the Alessandri formula were at best problematical; (c) "reliablest" sources in Santiago caution to proceed slowly, not to panic; (d) it would be possible to negotiate directly with Allende with respect to the company's properties; and (e) "strong outside political and economic pressures resulting in unemployment and unrest internally will certainly strengthen the hand of the left wing extremists and will convert Allende into merely a puppet of a machine dedicated to violent anti-U.S. revolution on a hemisphere scale." . . .

During the week of September 14th, following the Washington activities of Mr. McCone and Mr. Neal, Mr. Hendrix joined Mr. Berrellez in Santiago. On September 17th, they cabled a joint report to ITT in the United States which carefully explored the chances of blocking Dr. Allende's election by the Chilean Congress. The report also contained specific recommendations for supporting Chileans working to block Dr. Allende's election.

One paragraph written by Mr. Hendrix said, "Late Tuesday night (September 15), Ambassador Edward Korry finally received a message from State Department giving him the green light to move in the name of President Nixon." The message gave him maximum authority to do all possible—short of a Dominican Republic type action—to keep Allende from taking power." . . .

According to Mr. Hendrix, the source of the information was a Chilean national, described as an intimate political associate of Frei. (Hendrix testimony.) Mr. Hendrix said his informant told him that a very hard message—"muy duro"—had been received at the U.S. Embassy from a very high—"muy alto"—source. (Hendrix testimony.) The discussion took place at a coffee bar next to the presidential palace.

The Chilean source, according to Hendrix, never specifically named President Nixon or made reference to the Dominican Republic. These references, he said, were his own embellishment of what he had been told. Hendrix denied that the information on which the paragraph was based came from sources within the United States Embassy or the Central Intelligence Agency. (Hendrix testimony.)

Both Broe and Merriam testified that Mr. Merriam gave a copy of the cable to Mr. Broe and that Mr. Broe said that the report was accurate and the recommendations it contained were good.

These recommendations were the following . . . :

1. We and other U.S. firms in Chile pump some advertising into *Mercurio*. (This has been started.)

2. We help with getting some propagandists working again on radio and television . . .

3. Assist in support of a "family relocation" center in Mendoza or Baires [Buenos Aires] for wives and children of key persons involved in the fight. This will involve about 50 families for a period of a month to six weeks, maybe two months.

4. Bring what pressure we can on USIS in Washington to instruct the Santiago USIS to start moving the *Mercurio* editorials around Latin America and into Europe. Up until I left they were under orders not to move anything out of Chile.

5. Urge the key European press, through our contacts there, to get the story of what disaster could fall on Chile if Allende & Co. win this country.

These are immediate suggestions and there will be others between now and October 24 as pressure mounts on Frei and the Christian Democrats.

When Ambassador Korry was questioned about the "green light message" he refused to tell the Subcommittee what his instructions from Washington were. Assistant Secretary of State Meyer also refused to say what the Ambassador's instructions were and the Department refused to furnish copies of the cables it sent to Santiago. In the face of the refusal of the State Department to cooperate, it is impossible for the Subcommittee to determine definitely whether the Ambassador in fact received a cable substantially along the lines described by Hendrix. The reluctance of the State Department to assist the Subcommittee is indicated by the correspondence published as an appendix to the hearing volumes.

The latter part of the message was drafted by Mr. Berrellez and was based upon a further interview with Mr. Matte. In summing up this conversation, Mr. Berrellez noted that Mr. Matte told him "the leader we thought was missing is right there in the saddle (Frei) but he won't move unless he is provided with a constitutional threat; the threat must be provided one way or another through provocation; Matte did not mention money or other needs but at the end when it was mentioned we were, as always, ready to contribute with what was necessary, he said 'we would be advised.' "

Mr. Berrellez in his testimony attempted to explain this pledge of support as merely a polite leavetaking observation, general in nature, with no implication of political support, financial or otherwise. This explanation is belied by the context in which it was made. Mr. Berrellez had just finished a detailed discussion of the prospects of defeating Allende through the Alessandri formula, or by creating sufficient provocation, economic or otherwise, to bring about a constitutional crisis which would lead the Army to intervene and prevent Allende from being elected president. . . .

The cable is action oriented, specific in content and openly anti-Allende. Placed in context, it would be incongruous to construe Berrellez' offer of assistance as a stylized way of saying goodbye. The Subcommittee believes it was clearly an offer to back the anti-Allende effort then underway in Chile with financial or other resources. It was a logical complement to the offer that McCone and Neal made in Washington of a $1 million fund in support of any U.S. Government plan designed to form a coalition in the Chilean Congress to defeat Dr. Allende.

Messrs. Berrellez and Hendrix continued to file reports on the developing Chilean political situation which reflected the ardent desire to see Dr. Allende defeated. . . .

Contacts Between the ITT Washington Office and the CIA

A copy of the September 17th cable from Messrs. Hendrix and Berrellez was sent to William Merriam, head of the ITT Washington office. The cable was discussed at a staff meeting and became the basis for staff action. Mr. Merriam called Mr. Broe and arranged to meet him for lunch at the Metropolitan Club in Washington on September 22nd. Before the luncheon, Mr. Merriam sent Broe a copy of the September 17 cable. At lunch Mr. Merriam asked Mr. Broe for his judgment of the assessment and the workability of the recommendations. Broe confirmed the validity of the political analysis and approved the recommendations.

Acting on one of the recommendations in the cable, Bernard Goodrich, an ITT public relations man, visited the office of the United States Information Agency in Washington. Mr. Goodrich testified that he told the agency ITT was supporting *El Mercurio* with increased advertising and urged them to circulate *El Mercurio* editorials more widely in Latin America. He asked them whether there was anything ITT as a private company could do that the U.S. Government could not do. When USIA officials said the company should not do anything overt which might be interpreted as intervention, Goodrich "assured them that our people were well experienced in that field." . . .

Broe and Gerrity—September 29, 1970—and U.S. Government Policy

Prior to September 4, 1970, the policy of the U.S. Government, according to Assistant Secretary of State Meyer, was to not interfere in the Chilean electoral process. Mr. McCone testified that Mr. Helms had informed him that although the matter of the Chilean election had been discussed in June of 1970 at the "Forty Committee," the interdepartmental group which controls the covert operations of the CIA, nothing of consequence would be done to influence the outcome of the September 4 election.

In the aftermath of Allende's victory, however, this policy of allowing events to take their course in Chile without substantial U.S. intervention was the subject of high level review within the U.S. Government. Meyer testified that shortly after the September 4 election, the Forty Committee, at a meeting which he attended, met for the express purpose of discussing U.S. policy in connection with Chile; but he refused to inform the Committee what precisely was said at the meeting, what decisions, if any, were taken and what instructions were communicated to Mr. Korry, the U.S. Ambassador in Chile.

Mr. Korry did testify however that immediately after Allende won a plurality in the popular election of September 4, 1970, he sent a ten-point cable to the State Department indicating that an Allende presidency would not be in the best interests of the U.S. (Korry testimony.) Dr. Kissinger stated in an off-the-record briefing to a group of Midwestern newspaper editors in Chicago on September 16, 1970 that an Allende presidency would cause substantial problems for the United States as well as for Latin American countries bordering on Chile. (Korry testimony.) It is, accordingly, clear that both the U.S. Embassy in Santiago and high levels of the U.S. Government in Washington viewed with hostility the prospect of an Allende Government. It is within this context that Broe's visit to Mr. Gerrity of September 29, 1970 must be viewed.

On September 29th, for the first time in the course of the contacts between ITT and the United States Government, the Government took the initiative. Mr. Broe, at the instruction of CIA Director Richard Helms, called Mr. Gerrity in New York and arranged to meet him there on September 29th.

Messrs. Broe and Gerrity agreed substantially about what was said when they met. Mr. Broe proposed a plan to accelerate economic chaos in Chile as a means of putting pressure on Christian Democratic Congressmen to vote against Dr. Allende or in any event to weaken Dr. Allende's position in case he was elected. (Broe and Gerrity testimony.) As Gerrity summed it up, Broe made suggestions based on recommendations from "our representative on the scene" and analysis in Washington. The specific suggestions as recorded by Gerrity were the following:

1. Banks should not renew credits or should delay in doing so.

2. Companies should drag their feet in sending money, in making deliveries, in shipping spare parts, etc.

3. Savings and loan companies there are in trouble. If pressure were applied they would have to shut their doors, thereby creating stronger pressure.

4. We should withdraw all technical help and should not promise any technical assistance in the future. Companies in a position to do so should close their doors.

5. A list of companies was provided and "it was suggested that we approach them as indicated. I was told that of all of the companies involved ours alone had been responsive and understood the problem. The visitor added that money was not a problem." . . .

Broe testified that the plan to create economic chaos was a "thesis" which had been developed after analysis of the points of vulnerability of the Chilean society. Following Allende's victory in the popular election, many middle class Chileans were uneasy about the future of the economy and began to withdraw their money from banks. Also, many Chileans attempted to convert their Chilean currency to foreign currencies and to get it out of the country.

The CIA's thinking was that if additional pressure were placed on the Chilean economy, the deterioration would be accelerated and Christian Democratic Congressmen who were planning to vote for Allende would be shocked into changing their minds and following the Alessandri formula.

Mr. Gerrity told Mr. Geneen that he didn't think the plan would work. Mr. Geneen then consulted McCone who also told Geneen that the plan would not work. Mr. Geneen decided not to implement it.

Mr. Meyer attempted to explain Mr. Broe's proposal to Mr. Gerrity as merely the exploration of a possible policy option. Mr. Meyer was unwilling to inform the Subcommittee of the substance of the Forty Committee meeting. The Subcommittee is, accordingly, unable to say whether Mr. Helms' instruction to Mr. Broe to contact Mr. Gerrity and make proposals to Mr. Gerrity for creating economic dislocation in Chile were a direct outcome of the Forty Committee meeting which took place shortly after Allende won a plurality in the September 4 election. It is clear, however, that Mr. Broe's proposal of concrete measures designed to create economic difficulties in Chile for the purpose of influencing Christian Democrat Congressmen to vote against Allende in the Congressional election of October 24 was in striking contrast to the pre-September 4 U.S. Government policy of allowing events in Chile to follow their natural course without substantial interference from the U.S. Government.

The contacts between ITT and the CIA continued after Mr. Broe's meeting with Mr. Gerrity. On October 6th, Mr. Broe talked to the deputy head of ITT's Washington Office, John Ryan, about the prospects of stopping Dr. Allende. Mr. Ryan testified that his memorandum of the conversation was accurate, that Mr. Broe had urged ITT to keep the pressure on, and had suggested a run on the banks. (Ryan testimony.)

Mr. Merriam met Mr. Broe for lunch on several occasions after that and when cables arrived from Santiago he called Broe and arranged to have a CIA messenger pick up copies. In exchange, Mr. Broe kept Mr. Merriam informed about the CIA assessment of the situation. Mr. Merriam passed the information along to his superiors, and at Gerrity's specific request, to Mr. McCone.

The company's thinking is reflected in Mr. Merriam's October 23 letter to Dr. Kissinger. (Merriam testimony.) The letter, and the accompanying attachment, were the outgrowth of an October 16 conversation between Mr. Neal and Ambassador Korry. The Ambassador, Mr. Neal testified, advised him to get ITT's policy suggestions about Chile to Dr. Kissinger before October 24th.

The letter and memorandum proposed that the U.S. Government take a number of measures against the Allende government. For example, it suggested that, "without informing President Allende, all U.S. aid funds already committed to Chile should be placed in the 'under review' status in order that entry of money into Chile is temporarily stopped with a view to a permanent cut off if necessary. This includes 'funds in the pipe line'—'letters of credit' or any such." (Merriam testimony.)

Mr. Merriam's letter and the attachment were distributed to Mr. Gerrity. (Merriam testimony.) The only apparent dissent in the company came from Richard Dillenbeck of the ITT Legal Department who warned that the actions proposed by the company might jeopardize the investment guarantee which covered the company's properties in Chile. (Merriam testimony.)

The letter was acknowledged by Dr. Kissinger, but, although Mr. Merriam thought the acknowledgment was more than perfunctory, there apparently was no follow-up action or conversation with Kissinger or anyone on his staff. (Merriam testimony.)

The Banks—A Diverse Reaction

Because of the references in the ITT documents to "banks in New York and Califor-nia" and because the CIA suggestion to ITT was that they work to create economic chaos in Chile by causing a run on financial institutions, the Subcommittee invited testimony from the Chase Manhattan Bank, Manufacturer's Hanover Trust Company, First Na-tional City Bank, and the Bank of America. In addition, the Subcommittee staff inter-viewed officials of Morgan Guaranty Trust Company and Marine Midland National Bank.

All of the bank officials who testified or who were interviewed said they had not been approached by the Central Intelligence Agency, ITT, Chilean nationals or anyone else to cut back on their lending or to create economic chaos in an effort to block President Allende's election. The Subcommittee could find no evidence of involvement by Ameri-can financial institutions in a plan to block President Allende's election by the Congress or in a concerted effort to weaken him by creating "financial chaos."

Two of the banks, Chase Manhattan and Morgan Guaranty, cut their lines of credit because they thought Chile's economic prospects were poor. Two banks, Manufacturer's and Marine Midland, increased their outstanding loans in the period between the two elections. The Bank of America and First National City Bank carried on at existing loan levels. Thus, the financial community reaction to the Allende victory in the popular election was diverse.

Two of the large banks reported that they were approached by Chilean nationals with requests for campaign contributions to support the Alessandri candidacy and both re-ported turning the request down as a matter of long standing policy.

Several of the bank witnesses said that, from their perspective, creating economic chaos would have been counterproductive. The banks had large amounts outstanding in loans to the Chilean Government, as well as to Chilean businessmen. Economic chaos might have meant that the loans could not have been repaid.

A number of bank witnesses said that in order to operate in a large number of coun-tries around the world they have adopted strict policies of non-involvement in the political affairs of the countries where they do business. The bankers said they are located in countries with widely differing forms of government and widely differing political and economic systems. Involvement in host country politics would inevitably mean impair-ment of their ability to function.

The bank witnesses were unanimous in the view that the policy of non-involvement in host country politics is, in the long run, the best for business.

Part III. Allende in Power

On October 18, Alesandri withdrew from the Congressional run-off and, in the October 24 Congressional election Salvador Allende received 153 of the 195 votes cast. He was sworn in as President of Chile on November 4, 1970.

The Ad Hoc Committee on Chile

In early 1971, ITT began to follow a two-track strategy with respect to the Allende government. On the one hand, at the suggestion of Ralph Mecham, the Washington representative of the Anaconda Company, Mr. Merriam invited the Washington representatives of major U.S. companies having investments in Chile to form an Ad Hoc Committee on Chile. (Merriam testimony.) There were several meetings, the first of which took place in early January, 1971, in ITT's Washington offices. Representatives of Anaconda, Kennecott, Ralston Purina, Bank of America, Pfizer Chemical, and Grace and Company attended. (Merriam testimony.)

The purpose was described in a memorandum by Mr. Ronald Raddatz, the Bank of America representative: "the thrust of the meeting was toward the application of pressure on the (U.S.) Government, wherever possible, to make it clear that a Chilean take-over would not be tolerated without serious repercussions following." "ITT," said the memo, "believes the place to apply pressure is through the office of Henry Kissinger." "That is what we have been doing for the last year or so," said Mr. Merriam. One purpose of the pressure, Mr. Merriam confirmed, was to get the U.S. Government to block loans to Chile by institutions such as the World Bank and the Inter-American Development Bank. (Merriam testimony.) President Allende had not, at the time of the meeting, taken expropriatory action against any American concern.

Nevertheless, as explained by Merriam, the purpose of denying Chile credits in January 1971 was to produce economic problems for Chile. By confronting him with economic collapse, said Mr. Merriam, Dr. Allende could be made more willing to negotiate with ITT on terms satisfactory to the company. (Merriam testimony.)

The Anaconda Corporation may have shared this hard line approach toward Dr. Allende. Mr. Mecham, in reporting on the formation of the Ad Hoc group to Jay Parkinson, Chairman of the Board of Anaconda, noted that the purpose of the group was to "keep the pressure on Kissinger." (Mecham testimony.) The Ad Hoc Committee, Mecham testified, never considered the possibility that the application of such external economic pressure on Chile could, as Mr. Berrellez had warned in his cable of September 7, 1970, backfire and lead President Allende into a more aggressively anti-American posture. (Mecham testimony.)

William Foster, then the Washington representative of Ralston Purina Company, reported to his office in St. Louis on the first meeting of the Ad Hoc group and was directed not to attend any further meetings. (Foster testimony.) Ralston Purina was actively negotiating with the Chilean Government, saw a reasonable prospect of a satisfactory settlement and decided that participation in the Ad Hoc group would jeopardize the negotiations. Similarly, the Bank of America participated in two meetings to gather information but did not endorse an activist program because of its belief that a "hard line" position would compromise the banks' ability to negotiate. (Raddatz testimony.)

The Company's Stake and Negotiations

While Merriam was organizing the Ad Hoc Committee ITT was developing a strategy for negotiating with Allende. ITT's primary investment in Chile was a 70% interest in the Chilean telephone company (Chiltelco). The estimated book value of this ITT investment was placed at approximately $153 million. The remaining 30% of Chiltelco was held by the Chilean Development Corporation (Corfo) and individual Chilean private investors. $92.5 million of ITT's $153 million interest in Chiltelco was covered by investment guaranty agreements administered by the Overseas Private Investment Corporation (OPIC) which provided insurance, among other things, against expropriation.

Allende first mentioned the possibility of nationalizing Chiltelco in a campaign speech of September 2, 1970. The eventual Chilean ownership of Chiltelco was fully anticipated by ITT executives. In addition to the Chiltelco property, ITT had other lesser holdings in Chile, including two hotels, a telephone directory book service and an international cable company. The estimated book value of ITT's investments in Chile, including Chiltelco, amounted to approximately $160 million.

On October 20, 1970, Allende invited Benjamin Holmes, the Chiltelco local manager, to meet with him. At that meeting, Allende indicated that he had not definitely decided upon a course of action with respect to Chiltelco. . . . Hence, there was reason to believe that negotiations were possible with Allende.

ITT had successfully negotiated the sale of telephone properties to the Peruvian Government by persuading that Government that a satisfactory agreement with ITT would demonstrate that it was not inherently hostile to foreign investments. ITT persuaded the Peruvian Government that it could then argue that its decision to expropriate, without compensation, the property of the International Petroleum Company (IPC), a wholly owned subsidiary of the Exxon Corporation, was a special case and not an indication of general financial irresponsibility.

Mr. Guilfoyle summed up the strategy in a July 9, 1971 note to the ITT Board:

> When Allende signs the copper legislation and formally expropriates Anaconda and Kennecott, there must be increased international resentment against the Government of Chile, and, as in the case of Peru, on their expropriation of IPC, we were able to capitalize on this and eventually arrive at a deal which allowed them to announce internationally that copper and IPC were special cases and here is an arrangement we made in a reasonable negotiation with ITT. . . .

Through Mr. Holmes, a meeting was arranged with Dr. Allende on March 10, 1971 in Santiago, Chile, which was attended by, among others, Messrs. Guilfoyle and Francis Dunleavy of the New York Headquarters. ITT's memorandum about the meeting, prepared by Mr. Hendrix, described it as cordial. President Allende informed ITT that he had not decided whether the Government would nationalize Chiltelco or propose a joint venture with ITT. (Guilfoyle testimony.) Dunleavy told Allende that ITT was prepared to negotiate in good faith but that the day he "grabbed" the telephone company ITT would go to OPIC and invoke its investment guarantee agreement. (Guilfoyle testimony.)

On May 26, President Allende informed Mr. Guilfoyle that Chiltelco would be nationalized and that a commission to be headed by the Minister of the Interior would negotiate the terms of compensation. ITT responded that the terms of the contract required Chile to pay ITT the full book value of its interest in Chiltelco; i.e., $153 million. The Chileans offered $24 million for ITT's interest in Chiltelco. They also proposed valuation by international arbitration, but they insisted as well that the Government take over the management of the company pending the arbitration. Guilfoyle, however, opposed government management of the company while the arbitration was under way because he feared that the value of the property would deteriorate under Chilean Government management. This first phase of negotiations thus ended in impasse.

The October 1, 1971 Letter to Peterson

On September 29, the Chilean Government took over the management of Chiltelco, confiscating the books of the company. The government alleged that Chiltelco was deliberately allowing service to deteriorate. ITT denied the allegations.

A number of Chiltelco executives, all Chilean nationals, were arrested. The arrests were in connection with the activities of another ITT subsidiary which published telephone books.

Shortly after the intervention in Chiltelco by the Chilean Government, Mr. Merriam wrote to John Ehrlichman on the White House staff and requested a meeting for Mr. Geneen with Henry Kissinger and Peter Peterson, Assistant to the President for International Economic Affairs. A luncheon meeting was scheduled.

Because of the demands on Dr. Kissinger's time, General Haig, his deputy, joined Mr. Peterson at lunch with Mr. Geneen. Mr. Peterson testified that the luncheon meeting was brief and the discussion was a rather straightforward exposition of what had happened to the company in Chile. Mr. Peterson could not recall whether Mr. Geneen made specific suggestions but did remember Mr. Geneen saying he would send some ideas along.

Following the meeting, Mr. Geneen instructed Mr. Merriam to put ITT's suggestions in writing and forward them to Mr. Peterson. In response to the request, Merriam sent a letter to Peterson dated October 1, 1971, which had attached an 18-point action plan. Among other things the plan proposed the following specific measures to see to it that Allende would not "make it through the next six months": . . .

> Continue loan restrictions in the international banks such as those the Export/ Import Bank has already exhibited.
> Quietly have large U.S. private banks do the same.
> Confer with foreign banking sources with the same thing in mind.
> Delay buying from Chile over the next six months. Use U.S. copper stockpile instead of buying from Chile.
> Bring about a scarcity of U.S. dollars in Chile.
> Discuss with CIA how it can assist the six-month squeeze.
> Get to reliable sources within the Chilean Military. Delay fuel delivery to Navy and gasoline to Air Force. (This would have to be carefully handled, otherwise would be dangerous. However, a false delay could build up their planned discontent against Allende, thus, bring about necessity of his removal.)
> Help disrupt Allende's UNCTAD plans.
> It is noted that Chile's annual exports to the U.S. are valued at $154 million (U.S. dollars). As many U.S. markets as possible should be closed to Chile. Likewise, any U.S. exports of special importance to Allende should be delayed or stopped.

Thus, one year after Broe proposed a plan to accelerate economic chaos in Chile, Merriam on behalf of the company, was proposing to the President's Assistant for International Economic Policy a similar plan to exacerbate the Chilean economic situation. (Merriam testimony.) Peterson testified that he took no action to implement the Merriam plan. (Peterson testimony.)

In accordance with the company's usual distribution procedures, the Merriam letter and 18-point plan were distributed within the company. Neither Geneen nor Gerrity evidenced any disagreement with this plan to create economic chaos in Chile so as to prevent Allende from getting through the next six months.

Publication of the Anderson Columns and the Break-Off of Negotiations

In December 1971 negotiations were resumed between the company and the Allende Government. Allende agreed to move the locus of the negotiations from Santiago to Washington where they were to be conducted on behalf of the Chilean Government by

Chile's Ambassador to the United States, Orlando Letelier. Letelier and Guilfoyle were in active negotiations, according to Guilfoyle, pursuing the possibility of international appraisal of the company's assets, as a basis for determining compensation up until March 20, when Jack Anderson, syndicated columnist, published his first column dealing with ITT's activities in connection with Chile in the fall of 1970. Guilfoyle had been scheduled to meet with Letelier a few days after the publication of the Anderson column but that meeting was cancelled and the negotiations were broken off, following the publication of the Anderson columns. (Guilfoyle testimony; Geneen testimony.)

The Board of Directors of ITT

Felix Rohatyn testified that the Executive Committee of the Board of Directors, which is composed of the outside Directors including Rohatyn, was informed in April 1972, of McCone's and Geneen's 1970 offer of funds to the CIA, but had no knowledge of these fund offers at the time they were made. (Rohatyn testimony.) The Board's concern was whether the assets of ITT were likely to be depleted as a result of the actions of the management and McCone in connection with Chile. Opinion of outside counsel was obtained that the OPIC guarantees had not been jeopardized. No other investigation was undertaken as to the propriety of management's action. (Rohatyn testimony.)

Conclusions

In summary:

- On July 16, 1970, Geneen offered a substantial fund to the CIA to be used to support the conservative candidate Alessandri in the Chilean election of September 4, 1970. This offer was turned down, just as the CIA had rejected an offer of assistance made by ITT in connection with the 1964 Chilean election.
- In early September, 1970, McCone supported Geneen's offer of a $1 million fund in support of any U.S. Government plan designed to form a coalition in the Chilean Congress to prevent Allende from becoming president, and, at Geneen's request, communicated this offer to Kissinger and Helms.
- On September 13, 1970, Berrellez offered support, financial or otherwise, in Santiago to the key advisor of one of the principal political figures in Chile.
- On September 23, 1970, Goodrich urged the USIA to circulate throughout Latin America the editorials of an anti-Allende Chilean newspaper.
- Throughout September and October, 1970, Merriam provided Broe with, and received in return, detailed political intelligence in connection with Chile.
- Geneen, Gerrity and McCone, considering a plan proposed to them by the CIA on September 29, 1970, to create economic chaos in Chile, rejected it because they thought it "unworkable."
- In January, 1971, before there had been expropriation of the company's property, Merriam encouraged other American companies to form an Ad Hoc Committee on Chile for the express purpose of "pressuring Kissinger and the White House."
- Early in 1971 negotiations were undertaken with a view to convincing Allende that if he made a deal with ITT he could confiscate with impunity other U.S. companies in Chile.

• At the end of September, 1971, when negotiations seemed to have failed, and the Chilean Government moved to take over management of Chiltelco, Merriam proposed to Peter Peterson, then Special Assistant to the President, an 18-point plan designed to insure that Allende "does not get through the next six months." Peterson never acted upon this plan.

The attitude of the company perhaps was best summed up by Gerrity when he asked, "What's wrong with taking care of No. 1?" The Subcommittee limits its comments on this statement to the observation that "No. 1" should not be allowed an undue role in determining U.S. foreign policy and the Subcommittee will conclude with specific legislative recommendations on this point.

In order to appreciate the full meaning of ITT's activities, one need only consider the reaction in this country in circumstances similar to those prevailing in Chile.

Senator Church put the issue when he posed the following hypothetical situation to Mr. McCone:

Suppose we had an election in this country and the candidate receiving the largest number of votes fails to get either a majority of the popular vote or the electoral vote, with the result that the selection of the next President under our Constitution falls to the House of Representatives. Suppose, further, that the candidate getting the largest number of votes is one who has strongly favored very restrictive policies against foreign investment in the United States. Now we have a somewhat similar situation procedurally to that in Chile. The Congress of the United States is to make the choice of the next President. There is an interval between the popular election and the time that the Congress decides. Suppose British Petroleum, feeling that these restrictive policies will be inimical to its own interests in the United States, goes to the British Government and says, "If you can design a plan that will prevent this American candidate who received the most number of votes from being selected by the Congress, we are prepared to help support or finance that plan up to seven figures."

In response to Senator Church's question as to whether that would be an appropriate political action for a British company to take under these circumstances, Mr. McCone responded: "I would personally be very distressed if the British Government or any other government attempted to influence the Congress of the United States in their responsibility to select a President . . . I would be even more distressed if I learned that any corporation offered to support political action on the part of a foreign government." (McCone testimony.)

In the Chilean case, the consequences of ITT's proposed intervention in the Chilean electoral process could have been particularly severe. The company executives in New York City were warned by Berrellez, their top political reporter in Santiago, that support of the so-called "Alessandri formula" would result in bloodshed and near civil war, and that the application of external economic and political pressure would strengthen the hands of left wing extremists and convert Allende, whom Berrellez considered "a soft-lining Marxist," into an anti-American demagogue.

This is not to say that there was no reason for concern on the company's part over the fate of its investments in Chile. The company stake was large—investments of $160 million, book value, of which approximately $100 million was covered by OPIC investment guarantees. Allende was a dedicated Marxist, a member of the Socialist Party for 30 years. His electoral platform and public statements contemplated nationalization of Chiltelco. Whether compensation would be paid, or, if paid, whether such compensation would be adequate, was not clear from his utterances. So the company's concern was perfectly understandable.

So, too, was its desire to communicate that concern to the appropriate officials of the U.S. Government and to seek their judgment as to how the United States would view the possible eventuality of a seizure of company property without adequate compensation. It is also understandable that the company would wish to have the U.S. Government's assessment of the likelihood of an Allende victory, so that it could plan for such an eventuality in terms of negotiations, investment strategy, and corporate profitability targets.

But what is not to be condoned is that the highest officials of the ITT sought to engage the CIA in a plan covertly to manipulate the outcome of the Chilean presidential election. In so doing the company overstepped the line of acceptable corporate behavior. If ITT's actions in seeking to enlist the CIA for its purposes with respect to Chile were to be sanctioned as normal and acceptable, no country would welcome the presence of multinational corporations. Over every dispute or potential dispute between a company and a host government in connection with a corporation's investment interests, there would hang the spectre of foreign intervention. No sovereign nation would be willing to accept that possibility as the price of permitting foreign corporations to invest in its territory. The pressures which the company sought to bring to bear on the U.S. Government for CIA intervention are thus incompatible with the long-term existence of multinational corporations; they are also incompatible with the formulation of U.S. foreign policy in accordance with U.S. national, rather than private interests.

We hold no brief for President Allende's decision, in effect, to expropriate the property of U.S. owned corporations without adequate compensation. On the contrary, we condemn it. There should be no doubt in anyone's mind that this Subcommittee does not countenance the taking of the property of U.S. nationals without the payment of reasonable compensation. We consider that realistic negotiations, in good faith, over the amount of compensation to be paid for expropriated properties are essential to the maintenance of a healthy and constructive relationship between the United States and countries in which disputes arise over the property interests of U.S.-owned corporations.

The OPIC Guarantee

The Overseas Private Investment Corporation (OPIC) had a commitment in Chile of close to $500 million in investment guarantees against expropriation issued to American corporations with investments in that country. As previously noted, ITT's total investment in Chile amounted to a book value of $160 million of which approximately $100 million was covered by expropriation guarantees; thus, nearly two-thirds of ITT's total property interest in Chile was covered. Other large holders of such policies were the major U.S.-owned copper companies: Anaconda, Kennecott, and Cerro de Pasco.

The existence of OPIC guarantees did not deter ITT from seeking to influence the U.S. Government to intervene in the Chilean elections so as to preserve its property interests. On the contrary, the existence of the OPIC guarantees was used by McCone in his conversations with Helms as an argument, among others, for U.S. intervention in Chile: if OPIC had to compensate the companies under the guarantees, so the argument went, the cost would ultimately be borne by the U.S. taxpayer, since OPIC lacked adequate reserves to meet these potential liabilities.

Similarly, Ambassador Korry testified that in his post-September 4 election assessment for the Department of State, in which he noted that an Allende Government would not be in the U.S. national interest, he, too, used as one reason the potential cost to the U.S. taxpayer resulting from the OPIC exposure. Thus, at least in the case of Chile, OPIC insurance became an argument for American intervention "to protect the taxpayer."

The Subcommittee believes that this effect of OPIC insurance was not foreseen at the time the program was enacted. This issue, among others, will be considered in the Subcommittee's hearings on OPIC.

U.S. Government Policy

Mr. Broe arranged to meet with Mr. Gerrity in the ITT Headquarters in New York City on September 29, 1970. At that meeting Mr. Broe proposed a plan to Mr. Gerrity designed to create or accelerate economic chaos in Chile for the purpose of putting pressure on a number of Christian Democratic Congressmen to vote against Allende. Mr. Broe met with Mr. Gerrity and made his proposal with the express approval of Helms, the Director of the CIA.

Assistant Secretary of State Meyer attempted to explain Mr. Broe's proposal as merely an exploration of the feasibility of a possible policy option in connection with Chile which, he maintained, did not in itself constitute a change in policy. This explanation of Mr. Broe's proposal is weak. Even if we were to accept Mr. Meyer's theory that Mr. Broe's proposal was exploratory in nature, such an exploration, in and of itself, would indicate a major change in U.S. policy was under active consideration. Mr. Meyer testified that the pre-September 4 policy of the U.S. Government was to consider the popular election as an internal Chilean matter, which was to be allowed to run its course without interference from the United States. A decision actively to explore the feasibility of intervening in the Chilean electoral process so as to affect the outcome of the Chilean Congressional election of October 24 and deny Dr. Allende the presidency cannot be reconciled with this pre-September 4 policy, as stated to the Committee. On its face, Broe's proposal to Gerrity was a plan of action for specific concrete acts—stopping shipment of spare parts, cutting off credits, slowing down payments—and was so understood by Gerrity.

The record of the hearings calls into question the Administration's stated policy that it was willing to live with a "community of diversity in Latin America: we deal with governments as they are. Our relations depend not on their internal structures or social systems, but on acts which affect us in the inter-American system." (U.S. FOREIGN POLICY FOR THE 1970's, A REPORT TO THE CONGRESS by Richard Nixon, President of the United States, February 25, 1971, page 53.) A commitment to this policy would have been more convincingly evidenced by a willingness on the part of the State Department fully to disclose the content of the instructions which were communicated to the U.S. Embassy in Santiago.

The Forty Committee, Clandestine Operations of the CIA, and Multinational Corporations

The "Forty Committee" is the colloquial designation, taken from the serial number of the National Security Council document creating it, for the interdepartmental group within the executive branch which reviews clandestine operations of the CIA. The group is chaired by the Special Assistant to the President for National Security Affairs, Dr. Kissinger, and its members include the Deputy Secretary of Defense, the Under Secretary of State, the Director of Central Intelligence, and usually the Attorney General.

There are questions of concern in connection with the operations of the "Forty Committee" which bear directly upon this case. With what detail are instructions of the "Forty Committee" communicated to the CIA? Is the "Forty Committee" informed in advance of the modalities which the Agency contemplates using in carrying out an assignment? Specifically, in this case, was it informed by the CIA that in carrying out a mandate to explore means of influencing the political situation in Chile, use of U.S. companies was contemplated and specific proposals were being made to a particular corporation? Was the benefit to be potentially gained weighed against its overall negative consequences for U.S. business abroad by the "Forty Committee." Or was Helms merely given a general indication of what was desired, to be implemented as he saw fit?

It is clear from this case that there were significant adverse consequences for U.S. corporations which arose out of the decision to use ITT in the way it was used—willing as ITT may have been—and that it was not in the best interest of the U.S. business community for the CIA to attempt to use a U.S. corporation to influence the political situation in Chile.

There are further considerations which arise. Did the "Forty Committee" consider the consequences which would have ensued in the event that the plan to create or accelerate economic chaos in Chile had been successful? It had been the custom in Chile for the Congress to confirm as president the winner of a plurality in the popular election. There was ample evidence that an attempt to interfere with this custom would have led to bloodshed, and possibly, civil war. . . . There were also substantial doubts with respect to the capacity of the Chilean military to cope with this situation. . . . Did the members of the "Forty Committee" adequately consider the possibility that, once having launched the U.S. down the road of covert intervention, other, more direct, measures might have become necessary to insure the desired result: stopping Allende from becoming President of Chile?

The Subcommittee thinks the time is ripe for an in-depth review by the appropriate congressional committees, of the decisionmaking process in the authorization and conduct of CIA clandestine operations.

15 / Poverty Is the Product

Ronald Müller

Countries are called "less-developed" for specific reasons. Less-developed means a lack of adequately-trained government civil servants to examine and investigate whether or not commercial and business laws are being enforced, let alone complied with by multinational corporations (MNC's) or locally-owned companies. But this lack of expertise has even a deeper meaning because it indicates that the laws themselves are usually quite old, designed for times past, and too-long unrevised.

A basic part of being less-developed is having institutions which are either lacking or misfunctioning relative to similar institutions in industrialized societies. For those of us accustomed to life in the advanced nations, it is essential to understand this aspect of underdevelopment. The "bargaining power" of the MNC's is far greater in less-developed countries (LDC's) than in rich countries, because of this absence or weakness of institutional mechanisms to control the behavior of their subsidiaries. Stated in Galbraithian terms, Third World countries are characterized by an absence of the "countervailing" power of government and organized labor for setting limits on the power of the modern corporation.

Another aspect of underdevelopment further intensifies this power—the economic structure of these societies. There are two key characteristics of this structure which are important here: first, the need for and the sources of *technology;* and second, the need for and the sources of investment *financing*.

The Structure of Technology

Most Third World nations have already set in motion a process of industrialization highly similar to that found in more developed countries (MDC's). This industrialization is not only similar in terms of the output of industry, but also in terms of the technology and human skills needed for its implementation. In other words, the voluntary or involuntary institutionalization of MDC's consumption values as the goal of economic growth has, in turn, brought about the need for a technology which can satisfy this pattern of consumption.

From Ronald Müller, "Poverty Is the Product," by permission, from *Foreign Policy* 13 (Winter, 1973-1974), copyright © 1973, by National Affairs, Inc. Some notes have been omitted, and the remainder renumbered in sequence. Tables have been renumbered.

Given this need, what are the sources of this technology? Tables 15-1 and 15-2 below provide the answer.

Clearly, LDC's are virtually entirely dependent upon foreign sources for their technology. But not even these figures reflect the absolute dependency involved. First, if we look at the ownership of patents actually utilized for producing goods versus patents granted but not utilized in production we find that: "the so weighted patents belonging to their own nationals amount to a fraction of 1 percent of the total patents granted by" LDC's.[1]

Also, the foreign versus local control of technology does not indicate the actual concentration of control in the hands of a very few foreign corporations. Looking at the foreign countries involved we find that, for example, in the United States, of the 500 largest industrial corporations, the top 30 own 40.7 percent of the patents in their respective industries.[2] The mirror-image of this concentration of technology-control in the advanced nations is found to even a greater extent in the underdeveloped areas. For instance, in Colombia, in the pharmaceutical, synthetic fiber, and chemical industries, 10 percent of all patent-holders own 60 percent of all patents, and these 10 percent are all foreign MNC's.[3]

Such concentrated control of technology is one of the most effective means of establishing oligopoly power over the market place, restricting the development of local competition, and permitting an astounding rate of profits, the bulk of which leave the country. Once such a *process* is under way, it becomes cumulative and self-perpetuating, as can be seen in Table 15-2. The initial institutional purpose of patent rights, i.e., to stimulate

Table 15-1 Patents Granted to Foreigners as a Percentage of Total Patents Granted Between 1957 and 1961 Inclusive (in percentages)

"Large" Industrial Countries	
United States	15.72
Japan	34.02
West Germany	37.14
United Kingdom	47.00
France	59.36
"Smaller" Industrialized Countries	
Italy	62.85
Switzerland	64.08
Sweden	69.30
Netherlands	69.83
Luxembourg	80.48
Belgium	85.55
Developing Countries	
India	89.38
Turkey	91.73
United Arab Republic	93.01
Trinidad & Tobago	94.18
Pakistan	95.75
Ireland	96.51

Table 15-2 Percentages of Patents Registered in Chile and Owned by: (in percentages)

Year	Nationals	Foreigners
1937	34.5	65.5
1947	20.0	80.0
1958	11.0	89.0
1967	5.5	94.5

domestic inventiveness, is self-defeating, since the wherewithal—profits—to pursue research and development goes increasingly to foreign firms. Local business enterprises lose not only access to mechanical technology but perhaps more importantly to the human technical skills, accumulated only through experience, which allow further development. In the end, as is the case today in Latin America, domestic firms are either absorbed by the MNC's or must resort to the "licensing" of their technology, and with such licensing comes a number of significant restrictions.

The Structure of Finance

A similar set of vicious circles is also at play in the financial patterns of these countries. Of first importance is the expense of the technology being used. It is well known that in almost all LDC's there is a scarcity of local savings available for productive investments. This scarcity is not only due to the LDC's low level of income, but also to the fact that savings leave the country. Foreign firms repatriate a significant part of their profits and indigenous wealth-holders also channel a part of their savings out to MDC's (the latter is the so-called phenomenon of "capital flight"). Adding to this is the increasing debt-repayments to bilateral (e.g., AID) and multilateral (e.g., World Bank) aid agencies on loans granted in the 1960's. Together, the magnitude of these outflows have led a number of writers to comment that in aggregate terms the poor countries of the world are now ironically helping to finance the rich countries, i.e., the financial outflows from LDC's far exceed the inflows. [4]

There is thus a twofold dilemma in the financial structure of LDC's. On the one hand there is a growing gap between the supply of *available* local savings and the demand for investment funds to alleviate the growing poverty *and* the growing awareness of it by the people of these countries, via increased literacy, improved communications, and the ensuing demonstration effects. On the other hand, the particular technology which the industrialization process necessitates is not only expensive, but must be paid for in foreign, not local, exchange. The relative reduction in more developed countries' consumption of LDC's exports which has reduced the latter's ability to generate foreign exchange, plus the relative increase of foreign exchange outflows versus inflows, has now brought about the well-known problem of the "foreign exchange bottleneck": even when there are sufficient savings to finance needed investment projects, the investment may not take place because savings in local currency cannot be translated into foreign exchange for the purchase of the imported technology which the project requires.

The upshot of this twofold dilemma (inadequate amounts of local savings and foreign exchange), from the viewpoint of domestic enterprises, is a rather perverse form of non-competitive financing patterns in most LDC's. Contrary to the generally accepted notion, MNC's do not bring their own finance capital from abroad, but rather derive the over-whelming majority of their financing from local, host country sources. The subsidiaries of MNC's in LDC's borrow from local financial institutions with the credit-rating and financial resource back-up of the entire global network of their parent MNC. This is in contrast to the credit-rating and financial resource back-up of the smaller typical local business enterprise when it attempts to obtain finance capital. The vicious circle begins to close. The local financial institution, faced with limited loan capital relative to demand, and (like any other business) interested in risk-minimization, will inevitably be biased towards the subsidiaries of MNC's.

This is even more obvious when the local financial institution is, in fact, a branch or subsidiary of a so-called private multinational bank, such as the Bank of America, or the First National City Bank of New York. These banks are playing a powerful role in the financial structures of the Third World, where in many instances they control close to 50 percent of the private deposits of a country. [5] The LDC operation of a multinational bank will prefer lending to the subsidiaries of MNC's for the same reasons as locally controlled financial institutions. But there is more at stake than just the profitability of one loan in a single country. At work also is a worldwide client-customer relationship between multinational bank and corporation.

Our analysis of the economic structure of LDC's, with reference to technology and finance, has shown why MNC's have a relatively high and growing degree of oligopoly power in contrast to national firms in LDC's. A look at pre-1970 Chile will serve as an example for almost all LDC's in which MNC's operate. In the industrial sector between 1967 and 1969, foreign participation (in terms of assets owned) increased from 16.6 percent to 20.3 percent, while domestic participation diminished from 76.1 percent to 63 percent— the difference being made up of state-owned firms. Of the 100 largest industrial firms (on the basis of asset size) in the country, 49 were effectively controlled by MNC's. When the sampling was expanded to the largest 160 firms, over 51 percent were under the control of MNC's. Even these figures do not accurately convey the degree of concentration involved. When we look at control by industry, we see that in seven of the more important indus-tries in Chile, one to three foreign firms controlled not less than 51 percent of production in each industry. These figures are representative of most LDC's where MNC's are currently operating, and demonstrate the degree of oligopoly power of MNC's in the Third World as well as their ability to increase it over time. [6]

If the nonbusiness institutions of government and organized labor cannot act as a sufficient countervailing power on the MNC in a Third World country, there still remains the check of other business institutions, namely, domestic competition. The nature of the economic structure of underdevelopment, however, makes it highly unlikely that domestic business institutions will be able to act as a sufficient check on the power of the MNC. What is the resulting impact on the people of these countries?

Our evaluation criterion shall be different from that most frequently assumed in neo-classical analysis, although we shall employ the analytical tools of the latter. Instead of assuming that increases in average per capita income are, by definition, "development," we shall avoid the assumption and base our evaluation on the following: *An MNC activity and its impact will be judged a contribution to development if it results in an increase in the consumption potential of the poorest 60 percent of an LDC's population.* It is my judgment that unless economic

Table 15-3 Capital-Labor Requirements in Colombian Industries with Highest MNC Expansion: 1960-67

	1960	1961	1962	1963	1964	1965	1966	1967
Chemical Products	1.63	1.21	2.09	3.39	4.47	4.76	4.07	4.45
Paper & Its Derivatives	4.06	6.94	6.84	6.87	8.67	10.70	11.08	11.18
Rubber Products	4.37	4.07	4.07	3.99	4.31	4.36	4.52	16.09
Machinery & Electrical Products	1.20	1.18	1.38	1.50	1.66	1.96	1.86	3.95
Food Products	3.16	3.35	5.12	3.55	3.74	3.75	3.96	4.95
Industrial/Manufacturing Sector (Over-all)	2.94	2.92	3.24	3.32	3.49	3.49	3.55	4.30

growth brings some alleviation to those suffering most, such growth is not a contribution to development but rather to the continued underdevelopment of the Third World.

Employment: Impacts and Causes

It is well known that unemployment and underemployment in LDC's is very high and increasing sharply. It is now probably over 30 percent of the active labor force. Is there any hope for at least a partial diminution of the problem in the near future? If the past is any indication, the answer is no. With population growing at around 3 percent in many Third World countries, the Prebisch Report concluded that total output would have to grow by 8 percent per annum between 1970 and 1980 in order to absorb current unemployment as well as the new additions to the labor force. To maintain the 1960 unemployment levels, total output would have to grow at a yearly rate of 6 percent for 1970 to 1980, a rate higher than any yet achieved in Latin America.

An underlying cause of the unemployment crisis is the particular industrialization process used to bring about economic growth. The technology transferred to the Third World by the MNC's has been designed for the advanced industrialized nations where there is a relative abundance of capital and a relative scarcity of labor. Thus, the MNC drug companies use a technology in which only 3.4 percent of total costs are due to labor. There is, of course, an obvious contradiction in brining such technology to Third World countries where there is an abundance of labor and an acute scarcity of capital. Let us look at an example of the change in the employment capacity of the industries where MNC's have their most intensive expansion. Table 15-3 above shows an estimated index of the capital to labor requirements in the five industries in which MNC's concentrated most of their investments in Colombia between 1960 and 1967.

The index numbers shown are an approximation of the amount of fixed capital investment needed to employ a unit of labor. The table indicates that the increase in fixed investment was smaller for the industrial manufacturing sector as a whole, compared to the other specific industries where MNC's were concentrating their new investments.

It is this process of ever more intensive substitution of capital for labor in the technology transferred by the MNC's, which is one of the prime causes of the startling degree of unemployment in the Third World—a situation which Africa and Asia only recently have begun to face, but which has been gnawing at Latin America since the 1920's, given its earlier entry into "modern" industrialization. Thus between 1925 and 1960, the manufacturing sector was able to absorb only 5 million of the 23 million people who migrated into urban centers from the countryside in Latin America. And while the total output of modern manufacturing industries expanded relative to other activities, so that it increased its share of national product from 11 percent in 1925 to 25 percent in 1970, the work force which it employed actually decreased from 14.4 percent to 13.8 percent over the same time period. Or look at Mexico—one of the most successful in terms of economic growth rates and expansion of industrial output, and one of the largest recipients of investment by MNC's—where the manufacturing sector's rate of increase in production was about double its rate of increase in new jobs.

Yet statistics such as these are incapable of conveying the human tragedy of the millions upon millions of unemployed in the Third World. And it is difficult to understand why two of the most important reports underlying the Nixon Administration's foreign aid policy, the Rockefeller and Peterson Reports, almost totally ignored the unemployment problem.

With over 99 percent of the industrial technology of most of the Third World coming from the industrialized nations and controlled largely by MNC's, our conclusion is that the MNC's are eliminating more jobs than they are creating.

Income Distribution: Impacts and Causes

Unemployment is only one dimension of poverty; the other is income distribution.

In focusing on the relationship between MNC's technology and income distribution in LDC's the first question is the extent to which capital versus labor is used to produce output. We have seen that capital is replacing labor at a growing rate, so that the second and more important question is who receives the income generated by capital resources? Most LDC economies are based on the legal institutions of capitalism, meaning that the owners of capital resources receive the income generated by those resources. Where there are only a very small number of owners (and thus a very large number of non-owners) of capital, and where the technology used generates a larger proportion of income from capital than labor resources, then, by definition, income distribution will be highly unequal. In addition, where there is a relatively rapid change in technology biased towards laborsaving techniques, and where capitalist legal institutions are not modified via, for example, more progressive tax rates, to keep pace with this change, then, again by definition, income distribution will become even more unequal over time. This is the second dimension of the growing poverty in LDC's. Just how unequal is the distribution of national income in LDC's, and how has it been changing over time? The answer is very unequal and more unequal over time.

Irma Adelman and Cynthia Taft Morris, in a worldwide study of income distribution in Third World countries undergoing the industrialization process we have been describing, noted that from subsistence levels throughout the industrial "take-off," until an average per capita income level of about $800, there is a profound change in income distribution. During this "take-off," the richest 5 percent of LDC populations experience a "striking" increase in incomes compared to the poorest 40 percent of the population. While their countries are achieving what economists call rapid economic growth, as indicated by increases in output and the misleading term average per capita income, many people's actual intake of food, clothing, and shelter is declining! Latin-American countries, in the midst of industrialization, provide a dramatic verification of this finding. In the 1960's, for example, Chile's average per capita income was approximately $600, but the richest 10 percent were receiving 40 percent of the national income, or an actual per capita income of some $2,400—thus giving a family income higher than the majority of Western European families. In Mexico and Brazil, the situation is worse, and it is notable that these two countries have been by far the most favored investment targets of the MNC's in Latin America.

In Mexico in the early 1950's, the ratio of individual income of the richest 20 percent to the poorest 20 percent was ten to one. By the middle 1960's, the ratio had increased to seventeen to one. Yet even these figures obscure what is taking place in the urban industrial zones where MNC investment is concentrated. For example, in the Mexico City area, the richest 20 percent received 62.5 percent of the area's income while the poorest 20 percent attempted survival on 1.3 percent of this income. In Brazil, where unprecedented increases in industrial output are being achieved, almost all of the benefits of that increase are going to the richest 5 percent. In the short span of 10 years, their share of national income went from 27.8 percent (a U.S. government estimate) or 44 percent (a U.N. estimate), to a 1970 figure of 36.8 percent (U.S.) or 50 percent (U.N.). And what about the poorest 40 percent—some 40 million Brazilian people? Using the U.S. government figures as the conservative estimate, from 1960 to 1970 their income share dropped from 10.6 percent to 8.1 percent.

Perhaps the most dismal aspect of these figures, however, is the implication for the children of the poorest 40 percent of LDC populations. Although these families somehow survive, survival itself is a relative term. Scientists have confirmed that the undernourished children of these families suffer permanent brain damage severe enough to impair their mental and physical faculties, due to the fact that these families cannot afford food with adequate nutrients.

Thus, the income distribution of today's LDC will determine the lives and the productiveness of the greater bulk of its active labor force well into the beginning of the twenty-first century.

The investment incurred in establishing a subsidiary operation of an MNC is made up largely of the costs of the plant and equipment. On the average, anywhere from 50 to 65 percent represents the cost of the subsidiary's technology, as valued by and received from the parent MNC. Thus the dollar value placed on this technology is crucial to the over-all investment figure claimed to have been made by the MNC. This value of fixed investment is important to the parent for both economic and political reasons. For example, in many LDC's the tax rate on profits and/or excess profits is based on the dollar sum of profits calculated as a percentage of the value of fixed investment. This is the "rate of return"; it will be lower, as will the tax liability of the subsidiary, the higher the value of fixed investment claimed. In addition, many LDC's place limitations on the amount of profits that can be repatriated by an MNC subsidiary in any given period. Again this limit is based on the value of the fixed investment; thus, the higher the fixed investment, the greater the dollar amount of profits that can be transferred from the LDC.

The declared fixed investment via the declared rate of return also has political significance to the managers of the MNC's. A key operational criterion is to avoid charges of "exploitation" or—in the parlance of Western economists—charges of "excess profits."

Since the empirical basis of such charges relies on the rate of return in the first instance, it is wise to keep that rate as "normal" as is possible. The point here is to emphasize the motivations of MNC's to keep their declared values of transferred technology, and therefore fixed investment, as high as possible.

We can now look at some of the evidence on the actual values of MNC's transferred technology. From Mexico there have been numerous reported cases of secondhand technology being transferred to subsidiaries, declared as either new equipment or valued at prices much higher than could have been obtained on independent markets.[7] In Colombia, where detailed investigations have been undertaken, in *all* cases substantial overvaluation of the technology was found. For example, a parent MNC was selling machinery to its own subsidiary at prices 30 percent higher than it was charging for the identical items to an independent Colombian firm. In another case, investigation revealed that the value of machinery declared at $1.8 million was in fact overstated by 50 percent, the true figure being $1.2 million. In the paper industry, an MNC subsidiary applied for an import permit for *used* machinery which it claimed had a value in excess of $1 million. The government agency then asked for competitive bids internationally on *new* models of the same machinery. The MNC's declared value for the used machinery was found to be 50 percent greater than bids received on the new machinery. Finally, in research being conducted by the present author for a forthcoming book, interviews with managers of subsidiaries in LDC's were held. In a number of cases these managers admitted that overvaluing their technology was a common practice.

Financial Contribution of Domestic Firms

A traditional argument in favor of MNC expansion in the Third World has been that they bring much needed finance capital. The key assumption here is, of course, that the MNC's in fact do utilize foreign savings to finance their LDC operations. This assumption, incidentally, is also made by Marxist scholars who have held that MNC's expand from their home countries because of an excess of surplus finance capital. Upon investigation, however, the assumption proves to be incorrect. Table 15-4 below shows just how far from reality this argument is.

Table 15-4 shows that only 17 percent of the total finance capital used by MNC's in their gross investments came from nonlocal savings. In the last three years of the 1957-65 period, the figure dropped to 9 percent. Of more importance is the use of local savings in manufacturing, the most rapidly expanding of the three sectors. Here the figure of 78 percent of total financing being derived locally has been constant since 1960. Individual country studies covering the latest years of 1965-1970 also have shown no change.

In manufacturing, we see that 38 percent of the finance capital used by MNC subsidiaries comes from local "internal" sources (largely reinvested earnings) and 40 percent from local capital markets. While in an official accounting sense, reinvested earnings are classified as funds from the home country, such a classification misses the real economic meaning, as they were generated by the use of largely local resources to start with—both local financial and other resources. These reinvested earnings are local savings in the same sense that they are for a 100 percent domestically owned and controlled corporation, with one major exception. Whereas the future net profits (after taxes) from earnings reinvested today constitute, in the case of local firms, a net gain to the income of the LDC that most likely will stay *internalized* to the country, this is not the case for an MNC subsidiary.

Table 15-4 U.S. MNC Gross Investments in Latin America Financed from Local vs. Foreign Savings (in percentages)

Area & Sector	U.S.	Origin of Finance Capital 1957-1965		
		Reinvested Earnings & Depreciation (1)	Local, Host Country (2)	Total Local (1+2)
Latin America, Total	17	59	24	83
Mining & Smelting	8	78	14	92
Petroleum	13	79	8	87
Manufacturing	22	38	40	78
		Origin of Finance Capital 1963-1965		
Latin America, Total	9	60	31	91
Mining & Smelting	− 17	104	13	117
Petroleum	− 10	96	14	110
Manufacturing	22	38	40	78

Although the MNC subsidiary's future profit represents a net gain in income for itself, it will be largely *externalized* out of the LDC, and therefore not for the consumption or investment benefit of the local citizenry. This is borne out by the fact that, from 1960 to 1968, MNC's repatriated an average of 79 percent of their net profits, not to mention their additional remissions of royalties, interest, and other fees. In manufacturing, repatriated profits were somewhat lower but increasing, going from 42 percent of net profits in 1960-1964 to 52 percent in 1965-1968.[8] In the manufacturing sector, for each dollar of net profit earned by an MNC subsidiary, 52 cents will leave the country even though 78 percent of the investment funds used to generate that dollar of profit came from local sources. If we look at all sectors in which MNC's operate in Latin America, the inflow-outflow accounting gets even worse. Each dollar of net profit is based on an investment that was 83 percent financed from local savings; yet only 21 percent of the profit remains in the local economy.

Do the MNC's make a financial contribution to LDC's; i.e., do they make a net addition to the supply of available local savings over time? The answer is no. Although we cannot make an exact quantitative estimate of this loss, from the magnitudes of the above indicators it is clear that there is a net decrease in the amount of local savings being utilized for the benefit of either indigenous consumers or investors in local LDC's.

The Buying-Out of Domestic Firms

We now turn to the specific uses to which MNC's put finance capital. It is commonly held that when an MNC invests in an LDC, even if it uses largely local savings, it at least channels that investment into the creation of *new* production facilities; facilities which otherwise could have been absent from the local economy, i.e., a net addition to the productive assets of the LDC.

Again, reference to the facts shows this notion to be more myth than reality.

This conclusion can be demonstrated by the data now available on the 187 largest U.S. MNC's, which account for some 70 percent of all U.S. foreign investment in Latin America.[9] From 1958 to 1967 these firms established 1,309 subsidiaries. Of this number there are 173 cases for which no information was available on method of entry. Of the remaining 1,136 subsidiaries, 477, or more than 42 percent of these subsidiaries, were formed by buying out local enterprises. The figures become even more convincing when we examine the method of entry of new subsidiaries in the manufacturing sector in which the majority of the total were established and in which the MNC's are expanding fastest. For the 717 known new manufacturing subsidiaries, 46 percent or 331 did not establish new production but rather purchased existing domestic firms. Compared to the percentage of finance capital devoted to such acquisitions since 1929, the rate of increase is notable throughout. In addition, it was observed that in industries where the percentage of foreign investment going to acquisitions had decreased, the decline was "probably attributable in part to the scarcity of local firms (remaining) in these industries."

The implications are clear. In the manufacturing sector, currently the most important to the future development of Latin America, 78 percent of MNC's foreign investments are financed in actuality from local savings. With this finance capital, an estimated 46 percent is used to buy out existing locally controlled firms, whose profits would otherwise have been retained domestically and would thus have contributed to either local consumption and/or savings. But from the date of the acquisition and henceforth, some 52 percent of those profits will leave the country, resulting in a net decrease in the LDC's savings which would have been otherwise available *and* a net increase in their already acute shortage of foreign exchange. Given these results, it is impossible to see how the MNC's financial impact on Third World countries could possibly assist in the alleviation of their underdevelopment.

It is well known that Latin America, due to its head start into industrialization relative to Asia and Africa, is experiencing the severest of difficulties in maintaining its ability to pay off foreign debts. Besides the increasing negative gap between exports and imports, the region's foreign debts are growing at a rapid rate due to repayments of past public and private loans; concomitantly, outflows continue to mount on payments of profits, royalties, and interest for past MNC direct investment. While in the period 1951–1955 these latter items accounted for some 13 percent of the annual export earnings of the Latin-American countries, by the 1966–1969 time period, they took 21 percent.[10]

It is not surprising therefore that experts in both the offices of Wall Street and the government buildings of the Third World are taking an intense interest in the balance-of-payments impact of the MNC's. And it is also not surprising that different experts come to different conclusions on the matter.

Beyond an analysis of the sources of MNC's financial capital, there is a second dimension: the export and import behavior of these global corporations as well as their remittances of royalties and service fees. The latter item is the so-called managerial fee paid to the parent MNC for technical assistance rendered to its own subsidiaries and joint ventures, as well as to licensees of technology. These royalty and fee payments have reached significant proportions, accounting for some 25 percent of the total returns from all U.S. MNC's foreign investments in 1970. As for the significance of MNC's export and import operations, it should be noted that in 1968, U.S. MNC's were responsible for 40 percent of Latin America's manufacturing exports, and in 1966, some 33 percent of its total exports, while accounting for more than a third of the region's imports from the United States. We should emphasize here that these percentages refer largely to so-called *intracompany transactions:* exports and imports between subsidiaries of the same parent network. From the U.S. side, these intracompany transactions were very important, reflected by the fact that U.S. MNC's shipped some 58 percent of total U.S. manufactured exports directly to their subsidiaries in 1970.

It has been claimed that the MNC's can make a significant contribution to raising the foreign exchange earnings of Third World countries through their ability to export (particularly manufactured goods). On the surface this argument would appear correct given the competitive advantages of the technology and worldwide marketing systems of the MNC's compared to local firms. There are a number of considerations, however, which this argument overlooks. First, if MNC's have subsidiaries manufacturing similar products in many countries, as most of them do, would these subsidiaries want to compete with each other through exports? Second, even where the parents have complementary production between subsidiaries so that intersubsidiary exports and imports are desirable, what are the prices on such exports and imports, since as nonmarket transactions they are not subject to competitive pressures? Third, what are the tax and other financial criteria which would make these prices different from those received or paid by local firms dealing with independent buyers and sellers on the international market? Fourth, what does the available empirical evidence tell us concerning the initial argument and the considerations we have introduced? Fifth, besides the exporting by MNC subsidiaries, what impact does the licensing of their technology to local firms have on the latter's ability to export?

The MNC's and Exports: Restrictions

We shall start with the last question first. In detailed investigations of the licensing agreements between local firms in LDC's and the MNC's, it has been found that in most cases there are total prohibitions on using this technology in the production of exports. These findings can be seen below in Table 15-5 where they are classified by local firms versus MNC subsidiary, by industry of activity, and by country. The table is based on the results of a study of 409 "transfer of technology" contracts in the five countries of the Andean Group: Bolivia, Colombia, Chile, Ecuador, and Peru.

As telling as these figures are, they are, nevertheless, biased downwards. In many of the contracts which permitted some exporting, the effect was really a total prohibition, since they limited the firms to either a small neighboring market in which the MNC's had no interest, or they limited exports to distant countries which local firms could virtually not hope to penetrate. And these practices are not unique to the Andean countries. Similar results have been revealed by government and UNCTAD studies in India, Pakistan, the Philippines, Mexico, Iran, etc. The impact of these "restrictive business practices" (to use the formal language of the U.N.) on the export capacity of domestic firms and their LDC economies is profound. For at a time when the political leaders of the MDC's are encouraging Third World countries to export more, their own MNC's are making it virtually impossible for them to enter the one export market which in the long run is viable—namely, manufactured exports.

We turn now to the question of the export performance of the MNC subsidiaries themselves. It does not necessarily follow that the MNC's will export from LDC locations even though they may have the technology and marketing prerequisites. In the Andean Group,

Table 15-5 Export Prohibitions in Technology Contracts: Andean Group Countries

By Ownership of Firms	Percentage with Export Prohibitions
Wholly owned MNC Subsidiaries	79
Nationally owned Firms	92
By Industry of Firms	
Textile	88
Pharmaceuticals	89
Chemicals	78
Food & Beverages	73
Other	91
By Country-Location of Firms	
Bolivia	77
Chile	72
Colombia	77
Ecuador	75
Peru	72
Number of contracts for which information available = 409	

79 percent of the MNC subsidiaries were prohibited by their parents to engage in exporting, and these findings are not unique to these countries. In fact, studies for Latin America have found that manufacturing MNC's on the average export less than 10 percent of their total sales, while in Europe, U.S. firms average about 25 percent.[11] There are exceptions, however. Some MNC subsidiaries do export significant *volumes* depending on the industry and country in which they are located.

Performance and Pricing

We have already alluded to the fact that U.S. MNC's account for some 40 percent of Latin America's manufactured exports, and they have achieved this level of export participation within the span of the past 20 years. Yet the figure is a deceptive one if it is intended to imply that MNC's are therefore making a significant positive impact on the balance of payments of Third World countries. First, manufactured exports constitute only 16.6 percent of the region's total exports, and well over half of these exports come from only 3 of the 21 countries: Argentina, Brazil, and Mexico. The above-cited detailed econometric analysis has determined that, relative to local firms, MNC subsidiaries performed significantly better only in these three countries and only in terms of export sales to other Latin-American countries. In contrast, for exports to the rest of the world, where one would expect the technological and marketing superiority of the MNC's to be most crucial, their export performance was not significantly different from domestic enterprises. For the remaining countries of the region, the MNC's were outperformed on exports to the rest of the world by firms which had substantial domestic participation, while on exports to other Latin-American countries, the MNC's performed no differently than their domestic counterparts.

The price put on an export or import between MNC subsidiaries of the same parent is termed a "transfer price." Frequently, transfer prices deviate sharply from the market price of these goods. For example, if a subsidiary exporting in country X is faced with higher corporate tax rates than the importing subsidiary of the same parent in county M, then the parent will pay less *total* taxes for both subsidiaries and earn more *total* net profits by directing the exporting subsidiary to undervalue its exports. Another variant of this pricing technique, even more profitable, is to direct the underpriced exports first to a tax-free port (so-called tax havens) and then re-export the goods at their normal market value (or perhaps now overvalue) to the subsidiary of final destination. There is an obvious impact on the economy of the LDC in which such exports originate: the LDC governments, seriously short of needed tax revenues, are now deprived of that much more, so that an MNC can "maximize" their global profits.

In looking at the export pricing of MNC's in Latin America, the above-cited study found that 75 percent of these firms sold exports only to other subsidiaries of the same parent and, on the average, *underpriced their exports by some 40-50 percent* relative to the prices being received by local firms.

We should also mention an additional "restrictive clause" in the transfer of technology contracts negotiated between MNC parents and their subsidiaries and licensees. This is the so-called "tie-in clause," which requires the subsidiary or the licensee to purchase intermediate parts and capital goods from the same parent MNC which supplied the basic technology. This practice is common operational behavior for MNC's in the Third World. For example, in the Andean Group study, 67 percent of the investigated contracts had tie-in clauses. The results were no different in other countries such as India or Pakistan. [12]

The irony is that these types of clauses are in basic violation of the antitrust laws of the home countries of the MNC's which practice them in LDC's. In the United States, tie-in clauses are prohibited by Section 1 of the Sherman Act and Section 3 of the Clayton Act. Whether or not these laws are applicable to the MNC's in their overseas operations is still a moot question, but the fact that underdeveloped legal institutions of LDC's do not yet deal with these restrictions strongly underlines the differences in the oligopoly power of MNC's in advanced industrialized *versus* Third World countries.

Import Overpricing

We can now introduce evidence on import overpricing. Since this information is relatively unknown to economists and noneconomists alike, we shall devote some detail to it in Tables 15-6 and 15-7 below, drawing in large part on the important work at Harvard of Constantine Vaitsos, now a leading economist and planner in Peru for the Andean Common Market.

Overpricing is not unique to Colombia. Similar results have been discovered in other parts of Latin America and in other regions such as the Philippines and Pakistan. In Chile, overpricing ranges from 30 percent to more than 700 percent, in Peru from 50 percent to 300 percent, and in Ecuador from 75 percent to 200 percent. Apparently the techniques for extralegally transferring funds out of LDC's does not stop short of overpricing actual imports. During a two-day interview with the head of a European MNC subsidiary in a South-American country, I was shown shipping crates which had just cleared local customs. In this isolated case, the shipping crates contained less than 30 percent of their

Table 15-6 Overpricing of Imported Intermediate Parts by Foreign Ownership Structure: Colombia 1968 (in percentages)

Ownership Structure	Pharmaceutical Industry			Rubber Industry			Chemical Industry			Electronics Industry		
Structure	a	b	c	a	b	c	a	b	c	a	b	c
Foreign Owned	50	25	155	33	60	40	30	12	25.5	40	90	16-60
Joint Ventures	n.a.	n.a.	n.a.	n.a.	n.a.	n.a.	45	37	20.2	50	90	6-50

Code: a: approximate percentage of sales of sample-firms relative to total sales of firms with similar ownership structure
b: total volume of imports sampled and evaluated as a percentage of the firm's total imports
c: weighted average of overpricing of evaluated imports
n.a.: not available

Table 15-7 Selected Samples of Overpricing of Intermediate Imported Parts[a] By Specific Industry and Product: Colombia 1968

Specific Industry & Product:	Percentage Overpricing
Drug Industry	
Ampicillin	136
Tetracycline Hydrochloride	987
Tetracycline (base)	948
Valium[b]	8200
Clordiazepoxide (librium)[b]	6500
Electronics Industry	
1st TV Amplifier	258
U.S. Detector Transistors	1100
4 Pole Motor	404
Chemicals Industry	
Shellac	34.3
Acetic Acid	19.8
Nitrocellulose—30 percent I.P.A.	59.32

[a] Percent overpricing   (Import Price FOB Colombia-International Price Quotations FOB) ÷ International Price Quotations FOB
[b] From the Colombian (Bogotá) daily newspaper, "El Espectador," February 6, 1970, p.1A, reporting on the official government investigation

declared contents, although the payment to an offshore subsidiary of the parent was for 100 percent of the declared contents at a unit overpricing of 2,500 percent. One can only speculate as to what extent this represents the day-to-day behavior of MNC's in the Third World.

The total value of the overpricing for *actually sampled* items in four industries was more than $4 million. If the average overpricing is extended and assumed to hold for the rest of the products and MNC's in the drug industry, then the total loss to the 1968 Colombian balance of payments was on the order of $20 million with a loss in government tax revenues of some $10 million . . . this from one industry alone!

The Triangular Trade

In the Colombian investigation, it was found that a large proportion of the overpriced imports involved a "triangular trade." That is, they were shipped from a U.S.- or European-based parent or subsidiary of the parent to a holding company in Panama. In Panama, a tax haven, the prices of these articles were raised to their stated overpriced levels and then re-exported on to Colombia. Thus, the MNC's involved avoided tax payments on their true profits in *both* the country of export origin and in Colombia.

Panama serves still another function. MNC subsidiaries in Panama often hold the registration for many of the parent companies' other foreign investments in Latin America. In Peru, for example, Panama is the second largest foreign country in which foreign investments are registered. This procedure permits the channelling of royalty and fee payments to Panama, thereby giving the MNC's a substantial flexibility as to where they ultimately report their income. The income from royalties and fees alone is large and in fact, most often considerably greater than reported profits received from subsidiaries. In the Andean Group, for example, MNC subsidiaries' royalties paid to the parent are fixed at anywhere from 10 to 15 percent of gross or net sales, depending on the particular company. Since a considerable part of the final sale price is based on imported intermediate parts, which are overvalued, the MNC's multiply their unearned profits, first via the import overpricing and second through that component of royalties derived from an inflated sales price due to the overpricing. The earnings thus generated are impressive both relative to the MNC's reported profits and to the foreign exchange shortages of these countries. Thus in Chile the outflow of royalties is three times greater than profit remittances.

Reported vs. Actual Rates of Return

Taken together, overpricing of imports plus reported profits, royalties, and fees gives the total dollar value of profits generated by a subsidiary in a given year. This total dollar value of "effective profits" can then be divided into the subsidiary's declared net worth of its investments (including reinvested earnings). The resulting answer is what we call the "annual rate of return on investment." Vaitsos and his group performed this exercise for 100 percent parent-owned MNC drug subsidiaries in Colombia. The results showed an annual rate of investment return by wholly-owned MNC drug subsidiaries in Colombia in 1968 ranging from a low of 38.1 percent to an astonshing high of 962.1 percent. The average of declared returns to Colombia tax authorities was 6.7 percent, while the average effective rate of return was 136.3 percent.

As high as these rates of return are, they undoubtedly *understate* the actual sums earned by these MNC's. First, if any of these firms exported, the above calculations do not include the probability of export underpricing, which as shown earlier is quite high. Second, and more important, these returns are based on the net worth of investment as declared by the subsidiaries. As pointed out previously, all evidence to date indicates there is substantial overvaluation of declared investment of approximately 30 to 50 percent. One Colombian economist, Dario Abad, has commented on the fact that between 1960 and 1968 the average *reported* rate of return for MNC's in all manufacturing sectors of the country was 6.4 percent. He found it "difficult to accept" that these MNC's would continue to enter Colombia at this rate of reported profitability while national firms were showing higher returns and the interest rate in financial markets was running between 16 and 20 percent.

Conclusions

My over-all conclusion concerning the impact of MNC's on Third World countries is clear. With respect to the 1950-1970 period investigated, I have found more myth than reality in the claims made about the three most important contributions of MNC's. My analysis of the technology contribution revealed instead a basic cause of further unemployment and a further concentration of already extremely unequal income distribution, while noting the excessive prices being charged by the MNC's in transferring this technology. Upon examination, the financial contribution turns out to be a financial drain, thereby decreasing both current consumption and available local savings and thus future consumption for the vast majority of LDC inhabitants. In contrast to a balance-of-payments contribution, the data showed no superior export performance by MNC's relative to local firms unless it was accompanied by export underpricing. Concomitantly, exports were further limited via restrictions placed on their technology by the MNC's. While potential inflows were minimized, the balance-of-payments outflows were accentuated through import overpricing and inflated royalty payments.

Such an impact can only contribute to the further impoverishment of the poorest 60 to 80 percent of Third World populations. Summing up the specific consequences thus far analyzed, however, leads to an over-all consequence which should be given at least brief mention. In the Third World, the MNC's are involved in a structural process which cannot be ignored. I have already referred to the fact that this process permits an ever greater control over the technology and finances of the majority of LDC's, resulting in what Celso Furtado, among others, has shown to be an ever growing external dependence of the poor nations on the few rich nations of the world. Besides the transfer-in of inappropriate technology and the transfer-out of financial resources, this process includes one further destabilizing force.

The MNC's are also involved in the transfer of a consumption ideology, the goals of which only, at best, 30 percent, and more realistically 20 percent of LDC populations, can hope to achieve in the foreseeable future. Still, these consumption goals do not go unheeded by the greater majority in these countries. There is a rather blatant contradiction at work here. The new structure of consumption is in serious imbalance with the inadequate consumption capacity generated by the very production structure which the MNC's have largely helped to create, and which negates any possibility of attaining the new consumption goals by any except a small minority. Perhaps here we can find a major cause for the profound and growing frustration in many underdeveloped countries. When many share the same frustration, the problem goes beyond the realm of economics and becomes social and political.

Latin America, the region which has nurtured this frustration relatively longer than any other Third World area, has already witnessed three patterns of political response to this problem. The decision of Brazil and Mexico has been to continue the present reliance on the MNC's via the expedient of growing political oppression. Cuba is attempting to detach itself from industrialization via the MNC's by establishing socialist institutions. And the Peruvian military appears to be in the midst of deciding to what extent it desires, let alone is able, to minimize and/or modify the role of the MNC's to pursue a new form of national development. What the long-run viability of any of these three responses will be cannot be dealt with here. There is, however, a clear message. The continued and unaltered expansion of the MNC's into the Third World will increase the instability of these societies and will bring about significant political change.

To the extent that such political change will reduce the bargaining power of the MNC's in these countries and thereby diminish the transfer of income to MNC's, the result could be a drop in the general level of affluence in advanced nations. Such an interpretation could, in fact, be given to the creation of the Organization of Petroleum Exporting Countries (OPEC) and the "Energy Crisis" being faced in the United States and other MDC's. OPEC has succeeded in significantly reducing the flow of petroleum-generated income from poor to rich nations; so that by the late 1970's the rising price of energy—the backbone of modern industrial society—will have negatively affected the consumption levels of the majority of people residing in MDC's.

If new mechanisms for increasing Third World bargaining power over MNC's in the manufacturing sector are found, then there will be even more profound implications on maintaining present consumption styles in the rich nations. Whether or not the United States, Japan, and Western Europe will permit such mechanisms to become reality can only be speculated upon.

NOTES

1. *Constantine V. Vaitsos, "Patents Revisited,"* The Journal of Development Studies, *1973, p. 7.*

2. *John M. Blair,* Economic Concentration: Structure, Behavior and Public Policy, *1972, p. 205.*

3. *Vaitsos, op. cit., p. 12.*

4. *R. Prebisch,* Change and Development: Latin America's Great Task, *1970, or United Nations Survey for Latin America (ECLA), 1971, 1972.*

5. *Miguel Wionczek, "La Banca Extranjera en America Latina," presented to Novena Reunión de Técnicos de los Bancos Centrales del Continente Americano, Lima, November 1969; and Aldo Ferrer, "El Capital Extranjero en la Economia Argentina,"* Trimestre Economico, *No. 150, Abril-Junio 1971.*

6. *The figures for Chile are taken from Luis Pacheco in* Proceso a la Industrialización Chilena, *1972, and from Corporación de Fomento de la Producción (CORFO), Las Inversiones Extranjeras en la Industria Chilena Periodo 1960-69, 1971.*

7. *See citations in Leopaldo Solis, "Mexican Economic Policy in the Post-War Period: The Views of Mexican Economists,"* American Economic Review, *June 1971, Vol. 16, No. 3 p. 22, and also Miguel Wionczek in* Comercio Exterior, *December 7, 1967.*

8. *Fernando Fajnzylber,* Estrategia Industrial y Empresas Internacionales, *1970.*

9. *J. W. Vaupel and J. P. Curhan,* The Making of Multinational Enterprise, *1969, pp. 254–265.*

10. *Felipe Pazos in* Trimestre Económico, *No. 150, Abril-Junio 1971.*

11. *Ronald Müller and Richard Morgenstern, "Econometric Evidence on Multinational Corporate Behavior: Transfer Pricing and Exports in Less Developed Countries," paper presented to the American Economics Association, Toronto, December 28, 1972. For aggregates on Latin America and Europe see R. D. Belli, "Sales of Foreign Affiliates of U.S. Firms," in* Survey of Current Business, *L, No. 10, October 1970, p. 20.*

12. *UNCTAD,* Transfer of Technology. . . . *December, 1971, pp. 14–15, and Restrictive Business Practices, op. cit., pp. 44–45. These technology contracts also include many other restrictions, e.g., the MNC can determine final selling prices and volume, select key personnel in the licensee's business, etc.*

PART **IV**
REGULATION

INTRODUCTION

As should now be obvious, transnational enterprises both face and create numerous problems. A simple balance sheet of credits and debits to the account of world order cannot be drawn at this stage; and no single balance sheet would in any case suffice. We now know enough to say that such an inventory would include, on the credit side, efficiency in the performance of global functions and contribution to consolidating the foundations of a world economic system, possibly even a world society. But the list of complaints on the debit side cannot be ignored (see Part III). What measures and policies are needed to minimize these debit entries and to enhance the positive effects?

One policy that has been advocated is "unfettered free enterprise." The argument is that transnational corporations perform their functions best if left to themselves and if allowed to govern their own affairs in pursuance of their own interests, for they are clusters of useful social activity, and such activity flourishes when there is no interference. The public interest would indeed suffer if the economic efficiency of transnational corporations were to be decreased as a result of excess governmental meddling.

This type of argument seems to be implicit in Tannenbaum's article, reviewed in Part III. In Tannenbaum's view, the international corporate body would provide not only indispensable international services, such as communications and the manufacture and distribution of key products, but also some of the basis services of government, this makes redundant the security problems that have engaged the attention of nation-states and becomes the critical component of world order. Spokesmen for business generally take the same position without feeling it necessary to explain such elaborate reasoning, and argue persuasively for freedom from outside interference, resentful of anything that would be likely to slow down the progress of the work at hand.

Granted that transnational corporations need a certain degree of autonomy, the case for "unfettered" free enterprise is weak. The operations of large corporations tend not to be self-correcting because of the imperfections of the markets and the societies in which they function. The services of large firms do not fulfill the needs and requirements of all the world's peoples; other organizations are therefore needed. The degree to which any organizations and institutions are capable of serving these purposes is an open question, too; their activities must be monitored and justified. For if it is agreed that large international firms are only one of the elements out of which a viable world order may be built, then there is a case for coordinating these various elements and relating each to the other both in a supportive and in a mutually restrictive fashion.

That is why the transnational enterprise, like any modern enterprise, must be viewed as subject to three broad kinds of control.[1]

1. *Economic controls:* "the controls exercised by other enterprises and economic suppliers, consumers, rivals . . . sometimes through complex mechanisms of the market, sometimes through bargaining, collusion, collaboration. . . ."

2. *Internal controls:* "exercised by those who directly manage or run the firm."

3. *Governmental controls:* "exercised by the various governments at the state, local, provincial and national" levels, and we might add, at the international public level.

All that we know about the large international firm tends to suggest that the *economic controls* upon it tend to be light. As shown in Part II, the chief characteristics of monopolistic or oligopolistic firms are their market power, bargaining strength, size, and activity. They are also firms upon whom the restraints normally expected to operate in a competitive market have less impact. John Galbraith has strikingly portrayed the powerful firm skillfully manipulating markets, consumers, small firms, and even households and established social institutions, to its own advantage (see, for example, *The New Industrial State,* 1967, or *The Economics of Public Purpose,* 1973). This is not to say that large firms are totally exempt from economic controls. Their power and self-confidence may fatally retard the adjustment to secular and long-range trends that smaller firms must make much sooner. Even large firms find that in the normal course of economic life, they encounter considerable risks (such as the occasional case of bankruptcy) and uncertainty (mergers, and the like). Hence it is a fundamental condition of a sound system of large corporations that free-market competition (the "invisible hand") exercises a significant influence over the decisions of these firms and in fact, over the decisions of all economic units. Such influence may be enhanced by maintaining free entry into all industries, and even promoting divestiture in cases where excessive size interferes with the functioning of markets. It is true nonetheless that as a general rule, economic controls are less effective where large firms are concerned and hence that in these situations, stricter internal and governmental controls are necessary.

In an article entitled, "Governing the Large Corporation," Robert Dahl[2] spelled out some of the problems involved in *internal control* of such an enterprise. He was not concerned specifically with the transnational corporation but only with the 200–500 largest American firms. Yet because large firms generally have high international content, his analysis also has implications for our own field.

Dahl pointed out that the large firm should be thought of both as a social enterprise (an entity that can gain legitimacy only insofar as it serves public or social purposes) and also as a political system whose governance requires close scrutiny, which it does not normally receive. Like other political systems, it must meet the requirements of being responsible and accountable, competent and economical. For the internal government of a large firm a number of alternate constitutional forms need to be considered (stockholder democracy, control by employees, representation of interest groups—such as investors, consumers, and the general public—and codetermination). Their respective advantages should be ascertained and kept distinct from questions of ownership—of which a number of alternate forms also are conceivable.

The focal point of the governance of a large firm is the board of directors, and altering the composition of that board is one way to control a corporation. With regard to multinational firms, some attention has been given to rotating the nationality of board members as a way of promoting international responsiveness and accountability. Yet at the central level there is little evidence of a trend toward multinational board membership, and if it did exist in more than token form, its significance would be unclear. (A survey of 150 United States companies in 1965 showed that 1.6 percent of the top corporate positions, including directorships, were held by non-Americans. In that year 20 percent of the total work force was non-American.[3]) Subsidiary and affiliate boards, on the other hand, frequently, and often by law, have foreign membership, but the influence of these boards is open to question. Recent years have seen some broadening of the participation of minority interests on the central boards of directors of American corporations, essentially in the form of voluntary interest group representation. Were such participation to include transnational interest groups, some new developments might ensue. Minority representation has not been without effect. A prominent black clergyman who serves on the Board of Directors of General Motors was recently instrumental in securing the agreement of twelve major corporations on a set of principles aimed at ending segregation and promoting fair employment practices at these corporations' plants in South Africa.[4]

There are a number of questions regarding the internal governance of all large corporations that need to be answered more fully, and they are particularly relevant for students of transnational enterprise. Important too is the need to emphasize the separability of questions of ownership from those of control, a subject that is discussed in selection 12. Viewed as a means of changing the ownership of a firm's assets, nationalization may in fact not be incompatible with the retention of a large degree of operational control, as the oil companies have found in Iran, Kuwait, and Saudi Arabia. But in some cases, expropriation and nationalization are, of course, methods not only of changing ownership but also of imposing new controls; they are a form of revolutionary overthrow of a firm's government.

Although the internal government of a multinational firm has received only limited attention, the question of *governmental controls,* especially at the international level, has become an increasingly important subject in the literature. How-ever, an international regulatory system for large international firms seems to be evolving along not one, but two separate tracks: one for the developed, or indus-trial countries, under the aegis of the Organization for Economic Cooperation and Development (OECD); and the other for the developing countries, which has been evolving since 1972 in the United Nations, where political leadership is now with the Third World majority. (A third track could conceivably develop for the East European countries, and would be tied closely to East-West trade relations.)

Robert Keohane and Van Doorn Ooms (a political scientist at Stanford Univer-sity and an economist at Swarthmore College, respectively) mention this bifurca-tion in their discussion of regulatory problems. They present a broad and general review of the governmental controls that are relevant to multinational corpora-tions, and their survey includes measures for the promotion of such activity, partic-ularly by home governments, and also policies for the regulation of such controls, chiefly by host countries. They distinguish clearly among the two tracks that inter-national controls are now following: one developing through the instrumentality of the OECD and consisting of efforts toward policy harmonization among the industrial countries, and the other evolving chiefly through the instrumentality of the United Nations and characterized by efforts toward altering the bargaining situation in favor of the governments of developing countries. Keohane and Ooms describe the evolution not of a regulatory system that has one new and powerful international organization at its center and is dominated by one superpower, but rather one that, in response to a number of specific problems, accommodates a variety of national and international interests and activities.

In 1976 the OECD, a Paris-based intergovernmental agency comprised of twenty-four mostly industrial countries (including the United States, Canada, Brit-ain, France, Japan, and West Germany), issued a "Declaration on International Investment and Multinational Enterprises," together with provisions for mutual consultation and review, and these may now be regarded as the basic documents regulating the activities of First World international firms. The documents, which are reproduced in selection 16, include provisions requiring greater disclosure and encouraging better labor-management relations, and they state that enterprises "should not render . . . any bribe . . . to any public servant or holder of public office." Multinational corporations took part in the drafting of these documents (as members of the Business and Industry Consultative Committee), as did labor, and they seem to be generally happy with it. In its annual report for 1976, IBM an-nounced its "full support" for the declaration and, although it commended the "voluntary" nature of the guidelines, it expressed the intention to give them "full consideration" when formulating company policies.

Although he covers some of the same ground as Keohane and Ooms, Francisco Orrego Vicuña, a law professor at the University of Chile, presents a somewhat different point of view—his is an analytical legal perspective. He comments exten-sively on the experience of United States corporations and the writings of North American scholars, but his analysis is oriented to the needs of the developing countries. He classifies controls according to whether they are applied unilaterally or bilaterally, by one or two countries; regionally, by a number of governments acting in unison; or internationally, through the United Nations. Unlike Keohane and Ooms, he argues that unilaterial national action (especially on the part of the developing countries) has accomplished little; but he does expect national regulation to remain an important element, for to him regional and international forms of control are the hope of the future. The only lasting solution to the problem of unequal development posed by multinationals may be a system of taxation of the international production of such firms, to bring about a more equitable distribution of world income. Like Sunkel (selection 13), Orrego believes that the problems posed by multinational corporations will be resolved by structural changes made at the global level, giving rise to a new international economic order.

The Report of the Group of Eminent Persons to Study the Impact of Multinational Corporations on Development and on International Relations, issued in 1974, follows Orrego's trend of thought. The group consisted of twenty government officials, business leaders, and academic leaders, about evenly divided between the developed and the developing countries. Its chairman was L. K. Jha, an Indian banker and diplomatist, and its rapporteur was Juan Somavia of Chile. Its members were appointed by the Secretary General of the United Nations pursuant to a resolution of the Economic and Social Council in 1972 that was the direct consequence of the revelations about ITT involvement in Chile (noted in Part 3). But the group's deliberations also coincided with the rise to prominence of the OPEC and the consequent increase in the activity and strengthening of the influence of the developing countries in the United Nations, as reflected by the passage of such General Assembly resolutions as those on the Declaration on the Establishment of a New International Economic Order (May 1, 1974) and the Declaration of the Economic Rights and Duties of States (December 12, 1974). Hence the report, like the Orrego article, generally favors the views of the developing world; it expresses the desire to augment the bargaining power of Third World governments through action taken at the international level.

Part One of the report, reprinted here as selection 19, broadly outlines the issues the group was charged to examine. The Report begins with a description of the problems created by multinational enterprises and the problems created by inequalities of bargaining power between the corporations and some nation-states. Chapter I explains the role of the multinational firm in the development process and the conditions that would maximize their contribution to a reduction in world inequalities. Chapter II analyzes the impact of multinational corporations on international relations, condemns "subversive intervention" and the use of firms as instruments of foreign policy, and recommends that "home countries should refrain from involving themselves in differences and disputes between multinational corporations and host countries." Chapter III recommends the regular review of the subject of multinational corporations by the Economic and Social Council and the establishment of new international machinery.

The group did not unanimously approve the report; Part Three includes comments and reflections by individual members. Among the most critical and explicit expressions of dissent from a "significant number of recommendations" are those by Senator Jacob Javits of New York, one of the two American members of the group. Although he approves of the organizational proposals contained in Part One, the senator expresses certain basic reservations about the report as a whole because of its high level of generalization, its tendency to give expression to a variety of fears concerning multinational corporations because they have not been the object of a thorough investigation, and its lack of balance in the treatment of the subject as a whole. He rejects as "unrealistic" the recommendation that the home countries should refrain from pressure on behalf of corporations and argues that "it is entirely proper for a home country to review its aid programme, for example in the case of a country that has expropriated unfairly the property of home country nationals."

As previously mentioned, the evolving United Nations regulatory system for transnational corporations is part of efforts by the developing countries to alter in their favor the "rules of the game" of the international economic system.[5] The Programme of Action on the Establishment of the New International Economic Order (3202-S-VI), a companion to the Declaration passed on May 1, 1974, by the Sixth Special Session of the General Assembly, has a section on "Regulation and Control over the Activities of Transnational Corporations." The program urges that all efforts should be made to formulate, adopt, and implement an international code of conduct for transnational corporations, in order to prevent their interference in the international affairs of the countries in which they operate and their collaboration with racist regimes and colonial administrations," "to eliminate restrictive business practices . . .," and "to bring about assistance, transfer of technology and management skills to developing countries on equitable and favourable terms. . . ."

On December 5, 1974, the Economic and Social Council largely accepted the organizational recommendations of the Group of Eminent Persons, resolved to establish an intergovernmental Commission on Transnational Corporations as an advisory body to assist it in dealing with transnational corporations, and established the guidelines for the Information and Research Centre on Transnational Corporations (since renamed the Centre on Transnational Corporations). Resolution 1913 (LVII) is the fundamental charter of the new United Nations machinery in this field and is reproduced here in selection 20. It diverges from the group's recommendations inasmuch as the commission it launched is larger (forty-eight members, versus twenty-five originally proposed) and is composed of government representatives and hence not necessarily of "individuals with a profound understanding of the issues and problems involved." Both changes reflect the views of the developing countries.

A United Nations code of conduct for transnational corporations became part of the program of work of the newly established Commission on Transnational Corporations. A principal issue that arose in the course of discussion was whether the proposed code should be mandatory or voluntary. The developing countries had come around to the position that the code should be binding in nature; the other countries held the view that the new international machinery required to ensure compliance would take a long time to evolve and would require the concurrence of all the affected governments. Another issue was whether the code should apply to transnational corporations alone or to both nation-states and corporations. In addition to the general code, more specialized codes were being drafted on such matters as taxation, accounting standards, disclosure of information, and corrupt practices. (The last was proposed by the United States.)

When finally drawn up the code may be less favorable to corporations than the OECD guidelines. A framework within which such a code is likely to be drawn is the Charter of the Economic Rights and Duties of States, passed at the end of 1974 over the vigorous opposition of the United States. The final vote on the charter was 120 for, 6 against, and 10 abstaining. The United States was joined in its negative vote by Britain, Belgium, Denmark, the G.F.R., and Luxembourg; the abstainers included Canada, France, Italy, Japan, the Netherlands, and Spain.

This wide-ranging document, originally proposed in 1972 by then President of Mexico Echeverria, has, when strictly interpreted, no legal force, but its supporters hope that it will exercise a moral influence not unlike that of the Declaration of Human Rights. A less strict interpretation could claim for it the expression of a broad consensus of what the law now is. Only some of its provisions have direct relevance to transnational corporations and these have been reproduced here. Article 2 defines the state's right to regulate and supervise the activities of such corporations, including the right of expropriation without a guarantee of equitable compensation. Article 5 upholds the right to organize commodity cartels (such as OPEC). Article 13 pertains to access to technology. Article 16 declares that it is the right and duty of all states "to eliminate colonialism, *apartheid,* [and] racial discrimination . . ." and that no state has the right to promote investments that may constitute an obstacle to national liberation.[6] Although the precise effect of such declarations of principle is hard to determine, one of their consequences is likely to be creation of a climate of opinion in which the bargaining power of developing countries and the legitimacy of their positions are augmented. However, spokesmen for corporations claim that the document will seriously deter, if not needlessly hamper, foreign private investment.

Codes of conduct for multinational business have become popular in recent years, for in addition to the two general codes just discussed (those of the OECD and of the United Nations), other, more specialized codes were being drafted on technology transfer[7] and (as mentioned) on restrictive measures and "unethical practices." The effectiveness of such detailed prescription is difficult to predict. Much of the work of the large corporations must be understood on a case-by-case basis, and solution of their problems requires negotiation rather than the formulation and enforcement of rules of conduct. But it can be said in favor of such attempts that the process of formulating rules undoubtedly helps to crystallize views, and may lead to a consensus on what the conduct of multinational corporations should be. It is useful at this point to consider some of the practical difficulties of regulating the conduct of multinational corporations, especially those in the developing countries.

Franklin B. Weinstein (a political scientist at Stanford University), in discussing Japanese firms in Southeast Asia, echoes Orrego's concern over the weaknesses of governmental machinery (hence the strength of the possible "domination effect") in the Third World. He argues that the basic problem resides in the "softness" of underdeveloped states, which renders ineffectual the regulations intended to control the multinational firm. In fact, he suggests that the corporations themselves may, in a variety of ways, be contributing to that "softness" and inhibiting the process of building more viable indigenous institutions.

NOTES

1. Robert A. Dahl, *After the Revolution: Authority in a Good Society* (New Haven, Conn.: Yale University Press, 1970), p. 121.
2. In Ralph Nader and Mark J. Green, eds., *Corporate Power in America* (New York: Grossman, 1973), pp. 10–24.
3. See K. Simmonds, "Multinational? Well, Not Quite," in Courtney C. Brown, *World Business: Promise and Prospects* (New York: Macmillan, 1970), pp. 43–56; see also the section of "International Control" in selection 3.
4. *New York Times,* March 2, 1977, p. 45.
5. See also George Modelski, "United Nations and the Regulation of Transational Corporations," *Journal of Contemporary Business* (Autumn 1977). A convenient digest of United Nations activities in this field is the *CTC Reporter,* the first issue of which appeared in December 1976.
6. In May 1977, at its third session, the Commission on Transnational Corporations adopted (by a vote of 36 to 4 with 7 abstentions) a resolution "strongly" condemning "the actions of those transnational corporations which continue to collaborate with the racist minority regimes in southern Africa."
7. A basic work is United Nations Conference on Trade and Development, *Guidelines for the Study of Transfer of Technology* (New York and Geneva: The United Nations, 1972).

16 / The Multinational Firm and International Regulation

Robert O. Keohane and Van Doorn Ooms

International Measures to Promote Direct Foreign Investment

It has long been recognized that consistent and predictable legal infrastructure promotes the development of business activity, and arrangements that simply extend such consistency and predictability across national boundaries should therefore promote DFI and reinforce the impact of the multinational firm, indeterminate though that may be. The existing international legal environment, to the extent that it has an impact on direct investment, was generally designed to provide such consistency and predictability. [1] Schemes to accomplish this purpose more systematically have also been proposed from time to time.

Existing Arrangements

The most common existing arrangements are bilateral, such as United States treaties of friendship, commerce, and navigation (of which over 130 have been signed since the eighteenth century) and bilateral tax treaties dealing especially with double taxation. Of growing importance in recent years have been bilateral agreements on investment protection negotiated between source and host countries in conjunction with the development of investment-guarantee programs in the former. Such bilateral arrangements have in some cases been facilitated by multilateral action: the Organization for Economic Cooperation and Development (OECD) has drawn up a Draft Convention on Double Taxation (1963) and a Draft Convention on Protection of Foreign Property (1967). There are also, of course, multilateral arrangements for the protection of industrial property rights, some of them long standing, such as the Convention of Paris (1883) and the Inter-American Convention on Inventions, Patents, Designs and Models (1910), and others more recent, such as the European Patent Convention (1972). Of multilateral agreements directed specifically at direct investment, however, two are particularly noteworthy.

On 12 December 1961, OECD adopted the Code of Liberalization of Capital Movements, which has been revised several times since then but is still in force, with various

From Robert O. Keohane and Van Doorn Ooms, "The Multinational Firm and International Regulation," *International Organization*, Vol. 29, No. 1 (© 1975 by the Board of Regents of the Universtiy of Wisconsin System), pp. 186–206. Some notes have been omitted, and the remainder renumbered in sequence.

reservations. Canada does not adhere to the code, and its liberalization obligations do not apply to Greece, Iceland, Turkey, or to Portuguese overseas provinces. But for the other states of OECD, the code represents an attempt to induce members, in the language of the code, to "progressively abolish between one another . . . restrictions on movements of capital to the extent necessary for effective economic cooperation." Related to this code is the OECD Code of Liberalization of Current Invisible Operations, also adopted in 1961 and more recently amended.[2]

These OECD arrangements are not focused specifically on direct foreign investment, although they serve to facilitate that as well as other types of transnational economic activities. The International Bank for Reconstruction and Development (IBRD), however, took the initiative in the middle 1960s of sponsoring the Convention on the Settlement of Investment Disputes between States and Nationals of Other States, which came into force on 14 October 1966. A new international organization, the International Centre for Settlement of Investment Disputes (ICSID), located at the headquarters of the IBRD, was created in that year for the purpose of facilitating the flow of funds from developed to less developed countries by providing arbitration facilities equipped to deal with disputes between states and nationals of other states, particularly multinational firms. Previously, parties to a dispute would have had to have recourse to local courts or to private arbitration facilities, such as those provided by the International Chamber of Commerce, unless they wished to take the dispute to the Permanent Court of Arbitration at the Hague. Few less developed countries belong to that court, and in any case its rulings are not binding on the parties involved.[3]

As of 30 June 1973, the Convention on the Settlement of Investment Disputes between States and Nationals of Other States had 68 signatories. Most Latin American governments refused to sign, on the grounds that the convention would give preference to foreign over domestic investors and that both sets of investors should be equally subject to domestic law and domestic courts. With the exception of Yugoslavia, socialist states have also not signed the convention, nor has Australia, Canada, India, Iran, or Saudi Arabia. Apart from the major capital-exporting states, most members are small and economically unimportant. Most major capital importers, for which the convention was apparently designed, have decided that they would rather retain sole domestic jurisdiction over investment activities within their borders.

Under the best circumstances, the arbitration and conciliation procedures of ICSID would be better suited to handling relatively minor disputes, such as disagreements over the interpretation of contracts, than to dealing with politically explosive questions of nationalization and expropriation.[4] Yet the efficacy of ICSID in handling even those secondary matters is called into question not only by its limited membership but by the fact that it can consider only certain disputes between the members. The convention does not provide for automatic ICSID jurisdiction in the event of a dispute; on the contrary, consent to ICSID jurisdiction must be specified in writing by the parties before arbitration can begin. This consent, however, may be given before disputes arise, after which consent cannot be unilaterally withdrawn by either party. Arbitration rulings are legally binding once given.

Until 1974, only one case had come to arbitration, and it seemed hard to disagree with the conclusion of one observer that "the lack of use of the convention to date further attests to the lack of enthusiasm of the less developed countries for this appoach to private investment problems."[5] During the first half of 1974, however, four more disputes were registered, three of which involved requests for arbitration by US-based aluminum companies operating in Jamaica. The government of Jamaica, like other governments, can hardly be expected to be enthusiastic about having its discretion limited by an international tribunal, even one to which it once agreed to refer certain types of disputes. The efficacy of the ICSID procedures and the extent to which governments can be expected to abide by ICSID rulings are likely to be severely tested during the next few years.

Proposals for International Action

The United States has had bilateral investment guarantee programs with selected countries since the Marshall Plan period, and other major countries followed suit in the 1950s and 1960s. Around 1960, a number of proposals were made to supplement these arrangements with schemes for multilateral investment insurance. This was formally taken up by the World Bank at the request of the Development Assistance Group (later, the Development Assistance Committee) of OECD. In July 1961, in conjunction with the International Chamber of Commerce, the Bank undertook a survey and made some suggestions about arranging a multilateral insurance program in a staff report.[6] In 1965, an OECD group of experts transmitted to the IBRD, with the approval of the OECD Council, the "Report on the Establishment of a Multilateral Investment Guarantee Corporation," which was used by the IBRD staff and executive directors to prepare a draft set of "Articles of Agreement of the International Investment Insurance Agency" (IIIA) in 1966, a second draft set of articles in 1968, and still a third set in 1972.

From an economic point of view, the effect of successful investment guarantee schemes is to narrow the differential between private and social risk.[7] To the extent that such a differential exists, there is an efficiency argument for reducing political risk to the same degree for different lenders through multinational arrangements, which would also be able to effect guarantees for multinational consortia, which are presently inelegible for national guarantee. Administrative simplification could also result from multilateralization.

The rub comes on the political side. Source country governments tend to gain in a double sense. On the one hand, multilateralization provides a vehicle for coordinating policy, to avoid mutually costly competition to maintain the positions of their national firms. On the other hand, such an arrangement will tend to weaken host country positions, since multilateral threats of coercion may be more effective than bilateral ones. As the IBRD staff report commented, with reference to the insurance scheme: "Whereas under a bilateral program the action of one party could offend only the other party, in the context of a multilateral program the act of a capital-importing participant could bring that country into disfavor with the community of industrialized nations as well as with the other capital-importing nations."[8] In the light of the political bias of this sort of proposal, it is not surprising that it has not been accepted by the executive directors of the World Bank. All indications are that the proposal is, if not quite dead, certainly dormant.

Following a French initiative in 1969, the European Commission, in July 1971, suggested a number of steps "to further an active, coherent private investment policy in developing countries," including instituting a community system of guarantees for private investment. However, a subsequent "initial action program" for development cooperation, released in February 1972, included no reference to this proposal. Thus, although the sixth general report of the European Commission lists this proposal as pending, little has apparently been done about it.

In view of the difficulties states have had in agreeing on multilateral investment guarantees or insurance schemes, it is hardly necessary to comment on the political feasibility of proposals such as that by George Ball, for the creation of an international companies law, administered by a supranational regulatory body, facilitating the development of stateless corporations, or Cosmocorps. Even Ball agrees that it "may seem utopian and idealistic." The mixture of motivations for direct foreign investment, however, and the variety of effects that such investment may have throw doubt also on Ball's notion that such an arrangement would tend to assure "the most economical and efficient use of the world's resources."9 In any case, such a proposal neglects a primary political requirement for any international scheme—providing for accountability. When perceived interests diverge widely, they can be reconciled only through mechanisms that are accountable to those interests and that are therefore perceived as legitimate, and the Cosmocorps and their regulators will hardly meet the test.

International facilitation of direct foreign investment is not where the action is. Governments see little incentive in the present environment to commit themselves further to protection of multinational firms, particularly when this could mean sacrificing powers to outside authority. The multinational firm is unlikely soon to be the beneficiary of an international rescue operation.

International Regulation of Direct Foreign Investment

The primary subject of this article is international regulation of direct foreign investment, yet our discussion so far has focused primarily on national concerns. Governmental attention to these issues is clearly a necessary condition for international action, and the effects of DFI that are perceived as important by national policymakers will influence heavily the nature of any international regulation that may appear. This explains our decision to emphasize the national perspective so strongly. Nevertheless, national concern is by no means a sufficient condition for international action. Governments must perceive common interest with one another, and must be able to communicate. Their interests in collaborating must be great enough to overcome the barriers of organizational inertia and reluctance to become constrained in their own policies by the policies and practices of others.

In a period of rising national regulation of multinational firms, the relative underdevelopment of international measures is striking. This may suggest that national regulation is generally effective, or that much of what is often seen as conflict between firms and governments in fact reflects deeper conflicts between governments or the societies that they represent. 10 Both of these explanations may contain some truth. But it is also possible that international regulation has lagged for other reasons, such as the difficulty in getting cumbersome governments to develop coherent positions and to act on issues that are not urgent at the moment. In that case, further international regulation may be desirable, whether or not it is politically feasible.

For analytic purposes, we make a distinction between two kinds of international arrangements designed to regulate direct investment. We refer to *policy coordination*, discussed in the following section, where the governments involved are from highly developed capitalist countries and have favorable orientations toward multinational firms in general. Here there is characteristically considerable overlap between governmental and business elites, and a general sense of common interest between them. Yet to some extent the governments may find their attempts to regulate multinational enterprises thwarted by the firms' abilities to evade governmental jurisdiction by operating abroad. An extension of governmental jurisdiction through international measures—to encompass as wide an area as the decision domain of the firm—seems the natural course of action. Nevertheless, as we will see, policy conflicts between governments may complicate the issue.

Policy coordination is distinguished from *alteration of bargaining power* as a motive for international action. In the latter case, governments of less developed countries or groups (such as labor organizations) that consider themselves disadvantaged by DFI use international measures—through regional groupings, producers' cartels, or international organizations—to increase their bargaining power vis-à-vis multinational firms. Here there is generally much less sense of common interest between the regulators and those they hope to regulate. Furthermore, situations such as these frequently involve conflicts between host governments, banded together to increase their political leverage, and source country governments, as well as between host governments and multinational firms.

Policy Coordination as an International Strategy

It is within common markets that the mobility of multinational firms often poses the most severe problems for advanced-country goverments, since traditional national means for coping with such problems, particularly the erection of trade barriers, are proscribed. Thus, in the 1960s France found itself quite disadvantaged in its attempt to regulate American firms, which could, if displeased by French policies, simply locate across the borders in Belgium or Germany and export freely to France. The fact that the firms in question were American is significant: it has often been remarked that the most "European" firms, in the sense of having a continent-wide outlook, during the 1960s were based in the United States.

It was therefore natural that some attempts would be made to use the institutions of the European Community in developing regional policies to strengthen European enterprises, primarily through transnational mergers. The policies to be involved in the effort are fiscal harmonization, unification of capital markets, public sector support for research and development activities, and the creation of a European company law.[11] Yet, to date, progress in these areas has been very slow. Although the European Commission has prepared proposals on tax standardization, harmonization of capital market structures, industrial development contracts, and a European company law, political agreement in the European Economic Community (EEC) Council has not been forthcoming. Not altogether surprisingly, it has been precisely in those key sectors involving high technology, where the need for regional cooperation is argued to be strongest, that national resistance to the surrender of any control has been most adamant. As the European Commission remarks rather ruefully with respect to one of these areas:

> although in the case of standard supplies the liberalization of public contracts in the Community shows some progress . . . the same cannot be said of certain capital goods and advanced technological items such as computers, aircraft, conventional and nuclear power plant equipment, railway and telecommunications equipment.[12]

It would appear to remain the case that "European governments have *not* decided that the loss of sovereignty to other Europeans is better than a loss to U.S. enterprises."[13]

Indeed, the feeling of the EEC Council seems to be that regulating multinational enterprises is properly a problem for all developed countries, rather than for Europe alone:

> The phenomenon of the multinational corporation must be viewed in a wider context than the Community, even the enlarged community. It should really be viewed in a world context. This is why the Commission is participating in the work of certain international organizations, such as the OECD in Paris, which are trying to establish a code of good conduct for these companies and possibly to find a more efficient method of control.[14]

Thus the issues have primarily been Atlantic ones. And as David Leyton-Brown has recently shown, interstate conflicts arising from activities of multinational firms in Britain, Canada, and France since World War II have arisen primarily from extraterritoriality problems.[15] Although a number of notorious cases are repeatedly cited in the literature, the number of severe intergovernmental policy conflicts has been small.

Among the OECD countries, there have been significant efforts to coordinate various policies affecting multinational firms, in areas such as antitrust policy, export controls, and securities regulation, where extraterritorial application of United States law has given rise to issues. OECD has a working party of experts within its Industry Committee to study on a continuing basis problems related to multinational enterprises.[16] OECD has also attempted to coordinate antitrust policy through a committee of experts on restrictive business practices, which periodically issues descriptive reports as well as recommendations to member governments to take measures against practices found to be harmful. Issues revolving around the American Trading with the Enemy Act, which produced twelve of the sixteen conflicts cited by Jack N. Behrman as arising from activities of US corporations in the Atlantic area during the 1960s, were dealt with in special committees established for that purpose.[17] Except for these export control issues (which now seem to focus on mighty Cuba due to changes in American trade policy toward the Soviet Union and China), the most striking fact about questions of extraterritoriality is the apparent success of quiet negotiation and intergovernmental coordination. This leads us to agree with a close observer of the legal-economic scene, Seymour Rubin, who has argued with respect to problems of extraterritoriality that "governments having a reasonably similar polity are increasingly desirous of avoiding conflicts and increasingly accustomed to the consultative procedures that can accomplish that purpose."[18]

Taxation and capital controls raise more difficult issues. Here the macroeconomic effects of policy can be considerable. What is at stake for policymakers is not merely the existence of a firm or the legitimacy of some of its practices but the flows of taxes across borders and into government coffers, and the inexorable imperatives of the balance of payments. Robbins and Stobaugh have argued that enterprises do a suboptimal job of managing their financial assests, both in realizing returns on liquid assests and in avoiding excessive taxation.[19] As these firms move toward optimal financial policies, effects on government tax revenue will be substantial, and there will be greater yearly variation in tax receipts.

At a conference held in 1973 on international regulation of the multinational firm, a number of speakers, including Fernand Braun from the EEC and Nicholas deB. Katzenbach of International Business Machines (IBM), focused on taxes as an area in which further international harmonization of government policy could take place. With respect to questions of tax havens, Charles Kindleberger was quite explicit:

From the viewpoint of economic efficiency, taxes should be neutral. In the real world, without harmonization of tax systems, they are distortionary. Tax havens continue to distort resource allocations despite the limitations on them in the 1962 Revenue act in the United States and the Swiss-German double taxation agreement. In the long run, the Netherlands Antilles, Lichtenstein, Luxembourg, Andorra, San Marino, Zub, and Appenzell are going to have to stop trying to entice tax evaders. It is not attractive for the big countries to push around the little entities, but it is strongly dysfunctional to continue them. Like Delaware and Hoboken in the United States, in the long run they will have to give up exploiting gaps in the system.[20]

Since the benefits could be significant and the entities to be regulated are weak, tax neutrality would appear to be a suitable subject for international policy coordination.

The situation with regard to capital movements has recently been more pressing. Particularly in the years before 1971, transfers of funds by multinational enterprises became a source of great concern to governments wrestling (for the most part unsuccessfully) with the contradictions between freedom of short-term capital flows and the requirements of fixed exchange rates. It has been estimated that in 1971 as much as $268 billion in short-term assets were held by principal institutions in the international money markets, that a "dominant share" ($190 billion) of this was held by multinational corporations, and that a 1 percent flow would therefore be "quite sufficient to produce a first-class international financial crisis."[21] Robbins and Stobaugh estimate that approximately 100 multinational firms control about $25 billion in cash and marketable assests, overshadowing the reserves of any single country except Germany. They point out that financial decisions by multinational managers can collectively have drastic effects on international reserve positions; if all debts to United States parents by foreign affiliates were paid immediately, the US official reserves could triple.[22] In the Schydlowsky simulation model which the authors employ, balance-of-payments swings produced by short-term capital transfers under optimal multinational enterprise policies are very substantial.

Clearly, the potential for disruption represented by these funds poses an important policy problem. Governments will probably be under pressure to regulate and restrict capital transfers further. Robbins and Stobaugh go so far as to argue:

> Sooner or later government action will severely limit the multinational enterprise's use of credit tools in shuttling funds throughout its system; thus the enterprises will be shackled in their ability to protect against currency changes. As a result, multinational enterprises may come to accept losses and gains from devaluations and revaluations as a routine element in operating internationally. As long as all multinational enterprises are faced with the same rules, no one enterprise will suffer unduly. In fact, such rules will remove a major tension between firms and national governments and thereby make multinational enterprises more welcome than they might otherwise be.[23]

Clearly, national regulation of short-term capital movements may involve heavy costs to individual governments, as testified by recent events in Germany and Japan. Such controls would fall disproportionately on a country's own firms, putting them at a competitive disadvantage, at the same time that it diverted direct investment away from the country in question to other host countries. The argument for international agreement on control policies therefore becomes persuasive.

The importance of achieving such agreement is reinforced by the dangers of intergovernmental conflict in this area. . . . The international monetary situation carries continual dangers of destructively competitive national action. National attempts to impose controls on capital movements for balance-of-payments or exchange-rate purposes may well collide. This is widely recognized: the *First Annual Report of the U.S. Council on International Economic Policy*, for instance, stressed capital controls as an area of international investment policy needing review of OECD.

The political problems in this area, however, are immensely complicated by the fact that conflicts over capital movements and exchange rates frequently pit major governments against one another, as well as against mini-jurisdictions, banks, or corporations. The behavior of firms may stimulate or compound intergovernmental conflict, but this does not make the national conflicts of interest any less real. From governments' point of view, the game is non-zero-sum; great losses are possible and the stakes are therefore very high. Indeed, the question is so complex that we cannot discuss it adequately here. . . .

When a case for the desirability of international policy coordination has been made, the question immediately arises: How institutionalized should the regulation be? In a well-known article, Paul Goldberg and Charles Kindleberger have called for a "General Agreement for the International Corporation" (GAIC), modeled after the GATT, which would establish an international agency to deal with five important problems involving foreign investment; taxation, antitrust policy, foreign exchange controls, export controls, and securities regulation. Their goal is the "creation of an international agreement based on a limited set of universally accepted principles. This agreement would be structurally similar to GATT." The agency's role would be to investigate facts and issues and to make recommendations, which would not be binding but would be accepted voluntarily if the agency "succeeded in acquiring a reputation for thorough analysis and impartiality . . . As its status in the world community improved, the agency could act as an ombudsman for corporations and countries seeking relief from oppressive policies."

The agency's findings would be based on a set of legal agreements:

> A contractual arrangement could be developed from agreement on a few fundamental concepts of substance and procedure. Then, as a seminal body of accepted principles emerge, broader and deeper agreement as to foreign investment practices would be generated. Perhaps after a guarded and gradual start gathered momentum, an international treaty of substantial coverage could be accepted by the nations of the world.[24]

In considering the GATT as a model for the proposed GAIC, it is useful to recall that the GATT operates in two rather different ways. It is primarily a contractual agreement in which members (or those countries that accede to it) are governed by rules that set out specific rights and obligations. It also "creates in a flexible and pragmatic way committees, working parties, and informal discussion groups to explore new problems and to settle conflicts in relation to the rules and obligations set out in the GATT agreement."[25] It is clearly the former, legalistic structure that Goldberg and Kindleberger have primarily in mind in calling for a *new* multilateral organization, with the massive political task of negotiation and institution building that this imples. The proposal raises rather sharply, then, the relative merits of such a legalistic model and the more informal consultative framework that, while applied in a limited way by the GATT, is employed by OECD. The key question is whether formal codification would have more advantages than liabilities.

Assuming a high degree of consensus on substantive principles, the codified rights and obligations of the proposed GAIC might, like those of the GATT, have the advantage of legally committing governments to the common interest of capitalist countries by providing for liberal, equitable arrangements for direct investment. This commitment would then serve the purpose of protecting such arrangements, and the general interests they serve, from the erosion to which less public and formal arrangements are subject due to the pressures of special interests or the temptation to use ad hoc measures in one area to avoid adjustment costs in another, as in the use of investment controls to improve the balance of payments. Such arrangements, if feasible, have the related advantage of adding an element of stability and predictability to policy.

But all this begs the question of whether such consensus exists. While the OECD countries cannot be said to be in fundamental disagreement on these questions, problems in Canada, Japan, and France notwithstanding, it seems unlikely that consensus is wide enough to negotiate an agreement or use one successfully. Nor is there much enthusiasm for making the effort. A 1973 conference of academics, businessmen, and officials of governments and international organizations, held on this subject, resulted in "a considerable unanimity of opinion as to result: that a GATT for investment, much less disinvestment agency, would be neither feasible nor desirable at present."[26]

In such a situation, attempts to negotiate a GAIC would probably come to nought. If negotiations became serious, however, there could be negative effects. A major negotiation would tend to politicize the direct investment issue further, through the increased involvement of legislatures and high officialdom, and through subsequent attention from the press and general public. The politics of direct investment would become increasingly nationalistic and symbolic. This would particularly be the case if Third World countries were involved, although, in view of the experience of the International Investment Insurance Agency noted above, and as Goldberg and Kindleberger admit, this seems most unlikely. Because negotiators at relatively high levels would need to adopt coherent positions and maximize bargaining leverage, more linkages would be drawn between issues in the direct investment area, and further linkages with other economic or political issues would become likely. For all of these reasons, it would probably become more difficult to reach workable agreements, even on narrowly defined issues on which some degree of consensus now exists.

There are situations where wide-sweeping negotiations and a high degree of politicization are desirable, and even necessary—Bretton Woods, the Treaty of Rome, and the Kennedy Round come to mind. But at the moment, as Katzenbach has argued, "governments are unsure of what their positions are. . . . There are just too many problems. There is too much dispute, too much dissension, too much uncertainty."[27] Until direct investment issues become much more politically salient in OECD countries, and until positions become clearer, an attempt to negotiate a comprehensive agreement seems premature.

Thus those international arrangements among OECD countries that develop over the next few years will probably be relatively informal and issue specific. Since OECD is not a powerful organization, and since the difficulties of coordinating policies are extensive, there can be no guarantee that the informal measures that evolve will be sufficient to cope effectively with the problems. At a minimum, OECD policy coordination represents a holding action, until the point at which pressure for more far-reaching agreements becomes sufficient to produce action by governments.

Yet it may be possible to be more optimistic. As we pointed out above, OECD has developed a number of special committees for policy coordination in areas related to direct investment, and on issues of extraterritoriality these have had some success. Other issues have also been considered; in particular, the Fiscal Committee has concentrated some attention on transfer pricing and tax revenues. Over the past two decades, in a variety of issue areas, OECD governments have developed a remarkable number of relatively informal methods of intergovernmental policy coordination, which are feasible because of the highly specialized nature of those governments and the close communication among them at working levels, and which are rendered necessary by the inability of high-level decision makers, in highly complex and bureaucratized governments, to oversee detailed decisions and to coordinate policies effectively among many branches of government. Where political agreement exists, these informal procedures may be quite effective.

Having considered the feasibility of international policy coordination, we turn now to its likely effects. It is important to note that not all international policy coordination will restrict enterprise behavior. Agreements to observe national self-restraint in matters of antitrust, exchange controls, and export prohibitions would increase the freedom of action of firms, while arrangements on the necessity, ends, and means of regulation in these areas would tend to narrow it. But even if the direction of coordination were clear in these terms, the economic effects would remain obscure, and it is partly this obscurity that makes a rapid or comprehensive convergence of views on these matters unlikely. Where firm behavior presently reduces efficiency or intended distributional arrangements, as in the use of transfer pricing to bar entry or avoid taxation, coordinated regulation would be beneficial. Where the same practice is presently used to avoid exchange controls, regulations might have efficiency costs, at least in this partial sphere.

In other areas, regulatory activity would have to face squarely the efficiency and distributional conflicts generated by multinational corporation activity, as in the imposition of short-term adjustment costs in securing (presumably) efficient location of the firm. The regulatory effects of certain policies may appear relatively clear, such as the use of standard disclosure requirements for security issues to lower information costs and improve markets. But there are others, such as antitrust policies to limit market concentration, where different states are in fundamental disagreement on the presumptive effects of current practice and the appropriate degree of regulation. It is therefore difficult to reach any settled conclusions in this area. Since progress, in whatever end, is likely to be gradual in the best of circumstances, one should at least hope that these problems are put in proper perspective by removing them from the arena of balance-of-payments conflict through reform of the monetary adjustment mechanism.

Altering Bargaining Power

Problems, Plans, and Prospects

When one set of actors in a relationship believes itself to be at a fundamental and systematic disadvantage, it is unrealistic to believe that measures to institutionalize the relationship or to coordinate policy more closely with the more powerful actors are likely to alleviate the situation for the actors that perceive themselves to be disadvantaged. On the contrary, these actors are likely to be inclined either to seek assistance from outside organizations or to concert policy more closely with one another in order to increase their joint bargaining power with the outsider. With respect to the modern multinational enterprise, both international trade unions and less developed countries find themselves in this general position.

International trade unions have attempted, in some instances, to coordinate their behavior vis-à-vis particular firms, although with indifferent success.[28] They have also turned to their most familiar and friendly international organization, the International Labour Organization (ILO), among others, for help. Here the emphasis has been on securing a code of conduct that would ensure the firms' respect for trade union rights. The International Confederation of Free Trade Unions (ICFTU) has adopted resolutions specifying that multinational enterprises should follow relevant ILO conventions, and both the International Metalworkers' Federation and the Miners' International Federation have called for a code of conduct whose provisions would include the requirement that companies abide by such conventions.[29]

A number of proposals emanating from the less developed countries or from individuals and groups sympathetic to their interests have stressed the need for concerted international action to alter economic power relationships. This is one of the major themes of a recent United Nations report, *The Impact of Multinational Corporations on the Development Process and on International Relations*, by a Group of Eminent Persons working under the authority of Economic and Social Council (ECOSOC) Resolution 1721 (LIII). This report makes three major institutional proposals: (1) the establishment of an information and research center on multinational corporations within the United Nations Secretariat; (2) the formation of a commission on multinational corporations, composed of individuals rather than government representatives, which would "act as the focal point within the United Nations system for the comprehensive consideration of issues relating to multinational corporations," and which would direct the activities of the information and research center; and (3) regular arrangements for at least annual meetings of ECOSOC on issues related to multinational firms, at which reports by the commission on multinational corporations would be considered.

It seems clear that United Nations agencies are moving toward serving, not only as sources of support for governments dealing with particular enterprises, but as catalysts for policy harmonization among less developed countries seeking to strengthen their general position and to avoid competitive actions that benefit none of them in the long run.[30] This does not mean that a grandiose new UN operating agency to deal with multinational firms is likely to arise: due to opposition to such a development by existing agencies, as well as the efficiency costs, it is more likely that an attempt will be made to coordinate various actions taken by a variety of UN bodies that bear on the direct investment problem.[31]

The information-sharing approach may be particularly relevant in helping governments decide on what terms to permit the transfer of technology from industrialized to less developed countries through multinational firms. Both UNCTAD and the Andean Common Market (ANCOM) have been concerned with rather stringent controls usually placed by parent companies upon the use of technology acquired under collaborative arrangements. Studies commissioned by UNCTAD on India, the Philippines, and the Andean countires indicate that export restrictions on goods produced with foreign-controlled technology are very widespread. A study by the Junta del Acuerdo de Cartagena, for instance, found that 81 percent of the technology transfer contracts for Bolivia, Columbia, Peru, and Ecuador prohibited exports entirely, and that 86 percent had some export restrictions.[32] An UNCTAD-sponsored study of the Philippines indicated that 65 percent of technical collaboration agreements involving local enterprises between 1965 and 1970 contained export restrictive clauses; a similar study of the Indian experience showed the approximately 40 percent of such agreements had export restrictions.[33]

These formal restrictions upon exports do not, of course, provide an adequate measure of the barriers to exports. Joint ventures or licensees may find themselves restrained from exporting, in the absence of any formal prohibitions, by the areas specified in licensing agreements, by considerations of market structure, and ultimately by the necessity of remaining on good terms with the licensor. Thus the problem of restrictive practices goes far deeper than formal export restrictions. Yet such restrictions, with their implication of economic and political dependence, have emerged as a highly visible symbol of the use of economic power by the monopolists of technology.

The fundamental problem here, as the reports point out, is that sellers of technology have great bargaining strength. Not only do purchasers not know exactly what they are buying until they have done so (since it is information that is for sale), they also do not know what the terms of sales were elsewhere. Furthermore, the transfer of technology commonly takes place between the subsidiary of a multinational firm and its parent, where the transfer price is matter of internal firm policy. The manipulation of transfer prices may be used to transfer profits out of the country, escaping the local tax collector as well as exchange controls. The study of the experience of the Andean countries referred to above found, in support of this suspicion, that foreign subsidiaries of multinational firms pay much more for technology than do national firms.

It is thus not surprising that UNCTAD is moving toward providing "action-oriented research, training, and advisory services and the formulation of appropriate policies in the context of UNCTAD's activities."[34] In its report, the Junta del Acuerdo de Cartagena proposes, as a remedy, regional cooperation in the technology-bargaining process. The Junta's report looks toward the day when exchanges of information are effective enough among countries that a most-favored-nation principle in technology would take effect: discriminatory pricing or restrictions on the basis of variations in bargaining power would be outlawed. Information may not be a sufficient weapon for the weak, but it is surely a necessary condition for effective bargaining by small countries or groups of countries attempting to deal with large multinational firms.

The Andean Common Market itself has moved further than the recommendations of the Junta, its technical secretariat, to UNCTAD. If fully implemented, the ANCOM foreign investment rules, drafted in 1970, would fundamentally change the nature of foreign direct investment, particularly in the industrial sector, by making majority owner-ship by foreigners a temporary, rather than a permanent, result of successful direct invest-ment. After fifteen years (twenty in Bolivia and Ecuador), a majority of the stock of any new firm or of any preexisting firm that wishes to enjoy the benefits of trade liberalization within the Andean Group must be owned by local investors. Stricter provisions have been developed for banks, which must sell 30 percent of their capital to Andean sources within three years, and which, along with the mass media, internal transportation, and domestic marketing, may not receive new direct foreign investments. Restrictions are also placed on the transfer of profits outside of the region, but it is the divestment provisions of the code that are the most innovative and structurally far-reaching.[35] If the Andean arrangements work as the group's membership hopes (despite grumblings of opposition from foreign investors), one of the most disturbing aspects of direct foreign investment—the perma-nence of foreign control—will have been eliminated. But the economic risks will be sub-stantial, as we note below.

Even more decisive action directed at changing bargaining positions has come from the Organization of Petroleum Exporting Countries (OPEC), a producer's cartel, which at the time of writing had succeeded in increasing the price of crude oil about fivefold over the last three years. Little that is intelligent can be said in a short space about the many issues involved here, or about the future of producers' cartels in such commodities as copper, cocoa, or coffee. In view of the unique importance of petroleum to industrialized economies and of the political affinity of many of its suppliers, it would seem unwise to generalize OPEC's experience too readily. The failures of international cartelization are legendary, and very much the stock-in-trade of liberal economists. Such cartels may, as one Third World proponent has described it, "give us some equity in a world of wolves," but they are unlikely suddenly to effect drastic changes in bargaining relationships on a larger number of important commodities.[36]

As governments attempt increasingly to use international organizations to alter bargaining power in their favor, we should expect to see two types of organizational action. Specific, programmatic action is most likely from organizations, such as OPEC or ANCOM, that are partisan and either regional in scope or product or sector specific. Even with respect to a commodity as critical as oil, concentrated action is difficult in an organization as large and diffuse as OECD. Nevertheless, OECD countries have enough common interest that cooperation on some issues, although not on all, may be expected. At another level, rhetorically oriented organizations, such as UNCTAD, ECOSOC, and perhaps the UN General Assembly, will examine developments, but strongly coherent and concerted positions are unlikely to emerge, given the wide diversity of interests. (Within UNCTAD, for instance, the conflict between oil-importing LDCs and the oil exporters will be sharply drawn.) Both the rhetoric from the incoherent organizations and the action from the coherent ones will generate and exacerbate, rather than ameliorate, conflict. For international politics, and particularly North-South politics, these organizations will constitute a continuous irritant rather than a soothing balm.

Economic Effects of Measures to Alter Bargaining Power

Several types of action to alter bargaining power would seem to imply rather high efficiency costs. The development of producer (or consumer) cartels raises the issue in sharpest form, as well as creating severe distributional problems, as reflected in the difficulties of poor, oil-importing countries such as India. Yet the issue is also raised in the international labor area. Union goals of "wage parity and harmonization of conditions of work," and of preventing the "exploitation of wage differentials,"[37] imply restrictions on efficiency as well as distributional effects favoring the interest of labor in developed countries and of skilled unionized labor in less developed countries over those of the unemployed or other workers in poor lands.

In some cases, international regulation could increase efficiency as well as serve other goals. One example is provided by the attempts made by less developed countries to obtain imformation through international organizations in order to bargain more effectively with enterprises on questions such as technology transfer. Lower information costs should help to improve efficiency as well as have desirable distributional effects. Another case in point might be the exercise of restrictions by less developed host countries on the granting of patents and copyrights to foreigners, since the social cost to them of such monopoly power is large, and the contribution to innovative activity in the industrial countries is probably negligible.

The most interesting case on which to speculate, however, is that of the Andean Common Market. *If* implemented collectively and enforced stringently, the 1970 ANCOM foreign investment rules are likely to have far-reaching economic implications for the development of the countries involved. These provisos must be entered, since even countries with highly organized bureaucracies have been known to modify well-established restrictive policies under the pressure of circumstances, and such flexibility might have a strong tendency to become nationally competitive among the Andean countries.[38] As of late 1973, the Andean countries had by no means consistently implemented the ANCOM code; this was particularly true for Bolivia, Ecuador, and Colombia.[39]

It seems very likely that the restrictions placed on profit transfer and reinvestment in the manufacturing sector, the more stringent regulations and prohibitions in other sectors, and in particular the divestment requirements will have substantial costs in terms of investment foregone, but the size of the costs is difficult to estimate. There have been protestations of alarm from organs of international business, and individual executives have also voiced pessimism about the reactions of foreign investors. There was also, in 1972 and 1973, a falloff in foreign investment in the ANCOM countries.[40] ANCOM is not an inconsiderable market, with GNP roughly equal to that of Brazil. The long-term attractions of an integrated and protected market offer something of a counterweight to restrictions on behavior and ownership, and existing companies may well "adopt a strategy of divestiture in order to maintain a foothold in the area."[41] This will, however, depend to some extent on ANCOM's apparent prospects: the better its chances seem of holding together, the more incentive firms will have to cooperate.

New investment, however, is far more problematical. Stopford and Wells note a tendency for firms with a strong preference for wholly owned subsidiaries to avoid countries with "insistent" policies on local equity participation, but the effect is hardly dramatic.[42] If firms really maximized present net worth, one might not expect divestment requirements at some distance in the future to have large effects; but since firm growth and long-term market strategy are undoubtedly extremely important, one must be less sanguine about the prospects.

The *type* of investment that would be discouraged is perhaps a more important concern than the overall total. Stopford and Wells have found that firms that emphasize marketing techniques, the international rationalization of production, control of raw material sources, and product innovation tend to avoid local equity participation.[43] The loss of new investment in the first three areas may not be viewed as especially costly, and in some cases may be welcome; but the loss of technology transfer by firms in the last category is a matter for greater concern: even countries of the size of India and Japan have discoveered that IBM comes in on its own terms or not at all.[44] As Vernon has pointed out, there is a fundametal difference between firms that do not continuously innovate (for which divestment may be well suited as nationals acquire capabilities over the standardized products and processes involved) and those that maintain a stream of innovations.[45] The latter are likely to make a significant contribution to efficiency and growth, where innovations are not the results of trivial product differentiation or of a demand structure based on highly unequal income distribution, and they will be especially costly to lose.

A further source of concern is possible changes in the behavior of existing firms. There will be greater incentives to take short-term profits instead of concentrating on long-term growth objectives, and one may also expect the use of transfer pricing and other accounting techniques to repatriate capital in anticipation of divestment.[46] Effective control over such behavior will present severe challenges to the limited administrative capabilities of the countries involved.

Given some of these probable costs, the net economic effects, over the long run, are likely to depend very much on whether this attempt at integration will have significant effects on the mobilization of domestic resources, and in particular entrepreneurship, as argued by Hirschman.[47] But on that critical question not much can be usefully said. There may also be some positive effects generated by the pressures for regional planning which result from the restriction of DFI; resource scarcity can be a severe taskmaster, and it could lead either to a higher regional "rationality" in investment planning or to competitive nationalistic retreats into small markets. The Andean Agreement contains provisions for sectorial planning of industry which go well beyond the complementarity agreements of the Latin American Free Trade Association (LAFTA) and the integrated industry provision of the Central American Common Market (CACM), and these, in conjunction with a flexible application of DFI regulation, could lead to more efficient investment allocation. But the aborted development of the other two Latin American attempts to integrate industrial planning does not provide the basis for much optimism, despite the fact that such failures may have been due more to external than to internal causes.[48]

. . .

NOTES

1. For a brief summary, see Stefan H. Robock and Kenneth Simmonds, *International Business and Multinational Enterprises* (Homewood, Ill.: Richard D. Irwin, 1973), chapter 14, "The Legal Environment."

2. The basic sources are OECD, *Code of Liberalization of Capital Movements* (Paris, Janurary 1969) and *Amendments* thereto (Paris, April 1972); and *OECD Code of Liberalization of Current Invisible Operations* (Paris, March 1973). *The OECD Observer* 55 (December 1971) provides a useful summary.

3. Paul C. Szasz, "Using the New International Centre for Settlement of Investment Disputes," *East African Law Journal* 7 (June 1971).

4.. P. K. O'Hare, "The Convention on the Settlement of Investment Disputes," *Stanford Journal of International Studies* 6 (1971).

5. Stanley D. Metzger, "American Foreign Trade and Investment Policy for the 1970's: The Williams Commission Report," *American Journal of International Law* 66, no. 3 (1972): 548.

6. IBRD, *Multilateral Investment Insurance,* a staff report (Washington, D.C., March 1962).

7. Marina von Neumann Whitman, *Government Risk-Sharing in Foreign Investment* (Princeton, N.J.: Princeton University Press, 1965), chapter 2.

8. IBRD, *Multilateral Investment Insurance,* p. 21.

9. George W. Ball, "Cosmocorp: The Importance of Being Stateless," *Columbia Journal of World Business,* November-December 1967, p. 27.

10. For an interesting argument that problems in the area of private international financial flows fundamentally reflect conflicts of governments with one another rather than with multinational enterprises, see Robert W. Russell, "Public Policies Toward Private International Financial Flows," paper prepared for the Fifteenth Annual Meeting of the International Studies Association, St. Louis, Mo., March 1974.

11. Behrman, *National Interests and the Multinational Enterprise,* pp. 161-72.

12. Commission of the European Communities, *Sixth General Report on the Activities of the Communities,* 1972 (Brussels-Luxembourg, February 1973), pp. 65, 204, 78-79.

13. Behrman, *National Interests and the Multinational Enterprise,* p. 169.

14. Statement by Mr. Albert Borschette, member of the Commission, to the European Parliament, 12 February 1973, in *Bulletin of the European Communities,* 2-73, p. 35.

15. David Leyton-Brown, "Governments of Developed Countries as Hosts to Multinational Enterprise: The Canadian, British and French Policy Experience" (Ph.D. dissertation, Harvard University, 1973), p. 423, . . .

16. Cited in Jack N. Behrman, "Sharing International Production Through the Multinational Enterprise and Sectoral Integration," *Law and Policy in International Business* 4, no. 1(1972): 1-36.

17. The Computation is from Nye, "Multinational Corporations in World Politics," and from Behrman, *National Interests and the Multinational Enterprise.* For discussions of the US embargo policy and the activities of the relevant committees, see Gunnar Adler-Karlsson, *Western Economic Warfare,* 1947-1967 (Stockholm: Almquist and Wiksell, 1968).

18. Seymour J. Rubin, "The Multinational Enterprise and National Sovereignty: A Skeptic's Analysis," *Law and Policy in International Business* 3, no. 1 (1971): 14.

19. Sidney M. Robbins and Robert B. Stobaugh, *Money in the Multinational Enterprise: A Study in Financial Policy* (New York: Basic Books, 1973).

20. Charles P. Kindleberger, "Comment," in *International Control of Investment: The Dusseldorf Conference on Multinational Corporations,* ed. Don Wallace, Jr., assisted by Helga Ruof-Koch (New York: Praeger, 1974), p. 64.

21. US Congress, Senate, Committee on Finance, *Implications of Multinational Firms for World Trade and Investment and for US Trade and Labor, Report to the Committee on Finance by the US Tariff Commission,* 93d Cong. 1st sess. (Washington, D.C.: Government Printing Office, 1973), p. 539.

22. Robbins and Stobaugh, pp. 178-83.

23. Ibid., p. 186.

24. Paul M. Goldberg and Charles P. Kindleberger, "Toward a GATT for Investment: A Proposal for Supervision of the International Corporation," *Law and Policy in International Business* 2 (Summer 1970): 295-323.

25. Harald B. Malmgren, "The International Organizations in the Field of Trade and Investment," in *United States International Economic Policy in an Interdependent World,* vol. 2, p. 429.

26. Seymour Rubin, "Report on the Conference," in *International Control of Investment,* p. 9. Even Kindleberger seemed to agree: "I am a little embarassed by the occasional reference to the fact that I have suggested that we need international rules for the international corporation, a sort of GATT. I do not feel very strongly about this: I just threw out the suggestion" (ibid., p. 249).

27. Nicholas deB. Katzenbach, "The Realistic Prospects for Greater Political Integration and Organization of Developed Countries Related to Investment," ibid., p. 69.

28. David H. Blake, "Trade Unions and the Challenge of the Multinational Corporation," *Annals of American Academy of Political and Social Science,* no. 403 (September 1972): 34-45.

29. ILO, *Multinational Enterprises and Social Policy.*

30. See the discussion of this question in United Nations, Department of Social and Economic Affairs, *Multinational Corporations in World Development* (UN Document ST/ECA/190), New York, 1973, p. 90.

31. This sentence was written before the publication of the report by the Group of Eminent Persons, but its conclusion seems to be supported by that report. The group did suggest that as a "longer term objective," a "general agreement on multinational corporations" should be negotiated, but it argued that serious steps in this direction were premature at this time.
    For a previous elaboration of the argument that vested interests of established international organizations would create pressures for coordination machinery rather than a powerful new operating agency to deal with multinational firms, see Robert W. Walters, "International Organizations and the Multinational Corporation: An Overview and Observations," *Annals of American Academy of Political and Social Science,* no. 403 (September 1972): 127-38.

32. See the UNCTAD study by the Junta del Acuerdo de Cartagena, *Politics Relating to the Technology of the Countries of the Andean Pact: Their Foundations* (UN Document TC/107).

33. UNCTAD, *Restrictions on Exports in Foreign Collaboration Agreements in India* (New York: United Nations, 1972), pp. 1-18; and UNCTAD, *Restrictions on Exports in Foreign Collaboration Agreements in the Philippines* (New York: United Nations, 1972), pp. 1-13. See also a discussion of these in the context of African countries' bargaining problems in Robert L. Curry, Jr., and Donald Rothchild, "On Economic Bargaining Between African Governments and Multinational Companies," paper presented at the Sixteenth Annual Meeting of the African Studies Association, Syracuse, New York, November 1973.

34. *Report of Secretary-General of UNCTAD to Secretary-General of United Nations* (UN Document TC/179), 30 June 1972, p. 10, paragraph 35.

35. See William P. Avery and James D. Cochrane, "Innovation in Latin American Regionalism: The Andean Common Market," *International Organization* 27 (Spring 1973); 181-224. See also the UN Secretariat study, *Multinational Corporations in World Development*, p. 77; and Ralph A. Diaz, "the Andean Common Market: Challenge to Foreign Investors," *Columbia Journal of World Business,* July-August 1971, pp. 22-28.

36. The quotation is from the *New York Times,* 31 December 1973, p. 2. For an opposing view, see C. Fred Bergsten, "The New Era in World Commodity Markets," *Challenge,* Sept./Oct. 1974, pp. 32-39. A symposium on this subject, with contributions by C. Fred Bergsten, Stephen Krasner, and Zuhayr Mikdashi, can be found in *Foreign Policy,* no. 14 (Spring 1974).

37. See ILO, *Multinational Enterprises and Social Policy*, p. 65. Also see the statement of Herbert Maier, director of the Economic, Social and Political Department of the International Confederation of Free Trade Unions, in US Congress, Joint Economic Committee, *A Foreign Economic Policy for the 1970's,* p. 824.

38. John M. Stopford and Louis T. Wells, Jr., *Managing the Multinational Enterprise* (New York: Basic Books, 1972), chapter 11. One senior executive of a US manufacturing concern noted of Decision 24 of the Andean Pact: "I won't be surprised if it passes, but then I won't be surprised if it stretches like an accordion with all the clauses." See "How Will Multinational Firms React to the Andean Pact's Decision 24?," *Inter-American Economic Affairs* 25 (Autumn 1971):57.

39. Council of the Americas, *Andean Pact: Definition, Design, and Analysis* (New York: Council of the Americas, no date, but contextually set in late 1973 or early 1974); particularly, "Implementing Legislation and Juridical Trends of ANCOM Members," by Dr. Mary Mercedes Martix. Her conclusion is that the ANCOM code "will be much milder than it looks on the books" (part 3, p. 39).

40. John R. Pate, Jr., "Activities of Non-U.S. Companies and Governments in Peru," in ibid., part 4, p. 4.

41. "How Will Multinational Firms React to the Andean Pact's Decision 24?," p. 62.

42. Stopford and Wells, pp. 152-53.

43. Ibid., chapter 8.

44. Ibid., p. 154.

45. Vernon, *Sovereignty At Bay,* pp. 266 ff.

46. Reuber discusses two cases in which firms were forced into a minority ownership position at the insistence of the host country. "Agreements were finally signed allowing managerial fees, royalties for technology, and guaranteed dividends which, in combination, far exceeded anything that . . . the firms had repatriated from these projects up to that time or hoped to repatriate later; . . . they were no longer prepared to reinvest earnings on the basis of future growth potentials. Lack of control over the direction of growth and the distribution of potential profits changed the fundamental purpose of the companies' involvement." [Grant L.] Reuber, [*Private Foreign Investment in Development* (London, 1973),] pp. 86-87.

47. Albert O. Hirschman, *How to Divest in Latin America, and Why,* Princeton Essays in International Finance, no. 76 (Princeton, N.J.: Princeton University Press, 1969), pp. 4-9.

48. See Miguel S. Wionczek, "The Rise and the Decline of Latin American Economic Integration," *Journal of Common Market Studies* 9 (September 1970): 49-66; Gary W. Wynia, *Politics and Planners: Economic Development Policy in Central America* (Madison, Wis.: University of Wisconsin Press, 1972).

17 / Declaration
on International Investment
and Multinational Enterprises
and Guidelines
for Multinational Enterprises

Organization for Economic Co-operation
and Development

Declaration on International Investment and Multinational Enterprises

The Governments of OECD Member Countries

CONSIDERING

- that international investment has assumed increased importance in the world economy and has considerably contributed to the development of their countries;
- that multinational enterprises play an important role in this investment process;
- that co-operation by Member countries can improve the foreign investment climate, encourage the positive contribution which multinational enterprises can make to economic and social progress, and minimise and resolve difficulties which may arise from their various operations;
- that, while continuing endeavours within the OECD may lead to further international arrangements and agreements in this field, it seems appropriate at this stage to intensify their co-operation and consultation on issues relating to international investment and multinational enterprises through inter-related instruments each of which deals with a different aspect of the matter and together constitute a framework within which the OECD will consider these issues:

DECLARE:

Guidelines for Multinational Enterprises

I. that they jointly recommend to multinational enterprises operating in their territories the observance of the Guidelines as set forth in the Annex hereto having regard to the

From a pamphlet issued by OECD containing the Declaration of June 21, 1976, by Governments of OECD Member Countries on International Investment and Multinational Enterprises, together with the Guidelines for Multinational Enterprises (an annex to the Declaration).

considerations and understandings which introduce the Guidelines and are an integral part of them;

National Treatment

II. 1. that Member countries should, consistent with their needs to maintain public order, to protect their essential security interests and to fulfil commitments relating to international peace and security, accord to enterprises operating in their territories and owned or controlled directly or indirectly by nationals of another Member country (hereinafter referred to as "Foreign-Controlled Enterprises") treatment under their laws, regulations and administrative practices, consistent with international law and no less favourable than that accorded in like situations to domestic enterprises (hereinafter referred to as "National Treatment");

2. that Member countries will consider applying "National Treatment" in respect of countries other than Member countries;

3. that Member countries will endeavour to ensure that their territorial subdivisions apply "National Treatment";

4. that this Declaration does not deal with the right of Member countries to regulate the entry of foreign investment or the conditions of establishment of foreign enterprises;

International Investment Incentives and Disincentives

III. 1. that they recognise the need to strengthen their co-operation in the field of international direct investment;

2. that they thus recognise the need to give due weight to the interests of Member countries affected by specific laws, regulations and administrative practices in this field (hereinafter called "measures") providing official incentives and disincentives to international direct investment;

3. that Member countries will endeavour to make such measures as transparent as possible, so that their importance and purpose can be ascertained and that information on them can be readily available;

Consultation Procedures

IV. that they are prepared to consult one another on the above matters in conformity with the Decisions of the Council relating to Inter-Governmental Consultation Procedures on the Guidelines for Multinational Enterprises, on National Treatment and on International Investment Incentives and Disincentives;

Review

V. that they will review the above matters within three years with a view to improving the effectiveness of international economic co-operation among Member countries on issues relating to international investment and multinational enterprises;

NOTE

The Turkish Government did not participate in the Declaration and abstained from the Decisions.

Guidelines for Multinational Enterprises

1. Multinational enterprises now play an important part in the economies of Member countries and in international economic relations, which is of increasing interest to governments. Through international direct investment, such enterprises can bring substantial benefits to home and host countries by contributing to the efficient utilisation of capital, technology and human resources between countries and can thus fulfil an important role in the promotion of economic and social welfare. But the advances made by multinational enterprises in organising their operations beyond the national framework may lead to abuse of concentrations of economic power and to conflicts with national policy objectives. In additions, the complexity of these multinational enterprises and the difficulty of clearly perceiving their diverse structures, operations and policies sometimes give rise to concern.

2. The common aim of the Member countries is to encourage the positive contributions which multinational enterprises can make to economic and social progress and to minimise and resolve the difficulties to which their various operations may give rise. In view of the transnational structure of such enterprises, this aim will be furthered by co-operation among the OECD countries where the headquarters of most of the multinational enterprises are established and which are the location of a substantial part of their operations. The guidelines set out hereafter are designed to assist in the achievement of this common aim and to contribute to improving the foreign investment climate.

3. Since the operations of multinational enterprises extend throughout the world, including countries that are not Members of the Organisation, international co-operation in this field should extend to all States. Member countries will give their full support to efforts undertaken in co-operation with non-member countries, and in particular with developing countries, with a view to improving the welfare and living standards of all people both by encouraging the positive contributions which multinational enterprises can make and by minimising and resolving the problems which may arise in connection with their activities.

4. Within the Organisation, the programme of co-operation to attain these ends will be a continuing, pragmatic and balanced one. It comes within the general aims of the Convention on the Organisation for Economic Co-operation and Development (OECD) and makes full use of the various specialised bodies of the Organisation, whose terms of reference already cover many aspects of the role of multinational enterprises, notably in matters of international trade and payments, competition, taxation, manpower, industrial development, science and technology. In these bodies, work is being carried out on the identification of issues, the improvement of relevant qualitative and statistical information and the elaboration of proposals for action designed to strengthen inter-governmental co-operation. In some of these areas procedures already exist through which issues related to the operations of multinational enterprises can be taken up. This work could result in the conclusion of further and complementary agreements and arrangements between governments.

5. The initial phase of the co-operation programme is composed of a Declaration and three Decisions promulgated simultaneously as they are complementary and inter-connected, in respect of guidelines for multinational enterprises, national treatment for foreign-controlled enterprises and international investment incentives and disincentives.

6. The guidelines set out below are recommendations jointly addressed by Member countries to multinational enterprises operating in their territories. These guidelines, which take into account the problems which can arise because of the international structure of these enterprises, lay down standards for the activities of these enterprises in the different Member countries. Observance of the guidelines is voluntary and not legally enforceable. However, they should help to ensure that the operations of these enterprises are in harmony with national policies of the countries where they operate and to strengthen the basis of mutual confidence between enterprises and States.

7. Every State has the right to prescribe the conditions under which multinational enterprises operate within its national jurisdiction, subject to international law and to the international agreements to which it has subscribed. The entities of a multinational enterprise located in various countries are subject to the laws of these countries.

8. A precise legal definition of multinational enterprises is not required for the purposes of the guidelines. These usually comprise companies or other entities whose ownership is private, state or mixed, established in different countries and so linked that one or more of them may be able to exercise a significant influence over the activities of others and, in particular, to share knowledge and resources with the others. The degree of autonomy of each entity in relation to the others varies widely from one multinational enterprise to another, depending on the nature of the links between such entities and the fields of activity concerned. For these reasons, the guidelines are addressed to the various entities within the multinational enterprise (parent companies and/or local entities) according to the actual distribution of responsibilities among them on the understanding that they will co-operate and provide assistance to one another as necessary to facilitate observance of the guidelines. The word "enterprise" as used in these guidelines refers to these various entities in accordance with their responsibilities.

9. The guidelines are not aimed at introducing differences of treatment between multinational and domestic enterprises; wherever relevant they reflect good practice for all. Accordingly, multinational and domestic enterprises are subject to the same expectations in respect of their conduct wherever the guidelines are relevant to both.

10. The use of appropriate international dispute settlement mechanisms, including arbitration, should be encouraged as a means of facilitating the resolution of problems arising between enterprises and Member countries.

11. Member countries have agreed to establish appropriate review and consultation procedures concerning issues arising in respect of the guidelines. When multinational enterprises are made subject to conflicting requirements by Member countries, the governments concerned will co-operate in good faith with a view to resolving such problems either within the Committee on International Investment and Multinational Enterprises established by the OECD Council on 21st January 1975 or through other mutually acceptable arrangements.

Having regard to the foregoing considerations, the Member countries set forth the following guidelines for multinational enterprises with the understanding that Member countries will fulfil their responsibilities to treat enterprises equitably and in accordance with international law and international agreements, as well as contractual obligations to which they have subscribed:

General Policies

Enterprises should

1. take fully into account established general policy objectives of the Member countries in which they operate;
2. in particular, give due consideration to those countries' aims and priorities with regard to economic and social progress, including industrial and regional development, the protection of the environment, the creation of employment opportunities, the promotion of innovation and the transfer of technology;
3. while observing their legal obligations concerning information, supply their entities with supplementary information the latter may need in order to meet requests by the authorities of the countries in which those entities are located for information relevant to the activities of those entities, taking into account legitimate requirements of business confidentiality;
4. favour close co-operation with the local community and business interests;
5. allow their component entities freedom to develop their activities and to exploit their competitive advantage in domestic and foreign markets, consistent with the need for specialisation and sound commercial practice;
6. when filling responsible posts in each country of operation, take due account of individual qualifications without discrimination as to nationality, subject to particular national requirements in this respect;
7. not render—and they should not be solicited or expected to render—any bribe or other improper benefit, direct or indirect, to any public servant or holder of public office;
8. unless legally permissible, not make contributions to candidates for public office or to political parties or other political organisations;
9. abstain from any improper involvement in local political activities.

Disclosure of Information

Enterprises should, having due regard to their nature and relative size in the economic context of their operations and to requirements of business confidentiality and to cost, publish in a form suited to improve public understanding a sufficient body of factual information on the structure, activities and policies of the enterprise as a whole, as a supplement, in so far as necessary for this purpose, to information to be disclosed under the national law of the individual countries in which they operate. To this end, they should publish within reasonable time limits, on a regular basis, but at least annually, financial statements and other pertinent information relating to the enterprise as a whole, comprising in particular:

i) the structure of the enterprise, showing the name and location of the parent company, its main affiliates, its percentage ownership, direct and indirect, in these affiliates, including shareholdings between them;

ii) the geographical areas[1] where operations are carried out and the principal activities carried on therein by the parent company and the main affiliates;

iii) the operating results and sales by geographical area and the sales in the major lines of business for the enterprise as a whole;

iv) significant new capital investment by geographical area and, as far as practicable, by major lines of business for the enterprise as a whole;

v) a statement of the sources and uses of funds by the enterprise as a whole;

vi) the average number of employees in each geographical area;

vii) research and development expenditure for the enterprise as a whole;

viii) the policies followed in respect of intra-group pricing;

ix) the accounting policies, including those on consolidation, observed in compiling the published information.

Competition

Enterprises should, while conforming to official competition rules and established policies of the countries in which they operate,

1. refrain from actions which would adversely affect competition in the relevant market by abusing a dominant position of market power, by means of, for example,

a) anti-competitive acquisitions,

b) predatory behaviour toward competitors,

c) unreasonable refusal to deal,

d) anti-competitive abuse of industrial property rights,

e) discriminatory (i.e. unreasonably differentiated) pricing and using such pricing transactions between affiliated enterprises as a means of affecting adversely competition outside these enterprises;

2. allow purchasers, distributors and licensees freedom to resell, export, purchase and develop their operations consistent with law, trade conditions, the need for specialisation and sound commercial practice;

3. refrain from participating in or otherwise purposely strengthening the restrictive effects of international or domestic cartels or restrictive agreements which adversely affect or eliminate competition and which are not generally or specifically accepted under applicable national or international legislation;

4. be ready to consult and co-operate, including the provision of information, with competent authorities of countries whose interests are directly affected in regard to competition issues or investigations. Provision of information should be in accordance with safeguards normally applicable in this field.

Financing

Enterprises should, in managing the financial and commercial operations of their activities, and especially their liquid foreign assets and liabilities, take into consideration the established objectives of the countries in which they operate regarding balance of payments and credit policies.

Taxation

Enterprises should

1. upon request of the taxation authorities of the countries in which they operate, provide, in accordance with the safe-guards and relevant procedures of the national laws of these countries, the information necessary to determine correctly the taxes to be assessed in connection with their operations, including relevant information concerning their operations in other countries;

2. refrain from making use of the particular facilities available to them, such as transfer pricing which does not conform to an arm's length standard, for modifying in ways contrary to national laws the tax base on which members of the group are assessed.

Employment and Industrial Relations

Enterprises should, within the framework of law, regulations and prevailing labour relations and employment practices, in each of the countries in which they operate,

1. respect the right of their employees, to be represented by trade unions and other bona fide organisations of employees, and engage in constructive negotiations, either individually or through employers' associations, with such employee organisations with a view to reaching agreements on employment conditions, which should include provisions for dealing with disputes arising over the interpretation of such agreements, and for ensuring mutually respected rights and responsibilites:

2. *a)* provide such facilities to representatives of the employees as may be necessary to assist in the development of effective collective agreements,

   b) provide to representatives of employees information which is needed for meaningful negotiations on conditions of employment;

3. provide to representatives of employees where this accords with local law and practice, information which enables them to obtain a true and fair view of the performance of the entity or, where appropriate, the enterprise as a whole;

4. observe standards of employment and industrial relations not less favourable than those observed by comparable employers in the host country;

5. in their operations, to the greatest extent practicable, utilise, train and prepare for upgrading members of the local labour force in co-operation with representatives of their employees and, where appropriate, the relevant governmental authorities;

6. in considering changes in their operations which would have major effects upon the livelihood of their employees, in particular in the case of the closure of an entity involving collective lay-offs or dismissals, provide reasonable notice of such changes to represeentatives of their employees, and where appropriate to the relevant governmental authorities, and co-operate with the employee representatives and appropriate governmental authorities so as to mitigate to the maximum extent practicable adverse effects;

7. implement their employment policies including hiring, discharge, pay, promotion and training without discrimination unless selectivity in respect of employee characteristics is in furtherance of established governmental policies which specifically promote greater equality of employment opportunity;

8. in the context of bona fide negotiations[2] with representatives of employees on conditions of employment, or while employees are exercising a right to organise, not threaten to utilise a capacity to transfer the whole or part of an operating unit from the country concerned in order to influence unfairly those negotiations or to hinder the exercise of a right to organise;

9. enable authorised representatives of their employees to conduct negotiations on collective bargaining or labour management relations issues with representatives of management who are authorised to take decisions on the matters under negotiation.

Science and Technology

Enterprises should

1. endeavour to ensure that their activities fit satisfactorily into the scientific and technological policies and plans of the countries in which they operate, and contribute to the development of national scientific and technological capacities, including as far as appropriate the establishment and improvement in host countries of their capacity to innovate;

2. to the fullest extent practicable, adopt in the course of their business activities practices which permit the rapid diffusion of technologies with due regard to the protection of industrial and intellectual property rights;

3. when granting licences for the use of industrial property rights or when otherwise transferring technology do so on reasonable terms and conditions.

NOTES

1. For the purposes of the guideline on disclosure of information the term "geographical area" means groups of countries or individual countries as each enterprise determines is appropriate in its particular circumstances. While no single method of grouping is appropriate for all enterprises or for all purposes, the factors to be considered by an enterprise would include the significance of operations carried out in individual countries or areas as well as the effects on its competitiveness, geographic proximity, economic affinity, similarities in business environments and the nature, scale and degree of interrelationship of the enterpises' operations in the various countries.

2. Bona fide negotiations may include labour disputes as part of the process of negotiation. Whether or not labour disputes are so included will be determined by the law and prevailing employment practices of particular countries.

18 / The Control
of Multinational Enterprises

Francisco Orrego Vicuña

. . .

The Efforts Toward Unilateral Control and Their Limitations

The alternatives for control of the multinational enterprise are the following: (1) unilateral action, either by the host country or the home state; (2) bilateral action, by two host countries or by the host country and the home state; and (3) multilateral action on a universal or semi-universal basis (which would include the host as well as the home country) or on a regional basis, from groups of countries. It is also possible to combine these various alternatives.

The first difficulty in every type of control is that the legal framework applicable to the multinational enterprises has not yet been sufficiently refined, either at the level of national law or that of international law. At the present state of development of this framework, only the multinational enterprise formed in pursuance of a treaty or other type of intergovernmental agreement may be so called. However, this is not the kind of public enterprise most in need of control, at least not as a rule. As D. F. Vagts observes, the "law of the multinational enterprise" has serious deficiencies. In the first place, it is divided into categories dealing with different aspects separately and does not view the phenomenon as a whole; in the second place, it is basically obsolete, inspired by an outdated situation; third, the forms and actions of the corporation are so atypical that they preclude the establishment of stable precedents which are regular and similar enough to become the basis of the necessary juridical norms; and finally, one cannot think about legal control without also dealing with the underlying economic problems, which have not yet been clearly understood.[1]

In spite of these difficulties, systems of control of the unilateral level have gradually emerged involving both host and home governments. A first requisite for the effectiveness of these systems is adequate information on the multinational enterprise to be controlled, its mode of action and its strategies—a requisite that, although obvious, may be most difficult to impose. This assumes, of course, that there also exists the professional capacity to obtain and to process the information and to formulate the corresponding conclusions, a capacity that may not be available to many developing nations. Significant tests of this

From Francisco Orrego Vicuña, "El Control de las Empresas Multinacionales," *Foro Internacional* (Mexico City), Vol. XIV, No. 1 (July–September, 1973), pp. 109-128. By permission of the publisher. Translated by Sylvia Modelski. Some notes have been omitted, and the remainder renumbered in sequence.

capacity have been made by introducing the "obligation to inform" in Canada and the European Economic Community.

Methods of Control by the Host Country

The most important weapon at the disposal of every state is the power to accept or reject the intrusion of a multinational enterprise in its economy. However, as well as being the most important it is the most difficult to manage for various reasons. The first of these is that a developing country faces a conflict of interests: the fear of associating itself with a powerful entity and the necessity to encourage investments and technology for its development. This situation is precisely the one which the multinational enterprise knows how to exploit through its enormous capacity for negotiation. Another reason why the use of this power by the host country is impeded is that normally its decision is based on the application of legislation relating to foreign investments which is not yet sophisticated enough to distinguish efficiently between traditional foreign investment and the investment of the multinational enterprises, which often have a radically different effect.

This leads to the conclusion that the efficiency of the system of control adopted by the host country will depend basically on two factors. The first is the development of its own capacity to negotiate deals which are not disadvantageous to itself. (The policy of developed countries which have been faced with the problem, such as Canada, France and Japan, is based to a large extent on this capacity, which explains why they have not found it necessary until now to adopt or put into practice regulations of a restrictive type.[2]) The second factor is the refining of the legislation on foreign investments and of the procedures of registration and selection and, above all, the abrogation of restictive trade practices though efficient regulations.[3]

Closely related to these policies are proposals for further measures to be initiated by the host country, such as creating competing corporations within the host country itself, developing a policy for building up the national private sector, entering into joint ventures and drawing up effective accords on licensing and management. All of this may be relevant when the host country is Canada, Japan or France, but if one is thinking of the developing countries (say, in Africa or Latin America), with some exceptions, these measures are utopian and their real use for resolving the problem is very slight. Perhaps within a regional context, which will be examined later, they may have more viability, but they certainly do not within a context of unilateral control.

Apart from the problems examined, the major weakness of unilateral control by the host country is the fact that the multinational enterprise, by its very structure, will normally be able to evade many aspects of the controls because its operations extend beyond the frontiers of the host state in question. Two possible remedies for this situation are: either an extremely efficient form of national control, which to this day does not exist, or control by more than one country, i.e., control which ceases to be unilateral.

For the same reasons we must dismiss the favorite alternative of the multinational enterprises themselves: the code of "good conduct," of "rights and obligations" of the multinational enterprise or of "good corporate behavior"—a proposal based on the idea of self-imposed discipline by the corporations and of directives that they will voluntarily undertake to respect.[4] If the developing countries have any experience at all in this matter of international economic relations, the most frustrating is that good intentions are no guarantee at all of their rights and interests.

Methods of Control by the Home Country

The country in which the multinational enterprise has its principal base, which in 90 percent of the cases will be the United States, also faces the possibility, and in many cases the necessity, of controlling such companies. In the present study we are not interested in the controls that the home country exercises over the activities of the company within its own borders, for this is an internal problem. What we are concerned with are the controls applicable to the company's activities abroad, whether directly or through its subsidiaries. The extraterritorial application of national legislation causes acute conflicts of sovereignty, but it also could mean a type of unilateral action that would lead to saner commercial practices.

It is perhaps in this field that the obsolescence of the classic law is best in evidence, especially when the question is to determine the nationality of the company to be controlled. Frequently, the subsidiary operating abroad will have a different nationality from that of the parent company, and thus it is difficult to submit the subsidiary to the same rules as the parent company. For certain purposes, such as the confiscation of enemy property in times of war, the nationality of the corporation is determined by that of its owners or controllers, but this has not been the rule for multinational enterprises. This illustrates well the necessity of adopting clear norms for particular cases and the necessity of focusing on the phenomenon as a whole.

The Extraterritorial Application of Antitrust Legislation

One type of control the United States has used is the extraterritorial application of antitrust legislation, a matter which has generated considerable controversy. In the celebrated case *British Nylon Spinners Ltd.* vs. *Imperial Chemical Industries Ltd.*, an English tribunal in 1955 refused to apply the decision of an American court requiring a reassignment of patents from the latter enterprise, since the situation, which might have been illegal in the United States, was not illegal in England. The *Swiss Watch* case was a similar controversy. The imposition of fines by the Commission of European Communities on Swiss, English and even Community companies for price fixing led to a protest from the English government, for whom this extraterritorial imposition exceeded "the limits established by recognized principles of International Law." Such jurisdictional conflicts have shown that this system of control does not function efficiently and at the same time explains why, except in the case of members of the European Economic Community, international and antitrust cooperation is virtually nonexistent or of very little significance.[5] Furthermore, various countries have even adopted laws prohibiting the application of foreign antitrust measures.

Other Types of Extraterritorial Control

The same thing happened when export controls were tried. In a famous case the *Fruehauf* case, the United States Treasury Department caused the prohibitions of the Trading with the Enemy Act to be applied to a French subsidiary of the Fruehauf Company with the intention of impeding certain exports to mainland China, which in fact were thwarted. This also happened in the case of exports to Cuba.

It should also be mentioned that other areas offer opportunities for extraterritorial control and potential conflict. Among them are tax legislation, securities regulation and, more recently, balance of payments controls.

Balance of payments controls illustrate the effect of the multinational enterprise on the balance of payments of developed countries, particularly with reference to the weakening of the pound sterling and the dollar. In the United States such controls were initiated as "voluntary directives" in 1965, calling for moderation in the export of capital and diligence in the repatriation of profits. In 1968 these measures had to be changed to "mandatory controls," but institution of these measures proved that the companies' system of voluntary "good conduct" was ineffective. Anyway, the efficacy of even these controls has proven quite limited, as evidenced by the gradual strengthening of the Euro-dollar and Euro-bond markets, which escape these measures.

This also shows the beginning of a conflict of interest between the United States and the multinational enterprise, which has led Vagts to suggest that "it could well be that to the degree to which the United States finds it difficult to maintain its relative position in fiscal and economic terms, it will be a less suitable base for multinational operations."[6] In the light of these problems, it may not be too bold to think that the United States itself might in the future take the initiative in controlling multinational enterprises, as has been proposed by an important section of the American academic community.

Finally, other proposals must be mentioned which, although they do not aim to establish controls, have as their objective the avoidance of conflicts in the investment field. Hirschman suggested some time ago, particularly in relation to Latin America, the idea of proceeding toward gradual "disinvestment" in certain sectors, with the help of a system of guarantees and of a "corporation for disinvestment," which could be the Inter-American Bank for Development.[7] His proposal is based on the idea that a temporary suspension of foreign private investment would be more beneficial than harmful to the growth of Latin America. Vernon and Rosenstein-Rodan too, have also suggested a "fade out." Even if, in the light of the different economic requirements of the Latin American countries, such ideas were arguable, the multinationals must remain present at least as regards those sectors that are of primordial interest for the national economy. On this subject the experience to be gained by decision 24 of the Andean group and the Mexican legislature's recent proposal on foreign investment, which contemplates the regulation by sectors and the gradual transfer of ownership in certain investments, might be a brave precedent by which to judge the efficacy of these initiatives and proposals.[8]

The conclusion to be drawn from the totality of controls exercised by the home country is that they have proven largely inefficient; furthermore, even if they could be perfected and standardized, their effect on the total volume of activity of the multinational enterprise would always remain minimal, from which it follows that rather than having a real significance, they are symbolic of the pressing need to achieve some degree of control. Thus in practice the multinational enterprise continues to operate in large measure outside the purview of effective regulation; hence, also the need for controls other than unilateral.

The Experiments in Regional Control

Apart from the efforts at unilateral control just mentioned, the tendency has been toward the establishment of regionally based multilateral mechanisms between countries sharing certain interests. In this sense, cases of bilateral cooperation have been few and of minor significance,[9] except perhaps in the area of taxation and double taxation.

The Control Policy of the European Communities

The most elaborate instance of regional control today is that of the European Community, manifested by the regulation of competition by means of the antitrust policy, as well as by efforts to strengthen the European firm (for example, by implementation of such projects as the European incorporation and the encouragement of mergers). Nevertheless, the object of such control is limited almost exclusively to activities taking place within this economic community, and does not include activities outside it except very rarely. Hence the significance of this control for other countries and especially for developing countries is very limited and indirect.

The antitrust policy of the Community, based on articles 85 and 86 of the Treaty of Rome, was designed with intra-European competition in mind and for the control of cartels that reached their apogee before the Second World War. It did not anticipate that, in the era of the Treaty of Rome, the presence of American multinational enterprises would become a major concern. Keeping things in their correct proportions, it can be asserted that this antitrust policy is aimed mainly at the regulation of traditional economic competition, not at solution of the new problems generated by the multinational enterprise.

The increasing presence of North American, English and Japanese multinational enterprises within the Community has had a strong impact on traditional policy. Since 1965 the preoccupation has definitely been with strengthening the competitive power of European enterprises in relation to that of these multinationals, and this requires thinking in terms of company mergers at the national and community levels, even though the compatibility of such a policy with articles 85 and 86 of the Treaty may be in doubt. The economic strength of the Community must be given credit for the fact that the multinational phenomenon was squarely met, not through restrictive measures, but through the creation of competitive mechanisms.

The Control Policy of the Andean Group

A second kind of regional control worth mentioning is the system created by the Andean group. This system is made up of a complex network of decisions based on two main ideas: first, the strengthening of the competitive power of the local company, whether national or subregional; second, in order to achieve this objective, the imposition of certain restrictions on foreign capital. Here we observe a fundamental difference between this group and the European Economic Community, namely, that whereas the latter based its policy entirely on its competitive capacity, the Andean group had, in addition, to introduce restrictions because of the inablility of its developing member countries to meet foreign companies on equal terms.

The objective of strengthening competitive potential is underwritten by the subregional Accord, which aims at establishing a bigger market and special mechanisms such as the regulation of competition, subregional investment and a regime for multinational enterprises.[10] The restrictive policy aimed at securing this objective is expressed by a common tariff, which regulates imports from outside the region, and above all by Decision No. 24

on the treatment of foreign investments, which covers investments within the region.[11] As is known, that decision not only regulates the situation in different sectors and in both existing and future investments; it establishes related measures for the gradual transfer of property rights and for the elimination of restrictive practices as well as measures for strict control in matters of patents and technology transfer.

There is no doubt that the system has been well designed and, even though its operation may have encountered serious difficulties,[12] it is reasonable to expect that to the extent to which the member countries consistently follow the rules, it will have results. Doubtless the current opposition from the multinational enterprises is the clearest evidence that it is an efficient system of control; had it been otherwise, it would perhaps not have attracted such criticism or merited such attention.

Limitations of Regional Control

In spite of what has just been said, the problem must be examined from an even wider perspective. Even supposing that a control system such as the Andean group's were completely successful, we must ask whether it fully serves the interests of the developing countries. A prime factor to take into account is the risk of the multinational investment moving to other developing countries in the same region that are not participants in the control system. As a concrete example, with respect to the Andean group, the argument is frequently made that Decision No. 24 is the best stimulus for the orientation of the multinational enterprise toward other Latin American countries, usually Brazil. At the moment the criteria for judging the validity of this argument do not exist, but it can in principle be assumed that the argument does not have a firm basis because, first of all, given the level of competition between multinational enterprises themselves, none of them is inclined to abandon a potentially lucrative market; second, the corporation normally can embrace yet another profitable market without abandoning the first; and finally, what the corporation is looking for more often than not is precisely the clarity of the principles governing it and the security of its investment, a need that can be met more effectively within a multilateral system than within a unilateral system. In any case, even if the argument were valid, the solution is not to abandon control but to seek a broader system of control.

But there is an even more serious factor to be considered. Given that the multinational enterprise has constituted itself as a new agent for the international division of labor and given that its major capacity for action is in the market of the developed areas, the achievement of control over the branch located in a developing country does not necessarily mean that the interest of that country in terms of its export needs or preferential access to the big markets will be secured. It will in the greatest measure continue to depend on the global policy of the corporation as a whole; and as long as control cannot be achieved on that higher level, the problem will remain. In other words, when a developing country pins its hopes on the contribution that a multinational enterprise can make toward the growth of exports which this country or group of countries needs, the control of the subsidiary does not secure the accomplishment of the objective pursued; the outcome depends on the parent company and its policy, which could be indifferently oriented either toward international trade or toward local production.

Regional control is certainly a positive step, above all by comparison with the limitations of unilateral control, as is shown not only by case studies but also to a certain extent by the experience of the Central American Convention on Tax Incentives to Industrial

Development and the Regime of Central American Integration Industries. Nevertheless, the truly international dimension of the multinational enterprises imposes strong limitations even on this type of control, at least when it is exercised by developing countries.

Proposals for a System of International Control

The limitations of the control systems thus far examined and the ineffectiveness of GATT (General Agreement on Tariffs and Trade) consultative procedures in matters of restrictive practices have led to the initiation of a search for genuinely international forms of control. The uneasiness concerning this problem, which can be observed even in the developed countries themselves, has further contributed to this movement. Moreover, the multinational corporations themselves have shown some interest in disconnecting themselves from the nation-state, not in order to submit themselves to international control but rather to liberate themselves even more in their operations, which has led to certain proposals which will be examined. Common as this tendency toward international control may be in the field of academic writing, there is also, as will be seen, a considerable body of official opinion moving in the same direction.

Among the objectives which an international system must set for itself, Vagts notes the following: (1) avoiding the exacerbation of conflicts between countries, particularly those that might lead to a breach of the peace; (2) maximizing production of the necessary material goods; (3) minimizing the costs of production, including the external ones relating to environmental and social cost; (4) equalizing the distribution of wealth and opportunity between nations and individuals; and (5) bringing the maximum degree of autonomy to the individual, the family and the community, be it in respect to working conditions or in respect to the political and social life, with particular regard to protecting freedom from the actions of an insensitive, regimenting and remote authority.[13] These objectives reveal not only the political and economic dimension of multinational corporation activity, but also the complex human factors affected by this new phenomenon.

The Autonomous Development of the Multinational Enterprise

The first series of proposals to be discussed is that which to some extent provides for the preservation or perfecting of the *laissez-faire* of the multinational enterprise. Some authors have tried to maintain that the best solution is to do nothing at all in this matter, since it concerns problems of secondary importance which can be resolved through the normal channels of diplomacy.[14] To say the least, this position purposely ignores the reality of the contemporary world. Another type of proposal is for an international system designed to facilitate the activity of the multinational enterprise. In effect, for George W. Ball, the multinational enterprise is a blessing for mankind and its growth should be promoted; to this end, to obviate the obstacles to it created by conflicts with the nation-state, the corporation should be brought under international jurisdiction. In his opinion this can be achieved through:

> The establishment by treaty of an international companies law, administered by
> a supranational body, including representatives drawn from various countries, who
> would not only exercise normal domiciliary supervision but would also enforce

antimonopoly laws and administer guarantees with regard to uncompensated expropriation. An international companies law could place limitations, for example, on the restrictions nation-states might be permitted to impose on companies established under its sanctions. The operative standard defining those limitations might be the quantity of freedom needed to preserve the central principle of assuring the most economical and efficient use of world resources.[15]

The basic objective of this proposal is the control of the state and not the corporation, except for such aspects as monopoly control. But this is unrealistic and has been unanimously criticized for being impossible to put into practice. As Vagts notes, the autonomous development of the multinational enterprise, which is what this and other proposals favor,[16] involves the dissolution of at least five links: (1) the corporation would not be set up in any particular country; (2) the corporation would diversify its activity in such a way that it would not have a home state; (3) the stockholders would also belong to many countries; (4) management would be internationalized; and (5) no state would be able to claim control over the activities of the corporation outside its territory. However eagerly the multinational enterprises endeavor every day to dissolve more and more of these ties, establishing themselves, for example, in Luxemburg or Bermuda, internationalizing their personnel, issuing stocks in the major markets of the world and diversifying their operations, the possibility of doing without the nation-state remains very remote, contrary to what the above proposals maintain.

Deconcentration and Restructuring

A second series of initiatives have aimed at the establishment of measures for the international control of specific problems, which would not necessarily mean the adoption of global controls, although in some cases this is not excluded either. Vagts notes two lines of action in this direction: deconcentration and the restructuring of the multinational enterprises. Deconcentration would basically consist of international antitrust legislation, which the author calls the international version of the Sherman and Clayton Acts.[17] Ideally this should lead to an international antitrust agency which would distinguish between mergers that create enterprises that would benefit from economies of scale and those which only create mammoths of power. Action on a supranational level would be required to achieve that end, since no government, by itself, could do more than control the local tentacles of a world-wide operation. The restructuring of the multinational enterprise would aim at forcing it to take into consideration other factors besides the purely commercial ones, such as the impact of its activity on foreign cultures and societies. The author suggests the integration of the foreign element in the administrative structure and the personnel of the enterprise. This type of regulation is becoming urgent, especially since the international merger of companies is daily creating ever more powerful conglomerates.

Methods of General Control

Within the confines of the academic proposals just examined, one must finally refer to those which envisage a global scheme, though with varying degrees of authority. In general terms, these proposals can be classified in the following categories: (1) An agency entrusted with the task of collecting, processing and systematizing information about the multinational enterprises, with power to require the presentation of the needed information. On this basis, adequate control measures will eventually take shape. (2) A consultative organization formed by interested countries for an exchange of views on problems caused by multinational enterprises, from which will eventually emerge rules of conduct and procedures for the resolution of disputes. (3) A genuinely controlling organization, with direct authority over multinational enterprises.

The best-known proposal is that of Goldberg and Kindleberger for the establishment of a forum where the problems of the multinational enterprises can be discussed, and where disputes may, eventually, also be resolved. This forum would fill a function similar to that of GATT in the commercial world; it would be given a similar administrative structure and aim at an international agreement which would rest on a limited number of acceptable basic principles. The proposed title is: General Agreement for the International Corporation. The functions of this instrument would be limited, since it would only investigate those operations and problems brought to its attention by countries and corporations themselves, issue recommendations with no powers of enforcement, and rely on the prestige of an impartial body. Its basic role would be that of ombudsman for the corporations and the countries.[18]

Because the analogy with GATT might be misleading, another author has proposed the creation of a Consultative Center for the International Corporation (CCIC), which could function within the bounds of the OECD (Organization for Economic Cooperation and Development) or, to facilitate the participation of developing nations, within the bounds of the World Bank. This author rejects the idea of a link with UNCTAD (United Nations Conference on Trade and Development) or UNIDO (United Nations Industrial Development Organization) because of the ideological diversity represented in these organizations. The eventual application of this idea on a regional basis is also suggested, using the channels of OAS, Inter-American Committee on the Alliance for Progress (ICAP), or Inter-American Development Bank (IDB). The Consultative Center would be a forum for the analysis and discussion of problems, particularly those relating to the growth of international production. It would have the right to issue recommendations but no controlling power. One of its functions would be to separate the problems of the multinational enterprise in relation to developed countries from those relating to developing countries, taking into account the different levels of development in the latter.[19] The limited function assigned to the Center is closely related to the function described in previous writings of the same author, in whose opinion the more adequate solution would be to do nothing.

Sectoral International Integration

Recently, Jack N. Behrman has brought an important point of view to bear on the subject. Without prejudice to the more traditional types of control measures used by states, he proposes the creation of an agency to assign to the multinational enterprise responsiblities in particular sectors of economic activity, viewing each sector separately and following clear directives. Due to the difficulty of adapting this function to organizations such as OECD or GATT, Behrman proposes the creation of the Organization for International Industrial Integration (OIII), which would be charged with the task of organizing equal participation in the different sectors, particularly through the development of international coproduction projects, the exchange of information, the control of industrial promotion policies and the execution of directives for the participation of multinational enterprises in these projects. All this with the aim of increased efficiency and the better use of available resources and enterprises, which would stimulate the interdependence and the coordination of the economic policies of member states.[20]

This proposal deals with a fundamental problem much more than do any of the previous ones because it suggests a greater measure of control over the multinational enterprise. However, it basically takes into account the interests and the potential of the developed countries and only secondarily focuses on the problems besetting the developing nations. In particular, it is inspired by a scheme of cooperation with the other developed countries having market economies—based to some extent on the experience in military coproduction of NATO—and goes on to explore the possible alternatives of coproduction between the said countries and the socialist countries, mainly the Soviet Union and China. As we shall soon see, all these proposals in large measure ignore the problems of the developing countries; thus the practicality and equity of the control measures are greatly weakened.

The Initiatives for International Action

In view of the progressive expansion of the multinational enterprise, the desire for some means of control has also spread in an increasing number of sectors. One of the important sectors expressing this uneasiness is that of labor. In this respect it must be observed that the powerful American labor union organizations have begun to see the multinational enterprise as a serious threat to their own interests, due to the fact that United States-based enterprises, availing themselves of cheaper labor, are producing more and more in other countries, and then shipping those products to the American market, which in turn affects employment opportunities in that country. The AFL-CIO has proposed that in this case the products should be taxed with special duties to protect the American labor market. In response to this uneasiness, the ILO (International Labor Organization) at the 56th session of its 1971 Conference passed a resolution on "social problems caused by the multinational enterprise," recommending the initiation of studies and the convocation of a meeting to examine the relationship between the multinational enterprise and social policy.

In the meantime, the 1972 third session of the UNCTAD, in its Resolution 73 (III) on restrictive trade practices, referred expressly to those involving multinational enterprises, and established a Group of Experts to study such practices. We must also mention that the United Nations Secretariat in 1972 called attention to the necessity of the international community formulating a policy and setting up the effective mechanism to deal with the problems caused by the multinational enterprises.

The first initiative for systematic study and the formulation of recommendations for action was presented in the name of Chile by Ambassador Hernán Santa Cruz in the 53rd session of the United Nations Economic and Social Council in 1972. On the basis of this initiative, Resolution 1721 (LIII) was passed which, instead of following up the other proposals mentioned, asked the United Nations Secretary General to name, after consultation with the governments, a study group consisting of eminent persons to inquire into the role of multinational enterprises, their impact on the development process—especially that of developing nations—and the implications of that process for international relations. At the same time they would draw up guidelines for use by governments in the planning of their national policies and submit recommendations for appropriate international action. Thus, the first step has been taken toward official action at the international level, which surely will contribute to the formulation of a control policy in the near future.

The necessity for action of this nature found strong expression in the proposal of President Echeverría of Mexico for a Charter of Economic Rights and Duties of States, made in the joint communiqué of the Presidents of Mexico and Chile on the 3rd of December 1972 and in the latter's speech to the United Nations General Assembly on the 4th of December 1972. The same preoccupation was also in evidence at the regional level. The theme of the multinational corporations was placed by the OAS Council on the agenda of the Special Inter-American Conference on International Private Law, meeting in 1974.

Prospects for a System of Control:
Toward the Redistribution of International Income

Since the multinational enterprise has demonstrated its capacity to elude the methods of unilateral control available to a state, it can reasonably be said that these methods are inadequate as a future solution. This is surely true for the developing countries and, to a lesser extent, it is also true for the developed countries. Of course, national control will remain an important element in any system, but everything points toward forms of regional and international control.

The Interests of the Developing Countries

The most serious weakness of practically all the proposals or systems which have been examined has been that the interests of the developing countries were not taken into account at all or only as an afterthought. Practically all the proposals aim at perfecting competition in the economic relations between developed countries, but in respect to the activity of those same firms in the developing world no serious effort to control them has been made. Whatever these proposals might be, activity in developing countries is governed by different principles, which are those of the international division of labor. This applies to private as well as state enterprises, since each aims at satisfying the interests of its own economy.[21]

The growing economic and political integration of the industrialized world is the reason for this lack of concern. But if a system of control emerges which does not duly take into account the interests of the developing countries, the result will be an aggravation of the present conditions because those countries will have to face the solid front of united enterprises without the advantage of the alternatives offered today by competition between big corporations.

Thus, from the point of view of the developing countries, a consultative system is not enough, nor, for the time being, are there real possibilities for the development of the potential for competition. These alternatives are only viable for the developed countries. Behrman is the one who has gone to the root of the problem. He maintains that it is necessary to distribute equitably the process of international production. Nevertheless, the schemes for sectoral integration and coproduction that have been proposed to attain these objectives can only work if consideration is given to the participation of the developing world. Within the latter, only those countries having major economic potential or those endowed with special natural resources could eventually draw satisfactory benefits. This might be the case in certain specified sectors, but in no way can it be thought of as a general rule.

The Redistribution of Income

The root of the problem goes deeper than the simple rearrangement of the physical process of production; the question essentially is that of the distribution of the income derived from international production. To attain this objective it is necessary that the control procedure should basically aim at the establishment of an international redistributive mechanism that would allow the transfer in just proportion of the income from one sector to another, not in terms of partnership but in the name of justice, as occurs in a well-organized national society.

Our own proposal in this matter is to look for a system of international taxation, applicable to the facilities made available to the multinational enterprises and other entities in the process of international production and trade, as a kind of international value-added tax—the international version of the (European) value-added tax. The revenue from this tax would be distributed among the countries, perhaps in inverse proportion to their national production, or else it could contribute to the financing of development projects carried out by international agencies. In this way the redistribution would benefit all the developing countries without exception. Such a system naturally presumes an international authority with strong and very direct powers of control and investigation.

Whatever the difficulty in establishing a system of this kind, beginning with the definition of international production or the types of activity taxed, and with the relationship of that tax to the national tax system, we are firmly convinced that it is the only solution that could lead to an effective process of even development, given the known statistics on the increasing role of the multinational enterprise in world production. Those who think that this is a utopian solution should remember that the United Nations has made considerable progress toward the design of a similar mechanism for the redistribution of income from the exploitation of the sea and ocean floors outside national waters. The "common heritage of mankind" need not limit itself to the sea bottom; it can also be applied to international investment, production and trade.

NOTES

1. Detlev F. Vagts, "The Multinational Enterprise: A New Challenge For Transnational Law," *Harvard Law Review* 83 (1970):743-744.
2. The regulations adopted by countries such as France and Japan have been of extremely limited use. See Vagts, op. cit., pp. 777-779. See also Jack N. Behrman, "The Multinational Enterprise: Its Initiatives and Governmental Reactions," *Journal of International Law and Economics* 6 (1972):230-231.
3. For an examination of such possible measures and notes on various national legislations, see UNCTAD, *Restrictive Trade Practices*, TD/122/Supp. 1, January 7, 1972, pp. 87-95. See also the draft bill and address presented on December 26, 1972, by the President of

Mexico on the promotion of Mexican investment and regulation of foreign investment. In *Commercio Exterior,* January 1973, pp. 16–25.

4. Sidney E. Rolfe, *The International Corporation* (Paris: International Chamber of Commerce, 1969), pp. 141–144; J. Behrman, *U.S. International Business and Governments* (New York: McGraw-Hill, 1971), Chap. 5.

5. In 1960, GATT adopted a fragile consultative procedure for restrictive practices, which up to now has had no influence at all (GATT Decisions of the Seventeenth Session, December 5, 1960). For a discussion of the limitations of GATT in this area, see John H. Jackson, *World Trade and the Law of GATT* (Indianapolis: Bobbs-Merrill, 1969), pp. 522–527.

6. Detlev F. Vagts, "The Global Corporation and International Law," *Journal of International Law and Economics* 6 (1972):249.

7. Albert O. Hirschman, "How to Divest in Latin American, and Why," *Essays in International Finance,* Princeton University, Vol. 76 (November 1969), pp. 3–24.

8. The draft Bill proposed in Mexico by the President of the Republic (cited in note 3 above) reserves exclusively for the State certain sectors of prime importance for the country's economy. In other sectors the participation of foreign capital is limited to given percentages, which fluctuate between 43 percent and 49 percent according to the case. As a general rule, 49 percent is the maximum percentage of participation allowed, barring special authorizations. The foreign participation in the administration of the corporation is not to exceed its contribution of capital. Also, a national register of foreign investments is to be established.

9. An example of bilateral cooperation is the agreement signed on January 29, 1959, by the Canadian Minister of Justice and the United States Attorney General, on consultations about the application of antitrust legislation to the two countries. See R. Stevenson, "Extraterritoriality in Canadian-United States Relations," *Department of State Bulletin* 63 (1970):425, 427.

10. On the Subregional Agreement, see Bernardo Nun's *El acuerdo subregional andino* (Santiago: Andres Bello, 1972). On the regime for multinational enterprises, see Gustavo Fernandex Saavedra, "El régimen de la empresa multinacional en el Groupo Andino," *Derecho de la Integración* No.11 (October 1972), pp. 11–38.

11. See Covey T. Oliver, "The Andean Foreign Investment Code: A New Phase in the Quest for Normative Order as to Direct Foreign Investment," *Americàn Journal of International Law* 66 (1972):763–784.

12. An examination of these difficulties may be found in articles by the author on the cases of Chile and Colombia, in *Derecho de la Integración* No. 7 (October 1970) and No. 11 (October 1972).

13. Vagts, *loc. cit.,* note 6, pp. 256–257.

14. Seymour J. Rubin, "The International Firm and the National Jurisdiction," in C. Kindleberger, ed., *The International Corporation* (Cambridge, Mass: The M.I.T. Press, 1970), p. 179.

15. George W. Ball, "Cosmocorp: The Importance of Being Stateless," in C. Brown ed., *World Business: Promise and Problems* (New York: Macmillan, 1970), p. 337.

16. For other proposals in the same direction, see Selections 2 and 10.

17. Vagts, *loc. cit.,* note 6, pp. 257–260.

18. P. Goldberg and C. Kindleberger, "Toward a GATT for Investment: A Proposal for Supervision of the International Corporation," *Law and Policy in International Business* 2 (1970), pp. 321–323.

19. Seymour Rubin, "Multinational Enterprise and National Sovereignty: A Skeptic's Analysis," *Law and Policy in International Business* 2 (1971):2–6.

20. J. N. Behrman, "Sharing International Production through the Multinational Enterprise and Sectoral Integration," *Law and Policy in International Business* 4, No. 2 (1972).

21. For an examination of this aspect, see the article by this author in *El Commercio de Estado: alternativa de la clausula de la nacion mas favorecida en la estructuración juridica del comercio internacional?* Carnegie Endowment, Interamerican Study Group, 1972.

19 / Report of the Group of Eminent Persons to Study the Impact of Multinational Corporations on Development and on International Relations

United Nations

Introduction

Multinational corporations are important actors on the world stage. The report entitled, *Multinational Corporations in World Development*, aptly describes their current significance and recent trends. The total value of international production controlled by such corporations now exceeds that of international trade. Their spread and growth has been one of the outstanding phenomena of the last two decades, and in many countries, outside the centrally planned economies, they have significantly increased their share of national output.

Multinational corporations are enterprises which own or control production or service facilities outside the country in which they are based. Such enterprises are not always incorporated or private; they can also be co-operatives or state-owned entities.[1]

Most countries have recognized the potential of multinational corporations and have encouraged the expansion of their activities in one form or another within their national borders. The role of foreign private investment in development is indeed acknowledged in the International Development Strategy for the Second United Nations Development Decade. At the same time, certain practices and effects of multinational corporations have given rise to widespread concern and anxiety in many quarters and a strong feeling has emerged that the present *modus vivendi* should be reviewed at the international level.

Opinions vary on the contribution of multinational corporations to world economic development and international relations, on the problems created by them and on the ways in which they should be treated. This was amply borne out in the discussions of the Group and in the views expressed during the hearings by representatives of Governments, labour and consumer organizations, by executives of multinational corporations and by

From United Nations Department of Economic and Social Affairs, *The Impact of Multinational Corporations on Development and on International Relations* (New York: United Nations, 1974), pp. 25-57. Some notes have been deleted, and the remainder renumbered in sequence.

members of the academic community. All, including the multinational corporations themselves, expressed concern of one kind or another.

Home countries are concerned about the undesirable effects that foreign investment by multinational corporations may have on domestic employment and the balance of payments, and about the capacity of such corporations to alter the normal play of competition. Host countries are concerned about the ownership and control of key economic sectors by foreign enterprises, the excessive cost to the domestic economy which their operations may entail, the extent to which they may encroach upon political sovereignty and their possible adverse influence on socio-cultural values. Labour interests are concerned about the impact of multinational corporations on employment and workers' welfare and on the bargaining strength of trade unions. Consumer interests are concerned about the appropriateness, quality and price of the goods produced by multinational corporations. The multinational corporations themselves are concerned about the possible nationalization or expropriation of their assets without adequate compensation and about restrictive, unclear and frequently changing government policies.

From all these expressions of concern, one conclusion emerges: fundamental new problems have arisen as a direct result of the growing internationalization of production as carried out by multinational corporations. We believe that these problems must be tackled without delay, so that tensions are eased and the benefits which can be derived from multinational corporations are fully realized.

Although international, intergovernmental and governmental bodies have been devoting themselves to the issue for some time, most efforts concentrate on the problem as seen in certain countries or groups of countries, or with respect to particular subjects, rather than taking up the total international implication of multinational corporations. It is in this context that the present involvement of the United Nations acquires particular significance and leads the way for pioneering work within the Organization.

In our report, we seek to identify and analyze the most urgent areas of concern and to propose action for political decision making. We regard our recommendations, which are addressed to Governments and to intergovernmental bodies, as the first step towards a programme for harnessing the capacities of multinational corporations for world development while safeguarding the legitimate interests of all the parties involved. Because of their major importance, our time was devoted primarily to an examination of the problems that arise from the operations of multinational corporations in the manufacturing and resource-based sectors. Further studies are certainly required on the role of multinational corporations in the service sector, that is to say in banking, tourism, land development, transport and communications. Special consideration has been given to the concerns of developing countries. To a large extent our proposals are directed towards tackling the problems these countries are facing. To implement the action proposed, we feel strongly that some permanent machinery within the United Nations is necessary.

There are frequently alternative ways which should be actively explored of obtaining the benefits provided by multinational corporations. These enterprises are not the only vehicles for the internationalization of production. In the socialist countries of Eastern Europe, for example, where planned economic integration is the counterpart of regional integration among market economies, this process is carried out at the public and inter-state level through, *inter alia*, joint state-owned undertakings established by the member States of the Council for Mutual Economic Assistance. Moreover, these countries follow a selective, centrally planned, approach as regards the objectives, areas and forms of co-operation with multinational corporations—for example, co-production arrangements—

employing the modalities of their economic and social system to protect national interest. In addition, there are countries which, on the basis of their political and social choices, may opt for different, self-reliant styles or models of development which leave little or no room for the participation of multinational corporations as they are currently organized.

I. Impact on Development

Economic growth in this century has been to a large extent the result of the technological explosion, the development of management systems which permit increasingly effective mobilization and utilization of human and other resources, and of the new skills of marketing and world-wide distribution. Constantly developing technology, management systems, and distribution skills are the major assets of multinational corporations. It is therefore understandable that developing nations turn to multinational corporations for some of the inputs needed for accelerated economic growth.

With the exception of those operating in the field of extractive industries, multinational corporations are not necessarily equally attracted to all developing countries. They tend to enter countries possessing large or expanding markets, high *per capita* income, abundant and relatively skilled labour, stable political conditions as well as ancillary skills and services that multinational corporations need. This is why the bulk of foreign direct investment goes to developed countries. Consequently, many developing countries have offered special inducements to attract multinational corporations, in the form of tax holidays, protective tariffs or export and other subsidies. The merits of such policies are discussed more fully in part Two.

While the importance of multinational corporations in economic development is acknowledged by most developing countries, it is equally recongized that their role in the development process is usually a limited one. Indeed no single device is sufficient for achieving development or is equally suitable.

In view of their scarce resources, developing countries should endeavour to allocate them efficiently on the basis of both short-term and long-term priorities. Recognizing this fact we have laid particular emphasis throughout this report on the importance of national planning and the formulation of priorities, as well as on the need to ensure that multinational corporations are sought after and admitted in accordance with predetermined goals and in harmony with existing plans. In this way the process of development will be advanced with greater certainty, and multinational corporations could be more willing to enter developing countries on terms more favourable to the latter.

In examining the impact of multinational corporations it should be recognized that these enterprises are of many different kinds and that host countries may react very differently to their presence. The skills and know-how provided by multinational corporations in resource-based industries are different from those provided in manufacturing industries. The control mechanisms of multinational corporations which adopt an integrated production or marketing strategy towards their affiliates are not the same as those which treat their affiliates as largely autonomous units.

Similarly, developing countries which are large, comparatively prosperous, and possess strong indigenous industries, may view foreign direct investment in a very different light from those which are smaller and poorer and which have little local industry.

Nevertheless, we believe that there are certain aspects of international production common to all multinational corporations wherever they operate. These are relevant to a large enough number of countries and multinational corporations to call for world atten-tion, and it is on these aspects that this chapter concentrates. The main focus is on multinational corporations as industrial producers in the resource and manufacturing sectors in developing countries.

The Impact: Some Problems

Generally speaking, multinational corporations introduce into a host country a package of resources and capabilities which they continue to own or control. They also tap resources on a world-wide basis and syphon them off to markets where profitable possibilities exist. Their impact depends on the one hand on the nature of the package and the attitude and strategies of the multinational corporations, and on the other hand on the environment in which they operate. For example, foreign capital may augment the resources of the host country and relieve bottle-necks in foreign exchange; but it may also generate a series of large outflows in dividends and service payments. New technology may improve the utilization of resources, but may not always be appropriate for local needs such as for employment creation. Managerial and marketing skills may enhance productivity and the availability of goods, but they may also divert resources from where they are most needed to where they are most profitably sold.

However, it is often the less tangible elements in the package that carry with them the most far-reaching effects. Indeed, the package in its entirety is more than the sum of the individual components. Similarly, the impact as a whole is often more than the sum arising from each component.

The significance of the package is that the components are assembled so that they are mutually complementary. It is not only what is actually brought into the host country that counts; the potential access to the capital, technology, skills and markets of the global network of the multinational corporation is equally important. It is not only the number of people that the affiliates employ that must be considered, but also the possibility of employment creation or labour displacement elsewhere in the economy. It is not only the foreign exchange brought in and out that matters, but also the long-term repercussions on the balance of payments. It is not only the increment of national income that is relevant, but also the possible effect on the direction and path of development. Multinational corporations may serve as carriers of modernization and agents for linking host developing countries and the world economy, or they may place the host countries in a situation of even greater dependency.

The non-economic impact is frequently as important as or even more important than the economic impact. The effect of multinational corporations on the social institutions and cultural values of host countries may be especially striking if the tenor, tradition and stage of development of these countries differ considerably from those of the home coun-tries. For example, the "business culture," with its emphasis on efficiency, may be consid-ered too impersonal in traditional societies. The very cultural identity and the entire social fabric may be at stake, especially if multinational corporations attempt to trans-plant their own models of social development to the host country.

These problems are more pronounced in developing countries because most multina-tional corporations originate in countries with very different social and cultural back-grounds. Multinational corporations feel they can count on the support of a powerful home country or on the co-operation of a broad service network might behave differently from others. [*sic*] Those which operate on a relatively modest scale may be less inclined to exert their influence and may generate fewer stresses and strains in the process.

Even in strictly economic terms, a wider vision and deeper probing beneath the surface is essential. Spurs by multinational corporations to productive activities do not always provide a basis for sustained and sound development. Isolated foreign enclaves have few linkages with the domestic economy. The extraction of natural resources may generate few processing industries or do little to raise the level of local skills. Branch plants which operate purely as off-shoots of their parent companies, such as component manufacturers, are unlikely to integrate fully into the local economy. Restrictions to competition may benefit the enterprise but not the individual countries in which its affiliates operate. Export market allocation and tied purchases affect the foreign exchange gained or saved by the host country. The attempts of host countries to raise taxes or to place limitations on foreign exchange remittances can be negated by vertically or horizontally integrated multinational corporations through transfer pricing and the use of tax havens.

Some host countries attempt to tackle such problems by insisting on participating in the decision making of the affiliates. Local ownership through joint ventures does not always affect the control mechanism. On the other hand if the multinational corporation loses effective control over the affiliate, some of the benefits stemming from its multinational character may be lost; technology flows may be reduced, made too costly or made subject to export restrictive clauses. Or again, if a host Government tries, through policy measures, to influence the activities of the affiliates of the multinational corporations and exerts a measure of control over their decision making, it may see its efforts frustrated by evading behaviour on the part of the corporations or by the lack of co-ordination of policies among host countries.

In all these processes, the host country's share of the benefits from the operation of the affiliate is affected. The generation of income, the provision of foreign exchange and the collection of tax revenue are influenced by the strategy of the multinational corporation and its response to governmental and international policies. At the same time, even if a host country increases its share of benefits from the activities of multinational corporations and enjoys high rates of growth, its income distribution may not improve or may even deteriorate. Welfare standards for workers may be kept low, owing to weak or non-existent trade unions. Consumers may not benefit from low prices. High income obtained locally from the activities of multinational corporations may accrue largely to domestic élites associated with foreign interests. The vigorous sales efforts of the affiliate on behalf of products usually consumed in high-income countries may cater largely to upper income groups and promote consumption habits beyond the means of a poor country and unsuitable for the development of local industries. Basic needs of the population, such as food, health, education and housing, may be left unattended. The location of activities of multinational corporations in the developing countries may be influenced by more stringent requirements for protection of the environment in development countries. As a result, there may be some apprehension that pollution may be transferred to developing countries, even though multinational corporations can also be instrumental in introducing new means of combating pollution.

These are some of the factors that shape the impact of multinational corporations on development. They are discussed in greater detail in part Two. Nevertheless, it is already apparent that their impact on development does not relate simply to the division of gains between multinational corporations and developing countries. It relates to the whole development process and the purpose of development itself. In this connection, we believe it is necessary for host countries—both developed and developing—to be certain of the degree to which they wish to rely on foreign enterprises for their growth and prosperity.

Because of the nature and orientation of multinational corporations, developing countries will not want to rely solely or excessively on them for their development, but will strive to create internal forces and institutions for development. This is all the more essential in a situation where "dependencia" already characterizes the economy, while the basic purposes of development, in terms of providing the minimum requirements of human life, are not being fully met. The contribution of multinational corporations will be enhanced by appropriate policies and institutions, but at the same time the international community must rededicate itself to providing increased public aid to developing countries. Where such countries consider it appropriate to develop indigenous industries, in competition with the affiliates of the multinational corporations, international aid-giving bodies should help to finance such ventures.

> *The Group therefore recommends* that international public aid should be increased, as recommended by the International Development Strategy, and directed to the basic needs of the poorest part of the population in developing countries, especially with regard to food, health, education, housing, and social services, as well as the development of indigenous industries.

Improving the Impact

The impact of multinational corporations on economic development, whether actual or just perceived, can be influenced in various degrees by the policies pursued by host Governments, and by the international economic environment in which the corporations operate. In this section the policies of host Governments, especially those of developing countries, are dealt with first, regional policies second and the international economic system third.

National Policy Framework

Host Governments may affect the contribution of multinational corporations to development by their specific policies towards and their treatment of foreign direct investment, as well as by their general economic and social policies.

NEGOTIATING WITH MULTINATIONAL CORPORATIONS   The terms on which multinational corporations gain entry into a host country are obviously a matter of considerable importance. Influenced by the view once widely held that developing countries should open their doors wide to foreign capital to enhance their development, many of these terms were not sufficiently carefully negotiated.

Many developing countries have felt that their bargaining position in dealing with multinational corporations is weak. There has been the assumption that multinational corporations, with the exception of certain resource-based industries, can choose their location for production according to the country offering them the most attractive environment and most favourable terms. The initial agreement concluded with multinational corporations thus tends to include a large number of special concessions. Later, as circumstances change, the concessions appear to be too onerous and the host country may deem it necessary to redress the situation. In such cases foreign affiliates could be treated in a discriminatory fashion or could even be expropriated. Such treatment, though it may be directed towards particular multinational corporations, inevitably creates an atmosphere of distrust which operates against the long-term interests of both host countries and corporations. Moreover, concern about future unfavourable treatment may lead multinational corporations to attempt to extract the most out of their investment in the least possible time. These, and other uncertainties, make multinational corporations reluctant to invest in some developing countries unless their prospects are distinctly more attractive than those expected in developed countries.

In fact developing countries are not always, in the initial negotiations, in such a weak position. Those which possess valuable natural resources, for example, are beginning to realize their vital importance to multinational corporations and their increased bargaining power. Several others, by forming regional groups among themselves and enlarging their markets, have been able to secure the collaboration of multinational corporations on more advantageous terms. The abundance of relatively skilled labour is also being used to induce multinational corporations to set up export-oriented, labour-intensive manufactures. Finally, a number of developing countries have evolved careful planning policies and foreign investment regulations which not only enable them effectively to control and monitor the operations of multinational corporations, but also offer those enterprises a stable and balanced environment.

However, a number of further steps must be taken. Developing countries should indicate precisely, as an increasing number of them are already doing, what, in general, they expect of multinational corporations. They need to elaborate the ways in which multinational corporations can fit into their over-all plans and priorities, and to identify the areas in which those enterprises should make a contribution. Governments should clarify questions of ownership and control as well as specify policies in respect of the activities of multinational corporations pertaining to the political field. When negotiating with a particular multinational corporation they should indicate more precisely the kind of policy that the affiliate should follow with respect to such matters as the choice of products to be manufactured, the degree of local processing, the employment of nationals, wage policy and other similar matters.

Among the particular points which should be covered in such an understanding is whether the multinational corporation should be treated differently from a national enterprise; for example whether special regulation will be introduced governing such activities of the corporation as the production and marketing of new products, the sources and ways of finance, remittances of profits, royalties and capital, and the employment of expatriates. Maximum clarity on both sides is essential for better understanding and future good relations.

The Group recommends that host countries should specify as precisely as possible the conditions under which multinational corporations should operate and what they should achieve. They should also indicate the ways in which the activities of multinational corporations should be integrated into the local economy and fit into the over-all priorities of the country.

In considering specific investment projects, developing countries should take the initiative in exploring possibilities of obtaining the kind of external contribution they want in the selected sectors. This means seeking competitive offers from multinational corporations which seem to have the requisite technology and skills. Simultaneously, alternative forms of foreign co-operation with international institutions or public or private entities should be considered.

In evaluating the terms proposed by multinational corporations, the ostensibly most attractive offer may not be the most advantageous, since the impact of these corporations on the local economy can be far-reaching. Therefore their true costs and benefits should be carefully analysed.

Experience and expertise are crucial elements in conducting negotiations of this kind successfully. Yet those elements are often lacking in developing countries. Experience can be gained more quickly if the same group of people handle all such negotiations. And the international community should assist developing countries in strengthening their expertise.

The Group recommends that host countries should consider setting up centralized negotiating services or co-ordinating groups to deal with all proposals for foreign investment, especially from multinational corporations.

The Group recommends that the United Nations should strengthen its capacity to assist host countries, at their request, in such negotiations with multinational corporations, as well as to train their personnel in the conduct of such negotiations (see chap. III).

While a clear understanding on various issues at the time of entry is vital, it has to be recognized that conditions change, and that what may have seemed to be adequate and fair at the time of entry may prove unsatisfactory to either party over time.

A large number of agreements made in the past lack comprehensiveness and contain no provision for renegotiation. Developing countries have, of course, the power, through legislation, to modify the terms of agreements. But sometimes such actions, if carried out unilaterally, entail disproportionately high costs in terms of the future flow of investment. A willingness on both sides to renegotiate agreements which have been in force for more than, say, 10 years could help to avoid recourse to extreme measures.

The Group recommends that in the initial agreement with multinational corporations, host countries should consider making provision for the review, at the request of either side, after suitable intervals, of various clauses of the agreement. The review by the host country should be carried out by the negotiating services or co-ordinating groups recommended above.

In recent years, the multinational corporations themselves have done a great deal of rethinking about their role in developing countries. Many of them no longer insist on operating only through wholly owned subsidiaries, or even on a majority share-holding basis in the enterprises they set up. Yet many of them do wish to retain effective control over management, especially in the initial years.

The Group recommends that developing countries should consider including provisions in their initial agreements with multinational corporations which permit the possibility of a reduction over time of the percentage of foreign ownership; the terms, as far as possible, should also be agreed upon at the very beginning, in order to minimize the possibilities of future conflict and controversy.

Not only is there a need to review the terms and conditions of entry in the light of changing circumstances, it is also essential to keep under review the policies and performance of the multinational corporations. Knowledge of such conduct and performance would help to dispel mystery and distrust and contribute to credibility. An evaluation of such conduct and performance would constitute a basis on which developing host countries could formulate their policy.

The first requisite for a proper evaluation is the availability of information on a continuing basis. We make our recommendations on the subject in chapter XII.

We wish to make one final point in this subsection. The negotiating position of host countries is strengthened if broader options or alternatives are open to them. One alternative to the "package deal," implicit in foreign direct investment, is for the individual components of the package to be purchased separately. There is evidence that some multinational corporations are ready to accept new forms of operation in which ownership rights are reduced. Management and service contracts, turnkey operations, limited-life joint companies, are all being actively explored.

The agreements that multinational corporations have made with several socialist countries of Eastern Europe are also worthy of consideration. Contractual joint ventures, or co-production agreements, are based on national ownership, limited duration and explicit provision for renegotiation, and involve a reduction of many of the risks usually attached to foreign direct investment.

Developing countries would also enhance their bargaining power if they identified alternatives outside the realm of the multinational corporations. Enterprises jointly owned by Governments or firms of several developing countries or joint enterprises with Governments of developed market or centrally planned economies are possibilities which could be further explored.

Each of these arrangements may or may not be a suitable alternative to the package provided by the multinational corporation. Each case should be assessed on its own merits.

TREATMENT OF FOREIGN INVESTMENT As a general principle, we believe that the affiliates of multinational corporations should be encouraged to identify, as closely as possible, with the interests of host countries, developed and developing. The links that multinational corporations maintain with their parent companies and home Governments should not lead them to act in a way which conflicts with the national policy of the host countries. An essential counterpart is that the policies of host Governments towards foreign affiliates should be fair, and as closely as possible similar to those which they apply to their national enterprises.

The phrase "as closely as possible" is used because we recognize that there are many respects in which both the rights and obligations of multinational corporations or their affiliates cannot be identical with those of the national firms. Multinational corporations expect the right to repatriate their profits and, in certain circumstances, their capital. A national firm cannot be given the facility of transferring its profits abroad by countries which cannot afford the free outflow of funds.

Likewise, there may be areas in which host Governments might find it desirable to introduce policies which are favourable or unfavourable to multinational corporations. Such discriminatory policies may be necessary because of the special features of foreign direct investment. For example, since a country can protect its infant industries from foreign competition through international trade, it cannot totally deny itself the possibility of sheltering such industries from competition by foreign affiliates established by multinational corporations. It may consider that mergers and acquisitions involving domestic firms should be allowed, or even actively promoted, while those involving foreign firms should be prohibited. On occasion, the host country may deem it justified to impose special requirements on its foreign affiliates, for example, in respect of profit remittances, access to capital markets, or labour conditions.

We believe that the cases in which relationships between multinational corporations and host Governments have deteriorated sharply over time are often those in which clarity was lacking in host country policies or, no less important, those in which special exemptions from prevailing regulations and policies were sought and given as a price for the entry of the corporation. In general, we believe that if the framework of a country's policies is not acceptable to a multinational corporation, it may be better for it to stay out than to gain entry on exceptional terms.

To avoid these negative impacts, no less than to promote fruitful co-operation between themselves and multinational corporations, it is desirable for host Governments to treat the affiliates of the corporation as indigenous companies, unless specific exceptions are provided.

The Group recommends that host countries should adopt policies towards affiliates of multinational corporations similar to those applied to indigenous companies, unless specific exceptions are made in the national interest.

GENERAL POLICIES   The capacity to deal effectively and successfully with multinational corporations depends on the total development effort, of which direct measures concerning those corporations, or their alternatives, form only a part.

The kind of products produced by multinational corporations are obviously influenced by import substitution measures, as well as income distribution policies, or the lack of such policies, in the host country. The balance of payments impact of multinational corporations is influenced by trade policy. If protective tariffs are levied, a high cost structure may be encouraged, and exports may be inhibited. The type of technology introduced and the employment impact may be adversely affected by inappropriate interest rate and tax policies or by veiled subsidies to imported capital goods. The incidence of transfer pricing depends, to a large extent, on the efficiency of exchange controls and rules concerning remittances, as well as intercountry differences in tax rates and systems.

Some of these specific issues are discussed in part Two. Here we would simply emphasize that a proper policy by host countries towards multinatinal corporations cannot be evolved in a vacuum, but must form part of a network of policies which is based upon a well-conceived development strategy with adequate support from national institutions.

This, in turn, will only be possible if the host country possesses the technology of choice (as discussed in chapter VI), in other words, the ability to make the appropriate decisions based on adequate information about the alternative policies open to it and the costs and benefits involved in adopting one policy rather than another. The misuse of these resources may well be the most serious true cost of development. The importance of choosing wisely is especially crucial today, since the assets with which many developing countries find that they can bargain best with the developed world and with the multinational corporations are non-renewable natural resources. It is thus not only important for developing countries to obtain a just price for their resources, but to spend the proceeds in a way which will generate long-term and continuing economic and social progress.

The general environment which host countries provide is sometimes influenced by the actual implementation and administration of policies as much as by the nature of the policies themselves. We are very conscious of the fact that ostensibly sound policies may be undermined by bureaucratic red-tape or even rampant corruption. Regulatory machineries and discretionary administrative powers, including those concerning multinational corporations, may be used as avenues for bribery. Vigorous anti-corruption measures should be introduced by all Governments. Host countries, both developed and developing, should examine carefully the possibilities of corruptive practices in granting special permissions or concessions to multinational corporations. In particular, multinational corporations should not be allowed to give direct or indirect gratuities to office holders of host Governments and trade unions. Home countries could assist in this regard by strict measures against bribery committed by their nationals elsewhere. International efforts for exchange of experiences in the harmonization of anti-corruption provisions would also help.

Regional Co-operation

Developing countries have a great deal to gain from measures of regional co-operation among themselves. Such measures would also greatly assist them in their dealings with multinational corporations.

The bargaining power of developing countries may be strengthened by co-operative action. Many of them in the past have engaged in competitive granting of tax concessions to multinational corporations and other incentives to attract foreign investment. Often these concessions, which involve a measure of sacrifice on the part of host countries, are not necessary to augment the flow of investment. Even the tax concessions, as is pointed out in chapter XI, transfer resources from poor host countries to rich home countries. In other instances, they only reduce the benefits which could be expected to flow from the operation of multinational corporations.

Regional co-operation not only strengthens the bargaining position of developing countries but also helps them to evolve appropriate techniques for dealing with the problems to which the activities of multinational corporations often give rise. Where regional co-operation enlarges the market to which the multinational corporation gains access, the inducement to invest is enhanced. In order to gain access to large regional markets, multinational corporations have been willing to accept terms and conditions which they would reject from small countries. Developing countries in such conditions not only secure the co-operation of the corporations on better terms but can also benefit from the economies of scale. A number of developing countries have attempted to achieve these purposes by regional co-operation of various forms and degrees of comprehensiveness, although progress has been uneven on the whole.

The Group recommends that developing countries should intensify their efforts for regional co-operation, in particular the establishment of joint policies with regard to multinational corporations. The United Nations should study the experience of existing regional groups as it relates to multinational corporations and should disseminate relevant information to developing countries and provide technical assistance to them.

The International Economic System

The multinational corporations in their present form and dimension are products of the international economic system within which they operate. Their basic strategies evolve in response to the existing world situation as well as to policies at national or regional levels. The rules of the game of the international system thus affect the activities of the multinational corporations, as well as national and regional policies. The growing importance of these corporations has in turn affected the functioning of the entire system.

The response of multinational corporations to the basic orientation of the existing system is most apparent in regard to trade. When capital and technology are mobile but labour is not, they tend to turn to countries where relatively skilled labour is abundant and inexpensive. Whether this will generate much employemnt in many developing countries where unemployment is endemic depends on the readiness of the developed countries to accept their products. If instead they choose to raise tariff and non-tariff barriers against such exports from developing countries, the potential of multinational corporations to contribute in this regard will necessarily be reduced. Improvements in the existing international trade régime will thus enhance the potential of the multinational corporations to contribute to development.

The international monetary system also has an important bearing on the operations of multinational corporations, in areas such as choice of location and financial flows. Apart from its influence on national and regional policies on production and trade, the degree of stability of exchange rates and the adjustment mechanism provided by the system evidently affects the policies of multinational corporations. Events in the recent monetary crisis have directed attention to the possible role of multinational corporations in the volatile short-term movements that have occurred, in addition to the fundamental disequilibria in the balance of payments of several major industrial countries. Although the current convulsions in the international monetary system may not be caused by speculative activities of multinational corporations, the ability of these enterprises to move massive amounts of funds across borders is unquestionable and such movements can undoubtedly aggravate the situation. This potential has been greatly enhanced by dramatic changes in international banking and consortia arrangements. A vigilant monitoring or surveillance by central banks of movements of funds of multinational corporations across borders is thus indicated. Moreover, in evolving a new monetary system, the role of multinational corporations will need to be taken seriously into account, in contrast to the benign neglect it has received so far.

While the international division of labour is influenced by the existing international trade and monetary régimes, it may be strongly affected, intentionally or unintentionally, by multinational corporations. Their large capabilities for moving products and inputs across borders are important instruments in affecting the actual division of labour. At the same time, the apprehension that host countries may be turned into "branch-plant" economies may not be limited to developing countries. The organizational, productive and distributive networks created by multinational corporations often assign a peripheral and dependent role to affiliates in many host countries, while the centers of top decision making and scientific research remain in a few highly industrialized countries. Although the locational pattern of multinational corporations reflects the uneven distribution of the factor endowments, it is also moulded in many cases by artificial administrative devices employed by home and host Governments (tariffs, subsidies, etc.) as well as by the corporations themselves. There is no indication, as is sometimes suggested, that multinational corporations are evolving into real internationalized entities whose ownership, management and objectives are truly global, and within which all nations and their citizens are treated equitably and world welfare is truly maximized.

In today's complex economy, the "invisible hand" of the market is far from the only force guiding economic decisions. To a considerable extent, conscious planning, both public and private, has played an increasing role in decision making. Increasingly, basic decisions on the allocation of resources with respect to what, how and for whom to produce are being concentrated in corporate planning mechanisms. The growth of multinational corporations gives them increasing control over resources and thus augments their capacity to re-allocate them. Such decisions, when taken exclusively from the point of view of an interest of enterprise, again pose serious problems. The question of establishing public mechanisms, both national and international, to orient the planning of consumption, to choose among different alternatives and to generate awareness in respect of their implications for the strategy of development of a given country, or region, appears to be a basic problem demanding a solution.

Decisions regarding the rules of the game and the creation of institutions and machinery to deal with the operations of multinational corporations must therefore be made in addition to, as well as in the context of, current negotiations for the improvement of the existing international trade and monetary systems. For unless a serious and united effort is made to formulate policies and programmes in respect of multinational corporations, which are most directly related to the actual international division of labour, considerations of money and trade reform appear to be somewhat empty and the world economic order lacks any firm foundation. There is no substitute for consideration of the various parts of the system in the context of the entire interdependent network.

II. Impact on International Relations

Concern over the impact of multinational corporations on the domestic and international affairs of nation-States has been voiced at the highest government levels, for example at the Fourth Conference of Heads of State or Government of Non-Aligned Countries held at Algiers in 1973, at the Conference of Commonwealth Heads of Government held at Ottawa in August 1973, at the meeting of Latin American foreign ministers at Bogotá in 1973, at the intra-American meeting of foreign ministers held at Mexico City in February 1974, and in various forums of the United Nations. While, in the main, the role of multinational corporations is economic in character and influence, it often extends in various forms into the political area, affecting in the process international relations. It is to these issues that this chapter is addressed.

On the positive side, multinational corporations may promote the exchange of knowledge among peoples and countries and contribute to co-operation among Governments. They can also influence, for good or ill, the mode of life, the socio-cultural fibre and political development within a country, as well as relations among countries. This report will concentrate on some of the areas in which multinational corporations can create, or be agents in creating—voluntarily or involuntarily—political tensions within countries or between home and host countries.

Political Intervention

One of the reasons the subject of multinational corporations came to world-wide attention was the exposure of an attempt by one of the largest corporations to overthrow the elected Government of a developing country. Such incidents are uncommon but, in a number of cases, multinational corporations have actively promoted political intervention in the domestic affairs of host, particularly developing, countries. Many multinational corporations have themselves condemned such activities. But the bringing to light of such incidents has in general laid them open to suspicion, and has lent support to ideological objections to, and distrust of, their influence—especially that of multinational corporations originating in the major developed countries. It is obvious that such intervention is incompatible with the long-term existence of multinational corporations in host countries and clearly infringes upon national sovereignty.

Action by multinational corporations in the political field can take less direct and obvious forms. In home countries, they may attempt to influence foreign and domestic policy by utilizing their broad financial power and their often close relationship with government cadres. They can lobby for or against Governments of host countries, depending on whether or not they receive specially favourable terms of treatment.

In host countries, the affiliates of multinational corporations can seek to influence government policies in undesirable ways. Being closely connected with domestic groups favouring foreign investment, they can use their own or their parent company's resources to support particular political parties of their choice, and they can rally against groups advocating social reforms.

It is in the interest of the multinational corporations to avoid engaging in activities that would embroil them in indigenous political controversies, or identifying themselves with any political side. Nor should they lose sight of the fact that domestic policies for social and structural change which appear onerous to them may well be in their interest in the longer run, as well as that of host and home countries.

We believe that this is not a matter to be left solely to the multinational corporations acting on their own judgement. They must have a clear indication from the host Government of the type of public activity from which they must refrain. We feel that, as a general principle, their public activities should be confined to those having a direct relationship to the objectives set out for the corporation upon its entry into the host country; for example, representing their views to local authorities regarding policies that may affect their own companies. In order to avoid misunderstandings, host developing countries would be well advised to impose strict limitations and to make governmental policy quite clear. In case of infringements, sanctions should be established according to due process of law of the country concerned.

The Group recommends that host countries should clearly define the permissible public activites of the affiliates of multinational corporations and also prescribe sanctions against infringements. The financial contributions of multinational corporations as well as of others to interest groups should be regulated and disclosed.

If permissible limits exist and multinational corporations overstep them, they naturally expose themselves to penal action. Multinational corporations which engage in illegal activities do so at their own risk.

Although in this report no reference is made to specific multinational corporations, it is not possible to refrain from mentioning by name the actions of the International Telephone and Telegraph Corporation in Chile. Such actions can only bring discredit to the business community and negatively affect the image of those corporations which do not resort to such unjustifiable methods. We feel very strongly that, where unquestionable evidence exists of such activities, strict sanctions should be imposed according to due process of law of the country concerned. We also feel that no distinction should be made for this purpose between national and multinational companies. The existence of home country investment guarantee schemes can have the result of making the burden of the sanction fall on the country's taxpayers rather than specifically on the multinational corporation itself. Thus, in order for sanctions to be effective, home countries should consider withholding investment insurance payments where warranted by adequate proof of political intervention, as was done in the case of the International Telephone and Telegraph Corporation.

> *The Group unequivocally condemns* subversive political intervention on the part of multinational corporations directed towards the overthrow or substitution of a host country's Government or the fostering of internal or international situations that stimulate conditions for such actions, and *recommends* that, in such an eventuality, host countries should impose strict sanctions in accordance with due process of law of the host country concerned. Home countries are encouraged to consider ways of ensuring that their investment guarantee schemes do not make these sanctions ineffective.

The responsibility for political action by multinational corporations lies sometimes with Governments, especially home country Governments, which have on occasion used the corporations as instruments of their foreign policy and even for intelligence activities. This applies in particular to home countries which, through investment, trade, or post-colonial ties, occupy a dominant position in certain host countries or regions. As long as the fear persists that multinational corporations may be tools in the hands of Governments and that they may, through their affiliates abroad, seek to fulfill foreign policy objectives, for example through the supply of information and the promotion of political ideas and changes in policy orientations and Governments, the relationship between developing host countries and multinational corporations belonging to powerful countries will be uneasy.

> *The Group recommends* that the Economic and Social Council, in the application of the concept of non-intervention, should call upon countries not to use multinational corporations and their affiliates as instruments for the attainment of foreign policy goals.

Intergovernmental Confrontations

It is important to ensure that the activities of multinational corporations do not affect relations between countries or lead to confrontations among them. It is equally important that affiliates of multinational corporations should not become the vicitms of disputes between home and host countries.

The most frequent cause of acute bilateral tension between home and host countries is a situation in which the host country nationalizes the investment of a multinational corporation and the latter turns to the home country for protection and help. The right of a country to nationalize the assets of any company should not be questioned. The real bone of contention is the amount of compensation to be paid, the manner in which it should be determined, and the extent to which home countries should involve themselves in the issue.

It is clearly necessary for host countries to pledge themselves to pay fair compensation. The denial or reduction of compensation as a result of the violation by multinational corporations of particular regulations should be arrived at through due process of law of the country concerned. It is here that a clear enunciation by the host country of what the multinational corporation is expected to do or not to do assumes importance from the international point of view. While it is not possible to lay down any single yardstick regarding the amount of compensation, all factors relevant to the interests of the country and the multinational corporation should be taken into account and any impression of arbitrariness must be avoided. Ideally, the compensation should be determined by mutual agreement. Failing agreement, recourse should be had to appropriate host country legislative and judicial processes.

In actual experience—except where host countries have formed the conviction that the activities of a particular multinational corporation have been such as to cause them deliberate political or economic damage—host countries have been conscious of the importance of paying fair compensation in cases of nationalization. One of the factors that weighs with them is the knowledge that otherwise further investment would be jeopardized in most cases. Although transferable payment should be made within a short period of time wherever possible, there may be cases where serious balance of payments problems call for a prolongation of the period or for the reinvestment of part of the compensation in the host country. In such cases, international lending agencies should consider making soft long-term loans available to countries facing this difficulty.

We have given careful consideration to the suggestion that investment disputes should be settled through international arbitration. If the parties agree, arbitration can be a good method of settling the matter. Sixty-five countries have joined the Centre for the Settlement of Investment Disputes established by the International Bank for Reconstruction and Development some years ago. Some host countries, however, both developing and developed, object to international arbitration on grounds of principle. They note that these disputes are not between nations. They relate to property situated within the national boundaries of a State. Often the same act of nationalization may affect both foreign and domestic investment. They maintain, therefore, that only national courts can have jurisdiction over such disputes. As a result, a number of countries have decided not to join the Centre for the Settlement of Investment Disputes.

> *The Group recommends* that whenever there is occasion to nationalize the assets of a multinational corporation, host countries should ensure that the compensation is fair and adequate and determined according to due process of law of the country concerned, or in accordance with any arbitration arrangements existing between the parties.

The question arises as to what the role of the home country should be in cases of nationalization or of other serious disputes between the multinational corporation and the host country. Many countries in Latin America have adopted the doctrine of the Argentinian Carlos Calvo, according to which host Goverments deny all local rights and remedies to foreign affiliates which, in cases of dispute, call for the support of their home Governments. They make acceptance of the Calvo doctrine by investors a condition of their entry. Some home Governments, however, have maintained that their rights cannot be written off by commitments made by investors on their own account and that States have an inherent duty and right to protect the interests of their nationals.

We feel that a national of any country has the right to request the assistance of his Government when confronted with problems in a foreign land and that indiscriminate support by home Governments for their multinational corporations regardless of the merits of the case should be discouraged, as should some of the ways in which such support may be provided by powerful countries. Although it may be hoped that the days are over when even military force was employed in such circumstances, some of the measures which home Governments seek or threaten to employ go well beyond the limits of normal diplomatic representation and amount to the exercise of political pressure. As a result, international tensions are generated which, even from the point of view of multinational corporations in general, create more problems than they solve.

It is not easy to define in precise terms the limits of what home countries should do to protect the interests of their nationals. Trade or financial sanctions, particularly when applied by powerful countries against weaker ones, may prove effective in the short run, but will inevitably generate feelings of frustration and create unstable conditions for the future. In general, they should be ruled out. We strongly feel that in any case no attempt should be made to use international agencies as channels for exerting pressure.

> *The Group recommends* that, in such contexts, home countries should refrain from involving themselves in differences and disputes between multinational corporations and host countries. If serious damage to their nationals is likely to arise, they should confine themselves to normal diplomatic representations. No attempt should be made to use international agencies as means of exerting pressure.

We believe that disputes of the kind discussed above are easier to prevent than cure. What is needed is a change in the whole environment in which multinational corporations operate in developing countries. Such a change will be helpful to both. The recommendations that we make in various chapters of this report will, we trust, go some way towards developing a sound, long-lasting relationship between multinational corporations and host countries, which must in the last analysis depend upon both parties finding the relationship rewarding. Here we believe that international bodies, such as the commission on multinational corporations proposed in this report, can be helpful in promoting understanding at the international level. As a starting point, a resolution by the Economic and Social Council would help greatly in clearing the air and making a break from the past.

Conflicts and Jurisdiction

Quite often, problems affecting international relations arise out of a conflict of jurisdiction between home and host Governments. Legislation enacted by the home Government may be such as to compel a certain type of behaviour by the affiliates of the multinational corporation. Such behaviour may not be in the interest of, or otherwise acceptable to, the host country.

Thus, if the home country's legislation restricts the freedom of affiliates to export to particular countries, host countries may legitimately feel aggrieved. If home country legislation prohibits a merger between a foreign affiliate of one of its companies with an indigenous firm, this also may cause friction.

We recognize that the problem of jurisdiction is complex. As a start, however, we believe that one general principle should be accepted. Home country jurisdiction should apply until the multinational corporation enters the host country. Home country legislation should cover the prohibition of investment in countries upon which sanctions are imposed by the United Nations Security Council, for example, those which violate human rights and follow racist policies. These sanctions can be circumvented if multinational corporations are allowed to produce in those countries the very goods which are denied to them under the sanctions.

The Group recommends that home and host countries should ensure, through appropriate actions, that multinational corporations do not violate sanctions imposed by the United Nations Security Council, for example, on countries suppressing human rights and following racist policies.

On the other hand, once an affiliate of a multinational corporation is established in another country, home country laws should cease to govern its behaviour, and only host country laws should apply. This broad division would avoid many of the conflicts of jurisdiction which currently arise, but would certainly not solve all of them. The question of what country's jurisdiction should apply for certain activities of a parent or affiliate would remain. Important disputes of jurisdiction also arise because Governments do not agree on whether a certain activity of a corporation in one country affects other countries or not.

Also, there are areas in which, if the economic policies of the home country are to be effective, collaboration with other Governments becomes necessary. This is the case of anti-trust legislation, which is discussed more fully in chapter IX. In such circumstances, consultations should be held between the countries concerned in order to avoid misunderstandings and recriminations. We believe that home and host countries should refrain from extraterritorial application of their domestic legislation, unless it is exercised under bilateral or, preferably, multilateral agreements. Home countries should recognize that affiliates are under the jurisdiction of the host country.

The Group recommends that home and host countries should explore, with the help of the appropriate United Nations body, the possibility of concluding an international agreement regulating the issue of extraterritoriality of jurisdiction. As an interim measure, formal consultative machinery should be established in cases of conflicts of jurisdiction.

Considering the nature of the issues discussed in this chapter and the importance of creating a proper international framework and atmosphere in which multinational corporations can operate without causing strains on international relations, we feel that it would be appropriate for the Economic and Social Council to consider these issues and the views we have expressed.

The Group recommends that the Economic and Social Council should give consideration to the adoption of the resolution embodying the recommendaitons in this chapter.

III. International Machinery and Action

In this report we have analyzed broad as well as specific issues and problems related to the activities of multinational corporations. On the basis of this analysis, we have made a number of recommendations. While the primary responsibility for taking action rests with individual Governments, we have pointed out on numerous occasions that many of the measures that we think necessary will be ineffective and frustrated unless they are accompanied by action at the international level which promotes co-operation and harmonization. Furthermore, on a number of issues, effective action can only be taken at the international level.

While multinational corporations are subject to the jurisdiction of individual Governments in respect of their activities within specific countries, the global character of these corporations has not been matched by corresponding co-ordination of actions by Governments or by an internationally recognized set of rules or a system of information disclosure.

Even though international production has become as important a fact of life as international trade, there exist today no international institutions dealing with the activities of multinational corporations comparable with the General Agreement of Tariffs and Trade (GATT) and the United Nations Conference on Trade and Development (UNCTAD) which are concerned with international trade. The absence of an international forum makes it very difficult to work towards the international arrangements and agreements which would harmonize relevant national policies and laws and provide a framework within which the global strategies of multinational corporations should operate.

The need to begin work promptly toward these goals has been recognized not only by the members of the Group, but also by the overwhelming majority of those who appeared before us at the hearings. It is widely felt that more information and analysis, as well as the gradual elaboration of internationally accepted "rules of the game", will not only help to remove misunderstandings and frustrations but will be of benefit to all concerned.

We have also repeatedly brought out the need to analyse this subject in a comprehensive framework and the necessity of viewing it within the context of the development process as a whole. It is only in this way that the role of the multinational corporations and alternatives to the resources provided by them can be properly appreciated, and that appropriate measures can be devised to maximize the positive effects of the presence of these corporations and to bring under control its undesirable consequences.

To fulfill these functions at the international level it is not necessary to create a new institution. The existing institutions can be geared and strengthened to respond to the requirements. Given the functions and responsibilities vested in the United Nations in Chapters IX and X of the Charter, and the methods of conceptualization and negotiation that it has developed over the years, we believe that the Economic and Social Council itself, being fully representative of the membership of the United Nations, is the intergovernmental body in which, on the basis of adequate support, the subject of multinational corporations in all its ramifications should be considered and negotiated on a regular basis.

We are convinced that the deliberations and decision-making process of the Economic and Social Council would be greatly facilitated and enhanced if the Council were supported in its work in this field by a body specifically designed for this purpose. The complexity and breadth of the issues involved are such that effective action by the Council must flow out of a continuing elucidation and analysis of the problems involved, based on more information, professional studies and consultations with the various parties concerned. This is a formidable task that requries continuous and systematic attention.

We have carefully considered the kind of body which could best assist the Council in fulfilling its responsiblity in this field, including the respective advantages of an intergovernmental body and one composed of persons acting in their individual capacity. We have come to the conclusion that the functions which need to be performed can best be carried out by a group of persons acting in their individual capacity. Our reasons are the following. First, the complexity of the subject requires that the members be selected on such a basis that together they possess a broad and varied experience and deep knowledge and understanding of the many aspects of the subject so that the question of multinational corporations can be covered in a comprehensive manner; secondly, experience indicates that members of a group selected in their individual capacity are able to devote more time and attention on a continuing basis to the questions under consideration by the group; thirdly, experience also suggests that a group constituted in this way may facilitate the consultation process which is necessary for it to discharge effectively its responsibilities to the Council.

Under the direction of the intergovernmental body (namely, the Economic and Social Council) the commission on multinational corporations proposed here would provide a forum for airing views and discussing issues, would guide and co-ordinate the programme of work and action that is required at the international level, and would provide a basis for further measures and the evolution of institutions.

The Group recommends that a full discussion on the issues related to multinational corporations should take place in the Economic and Social Council at least once a year, in particular to consider the report of the commission on multinational corporations.

The Group recommends that a commission on multinational corporations should be established under the Economic and Social Council, composed of individuals with a profound understanding of the issues and problems involved. . . .

The Group regards this report as being the first step in a comprehensive programme of study, discussion, negotiation and practical action which will unfold in the years to come. It remains for the commission on multinational corporations, under the Economic and Social Council, to consider and give expression to the recommendations made by the Group.

In a number of specific fields, such as the transfer of technology, restrictive business practices, labour and legal questions related to multinational corporations and international trade law, work is already going on in a number of United Nations bodies. Such work represents an important part of the programme of action proposed by the Group and should be encouraged and intensified. In a number of other fields, such as information, new initiatives are required.

In addition, research is required to cover those areas mentioned in this report in which multinational corporations are active but which the Group was unable to deal with adequately. These include international banking, tourism and land development. Research is also required to clarify certain specific issues and to bring out more sharply their implications and interrelationships.

As one of its first tasks, the commission should review the kind of technical co-operation which may be most needed, the form in which it could best be provided, and the capacity of the various United Nations organizations concerned to provide such assistance at the request of Governments.

Information and Research Centre on Multinational Corporations

Just as we believe that a specifically designed body is required to assist the Council, so too at the secretariat level special arrangements are required to provide the necessary and continuous support.

Throughout its work, the Group was struck by the lack of useful, reliable and comparable information on many aspects of this subject. The availability of pertinent information is central to many issues, such as restrictive business practices, transfer pricing and taxation. Making available the right kind of information could well be a most important first step in assisting developing countries in their dealings with multinational corporations. Broad areas in which information should be gathered, analysed and disseminated to all interested parties should include legislation and policies of home and host countries; geographical and industrial distribution of activities of multinational corporations; transmission of technology and financial flows; organization, structure, ownership and global strategies of multinational corporations; the effects of the activities of multinational corporations on national and international development. In carrying out the work, the centre would have to devote considerable attention to reporting procedures. . . . In addition, the centre would carry out research as requested by the commission on multinational corporations.

Technical Co-operation

While the work of the Commission itself should contribute significantly to improving the possibilities of host countries, particularly developing countries, the Group believes that direct technical co-operation with Governments requesting it is an important component of the total effort. Particular attention should be given to providing assistance to requesting Governments for strengthening their relevant machinery and for training local personnel through national or regional training programmes in negotiation and administration of governmental policies on foreign direct investments. Increasing their capacity to use information is another area where assistance should be provided. In addition, advisory teams (including economists, engineers, lawyers, social scientists and others) should be made available to requesting Governments to assist them in evaluating investment proposals, and in analysing proposed contracts and arrangements and, if desired, to provide technical advisory support to Governments in connection with their negotiations with multinational corporations.

In view of the mutually reinforcing characteristics of the informational, research and technical co-operation functions, the Group considers it advisable to incorporate the technical co-operation function within the information and research centre on multinational corporations.

> *The Group recomends* that an information and research centre on multinational corporations should be established in the United Nations Secretariat or closely linked with it, which, under the general guidance of the commission on multinational corporations, would perform the following functions:
>
> (a) Provide substantive and administrative services for the commission on multinational corporations;
>
> (b) Collect, analyse and disseminate information, and undertake research along the lines recommend above.
>
> *The Group recommends* that the technical co-operation capacity of the United Nations in matters related to multinational corporations should be significantly strengthened and expanded in the areas of training and advisory services.

Programme of Work

The Group considers an appropriate longer term objective to be the conclusion of a general agreement on multinational corporations having the force of an international treaty and containing provisions for machinery and sanctions. The need for such an agreement was perceived as early as 1948 in the drafting of the Havana Charter for an International Trade Organization, which contained elements still being sought today.

We recognize that it is premature to propose serious negotiations on such an agreement and the machinery necessary for its enforcement. This requires careful and extended preparation and discussion. However, the world community should not have to wait until such a general agreement is finally concluded; in the meantime, many specific issues can be tackled and resolved. On certain specific aspects such as technology, competition and market structure, taxation and labour, the work going on in various United Nations bodies should be encouraged and intensified in line with the recommendations below.

Code of Conduct

The Group has discussed extensively the now widespread notion of a code of conduct which would be addressed to both multinational corporations and Governments. It is recognized, however, that the term "code" itself is full of ambiguity.

A code may be the assembling in one document of laws, decrees and rules which are already adopted and being enforced. A comparable attempt would be the drafting of an international agreement which, as mentioned above, we hope can be ultimately negotiated and ratified. The same term is also used for a set of rules established by negotiations in international organizations such as the Organisation for Economic Co-operation and Development (OECD) and the International Labour Organisation (ILO), all or only some of which each country chooses to accept and apply. This apparently strong, but, in effect, loose notion does not represent what we are aiming at. Finally, a code of conduct may be a consistent set of recommendations which are gradually evolved and which may be revised as experience or circumstances require. Although they are not compulsory in character, they act as an instrument of moral persuasion, strengthened by the authority of international organizations and the support of public opinion.

It is the last-mentioned form of code of conduct that the Group has in mind; namely, a set of recommendations which could be prepared by the commission, and considered and approved by the Economic and Social Council. They should be addressed to both Governments and multinational corporations. The Economic and Social Council may wish to consider, with the assistance of the commission, the desirability of preparing a series of recommendations attuned to particular sectors or categories. The commission could keep under review not only how far Governments and multinational corporations abide by them, but also whether changing circumstances may render some of them obsolete or call for additional or revised recommendations to be devised.

Information and Reporting Procedures

We have noted in Chapter XII the serious lack of both financial and non-financial information, in usable form, and the desirability of working out agreed international reporting standards in this connection. To achieve this goal, the commission on multinational corporations should give consideration to the convening of an expert group on international accounting standards. The task of the expert group would be to identify the information needed, determine how and in what form it should be collected, and decide how it could best be used by all concerned. The proposed information and research centre on multinational corporations would provide the supporting work for the expert group and would subsequently be responsible, under the direction of the commission on multinational corporations, for collecting, analysing and disseminating information in the agreed form.

Technology

The importance of technology and the problems faced by host developing countries in this connection was brought out in chapter VI. In particular, we have noted the difficulties faced by developing countries in obtaining technology that is appropriate for their needs at a reasonable cost. To this end, we believe the current work by such United Nations bodies as UNCTAD, UNIDO, UNESCO and ILO, should give special consideration to ways of improving the machinery for producing technology in both developed and developing countries which is appropriate for and readily available to the latter. The international organizations concerned should work towards revising the patent system and evolve an over-all régime under which the cost of technology provided by multinational corporations to developing countries can be reduced. Consideration should also be given to establishing a world patents (technology) bank to which public institutions could donate for use in developing countries patents which they own or purchase for this purpose; and to finding ways of providing financial assistance, for example through existing international financial institutions, to developing countries for the acquisition of technology.

Employment and Labour

The important impact which multinational corporations may have on employment, labour relations and labour standards has been stressed in chapter VII. Consideration should be given to ways of concerting national action at the international level, thereby rendering it more effective. Studies should be carried out to examine various forms and procedures for the participation of workers' representatives in the decision-making process of multinational corporations. To ensure that minimum health and safety standards are applied universally, the ILO and WHO should develop and keep under review international safety and health standards which should be ratified by Governments.

Consumer Protection

As is made clear in chapter VIII, to achieve better consumer protection, we believe that consideration should be given to working out minimum international health and safety standards for various types of products, as well as international standardized labelling.

Competition and Market Structure

In chapter IX two areas are noted, market allocation and market structure, in which action at the international level is required to help in solving existing difficulties. As regards the former, an international agreement should be sought to prohibit unjustified export market allocations and provide the framework within which revisions of existing arrangements should be effected. With respect to market structure, an agreement should be sought which would harmonize existing anti-trust policies and national jurisdictions that may be in conflict.

Transfer Pricing

In chapter X the problems raised by intracorporate transfer pricing across national boundaries and the need to evolve sound policies and practices to control them are noted. To this end, consideration should be given to preparing an international agreement on the rules concerning transfer pricing for purposes of taxation.

Taxation

In chapter XI is noted the variety of practices in taxation, which have created an unreasonable situation for home and host Governments as well as multinational corporations. Furthermore, unco-ordinated efforts by host developing countries to give tax incentives can result in unnecessary loss of tax revenues. While, in the short run, we believe that bilateral treaties should be negotiated in accordance with the guidelines recommended by the United Nations Group of Experts on Tax Treaties, it also urges that work should be initiated by the commission on multinational corporations towards reaching an international agreement on taxation in order to harmonize taxation and protect the interests of developing countries.

. . .

NOTE

1. There is general agreement in the Group that the word "enterprise" should be substituted for corporations, and a strong feeling that the word transnational would better convey the notion that these firms operate from their home bases across national borders. However, the term "multinational corporations" is used in this report in conformity with Economic and Social Council resolution 1721 (LIII). See also alternative definitions in Multinational Corporations in World Development.

20 / Resolution Establishing the Commission on Transnational Corporations *and* Charter of the Economic Rights and Duties of States

United Nations

Resolution Establishing the Commission on Transnational Corporations

1913 (LVIII) The Impact of Transnational Corporations on the Development Process and on International Relations

The Economic and Social Council,

Recalling its resolution 1721 (LIII) of 28 July, 1972,

Recalling also its resolution 1908 (LVII) of 2 August 1974,

Recalling further General Assembly resolutions 3201 (S–VI) and 3202 (S–VI) of 1 May 1974, including the provisions relating to transnational corporations,

Having given preliminary consideration to the report of the Group of Eminent Persons to Study the Impact of Transnational Corporations on Development and on International Relations, as well as the report of the Secretary-General,

Recognizing that further detailed consideration of the issues contained in the report of the Group of Eminent Persons should take place at a later date,

Having further considered the reports of the Secretary-General on the activities of the United Nations system closely related to the subject of transnational corporations and on the views of States on the report of the Group of Eminent Persons, and having heard the views expressed by Governments at the Special Intersessional Committee on transnational corporations,

Desirous of establishing effective machinery for dealing with the full range of issues relating to the activities of transnational corporations in order, *inter alia,* to recommend to the Economic and Social Council a detailed programme of work for formulating policies,

Bearing in mind its decision to keep the full range of issues relating to transnational

From a print issued by the United Nations, containing the Resolution of December 5, 1974, Establishing the Commission on Transnational Corporations, together with excerpts from the Charter of December 12, 1974, of the Economic Rights and Duties of States. All notes except one have been omitted, and that note has been renumbered.

corporations, and in particular the subject of the regulation of and supervision over their activities, under close consideration on a continuing basis,

1. *Decides* to establish an intergovernmental Commission on Transnational Corporations as an advisory body to the Economic and Social Council to assist it in dealing with the issue of transnational corporations:

(a) The Commission on Transnational Corporations shall be composed of 48 members from all States, elected by the Economic and Social Council on a broad and fair geographical basis;[1] each State shall appoint a high-level expert taking into account his knowledge of the issues involved; the States may also appoint alternates;

(b) Elected States may consult with the President of the Economic and Social Council before they finally appoint their experts so as to ensure as far as possible a balanced representation reflecting the various fields of activities covered by the Commission so that it may discharge its functions effectively;

(c) The term of office of the members of the Commission shall be three years and members shall be eligible for re-election;

(d) The Commission, as required by its programme of work, and in consultation with the Secretary-General, shall select persons on the basis of their practical experience, particularly from trade unions, business, public interest groups and universities, from both developed and developing countries, who, in a private consultative capacity, will assist the Commission and participate in its discussions in a manner to be decided by it;

2. *Decides also* that the Commission on Transnational Corporations shall meet annually and shall submit an annual report to the Economic and Social Council at its summer session, unless the Council decides otherwise;

3. *Decides further* that the Commission on Transnational Corporations will assist the Economic and Social Council in fulfilling its responsibilities in the field of transnational corporations by:

(a) Acting as the forum within the United Nations system for the comprehensive and in-depth consideration of issues relating to transnational corporations;

(b) Promoting the exchange of views among Governments, intergovernmental and non-governmental organizations, trade unions, business, consumers and other relevant groups through the arrangement, *inter alia,* of hearings and interviews;

(c) Providing guidance to the Information and Research Centre on Transnational Corporations, referred to in paragraph 4 below, on the rendering of advisory services to interested Governments and promoting programmes of technical co-operation;

(d) Conducting inquiries on the activities of transnational corporations, making studies, preparing reports and organizing panels for facilitating discussions among relevant groups;

(e) Undertaking work which may assist the Economic and Social Council in evolving a set of recommendations which, taken together, would represent the basis for a code of conduct dealing with transnational corporations;

(f) Undertaking work which may assist the Economic and Social Council in considering possible arrangements or agreements on specific aspects relating to transnational corporations with a view to studying the feasibility of formulating a general agreement and, on the basis of a decision of the Council, to consolidating them into a general agreement at a future date;

(g) Recommending to the Economic and Social Council the priorities and the programmes of work on transnational corporations to be carried out by the Information and Research Centre on Transnational Corporations;

4. *Decides* that the Information and Research Centre on Transnational Corporations, established under Council resolution 1908 (LVII), shall conduct its activities under the guidance of the Commission on Transnational Corporations with the following terms of reference:

(a) To provide the necessary support to the Economic and Social Council and to the Commission on matters related to transnational corporations;

(b) To develop a comprehensive information system on the activities of transnational corporations by gathering information made available by Governments and other sources, and by analysing and disseminating such information to all Governments;

(c) To organize and co-ordinate at the request of Governments, programmes of technical co-operation on matters related to transnational corporations, through existing organs of the United Nations system, aimed at strengthening the capacity of host countries, in particular of developing countries, in their dealings with transnational corporations;

(d) To conduct research on various political, legal, economic and social aspects relating to transnational corporations, including work which might be useful for the elaboration of a code of conduct and specific arrangements and agreements as directed by the Economic and Social Council and the Commission;

5. *Requests* the Secretary-General to ensure that the Information and Research Centre on Transnational Corporations is constituted early in 1975 in accordance with Article 101 of the Charter of the United Nations, so that it may become fully functional at the earliest possible date, bearing in mind the provision regarding budgetary support for the Centre in paragraph 6 of Council resolution 1908 (LVII); and to report to the Economic and Social Council at its fifty-ninth session on the progress made;

6. *Further requests* the Secretary-General to ensure the co-ordination of the activities of the Information and Research Centre on Transnational Corporations with those of other organizations and agencies of the United Nations system which undertake activities closely related to the subject of transnational corporations;

7. *Requests* the Commission on Transnational Corporations, in fulfilment of paragraph 8 of Council resolution 1908 (LVII), to submit to the Economic and Social Council at its sixtieth session a detailed draft programme of work on the full range of issues relating to transnational corporations, including a statement of its proposed priorities within the framework of the following guidelines: the development of a comprehensive information system; preliminary work with the objective of formulating a code of conduct; the undertaking of studies, especially case studies, on the political economic and social impact of the operations and practices of transnational corporations which seem most urgent; and the definition of transnational corporations; the draft programme should be without prejudice to the work undertaken within the United Nations system in related fields.

NOTE

1. The member States of the Commission shall be elected according to the following pattern: 12 members from African States; 11 members from Asian States; 10 members from Latin American States; 5 members from Socialist States of Eastern Europe; and 10 members from Western European and other States.

Charter of the Economic Rights and Duties of States

[Excerpts From United Nations General Assembly Resolution 3281 (XXIX).]

Article 1

Every State has the sovereign and inalienable right to choose its economic system as well as its political, social and cultural systems in accordance with the will of its people, without outside interference, coercion or threat in any form whatsoever.

Article 2

1. Every State has and shall freely exercise full permanent sovereignty, including possession, use and disposal, over all its wealth, natural resources and economic activities.

2. Each State has the right:

(a) To regulate and exercise authority over foreign investment within its national jurisdiction in accordance with its laws and regulations and in conformity with its national objectives and priorities. No State shall be compelled to grant preferential treatment to foreign investment;

(b) To regulate and supervise the activities of transnational corporations within its national jurisdiction and take measures to ensure that such activities comply with its laws, rules and regulations and conform with its economic and social policies. Transnational corporations shall not intervene in the internal affairs of a host State. Every State should, with full regard for its sovereign rights, co-operate with other States in the exercise of the right set forth in this subparagraph;

(c) To nationalize, expropriate or transfer ownership of foreign property, in which case appropriate compensation should be paid by the State adopting such measures, taking into account its relevant laws and regulations and all circumstances that the State considers pertinent. In any case where the question of compensation gives rise to a controversy, it shall be settled under the domestic law of the nationalizing State and by its tribunals, unless it is freely and mutually agreed by all States concerned that other peaceful means be sought on the basis of the sovereign equality of States and in accordance with the principle of free choice of means.

Article 3

In the exploitation of natural resources shared by two or more countries, each State must co-operate on the basis of a system of information and prior consultations in order to achieve optimum use of such resources without causing damage to the legitimate interest of others.

Article 4

Every State has the right to engage in international trade and other forms of economic co-operation irrespective of any differences in political, economic and social systems. No State shall be subjected to discrimination of any kind based solely on such differences. In the pursuit of international trade and other forms of economic co-operation, every State is free to choose the forms of organization of its foreign economic relations and to enter into bilateral and multilateral arrangements consistent with its international obligations and with the needs of international economic co-operation.

Article 5

All States have the right to associate in organizations of primary commodity producers in order to develop their national economies, to achieve stable financing for their development and, in pursuance of their aims, to assist in the promotion of sustained growth of the world economy, in particular accelerating the development of developing countries. Correspondingly all States have the duty to respect that right by refraining from applying economic and political measures that would limit it.

. . .

Article 13

1. Every State has the right to benefit from the advances and developments in science and technology for the acceleration of its economic and social development.

2. All States should promote international scientific and technological co-operation and the transfer of technology, with proper regard for all legitimate interests including, inter alia, the rights and duties of holders, suppliers and recipients of technology. In particular, all States should facilitate the access of developing countries to the achievements of modern science and technology, the transfer of technology and the creation of indigenous technology for the benefit of the developing countries in forms and in accordance with procedures which are suited to their economies and their needs.

3. Accordingly, developed countries should co-operate with the developing countries in the establishment, strengthening and development of their scientific and technological infrastructures and their scientific research and technological activities so as to help to expand and transform the economies of developing countries.

4. All States should co-operate in research with a view to evolving further internationally accepted guidelines or regulations for the transfer of technology, taking fully into account the interests of developing countries.

. . .

Article 16

1. It is the right and duty of all States, individually and collectively, to eliminate colonialism, *apartheid,* racial discrimination, neo-colonialism and all forms of foreign aggression, occupation and domination, and the economic and social consequences thereof, as a prerequisite for development. States which practise such coercive policies are economically responsible to the countries, territories and peoples affected for the restitution and full compensation for the exploitation and depletion of, and damages to, the natural and all other resources of those countries, territories and peoples. It is the duty of all States to extend assistance to them.

2. No State has the right to promote or encourage investments that may constitute an obstacle to the liberation of a territory occupied by force.

21 / Underdevelopment and Efforts to Control Multinational Corporations

Franklin B. Weinstein

Many of the difficulties which Third World states encounter in their efforts to control MNCs are rooted in the fact, often neglected in accounts of rising Third World power, that these countries are not only poor but underdeveloped. It will take much more than "information" about the techniques and benefits of bold and concerted action to overcome these difficulties.

Underdevelopment has, of course, many dimensions. Of central importance is the inadequacy of political and economic institutions, which leads, as Huntington has noted, to a general inability to implement policies. Most striking is the ineffectiveness of governmental efforts to extract resources from the populace by taxation. Gunnar Myrdal has described underdeveloped countries as "soft states," in which laws are generally ignored and often unenforceable.[1] Corruption is a most serious condition in these countries less for moral reasons than for its reflection of the anarchy pervading both the political and economic arenas; it so pervades both public and private sectors and introduces such a high degree of unpredictability into decision making that it virtually precludes consistent implementation of policies in most fields. Increasing functional specialization and expertise, presumed to be important characteristics of development, find few rewards where decision making is capricious. An underdeveloped state may have abundant resources, but it lacks the means to mobilize them to achieve desired ends.

That underdevelopment is more than a matter of poverty has been graphically demonstrated by the experience of Indonesia, Southeast Asia's only beneficiary of the oil bonanza. The state oil company, operating with virtually no accountability to any government agency, overextended itself with a host of questionable projects. In 1975 the government had to arrange massive loan packages from Japanese and American banks in order to meet the company's enormous ($1.5 billion due within 12 months) short-term debt. Because of the company's financial condition, a projected budget surplus for Indonesia has failed to materialize. Meanwhile, with expectations raised high in the euphoria occasioned by the quadrupling of oil prices, government agencies made ambitious plans, many

From Franklin B. Weinstein, "Multinational Corporations and the Third World: The Case of Japan and Southeast Asia," *International Organization*, Vol. 30, No. 3 (© 1976 by the Board of Regents of the University of Wisconsin System), pp. 387–396, 403–404. Some notes have been omitted, and the remainder renumbered in sequence.

of which have had to be scrapped. Prices of domestic oil, including kerosine for cooking, have risen sharply. The inflated cost of imported products has reduced the increment to per capita GNP resulting from the oil price rise from \$20 to \$6 (at 1972-73 prices). Because of declining demand in the industrial economies, Indonesia's traditional exports, some of which are the product of relatively labor-intensive smallholder activity, fell in value by 41 percent from mid-1974 to early 1975. The principal use to which the augmented oil revenues have been put is the stockpiling of rice and fertilizer, so as to hold down inflation and enhance the prospects of stability. Now there is concern that those stocks may be depleted through deterioration and pilferage. The situation has been described as confused. The institutions needed to make effective use of the oil bonanza simply are not there.

The softness of underdeveloped states continually frustrates their efforts to regulate MNCs. It is often assumed that the most effective way to bring MNCs under control is to require that the subsidiaries they establish in the Third World be joint ventures with some provision for transfer of shares to local hands within a reasonable period. Those who discern a rising nationalist tide in the Third World usually cite regulations restricting foreign ownership. There are now many such regulations in Southeast Asia.[2]

The author's research on Japan-based MNCs operating in Southeast Asia revealed that majority ownership can be very misleading as an indicator of control. Japanese, like other foreign businessmen, usually prefer to hold a majority of the shares in any investment venture. Like other foreign businessmen, they deplore regulations restricting alien ownership as a sign of a political climate growing less hospitable toward foreign investment. But most of those interviewed were not really alarmed at the prospect of greater local ownership. The principal representative of a major Japanese trading company in Bangkok was asked whether he did not fear that the Thai, once they had a majority of shares in the joint ventures in which his company was involved, might undertake policies which the Japanese side considered unwise. Reflecting a common attitude among Japanese executives in Southeast Asia, he indicated his lack of concern at such a prospect, pointing out that the joint ventures were so dependent on Japanese assistance in procuring raw materials, equipment, spare parts, financing, and marketing services that the local owners would be able to disregard Japanese advice only if they were prepared to sabotage the entire venture.

There are, in fact, numerous ways in which the foreign partner in a joint venture can retain control even in the face of majority shareholding by local nationals. "Nominal" or "dummy" shareholding has long been a common practice in Southeast Asia. In Indonesia, for example, there is a long tradition of "Ali-Baba" relationships, in which an indigenous Indonesian "Ali" is the nominal owner of a firm, while the real capital and direction come from the Chinese "Baba." The Japanese, it should be noted, are often far more willing to permit local ownership than are some American firms, which still insist on maintaining wholly owned subsidiaries, rather than joint ventures. But Japanese businessmen and government officials explained how difficult it is to find Thai and Indonesian nationals with sufficient capital to purchase even a respectable minority of the shares. And when a decision is made to expand the venture, actual shareholding on the local side sometimes decreases, because the latter may find it impossible to raise the additional capital needed to maintain the existing level of share participation.

Nominal shareholding takes various forms. In many cases, the Japanese lend the partner money with which to buy shares; the loan may be repaid out of future dividends. Sometimes the local partner contributes land or an old factory, which may be taken as the basis for placing in his name a quantity of shares far exceeding the value of his contribution. One Indonesian army general involved in numerous joint ventures asserted that his actual "capital" contribution was his ability to see the President on a day's notice. As he observed, that is indeed worth a good deal. The Japanese may simply purchase shares in the name of the local partner. According to Japanese embassy sources, it is not uncommon for under-the-table money to be paid to local nationals for the use of their names. In the Philippines, mention was made of arrangements whereby representatives of the Filipino shareholders are actually selected by the Japanese side and invariably vote according to the instructions of the Japanese.

Thus, the immediate effect of regulations in Thailand requiring 51 percent local ownership of joint ventures was, according to the Japanese partners in some of those ventures, likely to be a dramatic increase in the incidence of nominal shareholding. Under these circumstances, it may well be that from the standpoint of the underdeveloped countries these ostensibly nationalist regulations are worse than none at all, because they may create a false impression of local control and thereby defuse further pressure to make the MNCs serve local purposes.

A second technique for maintaining control in the face of 51 percent shareholding by local nationals is through the maintenance of unusually high debt to equity ratios. In order to satisfy the requirement that local shareholders hold a majority of equity in a joint venture, the two sides agree to keep the equity capital very low. Then heavy reliance is placed on loans for the import of plant, equipment, raw materials, and even for day-to-day operating expenses. These loans normally are procured by the Japanese side and sometimes are possible mainly because the parent Japanese company stands behind them. Often the loans come directly from the parent company itself, which enables the company to earn interest at the expense of its subsidiary. Heavy use is also made of supplier's credits. The venture's indebtedness and likely need for future Japanese support in procuring additional loans may constitute a substantial source of leverage in the hands of the Japanese side.

Another device is the use of "basic agreements" between the two parties to a joint venture which delineate explicitly the division of responsibility, and this division may hold regardless of changes in shareholding. Typically such agreements make the Japanese side responsible for operation of the factory, procurement of raw materials, and marketing of the product. To the local partner is normally consigned responsibility for employee relations, payroll, and similar noncritical functions. In Thailand not only export sales but domestic as well are frequently handled by the Japanese side—that is, the manufacturing venture sells the product to a Japanese trading company which then sells it to local merchants. When asked why they rely on the Japanese in this fashion, Thai businessmen responded by pointing out that the Japanese are in a much better position to extend credit and assume the risk of nonpayment. In the words of one leading Thai businessman involved in numerous joint ventures with the Japanese: "It is a guarantee against loss. We collect the money from the Japanese, and then they have all the worries."

In Indonesia there is a regulation prohibiting aliens from engaging in domestic trade, so the responsibility for local sale of the product is assigned to the Indonesian partner. Sometimes, when the latter is an overseas Chinese with heavy experience in marketing and ample resources, he actually carries out this function. In other companies, marketing responsibility is only nominally vested in the local partner.

Sometimes the basic agreement takes account of anticipated shifts in the balance of shares by reassigning functions. For example, one Japanese-Indonesian basic agreement (described as a model for future agreements) made available to the author stipulated that as the balance shifted from the present 70-30 Japanese majority to 51-49 in favor of the Indonesians after eleven years, the Japanese would yield their 4-3 majority on the board of directors and reduce the number of directors to six, with each side holding three. But by combining some categories of responsibility, the Japanese managed to keep the key positions for themselves.

The assignment to the Japanese side of key functions, such as the import of raw materials and sale of the product in export markets, is particularly important because many of the Japan-based MNCs find that it is these transactions, rather than the overall profitability of the joint venture, that provide the principal reward. Because the Japanese trading companies, which are the dominant force in Japanese investment in Southeast Asia, are involved in such diverse activities, it is normal for these transactions to take place entirely within the parent company's empire. Thus the MNC makes a profit when it sells equipment and raw materials to its joint ventures. One Japanese manager in Bangkok indicated that it is not uncommon to pay up to 5 percent above the price that would prevail if raw materials were procured in a competitive situation. This practice has, of course, irritated some of the local partners. Thai businessmen have, on occasion, alleged that where Thai partners have proved less cooperative than anticipated, the Japanese intentionally have forced the joint venture to run at a loss, so that they could then call for the issuance of additional shares, which the Thai lack the capital to purchase. The Japanese, on the other hand, contend that the Thai, discouraged by the initial unprofitability of a venture, are sometimes eager to extricate themselves and leave the enterprise to the Japanese. In any case, the result is a diminution of the Thai share.

Basic agreements also limit the decision-making authority of the joint venture by stipulating restrictions on export of the product, so as to avoid possible competition with the parent MNC. Although these restrictions can be modified in extreme circumstances— for example, a Thai glass producer was grudgingly allowed to export to Japan when it was able to show that because of a domestic surplus failure to do so would have dire economic consequences—this remains an area in which some of the most bitter controversies between local partners and MNCs have occurred.

Perhaps of most direct relevance to the question of whether OPEC's experience portends a decisive shift in the ability of Third World countries to control MNCs is the case of Pertamina, the Indonesian national oil company. Legislation passed in 1960 prohibited foreign oil companies from maintaining their concessions. In 1963 Sukarno induced the companies to operate in Indonesia under "work contracts," in which the companies served as contractors to the Indonesian government, which received a share of the profits. In 1966 companies entering the Indonesian field were required to operate under production sharing contracts, which explicitly gave management control to the Indonesians and required that the companies make available raw data to them.

This, then, was a case of total Indonesian ownership and explicit assertion of Indonesian management. The companies considered themselves, in effect, to have been nationalized. Yet the companies have in fact lost very little of their power. Because of their lack of technical expertise and organizational skills, as well as their desire to attract additional foreign investment, the Indonesians have not been in a position to exercise effective management, though there is one reported case in which the Indonesians successfully overruled a company on a production decision. In fact, a top official of Pertamina complained to the author about the unwillingness of the oil companies to make available "secrets" of oil exploration. Businessmen with experience in both Indonesia and the Middle East have asserted that the companies were under fewer actual restrictions as contractors in Indonesia than as concession-holders in the Arab countries.

Local ownership is thus by no means an indication that power has passed into local hands. But what about those cases in which regulations have been enacted requiring that jobs and training be made available to local nationals? Thailand, Malaysia, and Indonesia all have in recent years enacted regulations imposing obligations on foreign investors with respect to the employment and training of local nationals. The problem, in each case, has been that such regulations are rarely enforced.

The Thai, for example, have sought through immigration regulations to limit the number of foreign businessmen active in joint venture companies. But many foreigners have found that Thai immigration officials can with relative ease be induced to approve visa extensions. Where there have been limits imposed on the number of Japanese businessmen who may be assigned to a particular joint venture, personnel have been nominally assigned to the trading company office in Bangkok, though in reality they function as staff members of a particular joint venture. Sometimes the Japanese are listed as "technical advisers," while responsible managerial positions appear to be held by Thai personnel. But an hour in a Japanese-Thai textile company, observing the demeanor and authoritativeness of the "advisers," leaves no doubt as to who is actually in charge.

In Malaysia there are requirements that indigenous Malays be hired in managerial positions, but it is often hard to locate Malays with the requisite skills. When such people are identified they are eagerly sought by the foreign companies, which leads them to switch from one company to the next, falling into a role that is more symbolic than substantive. The companies regularly inform the government that they have been unable to comply with these requirements; it is the government's policy to accept this, so long as there is some evidence that a bona fide effort has been made to locate competent Malays. Musa Hitam, Minister of Basic Industries and a man clearly committed to a more nationalist course, told the author that the Japanese must make a real effort to hire Malays, but "if they come to us for people and we don't have any to offer, then we can't blame them."

The situation is most difficult in Indonesia. There Japanese executives told the author that they had come to Jakarta with the expectation of turning over operations to local staff in three or four years, but now they felt they would be lucky to find competent Indonesians in 15 or 20 years. Many of the companies have government approval to operate in Indonesia for 30 years, at which time complete control is to have passed to the Indonesians. When asked what they envisaged as the long-term future of their companies, several of the Japanese indicated that they had been encouraged by Indonesian officials to believe that they could apply for another 30 years at the conclusion of the first period. And a top-level Indonesian with jurisdiction over foreign investment affirmed to the author that such applications might well be approved.

Training and promotion are, to some extent, especially difficult problems for the Japanese. Concepts of seniority and company loyalty prevalent in Japan make it hard for Japanese executives to understand why they should train local people. Recipients of training, they find, are likely to demand high-level positions which it would take many years for a Japanese to attain; even worse, they may switch to another company. Two executives recalled that some Indonesians sent to Japan for training had instigated a strike almost immediately on their return. "What's the point of sending them to Japan for training, if all they're going to learn is how to strike," complained one of the Japanese businessmen. As a result, there is relatively little training in managerial and organizational skills given to employees of Japanese joint ventures in any of the Southeast Asian countries visited.

There are similar gaps in compliance with regulations concerning the establishment of processing industries and the fulfillment of "local content" requirements in assembly industries. Most of the commitments undertaken by foreign investors are explicitly or implicitly accompanied by the "escape clause" that the commitment is contingent on its economic feasibility when the time for implementation arrives. Where local content requirements were set up in the automobile assembly industry in Thailand and the Philippines, there was pessimism, especially in Thailand, about the prospects of meeting those requirements. The secretary-general of the foreign investment board in Bangkok predicted that the companies would fail to fulfill the requirement that by the end of 1974 automobiles assembled in Thailand contain locally produced parts accounting for 25 percent of the vehicle's value. When the deadline passed, he added, the Thai government would simply have to lower the requirement. Even when such requirements are met, it can be somewhat misleading. In the Philippines, the value of locally produced parts is computed as if they were sold as spare parts, which generally runs about double the price of the same item as original equipment on a new car. Thus a car may contain locally produced equipment said to account for 25 percent of the vehicle's value, when in reality the figure is only about 13 percent if one were to assume that all the components were produced as original eqiupment, not spare parts.

Nor does a commitment from MNCs to construct major industrial processing facilities necessarily mean that such projects will ever reach fruition. In Indonesia the massive Asahan aluminum smelting and electrification project, after many years of on-again off-again negotiations between Jakarta and Tokyo, now seems destined to become a reality. But in Thailand a very large petrochemical project was abandoned some five years after it had received government approval. Thai officials were skeptical about the seriousness of the Japanese in making the commitment. The Japanese, who held a dominant position in the sale of those items which the new factories would have produced, were believed to have outbid their competitors mainly because they were determined to ensure that no one else moved into the field. According to a top-level Thai official, a European company was persuaded to drop out of the bidding by intimations that entry into the Thai market would jeopardize the European firm's more important business operations in Japan itself. After years of haggling over details, the project finally collapsed. The Japanese insisted that they had been sincerely committed to the project; the Thai, noting the depressed state of the petrochemical industry in Japan and the fact that the years of delay had at least kept others out of the field, were unconvinced.

A major concern of the Southeast Asian governments has been to encourage MNCs to locate their manufacturing facilities in those regions where an economic stimulus is most needed. In this connection, incentives, usually in the form of tax holidays, have been extended to companies willing to locate in remote areas. But these incentives have been extremely ineffective. For most companies, tax holidays are less important than proximity to necessary infrastructure and to markets, urban amenities for their staffs, and the like. Thus MNC investment in Southeast Asia, except for the mining and logging fields, has been overwhelmingly concentrated near the principal urban areas, and there seems little the local governments can do to change this.

The inability of Southeast Asian governments to influence the behavior of MNCs in the areas described above is not to be explained simply as the result of a lack of will or boldness on the part of the governments concerned. A basic problem is that despite forthright government statements and regulations, the local partners of the Japanese do not, as a rule, seek to exercise a significant managerial role. In fact, a Japanese business-man with extensive knowledge of the situation in Thailand declared that he had never heard of a case in which the Thai side had demanded managerial authority, even where the Thai held a majority of shares. The Thai, he observed, prefer to let the Japanese run the company.

This situation stems from the motivations of local partners for entering a joint venture. There are essentially two kinds of partners. In the majority of manufacturing enterprises, the partners of the Japanese are overseas Chinese businessmen, often individuals who have long been associated with them as importers of Japanese manufactured products. Seeing that the Japanese intend to assemble or produce locally, they form joint ventures in order to gain the right to sell at least a part of the output in the local market. In other cases, the partners are businessmen who simply choose to join, rather than compete with, the Japanese. Or they see an opportunity for profit with little risk. Outside the manufac-turing industries (that is, in logging or mining), the Southeast Asian partners tend to be politicians, army generals, or other prominent figures well connected to the local centers of power. These people are expected to use their influence to handle the government officials who must be dealt with if the enterprise is to function smoothly.

Whether Chinese businessmen or army generals, the local partners have little to gain from demanding a role in management. Often they are paid a monthly retainer to serve as president or in another capacity, and some of them have taken pains to assure the Japanese that they would not interfere with the running of the company. The top-level executives of most joint ventures on the local side are men who have numerous business interests—some of them occupy key positions in 10 or 20 companies. They normally try to visit each of the joint ventures once a week. Their chief interest is that the company run smoothly, so as to maximize their profits, and they generally assume that operations will run most smoothly if the Japanese are permitted to manage the company undisturbed. They have little desire to press for training programs, promotion of local managers, and other measures which, at least in the short run (which is the chief concern of most businessmen) can only reduce profits. In one case, the Indonesian partner in a logging venture had never even been to visit the site. When asked why, he replied: "If I went there, I'd probably have to sleep in a tent. Who wants to do that?"

The inability of Southeast Asian governments to control MNCs is a product of factors a good deal more subtle than a shortage of boldness or a lack of information. The failure of these governments to enforce laws and regulations, and the disinclination of local partners to press for control of joint ventures, should not be taken to mean that these laws or these individuals are peculiarly wanting. Rather, an inability to enforce laws is but a manifestation of the more basic condition of underdevelopment, and the behavior of these individuals is quite rational given the circumstances prevailing in an underdeveloped country. To chastise citizens of a soft state for failing to live up to norms appropriate to a more developed society is to ignore the awesome obstacles which underdevelopment does in fact impose on a society. Nor is it reasonable to cast the Japanese as villains. They too are merely acting rationally, given the perspective they bring to the situation. Certainly their behavior differs little from that of American businessmen in the Third World.

In assessing these problems, it is, of course, important to avoid falling into the assump-tion that the future must be like the past. Nor can we conclude that merely because MNCs do not achieve the goals set for them by local governments that nothing at all is being accomplished along those lines. But progress is likely to remain extremely limited until the Southeast Asian nations have managed, through a process of internal change, to overcome the obstacles which a soft state imposes on them.

MNCs as "Engines of Development"

The remaining question is whether MNCs are likely to contribute to development—that is, to the process of change by which the characteristics associated with the soft state might be eliminated. The irony of this question is immediately apparent. We are really asking whether MNCs are likely to contribute to the process by which Third World states may become better able to control MNCs. For to foster development means, among other things, to help the state create institutions capable of sustaining the enforcement of its laws and regulations (including those concerning MNCs) and the mobilization of its own national resources, both human and material (which would make it less dependent on MNCs).

Development, then, is not merely a matter of industrialization or the acquisition of wealth; it involves as well the creation of institutions capable, on a self-sustaining basis, of channeling resources into more productive uses and distributing the output of that process to the populace in a way that will win sufficiently diffuse support to maintain the system. This means, among other things, the establishment of a bureaucracy which can be relied on to implement policies with a reasonable degree of consistency; the cultivation of a broad base of entrepreneurial, managerial, and technical skill; development of a capacity to raise capital internally through an effective tax system; and, most pressing given the seriousness of the unemployment problem, the creation of jobs that will enable the majority of the populace not only to survive but to be productive.

A definitive answer concerning the impact of MNCs on development is probably not possible, for many of the claims made on their behalf look to the long run. Some advocates of reliance on MNCs are prepared to admit that certain short-term effects will be negative, but, they maintain, the benefits will become apparent in time. There are really two questions. First, are MNCs likely to foster development in the long run? Second, if there are significant negative effects in the short term, is it likely to prove possible, from a political standpoint, for MNCs to continue operating in the Third World until the day arrives when the promised benefits are to be realized?

• • •

While there may not be sufficient evidence on which to base a conclusive judgment about the impact of MNCs on the Third World, there is certainly reason to suspect that on balance they may do more to impede than to stimulate development, at least in the softer Third World states. As outlined in the preceding pages, reliance on MNCs inhibits in certain key areas the process of building viable indigenous institutions, and this process is central to development. MNCs help to keep the soft states soft. The benefits which MNCs have to offer, such as capital and productivity-raising technology, may indeed stimulate the further development of a country that already possesses a sound institutional base. In a soft state, however, MNCs tend to exacerbate social inequities, heighten frustrations, and undermine the legitimacy of the government. Whether increased productivity will ultimately solve those problems is at least open to question.

If this picture is accurate, then it is reasonable to ask what alternatives there may be. Are there ways for these states to extract benefits from MNCs without suffering a perpetuation of the characteristics associated with the soft state? Perhaps there are, but the foregoing analysis leaves little room for optimism, since it is precisely their softness that prevents these governments from establishing a more beneficial relationship with MNCs. What, then, would be the prospects for development if the role of MNCs were to be sharply circumscribed, perhaps as part of a broader strategy of temporary isolation?[3] The answers to these questions are by no means apparent. But if there is even a reasonable possibility that our skepticism about the potential contribution of MNCs will prove justified, then these would seem to be questions deserving considerably more study than they have yet received.

NOTES

1. Gunnar Myrdal, *The Challenge of World Poverty* (Penguin Books, 1970), Chapter 7. See also Samuel P. Huntington, *Political Order in Changing Societies* (New Haven: Yale University Press, 1968), p. 1.

2. For example, the Thai government declared at the end of 1972 that foreigners could no longer own a controlling interest in companies in certain fields. In the Philippines, foreign shareholding has been limited to 30 percent in particular fields, and Indonesia, where the shortage of local capital has been most severe, announced recently that 51 percent of the shares in all joint venture companies must be in the hands of Indonesians within 10 years.

3. For a discussion of the advantages of "voluntary quarantine," see Tibor Mende, *From Aid to Re-Colonization: Lessons of a Failure* (New York: Pantheon, 1973), pp. 194–212.

PART V

FUTURES

INTRODUCTION

Indispensable to our thinking about transnational corporations is an ordering of ideas about what their future might be or ought to be. In this regard, images (or models) of the future world order are useful. Such world order models are concise summaries of the characteristics of the global system of the future, with particular reference to the subject that has been the focus of our interest in this volume: the extranational corporate body (to borrow Tannenbaum's expression).

Alternative images (or models) of the future are a basic tool for clarifying social trends or the choices that are implicit in public policies. As aids to policy analysis, images of the future are statements of the consequences of such trends or of policy decisions. For example, in "The Survival of the Fittest" (Part III), Frank Tannenbaum in effect draws an image of the corporate-dominated, peaceful world that might exist if corporations were to wield greater political power than they do at the present time. It might fairly be said to be an image that appeals to the corporate world because it may well be favorable to their interests. But such an image might be analytically incomplete inasmuch as the consequences of some trends or policies may in fact be incompletely or incorrectly portrayed. (Tannenbaum, for example, does not specify how the extranational corporate body will assume political functions.) And yet such images remain part of our intellectual currency; they are shorthand terms that are necessary for any discussion of the basic traits of a complex future.

Two basic components of images of the future might be distinguished: (1) the predictive component—the "is" or "will be" component, and (2) the value or preferential component—the "ought to be" component. In studies of human af-

347

fairs, the "is" and the "ought to be" components are notoriously hard to separate, especially when speculating about the future, which is, by definition, fluid and uncertain. But an attempt must obviously be made to keep distinct what we would like to happen and what would be in our interest to happen, from what is likely to happen whether we like it or not.

The predictive component of future images is exemplified by forecasts of the prospects of multinational corporations relative to other forms of enterprise. In the mid- and late 1960s, a brilliant future was forecast for these firms. The then current growth rates were projected two to three decades hence, and such extrapolations gave rise to confident statements that the future would be dominated by a small number of very large corporations.[1] Howard Perlmutter advanced the "300 Hypothesis—a prediction that the global system of the future will contain 300 or so super-giant companies, . . . hundreds of thousands of small flexible companies of the one man show variety," and a relatively weaker sector of medium-sized forms.[2] By "future" Perlmutter meant 1985 or 1988. That "future" will soon be upon us, yet there is little sign that the large firms are any more dominant than they were one decade ago—if anything, they seem less so.

As for the preferential component of images of the future, four principal sources immediately come to mind: (1) the corporation itself; (2) corporate employees, in particular the workers, as distinct from top management; (3) the home state; and (4) the host state. Expressions of the opinions of these interest clusters abound in the literature on international business and have already been encountered in this volume. Robert Gilpin's "Three Models of the Future" is a good example of an analysis that seeks to impose an order on such diverse opinions. Gilpin distinguishes three such models: (1) sovereignty-at-bay, (2) *dependencia,* and (3) mercantilism. Each of them repays close study. The classification Gilpin proposes is not identical with the four interest clusters just mentioned but it is closely related to it. The "sovereignty-at-bay" school (which asserts that dynamic business enterprises are putting in jeopardy the nation-state) is broadly expressive of corporate concerns. Gilpin terms it liberal in the sense that it tends to minimize the need for political restraints and to assume that if business is unrestrained, the world will be a better place to be in. One of the principal expositions of this view is Tannenbaum's article, mentioned earlier. Another is an imaginative article (selection 23) by Norman Macrae, an editor of the London *Economist,* that is alluded to in Gilpin's article. Macrae believes that technology, and "information technology" in particular, offers some splendid opportunities for international business, even though the precise characteristics of such firms are yet to be defined.

But "sovereignty-at-bay" views also tend to be held by home-country spokesmen, especially if national interests are perceived as being identical with those of the multinational corporations domiciled in those countries. The countries of the world differ according to whether they are principally senders of (home bases for), or recipients of (hosts for), multinational enterprises. Most countries are either one or the other, and only a few (such as West Germany) are about equally important as both. The United States sends out more foreign investment than it receives (in 1971 the proportions were about 6.3:1.0), and its international posture tends to be reflective of corporate views (especially under Republican administrations); hence it is an example of the "sovereignty-at-bay" model. But the preferences of the home country may reflect more than merely corporate interests. The home country may view international business activity as an appropriate component of a stable world order, hence also of the national interest. For the United States after 1945, multinational corporations were one of the important components of a world that was being built. To the extent that the United States as a world power created such a world order, it also created a political framework for the expansion of multinationals.

The great majority of the world's countries, especially those in the Third World, tend to be host countries, that is, recipients of corporate activity that is seen as extraneous. Among the top-fifty industrials, only ten countries are represented as home countries out of some 150, and even though the top-fifty include two Third World corporations (from Iran and Brazil) now commencing transnational activity all over the world, it is still true that most countries in the world are host countries. Hence, the majority view internationally tends to accept theories of domination, imperialism, or dependency. These theories are characteristic of Gilpin's second model, *dependencia*. Because dependency theorists attribute the underdevelopment of their countries to dependency upon the center, and see the multinational enterprise as one of the mechanisms maintaining that dependency, their desired future world is one in which the interests of the host countries of today would be maximized as a result of the independence of those countries from the center. The principal objective of the dependent host country is to obtain adequate international and national control over external corporate activity; whereas, of course, the principal objective of corporations is the liberalization of controls, and that of home countries is retention of their ability to support the overseas activities of their corporations.

That is why Gilpin's dependency model is in fact closely related to his mercantilist model. True, there are differences of style (dependency literature draws in part on Marxist analysis), of origin (dependency theorists hail mostly from developing countries, and originally from Latin America), and of substance (dependency models tend to adopt a systemic (as distinct from a national) perspective and see importance in influencing the rules of the game of the international economic system), but insofar as the image of the future is concerned, dependency theorists, just like mercantilists, want "independence"; they want viable and developed nation-states capable of manipulating economic arrangements with a view to maximizing national interests. In practice, though, the ranks of mercantilists are likely to be filled by recruits from the industrialized nations, because those nations are more capable of controling their own economic environment; the "dependistas" have yet to reach this point, but their goals seem quite similar to those of industrialized nations.

We have two other examples of analysis that reflects host-country concerns and spans the dependency-mercantilist continuum. Stephen Hymer (an MIT-trained economist who died in 1974) was one of the seminal writers in this field. In his much-quoted paper, "The Multinational Corporation and the Law of Uneven Development," he gave expression to the widely felt apprehension of people unwilling to live their lives in "branch plant countries." He stressed that the nation-state is the center and the coordinator of economic activity. Hymer strongly suggested that the multinational enterprise is not the preferred engine for the development of poor countries; the task must be undertaken by the countries themselves. He was less clear about other functions that international firms might be capable of performing.

Samir Amin, Director of the United Nations Institute for Economic Development and Research at Dakar, Senegal, holds a similar view of the future. He discusses the objectives that Third World countries ought to pursue in the United Nations system, and he strongly voices the concerns of the least developed of the Third World countries, particularly those in Africa. Amin is critical of those who try to "get along" with contemporary international economic arrangements by tinkering with some of the rules of the game and argues that real change in less developed countries can come about only as a result of what he terms "auto-centered development," that is, the development of self-reliance. (In this respect his view is similar to that of Hymer.) In Samir Amin's scheme of things, multinational corporations do play a role as purveyors of technology, but it is clearly a minor role and one that needs strict control—auto-centered development is achieved largely through indigenous effort.

In discussing the four preference clusters, Gilpin focuses only indirectly on the interests of labor. Richard Cox, formerly of the staff of the International Labor Organization and now a professor at York University, provides that missing perspective. His views are broad, and unlike some writers on this topic, he describes not only the concerns of employees of transnational corporations (who tend to make up a relatively small proportion of the total labor force) but those of labor in general. He discusses the relative merits of the transnational strategies and the national strategies for maximizing labor interests and sees the national strategy, which asserts that home-country interests are not identical with those of large corporations, as the principal weapon in labor's future arsenal.

Gilpin's analysis also includes a prediction of trends in world politics that will affect the future of the world economy. His two principal models of the global political system are (1) the United States' leadership, or hegemonial, model, and (2) the multipolar (triangular, or five-power) model. Broadly, he sees the first as losing strength and the second as gaining ground, in a manner that recalls to him the movement of the nineteenth-century system of world order, after 1880, into a phase of economic tensions, protectionism, and imperialism. Such a phase, with its attendant multipower animosities, tensions, and confrontations, lends strength to the view that the mercantilist image is the dominant one for the future; in a world of warring powers each nation-state will want to take charge of its own economic destinies, leaving less room for the global planning system of the multinationals.

On the whole, then, the prospects for transnational enterprise appear to be less than favorable. Writing in 1968, at the peak of the multinational boom, Tannenbaum came nearest to foreseeing a bright future for the "extra-national corporate body." Macrae is bullish on international business and the contribution it can make to the world economy by transferring manufacturing operations to the developing countries (a prospect that disturbs Hymer and Amin), but Macrae expects to see the small firm, rather than the very large enterprise, flourish. Hymer, Amin, and Cox would each opt for limiting, if not eliminating completely, the multinational.

One decade ago, Edith Penrose, a British economist, was similarly (if more judiciously) doubtful.[3] Without putting into question the real contributions made by large firms, she also saw some difficulties inherent in the dual commitment and the divided loyalties such firms inevitably must suffer despite their rhetoric of global mission. At the root of the problem she saw the failure of international firms to find a way of operating in the modern world that would make them generally acceptable as international institutions. The managers of many of these firms had made no progress toward a world outlook, and although some were aware of the problem of acceptability, few had gone beyond rhetoric and cosmetic change. For, as Penrose correctly pointed out, solution of the problem was beyond the reach of the firms, for they had to conduct their operations in a system of nation-states lacking accepted and well-established central institutions. The firms could not avoid allocating income and investments among these states in a discriminatory manner; yet, a global system of taxation that could compensate for such discrimination was not in sight.

The more fundamental of Penrose's strictures, the difficulty of operating multi-national business in a nation-state system, is still with us and will probably continue to be a source of tension. But in the decade since she wrote, some new problems have arisen, and other trends are also evident. The managers of transnational firms are more careful today than they were in the 1950s and 1960s; they know they are under more careful scrutiny than ever before. The characteristics of multinational firms are changing too. More firms are entering the world arena and are becoming more fully multinational. If the world oil industry is a reliable indicator of the general situation, then transnational business is becoming less concentrated. Hence the power of transnational firms may loom less heavily over the world economy, and the worst of the problems of multinationals could be over.

Corporations, corporate employees, and home and host countries are not the only interests affected by transnational corporations. The ideas of consumers and environmentalists about the shaping of the future must also be heard. As previously observed, the value of alternative images of the future is that they make clear the consequences of public choices and the range of available alternatives. But definition of the global public interest out of the clamor of such varied and sometimes discordant voices is not an easy task. For although each of them has some claim to speak for the common good (most especially perhaps the corporations because they claim to advance both universal welfare and peace, and the host countries because they claim to speak for the majority of the world's peoples), in each instance the case advanced bears the marks of special pleading.

A student of transnational corporations thus cannot avoid asking, what are the elements of the global public interest in this matter? Can we go beyond saying that we need to strike a balance between all the interests involved, a balance that will need to be adjusted as new developments alter the positions and expectations of the various parties, yet in such a manner that the best interest of none should suffer irreparable damage?

Two general propositions may serve as guidelines for the definition of the global public interest. First, since international business is serving important global functions, and since such functions will continue to be required, the effective performance of these functions requires conditions of considerable autonomy. Second, since the precise form assumed by international business and the precise functions performed by such business may change and may need to change from time to time, these functions will need to be coordinated with each other and with other public functions, and will need to be adjusted both in form and in substance.

The public interest is generally protected by public organizations of the appropriate scope and level. The activity of transnational business would normally be monitored and coordinated by a public international organization such as the United Nations. But the multinational enterprise has as yet little tie-in of interest or substance with the world organization. Unlike nation-states, the United Nations has little to offer the multinational enterprise in the way of contracts or purchasing arrangements, nor does the United Nations receive from it taxes or contributions in any form.[4] That organization has functioned primarily as a forum for critical comment and adversary confrontation.

Yet as organizations of global scope and function, transnational enterprises need a reliable political framework of global dimensions to ensure secure and predictable operations. Such a framework has in the past been provided by the world powers: in the seventeenth century, by the Dutch Republic; in the eighteenth and nineteenth centuries, by Great Britain; and for long periods in the twentieth century, by the United States. These have been home-state, world-order frameworks, favorable to international business in their expanding phases but ultimately facing almost inevitable contraction. The multipolar alternative of mercantilist nation-states is a less favorable context for global enterprise.

It is therefore reasonable to suggest that the future context of world politics should not be characterized by a cyclical alternation between home-state world orders and mercantilist multipolarity. Students of world order need to give thought to ways to build a system that avoids such dangerous fluctuations and that affords a more stable political framework for the conduct of world business.

NOTES

1. R. J. Barber, *The American Corporation* (New York: E. P. Dutton, 1970), Part Five.
2. "Some Management Problems in Spaceship Earth: The Megafirm and the Global Industrial Estate," *Academy of Management Proceedings,* Chicago, 1969, p. 67.
3. *The Large International Firm in Developing Countries: The International Petroleum Industry* (London: George Allen & Unwin, 1968), especially Chap. X.
4. In the mid-1970s the funds disbursed by the United Nations system (including the Development Program, the World Bank, and the International Monetary Fund) approximated $6 billion annually. Less than 1 percent of that amount may have involved multinationals, mostly in the form of loan arrangements for development projects, supported by multinational corporations—lesser amounts were used for procurement contracts.

22 / Three Models of the Future

Robert Gilpin

Edward Hallet Carr observed that "the science of economics presupposes a given political order, and cannot be profitably studied in isolation from politics."[1] Throughout history, the larger configurations of world politics and state interests have in large measure determined the framework of the international economy. Succeeding imperial and hegemonic powers have sought to organize and maintain the international economy in terms of their economic and security interests.

From this perspective, the contemporary international economy was the creation of the world's dominant economic and military power, the United States. At the end of the Second World War, there were efforts to create a universal and liberal system of trade and monetary relations. After 1947, however, the world economy began to revive on the foundations of the triangular relationship of the three major centers of noncommunist industrial power: the United States, Western Europe, and Japan. Under the umbrella of American nuclear protection and connected with the United States through military alliances, Japan and Western Europe were encouraged to grow and prosper. In order to rebuild these industrial economies adjacent to the Sino-Soviet bloc, the United States encouraged Japanese growth, led by exports, into the American market and, through the European Economic Community's (EEC) common external tariff and agricultural policy, also encouraged discrimination against American exports.

Today, the triangular relationship of the noncommunist industrial powers upon which the world economy has rested is in disarray. The signs of decay were visible as early as the middle 1960s, when President John F. Kennedy's grand design failed to stem the coalescence of an inward-looking European economic bloc and to achieve its objective of an economic and political community extending from Scandinavia to Japan and pivoted on the United States.

Believing that the world trading and monetary system was operating to America's disadvantage, the administration of Richard Nixon took up the challenge with a completely different approach. On 15 August 1971, former President Nixon announced a new foreign economic policy for the United States. In response to the first trade deficit since 1893 and to accelerating attacks on the dollar, the president imposed a surcharge on American imports, suspended the convertibility of the dollar, and took other remedial actions. Subsequently the dollar was devalued twice (December 1971 and February

From Robert Gilpin, "Three Models of the Future," *International Organization*, Vol. 29, No. 1 (© 1975 by the Board of Regents of the University of Wisconsin System), pp. 37-60. Some notes have been omitted, and the remainder renumbered in sequence.

1973); the world moved toward a system of flexible exchange rates; and intense negotiations were initiated to create a new international monetary and trading system.

A new economic policy was necessary for several reasons. The United States believed an overvalued dollar was adding significantly to its unemployment rate. American expenditures abroad for military commitments, foreign direct investment, and goods and services required, in the 1970s, greater outlays of foreign exchange than the United States could earn or wished to borrow. The US rapprochement with China, its moves toward détente with the Soviet Union, and President Nixon's announcement of the New Economic Policy appeared to signal the end of the political order that American economic and military supremacy had guaranteed; this political order had been the foundation for the post-World War II world economy. All these policy initiatives were efforts to adjust to the growing economic power of America's partners, Europe and Japan, and to the growing military power of its primary antagonist, the Soviet Union. In terms of the present article, these economic and political changes raised the question of whether the interdependent world economy could survive in the changing political environment of the 1970s and beyond.

In this brief article I make no attempt to give a definitive answer to this question. Rather, my purpose is to present and evaluate three models of the future drawn from current writings on international relations. These models are really representative of the three prevailing schools of thought on political economy: liberalism, Marxism, and economic nationalism. Each model is an amalgam of the ideas of several writers who, in my judgment (or by their own statements), fall into one or another of these three perspectives on the relationship of economic and political affairs.

Each model constitutes an ideal type. Perhaps no one individual would subscribe to each argument made by any one position. Yet the tendencies and assumptions associated with each perception of the future are real enough; they have a profound influence on popular, academic, and official thinking on trade, monetary, and investment problems. One, in fact, cannot really escape being influenced by one position or another.

Following the presentation of the three models, I present a critique that sets forth the strengths and weaknesses of each. On the basis of this critique, I draw some general conclusions with respect to the future of international economic organization and the nature of future international relations in general.

The Sovereignty-at-Bay Model

I label the first model *sovereignty at bay*, after the title of Raymond Vernon's influential book on the multinational corporation. According to this view, increasing economic interdependence and technological advances in communication and transportation are making the nation state an anachronism. These economic and technological developments are said to have undermined the traditional economic rationale of the nation state. In the interest of world efficiency and domestic economic welfare, the nation state's control over economic affairs will continually give way to the multinational corporation, to the Eurodollar market, and to other international institutions better suited to the economic needs of mankind.

Perhaps the most forceful statement of the sovereignty-at-bay thesis is that of Harry Johnson—the paragon of economic liberalism. Analyzing the international economic problems of the 1970s, Johnson makes the following prediction:

In an important sense, the fundamental problem of the future is the conflict between the political forces of nationalism and the economic forces pressing for world integration. This conflict currently appears as one between the national government and the international corporation, in which the balance of power at least superficially appears to lie on the side of the national government. But in the longer run economic forces are likely to predominate over political, and may indeed come to do so before the end of this decade. Ultimately, a world federal government will appear as the only rational method for coping with the world's economic problems.

Though not all adherents of the sovereignty-at-bay thesis would go as far as Johnson, and an interdependent world economy is quite conceivable without unbridled scope for the activities of multinational corporations, most do regard the multinational corporation as the embodiment par excellence of the liberal ideal of an interdependent world economy. It has taken the integration of national economies beyond trade and money to the internationalization of production. For the first time in history, production, marketing, and investment are being organized on a global scale rather than in terms of isolated national economies. The multinational corporations are increasingly indifferent to national boundaries in making decisions with respect to markets, production, and sources of supply.

The sovereignty-at-bay thesis argues that national economies have become enmeshed in a web of economic interdependence from which they cannot easily escape, and from which they derive great economic benefits. Through trade, monetary relations, and foreign investment, the destinies and well-being of societies have become too inexorably interwoven for these bonds to be severed. The costs of the ensuing inefficiencies in order to assert national autonomy or some other nationalistic goal would be too high. The citizenry, so this thesis contends, would not tolerate the sacrifices of domestic economic well-being that would be entailed if individual nation states sought to hamper unduly the successful operation of the international economy.

Underlying this development, the liberal position argues is a revolution in economic needs and expectations. Domestic economic goals have been elevated to a predominant position in the hierarchy of national goals. Full employment, regional development, and other economic welfare goals have become the primary concerns of political leadership. More importantly, these goals can only be achieved, this position argues, through participation in the world economy. No government, for example, would dare shut out the multinational corporations and thereby forgo employment, regional development, or other benefits these corporations bring into countries. In short, the rise of the welfare state and the increasing sensitivity of national governments to the rising economic expectations of their societies have made them dependent upon the benefits provided by a liberal world-economic system.

In essence, this argument runs, one must distinguish between the creation of the interdependent world economy and the consequences of its subsequent dynamics. Though the postwar world economy was primarily a creation of the United States, the system has since become essentially irreversible. The intermeshing of interests across national boundaries and the recognized benefits of interdependence now cement the system together for the future. Therefore, even though the power of the United States and security concerns may be in relative decline, this does not portend a major transformation of the international economy and political system.

The multinational corporation, for example, is now believed to be sufficiently strong to stand and survive on its own. The flexibility, mobility, and vast resources of the corporations give them an advantage in confrontations with nation states. A corporation always has the option of moving its production facilities elsewhere. If it does, the nation state is the loser in terms of employment, corporate resources, and access to world markets. Thus the multinationals are escaping the control of nation states, including that of their home (source) governments. They are emerging as sufficient powers in their own right to survive the changing context of international political relations.

On the other hand, it is argued that the nation state has been placed in a dilemma it cannot hope to resolve. It is losing control over economic affairs to transnational actors like the multinational corporation. It cannot retain its traditional independence and sovereignty and simultaneously meet the expanding economic needs and desires of its populace. The efforts of nation states to enhance their security and power *relative* to others are held to be incompatible with an interdependent world economy that generates *absolute* gains for everyone. In response to the growing economic demands of its citizens, the nation state must adjust to the forces of economic rationality and efficiency.

In the contemporary world, the costs of disrupting economic interdependence, of territorial conquest, and of risking nuclear warfare are believed to be far greater than any conceivable benefits. The calculus of benefits and risks has changed, and "the rational relationship between violence as a means of foreign policy and the ends of foreign policy has been destroyed by the possibility of all-out nuclear war." In contrast to the nineteenth century, the cost of acquiring territory is viewed as having simply become too great. In the contemporary world, there is more to be gained through economic cooperation and an international division of labor than through strife and conflict. Thus, in the opinion of Saburo Okita, formerly president of the Japan Economic Research Center, the exercise of force for economic gain or to defend economic interests in an anachronism:

> We are living in a century when such military action is no longer viable. To build up military power just to protect overseas private property is rather absurd in terms of cost-benefit calculations. The best course for the Government in case of nationalization or seizure of overseas private Japanese assets is to compensate Japanese investors directly in Japan rather than to spend very large amounts of money to build up military strength.

Just as the nuclear revolution in warfare now inhibits the exercise of military power, the revolution in economic relations now inhibits the national exercise of economic power by increasing the cost. Advances in transportation and communications have integrated national economies to the point where many believe it is too costly to threaten the severance of economic relations in order to achieve particular political and economic goals. Economically as well as militarily in the contemporary world, nations are said to be mutually deterred from actions that would disrupt the interdependent economy. This mutual vulnerability of necessity limits and moderates the economic and political struggle among nation states. It provides the necessary minimum political order where the multinational corporations of all the major industrial powers can flourish and bring benefits to the whole of mankind.

The sovereignty-at-bay view also envisages a major transformation of the relationships among developed and underdeveloped countries. The multinational corporations of the developed, industrial economies must not only produce in each other's markets, but the locus of manufacturing industry will increasingly shift to underdeveloped countries.[2] As the economies of developed countries become more service oriented, as their terms of trade for raw materials continue to deteriorate, and as their labor costs continue to rise, manufacturing will migrate to lesser-developed countries. United States firms already engage in extensive offshore production in Asia and Latin America. Western Europe has reached the limits of importing Mediterranean labor, which is the functional equivalent of foreign direct investment. Japan's favorable wage structure and undervalued currency have eroded. With the end of the era of cheap energy and of favorable terms of trade for raw materials, the logic of industrial location favors the underdeveloped periphery. Increasingly, the multinational corporations of all industrial powers will follow the logic of this manufacturing revolution. Manufacturing, particularly of components and semiprocessed goods, will migrate to lesser-developed countries.

This vision of the future has been portrayed most dramatically by Norman Macrae, in an issue of *The Economist*, who foresees a world of spreading affluence energized perhaps by "small transnational companies run in West Africa by London telecommuters who live in Honolulu?"[3] New computer-based training methods and information systems will facilitate the rapid diffusion of skills, technologies, and industries to lesser-developed countries. The whole system will be connected by modern telecommunications and computers; the rich will concentrate on the knowledge-creating and knowledge-processing industries. More and more of the old manufacturing industries will move to the underdeveloped world. The entire West and Japan will be a service-oriented island in a labor-intensive global archipelago. Thus, whereas the telephone and jet aircraft facilitated the internationalization of production in the Northern Hemisphere, the contemporary revolution in communications and transportation will encompass the whole globe.

"The logical and eventual development of this possibility," according to management consultant John Diebold, "would be the end of nationality and national governments as we know them."[4] This sovereignty-at-bay world, then, is one of voluntary and cooperative relations among interdependent economies, the goal of which is to accelerate the economic growth and welfare of everyone. In this model, development of the poor is achieved through the transfer of capital, technology, and managerial know-how from the continually advancing developed lands to the lesser-developed nations; it is a world in which the tide of economic growth lifts all boats. In this liberal vision of the future, the multinational corporation, freed from the nation state, is the critical transmission belt of capital, ideas, and growth.

The Dependencia Model

In contrast to the sovereignty-at-bay vision of the future is what may be characterized as the *dependencia* model.[5] Although the analysis underlying the two approaches has much in common, the dependencia model challenges the partners-in-development motif of the sovereignty-at-bay model. Its Marxist conception is one of a hierarchical and exploitative world order. The sovereignty-at-bay model envisages a relatively benevolent system in which growth and wealth spread from the developed core to the lesser-developed periphery. In the dependencia model, on the other hand, the flow of wealth and benefits is seen as moving—via the same mechanisms—from the global, underdeveloped periphery to the centers of industrial financial power and decision. It is an exploitative system that produces affluent development for some and dependent underdevelopment for the majority of mankind. In effect, what is termed transnationalism by the sovereignty-at-bay advocates is considered imperialism by the Marxist proponents of the dependencia model.

In the interdependent world economy of the dependencia model, the multinational corporation also reigns supreme. But the world created by these corporations is held to be far different from that envisaged by the sovereignty-at-bay school of thought. In the dependencia model the political and economic consequences of the multinational corporation are due to what Stephen Hymer has called the two laws of development: the law of increasing firm size, and the law of uneven development. The law of increasing firm size, Hymer argues, is the tendency since the Industrial Revolution for firms to increase in size "from the *workshop* to the *factory* to the *national* corporation to the *multidivisional corporation* and now to the multinational corporation."[6] The law of uneven development, he continues, is the tendency of the international economy to produce poverty as well as wealth, underdevelopment as well as development. Together, these two economic laws are producing the following consequence:

> . . . a regime of North Atlantic Multinational Corporations would tend to produce a hierarchical division of labor within the firm. It would tend to centralize high-level decision-making occupations in a few key cities in the advanced countries, surrounded by a number of regional sub-capitals, and confine the rest of the world to lower levels of activity and income, i.e., to the status of towns and villages in a new Imperial system. Income, status, authority, and consumption patterns would radiate out from these centers along a declining curve, and the existing pattern of inequality and dependency would be perpetuated. The pattern would be complex, just as the structure of the corporation is complex, but the basic relationship between different countries would be one of superior and subordinate, head office and branch office.[7]

In this hierarchical and exploitative world system, power and decision would be lodged in the urban financial and industrial cores of New York, London, Tokyo, etc. Here would be located the computers and data banks of the closely integrated global systems of production and distribution; the main computer in the core would control subsidiary computers in the periphery. The higher functions of management, research and development, entrepreneurship, and finance would be located in these Northern metropolitan centers. "Lower" functions and labor-intensive manufacturing would be continuously diffused to the lesser-developed countries where are found cheap pliable labor, abundant raw materials, and an indifference to industrial pollution. This global division of labor between higher and lower economic functions would perpetuate the chasm between the affluent northern one-fifth of the globe and the destitute southern four-fifths of the globe.

The argument of the dependencia thesis is that the economic dependence of the underdeveloped periphery upon the developed core is responsible for the impoverishment of the former. Development and underdevelopment are simultaneous processes; the developed countries have progressed and have grown rich through exploiting the poor and making them poorer. Lacking true autonomy and being economically dependent upon the developed countries, the underdeveloped countries have suffered because the developed have a veto over their development.

> By dependence we mean a situation in which the economy of certain countries is conditioned by the development and expansion of another economy to which the former is subjected. The relation of interdependence between two or more economies, and between these and world trade, assumes the form of dependence when some countries (the dominant ones) can expand and be self-sustaining, while other

countries (the dependent ones) can do this only as a reflection of that expansion, which can have either a positive or negative effect on their immediate development.[8]

Though this particular quotation refers to trade relations, much of the dependence literature is addressed to the issue of foreign direct investment. In content, most of this literature is of a piece with traditional Marxist and radical theories of imperialism. Whether because of the falling rate of profit in capitalist economies or the attraction of superprofits abroad, multinational corporations are believed to exploit the underdeveloped countries. Thus, Paul Baran and Paul Sweezy see the multinationals necessarily impelled to invest in lesser-developed countries.[9] Constantine Vaitsos has sought to document the superprofits available to American corporations in Latin America.[10] The message conveyed by this literature is that the imperialism of free investment has replaced the imperialism of free trade in the contemporary world.

The Mercantilist Model

A key element missing in both the sovereignty-at-bay and the dependencia models is the nation state. Both envisage a world organized and managed by powerful North American, European, and Japanese corporations. In the beneficial corporate order of the first model and the imperialist corporate order of the second, there is little room for nation states, save as servants of corporate power and ambition. In oppositon to both these models, therefore, the third model of the future—the mercantilist model—views the nation state and the interplay of national interests (as distinct from corporate interests) as the primary determinants of the future role of the world economy.[11]

According to this mercantilist view, the interdependent world economy, which has provided such a favorable environment for the multinational corporation, is coming to an end. In the wake of the relative decline of American power and of growing conflicts among the capitalist economies, a new international political order less favorable to the multinational corporation is coming into existence. Whether it is former President Nixon's five-power world (US, USSR, China, the EEC, and Japan), a triangular world (US, USSR, and China), or some form of American-Soviet condominium, the emergent world order will be characterized by intense international economic competition for markets, investment outlets, and sources of raw materials.

By *mercantilism* I mean the attempt of governments to manipulate economic arrangements in order to maximize their own interests, whether or not this is at the expense of others. These interests may be related to domestic concerns (full employment, price stability, etc.) or to foreign policy (security, independence, etc.).

This use of the term *mercantilism* is far broader than its eighteenth-century association with a trade and balance-of-payments surplus. The essence of mercantilism, as the concept is used in this article, is the priority of *national* economic and political objectives over considerations of *global* economic efficiency. The mercantilist impulse can take many forms in the contemporary world: the desire for a balance-of-payments surplus; the export of unemployment, inflation, or both; the imposition of import and/or export controls; the expansion of world market shares; and the stimulation of advanced technology. In short, each nation will pursue economic policies that reflect domestic economic needs and external political ambitions without much concern for the effects of these policies on other countries or on the international economic system as a whole.

The mercantilist position in effect reverses the argument of the liberals with respect to the nature and success of the interdependent world economy. In contrast to the liberal view that trade liberalization has fostered economic growth, the mercantilist thesis is that several decades of uninterrupted economic growth permitted interdependence. Growth, based in part on relatively cheap energy and other resources as well as on the diffusion of American technology abroad, facilitated the reintroduction of Japan into the world economy and the development of a closely linked Atlantic economy. Now both cheap energy and a technological gap, which were sources of rapid economic growth and global interdependence, have ceased to exist.

International competition has intensified and has become disruptive precisely because the United States has lost much of its technological lead in products and industrial processes. As happened in Britain in the latter part of the nineteenth century, the United States no longer holds the monopoly position in advanced technologies. Its exports must now compete increasingly on the basis of price and a devalued dollar. As was also the case with Great Britain, the United States has lost the technological rents associated with its previous industrial superiority. This loss of industrial supremacy on the part of the dominant industrial power threatens to give rise to economic conflict between the rising and declining centers of industrial power.

From the mercantilist perspective, the fundamental problem of modern international society has been how to organize an industrial world economy. This issue arose with the spread of industrialism from Great Britain and the emergence of several competing capitalist economies in the latter part of the nineteenth century. In the decades prior to the First World War, the issue of how to organize a world economy composed of several competing industrial economies was at the heart of international politics. The resulting commercial and imperial struggle was a major factor in the subsequent outbreak of the First World War.

The issue was never resolved during the interwar period. During the Second World War, the organization of the world economy was regarded, at least in the United States, as a central question for the postwar era. Would it be a universal liberal system or a fragmented system of regional blocs and preference arrangements? With the outbreak of the cold war and the undisputed hegemony of the United States over other capitalist economies, however, the issue faded into the background. Former President Nixon's 15 August 1971 speech signaled to mercantilist writers that with the easing of the cold war the issue has once again moved to the fore.

These mercantilist writers tend to fall into two camps of malevolent and benign mercantilism. Both tend to believe the world economy is fragmenting into regional blocs. In the wake of the relative decline of American power, nation states will form regional economic alliances or blocs in order to advance their interests in opposition to other nation states. International trade, monetary arrangements, and investment will be increasingly interregional. This regionalization of economic relations will replace the present American emphasis on multilateral free trade, the international role of the dollar, and the reign of the American multinational corporation.

Malevolent mercantilism believes regionalization will intensify international economic conflict. Each bloc centered on the large industrial powers—the United States, Western Europe, Japan, and the Soviet Union—will clash over markets, currency, and investment outlets. This would be a return to the lawlessness and beggar-thy-neighbor policies of the 1930s.

Benign mercantilism, on the other hand, believes regional blocs would stabilize world economic relations. It believes that throughout modern history universalism and regionalism have been at odds. The rationale of regional blocs is that one can have simultaneously the benefits of greater scale and interdependence and minimal accompanying costs of economic and political interdependence. Though the material gains from a global division of labor and free trade could be greater, regionalism is held to provide security and protection against external economic and political forces over which the nation state, acting alone, has little influence or control. In short, the organization of the world economy into regional blocs could provide the basis for a secure and peaceful economic order.

Benign mercantilism derives from the view of John Maynard Keynes and other Englishmen who were highly critical of an increasingly interdependent world economy. The loss of national self-sufficiency, this more benign view of mercantilism holds, is a source of economic-political insecurity and conflict. Liberalism, moreover, is detrimental to national cultural and political development. Therefore, this benign mercantilist position advocates a regionalization of the world economy as the appropriate middle road between a declining American-centered world economy and a global conflict between the capitalist economies. An inevitable clash between industrial economies can be prevented through the carving out of regional spheres of influence and the exercise of mutual self-restraint among them.

In the opinion of benign mercantilism, the thrust of much domestic and international economic policy, especially since the end of the First World War, has in fact been away from interdependence. Nations have placed a higher priority on domestic stability and policies of full employment than on the maintenance of international links; they have sought to exert national control over their monetary and other economic policies. This is what the Keynesian revolution and its emphasis on management of the domestic economy is said to be all about. The same desire for greater latitude in domestic policy underlies the increasing popularity today of flexible over fixed exchange rates and the movement toward regional blocs. Mercantilists point out that in many industrialized economies there is, in fact, a renewed questioning of whether the further benefits of trade liberalization and interdependence are worth the costs. Interdependence accentuates domestic economic adjustment problems as economic instabilities in one economy spill over into others. It causes labor dislocations, may accentuate inequalities of income distribution, and makes national planning more difficult. In short, according to these mercantilists, the world has reached the limits of interdependence and loss of national self-sufficiency.

A Critique of the Three Models

In this section of the article, I evaluate the three models and draw from each what I consider to be important insights into the nature of contemporary international economic relations. This critique is not meant to cover all points of each model but only those most directly relevant to this essay.

Sovereignty at Bay

Fundamentally, the sovereignty-at-bay thesis reduces to a question of interests and power: Who has the power to make the world economy serve its interests? This point may be best illustrated by considering the relationship of the multinational corporation and the nation state. In the writings I identified with the sovereignty-at-bay thesis, this contest is held to be most critical.

On one side of this contest is the host nation state. Its primary source of power is its control over access to its territory, that is, access to its internal market, investment opportunities, and sources of raw material. On the other side is the corporation with its capital, technology, and access to world markets. Each has something the other wants. Each seeks to maximize its benefits and minimize its costs. The bargain they strike is dependent upon how much one wants what the other has to offer and how skillfully one or the other can exploit its respective advantages. In most cases, the issue is how the benefits and costs of foreign investment are to be divided between the foreign corporation and the host economy.

The sovereignty-at-bay thesis assumes that the bargaining advantages are and always will be on the side of the corporation. In contrast to the corporation's vast resources and flexibility, the nation state has little with which to bargain. Most nation states lack the economies of scale, indigenous technological capabilities, or native entrepreneurship to free themselves from dependence upon American (or other) multinational corporations. According to this argument, the extent to which nation states reassert their sovereignty is dependent upon the economic price they are willing to pay, and it assumes that when confronted with this cost, they will retreat from nationalistic policies.

In an age of rising economic expectations, the sovereignty-at-bay thesis rests on an important truth: A government is reluctant to assert its sovereignty and drive out the multinational corporations if this means a dramatic lowering of the standard of living, increasing unemployment, and the like. But in an age when the petroleum-producing states, through cooperation, have successfully turned the tables on the multinational corporations, it becomes obvious that the sovereignty-at-bay thesis also neglects the fact that the success of the multinational corporation has been dependent upon a favorable political order. As this order changes, so will the fortunes of the multinationals.

This political order has been characterized by an absence of unity on the part of the economies that have been host to American and other corporations. The divisions between and within the host countries themselves, and the influence of the American government, left the host countries with little power to bargain effectively or to increase their relative benefits from foreign investments in their countries. Thus, in the case of Canada, the competition between the provinces and particularly between English Canada and Quebec greatly weakened Canada's position vis-à-vis American investors. Similarly, nationalistic competition for investment has weakened attempts, such as the Andean Pact, that have tried to develop a common policy toward foreign corporations. But the importance of political factors in the overseas expansion of American corporations may be best illustrated by the case of Western Europe and Japan.

American corporations coveted both the Japanese and Western European markets; they have been able to establish hundreds of subsidiaries in the latter but only a few in the former. The reason for this difference is largely political. Whereas the former has one central government controlling access to Japan's internal market of 100 million population, six (now nine) political centers have controlled access to the European Common Market. By interposing itself between powerful American corporations and intensely competitive Japanese firms that desired American capital and technology, the Japanese government has been able to prevent the latter from making agreements not desired by the government. As a consequence, the Japanese home market has been protected as the almost exclusive domain of Japanese industry. American firms have had, therefore, a strong incentive to license their technology to the Japanese or to form corporate arrangements in which the American firms were no more than a minor partner.

What the Japanese succeeded in doing was to break up the package of capital, technology, and entrepreneurship that foreign direct investment entails. The Japanese did not need the capital; they got the technology without managerial control by American corporations; entrepreneurship remained in the hands of Japanese. This Japanese example of untying the package and obtaining the technology, and in many cases the capital, required for development without loss of control has become an inspiration for economic nationalists in Latin America, Canada, and elsewhere.

In Western Europe, on the other hand, an American firm denied the right to establish a subsidiary in one Common Market country has had the option of trying another country and thereby still gaining access to the whole Market. Moreover, the strong desire of individual European countries for American investment has enabled American corporations to invest on very favorable terms. In certain cases, the firms have followed a divide-and-conquer strategy. Denied permission by President de Gaulle to invest in France, General Motors established in Belgium one of the largest automobile assembly plants in the Common Market. Through this route, the corporation gained access to the French market as well as to other European markets.

In response to this situation, de Gaulle sought to obtain West German cooperation against American investment in EEC countries. Together these two most powerful of the Six could dictate a policy the others would be forced to accept. Through the instrumentality of the Franco-German Friendship Treaty of 1963, therefore, de Gaulle sought to form a Bonn-Paris axis directed against American hegemony in Western Europe.

Although there was sentiment in West Germany favorable to taking measures to limit the rapidly growing role of American subsidiaries in EEC countries, the West German government refused to take any action that might weaken the American commitment to defend Western Europe. The United States government not only reminded the West Germans that a continued American military presence was dependent upon West German support of measures to lessen the American balance-of-payments deficit, but it also pressured West Germany to increase its military purchases from the United States and to avoid competitive arrangements with France. Largely as a result of these American pressures, the Friendship Treaty was, in effect, aborted. The first serious counteroffensive of the nation state against the multinational corporation collapsed. It is clear, however, that the outcome of this tale would have been altogether different if West Germany had desired greater military and economic independence from the United States. In short, the American corporate penetration of the European Common Market has been dependent upon the special security relationship of the United States and West Germany.

One could extend this type of analysis for the whole of American overseas investment. American investment in the Middle East, Africa, Latin America, Canada, and elsewhere has benefited from America's dominant position in the world. This position is now seriously challenged not only by the Soviet Union but by Japan, Western Europe, China, the Arabs, and Brazil in Latin America. Throughout these areas, economic nationalism is on the rise, threatening American investments and the income they bring to the United States. The thrust of this attack has been to break up the package of capital, technology, and management in order to acquire the first two without the third; the goal is greater local control through joint ventures, nationalization, and other policies. While the host countries are unlikely to "kill off" the American multinational corporations, they will increasingly make them serve local interests. This in turn will undoubtedly make direct investment abroad less attractive to American corporations.

A reversal of fortunes has already been seen in the case of the oil multinationals. The significance of the offensive by the oil-producing states against the large international oil companies is not merely that the price of oil to the United States and to the rest of the world has risen but also that the United States may lose one of its most lucrative sources of investment income. The oil crisis and Arab oil boycott which followed the 1973 Arab-Israeli war was a profound learning experience for Europe, Japan, and even the United States. The oil boycott and the behavior of the oil multinationals set into motion a series of events that cannot help but transform national attitudes and policies toward the oil multinationals. The sudden appreciation of how vulnerable governments were to the policies of the oil multinationals and how far their "sovereignty" had been compromised awakened them to the inherent dangers of overdependence on the corporations and their policies.

The French and, to a lesser extent, the Japanese responses to this experience have received the most attention. But perhaps more noteworthy was the reaction of the West German government—after the United States the nation most committed to a liberal world economy. It was the West German representative at the February 1973 Washington conference of oil-consuming nations who demanded that the United States and Western Europe undertake "a joint analysis of the price policies, profits, and taxes of oil-multinationals." While the proposal, which became part of the Washington Declaration, does not mean demise of the oil multinationals, it does suggest that the policies of nation states will increasingly impinge on the freedom of action of these particular multinational corporations.

This change in attitude toward the oil multinationals can be witnessed in the United States itself. The role of the companies as instruments of the Arab boycott has had a significant impact on American perceptions. Prior to that time, few probing questions about the oil multinationals had been raised in the press or in Congress. Other than a few "radicals," few had challenged the fact that Exxon, Gulf, and other oil multinationals paid virtually no taxes to the United States government and that they acted as sovereign entities in their dealings with the oil-producing countries. When the tables were turned, however, and the oil companies became the instruments of the Arab boycott against the United States, then even their staunchest defenders began to raise questions about tax avoidance. More importantly, the United States government took into its own hands some of the task of negotiating with the oil-producing states. Thus, when the multinationals were perceived as no longer supportive of the national interests of the United States, there was a reassertion of national sovereignty.

The case of oil and the oil multinationals is perhaps unique. Yet it does suggest that nation states have not lost their power or their will to act when they believe the multinational corporations are threatening their perceived national interests and sovereignty. The experience of the oil boycott and the role of the multinationals in carrying it out reveal the extent to which the operators and the success of these corporations have been dependent upon American power. With the relative decline of American power and the rise of governments hostile to American interests and policies, this case history at least raises the question of how the weakening of the Pax Americana will effect the status of other American multinational corporations throughout the world.

Dependencia

The weakness of the dependencia, or ultraimperialism, model is that it makes at least three unwarranted assumptions. In the first place, it assumes much greater common interest among the noncommunist industrial powers—the United States, Western Europe, and Japan—than is actually the case. Secondly, it treats the peripheral states of Asia, Africa, Latin America, Canada, and the Middle East solely as objects of international economic and political relations. Neither assumption is true. As the first assumption is considered in more detail in the next section, let us consider the second for a moment.

After nearly two centuries, the passivity of the periphery is now past. The Soviet challenge to the West and the divisions among the capitalist powers themselves have given the emerging elites in the periphery room for maneuver. These nationalist elites are no longer ignorant and pliable colonials. Within the periphery, there are coalescing centers of power that will weigh increasingly in the future world balance of power: China, Indonesia, India, Iran, Nigeria, Brazil, and some form of Arab oil power. Moreover, if properly organized and led, such centers of power in control over a vital resource, as the experience of the Organization of Petroleum Exporting Countries (OPEC) demonstrates, may reverse the tables and make the core dependent upon the periphery. For the moment at least, a perceptible shift appears to be taking place in the global balance of economic power from the owners of capital to the owners of natural resources.[12]

The third unwarranted assumption is that a quasi-Marxist theory of capitalist imperialism is applicable to the relationship of developed and lesser-developed economies today. Again, I illustrate my argument by considering the role of the multinational corporation in the lesser-developed countries, since its allegedly exploitative function is stressed by almost all dependencia theorists.

The dependencia theory undoubtedly has a good case with respect to foreign direct investment in petroleum and other extractive industries. The oil, copper, and other multinationals have provided the noncommunist industrial world with a plentiful and relatively cheap supply of minerals and energy. The dramatic reversal of this situation by the oil-producing countries in 1973-74 and the steady rise of prices of other commodities support the contention that the producing countries were not getting the highest possible price and possibly not a just price for their nonrenewable resources. But what constitutes the just price for a natural endowment that was worthless until the multinationals found it is not an easy issue to resolve.

With respect to foreign direct investment in manufacturing, the case is far more ambiguous. Even if technological rents are collected, does the foreign corporation bring more into the economy in terms of technology, capital, and access to world markets than it takes out in the form of earnings? The research of Canadian, Australian, and other economists, for example, suggest that it does. They find no differences in the corporate behavior of domestic and foreign firms; on the contrary, foreign firms are given higher marks in terms of export performance, industrial research and development, and other economic indicators.[13] Nonetheless, it would be naive to suggest that no exploitation or severe distortions of host economies have taken place.

On the other hand, it may not be unwarranted to suggest that a strong presumption exists for arguing that in terms of economic growth and industrial development, foreign direct investment in *manufacturing* is to the advantage of the host economy. A major cause of foreign direct investment is the sector-specific nature of knowledge and capital in the home economy.[14] In order to prevent a fall in their rate of profits through overinvesting at home or diversifying into unknown areas, American corporations frequently go abroad to guard against a lower rate of profit at home rather than because the superprofits abroad are attractive. Insofar as this is true, and there is sufficient evidence to warrant its plausibility, foreign direct investment benefits both the corporation and the host economy at a cost to other factors of production in the home economy. Thus, though the Marxists may be right in saying that there is an imperative for capitalism to go abroad, the effect is not to exploit but to benefit the recipient economy—a conclusion, by the way, that Marx himself would have accepted.[15]

While it is true that, in general, lesser-developed countries are economically dependent upon developed countries, the conclusions to be drawn from this fact are not self-evident. Are the countries underdeveloped because they are dependent, as dependencia theorists assume, or are they dependent because they are underdeveloped? China is underdeveloped, but it is not dependent upon any external power (though one could argue a historical case). As Benjamin Cohen has pointed out, the critical question is whether the poor are worse off economically because of this dependence.[16] Does dependence upon the developed countries entail a new loss, or foreclose opportunities of greater benefit to the economy of the undeveloped country? While the opportunity to exploit may be there, is it exercised? These are empirical questions to which no general answers can be given. Whether foreign direct investment is exploitative or beneficial depends on the type of investment, its terms, and the policies of the recipient economy itself.

The dependencia argument that foreign direct investment by multinational corporations preempts the emergence of an indigenous entrepreneurial middle class and creates a situation of technological dependence provides a clue to what is the central concern of dependence theory. Though most frequently couched solely in economic terms, the concepts of underdevelopment and dependence are more political than economic in nature. They involve an assessment of the political costs of foreign investment. They refer both to the internal political development of the recipient country and its external relations. As one of the better dependence theorists has put it, the problem "is not so much growth, i.e., expansion of a given socio-economic system, as it is 'development,' i.e., rapid and fundamental politico-socio-economic transformation."[17] In other words, foreign direct investment fosters an international division of labor that perpetuates underdevelopment and politico-economic dependencia.

This distinction between *growth* and *development* is crucial.[18] Economic growth is defined by most development economists simply as an increase in output or income per capita; it is essentially a positive and quantitative concept. The concepts of development and underdevelopment as used by dependence theorists are primarily normative and qualitative; they refer to structural changes internal to the lesser-developed economy and in external relations with the developed world. Dependencia theory really calls for a change in the current international division of labor between the core and the periphery of the international economy, in which the periphery is a supplier of raw materials and whose industries are branch plants of the core's multinational corporations.

Whatever its economic merits, the dependencia model will continue to generate opposition against the structure of the contemporary world economy and the multinational corporation throughout the underdeveloped periphery of the world economy. As these peripheral societies grow in power, one can anticipate that they will undertake initiatives that attempt to lessen their dependence upon developed countries.

Mercantilism

It seems to me that mercantilists either ignore or ascribe too little significance to certain primary facts. Although the relative power of the United States has declined, the United States remains the dominant world economy. The scale, diversity, and dynamics of the American economy will continue to place the United States at the center of the international economic system. The universal desire for access to the huge American market, the inherent technological dynamism of the American economy, and America's additional strength in both agriculture and resources—which Europe and Japan do not have—provide a cement sufficient to hold the world economy together and to keep the United States at its center.[19]

Furthermore, the United States can compensate for its loss of strength in one issue area by its continued strength in another. For example, the American economic position has indeed declined relative to Europe and Japan. Yet the continued dependence of Europe and Japan on the United States for their security provides the United States with a strong lever over the economic policies of each.

Thus, the fundamental weakness of the mercantilist model is the absence of a convincing alternative to an American-centered world economy. Western Europe, the primary economic challenger to the United States, remains internally divided; it is as yet unable to develop common policies in such areas as industry and energy or with respect to economic and monetary union. It is merely a customs union with a common agricultural policy. Moreover, like Japan, it continues to be totally dependent upon the United States for its security. As long as both Europe and Japan lack an alternative to their military and economic dependence on the United States, the mercantilist world of regional blocs lacks credibility.

The so-called energy crisis has affirmed this assessment. In the first place, the Arab oil boycott revealed the fragility of European unity. Threatened with the loss of vital supplies of Middle Eastern oil, every nation fended for itself. But subsequently, despite their reluctance, both Europe and Japan participated in the American-sponsored Washington energy conference. The American purpose in calling the conference was in part to reinforce its Middle Eastern diplomacy. But the purpose was also to reassert America's influence over its allies and to forestall policies such as competitive currency depreciation, creation of new trade barriers, and bilateral deals that would tend to fragment the world economy. No doubt, too, as the French and others charge, the United States hoped to find a solution to the energy crisis that did not threaten the position of the American oil multinationals.

Calling for cooperation from its European and Japanese allies, the United States reminded them that their security still rested on American goodwill. Moreover, in the event of a conflict over oil, America's economic weapons were far superior. Thus chastened and reminded where power continued to rest, all but the French fell into line. For the time being at least, the United States demonstrated that it retained sufficient power to maintain intact an American-centered world economy.

Yet sufficient tensions and conflicts of interests remain within this world economy to prevent one from dismissing so quickly the mercantilist thesis. Undoubtedly, the interstate conflict that will be the most vexing is the growing demand and competition for raw materials, particularly petroleum.[20] The loss of energy self-sufficiency by the United States and the growth demand for petroleum and other raw materials have already shifted the terms of trade against developed economies, and commodity prices have become major factors in world inflation. In the longer term, these changes have put the industrial powers in competition for these limited resources. They are also competing for export markets in order to finance these vital imports and for the capital the oil-producing states now have to invest. Thus, whereas in the past America's virtual control over the noncommunist world's supply of petroleum was a source of unity, today the United States is struggling with other industrial powers to insure its own position in a highly competitive environment.

In fact, one witnesses in the contemporary world the reemergence of the neo-Malthusian and Social Darwinist fears that swept industrial society and were so disruptive in the latter part of the nineteenth century. A common factor in the several imperialisms that burst forth after 1880 and fragmented the world economy was the growing fear of the potential consequences of exclusion from resources and markets. With expanding populations and productive industries believed to be dependent on foreign sources of food and raw materials, the insecurity of European states was magnified by the loss of their former relative self-sufficiency. The paradox of an interdependent world economy is that it creates sources of insecurity and competition. The very dependence of one state on another and the necessity for access to external markets and sources of raw materials cause anxieties and suspicions that exacerbate international relations.

The other reason for believing that there may be some validity in the mercantilist vision of the future is the weakening of political bonds between the United States, Western Europe, and Japan. During the height of the cold war, the foreign economic policies of these three countries were complementary. Potential conflicts over economic matters were subordinated to the necessity for political unity against the Soviet Union and China. The United States encouraged export-led growth and accepted anti-American trade discrimination in order to enable Japan and Europe to rebuild their shattered economies. Reciprocally, Japan and Europe supported the international position of the dollar. Through foreign direct investment, American corporations were able to maintain their relative share of world markets. Neither the Europeans nor the Japanese challenged America's dominant position with respect to the industrial world's access to vital raw materials, particularly Middle Eastern petroleum.

Until the early 1970s, the political benefits of this arrangement were regarded as outweighing the economic costs to each partner. With the movement toward détente and with the revival of the European and Japanese economies, however, the political benefits have receded in importance and the concern over costs has increased. As a consequence, the United States and its industrial partners now desire reforms of the world's trading and monetary systems that would enable each to pursue its own particular set of interests and to limit that of the others. For example, the United States has proposed reforms of the trade and monetary systems that would limit the ability of the Europeans and the Japanese to run up huge trade surpluses. Europe and Japan, for their part, desire to preserve this scope and to limit the privileges of the United States as world banker.

Regardless of the outcome of the negotiations over the future of the international monetary system, one thing is certain: whatever privilege is retained by the dollar will not be sufficient to enable the United States to behave as it has in the past. Gone are the days when the United States could run an immense balance-of-payments deficit in order to support foreign commitments, to buy up foreign assets, and at the same time pursue a full employment policy at home. It will no longer be able to expand overseas at a relatively low cost to the American standard of living. Having already lost its technological superiority and technological rents, the United States will have to finance its economic and military position abroad through currency devaluation and a current account surplus. Thus the cost of any effort to maintain US political and economic hegemony will bear upon the American people themselves. The weight and popular appreciation of this cost will profoundly alter American attitudes toward America's world role and toward its European and Japanese allies. These changes in political interests and perceptions cannot but help to push the world in a mercantilistic direction.

Implications for International Organization

What then do these three models and their relative merits tell us about the future of international economic organizations? As a consequence of the relative decline of American power and of other developments treated in this article, there is little reason to believe that many new international institutions will be created, but it is likely that the nature and functioning of existing institutions will be profoundly altered.

In a world of national states, international organizations tend to reflect the power and interests of the dominant states in the international system. From this perspective, the international organizations founded at the end of the Second World War reflected the then predominant states in the system. As the structure of the United Nations reflected the distribution of power between the United States and the Soviet Union, so the so-called Bretton Woods system and the institutions associated with it—the International Monetary Fund (IMF), the World Bank, and subsequently the General Agreement on Trade and Tariffs (GATT)—reflected the power and interests of the dominant world economy, the United States.

In both cases, the relative decline of American power over the past several decades has led to profound modifications of these political and economic institutions. Thus, with the growth of Soviet power in the United Nations Security Council and of the so-called nonaligned bloc in the General Assembly, the United Nation's role in American foreign policy and as an institution have been altered significantly. In terms of the major political issues of the world, the United Nations has moved from center stage to the sidelines. A similar transformation can be seen in the area of international economic institutions. This can be witnessed, for example, in the case of the IMF and the negotiations for the reform of the international monetary system which have taken place outside its aegis.

The transformation of the IMF began in the late 1950s with the gradual weakening of the dollar as an international currency. After 1958 the American balance-of-payments deficit began to assume major proportions. The moderate deficits of the previous decade became severe. A drain began on the large gold hoard the United States had accumulated before and during the Second World War. Between 1957 and 1963, US gold holdings fell from $22.8 billion to $15.5 billion, and foreign dollar holdings (official and private) rose from $15.1 to $28.8 billion. By 1968, American gold holdings fell to $10.9 billion, and foreign dollar holdings rose to $31.5 billion.

As Europeans and others began to turn dollars into gold, it became obvious that the United States could not continue to meet all gold claims. The immediate American response was to initiate numerous makeshift expedients—the gold pool, currency swap arrangements, the General Arrangements to Borrow, etc.—to reinforce the position of the dollar. Additionally, the United States undertook unilateral measures such as the Interest

Equalization Tax (1963), "voluntary" controls on the export of capital (1965), and, eventually, mandatory controls on foreign direct investment (1968) to stem the outflow of dollars.

Despite these and other measures, monetary crises continued to mount throughout the 1960s. In response to these crises, demands mounted for a fundamental reform of the international monetary system. In the ensuing monetary negotiations, as in trade negotiations, the Western powers divided into three positions. On one side were ranged the United States and Great Britain. On the other stood France. In the middle was West Germany, which attempted to reconcile the Common Market and the Atlantic powers.

Whereas the United States wanted a reform that would ensure the continued privileged position of the dollar, France under de Gaulle wanted a reform that would dethrone the dollar and thus would redistribute economic power in the West. This would allegedly be achieved if the world returned to what de Gaulle believed was the true measure of wealth and guarantor of political independence, namely, gold. A return to the gold standard would not only enhance the power of France, which had replenished its gold reserves, but the United States would have to expend real wealth in order to maintain and/or expand its hegemony. If other nations refused to accept any more dollars and demanded gold, the United States would be forced to bring its payments into balance and to liquidate its global economic and military position. In short, a shift from the dollar to gold as the world's reserve currency would mean a retrenchment of American power in Europe, Asia, and around the globe.

At the same time that the United States desired to maintain the privileged position of the dollar, the basic instability of the system was appreciated by all. An international monetary system and an expanding trade system that depended upon the deficits of the United States were prone to crisis. From the perspective of most countries, a return to gold was both politically and economically undesirable, however, In the late sixties, therefore, extensive IMF negotiations produced an "international money" called special drawing rights (SDRs).

The United States had desired the SDRs to relieve the pressure on the dollar while preserving its ultimate reserve role. France wanted nothing less than the reimposition of monetary restraints on the United States. Between the two of them stood West Germany and its desire to hold together the European and Atlantic powers. Due largely to German initiatives, a compromise solution was finally reached, which gave the Americans their SDRs in exchange for greater European voting power in the International Monetary Fund. Thus, while the IMF would have the power to "issue" SDRs as an international reserve on a limited scale, Europe (if it were united) could exercise a veto over American policy in the IMF.

In short, the internal structure and functioning of the IMF was reconstituted to reflect the redistribution of world economic and monetary power. The United States no longer ran the organization. Control over it was now shared by the European powers. Similarly, one can anticipate that the immense growth of Arab monetary balances will lead to a further internal transformation of the IMF. By one method or other, this redistribution of monetary power will be given an institutional form.

In the areas of trade and investment, the continuing redistribution of power among nation states will find a response in the nature and functioning of international economic organizations. In trade this has already begun to happen, as the United States and other industrial nations ponder the future of the GATT. Perhaps the German initiative at the

Washington energy conference in calling for an international investigation of the oil multinationals presages what many have long advocated—a GATT for investment. If so, it too will reflect the changes that have taken place in the world's distribution of economic and industrial power.

Conclusion

In conclusion, what does this redistribution of world power imply for the future of the interdependent world economy? Today, the liberal world economy is challenged by powerful groups (especially organized labor) within the dominant economy; the dominant economy itself is in relative decline. With the decline of the dominant economic power, the world economy may be following the pattern of the latter part of the nineteenth century and of the 1930s and may be fragmenting into regional trading and monetary blocs. This would be prevented, of course, if the United States, as it is presently trying to do, were to reassert its waning hegemony over Western Europe, Japan, and the rest of the noncommunist world economy.

In the wake of the decline of American power and the erosion of the political base upon which the world economy has rested, the question arises whether the wisest policy for the United States is to attempt to reassert its dominance. May not this effort in the areas of trade, money, investment, and energy exacerbate the conflicts between the United States, Western Europe, and Japan? If so, a future that could be characterized increasingly by benign mercantilism could well be transformed into its more malevolent relative. If this were to happen, the United States and its allies would be the losers.

This admonition suggests that the United States should accept a greater regionalization of the world economy than it has been wont to accept in the past. It implies greater representation and voice for other nations and regional blocs in international economic organizations. While such a policy of retrenchment would no doubt harm the interests of American corporations and other sectors of the American economy, the attempt to hold on to rather than adjust to the shifting balance of world power could be even more costly for the United States in the long run.

In a world economy composed of regional blocs and centers of power, economic bargaining and competition would predominate. Through the exercise of economic power and various trade-offs, each center of the world economy would seek to shift the costs and benefits of economic interdependence to its own advantage. Trade, monetary, and investment relations would be the consequence of negotiations as nation states and regional blocs sought to increase the benefits of interdependence and to decrease the costs. This in fact has been the direction of the evolution of the international economy, from a liberal to a negotiated system, since the rise of large and rival economic entities in the latter part of the nineteenth century.

Therefore, debate and policy planning today should not focus on economic independence or dependence but on the nature and consequences of economic interdependence. Economic interdependence may take many forms; it may affect the welfare of nations in very different ways. Some will emphasize security; others, efficiency, low rates of inflation, or full employment. The question of how these benefits and costs will be distributed is at the heart of the increasingly mercantilistic policies of nation states in the contemporary world.

NOTES

1. Edward Hallet Carr, *The Twenty Years' Crisis 1919-1939* (London: Macmillan and Co., 1951), p. 117.

2. John Diebold, "Multinational Corporations—Why be Scared of Them?," *Foreign Policy*, no. 12 (Fall 1973): 79-95.

3. "The Future of International Business," *The Economist*, 22 January 1972.

4. Diebold, p. 87.

5. The literature on dependencia, or underdevelopment, has now become legend. One of the better statements of this thesis is Osvaldo Sunkel, "Big Business and 'Dependencia': A Latin American View," *Foreign Affairs* 50 (April 1972): 517-31. For an excellent and critical view of the dependencia thesis, see Benjamin J. Cohen, *The Question of Imperialism— The Political Economy of Dominance and Dependence* (New York: Basic Books, 1973), chapter 6.

6. "The Multinational Corporation and the Law of Uneven Development," in *Economics and World Order—From the 1970's to the 1990's*, ed. Jagdish Bhagwati (New York: The Macmillan Co., 1972), p. 113 and passim.

7. Ibid., p. 114.

8. Quoted in Cohen, pp. 190-91.

9. *Monopoly Capital—An Essay on the American Economic and Social Order* (New York: Monthly Review Press, 1966).

10. Constantine Vaitsos, "Transfer of Resources and Preservation of Monopoly Rents," Economic Development Report No. 168, Development Advisory Service, Harvard University, 1970. (Mimeographed).

11. See, for example, David Calleo and Benjamin Rowland, *America and the World Political Economy* (Bloomington, Ind.: Indiana University Press, 1973). Mercantilism is also the real theme of Ernest Mandel's *Europe vs. America—Contradictions of Imperialism* (New York: Monthly Review Press, 1970).

12. See C. Fred Bergsten, "The Threat From The Third World," *Foreign Policy*, no. 11 (Summer 1973): 102-24.

13. See, for example, A. E. Safarian, *Foreign Ownership of Canadian Industry* (Toronto: University of Toronto Press, 1973).

14. This point is developed in US Congress, Senate Committee on Labor and Public Welfare, *The Multinational Corporation and the National Interest* (report prepared for the Committee), 93rd Cong., 1st sess., 1973, Committee print.

15. Karl Marx, "The Future Results of British Rule in India," in *Karl Marx on Colonialism and Modernization,* ed. Shlomo Avineri (Garden City, N.Y.: Doubleday, 1968), pp. 125-31.

16. Cohen, chapter 6.

17. This distinction is developed by Keith Griffin, *Underdevelopment in Spanish America* (Cambridge, Mass.: The M.I.T. Press, 1969), p. 117.

18. For a more detailed analysis of the distinction, see J. D. Gould, *Economic Growth in History* (London: Methuen and Co., 1972), chapter 1.

19. A forceful statement of this position is Raymond Vernon's "Rogue Elephant in the Forest: An Appraisal of Transatlantic Relations," *Foreign Affairs* 51 (April 1973): 573-87.

20. See Helmut Schmidt, "The Struggle for the Global Product," *Foreign Affairs* 52 (April 1974): 437-51.

23 / The Future of International Business

Norman Macrae

A Sudden Tomorrow

A revolution is coming in international business, and it is probable that we are all grossly underestimating what is in train. The paths ahead will depend on matters technological, matters organisational, matters political and probably only in small degree on matters financial. It is most honest to begin with a guess about the technological prospect, although this unfortunately means that this survey will start by sounding most extreme.

Man's material advance in the past two centuries has been based on his increase in control over matter and energy, at a pace that has accelerated in each of the past eight generations after having stayed remarkably stable even in the most advanced communities during the previous 3,000 to 10,000 years. To this post-1760 matter-cum-energy revolution there has been added in the past decade a breakthrough in the processing of information (computers, etc.) and a nascent breakthrough in the distribution of information (telecommunications by satellite, the beginnings of packaged and computerised "learning programmes," maybe even at last a start towards understanding of the learning process which we are at present instilling into both school-children and adult workers by the most labour-intensive, and therefore inefficient, possible means).

As is usual in the early years of extraordinary scientific advances, when producers who do not quite know what they are doing are trying to sell to consumers who do not understand what on earth they are about, a large number of the commerical pioneers of the new technologies have fallen flat on their faces. This has, again as usual, caused delight among the luddite majority of mankind. When many of the early car manufacturers were going bust in Edwardian days, *The Economist* won considerable plaudits from the then Establishment by publishing a well-reasoned article called "The Triumph of the Horse."

In fact, however, any predictions in the first decade of this century about the coming triumph of the horse were quite ineffably silly; and so are any business projections today which fail to pay central heed to the explosive changes which computer and telecommunicative technology are highly likely to bring about. My first four positive guesses, after wobbling a lot during research for this survey, are:

From Norman Macrae, "The Future of International Business," *The Economist* (January 22, 1972), pp. viii–xxx. Reprinted by permission of the publisher. Notes have been numbered.

(1) Some time in the period 1972-2012 we probably will make the breakthrough into genuinely intelligent use of computers, in place of today's damn silly use of them. The acceleration of both innovation (which is already advancing fast) and teaching capabilities (which for centuries have hardly advanced at all) will then become exponential.

(2) Even before the end of this century telecommunication may become virtually costless, and should certainly be in no way dependent on distance for its price. It should then become as cheap to ring China or Peru by picture-phone as to ring the office next door, with very large eventual consequences on where we think we have to live and work.

(3) It will then be discovered that the capacity for making basic materials, or unnecessary substitutes for them, exists practically everywhere. Today's prophets of a coming famine in basic materials—like their predecessors, yesterday's Malthusians—are probably going to be made to look more ludicrously wrong than their high innate intelligence really makes them deserve.

(4) Contrary to the present fashionable assumptions, these three trends will not increase the power of the big multinational business corporations. The most successful business organisations of the next 40 years are more likely to be fairly small but wholly transnational companies, of a rather new type. Some of today's biggest and best-known multinational companies may either have to be split into component parts by reverse takeover bids within the next four decades, or else may go bust.

At every stage of this survey it is necessary to say that there is no possibility that any of its forecasts will come out exactly right. My object at each stage is just to explain why I have come to think that it is more logical to hold the view propounded here than to hold the opposite view (which is usually the more conventional view).

If any of these first four technological and organisational forecasts proves to be even to that extent on beam, the social, political and financial consequences will be immense. In the following articles I turn to examining them in more detail. The emergence of events somehow recognisably something like them could bring about a very sudden tomorrow for all mankind.

Transglobal Teach In

The potentialities for computer-based learning systems were assumed to be obvious as long as ten years ago. Remember that a computer can beat even the brain of an Einstein at quickly deciding what is the best next information to give you, on the basis of the feedback from you to date; and most village schoolmarms are some way behind Einstein. In a surge of joint ventures between famous publishers and electronics manufacturers, a large number of American firms were created in the early 1960s to cash in on this huge opportunity for "educational technology." Many of them then went bust.

These failures overwhelmed both the respectable firms that tried to sell in America to school districts and universities (but found the market far too fragmented for what a mass system of educational technology really required) and the merchants of gimmicky and worthless packages peddled to individual dupes. Since teachers and educators almost everywhere have responded with a sad lack of imagination to other twentieth-century educational aids—from radio through television to new audiovisual devices—it is tempting to say that they will block computer-based methods for decades to come. There are three reasons why my own forecast is more optimistic.

Best for the Poorest

First, the advantages of computer-based learning systems are going to be very great. In a teaching profession where an urge for idealism really does break through more quickly than any urge for efficiency, the new technology will eventually win the decent do-gooders' vote, because it is going to be much more humane to the less able of our children than a purely human-based system can be. In a class of 25 kids today, there are up to 25 different learning patterns waiting to be dissatisfied in each non-automated lesson. When the teacher tries to proceed at a median pace, she creates small tensions for the brightest children whom she holds back, and cruel tensions for the least bright children whom she feels subconsciously obliged to chivvy (especially when she denies doing any such thing).

In sharp contrast to this, computer-based learning-systems will be able to bring an individually-tailored programme to each child and let him proceed at his own pace. To quote John Diebold, the American management consultant and computer expert:[1]

> Before the end of the 1970s, billion-bit computer memories will be relatively common, and it will be possible for a machine to keep records of every student's responses to key questions in instructional programmes. Thus each child's learning patterns will be discoverable and sequences of instruction can be made truly individual. Set in a heuristic configuration, drawing from recorded responses by other children with similar difficulties, the computer could by itself check out alternative ways of overcoming or circumventing the student's difficulties, vastly improving the efficiency of the energy the student applies to his education. In a very real sense, students in a future automated classroom could make "the system" serve their own needs and desires as no merely human system ever can.

Of course, one of the great things that will emerge from this in the best schools is that the teachers will then be freed from much of the rote and drill of teaching, and (to quote Charles Silberman) will be able increasingly to "become a diagnostician, tutor and Socratic leader rather than a drill master, the role he or she is usually forced to play." But the greater gain will be the effect in the worst schools. Computer-based instruction has already shown its worth in Negro ghetto schools in America, where—even in the present pathetically primitive state of the art—the disadvantaged child gets a feeling of adequacy for the first time as he acquires control over the computer through his console with its light pen attachment (and by 1980 there will be machines that respond to voice commands—ie, will be able to interpret and evaluate them).

Training the Underdeveloped

This leads to the second reason for optimism about the spread of computer-based learning systems, which is their effect on underdeveloped countries. The great economic tragedy of the past two centuries is that the process of enrichment which started so extraordinarily around 1760 has been confined only to the rich one-third of the world. The decisive barrier has lain in lack of facilities for communication with the other two-thirds: to a small extent communication in the transport of goods, but to a much greater extent communication of education and knowledge.

There have been two main difficulties here. The first has been the inelasticity of supply even of ordinary education in poor countries: especially while we have all laboured under the belief that we can instil the learning process even for literacy only over long years at school for small children taught in a labour-intensive way by scarce supplies of very skilled people. Poor countries have not had sufficient supplies of such skilled people, least of all those willing to go to live in the poorest areas where the need is greatest. Secondly, it has become apparent that there is a special difficulty of communicating in these countries the more multi-layered sort of knowledge which is generally called knowhow, and which requires two-way involvement in a teaching process of trial and error and retrial.

One of the great hopes for the world in 1972–2012 is that computer-based instruction ought to be especially well placed to break both these impediments down. In these circumstances, it will be surprising if international aid programmes some time in the next 40 years do not concentrate heavily on facilities for computer-based plus other audiovisual (cassette, televisual, etc.) learning systems. After the improvements in multi-processing and multi-programming capabilities expected over the next few years, it may be possible for computer time to be shared by many, perhaps hundreds of thousands, of students, each with an individually tailored programme, plugged into mass systems that are physically located thousands of miles away.

It is just arguable that richer countries, with good labour-intensive schools already, will have less need of such facilities; but as the cost of labour-intensive education will constantly mount, and the cost of computer-based education will steadily fall (as well as its quality dramatically improve), my own view is that richer countries will be very silly if they try to do without them.

The third reason why computer-based instruction should take off will lie in the increasing need of business for the quickest and most cost-effective methods of training and retraining. As we will see later, profitable investment by American and other multinational manufacturers has hitherto tended to go mainly to areas where knowhow has been easily teachable—which has tended to mean only either to other developed countries or to countries inhabited by the ablest (ie, expatriate) sorts of Chinese. Wages in these areas are going up. The world's economic situation will be changed indeed if it is going to be possible to teach knowhow for the manufacture of almost all transportable things—including the all-important capacity to organise and not merely the capacity to be nominally aware of facts—by two way, trial-and-error, heuristic (ie, serving to discover), computer-cum-cassette packaged learning programmes to very low wage areas. This will depend on the advance of telecommunicative as well as computer technology.

Costless Telecommunication?

My second main forecast . . . was that some time before the end of this century telecommunication could become virtually costless, and should certainly be in no way dependent on distance for its price. Once we have tossed enough and less transient communications satellites into frictionless space (and tossing them up will really become very cheap), it need put no more strain on the system if I ring up China by picturephone than I now put on our internal office telephone system if I ring up my secretary in the next room. Instead of commuting daily from Wimbledon to central London, it would then surely be more sensible for me (and anybody else with a non-manual job) to commute daily into central London by telecommunication from my chosen abode anywhere in the world, which would probably be a beach hut in some tropical island.

Even more important for industrial relocation than this growth of personal telecommunication, computers from all over the world will be talking across these costless airwaves to people and to other computers. Most of them will have more instructional, all of them will have more organised, things than I have to say.

There are two provisos. One is technical. We are going to have to be able to generate pure, coherent radiation, tightly and precisely controlled in frequency so that we produce separate signals side by side in the radio spectrum and thus open up many new channels for communications purposes. The odds are that this will be achieved. The other proviso is that market forces must be allowed to work efficiently in telecommunications. This is more doubtful. All over the world public and private monopolies in telecommunications are constantly seeking to protect old investments that they made in the 1920s against the more modern telecommunications which a freer market would bring in today.

Small Transnational Companies?

If this reform in telecommunications does come about, I suggested . . . that the industrial swing in 1972–2012 may be towards rather small but wholly transnational companies, organised in a totally new way.

As a prototype for the most successful sorts of firm in 30 or 40 years' time, it may be most sensible to visualise small groups of organisers of systems designers, all living in their own comfortable homes in pleasant parts of the world and communicating with others in the group (and with the systems designers) by picturephone: arranging for the telecommunication of the latest best computerised learning programme on how to make a better mousetrap (or, more probably, how to make the next-successor-but five to integrated circuits) rooftop to rooftop to about 2,000 quickly trainable, even if only newly literate, workers assembled before their two-way-teaching-in computer terminals by some just tolerably efficient organising sub-contractor (also taught by long-distance telecommunicated computer lessons) in west Africa or Pakistan.

One general forecast in this survey is that in the next 40 years the rich one-third of the world should concentrate more on the knowledge-creating and knowledge-processing industries, while more and more of the old manufacturing industries should move to any parts of the poorer two-thirds of the world which are politically stable. We shall be returning several times to this point. But the next question is: can a great surge in production in the poorer countries be ecologically afforded? How much heed do we need to pay to the old catchphrase that there cannot be infinite growth in a finite world?

The Poor Two-Thirds

One of my main arguments in this survey is that manufacturing industry will move increasingly to the poorer countries in the next four decades. Any really big and really new west European motor manufacturing complex that is established in the early 1980s, to make cars for sale in west Europe itself, is most likely to be situated in North Africa. Thereafter most manufacturing plants will probably be established even farther afield, while North America and west Europe and their contiguous areas concentrate increasingly on knowledge-producing and knowledge-processing—instead of goods-producing—forms of employment. Whenever one says this, somebody asks what the "knowledge-producing" and "knowledge-processing" jobs will be. The answer is that most of them have not yet been invented, in the same way as quite a lot of today's large appointments advertisements in, say, the *Daily Telegraph* would have been totally incomprehensible to anybody 15 (let alone 40) years ago. On the day on which I happen to be writing this, these advertisements include vacancies for a systems analyst to work in digital computer applications in process control, a chief security officer for a containerbase, a marina property development manager. . . .

In the poorer countries the great barrier to advance will be political instability, especially in countries that are industrialising and therefore perhaps turning urban. During the first 20 postwar years 17 of the 20 Latin American republics suffered from successful coups d'état, and since 1960 the pace and bloodiness of insurgencies in Africa and parts of Asia have become worse than that (although I have not regarded it as part of my necessary research for this survey to waste time counting them).

But the arguments on the other side, which I think will eventually outweigh this admittedly considerable disincentive to investment called fear of bloody revolution, are in order of importance:

(1) The learning process and training process for manufacturing skills are likely to become more automated, and cheaply importable over long distances by what might be called telecomputational methods.

(2) Many of the television sets now sold in America under American brand names are really already made in places like Taiwan, and the same areas of south-east Asia became the cheapest producers of integrated circuits within ten years of such things really being invented in an effective form.

(3) Note that electronics and some other modern products have thus led the migration to become poor countries' exporting manufacturing industries, taking over the lead from older (and largely women's) industries like textiles. One reason is admittedly that computers and electronics raced right through to become transnational industries before slow-moving domestic and protectionist organisations like trade unions and trade associations quite realised what was happening. But another reason is that these new industries have been intelligently designed from the start with fairly simple production systems that do not demand the use of much lengthily-taught craft labour.

(4) In transferring even trade-union-protected western industries to their own country, the Japanese have managed to break down production processes in the same modern way. Within a decade and a half they were then often exceeding the west in efficiency even at nearly western wage rates. Well within our period of 1972–2012 my guess is that it will become a much more systematic and common occupation to work out the best way in which 5,000 fairly primitive people in the middle of Africa could best make refrigerators there, and then set the system down in a packaged learning programme. Left-wing academics often complain that one of the great misfortunes of modern technology, as spread by western multinational corporations, is that it is geared towards the needs and capabilities of the rich countries both as producers and consumers, and may therefore be quite unsuitable for the poor two-thirds of the world. Actually, multinational companies are now slowly beginning to gear their technology towards the capabilities of the poor countries as producers, but left-wing trade unions

are the last people that they want to make aware of this. Mr. Jack Jones would not like it at all.

(5) Manufacturing has accounted for a sharply declining share of American employment since the mid-1950s. In continental west Europe, manufacturing industry has been kept up only by importing foreign labour from the south. Now the industries will move south instead. In labour-intensive industries, lower wage countries have an obvious advantage; while, in very capital-intensive industries, rich countries' workers will no longer do the night shifts now required for the capital equipment's full use.

(6) The organisational mechanism for transferring a lot of manufacturing production to lower wage countries now exists, thanks to the growth of multinational corporations. It is with the emerging world of and for the multinational companies that the next four articles in this survey will be mainly concerned.

Giants in the Late Afternoon

The biggest business development of the past two decades has been the growth of giant multinational corporations. . . . When I started on research for this survey, I was inclined to share the fashionable belief that by about 1992 the 300 biggest multinational corporations will totally dominate the world's business scene. I now believe that it is late afternoon for some of the giants instead. This conclusions arises from (a) looking at the lessons of industrial history; (b) looking at the forward prospects. Let us turn to the history lesson first.

• • •

The fashionable business of writing histories of multinationalism often begins with the trading companies of ancient Mesopotamia, the merchant bankers of the middle ages, or the East India Company and other British multinationals founded four centuries ago. Most of the analogies drawn with these are nonsense, but the story of the East India Company does contain two useful lessons, which go on being ignored today.

One was the familiar overemphasis on the importance of raw materials. The ambitious younger sons who enlisted in John Company thought that they would make their fortunes by sending rich spices back home, but those that prospered did so mainly by becoming much wider-ranging contractors on the spot.

Secondly, in so far as the colonial spice and other plantation companies did begin a species of multinational company operation—based on the assumption that the inferior local inhabitants would never learn to farm sugar, tea, rubber, etc, efficiently—their assumption has been ended in our lifetimes. As Vernon puts it, in Latin America: "The cultivation and sale of coffee may have seemed a formidable undertaking to the Yucate-can farmer of 1900; the management of a sugar plantation may have appeared beyond the reach of the Cuban poor of 1950. But these pursuits eventually lost their occult quality." In the same way the management of many manufacturing processes in underdeveloped countries will lose its occult quality in 1972-92, especially when the learning systems for such management are scientifically assembled on computer tape. The average new venture of a multinational company in a poor country in future may have something like the following life cycle: (a) a small initial period of loss; then (b) a slightly longer period of semi-monopoly profits: and then (c) the venture should be sold to local entrepreneurs just before other local imitators come along to undercut it. The organisations of today's big multinational companies, so far as I have seen them during research on this survey, are not yet well-oriented to operate in this way.

. . .

The conclusion from the history lesson so far is that the least successful multinational corporations may be those that seek merely to get close to some foreign market or to go hunting for raw materials. The most successful will be those that temporarily know how to use skilled labour, or perform some other managerial task, more efficiently than the local Establishment does.

. . .

Among definitions of a multinational corporation I have a special regard for that attributed by the *Daily Telegraph* to Hawker Siddeley's Sir Arnold Hall: "A multinational corporation is an American-registered company manufacturing its products where labour is cheapest, and channelling its profits to another country where taxation is lowest or preferably non-existent."

Sir Arnold's sort of multinational is the sort which I think will thrive in 1972-92. The next article discusses whether today's very big multinational corporations are well-placed to continue to play this role.

Ends of Some Roads

The general assumptions today are that the big multinational corporations will be the most efficient media in 1972-2012 for (a) training manufacturing labour in today's poorer countries; (b) standing up against possible expropriation by governments in those poorer countries; (c) spreading modern management techniques; (d) spreading technology; (e) exporting capital.

The first two of these arguments seem to me wrong, and the last three very dubious.

Labour and Multinational Unions

Until 15 years ago it was widely assumed that the migration of manufacturing industry (especially exporting industry) to poorer countries would be led by old-fashioned industries like cotton textiles. Instead, the most successful industries in Asian centres of multinational enterprises like Singapore and Taiwan have been rather modern industries like electronics; because (a) their production systems have been designed to be mobile from the start; and (b) they were rushed through to the transnational stage almost before trade unions in big manufacturing centres like America and Britain realised that they existed.

Redesigning of systems, and automation of the training process, will make it much easier over the next three decades to move even traditional manufacturing industries (up to and including export plants for automobiles) to the poorer countries. This time big international trade unions will realise what is happening, and they may co-ordinate strike actions against the home plants of giant international firms: with the cry that export-oriented plants can only be built in North Africa if North African workers are at once paid Detroit or Coventry wages, even while still only at North African standards of efficiency.

The last thing that the employing classes—including the socialist or military governments—in these poorer countries want is the entry of international trade unions into their territories, pushing up multinational firms' wage bills and thus spoiling their own local labour markets. This is one reason why these governments may increasingly prefer—if the chance arises—to import their technology through smaller transnational firms.

No Gunboats, but Some Scandals

Since most of the countries of the world have gnps smaller than the annual sales of the biggest 50 or so multinational companies, it is fashionable to say that many of them must be increasingly worried that the giant corporations will challenge their sovereignty. Actually, the heads of the biggest multinational manufacturing corporations are those who are most terrified of any accusation of dabbling in neo-colonial politics, and they certainly have no gunboats for hire; some are more liable to grovel disgustingly to the most odious local governments instead. Nevertheless, there is going to be a great *succès de scandale* against a lot of big multinational companies in the next ten years. Any day now some polemicist will make a lot of money with a hair-raising book revealing in detail the really very naughty things some of the biggest have been doing in their international accounts—while playing the two business games that are euphemistically called "tax planning" and "avoidance of exchange rate risk."

Since most foreign subsidiaries' accounts are those of unregistered companies, they do not have to be published in the full glare of an inquiring financial press. Some of the big multinationals have therefore taken full advantage of all the odd ways in which inter-subsidiary sales, loans, royalty and fee payments, service contracts, etc, can be priced. If the Mammoth Corporation's subsidiary in Avaricia (which taxes company profits very heavily) is doing some job for the Mammoth Corp's subsidiary in India (which taxes profits more heavily still), then this product or service may first be sold at an unprofitably low dollar price by Mammoth Avaricia to Mammoth's nil-taxpaying "central management services company" or "trading and finance subsidiary" in Liechstenstein; Mammoth Liechstenstein may then resell at a very high dollar price to Mammoth India, so that both Mammoth Avaricia and Mammoth India make a tax loss while Mammoth Liechstenstein has a profit that will be tax-free so long as it is being used for the whole multinational's finance (or is being lent on the Eurodollar market) and will just bear American corporation tax when it is finally brought back as a dividend to the United States.

Some European multinationals are even keener than American multinationals at playing this intellectually fascinating game, with its many side-issues (do not find yourself charging high prices on intra-company sales that pass through ad valorem customs duties, remember the timing of budgets, etc); but, when the exchange rates are foolishly fixed, the Americans are probably best at the game of the one-way exchange option. In Britain before 1967 a lot of foreign subsidiaries in London borrowed heavily from every British source they could, sent all liquid funds out of the country, and allowed their group's foreign subsidiaries in Germany enormously lengthy periods in which to settle their bills. Under floating rates a two-way risk is introduced into this branch of the game, which is what most multinational firms meant when they queued up between last August and

December to tell the world's finance ministers that "floating causes crippling uncertainties to business."

These devices are not so open to small multinational firms, but they are not going to be open to big ones for very much longer. It is pretty clear that some international regulations will be brought in, at least about proper publication of foreign subsidiaries' accounts. The best hope for the big multinational firms is that these rules will be drawn up by bodies like the European commission at Brussels, or by the central authorities of other sprouting free trade areas. They will then probably be responsible rules. If the counterattack against the big multinationals is less centrally organised, then the battles may just take place in individual countries in isolated acts of harassment and expropriation (perhaps sometimes by declaring a local subsidiary of a big multinational bankrupt, which, in technical terms, at some stage of the great financial game, some of the locally overborrowed ones legally are).

At present, the big multinationals are on the defensive in their efforts to please governments and public opinion, but are often still preparing to fight the last unnecessary war instead of the next necessary one. "We recognise the importance of promoting local staff to the very top posts especially in areas like Africa," say the big firms.

Awkwardly, this could be a crashing local mistake. The dictators who rule most African countries would view with the gravest suspicion the rise of local boss men over the local subsidiaries of really big multinational companies. The immediate post-independence rulers made the great error of Africanising or Asianising the general staffs of their armies, and those general staffs promptly ran coups d'état against them in a way that the original nice old English generals on loan from Aldershot would never have done. Projects for building up a powerful black corporate manager class for local subsidiaries of very big multinational corporations, with large payrolls, are not at present the black dictators' dearest desire. Originally, the rulers' demand to multinationals to "Africanise your staff" meant "give bribes to my brothers and cousins so that they can support me if I am democratically thrown out of power"; but now that few African rulers allow themselves to be democratically thrown out of power, they are becoming rather less interested in bribes and much more interested in thwarting the build-up of local power bases that are possible alternatives to themselves.

Does Maxi-Management Work?

There has been a revolution in managerial techniques in the past 20 years. The big multinational corporations certainly served to spread it around the world. The most obvious example of a big multinational's successful managerial system is that founded by the awe-inspiring Mr Hal Geneen, chief executive since the late 1950s of the now misleadingly named International Telephone and Telegraph (the world's largest conglomerate, running everything from Sheraton Hotels to Avis car rentals). Those who manage subsidiaries for Mr Geneen have to fill in his now famous reams of forms; every month there is a searching examination of whether the latest results from each subsidiary show that it is living up to the targets of growth and earnings per share that have been set for it, and suggestions will come for quick action if anything is even beginning to go wrong.

Is this sort of managerial revolution already beginning to eat its own children? After research during this survey, my own judgment is:

(1) A system like ITT's works when the genius who devised the forms also looks at the results filled in, and keeps changing the forms accordingly. It does not work when the system becomes institutionalised.

(2) Some small, and personally dominated, transnational firms, which have sprung up since the mid-1960s, now have rather better forms even than ITT's. The good ones would look incredibly anti-social if anybody ever published them (eg, a successful form for 1972 would probably say "In labour-intensive subsidiaries in the developed world this year, we should increase average selling prices by at least 8 per cent, but disguisedly. Give me your proposals for achieving this").

(3) In many of the big and established multinational companies (not including ITT), the reporting system has become institutionalised; and is accordingly disastrous.

I talked to several executives in the multinational which would probably have been voted by most people in the late 1950s (the pre-Geneen age) as the most brilliant of the big multinationals. Although the head office does not realise this, the managerial system there has now almost totally broken down. The forms that the executives in the subsidiaries have to fill in are basically of 1950s' vintage (in some respects even earlier). If they were filled in seriously, the planning consequences would now actually be perverse: because the forms pay insufficient attention to the movement in this corporation since 1958 to (a) a shorter average life for almost every product; (b) more capital-intensive types of production (because they are types that incorporate higher technology and thus higher development cost); (c) greater diversity of markets—eg, between consumer goods that are bought by 4 million customers and capital goods bought by four. So, of course, the forms are not filled in seriously, and whole sectors of the operations of this great and technologically advanced multinational corporation are really run by an old boy network as non-statistics-oriented as that which, by about 1968, was already evident in Rolls-Royce.

When institutional decay has reached this stage, the new fashion among some quite big multinationals is to say that executives should not be taught to pay attention to balance sheets anyway. They should concern themselves instead with something which is sometimes called "behavioural management": a concept that might originally have had some sense in it, but that is going to be adopted as a cloak by top managements that want to disguise their own inefficiency from themselves.

It was only after this survey was at an advanced stage that I read the best book on multinationals there is. . . . In six years of research Dr. Brooke and Dr. Remmers[2] interviewed executives from over 100 multinationals, on a scale that seems to have been about 50 times as intensive as the casual conversations which I held as my "research" for this survey. Although we differ in forecasts of the future, the most fascinating part of their research was the differentiation between:

"Type A" multinationals, where the main link in head office with the foreign subsidiaries is the chief executive and his central services (these tended to be small firms but growing fast).

"Type B" firms, where the main link is an "international division" (which therefore contains all the people at head office who are internationally minded). These firms often have good relations between head office and subsidiaries, but bad relations inside head office, where the product managements resent the urge of the international division to cut export sales by producing all the firms' best lines abroad.

"Type C" firms, which are organised on the basis of product groups. These often have poor communications between head office and subsidiaries, because the product group still has a built-in interest in concentrating manufacturing at home. "Type D" firms, which are often very large firms trying an elaborate combination of international division management and product group management, with the result that some executives in one subsidiary had as many as 19 reporting centres each to route papers through (and were probably going mad).

Brooke's and Remmers's book is read and known by people in the good multinationals, hardly known at all in the bad multinationals. I suspect that, accordingly, it has not had the very large sale it deserves. But it reinforces my belief that the wave of the future lies with "type A" firms, which should be ready to hive off affiliates after a certain stage of growth.

Importing Technology

There is no correlation between a country's expenditure on "Research and Development" (R and D) and its rate of growth in productivity. Nobody should expect there to be. No country except the United States invents more than 10 per cent of the new technology being incorporated each year into industry. A country's efficiency in absorbing the more than 90 per cent of new technology that will be imported is therefore bound to be far more important than its ability to invent an extra 1 or 2 per cent more of new technology itself.

Japan has created the most "absorptive" economy in this respect. If you find a way of making a better mousetrap, the whole world will still beat a path to your own door; but, at present, the first beater on your doormat will be a Japanese asking for a licensing agreement, and among the last will be the British (who will not believe much in these new-fangled mousetraps) and the communist countries (who are often not allowed to buy foreign technology, and have been interestingly inefficient in their devoted and expensive efforts to pinch it).

In the past decade there were two fashionable prophecies about the spread of technology. Both proved wrong:

(a) At the beginning of the 1960s it was fashionable to say that big companies would no longer license their technological knowhow, but would insist on setting up their own multinational companies; so that Japan's growth was bound to slow because its refusal to "liberalise capital imports" (ie, to allow multinationals to come in) was self-defeating. Japan accelerated its growth instead.

(b) By the mid-1960s the most scientifically minded prophets (the sorts who are most determinedly prophesying ecological disaster now) were saying that the growing "technological gap" made inevitable a perpetual tightening of American hegemony over the world business scene. Within a few years the dollar was devalued instead.

In the future, as in the past, technology will be transferred from country to country by whatever is the most profitable means. If the strictly patentable parts of new knowledge increase in importance compared with the less strictly patentable parts, and if (even in a world with freer access to huge computer data banks) the proportion of patentable inventions made in big corporations' often rather unattractive laboratories increases—both of which are propositions that I tend to doubt—then the price that will have to be paid for licensing agreements will rise because big corporations can adopt the alternative route of setting up their own multinationals. But some price mechanism will operate: it is nonsense to suppose that big firms (at least those sufficiently unmegalomaniac to stay in business) will not sell some licensing arrangements at some price.

A multinational corporation will be the most efficient means of exporting technology in at least two cases:

(1) The first is when the capacity of local entrepreneurs to "absorb technology" is much less efficient than the capacity of the multinational to utilise it: while there has been a "management gap" in favour of America, this has been a major advantage of American multinationals almost everywhere. For some time to come, there will go on being a "management gap" in favour of multinationals run from developed countries compared with local producers in the less developed countries; but the gap is not necessarily going to be in favour of the big multinationals compared with the smaller transnationals.

(2) In very new and expensive and complicated and still developing products, perhaps especially those sold to other businesses, there may be a tendency for one name to become regarded (rightly or wrongly) as the top and most "reliable" one. Probably this will be reinforced when the development process is of a sort that needs to be kept close to the firm's key decision-makers. In these cases a big multinational may have a golden period of swiftly snowballing growth. The obvious example is International Business Machines in computers; similarly, Xerox would probably have gained if it had struck out for multinationalism from the start, instead of allowing some joint -venture arrangements. But the signs are now that this advantage does not advance "inexorably" beyond a certain stage of development. Twenty years ago few people would have dared to forecast the inroads which Japanese cars have made into the American market, in the "unassailable" backyard of General Motors and Ford. All of the industries which think that they have unassailable home markets today will see the rise of new competitors in the next 20 years. That includes IBM.

NOTES

1. John Diebold, *Education, Technology and Business.* Praeger. 1971.
2. *The Strategy of Multinational Enterprise.* London: Longman, 1970.

24 / The Multinational Corporation and the Law of Uneven Development

Stephen Hymer

"The settlers' town is a strongly-built town, all made of stone and steel. It is a brightly-lit town; the streets are covered with asphalt, and the garbage-cans swallow all the leavings, unseen, unknown and hardly thought about. The settler's feet are never visible, except perhaps in the sea; but there you're never close enough to see them. His feet are protected by strong shoes although the streets of his town are clean and even, with no holes or stones. The settler's town is a well-fed town, an easy-going town, its belly is always full of good things. The settler's town is a town of white people, of foreigners.

The town belonging to the colonized people, or at least the native town, the Negro village, the medina, the reservation, is a place of ill fame peopled by men of evil repute. They are born there, it matters little where or how; they die there, it matters not where nor how. It is a world without spaciousness: men live there on top of each other, and their huts are built one on top of the other. The native town is a hungry town, starved of bread, of meat, of shoes, of coal, of light. The native town is a crouching village, a town on its knees, a town wallowing in the mire. It is a town of niggers and dirty Arabs. The look that the native turns on the settler's town is a look of lust, a look of envy . . . " Fanon, *The Wretched of the Earth.*

. . . This essay attempts to [look into the future towards the year 2000] in terms of two laws of economic development: the Law of Increasing Firm Size and the Law of Uneven Development.[1]

Since the beginning of the Industrial Revolution, there has been a tendency for the representative firm to increase in size from the *workshop* to the *factory* to the *national corporation* to the *multi-divisional corporation* and now to the *multinational corporation*. This growth has been qualitative as well as quantitative. With each step, business enterprise acquired a more complex administrative structure to coordinate its activities and a larger brain to plan for its survival and growth. The first part of this essay traces the evolution of the corporation stressing the development of a hierarchical system of authority and control.

The remainder of the essay is concerned with extrapolating the trends in business enterprise (the microcosm) and relating them to the evolution of the international economy (the macrocosm). Until recently, most multinational corporations have come from the United States, where private business enterprise has reached its largest size and most highly developed forms. Now European corporations, as a by-product of increased size, and as a reaction to the American invasion of Europe, are also shifting attention from national to global production and beginning to "see the world as their oyster." *If* present trends continue, multinationalization is likely to increase greatly in the next decade as giants from both sides of the Atlantic (though still mainly from the U.S.) strive to penetrate each other's markets and to establish bases in underdeveloped countries, where there are few indigenous concentrations of capital sufficiently large to operate on a world scale. This rivalry may be intense at first but will probably abate through time and turn into collusion as firms approach some kind of oligopolistic equilibrium. A new structure of international industrial organization and a new international division of labor will have been born.

What will be the effect of this latest stage in the evolution of business enterprise on the Law of Uneven Development, *i.e.,* the tendency of the system to produce poverty as well as wealth, underdevelopment as well as development? The second part of this essay suggests that a regime of North Atlantic Multinational Corporations would tend to produce a hierarchical division of labor between geographical regions corresponding to the vertical division of labor within the firm. It would tend to centralize high-level decision-making occupations in a few key cities in the advanced countries, surrounded by a number of regional sub-capitals, and confine the rest of the world to lower levels of activity and income, *i.e.,* to the status of towns and villages in a new Imperial system. Income, status, authority, and consumption patterns would radiate out from these centers along a declining curve, and the existing pattern of inequality and dependency would be perpetuated. The pattern would be complex, just as the structure of the corporation is complex, but the basic relationship between different countries would be one of superior and subordinate, head office and branch plant.

How far will this tendency of corporations to create a world in their own image proceed? The situation is a dynamic one, moving dialectically. Right now, we seem to be in the midst of a major revolution in international relationships as modern science establishes the technological basis for a major advance in the conquest of the material world and the beginnings of truly cosmopolitan production. Multinational corporations are in the vanguard of this revolution, because of their great financial and administrative strength and their close contact with the new technology. Governments (outside the military) are far behind, because of their narrower horizons and perspectives, as are labor organizations and most non-business institutions and associations. (As John Powers, President of Charles Pfizer Corporation, has put it, "Practise is ahead of theory and policy.") Therefore, in the first round, multinational corporations are likely to have a certain degree of success in organizing markets, decision making, and the spread of information in their own interest. However, their very success will create tensions and conflicts which will lead to further development. Part III discusses some of the contradictions that are likely to emerge as the multinational corporate system overextends itself. These contradictions provide certain openings for action. Whether or not they can or will be used in the next round to move towards superior forms of international organization requires an analysis of a wide range of political factors outside the scope of this essay.

Part I. The Evolution of the Multinational Corporation

The Marshallian Firm and the Market Economy

What is the nature of the "beast"? It is called many names: Direct Investment, International Business, the International Firm, the International Corporate Group, the Multinational Firm, the Multinational Enterprise, the Multinational Corporation, the Multinational Family Group, World Wide Enterprise, La Grande Entreprise Plurinationale, La Grande Unité Interterritoriale, La Grande Entreprise Multinationale, La Grande Unité Pluriterritoriale; or, as a French Minister called them, "The U.S. corporate monsters."

Giant organizations are nothing new in international trade. They were a characteristic form of the mercantilist period when large joint-stock companies, *e.g.*, The Hudson's Bay Co., The Royal African Co., The East India Co., to name the major English merchant firms, organized long-distance trade with America, Africa and Asia. But neither these firms, nor the large mining and plantation enterprises in the production sector, were the forerunners of the multinational corporation. They were like dinosaurs, large in bulk, but small in brain, feeding on the lush vegetation of the new worlds (the planters and miners in America were literally *Tyrannosaurus rex*).

The activities of these international merchants, planters and miners laid the groundwork for the Industrial Revolution by concentrating capital in the metropolitan centre, but the driving force came from the small-scale capitalist enterprises in manufacturing, operating at first in the interstices of the feudalist economic structure, but gradually emerging into the open and finally gaining predominance. It is in the small workshops, organized by the newly emerging capitalist class, that the forerunners of the modern corporation are to be found.

The strength of this new form of business enterprise lay in its power and ability to reap the benefits of cooperation and division of labor. Without the capitalist, economic activity was individualistic, small-scale, scattered and unproductive. But a man with capital, *i.e.,* with sufficient funds to buy raw materials and advance wages, could gather a number of people into a single shop and obtain as his reward the increased productivity that resulted from social production. The reinvestment of these profits led to a steady increase in the size of capitals, making further division of labor possible and creating an opportunity for using machinery in production. A phenomenal increase in productivity and production resulted from this process, and entirely new dimensions of human existence were opened. The growth of capital revolutionized the entire world and, figuratively speaking, even battered down the Great Wall of China.

The hallmarks of the new system were *the market* and *the factory*, representing the two different methods of coordinating the division of labor. In the factory entrepreneurs consciously plan and organize cooperation, and the relationships are hierarchical and authoritarian; in the market coordination is achieved through a decentralized, unconscious, competitive process.

To understand the significance of this distinction, the new system should be compared to the structure it replaced. In the pre-capitalist system of production, the division of labor was hierarchically structured at the *macro* level, *i.e.* for society as a whole, but unconsciously structured at the *micro* level *i.e.,* the actual process of production. Society as a whole was partitioned into various castes, classes, and guilds, on a rigid and authoritarian basis so that political and social stability could be maintained and adequate numbers assured for each industry and occupation. Within each sphere of production, however, individuals by and large were independent and their activities only loosely coordinated, if at all. In essence, a guild was composed of a large number of similar individuals, each performing the same task in roughly the same way with little cooperation or division of labor. This type of organization could produce high standards of quality and workmanship but was limited quantitatively to low levels of output per head.

The capitalist system of production turned this structure on its head. The macro system became unconsciously structured, while the micro system became hierarchically structured. The market emerged as a self-regulating coordinator of business units as restrictions on capital markets and labor mobility were removed. (Of course the State remained above the market as a conscious coordinator to maintain the system and ensure the growth of capital.) At the micro level, that is the level of production, labor was gathered under the authority of the entrepreneur capitalist.

Marshall, like Marx, stressed that the internal division of labor within the factory, between those who planned and those who worked (between "undertakers" and laborers), was the "chief fact in the form of modern civilization, the 'kernel' of the modern economic problem." Marx, however, stressed the authoritarian and unequal nature of this relationship based on the coercive power of property and its anti-social characteristics. He focused on the irony that concentration of wealth in the hands of a few and its ruthless use were necessary historically to demonstrate the value of cooperation and the social nature of production.

Marshall, in trying to answer Marx, argued for the voluntary cooperative nature of the relationship between capital and labor. In his view, the *market* reconciled individual freedom and collective production. He argued that those on top achieved their position because of their superior organizational ability, and that their relation to the workers below them was essentially harmonious and not exploitative. "Undertakers" were not captains of industry because they had capital; they could obtain capital because they had the ability to be captains of industry. They retained their authority by merit, not by coercion; for according to Marshall, natural selection, operating through the market, constantly destroyed inferior organizers and gave everyone who had the ability—including workers—a chance to rise to managerial positions. Capitalists earned more than workers because they contributed more, while the system as a whole provided all its members, and especially the workers, with improved standards of living and an ever-expanding field of choice of consumption.

The Corporate Economy

The evolution of business enterprise from the small workshop (Adam Smith's pin factory) to the Marshallian family firm represented only the first step in the development of business organization. As total capital accumulated, the size of the individual concentrations composing it increased continuously, and the vertical division of labor grew accordingly.

It is best to study the evolution of the corporate form in the United States environment, where it has reached its highest stage.[2] In the 1870s, the United States industrial structure consisted largely of Marshallian type, single-function firms, scattered over the country. Business firms were typically tightly controlled by a single entrepreneur or small family group who, as it were, saw everything, knew everything and decided everything. By the early twentieth century, the rapid growth of the economy and the great merger movement had consolidated many small enterprises into large national corporations engaged in many functions over many regions. To meet this new strategy of continent-wide, vertically integrated production and marketing, a new administrative structure evolved. The family firm, tightly controlled by a few men in close touch with all its aspects, gave way to the administrative pyramid of the corporation. Capital acquired new powers and new horizons. The domain of conscious coordination widened and that of market-directed division of labor contracted.

According to Chandler the railroad, which played so important a role in creating the national market, also offered a model for new forms of business organization. The need to administer geographically dispersed operations led railway companies to create an administrative structure which distinguished field offices from head offices. The field offices managed local operations; the head office supervised the field offices. According to Chandler and Redlich, this distinction is important because "it implies that the executive responsible for a firm's affairs had, for the first time, to supervise the work of other executives."

This first step towards increased vertical division of labor within the management function was quickly copied by the recently-formed national corporations which faced the same problems of coordinating widely scattered plants. Business developed an organ system of administration, and the modern corporation was born. The functions of business administration were sub-divided into *departments* (organs)—finance, personnel, purchasing, engineering, and sales—to deal with capital, labor, purchasing, manufacturing, etc. This horizontal division of labor opened up new possibilities for rationalizing production and for incorporating the advances of physical and social sciences into economic activity on a systematic basis. At the same time a "brain and nervous" system, *i.e.*, a vertical system of control, had to be devised to connect and coordinate departments. This was a major advance in decision-making capabilities. It meant that a special group, the Head Office, was created whose particular function was to coordinate, appraise, and plan for the survival and growth of the organism as a whole. The organization became conscious of itself as organization and gained a certain measure of control over its own evolution and development.

The corporation soon underwent further evolution. To understand this next step we must briefly discuss the development of the United States market. At the risk of great oversimplification, we might say that by the first decade of the twentieth century, the problem of production had essentially been solved. By the end of the nineteenth century, scientists and engineers had developed most of the inventions needed for mass producing at a low cost nearly all the main items of basic consumption. In the language of systems analysis, the problem became one of putting together the available components in an organized fashion. The national corporation provided *one* organizational solution, and by the 1920s it had demonstrated its great power to increase material production.

The question was which direction growth would take. One possibility was to expand mass production systems very widely and to make basic consumer goods available on a broad basis throughout the world. The other possibility was to concentrate on continuous innovation for a small number of people and on the introduction of new consumption goods even before the old ones had been fully spread. The latter course was in fact chosen, and we now have the paradox that 500 million people can receive a live TV broadcast from the moon while there is still a shortage of telephones in many advanced countries, to say nothing of the fact that so many people suffer from inadequate food and lack of simple medical help.

This path was associated with a choice of capital-deepening instead of capital-widening in the productive sector of the economy. As capital accumulated, business had to choose the degree to which it would expand labor proportionately to the growth of capital or, conversely, the degree to which they would substitute capital for labor. At one extreme business could have kept the capital-labor ratio constant and accumulated labor at the same rate they accumulated capital. This horizontal accumulation would soon have exhausted the labor force of any particular country and then either capital would have had to migrate to foreign countries or labor would have had to move into the industrial centers. Under this sytem, earnings per employed worker would have remained steady and the composition of output would have tended to remain constant as similar basic goods were produced on a wider and wider basis.

However, this path was not chosen, and instead capital per worker was raised, the rate of expansion of the industrial labor force was slowed down, and a dualism was created between a small, high wage, high productivity sector in advanced countries, and a large, low wage, low productivity sector in the less advanced.

The uneven growth of per capita income implied unbalanced growth and the need on the part of business to adapt to a constantly changing composition of output. Firms in the producers' goods sectors had continuously to innovate labor-saving machinery because the capital output ratio was increasing steadily. In the consumption goods sector, firms had continuously to introduce new products since, according to Engel's Law, people do not generally consume proportionately more of the same things as they get richer, but rather reallocate their consumption away from old goods and towards new goods. This non-proportional growth of demand implied that goods would tend to go through a life-cycle, growing rapidly when they were first introduced and more slowly later. If a particular firm were tied to only one product, its growth rate would follow this same life-cycle pattern and would eventually slow down and perhaps even come to a halt. If the corporation was to grow steadily at a rapid rate, it had continuously to introduce new products.

Thus, product development and marketing replaced production as a dominant problem of business enterprise. To meet the challenge of a constantly changing market, business enterprise evolved the multidivisional structure. The new form was originated by General Motors and DuPont shortly after World War I, followed by a few others during the 1920s and 1930s, and was widely adopted by most of the giant U.S. corporations in the great boom following World War II. As with the previous stages, evolution involved a process of both differentiation and integration. Corporations were decentralized into several *divisions*, each concerned with one product line and organized with its own head office. At a higher level, a *general office* was created to coordinate the division and to plan for the enterprise as a whole.

The new corporate form has great flexibility. Because of its decentralized structure, a multidivisional corporation can enter a new market by adding a new division, while leaving the old divisions undisturbed. (And to a lesser extent it can leave the market by dropping a division without disturbing the rest of its structure.) It can also create competing product-lines in the same industry, thus increasing its market share while maintaining the illusion of competition. Most important of all, because it has a cortex specializing in strategy, it can plan on a much wider scale than before and allocate capital with more precision.

The modern corporation is a far cry from the small workshop or even from the Marshallian firm. The Marshallian capitalist ruled his factory from an office on the second floor. At the turn of the century, the president of a large national corporation was lodged in a higher building, perhaps on the seventh floor, with greater perspective and power. In today's giant corporation, managers rule from the top of skyscrapers; on a clear day, they can almost see the world.

U.S. corporations began to move to foreign countries almost as soon as they had completed their continent-wide integration. For one thing, their new administrative structure and great financial strength gave them the power to go abroad. In becoming national firms, U.S. corporations learned how to become international. Also, their large size and oligopolistic position gave them an incentive. Direct investment became a new weapon in their arsenal of oligopolistic rivalry. Instead of joining a cartel (prohibited under U.S. law), they invested in foreign customers, suppliers, and competitors. For example, some firms found they were oligopolistic buyers of raw materials produced in foreign countries and feared a monopolization of the sources of supply. By investing directly in foreign producing enterprises, they could gain the security implicit in control over their raw material requirements. Other firms invested abroad to control marketing outlets and thus maximize quasi-rents on their technological discoveries and differentiated products. Some went abroad simply to forestall competition.

The first wave of U.S. direct foreign capital investment occurred around the turn of the century followed by a second wave during the 1920s. The outward migration slowed down during the depression but resumed after World War II and soon accelerated rapidly. Between 1950 and 1969, direct foreign investment by U.S. firms expanded at a rate of about 10 percent per annum. At this rate it would double in less than ten years, and even at a much slower rate of growth, foreign operations will reach enormous proportions over the next 30 years.

Several important factors account for this rush of foreign investment in the 1950s and the 1960s. First, the large size of the U.S. corporations and their new multidivisional structure gave them wider horizons and a global outlook. Secondly, technological developments in communications created a new awareness of the global challenge and threatened established institutions by opening up new sources of competition. For reasons noted above, business enterprises were among the first to recognize the potentialities and dangers of the new environment and to take active steps to cope with it.

A third factor in the outward migration of U.S. capital was the rapid growth of Europe and Japan. This, combined with the slow growth of the United State economy in the 1950s, altered world market shares as firms confined to the U.S. market found themselves falling behind in the competitive race and losing ground to European and Japanese firms, which were growing rapidly because of the expansion of their markets. Thus, in the late 1950s, United States corporations faced a serious "non-American" challenge. Their answer was an outward thrust to establish sales production and bases in foreign territories. This strategy was possible in Europe, since government there provided an open door for United States investment, but was blocked in Japan, where the government adopted a highly restrictive policy. To a large extent, United States business was thus able to redress the imbalances caused by the Common Market, but Japan remained a source of tension to oligopoly equilibrium.

What about the future? The present trend indicates further multinationalization of all giant firms, European as well as American. In the first place, European firms, partly as a reaction to the United States penetration of their markets, and partly as a natural result of their own growth, have begun to invest abroad on an expanded scale and will probably continue to do so in the future, and even enter into the United State market. This process is already well underway and may be expected to accelerate as time goes on. The reaction of United States business will most likely be to meet foreign investment at home with more foreign investment abroad. They, too, will scramble for market positions in underdeveloped countries and attempt to get an even larger share of the European market, as a reaction to European investment in the United States. Since they are large and powerful, they will on balance succeed in maintaining their relative standing in the world as a whole—as their losses in some markets are offset by gains in others.

A period of rivalry will prevail until a new equilibrium between giant U.S. firms and giant European and Japanese firms is reached, based on a strategy of multinational operations and cross-penetration. We turn now to the implications of this pattern of industrial organization for international trade and the law of uneven development.

Part II. Uneven Development

Suppose giant multinational corporations (say 300 from the U.S. and 200 from Europe and Japan) succeed in establishing themselves as the dominant form of international enterprise and come to control a significant share of industry (especially modern industry) in each country. The world economy will resemble more and more the United States economy, where each of the large corporations tends to spread over the entire continent and to penetrate almost every nook and cranny. What would be the effect of a world industrial organization of this type on international specialization, exchange and income distribution? The purpose of this section is to analyze the spatial dimension of the corporate hierarchy.

A useful starting point is Chandler and Redlich's[3] scheme for analyzing the evolution of corporate structure. They distinguish "three levels of business administration, three horizons, three levels of task, and three levels of decision making . . . and three levels of policies." Level III, the lowest level, is concerned with managing the day-to-day operations of the enterprise, that is with keeping it going within the established framework. Level II, which first made its appearance with the separation of head office from field office, is responsible for coordinating the managers at Level III. The functions of Level I— top management—are goal-determination and planning. This level sets the framework in which the lower levels operate. In the Marshallian firm, all three levels are embodied in the single entrepreneur or undertaker. In the national corporation a partial differentiation is made in which the top two levels are separated from the bottom one. In the multidivisional corporation, the differentiation is far more complete. Level I is completely split off from Level II and concentrated in a general office whose specific function is to plan strategy rather than tactics.

The development of business enterprise can therefore be viewed as a process of centralizing and perfecting the process of capital accumulation. The Marshallian entrepreneur was a jack-of-all-trades. In the modern multidivisional corporation, a powerful general office consciously plans and organizes the growth of corporate capital. It is here that the key men who actually allocate the corporation's available resources (rather than act within the means allocated to them, as is true for the managers at lower levels) are located. Their power comes from their ultimate control over *men* and *money* and although one should not overestimate the ability to control a far-flung empire, neither should one underestimate it.

> The senior men could take action because they controlled the selection of executive personnel and because, through budgeting, they allocated the funds to the operating divisions. In the way they allocated their resources—capital and personnel—and in the promotion, transferral and retirement of operating executives, they

determined the framework in which the operating units worked and thus put into effect their concept of the long term goals and objectives of the enterprise . . . Ultimate authority in business enterprise, as we see it, rests with those who hold the purse strings, and in modern large-scale enterprises, those persons hold the purse strings who perform the functions of goal setting and planning.

What is the relationship between the structure of the microcosm and the structure of the macrocosm? The application of location theory to the Chandler-Redlich scheme suggests a *correspondence principle* relating centralization of control within the corporation to centralization of control within the international economy.

Location theory suggests that Level III activities would spread themselves over the globe according to the pull of manpower, markets, and raw materials. The multinational corporation, because of its power to command capital and technology and its ability to rationalize their use on a global scale, will probably spread production more evenly over the world's surface than is now the case. Thus, in the first instance, it may well be a force for diffusing industrialization to the less developed countries and creating new centers of production. (We postpone for a moment a discussion of the fact that location depends upon transportation, which in turn depends upon the government, which in turn is influenced by the structure of business enterprise.)

Level II activities, because of their need for white-collar workers, communications systems, and information, tend to concentrate in large cities. Since their demands are similar, corporations from different industries tend to place their coordinating offices in the same city, and Level II activities are consequently far more geographically concentrated than Level III activities.

Level I activities, the general offices, tend to be even more concentrated than Level II activities, for they must be located close to the capital market, the media, and the government. Nearly every major corporation in the United States, for example, must have its general office (or a large proportion of its high-level personnel) in or near the city of New York because of the need for face-to-face contact at higher levels of decision making.

Applying this scheme to the world economy, one would expect to find the highest offices of the multinational corporations concentrated in the world's major cities—New York, London, Paris, Bonn, Tokyo. These, along with Moscow and perhaps Peking, will be the major centers of high-level strategic planning. Lesser cities throughout the world will deal with the day-to-day operations of specific local problems. These in turn will be arranged in a hierarchical fashion: the larger and more important ones will contain regional corporate headquarters, while the smaller ones will be confined to lower level activities. Since business is usually the core of the city, geographical specialization will come to reflect the hierarchy of corporate decision making, and the occupational distribution of labor in a city or region will depend upon its function in the international economic system. The "best" and most highly paid administrators, doctors, lawyers, scientists, educators, government officials, actors, servants and hairdressers, will tend to concentrate in or near the major centers.

The structure of income and consumption will tend to parallel the structure of status and authority. The citizens of capital cities will have the best jobs—allocating men and money at the highest level and planning growth and development—and will receive the highest rates of remuneration. (Executives' salaries tend to be a function of the wage bill of people under them. The larger empire of the multinational corporation, the greater the earnings of top executives, to a large extent independent of their performance. Thus, growth in the hinterland subsidiaries implies growth in the income of capital cities, but not *vice versa*.)

The citizens of capital cities will also be the first to innovate new products in the cycle which is known in the marketing literature as trickle-down or two-stage marketing. A new product is usually first introduced to a select group of people who have "discretionary" income and are willing to experiment in their consumption patterns. Once it is accepted by this group, it spreads, or trickles down to other groups via the demonstration effect. In this process, the rich and the powerful get more votes than everyone else; first, because they have more money to spend, second, because they have more ability to experiment, and third, because they have high status and are likely to be copied. This special group may have something approaching a choice in consumption patterns; the rest have only the choice between conforming or being isolated.

The trickle-down system also has the advantage—from the center's point of view—of reinforcing patterns of authority and control. According to Fallers, it helps keep workers on the treadmill by creating an illusion of upward mobility even though relative status remains unchanged. In each period subordinates achieve (in part) the consumption standards of their superiors in a previous period and are thus torn in two directions: if they look backward and compare their standards of living through time, things seem to be getting better; if they look upward they see that their relative position has not changed. They receive a consolation prize, as it were, which may serve to keep them going by softening the reality that in a competitive system, few succeed and many fail. It is little wonder, then, that those at the top stress growth rather than equality as the welfare criterion for human relations.

In the international economy trickle-down marketing takes the form of an international demonstration effect spreading outward from the metropolis to the hinterland. Multinational corporations help speed up this process, often the key motive for direct investment, through their control of marketing channels and communications media.

The development of a new product is a fixed cost; once the expenditure needed for invention or innovation has been made, it is forever a bygone. The actual cost of production is thus typically well below selling price and the limit on output is not rising costs but falling demand due to saturated markets. The marginal profit on new foreign markets is thus high, and corporations have a strong interest in maintaining a system which spreads their products widely. Thus, the interest of multinational corporations in underdeveloped countries is larger than the size of the market would suggest.

It must be stressed that the dependency relationship between major and minor cities should not be attributed to technology. The new technology, because it increases interaction, implies greater interdependence but not necessarily a hierarchical structure. Communications linkages could be arranged in the form of a grid in which each point was directly connected to many other points, permitting lateral as well as vertical communication. This system would be polycentric since messages from one point to another would go directly rather than through the center; each point would become a center on its own; and the distinction between center and periphery would disappear.

Such a grid is made *more* feasible by aeronautical and electronic revolutions which greatly reduce costs of communications. It is not technology which creates inequality; rather, it is *organization* that imposes a ritual judicial asymmetry on the use of intrinsically symmetrical means of communications and arbitrarily creates unequal capacities to initiate and terminate exchange, to store and retrieve information, and to determine the extent of the exchange and terms of the discussion. Just as colonial powers in the past linked each point in the hinterland to the metropolis and inhibited lateral communications, preventing the growth of independent centers of decision making and creativity, multinational corporations (backed by state powers) centralize control by imposing a hierarchical system.

This suggests the possibility of an alternative system of organization in the form of national planning. Multinational corporations are private institutions which organize one or a few industries across many countries. Their polar opposite (the antimultinational corporation, perhaps) is a public institution which organizes many industries across one region. This would permit the centralization of capital, *i.e.*, the coordination of many enterprises be one decision-making center, but would substitute regionalization for internationalization. The span of control would be confined to the boundaries of a single polity and society and not spread over many countries. The advantage of the multinational corporation is its global perspective. The advantage of national planning is its ability to remove the wastes of oligopolistic anarchy, *i.e.*, meaningless product differentiation and an imbalance between different industries within a geographical area. It concentrates *all* levels of decision-making in one locale and thus provides each region with a full complement of skills and occupations. This opens up new horizons for local development by making possible the social and political control of economic decision-making. Multinational corporations, in contrast, weaken political control because they span many countries and can escape national regulation.

A few examples might help to illustrate how multinational corporations reduce options for development. Consider an underdeveloped country wishing to invest heavily in education in order to increase its stock of human capital and raise standards of living. In a market system it would be able to find gainful employment for its citizens within its *national boundaries* by specializing in education-intensive activities and selling its surplus production to foreigners. In the multinational corporate system, however, the demand for high-level education in low-ranking areas is limited, and a country does not become a world center simply by having a better educational system. An outward shift in the supply of educated people in a country, therefore, will not create its own demand but will create an excess supply and lead to emigration. Even then, the employment opportunities for citizens of low-ranking countries are restricted by discriminatory practices in the center. It is well-known that ethnic homogeneity increases as one goes up the corporate hierarchy; the lower levels contain a wide variety of nationalities, the higher levels become successively purer and purer. In part this stems from the skill differences of different nationalities, but more important is the fact that the higher up one goes in the decision-making process, the more important mutual understanding and ease of communications become; a common background becomes all-important.

A similar type of specialization by nationality can be expected within the multinational corporation hierarchy. Multinational corporations are torn in two directions. On the one hand, they must adapt to local circumstances in each country. This calls for decentralized decision making. On the other hand, they must coordinate their activities in various parts of the world and stimulate the flow of ideas from one part of their empire to another. This calls for centralized control. They must, therefore, develop an organizational structure to balance the need for coordination with the need for adaptation to a patchwork quilt of languages, laws and customs. One solution to this problem is a division of labor based on nationality. Day-to-day management in each country is left to the nationals of that country who, because they are intimately familiar with local conditions and practices, are able to deal with local problems and local government. These nationals remain rooted in one spot, while above them is a layer of people who move around from country to country, as bees among flowers, transmitting information from one subsidiary to another and from the lower levels to the general office at the apex of the corporate structure. In the nature of things, these people (reticulators) for the most part will be citizens of the country of the parent corporation (and will be drawn from a small, culturally homogeneous group within the advanced world), since they will need to have the confidence of their superiors and be able to move easily in the higher management circles. Latin Americans, Asians and Africans will at best be able to aspire to a management position in the intermediate coordinating centers at the continental level. Very few will be able to get much higher than this, for the closer one gets to the top, the more important is "a common cultural heritage."

Another way in which the multinational corporations inhibit economic development in the hinterland is through their effect on tax capacity. An important government instrument for promoting growth is expenditure on infrastructure and support services. By providing transportation and communications, education and health, a government can create a productive labor force and increase the growth potential of its economy. The extent to which it can afford to finance these intermediate outlays depends upon its tax revenue.

However, a government's ability to tax multinational corporations is limited by the ability of these corporations to manipulate transfer prices and to move their productive facilities to another country. This means that they will only be attracted to countries where superior infrastructure offsets higher taxes. The government of an underdeveloped country will find it difficult to extract a surplus (revenue from the multinational corporations, less cost of services provided to them) from multinational corporations to use for long-run development programs and for stimulating growth in other industries. In contrast, governments of the advanced countries, where the home office and financial center of the multinational corporation are located, can tax the profits of the corporation as a whole, as well as the high incomes of its management. Government in the metropolis can, therefore, capture some of the surplus generated by the multinational corporations and use it to further improve their infrastructure and growth.

In other words, the relationship between multinational corporations and underdeveloped countries will be somewhat like the relationship between the national corporations in the United States and state and municipal governments. These lower-level governments tend always to be short of funds compared to the federal government which can tax a corporation as a whole. Their competition to attract corporate investment eats up their surplus, and they find it difficult to finance extensive investments in human and physical capital even where such investment would be productive. This has a crucial effect on the pattern of government expenditure. For example, suppose taxes were first paid to state government and then passed on to the federal government. What chance is there that these lower level legislatures would approve the phenomenal expenditures on space research that now go on? A similar discrepancy can be expected in the international economy with overspending and waste by metropolitan governments and a shortage of public funds in the less advanced countries.

The tendency of the multinational corporations to erode the power of the nation state works in a variety of ways, in addition to its effect on taxation powers. In general, most governmental policy instruments (monetary policy, fiscal policy, wage policy, etc.) diminish in effectiveness the more open the economy and the greater the extent of foreign investments. This tendency applies to political instruments as well as economic, for the multinational corporation is a medium by which laws, politics, foreign policy and culture of one country intrude into another. This acts to reduce the sovereignty of all nation states, but again the realtionship is asymmetrical, for the flow tends to be from the parent to the subsidiary, not *vice versa*. The United States can apply its anti-trust laws to foreign subsidiaries or stop them from "trading with the enemy" even though such trade is not against the laws of the country in which the branch plant is located. However, it would be illegal for an underdeveloped country which disagreed with American foreign policy to hold a U.S. firm hostage for acts of the parent. This is because legal rights are defined in terms of property-ownership, and the various subsidiaries of a multinational corporation are not "partners in a multinational endeavor" but the property of the general office.

In conclusion, it seems that a regime of multinational corporations would offer under-developed countries neither national independence nor equality. It would tend instead to inhibit the attainment of these goals. It would turn the underdeveloped countries into branch-plant countries, not only with reference to their economic functions but through-out the whole gamut of social, political and cultural roles. The subsidiaries of multina-tional corporations are typically amongst the largest corporations in the country of opera-tions, and their top executives play an influential role in the political, social and cultural life of the host country. Yet these people, whatever their title, occupy at best a medium position in the corporate structure and are restricted in authority and horizons to a lower level of decision making. The governments with whom they deal tend to take on the same middle management outlook, since this is the only range of information and ideas to which they are exposed. In this sense, one can hardly expect such a country to bring forth the creative imagination needed to apply science and technology to the problems of degrading poverty. Even so great a champion of liberalism as Marshall recognized the crucial relationship between occupation and development.

> For the business by which a person earns his livelihood generally fills his thoughts during the far greater part of those hours in which his mind is at its best; during them his character is being formed by the way in which he uses his facilities in his work, by the thoughts and feelings which it suggests, and by his relationship to his associates in work, his employers to his employees.

Part III. The Political Economy of the Multinational Corporation

The viability of the multinational corporate system depends upon the degree to which people will tolerate the unevenness it creates. It is well to remember that the "New Imperialism" which began after 1870 in a spirit of Capitalism Triumphant, soon became seriously troubled and after 1914 was characterized by war, depression, breakdown of the international economic system, and war again, rather than Free Trade, Pax Britannica and Material Improvement.

A major, if not the major, reason was Great Britain's inability to cope with the byprod-ucts of its own rapid accumulation of capital; *i.e.*, a class conscious labor force at home; a middle class in the hinterland; and rival centers of capital on the Continent and in America. Britain's policy tended to be atavistic and defensive rather than progressive, more concerned with warding off new threats than creating new areas of expansion. Ironically, Edwardian England revived the paraphernalia of the landed aristocracy it had just destroyed. Instead of embarking on a "big push" to develop the vast hinterland of the Empire, colonial administrators often adopted policies to slow down rates of growth and arrest the development of either a native capitalist class or a native proletariat which could overthrow them.

As time went on, the center had to devote an increasing share of government activity to military and other unproductive expenditures; they had to rely on alliances with an inefficient class of landlords, officials and soldiers in the hinterland to maintain stability at the cost of development. A great part of the surplus extracted from the population was thus wasted locally.

The new Mercantilism (as the Multinational Corporate System of special alliances and privileges, aid and tariff concessions is sometimes called) faces similar problems of internal and external division. The center is troubled: excluded groups revolt and even some of the affluent are dissatisfied with their roles. (The much talked about "generation gap" may indicate the failure of the system to reproduce itself.) Nationalistic rivalry between major capitalist countries (especially the challenge of Japan and Germany) remains an important divisive factor, while the economic challenge from the socialist bloc may prove to be of the utmost significance in the next thirty years. Russia has its own form of large-scale economic organizations, also in command of modern technology, and its own conception of how the world should develop. So does China to an increasing degree. Finally, there is the threat presented by the middle classes and the excluded groups of the underdeveloped countries.

The national middle classes in the underdeveloped countries came to power when the center weakened but could not, through their policy of import substitution manufacturing, establish a viable basis for sustained growth. They now face a foreign exchange crisis and an unemployment (or population) crisis—the first indicating their inability to function in the international economy, and the second indicating their alienation from the people they are supposed to lead. In the immediate future, these national middle classes will gain a new lease on life as they take advantage of the spaces created by the rivalry between American and non-American oligopolists striving to establish global market positions. The native capitalists will again become the champions of national independence as they bargain with multinational corporations. But the conflict at this level is more apparent than real, for in the end the fervent nationalism of the middle class asks only for promotion within the corporate structure and not for a break with that structure. In the last analysis their power derives from the metropolis and they cannot easily afford to challenge the international system. They do not command the loyalty of their own population and cannot really compete with the large, powerful, aggregate capitals from the center. They are prisoners of the taste patterns and consumption standards set at the center, and depend on outsiders for technical advice, capital, and when necessary, for military support of their position.

The main threat comes form the excluded groups. It is not unusual in underdeveloped countries for the top 5 percent to obtain between 30 and 40 percent of the total national income, and for the top one-third to obtain anywhere from 60 to 70 percent. At most, one-third of the population can be said to benefit in some sense from the dualistic growth that characterizes development in the hinterland. The remaining two-thirds, who together get only one-third of the income, are outsiders, not because they do not contribute to the economy, but because they do not share in the benefits. They provide a source of cheap labor which helps keep exports to the developed world at a low price and which has financed the urban-biased growth of recent years. Because their wages are low, they spend a moderate amount of time in menial services and are sometimes referred to as underemployed as if to imply they were not needed. In fact, it is difficult to see how the system in most underdeveloped countries could survive without cheap labor, since removing it (*e.g.*, diverting it to public works projects as is done in socialist countries) would raise consumption costs to capitalists and professional elites. Economic development under the Multinational Corporation does not offer much promise for this large segment of society and their antagonism continuously threatens the system.

The survival of the multinational corporate system depends on how fast it can grow and how much trickles down. Plans now being formulated in government offices, corporate headquarters and international organizations, sometimes suggest that a growth rate of about 6 percent per year in national income (3 percent per capita) is needed. (Such a target is, of course, far below what would be possible if a serious effort were made to solve basic problems of health, education and clothing.) To what extent is it possible?

The multinational corporation must solve four critical problems for the underdeveloped countries, if it is to foster the continued growth and survival of a "modern" sector. First, it must break the foreign-exchange constraint and provide the underdeveloped countries with imported goods for capital formation and modernization. Second, it must finance an expanded program of government expenditure to train labor and provide support services for urbanization and industrialization. Third, it must solve the urban food problem created by growth. Finally, it must keep the excluded two-thirds of the population under control.

The solution now being suggested for the first is to restructure the world economy allowing the periphery to export certain manufactured goods to the center. Part of this program involves regional common markets to rationalize the existing structure of industry. These plans typically do not involve the rationalization and restructuring of the entire economy of the underdeveloped countries but mainly serve the small manufacturing sector which caters to higher income groups and which, therefore, faces a very limited market in any particular country. The solution suggested for the second problem is an expanded aid program and a reformed government bureaucracy (perhaps along the lines of the Alliance for Progress). The solution for the third is agri-business and the green revolution, a program with only limited benefits to the rural poor. Finally, the solution offered for the fourth problem is population control, either through family planning or counterinsurgency.

It is doubtful whether the center has sufficient political stability to finance and organize the program outlined above. It is not clear, for example, that the West has the technology to rationalize manufacturing abroad or modernize agriculture, or the willingness to open up marketing channels for the underdeveloped world. Nor is it evident that the center has the political power to embark on a large aid program or to readjust its own structure of production and allow for the importation of manufactured goods from the periphery. It is difficult to imagine labor accepting such a re-allocation (a new repeal of the Corn Laws as it were), and it is equally hard to see how the advanced countries could create a system of planning to make these extra hardships unnecessary.

The present crisis may well be more profound than most of us imagine, and the West may find it impossible to restructure the international economy on a workable basis. One could easily argue that the age of the Multinational Corporation is at its end rather than at its beginning. For all we know, books on the global partnership may be the epitaph of the American attempt to take over the old international economy, and not the herald of a new era of international cooperation.

Conclusion

The multinational corporation, because of its great power to plan economic activity, represents an important step forward over previous methods of organizing international exchange. It demonstrates the social nature of production on a global scale. As it eliminates the anarchy of international markets and brings about a more extensive and productive international division of labor, it releases great sources of latent energy.

However, as it crosses international boundaries, it pulls and tears at the social and political fabric and erodes the cohesiveness of national states. Whether one likes this or not, it is probably a tendency that cannot be stopped.

Through its propensity to nestle everywhere, settle everywhere, and establish connections everywhere, the multinational corporation destroys the possibility of national seclusion and self-sufficiency and creates a universal interdependence. But the multinational corporation is still a private institution with a partial outlook and represents only an imperfect solution to the problem of international cooperation. It creates hierarchy rather than equality, and it spreads its benefits unequally.

In proportion to its success, it creates tensions and difficulties. It will lead other institutions, particularly labor organizations and government, to take an international outlook and thus unwittingly create an environment less favorable to its own survival. It will demonstrate the possibilities of material progress at a faster rate than it can realize them, and will create a worldwide demand for change that it cannot satisfy.

The next round may be marked by great crises due to the conflict between national planning by governments and international planning by corporations. For example, if each country loses its power over fiscal and monetary policy due to the growth of multinational corporations (as some observers believe Canada has), how will aggregate demand be stabilized? Will it be possible to construct super-states? Or does multinationalism do away with Keynesian problems? Similarly, will it be possible to fulfill a host of other government functions at the supranational level in the near future? During the past twenty-five years many political problems were put aside as the West recovered from the depression and the war. By the late sixties the bloom of this long upswing had begun to fade. In the seventies, power conflicts are likely to come to the fore.

Whether underdeveloped countries will use the opportunities arising from this crisis to build viable local decision-making institutions is difficult to predict. The national middle class failed when it had the opportunity and instead merely reproduced internally the economic dualism of the international economy as it squeezed agriculture to finance urban industry. What is needed is a complete change of direction. The starting point must be the needs of the bottom two-thirds, and not the demands of the top third. The primary goal of such a strategy would be to provide minimum standards of health, education, food and clothing to the entire population, removing the more obvious forms of human suffering. This requires a system which can mobilize the entire population and which can search the local environment for information, resources and needs. It must be able to absorb modern technology, but it cannot be mesmerized by the form it takes in the advanced countries; it must go to the roots. This is not the path the upper one-third chooses when it has control.

The wealth of a nation, wrote Adam Smith two hundred years ago, is determined by "first, the skill, dexterity and judgement with which labor is generally applied; and, secondly by the proportion between the number of those who are employed in useful labor, and that of those who are not so employed." Capitalist enterprise has come a long way from his day, but it has never been able to bring more than a small fraction of the world's population into useful or highly productive employment. The latest stage reveals once more the power of social cooperation and division of labor which so fascinated Adam Smith in his description of pin manufacturing. It also shows the shortcomings of concentrating this power in private hands.

Epilogue

Many readers of this essay in draft form have asked: Is there an alternative? Can anything be done? The problem simply stated is to go beyond the multinational corporation. Scholarship can perhaps make the task easier by showing how the forms of international social production devised by capital as it expanded to global proportions can be used to build a better society benefiting all men. I have tried to open up one avenue for explanation by suggesting a system of regional planning as a positive negation of the multinational corporation. Much more work is needed to construct alternative methods of organizing the international economy. Fortunately businessmen in attacking the problem of applying technology on a world level have developed many of the tools and conditions needed for a socialist solution, if we can but stand them on their head. But one must keep in mind that the problem is not one of ideas alone.

A major question is how far those in power will allow the necessary metamorphosis to happen, and how far they will try to resist it by violent means. I do not believe the present structure of uneven development can long be maintained in the light of the increased potential for world development demonstrated by corporate capital itself. But power at the center is great, and the choice of weapons belongs in the first instance to those who have them.

Theodor Mommsen summed up his history of the Roman Republic with patient sadness.

> It was indeed an old world, and even the richly gifted patriotism of Caesar could not make it young again. The dawn does not return till after the night has run its course.

I myself do not view the present with such pessimism. History moves more quickly now, the forces for positive change are much stronger, and the center seems to be losing its will and self confidence. It is becoming increasingly evident to all that in contrast to corporate capitalism we must be somewhat less "efficient" within the microcosm of the enterprise and far more "efficient" in the macrocosm of world society. The dysutopia of the multinational corporate system shows us both what is to be avoided and what is possible.

NOTES

1. See Marx, *Capital,* Vol. 1, Chapter XXV, "On the General Law of Capitalist Accumulation," Chapter XII, "Co-operation" and Chapter XIV, part 4, "Division of Labour in Manufacturing and Division of Labour in Society," and Vol. 3, Chapter XXIII.

2. This analysis of the modern corporation is almost entirely based on the work of Alfred D. Chandler, *Strategy and Structure* (New York, Doubleday & Co., Inc., 1961) and Chester Barnard, *The Functions of the Executive* (Cambridge, Harvard University Press, 1938).

3. Alfred D. Chandler and Fritz Redlich, "Recent Developments in American Business Administration and Their Conceptualization," *Business History Review,* Spring 1961, pp. 103–128.

25 / Toward an Alternative Strategy of Auto-Centered Development

Samir Amin

We propose to answer three questions:

1. What is the content of the objectives set by Third World countries in the UNCTAD (United Nations Conference on Trade and Development)? From what perspective (of development or not) must we view these objectives?

2. What has the Third World achieved? How effective has been the economic strategy implicit in its demands?

3. Is there an alternative strategy in case this one fails, as we think it will? And what is the content of this alternative?

The Objectives of the Group of 77 (The Charter of Algiers and the Lima Declaration)

The Third World governments' objectives, which were clearly formulated in the Charter of Algiers (October 1967) and in the Lima Declaration (October 1971), can be briefly stated as follows:

1. *On the question of international trade:* (a) negotiation of commodity agreements and the creation of buffer stocks financed by international agencies to limit price fluctuations; (b) liberalization of trade by removal of the developed countries' restrictions and taxes on imports from underdeveloped areas, guarantee of a minimum share by the latter in the former's markets when their products are competitive (e.g., oil seeds), abolition of preferences (such as those in the Yaounde agreement of Euro-African association) and removal of tariffs on manufactured products of underdeveloped countries (the extension of the Kennedy Round to the underdeveloped world).

2. *On the question of aid:* (a) transfer of 1 percent of the income of rich countries to the poor countries; (b) end of discrimination against the public sector, a frequent foreign aid practice; (c) elimination of the tied character of aid; (d) lightening of the foreign debt burden through its translation into long-term obligations.

From Samir Amin, "Per una Strategia Alternativa di Sviluppo Autocentrato," *Terzo Mondo* (Milan), Vol. VI, No. 19-20 (March-June, 1973), pp. 15-27. By permission of the publisher. Translated by Sylvia Modelski. Some notes have been omitted, and the remainder renumbered in sequence.

3. *On the question of international monetary reform:* recognition of the connection between the creation of additional liquidity and the financing of development.

4. *Finally, on various other questions:* (a) encouragement of maritime transport and insurance through the elimination of freight discrimination against the Third World, creation of merchant navies for these countries; (b) arrangements for the transfer of technology; (c) promotion of trade between underdeveloped countries; (d) adoption of special measures in favor of countries categorized as "least advanced."

As can be seen, the strategy behind these objectives coincides largely with that of the Pearson Report[1] in that it does not question the present international division of labor and limits itself to proposals for mere adjustments within that framework.

We have criticized elsewhere this strategy, which is a strategy for the development of underdevelopment, not a strategy of development. In fact, while it is true that the creation of buffer stocks may eliminate cyclical fluctuations in prices, it cannot stop the progressive deterioration of the relative price of products whose demand at the center grows less rapidly, which is the basic problem caused by the inequality of the international division of labor. This inequality will perpetuate itself if, advancing to a new stage of development, the underdeveloped countries have to concentrate on labor-intensive industries, leaving to the center the job of accelerating the development of future-oriented industries (atomic energy, space industries, electronics and automation). The Group of 77's objective of opening up the market in the developed countries to the manufactures of old industries (textiles, etc.) does not reflect a strategy of development, a prospect for the narrowing of the gap, but only a new stage in an always unequal specialization, inducing a widening of the gap. In fact, this can already be observed in certain underdeveloped countries where the multinational companies are establishing runaway industries (Hong Kong, Singapore, South Korea, Formosa). All this clamor for the "liberalization" of trade occurs within this context of wanting to deepen and revive modes of unequal specialization, not to do away with them. The same can be said about the "1 percent of aid" objective which does not challenge the fundamental structure of the world. A transfer from the rich to the poor which would genuinely be international aid can become a serious consideration only *after* the uneven international division of labor has been dealt with. In the meantime, *aid* is nothing but a means of support for this division of labor.

The Lesson from the Failure of UNCTAD: For an Alternative Strategy of Auto-Centered Development

One need not be overly pessimistic to note that the third session of the UN Conference on Trade and Development (Santiago, April 1972) ended as had the two previous meetings in Geneva (1964) and New Delhi (1968), with the utter refusal of the developed countries to satisfy even these modest Third World claims.

Nor is this the first failure. As is known, the Havana Charter on International Trade, drawn way back in 1947, never saw the light of day because of the opposition of the United States Senate. The allegedly liberal General Agreement on Tariffs and Trade (GATT) was set up in its place. At the Geneva meeting in 1964, the countries in the majority found themselves in the position of negotiating about what the "Great Powers" refused to concede, and of course they failed.

Does this obstinate rejection mean that the Third World's demands are unacceptable to the developed center and, therefore, that the objectives of the 77 reflect a correct strategy but that the methods used to attain them (i.e., international negotiations) are wrong?

Not at all. It only proves the incredible disdain with which the Great Powers behold the Third World. Indeed, changes which must come about anyway because they serve the objective tendencies of the system are made to look like "concessions" which the center is reluctant to make. The new version of uneven international specialization, which assigns to the periphery the role of supplier of labor intensive industrial products, takes its time in coming.

This is not the place to discuss these problems, in particular the role played by the United Nations in world diplomacy. For twenty years, the cold war between the two great powers relegated the United Nations to a subordinate place. One would have hoped that the end of that era might bring better prospects for international relations. The end of the United States' unchallenged superiority, the attendant gradual ascendency of Japan and Europe, the recognition of China, have replaced a diplomacy of two by a diplomacy of five (United States, Europe, Japan, U.S.S.R., China) with still nowhere for the Third World to go. Well, for the diplomacy of five as well as for the diplomacy of two, who needs the United Nations? The United Nations can only survive if it becomes, more than it has in the past, the mouthpiece of the Third World, provided the latter is capable of achieving a minimum of coherence through radical policy changes within itself.

If this were the case, certain objectives of the 77 could then be pursued by international negotiations. In fact, securing a better price for certain exports, opening up the market in developed countries to new industrial exports, the abolition of the tied character of "aid" and of discrimination against the public sector, reducing the "foreign debt," all this may bring some progress (not much, to be sure, but nonetheless genuine progress) while we wait for more drastic changes on the domestic and international levels. It would be useful, also, if the Third World were given a better role in the merchant marine and insurance areas. The value of these improvements within the existing system will depend on whether or not Third World countries will opt for the essential alternative of autocentered development.

This in fact is the main point. To the extent to which, by appropriate changes in their internal structure, the countries of the Third World commit themselves to autonomous and autocentered development, their foreign relations—serving the needs of development and no longer determining it—might be improved. In this context, international negotiations might reassume a certain place. But then they will be negotiations from positions of strength resulting from a radical challenge to the uneven international division of labor. In a world really "on the road to development," it is possible to foresee important improvements in the relative price of certain exports. It will then be easy to oppose to the monopoly of the developed countries an efficiently organized counter-monopoly of countries producing certain goods which are essential to the center. In a modest way, the experience of the oil producers has already proved it. But in fact it is well known that the prices of such products are in large measure conventional, expressing a balance of political power barely masked by the so-called economic laws of the famous "world market."

In expectation of such aggressive restructuring, the development of complementarity between Third World countries might have an important role to play. But this should not be confused with the expressions of pious intent for the development of trade between underdeveloped countries under the present structure of dependence. In the latter context, development is necessarily limited and also not very favorable to "least advanced" countries.

Finally, and the third session of UNCTAD confirms this, the Third World countries are not yet ready to carry out a systematic plan of autocentered development. This is why they are so weak and have failed to achieve anything, even minor "concessions" within the system. Vague resolutions about the reform of the international system, the transfer to technology or the "special measures in favor of least advanced countries" are in fact nothing other than pious and empty promises.

UNCTAD and the Reform of the International Monetary System

To assess the proposals of the Group of 77 for the reform of the international monetary system, it is first necessary to know what the crisis in the system consists of.

Since 1950, the connecting link between the volume of international liquidity and that of international trade has become more and more tenuous. Yet the crisis is not caused by an insufficiency in the volume of international liquidity since the necessary level of liquidity is not dependent on the level of trade but on the balances to be settled; as a matter of fact, after the world war, the structure of trade was very seriously off balance. But in reality, the crisis is due to an evergrowing disequilibrium in the distribution of reserves, that is, the accumulation of accounts in unwanted dollars which went from 4 billion in 1951 to 45 billion in 1970, while the US gold reserves continued to diminish. Hence the dollar crisis. The latter currency was accepted as the monetary basis of the international system because of the unchallenged economic superiority of the United States. The perennial surplus in the United States balance of payments, that is the "dollar famine" of other countries, reflected this superiority. But in the past ten years, the rapid progress of Europe (especially West Germany) and of Japan has been a challenge to that superiority. There has in fact been a reversal of the past trend: while the balance of payments of these countries chronically shows a surplus, due to the increasing competitiveness of their industries, that of the United States shows a deficit.

The advantage enjoyed by the dollar in its role as international currency—which allows the United States to settle in its own national money the deficit derived from its foreign relations, even though the other party does not want to increase its dollar reserves, is now being contested. Other national currencies, mainly the yen and the Deutsch mark today aspire to the privileges once enjoyed by the pound sterling which, since the Second World War have accrued to the dollar.

The "solutions" offered to the crisis invariably remain within the range bounded by the alternatives of flexible exchange rates or universal currency. But if the world system suffers from structural imbalances (and it was until recently always in favor of the United States, and now favors other countries such as Germany and Japan), flexible exchange rates are not enough to compensate for them. And the adoption of a universal currency issued by a supranational authority presupposes the settlement of conflicts of interest at that same supranational level. Here Triffin picks up Utopia at the point where Keynes defined it in 1945.

It is not as if the international system were unable to produce a universal currency and were thus forced to remain tied to gold and the reserve currencies. The IMF's drawing rights provide for the allotment of credit funds in these currencies, nothing more. As long as the dollar was the principal reserve currency, the IMF was nothing but an executive branch of the American Treasury. The crisis rests on a real conflict: that between the dollar, heir to a dominant position and its attendant privileges, and aspirants to a "more equitable distribution" of these privileges.

The underdeveloped countries have no voice in the international monetary system, hence they cannot hope to see their money become the international currency. Thus the solicitude of which they are the objects must be interpreted as just another ingredient in the monetary strategy of the Powers.

There are two precedents for this. When, after the war, the underdeveloped countries were "admitted" to the International Monetary Fund (IMF), the status of the pound sterling, as a legacy of the past, was still strong in Asia and Africa where many countries still belonged to a fairly centralized sterling area. This strength of the pound, reflecting Britain's place in the world economy, was the main reason why the IMF consecrated it as a reserve currency. Little by little, the dollar, through the IMF, dislodged the pound from its position. Similarly, certain proposals, which today seem to favor the developing countries, should be seen as elements in a strategy that was conceived elsewhere. One recalls how in 1967 the Rio decision favored the American cause. In the same way it is safe to assume that the move to create a Group of Twenty is inspired by the wish to counterbalance the stronger position of Europe and Japan in the Group of Ten.

Nevertheless, some Third World countries have real interests to defend in the international monetary system. The unequal relations from which certain central countries, whose currency is universally accepted, draw profit to the detriment of other central countries, are repeated on the global scale in the relations between the center and the periphery. Within the monetary zones which more or less formally govern the relations between certain countries in the center and their spheres of influence in the periphery, the privileges go only to the developed metropolitan countries. This is confirmed by the case of the franc zone, to cite the most obvious example.

In this situation, how can the Third World protect its interests? Perhaps by insisting on the creation of a universal currency based on raw materials, as the Kaldor plan proposes? This is unrealistic for at least two reasons: (1) the universal currency cannot rest on a sinking foundation and the gradual depreciation of the relative price of raw materials is an objective rule of the system; (2) it would reopen the question of the conflict of interests within the authority charged with issuing such money.

Instead of pursuing this unrealistic goal, the underdeveloped countries had better exploit the conflict to obtain reparations for the damages inflicted on them by the crisis. The devaluations, in effect, have reduced the value of their reserves by around 500 million dollars. Compensatory credits should be extracted from the Great Powers each time they devalue their money so as to guarantee the value of the Third World's reserves. This would be a prime example of the celebrated marriage between the creation of international currency and the financing of development championed by UNCTAD.

What are the means available to the Third World for extracting such reparations? True, these means are poor, but it is not at all unrealistic to believe that a concerted strategy might yield some result. A first measure could be taken unilaterally: withdrawal of the investments of the "rich" underdeveloped countries (the oil producers among them) from the developed financial centers: this amounts to some 20 or 25 billion dollars, or about 60 floating billion, and constitutes an additional gift the Third World bestows on the dominant centers.

UNCTAD and the Transfer of Technology
to the Developing Countries

The UNCTAD secretariat must be credited with having, finally, introduced on the agenda of international organizations the problem of technology transfer. But an aura of mystery, carefully maintained by the interested parties, surrounds this question. In a world where everything is bought and sold, we are asked to believe that to acquire know-how we must first consent to be entrapped by foreign capital. However, technology is a product that can be bought and sold just like any other. It is physically produced by: (1) machinery and raw materials; (2) skilled labor that has been trained to use the machinery; (3) information, principally on the market for the product and on inputs (prices, quantity, degree of competition, etc.). The UNCTAD secretariat must be praised for having finally begun to unravel the mystery of the monopoly of "technology markets."

We are dealing with a highly monopolistic market indeed. Plants are becoming ever more specialized, trained-on-the-job technicians are tightly bound to the suppliers of these plants, information is jealously guarded through "industrial secrecy." This monopoly power gives effective control over the users of the technology. Unexpected changes in the operation and maintenance of the machinery, the costly obligation to refer back to the firm which made the consignment, surprises in the delivery of specific inputs, spare parts, etc., patents and other ownership rights imposed in exchange for access to information, trade marks and markets, these are the methods by which the technology monopolists extract profits which are substantial enough to render obsolete former modes of sharing in the benefits gained from ownership of capital.

These monopolies, naturally concentrated in the more important countries of the developed world, are extremely costly to the Third World. To begin with, the price the underdeveloped countries pay to have access to advanced technology is already more than considerable and it is rising very fast. In fact, it already represents at least 1.5 billion dollars, is increasing at the rate of 20 percent annually, and, as far as can be foretold, will amount to 20 percent of the exports of the underdeveloped world by 1980. Second, and this is even more important, the technology of the developed countries does not meet the needs of the underdeveloped countries to which it is transferred. Research and development, pursued at the center as it is, does not deal in problems relevant to the development requirements of the poor countries. Its only aim is the resolution of the problems of the developed world. The consequences of this transfer of unsuitable techniques are well known: (1) growing unemployment in the Third World; (2) the industry of the Third World is put under foreign control (even when the multinational corporations do not directly acquire its capital).

Substituting these techniques for others now obsolete in the developed world does not solve the question because in this matter, as in the others, the Third World's problems are specific to it. Contrary to what the absurd Rostowian thesis asserts, the Third World's situation is not really in any way similar to that of the modern developed countries at a previous stage of their evolution.

In these circumstances UNCTAD III could only express a pious and ambiguous hope that the research and development of the developed countries be given the task of devising techniques appropriate to the underdeveloped world and that the wealthy nations endeavour to ease the transfer of these techniques at a less onerous cost. Which amounts to asking monopolies to act against their own interests, to abandon the methods of control upon which their monopoly profits depend!

It is obvious that the correct solution to the Third World's particular problems can only come from the Third World itself. The fair solution, in fact, lies wholly in the systematic organization of *autonomous* technological research there. This means a reversal of the traditional priorities according to which the poor nations should abstain from creating too "skilled" a labor force, which is a superfluous luxury for them. But the cost of this qualified labor must be reduced in order to cut off cultural and ideological ties which today create the problem of matching income levels with their counterparts at the center and the brain drain. It follows from this that the aims of autonomous research should no longer be to *imitate,* but rather to assimilate in order to *invent.* Undoubtedly, to plead the cause of autonomy in this matter means having the courage to confront those who draw their profits and influence from the present monopoly of technology. It means getting into conflict with the monopolists selling this technology; it also certainly means challenging a developed world which, through the suble channels of cultural and ideological structures, alienates the Third World *elites* in order to turn them into reliable servants of its dominance, transmission belts in the global system of asymmetrical division of labor.

UNCTAD and the Problem of the Least Developed Countries[2]

In recent years, the United Nations in general and UNCTAD in particular have launched a campaign on the problem of the least advanced countries. Their definition of these countries is simple: an annual per capita gross product of less than 100 dollars. As is known, the majority of these countries are found in Africa (Mali, Niger, Upper Volta, Chad, the Central African Republic, Ethiopia, Ruanda, Burundi, Tanzania, Lesotho, etc.) and have no access to the sea. The group also includes some Latin American countries (Bolivia, Paraguay, and Haiti) and some Asian ones (Afghanistan, the two Yemens, Nepal, and Laos).

Mainly in the course of session III of UNCTAD, "special measures" have been proposed in "favor" of these countries which can be summed up, in the final analysis, by a single concern: to increase the absolute and relative volume of foreign aid and, more specifically, of grants and public loans, made to them on easy terms. It is true that these countries, although poorer, have in general received less foreign "aid" than others. Public aid (mainly from France and Europe as far as the French-speaking African nations in the group are concerned) has been the same (or about the same) percentage of public expenditures, particularly of investments, for all the French-speaking African countries, "rich" and "poor." As the per capita gross product is not equally distributed among these countries, the result has been that the poor nations have received, per capita, about a third of the public aid sent to the group of "rich" countries. If one were to include the movement of private capital in the total external contribution, the gap would be even greater, since this capital is concentrated on the coastline. The external foreign contribution to the landlocked countries would then amount, per capita, to no more than 15 to 20 percent of that enjoyed by the "rich" countries. This may be observed in the case of Ruanda and Burundi as compared with Zaire, that of Lesotho and Tanzania as compared with Zambia or Kenya. Furthermore, the very unequally distributed external contribution is a decisive factor in uneven development. Since the latter process is cumulative, it reduces any return from foreign private investment in "poor" countries. That is why the United Nations wants to emphasize public aid for these countries.

In other words, UNCTAD really does not offer any change of strategy, but wants merely to do *more* in the old direction. This is a very questionable proposition. We think it doomed to certain failure. An increase of public aid for the least advanced countries would induce an unsustainable public deficit due to current spending, because the slower pace of production activities would not allow tax revenue to keep abreast of the debt. An objective relationship exists between the possible increase in public spending (therefore of public aid) and in production (partly generated by the movement of capital investments, which in its turn is determined by the economic return). This relationship is at the root of the famous "absorption capacity" which experience tells us is limited. Well, this relationship is even more unfavorable in the poor countries than it is in countries where the economic returns from production activity are greater. Which means that one cannot "increase aid" to the poorer countries without simultaneously facing a collapse of their structure.

This is the crux of the problem: what are these structures and how should they be transformed? Well, on this level, the United Nations literature has proved itself frustratingly inconsistent so far. It is enough to read the documents presented at seminars and conferences on the subject of the least advanced countries to become convinced of this. The total absence of structural analysis is compensated by pedantic enumerations of well-known descriptive banalities about less-advanced urbanization, the greater importance of subsistence agriculture, the lower level of education, etc.

The primary flaw consists in considering these least advanced countries as a homogeneous group which is not true in fact. This error in perception is due to the received conventional theory (Rostow's absurd theory of "stages of growth") according to which underdevelopment is *relative,* measurable by the per capita gross product, and which sees a continuous chain linking the countries where this index is lowest all the way through to the United States. This is sheer flight from reality, from the existence of *diverse structures.*

The center–periphery distinction belongs to the basic level of structures (domination-dependence) not to that of phenomenology, where one more or less finds the peculiar measurement called per capita gross product. The latter does not oppose the developed countries to the underdeveloped ones, but rather inscribes them on a continuous chain.

Within the peripheral group, we must deepen the analysis of their structures and study the *forms of dependence,* clarifying certain aspects ignored by the conventional analysis of "less advanced" countries.

Meantime, in the group of least advanced countries, we distinguish three different structural subgroups:

First, this grab-bag contains countries which do not belong to the periphery of the world system. Since they have no relations with the center of the system, exporting neither products nor capital to it, these countries *are not underdeveloped;* they should be called traditional or precapitalistic. Few countries today fit this category. But in 1935 Ethiopia was still predominantly of this type, as was Afghanistan and Northern Yemen. In contemporary Africa, Ethiopia, Ruanda and Burundi still possess strongly precapitalistic characteristics. But these are exceptions because the integration of the world system now extends over the whole planet. But if *today* no country belongs to the "pure" precapitalistic type, regions fashioned on this model still survive within the African continent. By virtue of their contribution to the gross national product or because of the size of their population, these regions occupy an unimportant place in the coastal countries which were developed by colonization. The same thing cannot be said of certain land-locked countries where these regions represent a high percentage of the total population. This is not the place in which to analyze the nature of the noncapitalistic means of production peculiar to these regions, but it must be said that precisely because we are dealing here with noncapitalistic means of production they cannot be reduced to a common denominator based on the per capita gross product.

In these circumstances, the gross per capita product *makes no sense in fact.* For example, if we were to give some of the products, which not being merchandise have no market value, a "subjective value" equal to their counterparts in the United States we would treble or quadruple this per capita gross product. These countries or regions have an essentially homogeneous or coherent character, not only on the economic level but also throughout the social system. Thus, for example, Ethiopia, Afghanistan and the Yemen exhibit an ethnic or national integrity which is generally not found in underdeveloped countries. The latter, in fact, stand out for the chaotic character of their structure (the so-called dualism) that is the consequence of their being part of the world system that having disfigured originally precapitalistic zones now subjects them to the imperatives of peripheral capitalism.

A second group consists of countries integrated with the world system and belonging therefore to the periphery; they are underdeveloped in the real sense of the term, but evolve specific functions within the context of *uneven development of the periphery* itself. These countries or regions supply either labor or merchandise to the main periphery.

Upper Volta and Lesotho are above all suppliers of labor to the coastal regions. We have shown elsewhere that, as far as Upper Volta is concerned, this supply of labor is equivalent to a *massive transfer* of value from that country to the coastal countries (Ghana, Ivory Coast), to the extent of 15 percent of its gross national product. The transfer is even greater in the case of Lesotho. These countries, therefore, are particularly "poor" because they are *overexploited.* Consequently, their structures show characteristics which are very different from those of countries not integrated in the world system.

Mali and Niger, for example, also belong to the second group. It has not been sufficiently noted that these countries are above all exporters of produce to the coastal countries (cattle and dried fish make up at least two-thirds of their exports). However, they import mainly goods made at the center, and obtain their imports through other peripheral countries. Thus they function under aggravated conditions of unequal exchange since they are forced to pay an additional premium to the intermediaries, i.e., the coastal countries. In sum, they are poor because they are *overexploited.* The theory of subimperialism, introduced by Ruy Mauro Marini sheds a more subtle light on the specific problems of these second echelon peripheries than does UNCTAD literature.

And finally there is a third group of least developed countries which possess completely different characteristics. These are the countries or regions which have been very rapidly and very thoroughly integrated in the world system and were *ruined and devastated by this process.* Haiti, the Antilles in general, northeastern Brazil, are the most glaring examples in Latin America, just as the Senegal River zone is in Africa. Characteristic of these countries or regions is not only that they are strongly integrated in the market, but more importantly, that they were once even more integrated. The mechanisms of the *transition bloc* (which we have analyzed elsewhere),[3] which are typical of dependence and are associated with the slowing down of the center's demand for some kinds of products, have ruined countries and regions which had once benefited from the "economic miracle" of very strong dependent growth. These countries are poor *because they have been overexploited.*

Sugar in the Antilles and the Brazilian northeast, rubber in the Senegal valley, have lost the privileged status they held in the eighteenth and nineteenth centuries respectively; but the structures which were then erected in the context of their dependent growth without development remain to give these countries a very different character than that of the other so-called "least advanced" regions.

We must now turn to what Suranda Patel calls the "depression areas of the Third World" whose exports since 1928 have had a rate of increase of less than 2 percent per annum, so that their share of global exports has fallen from 12 percent in 1928 to 3 percent in 1967. Though these depressed countries may not be part of the least advanced nations group (they are in fact some of the most important big countries of the Third World: Brazil, Argentina, India, Pakistan, Indonesia, Burma, Ceylon and Egypt) this deterioration in their position in world trade is the key to understanding their difficulties in development, at least so long as they do not question the fundamental principles of the world division of labor, as China has done. In discussing the Third World in global terms, one can get carried away and forget that the great increase in exports which characterizes the pattern of dependent development is actually limited to a small *elite* of fortunate ones, in particular the oil-producing nations who tomorrow (say, in thirty years?) will undoubtedly in their turn become the victims of the displacement of demand at the center to other products and will then join the long list of devastated areas.

Throughout this structural analysis, we found it difficult to speak in terms of countries and think it would have been easier to talk about regions. Because *uneven* development is, among other things, uneven on the spatial plane. In one area we have strong growth which seems a "miracle," in another this provokes the stagnation or devastation and decadence of an economy previously thought to be "flourishing." This is the kind of devastation that threatens all the underdeveloped countries.

NOTES

1. *Partners in Development,* Praeger, New York, 1969.
2. The distinction is between *less-* and *least-*developed countries—G.M.
3. Samir Amin: *L'Accumulation à L'Échelle Mondiale,* Paris, 1970.

26 / Labor and the Multinationals

Robert W. Cox

It is now generally accepted that the expansion of the multinational corporation is a major, perhaps *the* major, phenomenon of the international economy today. Large corporations with their headquarters in the United States, in other Western industrialized countries, and now increasingly in Japan as well, are expanding their activities both into industrialized countries, including the Soviet sphere, and into the less-developed world. Once heavily concentrated in mining and extractive fields, today is the manufacturing activities of the multinationals that command growing attention.

The political consequences of this transformation have now become the subject of a vast and growing literature. Much less attention, however, has been devoted to the impact of the multinationals on the work force within the affected nations.[1] Striving to come to grips with the rapidly changing pattern of production in the world, organized labor fluctuates between attempts to negotiate directly with the multinationals on their own ground wherever they may locate—a transnational strategy, if you will—and attempts to use their political leverage within their own nations in order to regulate and control the multinationals and thus to protect jobs within each nation.

In short, labor today has managed to generate only a confused, partial and lopsided response to the multinational corporation. To understand why this is so, it is necessary first to analyze the total impact of the multinational corporation (MNC) not merely on organized labor but on the total social structure and work force patterns of the affected nations. From such an analysis one can begin to grasp how truly drastic and dramatic the effect of the MNCs has already been and how over time that effect is likely to increase.

There emerges a reasonably clear conclusion that with rare exceptions organized labor henceforth is not likely to pursue the transnational strategy except in a minority of cases. Rather, the efforts of organized labor will be focused more and more heavily on moving national and international regulation of the multinationals in the direction of fuller control over their impact on jobs. The larger questions of what effect organized labor's response to the multinationals may have upon the direction and pace of social change and thus upon the welfare of the work force throughout the world remain open. But the options for labor can now be seen as bifurcating toward either a more egalitarian world or, alternatively, one determined by the protection of acquired positions.

II

The question of labor and the MNC has often been discussed as though the working people concerned were just the employees of the MNCs. This is far too restricted a perspective within which to evaluate the social consequences of MNC expansion. In the broader context required to assess social impact, the expansion of MNCs must be seen as a principal dynamic factor in a far-reaching transformation of the world economy which is affecting the whole world labor force. Among the workers affected, those directly employed by MNCs are a minority and on the whole a relatively privileged one.

The advocates of the MNC often describe it as an engine of development. What they usually mean by this is that MNCs can increase growth, measured in production and incomes. In aggregate terms, this is a defensible proposition, but it begs the question: what is development? Whatever precise meanings may be assigned to it, development is a normative and purposive concept, and can never properly be reduced to an accounting aggregate like Gross National Product.

Contrary to the engine-of-development thesis, it has also been cogently argued that the kind of growth promoted by MNCs produces dependency and underdevelopment.[2] The concept of development connotes an element of equity, of widespread partcipation both in the processes of production and in the enjoyment of the fruits of production. One criterion for judging whether or not MNCs are engines of development is to look at the consequences of their expansion as regards participation in employment and incomes for the labor force as a whole.

The expansion of the MNC can be directly associated with a change in the international distribution of economic activities. A major initial impetus to foreign direct investment was the desire to develop and control supplies of raw materials—minerals and tropical agricultural products—upon which the continuity of production in industrially advanced centers depended. This classic type (petroleum, bauxite, copper, and plantation crops) is no longer so characteristic as it once was of the MNC. The more recent and now much more characteristic aspect of the MNC's expansion has been the growth of international production—manufacturing in foreign-owned plants, which has been the world's fastest growing "economy" of the past decade, and has become the principal participant in international trade. In part, international production has taken the form of the creation or acquisition of plants by foreign owners to supply domestic markets, profiting from the monopolistic advantages of the big corporation (access to financing, knowledge of markets, product differentiation, a corner on some piece of technology) in competition with local industries and—as in the case of the European Economic Community (EEC)—operating within tariff walls. More recently, international production has taken the form of direct investment in "export platforms" provided by less-developed countries.

The importance of these changes can be seen in the auto industry: in 1950, 80 percent of world auto production was in the United States; by 1972, the United States accounted for only 32 percent, Western European production had risen from 15 percent to 35 percent of the world total, and Japan (with Brazil) had moved from one-third of one percent to 18 percent of the total. Since world production had expanded more than threefold during this time, there was no absolute drop in U.S. auto production, but the world distribution had shifted markedly.[3] All major automobile-producing companies had, by the latter date, become multinational producers. The shifting international distribution of production was reflected in significant intracorporate shifts in the location of production. Looking ahead, it seems likely that the international distribution of the industry will show an increased share going to the industrializing less-developed countries and to the U.S.S.R. and other socialist countries.

The automobile industry is characterized by high technology, though still relatively labor-intensive. In more labor-intensive lines of production, such as textiles or the manufacture of electronic components, the movement of industry toward the less-developed areas has been even more marked. Automobile production is geared rather more to domestic and regional markets than to distant exports, though Japanese and Russian automobiles have a share of the European market, and Europeans and Japanese currently a large share of the American market. But increasingly, in the most labor-intensive lines, MNCs have set up manufacturing plants in less-developed countries to build components or products primarily to export to their home country or other relatively rich-country markets.

The importance of the "export platform" for U.S.-based industries can be gauged by the fact that the aggregate of U.S. foreign subsidiaries by 1968 had become an exporter in world markets as large as Germany and twice as large as Japan, and that much of these exports of U.S. subsidiaries were coming into the United States as imports—to the extent of one-fourth of all U.S. imports.[4] The readiness of the U.S. government, under pressure from UNCTAD and Latin American countries, to reverse its opposition to the generalized system of preferences for manufactured exports from the less-developed countries may be critically appraised in the light of the fact that so substantial a part of these exports now entering the U.S. market are the produce of foreign subsidiaries of American companies.

In the most general terms, these trends show a shift of industrial manufacturing away from the most advanced economies toward those countries now in process of industrialization, while the control centers remain in the more advanced countries. European production expanded rapidly from the late 1950s, and more recently the mose rapid expansion has been in countries of the western Pacific and a few others like Brazil. Japan, once in the lead in pace of growth in the Pacific area, has become a relay furthering growth in less-developed countries like South Korea, Taiwan, Hong Kong and Singapore. The more advanced economies, meanwhile, turn toward a "post-industrial" structure of the labor force, with a declining proportion in manufacturing and an increasing emphasis on sophisticated services—on software rather than hardware.

For the labor force as a whole, the central issue posed by these changes in the structure of the world economy concerns employment. In the rich countries, can the growth of services compensate for the decline in manufacturing jobs? In the industrializing countries, will the growth of industry, rapid as it has been in countries like those of the western Pacific and Brazil, make a significant dent in widespread unemployment and underemployment? And will the poorest countries of all ever get some share of the action? These long-range questions are currently posed in a context of world recession outside the socialist countries, of a dramatic international shift in monetary reserves consequent on the increased cost of petroleum, with as yet unresolved implications for world monetary relations, and of a new awareness of the finite limits to the earth's ecosystem which cautions against thinking that all economic and social problems can be solved ultimately through economic growth.

In the more advanced industrial societies, organized labor has raised a number of alarm signals. In the United States, the AFL-CIO seeks government controls over MNCs that will limit the movement of production abroad by U.S. corporations so as to stop the "export of jobs." MNCs reply to organized labor that they are in fact creating more jobs at home. Many of these new jobs, however, are unlikely to be available to the displaced workers. Openings for systems analysts may not be very helpful to redundant auto assembly workers. Jobs lost and jobs created cannot be neatly balanced but have to be looked at in the more personal terms of the transferability of individuals with particular skills and habits—and in North America today, there is little confidence that the labor market is equipped to ease the transition of displaced workers satisfactorily.

Regarding the employment consequences of international changes in production, there appears to be a contrast between the United States and Japan, on the one hand, where corporate decisions are shifting the more labor-intensive production away from the home country into its external economic periphery (often to the same export platforms of the western Pacific and Latin America), and West European countries, on the other hand, in which less productive work has devolved to an imported lower wage category of immigrant labor from the Mediterranean countries, thus transforming a geographical periphery into an internal social periphery. Most of the concern voiced in Western Europe in recent years about this question has been over the issues of inter-ethnic relations and the encounter of contrasting cultures. This has led some West Europeans to argue for restriction of alien workers, while others point to inequities in their status and conditions. Until recently, the prospect of unemployment has not figured in the debate.

There are now, however, indications of a more acute concern about jobs. In part, this is because the recession has brought to Western Europe levels of unemployment less than those of the United States but still well above those regarded as politically safe. But in part the growing concern in Europe is with longer-term factors: with an outward flow of direct investment from the EEC countries and a fear that Europe may be but a temporary stopping place for U.S. capital in its secular movement toward lower labor cost areas.

In the less-developed countries, the employment prospects are even more pessimistic. The technology transferred from mature industrial countries has not expanded employment commensurate with increases in the labor force and declines in agricultural labor. Exhortations in favor of the development of more labor-intensive technology have not made much impression either on governments seeking new industrial investment or on potential investors who already have a stake in the technology they bring. The marginal populations of the Third World—those who have left rural pursuits without having found an established place in urban employment—now are estimated at close to one-third of the labor force, with no signs of their numbers abating.

Thus in all these different areas of the world, the employment consequences of the expansion of international production appear rather grim, accentuated by recession but traceable ultimately to continuing long-term structural changes. Unemployment, of course, hits some people more than others. Its social impact is differentiated by the structure of the labor force.

The concepts of primary and secondary labor markets, introduced by some labor economists, are useful in explaining this differential impact.[5] These economists observed that many workers are in enclosed internal labor markets, which they entered at an early stage in their employment history and within which they have some opportunities for career development. These may be big public or private corporations, or else an industry in which the conditions and status of workers are regulated by powerful unions, as in construction. These more established workers are in the primary labor market. They tend to be those with the higher skills, better pay and most effective union organization. The secondary labor market conforms more closely to the classical concept of a market in which the price of labor is determined by supply and demand. Employment for secondary labor-market workers is more unstable, there is greater turnover of jobs and little career development. These are the more expendable workers, less skilled and less well protected by unions. Ethnic discrimination and low social status frequently add to these disadvantages.

As is all too evident today, secondary labor-market workers are disproportionately hard hit by unemployment. In the United States, blacks, Puerto Ricans and Chicanos are numerically prominent among the unemployed. In Western Europe, the greatest impact of prolonged unemployment falls less heavily upon the industrialized center than upon the periphery—upon Portugal, Spain, Greece, Turkey and southern Italy, whence came Western Europe's secondary labor-market workers. This impact upon the southern rim of Europe only increases its political volatility.

Prevailing employment patterns also have political implications in other less-developed countries. The explosive potential of a large socially marginal population in these countries is now contained by two factors. One is the lack of any unifying consciousness of revolt among marginals themselves, who initially have been more susceptible to the consumption culture exported by more affluent societies, or to messianic illusions prompted by despair, than they have been to revolutionary action. The "wretched of the earth" have had their prophets from Michael Bakunin to Frantz Fanon. Revolutionary guerrilla bands like the Tupamaros have sought cover and support among them. Radical labor movements like anarcho-syndicalism have at times drawn support from them. But marginals generally have not been aroused as a social class with effective and sustained cohesion comparable to that attained by industrial proletariats in late nineteenth century Europe and America, although in some parts of the world they may now be approaching this threshold.

The other containing factor is the effectiveness of repressive techniques for the control and suppression of such overt discontent as does appear, in the hands of the authoritarian governments which have become the characteristic sponsors of industrialization by means of foreign investment. The connection between political authoritarianism and the promotion of economic growth through foreign investment derives more from the logic of political economy than from an iniquitous conspiracy of foreign big business with corrupt local politicians—although evidence of such conspiracies is not lacking of late. The pattern of growth promoted by private foreign investment has accentuated the discrepancy between geographical poles of growth and the hinterland—between the São Paulos and the Nordestes—and has exacerbated inequalities in the distribution of incomes between social groups within countries, in large part because of the very limited employment-creating effect of this kind of growth. Regimes which rely substantially upon MNCs to produce growth have consciously sacrificed the "less fit," among whom the social marginals loom larger and larger.[6] This is politically possible only if the less fit remain unable to protest effectively, and if such protest as they do make can be effectively repressed. Repression becomes a political condition for a pattern of growth which generates marginality. But the coercive state has its own autonomy, and the military-bureaucratic regimes born of this process acquire through it also in time the ability to exact greater concessions from the foreign investors they have admitted.

III

Thus, a consequence of the internationalizing of production is the emergence of a global class structure somewhat modified from that derived from nineteenth-century production

relations. The expansion of the MNC has been a major force in bringing this new structure of classes into being. Its outlines are as follows:

1. At the apex of the social configuration is a *transnational managerial class*. This
includes the administrators of MNCs, the associated economic diplomats, and many of
the technicians in research and development and control systems. These people are
transnationally mobile and may be expected to develop the kind of global outlook on
their work that Howard Perlmutter described as "geocentric." Sharing many of the
perspectives of this group and providing a framework of support for their activities are
officials of intergovernmental organizations, e.g., the World Bank, the International
Monetary Fund, U.N. Development Program, etc., and the larger network of experts
associated in their work. Further support is found among personnel within the public
policy-making institutions of national governments. Collectively, and despite rivalries
attributable to particular interests, the transnational class seeks to establish a liberal
world economic order in which stable and predictable conditions will be propitious for
the relatively free international movement of factors of production. The outlines of an
ideology expressive of these goals are already clear—an ideology that can be called
"transnationalism" or "globalism," which sees the MNC as the engine of global development, and economic nationalism as the obstructive reflex of an obsolescent nation-
state.

2. Beneath the transnational class stands a large class of *established labor*, established
in the sense that its members enjoy relatively secure employment and, corresponding
to this, a secure status in their local communities. These people do not move out of
their own countries and rarely out of their own communities, in which they have a
stake as more or less active citizens and often as small proprietors. They correspond to
the primary labor market. This group has been the main object and beneficiary of the
social institutions, the social legislation, and the institutionalization of conflict evolved
in the industrial societies during the nineteenth and twentieth centuries. As such, the
group has a high level of consciousness of its place and power in society. This consciousness has tended to take an instrumental form—a confidence in the group's ability to
make the institutions of industrial societies work for its own protection and advance-
ment.

3. At the bottom is a third group, varying in relative size, in some countries larger
than the class of established labor, in others somewhat smaller. This group can be
called the *social marginals*. (The designation of "class" may be disputed for this group,
on the ground that class presupposes not only a specific relationship to the means of
production, but also an awareness or consciousness of its position.) This group includes
both those—particularly in the less-developed countries—who have been unable to
find industrial employment, and also those—especially in the more industrialized
countries—whose precarious employment is in the secondary labor market. The marginals pay the higher social costs whether of industrial growth or of recession.

IV

It must be apparent that this description of the emerging social pattern, brought on
largely by the expansion of the multinational corporations, does not conform to the historical pattern of social structure on which the organized labor movement of the United
States and other industrialized countries is based. Clearly, if new social structures are, in

fact, developing rather rapidly, a serious question is raised whether the classic relationship of labor and management as it has evolved in mature industrial societies—in effect a procedure for institutionalized conflict[7]—is capable of containing the potential for social conflict inherent in the emerging class structure.

Keeping this question in the back of our minds, let us now look at the record of organized labor's response to the challenge of the multinational corporation. Ever since the early 1950s, the dramatic spread of production in the automotive industry had led trade unions to consider ways of making their response more effective. In particular, the International Metalworkers Federation organized a series of world company councils in the automotive industry, bringing together representatives of the unions that deal with a particular company in the different countries in which the company operates.

Another widely noted development was the consultation instituted between the management of the Philips electrical concern and unions, in regard to questions of production and job security. Then, in 1969, there occurred a highly publicized confrontation of the French multinational Saint Gobain Company by a multinational group of unions coordinated through the International Federation of Chemical and General Workers. This event was certainly of no greater intrinsic importance than a number of other similar multinational trade union initiatives in automotive, electronics, chemical and pharmaceutical, rubber, petroleum, and air transport industries, but it constituted a public relations breakthrough following as it did upon a widely publicized stock market battle for the takeover of Saint Gobain.

Such events seemed to suggest that the continuing global expansion of MNCs would be accompanied by the emergence of transnational collective bargaining through a restructuring of trade unions along the lines of the MNC. This particular image of labor's response could be spelled out in terms of the development of a series of instruments designed to strengthen unions in relation to the corporation. The first stage in putting these instruments together is acquisition, coordination and analysis of information about the MNC. Further instruments in the trade union arsenal are support for union organizing efforts in countries where unions are weak or nonexistent; pressure on corporate headquarters to recognize and bargain with unions in other countries in which the corporation operates; banning overtime and other increases in work schedules in other countries in the event of a strike in any one country in which the corporation operates in order to prevent shifts in production; organizing consumer boycotts of corporation products; coordinating the terminal dates of collective agreements in different countries; and ultimately collective bargaining at the level of the corporation as a whole.

Of course, when contemplating this particular image of future global labor management relations, unions recognized the relative advantages of MNCs and their own areas of relative weakness in the development of these different stages of response. The advantages enjoyed by MNCs derive from their size and the very fact that, operating within several national jurisdictions, they can minimize or avoid some of the controls and the checks and balances evolved within the national framework of industrial societies. MNCs can maximize their advantages among different national jurisdictions as regards such factors as fiscal and labor market conditions, and by intra-corporate transfer pricing and other accounting devices can determine where to show their profits. These advantages MNCs can exploit actively and aggressively because they have sophisticated and centralized information and decision systems, compared with which governments and *a fortiori* trade unions are in a more defensive posture, lacking adequate information on which to base their action, and—with regard to trade unions in host countries—frequently unable to deal directly with the real locus of decision-making authority in the MNC.

The principal weaknesses of unions in confronting the MNCs can also be readily catalogued. As between developed and less-developed countries, there are marked differences in the organized strength of unions. In some cases, the availability of abundant, docile and cheap labor is a major incentive for MNCs to establish manufacturing enterprises in certain developing countries. Furthermore, unions fear that MNCs' use of manipulative techniques of sophisticated personnel management may undermine union organization.

Differences in ideological orientation and political affiliation have also left bitter feelings of mutual suspicion among labor leaders in some countries that continue to obstruct concerted action. In addition, the distance between the rank and file on the shop floor and the union leadership and staff, which has become manifest in most industrialized countries in recent years in the form of wildcat strikes and shop steward movements, would likely be further widened by the introduction of transnational bargaining which would be even more remote from the individual worker. What guarantees would there be that a multinational union could hold all its members in different countries to a centrally negotiated agreement?

Union efforts to overcome these weaknesses include support in money and personnel for organizing drives abroad, public denunciation and the building up of pressure against governments that obstruct union organization in the interests of attracting foreign investment for export industries, and initiatives to bridge the ideological gap and to promote contacts among erstwhile hostile union leadership—such as the initiatives toward collaboration among social democratic, Communist and (former) Christian trade unionists through the recently formed European Confederation of Trade Unions (CES).

The image evoked here of future industrial relations is one of a growing power of multinational unions gradually overcoming these obstacles so as ultimately to balance the power of the global corporation. States do not figure prominently in this scenario, because those who have cultivated this vision have tended to regard the state as an obsolescent structure.

The United Automobile, Aerospace and Agricultural Implement Workers of America (UAW) has been the major single source of impetus behind this transnational strategy, though its exponents are now to be found well beyond the UAW itself. The UAW has been a preponderant influence upon the International Metalworkers Federation, which has become one of the principal vehicles for propagating and organizing the transnational approach from its headquarters in Geneva, Switzerland. And the leadership of the other international trade union body which has been most active in this direction—the International Federation of Chemical and General Workers—has at least an ideological affinity with the UAW. So striking is this point of origin of the strategy that the question must be asked whether the effort toward multinational bargaining is the extension abroad of a particular manifestation of U.S. trade union power, just as the expansion of MNCs was perceived abroad as an American challenge to weaker economies.

It would be an oversimplification, however, to think of the transnational strategy as the aggressive expansionism of American trade unions, and the national strategy as the defensive reaction of unions abroad. In the United States, only a minority of union leaders have been aligned with the UAW in practical support of the transnational strategy, while outside the United States the UAW has found some allies to participate in the strategy.

V

The alternative to this transnational strategy has been what might be called a *national* strategy, in which trade unions apply their political strength as pressure on the government to control MNCs in the interests of labor, as well as using their economic strength locally in bargaining with MNCs. The aim of this strategy is to ensure that state controls eliminate the special advantages MNCs enjoy because of their ability to operate in a number of countries. In countries where national entrepreneurship was hightly developed before MNCs became prominent, state controls may take the form of reducing the advantages MNCs have over national enterprises. In this respect, there is a basis for support of the national strategy by both organized labor and national entrepreneurs. But the national strategy may also be more radical and far-reaching, envisaging nationalization and a socialist structure of the economy.

Basically, the policy followed by the AFL-CIO in the United States has been along the lines of such a national strategy in the nonradical sense. To understand why different segments of organized labor in different countries opt either for the national or the transnational strategies, it is helpful first to look into certain characteristics of union organization, which differ significantly from country to country and from industry to industry.

The transnational strategy is most likely to be adopted where unions are strongly organized at the plant level and relatively autonomous of central trade union organizations at the national level. In other words, the transnational strategy requires a fragmentation of national labor organization so that the segments relevant to a particular MNC, or industry in which MNCs dominate, can be integrated transnationally. These conditions are facilitated when employment in an industry is characterized by relatively small numbers of relatively highly skilled workers in technology-intensive operations. Such groups of workers can readily perceive the advantage their strategic position in the industry gives to them. Even where the general pattern of trade union organization is centralized, such groups of workers may be inclined to go their own way, maximizing their advantage independently. National patterns of labor organization vary in respect to this factor of centralization. The plant-based strength of unions in North America and Britain opens the way toward a transnational strategy more readily than do the more centralized union structures of continental Europe.

Ideology is another factor in the choice between transnational and national strategies. The fact that a relatively small proportion of the work force is unionized in North America encourages an idealogy in which unions are regarded as instruments within an accepted economic system for protecting and advancing their members' particular interests. This essentially instrumental ideology is compatible with a transnational strategy. The much broader base of union membership found in Scandinavia and to a lesser degree in other countries of northern Europe tends on the other hand to sustain an ideology which sees unions as the vanguard of a movement to transform society in a spirit of solidarity with the least fortunate. Such an ideology of solidarity is a deterrent to the fragmentation necessary to the transnational approach. The discipline exercised by the central organization's control over the membership in Scandinavian labor organizations would obstruct any initiatives for independent transnationally coordinated bargaining in plants belonging to MNCs that could result in agreements out of line with the nationally negotiated agreements. For similar reasons, the powerful German metal workers union I.G. Metall has been less than eager to support the American UAW's initiatives toward using the IMF as a framework for implementing the transnational strategy.

A strengthening of shop floor movements, rebellious toward union leadership, which have become commonplace in Britain and increasingly so in other Western European countries, could bring about a loosening of central organization control in labor movements conducive to transnational confrontation of MNCs by plant-based révolts in several countries. Such a case did in fact occur in a simultaneous action by British and Italian employees of Dunlop-Pirelli. However, there are good reasons to believe such movements are unlikely to lead to formally structured multinational bargaining. Ideologically, shop floor movements have been more radical than the top union leadership and less likely to abandon the concept of solidarity in favor of instrumentalism. And structurally, local plant-based movements are likely to resist ceding their power to a multinational union with a company-wide base that would in effect remove labor relations from the direct workplace control which was the raison d'être of the shop floor movements in the first place.

The extent of trade union influence over the general economic environment of labor is a further factor. The chief objection by the AFL-CIO to the MNCs is that they export jobs from the United States. The same objection is not voiced by labor organizations in Scandinavia. The difference is explained by the degree of control Scandinavian labor has over the labor market. The effectiveness of adjustment assistance to displaced workers through active labor market policies in Scandinavian countries, achieved through a labor market system shaped and influenced very largely by the trade unions, enables the labor movement to give priority to economic modernization over the protection of specific jobs. Scandinavian trade union organizations have taken a benign view of the exporting of lower productivity types of employment to poorer countries. By contrast, American unions lack the same degree of confidence in the adjustment assistance measures written into U.S. trade legislation, and are more concerned to maintain existing jobs than to rely on upgrading and reemployment of displaced workers.

Both the Scandinavian and the American situations in this respect, it should be noted, are conducive toward the national strategy, the one in a spirit of confidence, the other of pessimism. The transnational strategy is more likely to be followed when unions are neither committed to national economic and labor-market policy nor feel especially threatened by job displacement to other countries. Since job displacement can become a threat under changed economic conditions, the propensity toward a transnational strategy may prove to be unstable and transitory. The recent history of the UAW offers a test case of a union which had led in promoting transnational action being driven as a consequence of massive layoffs in the automobile industry into a more defensive and protectionist national strategy.

Sometimes the rhetoric of union leaders and the language of tactical statements by trade union organizations about MNCs create confusion as to their basic strategic positions. The Communist-controlled World Federation of Trade Unions (WFTU) and the French Confédération Générale du Travail (CGT), for example, have issued statements asserting that the expansion of MNCs should lead to greater international collaboration among trade unions of different ideological persuasions—statements which seem to read like an endorsement of the transnational strategy. There is, however, a fundamental difference between the CGT, which sees the MNC as the highest form yet reached by the world capitalist system—a system which the CGT fundamentally opposes and seeks to transform into socialism—and the supporters of the transnational strategy who see the MNC as an efficient economic structure from which organized labor can extract greater benefits. The CGT's policy represents a radical variant of the national strategy; it proposes to attack capitalism through political and trade union action at the national level, while recognizing that the success of this enterprise within one country will be dependent upon the strength of the forces simultaneously opposing capitalism in many countries.

Weighing these various factors, the general conclusion emerges that at present the factors conducive to the national strategy predominate in labor movements in all parts of the world, and that a substantial development of transnational union bargaining with MNCs is an unlikely prospect, contrary to some recent speculation in this sense. The impetus behind the transnational strategy which came from the United States has been dampened at least momentarily by the recession, while the strength behing national strategies in the United States and elsewhere has grown.

This conclusion conforms with analyses which suggest that the relatively uncontrolled expansion of MNCs reached a peak on the threshold of the 1970s, and that the future is likely to see increased national controls over the MNCs by both host and home countries.[8] The image of a transnational countervailing power of trade unions arose at a time when states seemed to have let a good deal of control slip from their hands. With states in both home and host countries now more effectively back in the picture, trade unions are likely to direct both their economic and political power to influence state action.

Wherever the transnational strategy is maintained, it seems likely this will be by elite groups of workers who perceive their advantage in a symbiotic relationship with the MNCs. Insofar as such groups of elite workers are successful, the welfare implications for workers as a whole would be regressive; the gap between those within and those outside the symbiosis would widen. Thus the transnational strategy could provoke a reaction from the less favored group outside. The transnationalism of a new labor aristocracy would be confronted by the nationalism of the less favored majority of workers.

VI

If the main thrust of organized labor with respect to MNCs seems likely to be toward securing more effective public regulation, in ways that would protect and advance labor interests, the next questions to be considered are: What kinds of regulation of MNCs can be envisaged?[9] Which of these kinds of regulation is labor most likely to support?

At present, no international regime of rules or regulations exists for MNCs as such, much less in regard to the implications for labor of MNCs. International labor standards have, of course, been adopted through the procedures of the International Labour Organisation (ILO) which are applicable generally without distinction between MNCs and other employers. The ILO's standards are in the form of model provisions designed as guidelines for enactment through national legislation or practice; they do not constitute anything like an international jurisdiction administered by an international authority to which MNCs could be made accountable.

Since the MNCs operate beyond the jurisdiction of an individual state, the question of an *international regulatory authority* has been raised along with other more conventional proposals for regulation. This proposal envisages a supranational body which would register MNCs and give them an international legal personality—"cosmo-corps" according to the terminology of George Ball—and would apply such rules for the regulation of competition and guarantees against uncompensated expropriation as were agreed upon. The proposal is in effect intended to protect MNCs against the intervention of nation-states as a counterpart to the establishment of international regulation.

This proposal need only be noted in passing, for it lies clearly beyond the bounds of political feasibility. Given the present nature and authority of international organizations, the proposal must be accounted at best as utopian, at worst as a confidence trick which would remove MNCs very substantially from the only jurisdictions able effectively to control them, i.e., national jurisdictions with all the means of enforcement at their disposal, in order to allow them greater freedom under a facade of ineffectual international regulation. This suggestion for international regulation is mainly of interest as a manifestation of the ideology of transnationalism.

A possibly greater degree of feasibility attaches to suggestions for a *general agreement on foreign investments* analogous to the General Agreement on Tariffs and Trade (GATT) in the realm of commercial policy. Under this approach, states would remain the effective jurisdiction and enforcement agencies but would agree upon certain common principles of national action in such matters as taxation, regulation of competition, foreign exchange and export controls, expropriation conditions, etc. The general agreement might be supplemented by the setting up of an agency able to initiate investigation of related issues and to make recommendations which might become the basis for an extension of the scope of the agreement. Such a general agreement could be described as a code applicable to MNCs, and the notion of a "code of conduct" has also been suggested in looser forms and with less explicit machinery for accountability and enforcement.

The main proponents of the GATT-type approach to regulating the MNC have not usually given prominence to labor matters, although some labor organizations including the International Confederation of Free Trade Unions have advocated a "code of conduct" for MNCs in the labor field. The ILO has already begun—rather inclusively—to discuss the notion of such a code of conduct.[10] One obvious approach would be to include within a general agreement on investment certain of the more important existing ILO standards, such as those dealing with trade union rights and collective bargaining and certain basic conditions of work and safety provisions. (This idea encounters the objection that in some countries these norms would then apply to MNCs but not to national enterprises.)

This approach, like the foregoing, originates in a benign view of the potential role of the MNC in the global economy. Were any such agreement to be concluded, it would be most unlikely to be universal in scope but limited only to countries whose governments share such a view. Similarly, it would appeal mainly to those segments of the labor movements that opt for the transnational strategy. As with the international regulation proposal, the proponents of the general agreement have in mind to create certain guarantees for foreign investment as a counterpart to regulation, and thereby to provide a more predictable environment for the operations of MNCs. The general agreement approach does not respond so well to the desires of governments or of trade unions that see MNCs as a threat to their own control of the instruments essential to pursuing a welfare policy. Such governments would be disinclined to enter into international obligations that would restrict their means of control over foreign investors and the jobs they may create or withdraw. It is indicative that the Canadian government, which once favored the general agreement approach, has now moved away from it.

A further objection to the general agreement or code of conduct approach in the labor field is that it would apply only to workers employed directly by MNCs. The impact of the internationalizing of production on the welfare of people *outside* the MNC sector is a critical issue, with which the codes approach in no way comes to grip.

Any significant advance toward worker participation in management, advocated with growing vigor by part of the European Left, could alter the current balance between transnational and national strategies on the part of labor. This development could cut either way, depending upon the real nature of worker control. For many who advocate it, worker control in industry has become the current revolutionary myth heralding a transformation of the structure of power in society. Insofar as this vision approximates future reality, worker control, by ensuring that power remains on the shop floor, would crumble the centralized control structures of MNCs. The historical reality of worker participation in management has, however, been anything but revolutionary. Codetermination has co-opted worker elites into the social partnership. Union representation on the boards of management of MNCs, which has been advocated by some exponents of the transnational strategy, could well prove to be a step toward corporatist symbiosis in labor-management relations—a step which would confirm the neglect of and unconcern for the broader welfare issues which have characterized the process of internationalizing production.

An *information and reporting* approach to regulating MNCs seems likely to be widely adopted. The United Nations has lent its authority to this approach, which recognizes that national governments have the major responsibility for regulating MNCs, but frequently lack the information to make their attempts at regulation effective. The international aspects of this approach would identify the kinds of information governments should require MNCs to disclose, and would also provide expert assistance to governments which require it in order to set up the machinery to collect and use this information. Trade unions will support this approach since, even more than governments, they are aware that lack of information puts them at a disadvantage vis-à-vis MNCs.

The pattern of regulation most likely to emerge as dominant will come via a complex process of *intergovernmental bargaining over the application by home and host countries of national controls and requirements.* Looking backward, some countries like Japan took a highly restrictive attitude toward foreign investment, while other countries like Canada and many less-developed countries imposed few restrictions. Recently, the distance between these polar types has greatly diminished. Japan—and even the Soviet Union—admit MNC operations more readily but on their own conditions. Canada and less-developed countries increasingly require that foreign investors bring some specific benefit—in the form of jobs for nationals, new technology or investment, or an increase in exports—and that they conform to national industrial policies. Home countries are likewise under pressure to regulate MNCs from a variety of motives, e.g., to prevent the export of jobs, to curb an outflow of capital, to protect technological advantages in some fields, and to prevent shifts in the sourcing of exports entering world trade that could have long-term adverse balance-of-payments effects. The restrictions that both home and host countries now seek to apply to MNCs are more frequently coming into conflict with each other.[11] It is thus likely that governments of home and host countries will increasingly be negotiating with each other over what specific MNCs can do and the conditions under which they should do it. The issues at stake are not susceptible to generalization into norms or principles; they are questions of more or less. The resulting complex of regulations will be messier, more detailed, and probably more effectively administered than any generalized code of conduct. It will also be much less favorable to the MNCs.

From the perspective of labor, two main points must be noted. The first is that labor is very much concerned with these issues since they directly affect jobs. Organized labor will thus be prominent as a pressure group seeking to influence the outcomes both of national scrutiny and regulation of foreign investment and of intergovernmental negotiations about such regulation. The second point is that trade union action will take place within the national strategy. And in this process different national trade union strategies will frequently come into collision.

Canadian workers, for instance, have an interest in encouraging the establishment of a tire factory providing jobs in Canada, a factory designed to supply the North American market. Canadian workers would thus support a government offer of incentives to the foreign investors interested in establishing this factory in an area of Canada where unemployment is relatively high. U.S. organized rubber workers, on the other hand, see this Canadian action as potentially depriving their members of jobs, and petition their government to impose some restriction on the import of tires from Canada. Such cases will become increasingly common.

VII

The question remains: Even if organized labor, using the national strategy, is able to bring pressure on individual governments to improve national and international regulation of the multinational corporation, will this deal with the potential for social conflict inherent in the emerging class structure?

From the above, it seems clear that organized labor has not been able and seems unlikely to be able to deal equitably with the whole range of social issues raised by the changes in a world economy impelled forward by the expansion of MNCs. The transnational strategy—perhaps the most striking form of labor response—is in many ways the least equitable. It deals only with the employees of the MNCs themselves, and in practice only with the most favored of these. The transnational strategy offers little hope, for example, to the workers in "export platforms," whose governments frequently guarantee the conditions of low wages and freedom from strike actions which are so attractive to foreign investors. This union strategy would only increase the privileged position of a minority of workers.

The national strategy can have a broader social impact, but the danger is that where organized labor reflects primarily the interests of primary labor market workers, the class of social marginals will be neglected—and it is precisely this class whose claims rank highest by the criterion of social equity. At present, there is no sign of a response to the MNCs which would come effectively to grips with the condition of the social marginals. Yet economic trends continue to make this group increasingly numerous and increasingly vulnerable.

The extent to which social equity is an effective guide to policy is very much a matter of political structures, and the consequences of trends analyzed here are clear in their implications for political structures. Successful pursuit of the national strategy by strong trade union organizations in industrialized countries could lead toward a form of corporate state in which unions would exert a continuing influence along with business upon government intervention in the economy and upon foreign economic policy. The corporate state would provide the powerfully organized interests with protection and security, leaving the social marginals to the discretionary generosity of state welfare. In less-developed countries, the political consequence of growing marginality has more frequently been a less sophisticated form of coercive authoritarianism.

These political structures are not solutions to the problems posed but rather expedients to contain the conflicts inherent in the emerging class structure. In the broadest terms, we are moving from a period in which economic resources have by and large been sufficient to moderate social tensions, toward one in which political resources are being used to compensate for the growing inadequacy of economic resources. In retrospect, economic growth appears to have been the principal factor which allowed industrial conflict to become institutionalized and which diminished its intensity. Unions could dispute with employers over the division of increments to growth without attacking either the basic distribution of wealth or the structures for reproducing wealth. In consequence, established workers were able to improve their conditions progressively. The cult of growth—unquestioned as recently as the early 1960s—has now been displaced by an awareness that human survival requires some restraint in the rates of depletion of natural resources, of increases in population, and of the polluting effects of production. Superimposed upon this new perception of the finite character of the global ecosystem now comes a recession, bringing about a de facto decline in growth. Without actually embracing zero-growth as a policy for a world which has so much poverty to relieve, it does seem necessary to abandon the mental schema of the 1950s and 1960s in which all problems seemed to be resolvable or postponable through growth, with differential payoffs to the contending parties in proportion to their relative strength.

The new low-growth schema sees social classes as well as nations in an ongoing confrontation of a kind that Helmut Schmidt aptly described as the "struggle for the world product."[12] The form of the struggle is political though its object is economic. Power and bargaining strength now consciously replace the classical concept of the market as the way in which distribution is determined. The issues now have to be faced in terms of sharing and redistribution among social classes as well as among nations, no longer in terms of the division of increments. The issues thus become more intractable, more conflictual, and they place a very heavy, perhaps too heavy, strain upon national and international institutions which were devised upon the assumption of continuing growth.

Within this prospect of rising conflict and institutional stress, established labor and its union leaders are in a position to influence future directions in a crucial manner. They can acquiesce in the movement toward corporate states and coercive authoritarian regimes, or they can resist these tendencies. Some elements of self-regarding interest counsel acquiescence. It would be illusory to pretend the contrary. But established workers and at least some of their union leaders still recall the historic moral appeal to a worker solidarity in which the more powerfully organized demonstrate their responsibility to defend the weaker as well as themselves.

Thus, established labor confronts the critical ethical option: symbiosis or solidarity, either a corporatism with its coercive accompaniment or the pursuit of a broader and more egalitarian welfare at the sacrifice, for some more advantaged groups, of material gains they might have had. And if labor exercises the option for solidarity, the multinational corporation need appear neither as hero nor as villain. Rather, it would appear as an objective force in the movement of social history: both a generator of the class structure and a catalyst of labor's consciousness, provoking decisions on the future alignment of the classes into which labor has become divided.

NOTES

1. Several of the books which have dealt with this aspect are the products of symposia. The first in the field was Hans Günter (ed.), *Transnational Industrial Relations,* London: Macmillan, 1972. A more recent one is Robert J. Flanagan and Arnold R. Weber (eds.), *Bargaining Without Borders: the Multinational Corporation and International Labor Relations,* Chicago and London: University of Chicago Press, 1974. A recent analysis from a European trade union perspective is Ernst Piehl, *Multinationale Konzerne und internationale Gewerkschaftsbewegung,* Frankfurt-am-Main: Europa Verlags-Anst., 1974.

2. See for example Osvaldo Sunkel, "Big Business and 'Dependencia': A Latin American View," *Foreign Affairs*, April 1972. [Reprinted in this volume.]

3. These figures are derived from a table presented by Professor E. M. Kassalow in an unpublished manuscript on the International Metalworkers Federation. Professor Kassalow bears no responsibility for my use of his figures.

4. See Theodore H. Moran, "Foreign Expansion as an Institutional Necessity for U.S. Corporate Capitalism: The Search for a Radical Model," *World Politics*, April 1973, pp. 384–85.

5. These concepts have been used comparatively in Peter B. Doeringer, "Low Pay, Labor Market Dualism, and Industrial Relations Systems," (unpublished) Discussion Paper No. 271, Harvard Institute of Economic Research, Harvard University, January 1973.

6. Some Brazilian technocrats spoke of "Operation Euthanasia," i.e., neglect of the depressed areas and social groups. Cf. Marcio Moreira Alves, *A Grain of Mustard Seed: The Awakening of the Brazilian Revolution*, New York: Doubleday Anchor Press, 1973. In similar vein, some American theoreticians of economic assistance now speak of "triage," i.e., abandoning the hopeless cases to their fate while concentrating aid upon those who have demonstrated their fitness to survive by changing their cultural habits in line with externally perceived economic requirements. See "Triage: Who Shall Be Fed? Who Shall Starve?" by Wade Green, *The New York Times Magazine*, January 5, 1975, pp. 9–11 ff.

7. A brilliant analysis of the institutionalizing of conflict is given in Ralf Dahrendorf, *Class and Class Conflict in Industrial Society*, Stanford: Stanford University Press, 1959.

8. See for example, Peter P. Gabriel, "The Multinational Corporation in the World Economy: Problems and Prospects," in Flanagan and Weber, *op. cit.*

9. I am much indebted to the classification of proposals for international regulation for MNCs suggested by William Diebold, Jr. and Janice L. Murray, in an unpublished paper they prepared for the third Lester B. Pearson Conference on the Canada-U.S. Relationship, held at Niagara-on-the-Lake, Ontario, September 1974. The discussion at this conference was helpful in shaping some of the ideas expressed in this article. So was the Conference on International Rules for Multinational Corporations held at the OECD in Paris, in January 1975, under the auspices of the American Society of International Law and the Association Internationale du Droit Commercial et du Droit des Affaires. A useful analysis of the problem and prospects of regulating MNCs written from a standpoint of neoclassical economics while recognizing that politics may be more important than economics in this matter is by Robert O. Keohane and Van Doorn Ooms, "The Multinational Firm and International Regulation," *International Organization*, Winter 1975, pp. 169–209.

10. *Multinational Enterprises and Social Policy*, Geneva: ILO, 1973.

11. The point is discussed in C. Fred Bergsten, "Coming Investment Wars?," *Foreign Affairs*, April 1974.

12. Helmut Schmidt, "The Struggle for the World Product," *Foreign Affairs*, April 1974, pp. 437–51.

Glossary

Bilateral Monopoly Market relationship where a single seller faces a single buyer.

Cartel Combination of independent enterprises that agree to limit their competitive activities in the marketing of a similar commodity.

Center/Periphery Concepts descriptive of world dependency relationships between industrial states (center) and the Third World (periphery), the center exploiting the periphery. Recalls the earlier distinction between metropolis and colonies.

Concentration (industrial) Degree to which a few firms dominate the output of an industry; measured by the concentration ratio.

Contract Curve In bargaining relationships (bilateral monopoly), a locus of points where the benefits of exchange between two traders are maximized (that is, where the indifference curves of the two traders are tangent).

Contrat sans Combat A sale or deal closed without argument or haggling over the price, i.e., without bargaining.

Cost-Benefit Analysis Economic calculus to help in the making of choices among alternative courses of action.

Demand Curve Graphic illustration of the state of demand for a product, showing the volume of sales at each of a series of prices.

Direct Foreign Investment The process of creating a foreign affiliate or acquiring the controlling interest in a foreign firm; or the condition of having control over foreign affiliates or subsidiaries. Most d.f.i. is undertaken by transnational corporations.

Disinvestment Withdrawal of capital from investment, as by selling foreign affiliates of a transnational enterprise.

Duopoly A market (or industry) where supply is dominated by two producers.

Economies of Scale Lower unit cost of production due to large size of operation, allowing more intensive use of equipment, etc.

Elasticity of Supply or Demand   Relationship of responsiveness between changes in the quantity supplied or demanded and changes in price.

Equity Participation   A risk interest or ownership in a business venture.

Eurodollar Market   London-centered market in dollar-denominated debt instruments (such as bonds).

Exchange Parity   Equivalence of a commodity's price, expressed in one currency, to its price, expressed in another.

Factor of Production   A good or service (land, labor, or capital) used in the process of production.

General Equilibrium Analysis (as distinct from partial equilibrium analysis of a single market)   An approach that emphasizes the interdependence of all economic quantities in an economic system.

Geocentric   World-oriented (contrasted with ethnocentric or polycentric).

Group of 77   Caucusing group of more than 100 Third World countries in the United Nations, set up at the first UNCTAD meeting in 1964.

Home Country   The country where the headquarters of a transnational enterprise is located.

Host Country   The country where subsidiaries or affiliates of a transnational enterprise are located.

Imperfect or Monopolistic Competition; Imperfect Market   Market condition in which some firms produce a large enough proportion of the total output of a commodity for changes in their own output to have a perceptible effect on the price of that commodity.

Indeterminacy, Area or Margin of   Under bilateral monopoly, area where a unique outcome of the parties' bargaining cannot be predicted.

Indifference Curve   A measure of utility or value indicating a consumer's ratio of preference between two commodities. Move to higher indifference curve means improvement in welfare.

International Content   Degree to which an enterprise engages in operations outside the home country.

International Control   Degree to which ownership or managerial control of an enterprise is shared with non-nationals.

International Production   Production subject to foreign control or decision, measured by sales of foreign affiliates of transnational enterprises.

Laissez-Faire   Fundamental principle upholding a policy of least state interference in economic matters.

Macroeconomics   The study of an entire economy, using aggregate quantities (such as income, money, and prices), especially concerned with the problem of achieving the full employment of resources.

Marginal Productivity   Addition to the output of a firm arising from the hiring of one more unit of production (one worker, one drill). Contrast with average productivity, which is the total output divided by the number of units of production employed.

Marginal Return or Advantage Addition to the profits of a firm arising from the hiring of one more unit of production (labor, machinery) or the conclusion of one more sale. Contrast with average return, which is the total return divided by the number of units employed or sold.

Marginal Utility The amount of additional utility (or value) provided by an additional unit of an economic good or service.

Market Power Characteristic of a firm that has a significant degree of discretion about the prices it charges for its products.

Microeconomics The study of economics in terms of individual areas of activity (such as firms, households) and their allocation of resources among alternative uses. Contrast with macroeconomics.

Monopoly A market (or industry) where a seller is the sole supplier of an economic good that has no significant substitutes. Broadly, any market in which the behavior of sellers is other than purely competitive.

Net Return Net profit.

Oil Majors The seven largest multinational oil companies: Exxon, Mobil, Gulf, Texaco, Standard of California, Royal Dutch Shell, and British Petroleum (the Seven Sisters).

Oligopoly A market (or industry) diminated by a small number of producers. "Competition among the few."

Parameter In static economics, a variable (which is assumed to be constant) lying outside the mathematical model of an equilibrium situation—e.g., rainfall vis-à-vis the price and production of corn, or the international price of a product vis à vis the local supply and demand for it.

Pax Britannica British-dominated world order of the nineteenth century.

Perfect, Nonmonopolistic, or Pure Competition, Perfect Market Market situation in which each firm produces such a small part of the total output of a commodity that it cannot perceptibly influence its price by expanding or contracting its own supply. The price of the commodity is given and cannot be altered by the firm.

Poles of Development (Privileged) In a planned economy, favored centers of investment activity designed to stimulate and attract further economic development.

Portfolio Investment Transactions in, or holdings of, stocks, bonds, and money-market instruments involving independent firms or individuals.

Preferences The practice of giving some countries legal advantages over others in international trade—e.g., reduced tariffs.

Product Differentiation The use of trademarks and advertising to convince buyers that a certain product is different from and better than other similar products in the market, thus creating brand loyalty.

Putting-Out System; Verlagsystem A form of subcontracting to households whereby an enterpreneur provides materials for domestic work and pays for the product by the piece.

Rent (economic sense) A surplus accruing to a specific factor, the supply of which is fixed.

Rule of Nondiscrimination   Parties to the General Agreement on Tariffs and Trade (GATT, Art. XIII) accept the rule that trade restrictions will be applied among themselves in a nondiscriminatory manner.

Supply Curve   Graphic illustration showing the amounts of a product offered for sale at each of a series of prices.

Surplus Value   In Marxist theory, the difference between the contribution made by a worker and the subsistence wages paid him by his capitalist employer.

Synergy   Joint action by several units whose result is different from the mere sum of their separate actions.

Terms of Trade   The rate at which a country's exports are exchanged against imports.

Transfer Pricing   The prices at which intracorporate transfers of resources are made across national boundaries.

Vertical Integration   A combining into one interacting whole of firms in different phases of the manufacture and distribution of a product.

INDEX OF CORPORATIONS MENTIONED

INDEX OF NAMES AND TOPICS